Karibu Kenya
Accommodation Guide

Standard Chartered
Here for good

1 month of planning the perfect getaway

7 magical days on holiday

1 credit card that makes it possible

It's good when your Standard Chartered Credit Card is your perfect travel companion.

5% Cash Back
Get Cash Back anytime you spend on dining and fuel

Reward Points
Earn and redeem points for shopping vouchers, air tickets and more

Insurance
Lost card and purchase protection, travel insurance and more

Travel Benefits
Special airfares, hotel rates, airport transfers, lounge access and more

To know more, call 329 3900 or visit standardchartered.co.ke

Terms and conditions apply.

Accommodation Guide

by Tamara Britten

Imprint

First published July 2012

Author	Tamara Britten
Design & Layout	Marie-Claire Webner – Munich Design Ltd.
Logo Design	Marie-Claire Webner – Munich Design Ltd.
Photography	Andrew Nightingale, Sokomoto Images
Maps	Pat Kirby
Map of Kenya	Marie-Claire Webner – Munich Design Ltd.
Printing & Binding	Beijing Youwanji Printing Co., LTD, China

Copyright © Tamara Britten

The right of Tamara Britten to be identified as the author of this work has been asserted by her in accordance with the Copyright, Designs and Patents Act 1988.

ISBN 978-0-9573173-0-7

Published by Tamara Britten

Printed in China

All rights reserved. No part of this publication may be reproduced, stored in a retrieval system or transmitted in any form by any means, electronic, mechanical, photocopying, recording or otherwise, without the written permission of Tamara Britten.

This book is sold subject to the condition that it may not be circulated in any form of binding or cover other than that in which it is published.

The Karibu Kenya Accommodation Guide team has made every effort to make sure all information in Karibu Kenya Accommodation Guide is accurate. The team is not responsible for prices that change, telephone and fax numbers that alter and properties that open or close after publication.

Hotels, camps, lodges and resorts in Kenya that have not been included in Karibu Kenya Accommodation Guide are welcome to contact the team for inclusion in the next edition.

Hotels, camps, lodges and resorts that would like an amendment to their entry in Karibu Kenya Accommodation Guide are welcome to send the team the amended information.

Companies that would like to advertise in the next edition of Karibu Kenya Accommodation Guide, please contact:
tamara@karibukenya-accommodationguide.com.

Meet the Team

Tamara Britten
Author

Tamara Britten is the author and researcher of Karibu Kenya Accommodation Guide.

Tamara has a MA in Creative Writing from the University of East Anglia, UK. Her written work has won the Curtis Brown award for prose fiction, attained second place in the Yeovil Short Story Competition and been shortlisted in the Hookline Novel Competition.

Tamara taught English in language schools and state schools around Thailand, where she also created language courses and directed summer schools. She designed programmes and wrote course material at an adult education centre in Hong Kong. She coordinated research for a BBC radio series on livestock in Somalia. Tamara's work in the tourism field has included managing a restaurant in Thailand and managing safari camps and mobile tented safaris in Namibia and Kenya.

While researching Karibu Kenya Accommodation Guide Tamara travelled around Kenya locating camps, lodges, resorts and hotels, some of which have never before been listed in a guidebook. She carried out site inspections at the majority of properties profiled in the guidebook, and was in personal contact with the managers or marketing agents of the remainder.

Munich Design Ltd. – Marie-Claire Webner
Design & Layout

Munich Design Ltd. is a strategy and design oriented communications agency. We see ourselves as 'Architects' for Company and Brand Communication, as we plan, conceptualise, visualise and realise our clients' visions and communication strategies. We are a strong partner for all your graphic design needs, from the logo all the way to the sophisticated campaign. Contact us on **info@munichdesign.net**

Andrew Nightingale
Photography

Andrew Nightingale was born in Kenya and has spent his life exploring the country with his camera. He works as a location scout and fixer for film and television, and also guides fishing safaris around East Africa. He lives on his family's farm near Nakuru, on which he has a campsite and a collection of attractive holiday cottages, and where he offers a wide variety of activities. Documentary and film location scouting, fishing trips and holiday cottages are available at **www.kembu.com**

Sokomoto Images
Photography

Sokomoto showcases two Kenyan photographers, Mark Muinde and Teeku Patel, and features some of the most outstanding images from Africa. Sokomoto offers personal, high quality service to companies, publications and individuals, and helps them to find the most dynamic image to convey their visions, concepts and illustrations. Through its photos, Sokomoto aims to create enthusiasm for our world and promote awareness of our ecosystem. Commercial and documentary photography, photo workshops and photographic safaris are available at **www.sokomoto.com**

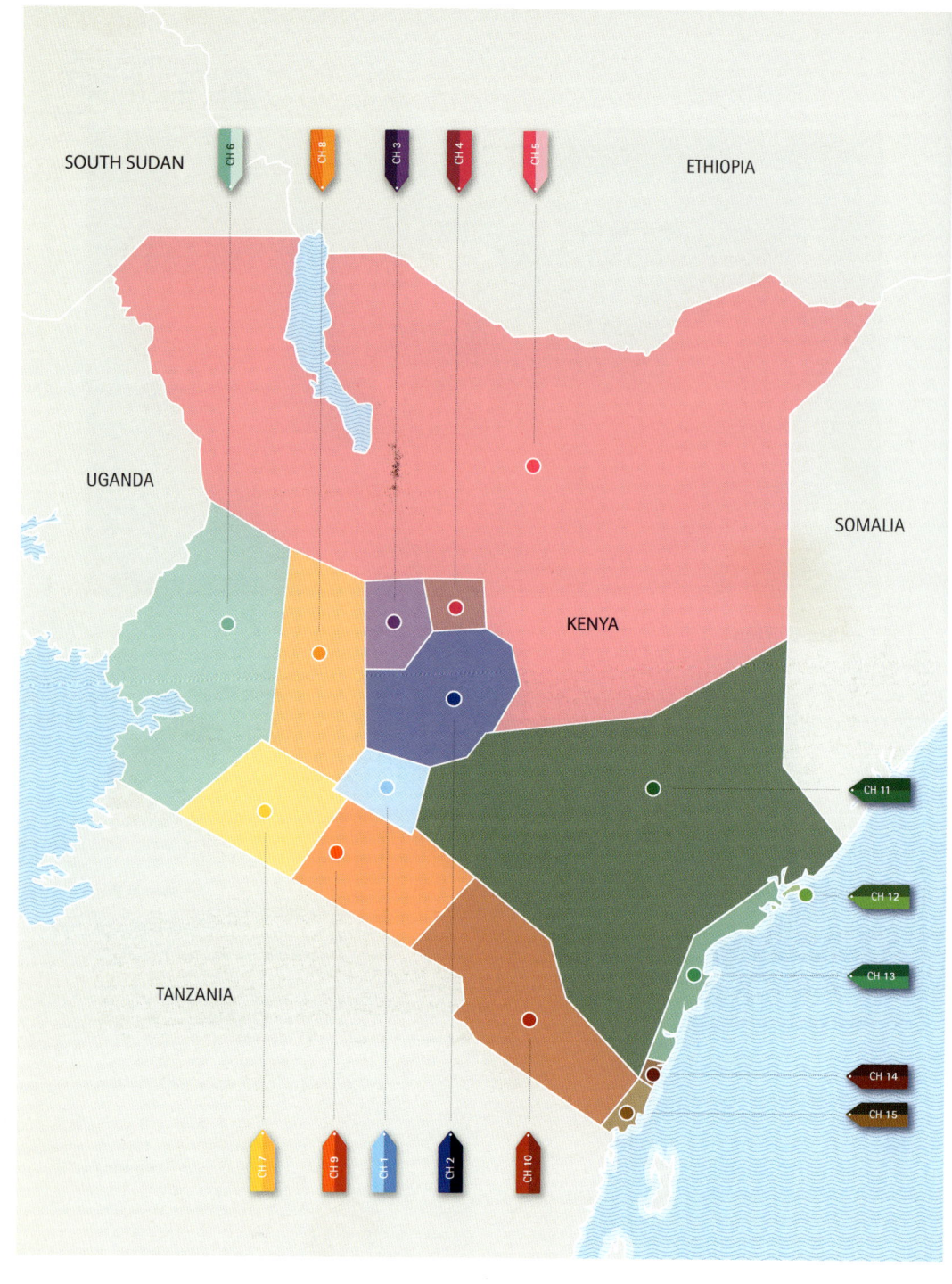

CONTENTS

	5	Meet the Team
	15	Karibu
	21	Icon Legend
Chapter 1	23	Nairobi
Chapter 2	69	The Central Highlands
Chapter 3	113	Laikipia
Chapter 4	131	Samburu, Buffalo Springs and Shaba National Reserves
Chapter 5	143	Northern Kenya
Chapter 6	159	Western Kenya
Chapter 7	209	Maasai Mara National Reserve
Chapter 8	271	The Lakes
Chapter 9	319	Amboseli National Park
Chapter 10	329	Tsavo West National Park
Chapter 11	343	Tsavo East National Park
Chapter 12	359	The Lamu Archipelago
Chapter 13	395	North Coast
Chapter 14	465	Mombasa
Chapter 15	477	South Coast
	525	Index to all camps, lodges hotels & resorts

Karibu Kenya
Accommodation Guide

A very warm jambo to you!

Kenya has a diverse and wide-reaching appeal as a holiday destination. Visitors come to visit our world-renowned game reserves, to experience the authentic safaris, to enjoy our palm-fringed beaches and for a taste of our vibrant town life. This remarkable variety provides visitors with the opportunity for safari, trekking, climbing, adventure sports and relaxation among others.

In line with diversification of our products, Kenya has invested in tourism; more and more regions have opened up with development of more properties to keep pace with the new tourism circuits.

We trust that this guide will act as a reference book for those involved in tourism business in Kenya from the tourists, to the local Kenya travel agents, ground handlers and for international travel agents around the world.

We have noted that the contents are divided into regions and on alphabetical index at the end to make it easy. Further that the guide covers hotels, lodges and camps in Kenya and that it also includes information on conservancies, national parks, game reserves, mountains, towns and beaches that are well illustrated by colour photography and maps.

As you navigate through this guide, we expect that you will learn the history of Kenya, her environment, cuisine and culture. A short report on Kenya's climate, geographical area and population has also been given. Further information on essential services such as the banking system and currency, medical facilities, domestic airlines, road and rail networks, the postal system, the telephone networks and dialling codes and internet have also been highlighted.

As Kenya Tourist Board (KTB) we have no doubt that this guide will add impetus to our marketing efforts and other initiatives aimed at making Kenya the preferred tourism destination.

Consequently KTB is happy to endorse this new Comprehensive Guide to Kenya.

Finally we wish to thank the producers of the guide for identifying this opportunity that will go a long way in supplementing KTB's marketing efforts.

Karibu Kenya!

Muriithi Ndegwa
Kenya Tourist Board

Kenya Tourism Federation is the umbrella body for the private sector in tourism. The federation represents the interests of seven mainstream tourism sector associations and seeks to promote a sustainable tourism sector through effective representation of private sector industry stakeholder interests through advocacy, information dissemination and promotion of sustainable use and development of natural resources and heritage among other activities.

This new guidebook provides the industry and other stakeholders with a much-needed reference book. It also provides tourists with a detailed introduction to the country and its facilities. We commend its producers for undertaking this important exercise which will ultimately promote Kenya's unique and diverse tourist attractions by making available information which is key in decision-making.

Sincerely,
for Kenya Tourism Federation

Agatha Juma
Chief Executive Officer

Kenya Professional Safari Guide Association was established in 1996. The association is an examining body whose aim is to improve the quality of driver guides for the Kenya tourist industry. KPSGA is committed to ensuring that visitors to Kenya are accompanied by qualified guides during their safari and throughout their stay. A number of tour companies now insist that their driver guides are certified by KPSGA.

KPSGA both improves standards within the industry and provides the possibility of career advancement for individuals.

There are three levels of examination: bronze, silver and gold. Between each level, candidates must attain three years' practical experience. By attaining certification, candidates prove they have a broad knowledge of wildlife, conservation and tourism, flora and fauna, as well as knowledge of ethics and standards relating to all aspects of tourism

This new accommodation guide to Kenya, provides tourists with much needed information about the accommodation available throughout Kenya, including those within the country's national parks and reserves. As well as providing details about camps and lodges, the guide includes an icon detailing the level of KPSGA certification of the guides employed by each property. KPSGA is therefore pleased to endorse this new guidebook.

Paul Kirui
Chairman | Kenya Professional Safari Guide Association (KPSGA)

Aberdare National Park - Photo © www.sokomoto.com

Orbit Chemical Industries Ltd.

| Agrochemicals |
| Industrial Chemicals | Soaps and Detergents |
| Sulphonation | Plastic packaging |
| Contract Manufacturing |

Mombasa Rd, Next to Mlolongo Weighbridge
Box 48870 00100, Nairobi
Fax: 020 821624
Wireless Fax: 0202014406, 0203540021
Cell: 0722 205502, 0733 333938
Tel: 020 6820060/1, 6821625, 6821646/7
Wireless: 020 2014407/8, 2338306, 3541925/6

Email: orbit@orbitchem.com | www.orbitchem.com

Crested Cranes – Photo © Tamara Britten

Karibu

HISTORY OF KENYA

Excavations in East Africa have uncovered a wealth of evidence that life in this region dates back millions of years. Dinosaur fossils found at Lokitang have been dated to 70 million years ago. Mammal remains including rhinos, bovidae and aquidae found at Lokipeda in West Turkana have been dated to 26 million years ago, and those found at Buluk in East Turkana and Kalahe in Pokot have been dated to about 20 million years ago.

The earliest evidence of human evolution has been found in the Rift Valley region of Africa. Discoveries in the Tugen Hills near Lake Baringo date to 6.8 million years ago, and precipitated the naming of a new species, the Orrorin Tugenensis. Excavations near Lake Turkana indicate that hominids like Australopithecus Anamensis lived in the area from around 4.1 million years ago. Homo Erectus found in the region have been dated to about 1.6 million years ago, while Homo Sapiens have been dated to 200,000 to 150,000 years ago.

The early Stone Age, dating from about 2 million years ago, is characterised by tools that consist of pebbles and stone blocks. Evidence of these tools has been found in the Koobi Fora region, east of Lake Turkana. A study of the fossil and animal remains at these sites indicates that the people of that period lived in small groups that depended on hunting and gathering, and were predominantly meat-eaters.

The middle Stone Age, dating from about 1 million years ago, is characterised by more advanced tools referred to as bifaces, such as hand axes and cleavers. These have been found in many areas of Kenya, including Olorgesailie near Lake Magadi, Kariandusi near Lake Elementaita, Kilombe near Eldama Ravine, Lewa Wildlife Conservancy near Isiolo, Isingya near Kajiado, Mtongwe near Mombasa, and the regions around Lake Victoria and Lake Turkana. Like their predecessors, people of this period lived by hunting and gathering.

The late Stone Age witnessed an emergence of the bow and arrow. More intricate techniques of stone tool manufacture produced microliths, such as blades, awls and scrapers, as well as artefacts such as grinding stones, pottery, bone harpoons and beads. These have been found in the Rift Valley between Naivasha and Nakuru, at Lukenya Hill near Athi River and in the Lake Victoria region.

The Neolithic period, from between about 6,000 and 1,000 BC, marked the origin of the domestication of plants and animals, and saw the emergence of agriculture and pastoralism. Tools found from this time include stone bowls, platters, wooden vessels and beads made of seed, bone and stone. Pottery became more varied in size and form. Burial sites from this era show that at Njoro River Cave and Keringet Cave the practice of cremation was common, while at Hyrax Hill burial graves were preferred.

The Iron Age, in the first few centuries AD, witnessed the emergence of iron technology. While little iron has been found because of its tendency to perish when exposed to the atmosphere, iron slag and bellows have been found. Other finds include stone artefacts, elaborate pottery and intricate beads. Sites from this era are in the Turkwell Basin, Siaya District, Kwale town, Gatunganga near Nyeri, South Nyanza, Bungoma District and Lanet near Nakuru.

In the 1st century AD, Cushitic-speaking peoples moved south from Ethiopia. These people settled along the route from Lake Turkana through Marsabit to Tana River. They are the ancestors of today's Rendille, Somali, Boran, Gabbra, Orma and Boni tribes. Shortly afterwards, Nilotic-speaking peoples moved from Sudan into the Western highlands and the Rift Valley. These are the ancestors of today's Maasai, Samburu, Teso, Turkana, El Molo, Njemps, Kalenjin, Marakwet, Tugen, Pokot, Elkony, Kipsigis and Luo.

The next wave of immigration was the Bantu-speakers moving from Central and Southern Africa. Kenya's largest linguistic group, these are the ancestors of today's Kikuyu, Akamba, Meru, Embu, Tharaka, Mbere, Gussi, Kuria, Luhya, Mikikenda, Pokomo, Segeju, Taveta and Taita.

KaribuKenya Accommodation Guide

From the 7th century AD, Arab dhows were docking at East African ports. Trading posts were established at Lamu, Gede and Mombasa and by the 9th century AD, there is evidence of Arabs settling and marrying the indigenous coastal people, producing the ancestors of the Swahili people who today inhabit much of the coastal region. Archaeological evidence shows signs of trade between the coastal people, the Near East and the Far East. Exports included leopard skins, tortoiseshell, rhino horn, ivory, gold and slaves. Ming Chinese porcelain and Persian glazed earthenware found from this time illustrate how extensive the trade routes were.

Cradle of Mankind

Vasco da Gama heralded the arrival of the Portuguese when he docked at Mombasa in 1498. Under the banner of Christianity, the Portuguese attacked the predominantly Muslim coast. They retained dominance of the coast through the 16th and 17th centuries, putting an end to Arab domination and taking over the trade routes. In the 18th century, the Omanis terminated Portuguese rule. Under their control, the caravan trade penetrated deeper into the centre of the continent.

The increasing rivalry between European nations was soon to overflow into Africa, and during what became known as the Scramble for Africa, Britain declared Kenya a British Protectorate in 1895. The British built the Uganda Railway, otherwise known as the Lunatic Express, between 1896 and 1901. Large numbers of Indian labourers were shipped in to assist with the railway's construction, many of whom remained in Kenya and are the ancestors of today's Indian Kenyans. During the next two decades the British extended their influence and imposed economic policies and taxation.

World War I saw bitter fighting in the Tsavo region of Kenya between the British and the Germans, who were based in what was then Tanganika, now Tanzania. The deaths of about 50,000 African porters during the war triggered the first wave of African resistance to British rule, spearheaded by Harry Thuku's Young Kikuyu Association. The British tightened their grip, proclaiming Kenya a colony in 1920, and formally defining the White Highlands in 1933.

After World War II, during which huge numbers of Kenyans were conscripted to fight in the British Army, Kenyan resistance to the British Colonial Administration gained momentum. Increasing waves of British settlers emigrating to Kenya exacerbated the land issue and intensified the pressure. Jomo Kenyatta, a local leader who had been studying in Britain, returned to Kenya and took over the presidency of the Kenyan African Union; the Mau Mau movement was born.

In 1952, a State of Emergency was declared. While the Mau Mau perpetrated attacks from their hideouts in forests and caves, lashing out at both British settlers and Kenyans who refused to take the Mau Mau oath of allegiance, the British administration enacted harsher and harsher retaliations and instigated a punitive system of detention and imprisonment. Finally, after a two-year handover period, Kenya became independent in 1963.

Jomo Kenyatta, Kenya's first president, led the country from independence until his death in 1978. His successor, Daniel arap Moi, was president until 2002, when the current president, Mwai Kibaki took power. After the 2007 elections, a power sharing agreement was signed between President Kibaki and Raila Odinga, the leader of the ODM opposition, producing Africa's first coalition government. Kenya's new constitution was voted in by referendum in 2010.

Vision 2030 is Kenya's new development plan. It aims to transform Kenya into a newly industrialising middle-income country providing a high quality of life to all its citizens by the year 2030. The project is based on three pillars: economic, social and political. Within these pillars, targets have been set in tourism, agriculture, trade, manufacturing, business, education, health, sanitation, environment, housing, rule of law, transparency, democracy and security.

Gede Ruins

KENYA'S LAND AND PEOPLE

Kenya straddles the equator. It has an area of approximately 582,650km². The country shares borders with five nations: Tanzania, Uganda, South Sudan, Ethiopia and Somalia. Variations in altitude are extreme, from sea level to 5,180 meters, producing extraordinary topological diversity and corresponding contrasts in climate.

There are four distinct geophysical features. The Rift Valley, a 5,000km fracture in the earth's crust filled with lakes, extinct volcanoes and geothermal activity, carves across the country. The Central and Western Highlands are rich agricultural lands blanketing striking mountain ranges, which produce coffee, tea, vegetables, fruits and flowers. The vast, semi-arid area that covers the rugged north and east of the country is home only to resilient nomadic peoples. And Kenya's coastline, a long stretch of attractive beaches and hot humidity, is fringed by coral reef.

Although the climate varies widely across the country, four main seasons can be noted. The hot, dry season covers December to March. The long rains come in April and May. The cool season covers June to October. And the short rains come in November.

There are three cities in Kenya: Nairobi, the capital, Mombasa, on the east coast, and Kisumu, on Lake Victoria.

Kenya has a population of about 40 million, of which almost 4 million live in Nairobi. There are 42 tribes. Although each tribe has its own language, there are three main linguistic groups. The Bantu-speaking tribes are the most numerous and live in the lush south of the country. These are Kikuyu, Akamba, Meru, Embu, Tharaka, Mbere, Gussi, Kuria, Luhya, Mikikenda, Swahili, Pokomo, Segeju, Taveta and Taita. The Nilotic-speaking tribes, living in the west of the country, are Maasai, Samburu, Teso, Turkana, El Molo, Njemps, Kalenjin, Marakwet, Tugen, Pokot, Elkony, Kipsigis and Luo. The Cushitic-speaking tribes, many of which are nomadic, live in the arid northeast and include Rendille, Somali, Boran, Gabbra, Orma and Boni.

There are three other racial groups of Kenyan nationality. The Kenyan Arabs are predominantly descended from the Yemeni, Omani and Persian traders who established early trading posts on the Kenyan coast. The Kenyan Asians are predominantly descended from the Indian labourers brought to Kenya by the British to build the railway. Kenyans of British origin are predominantly descended from the British who came during the Colonial Administration and took Kenyan nationality at independence.

The official languages of Kenya are Swahili and English.

TRANSPORT

There are three international airports in Kenya. Jomo Kenyatta International Airport, JKIA, is in Nairobi. Moi International Airport, MIA, is in Mombasa at the coast. Eldoret International Airport, EIA, is in Eldoret in the western highlands. Wilson Airport, in Nairobi, is the largest light aircraft airport in

Local Transport

Africa. A wealth of domestic airlines provide daily scheduled flights from Wilson Airport to domestic airports and airstrips around Kenya. Charter flights and helicopter flights are easily available, and can be booked directly with the airline or through a travel agent.

The railway links Nairobi to Mombasa. The train travels at night, leaving Nairobi and Mombasa alternate evenings. There are three classes: first class has 2-bed compartments, second class has 4-bed compartments, while third class has seats.

The roads linking major towns are suitable for 2WD vehicles. More remote roads, including all roads in northern Kenya, require 4WD vehicles. The roads in most national parks, reserves and conservancies also require 4WD vehicles.

BANKING

The currency of Kenya is the shilling. In tourist destinations, American dollars are accepted, although dollar bills printed before the year 2000 are not accepted in Kenya. British pounds and Euros are also widely accepted. Visa and MasterCard are the most extensively accepted credit cards, but other credit cards are accepted in some places.

Local and international banks operate in all major towns. Banking hours are between 9am and 3pm, and the first and last Saturday of each month between 9am and 11am.

A few banks also operate outside these hours. ATM machines are found at airports, banks and shopping centres, and operate 24 hours; many accept inter-

Karibu Kenya Accommodation Guide

national credit cards. Foreign exchange bureaus are found in most towns. All banks, and many hotels, also offer foreign exchange service.

Communication

Travellers are advised to convert any excess Kenya shillings into foreign currency at a bank or foreign exchange bureau before leaving the country. Anyone wishing to take more than 500,000 Kenya shillings out of the country requires written authorisation from the Central Bank.

COMMUNICATIONS
Mobile telephone network and internet service providers cover much of the country. Most hotels and lodges offer international telephone, fax and internet services. Business centres and cyber cafes are found in all major towns. The international country code is +254. There are post offices, known locally as posta, in most towns. Post restante services are available in Nairobi and Mombasa.

MEDICAL
There are a number of good hospitals in Nairobi. There are also hospitals in major towns, and medical clinics in rural areas. African Medical and Research Foundation, AMREF, provides an excellent air evacuation service for medical emergencies throughout the country. Contact www.amref.org for more details.

Malaria is found throughout the country, although malaria transmission at altitudes of over 1,520 meters is rare. Travellers should consult their doctor before travelling, for advice on the most recent prophylactics. Yellow fever vaccination certificates may be required at immigration, if visitors are entering Kenya from an infected country.

KENYA'S ATTRACTIONS
Although it is known worldwide for its safari industry, Kenya has much wider appeal than this would suggest. Other highlights include pre-historic excavations, well preserved ruins, cultural diversity, mountains, adventure sports and water sports. There are also a number of unique festivals that take place annually.

Kenya boasts one of the longest and most complete records of man's cultural development in the world. Excavations in the Tugen Hills near Lake Baringo have exposed some of the earliest fossil beds. Other fascinating sites are found in Sibiloi National Park on the shores of Lake Turkana, at Hyrax Hill and Kariandusi near Nakuru, on Rusinga Island in Lake Victoria and at Olorgesailie near Lake Magadi.

Striking and atmospheric ruins date back to earlier civilisations that flourished during the emergence of the Indian Ocean trade routes. Gede, near Watamu, was at the peak of its prosperity from the 13th to the 17th centuries, then was mysteriously abandoned. Stories abound of ghosts and inexplicable happenings in the area. Takwa, on Manda Island near Lamu, also thrived for centuries before being abandoned in the 17th century. Malindi, Lamu and Mombasa all have Old Towns which are both genuine historic towns and current-day functioning urban centres.

Each of the 42 tribes of Kenya has its own culture and traditions. The Maasai, Kenya's best known tribe, have a reputation for being warriors, and are recognised worldwide for their vivid red garments and exotic beaded jewellery. The El Molo are the least numerous of Kenya's tribes, and traditionally hunt fish, crocodile and hippo in Lake Turkana. The nomadic Rendille rely on camels for food, milk, clothing, trade and transport. The coastal Swahili have cultural ties to the Arabs and Persians. The Kalenjin are most famous for producing Kenya's marathon-winning athletes. A growing number of tour operators offer cultural safaris that include interaction, or volunteer work, with local people.

Kenya boasts two of Africa's five highest mountains. Mt Kenya, Africa's second highest mountain, offers spectacular trekking and climbing. Mt Elgon, Africa's fourth highest mountain, also has stunning viewpoints and interesting climbs. Other mountains and hills that offer exciting trekking and walking include Mt Longonot, the Aberdare National Park, the Cherangani hills and Marich Pass.

Adventure tourism is diversifying across the country. White water rafting is offered on both the Tana and Athi Rivers. Rock climbing, camel safaris, horse riding, game bird shooting, caving and fishing are available at a number of places. The coast provides a wealth of water sports, including scuba diving, water-skiing, kite surfing, windsurfing and jet skiing.

ANNUAL CULTURAL FESTIVALS

Maulidi Festival: Lamu
Prophet Mohammed's birthday
Maulidi is the popular name given to Milad-un-Nabi, an Islamic festival held during the third month of the Muslim calendar to celebrate the birth of the prophet Mohammed. The main religious celebrations take place in and around the Riyadha Mosque. This colourful festival also includes a swimming race and a donkey race.

Rhino Charge: variable locations
Last weekend in May
A cross-country off-road rally, Rhino Charge sees modified vehicles racing between checkpoints in harsh and challenging terrain. The chosen venue is announced only a few days before the event. The site has campsites, food stalls and bars, and hosts the infamous post-charge party. This charitable event supports the endangered rhino in the Aberdare National Park and around Kenya. www.rhinocharge.co.ke

Rhino Charge

Lewa Marathon: Lewa Wildlife Conservancy
Last weekend in June
A challenging, high altitude marathon, Lewa Marathon sees runners from around the world attempt the half or full marathon. This charitable event is sponsored by Safaricom, and supports education, health, community development and wildlife conservation projects across Kenya. www.lewa.org/support-lewa/safaricom-marathon

Maralal International Camel Derby: Maralal
First weekend in August
The finest camels in northern Kenya come together for this eagerly anticipated event. The weekend also has cycling races, children's donkey rides, traditional dancing displays and curio stalls.

Safari Sevens: Nairobi, Nyayo Stadium
First weekend in November
Africa's premier Rugby Sevens tournament, the Safari Sevens is an international event. www.safarisevens.kenyarfu.com

Lamu Cultural Festival: Lamu
Last weekend in November
Celebrating the history and culture of this unique Swahili island, the Lamu Cultural Festival showcases traditional dancing, poetry competitions, donkey races, dhow races, traditional handicrafts, photography exhibitions and a Swahili food bazaar.

RESPONSIBLE TOURISM

In order to ensure a high quality holiday with low environmental impact, it is recommended that transport, accommodation and activities are booked only with reputable operators and qualified safari guides.

The associations listed below provide vital certification that protects visitors to Kenya, conserves Kenya's environment and supports local communities.

THE KENYA ASSOCIATION OF TOUR OPERATORS, KATO
The Kenya Association of Tour Operators represents over 250 of the leading and most experienced professional tour operators in Kenya. The association provides a mechanism that ensures Kenyan tour operators maintain the highest standards of service and value.
Visitors to Kenya wishing to book travel, accommodation and safaris through a registered KATO member should go to www.katokenya.org

ECOTOURISM SOCIETY OF KENYA, ESOK
Ecotourism Society of Kenya certifies tourism establishments and community based tourism initiatives according to their sustainable tourism practices. The society promotes concern for the environment and the welfare of local populations. Certification is bronze, silver and gold.
Visitors to Kenya wishing to get the current list of ESOK-certified tourism establishments should go to www.ecotourismkenya.org

THE KENYA PROFESSIONAL SAFARI GUIDE ASSOCIATION, KPSGA
The Kenya Professional Safari Guide Association provides certification for safari guides, naturalists and individuals in the tourism sector. Individuals certified by KPSGA are not only knowledgeable in their own specific field, but in first aid, mechanical skills, etiquette and client safety. Certification is bronze, silver and gold.
Visitors to Kenya wishing to get the current list of KPSGA-certified guides should go to www.safariguides.org

SAFARI

Kenya's extraordinarily varied topology provides the range of habitats needed to support equally varied wildlife. The country is home to more than 100 species of mammals, more than 1,000 species of birds, and an incredible diversity of reptiles, insects and amphibians.

All the famous Big Five - lion, leopard, elephant, buffalo and rhino - are found here. Having attained notoriety during the hunting era for being the most prestigious trophies, the Big Five have retained their popularity into today's photographic safaris.

However, the diversity of mammal species in Kenya goes far beyond these. Carnivores found here include cheetah, wild cat, caracal, serval, hyena, civet, genet, jackal and fox. Primates include vervet monkey, blue monkey, sykes monkey, colobus monkey and bushbaby. Plains game includes wildebeest, hartebeest, zebra, giraffe, Grant's gazelle, Thomson's gazelle, bushbuck, waterbuck, eland, impala, reedbuck and dikdik.

The country has a high number of endemic species, as well as species found only in one specific location. Some national parks and reserves are the last remaining habitat of a particular species, such as the roan antelope in Ruma National Park, the sitatunga in Saiwa Swamp National Park and the Sable antelope in Shimba Hills National Reserve.

There are high numbers of endangered species. The current list of critically endangered species includes black rhino, hirola, Tana River red colobus, Cosen's gerbil and Macow's shrew. A number of sanctuaries have been established around the country to protect these species.

Many of Kenya's vast variety of birds are indigenous to specific regions of the country. Highland forest and moorlands such as Mt Kenya, Mt Elgon and the Aberdare National Park attract green ibis, Hartlaub's turaco, mountane oriole, alpine chat, Sharpe's longclaw and mountain buzzard. Savannah bush such as the Tsavo East and Tsavo West National Parks attracts ostrich, white-bellied go-away bird, green wood hoopoe, Taita fiscal, buff-crested bustard and martial eagle. Savannah grasslands such as the Maasai Mara National Reserve species include gabon nightjar, lilac-breasted roller, Livingstone's turaco, blue flycatcher and Pel's fishing owl.

Alkaline lakes attract such large numbers of lesser flamingo that their water appears pink. Freshwater lakes have a wider diversity, with white pelican, long tailed cormorant, goliath heron, squacco heron, African spoonbill, fish eagle and malachite kingfishers being but a few of the species found here.

Lowland forest attracts some very localised birds, including cuckoo hawk, red-tailed ant thrush and amani sunbird. Desert and semi-desert, particularly in the area of Lake Turkana, attracts the hardy fox kestrel, Abyssinian roller and Somali fiscal.

Kenya has a remarkable number of endemic or near endemic species, such as Clarke's weaver, found only in the Arabuko Sokoke Forest near Watamu and Hinde's pied babbler, found only in Kianyaga near Embu. Some birds even take their names from the regions of Kenya in which they are found, such as the grey-chested illadopsis, or Kakamega poliothorax, found only in Kakamega.

In addition to all the resident species, an estimated 6,000 migratory birds make the journey to Kenya each year during the winter in Europe.

The marine parks along Kenya's coast are home to a large array of marine species. Coral gardens, fringing reefs, mudflats, mangroves, sea grass and sea weed are all found here, and each provides habitat specific to certain species including dolphins, fish, crabs, sea urchins, sea cucumbers, starfish and jellyfish. Rare and vulnerable species include the dugong, humpback whale and sperm whale.

PARK FEES

Park fees are charged in all wildlife areas of Kenya. These contribute to conservation and wildlife protection projects. Park fees can be paid on entry, at either a gate or an airstrip, or can be included in the total package and paid prior to arrival.

Kenya's national parks are managed by Kenya Wildlife Service, KWS. A current list of KWS park fees can be found at www.kws.go.ke

Kenya's national reserves, conservancies and group ranches determine their own park fees and should be contacted individually for current rates.

THE WILDLIFE CODE

- Respect the privacy of the wildlife, this is their habitat
- Beware of the animals, they are wild and can be unpredictable
- Don't crowd the animals or make sudden noises or movements
- Don't feed the animals, it upsets their diet and leads to human dependence
- Keep quiet, noise disturbs the wildlife and may antagonise your fellow visitors
- Stay in your vehicle at all times, except at designated picnic or walking areas
- Keep below the maximum speed limit (40kph or 25mph)
- Never drive off-road, this severely damages the habitat
- When viewing wildlife keep to a minimum distance of 20 meters and pull to the side of the road so as to allow others to pass
- Leave no litter and never leave fires unattended or discard burning objects
- Respect the cultural heritage of Kenya. Never take pictures of the local people or their habitat without asking their permission. Respect the cultural traditions of Kenya and always dress with decorum
- Stay over or leave before dusk. Visitors must vacate national parks between 7pm and 6am unless they are camping overnight Night game driving is not permitted in national parks

 Karibu Kenya Accommodation Guide

Icon Legend

PRICE BRACKETS

- under 100 US $
- 100 – 250 US $
- 250 – 400 US $
- 400 – 600 US $
- 600 US $ and above

FACILITIES

- Credit cards
- Airstrip
- Swimming pool
- Spa - full
- Bush spa - limited treatments
- Hair and beauty salon
- Tennis courts
- Golf course
- Parking
- Aircon
- Laundry
- Gift shop
- Art gallery
- Library
- Safe
- Mini bar
- Fitness centre / Gym
- Conference facilities
- Business centre
- Internet
- WiFi
- Telephone
- Intercom in rooms
- Bureau de Change
- Weddings

- Disabled facilities
- 24-hour hot running water
- Bucket showers
- TV
- Satellite TV
- Children welcome
- Children's activities
- Babysitting facilities
- Yoga
- Beach access
- Medical clinic
- Flying doctors for guests
- Fly camp / Campsite
- Casino

SAFARI

- Game drives
- Game walks
- Night drives
- Visits to local villages
- KPSGA guides
- Scenic flights
- Helicopter
- Hide
- Bush meals
- 4WD vehicles
- Open sided vehicles
- Self drive game drives

ADVENTURE SPORTS

- Hiking
- Balloon
- Horse riding
- Camel riding
- Rafting / Canoeing

- Mountain climbing
- Mountain biking
- Bicycle hire

WATER SPORTS

- Scuba
- Water-skiing
- Fishing
- Kayaking
- Jetsking
- Kite surfing
- Boat trips
- Sailing
- Snorkeling
- Windsurfing
- Swimming in river / ocean
- Boating
- Boat rental

DINING

- A la carte
- Snack menu
- Seated all together, safari style
- Full board
- Half board
- Bed and Breakfast
- Buffet
- Self catering
- Room service
- Accommodation only

GREEN

- ESOK certified
- Eco-friendly
- Solar power
- Community development projects

 Accommodation Guide

Nairobi

Nairobi City Centre – Photo © Andrew Nightingale, kembu.com

Nairobi is a thriving, cosmopolitan hub of government offices, embassies, businesses, banks, churches, mosques, temples, shops, restaurants and markets. Attractions include the National Museum, Railway Museum, National Archives, Karen Blixen Museum and Bomas of Kenya. Nairobi is the world's only capital city to boast a national park within its boundaries.

Nairobi is derived from the Maasai word Ewaso Naiberi, meaning place of cool water. The town grew up around the railhead, during the building of the railway from Mombasa to Lake Victoria in the late 1890s. Nairobi was the centre of the British Colonial Administration, and since independence in 1963 has been the seat of Kenyan Government.

The Central Business District, CBD, is the pulsating heart of the city. Upper Hill is home to businesses and administrative offices. Gigiri is the site of the huge United Nations Regional Headquarters, and a number of embassies. Muthaiga, with its legendary colonial Country Club, is a prime residential area. Westlands is a vibrant hub of shopping centres, cinemas, galleries, restaurants and nightlife. Karen, named for Karen Blixen, borders Nairobi National Park.

Jomo Kenyatta International Airport, named for Kenya's first president, lies southeast of the city centre. Wilson Airport, Africa's largest light aircraft airport, is on Langata Road. Nairobi Railway Station is in the city centre. Public transport is by minibuses, known locally as matatus. Taxis are available throughout the city, and can be booked privately or called by any hotel reception.

The National Museum of Kenya was established in 1910 in a single room. It was relocated to its current site on Museum Hill in 1930, and completely refurbished between 2005 and 2007. There are excellent exhibitions on archaeological excavations, hominid fossils, ethnography, rock art, wildlife and birdlife. The Railway Museum details the building of the railway. Built between 1896 and 1901, the railway claimed the lives of nearly 2,500 labourers, earning it the nickname the Lunatic Express. Exhibits include a display on the notorious Man Eaters of Tsavo. The National Archives of Kenya houses historical documents dating back to Britain's colonisation of Kenya and the Mau Mau fight for independence. Contemporary art, historical photos and cultural artefacts are on display.

Karen Blixen, who farmed coffee in Kenya from 1913 to 1931, was most famous for her iconic memoirs Out of Africa. Her farmhouse and garden are now a well-preserved historical museum. Bomas of Kenya introduces visitors to Kenyan traditions and culture. Dancers and artists perform traditional dances and songs belonging to the various tribal groups.

Nairobi National Park was gazetted in 1946, and has grass plains, highland dry forest and a permanent river with riverine forest. Wildlife includes black rhino, lion, leopard, cheetah, hyena, buffalo, giraffe, zebra and wildebeest; over 400 species of birds have been recorded. Park gates are Main Gate, Langata, Cheetah and Maasai; picnic sites are at Mokoyiet, Kingfisher and Impala.

The David Sheldrick Wildlife Trust, on the edge of Nairobi National Park, raises orphaned elephants and black rhinos. Visitors are welcome at 11am; the site has an information centre and gift shop. The Giraffe Centre, in nearby Langata, is a breeding centre for endangered Rothschild giraffes. Giraffes can be fed by hand from a raised wooden structure.

KaribuKenya Accommodation Guide

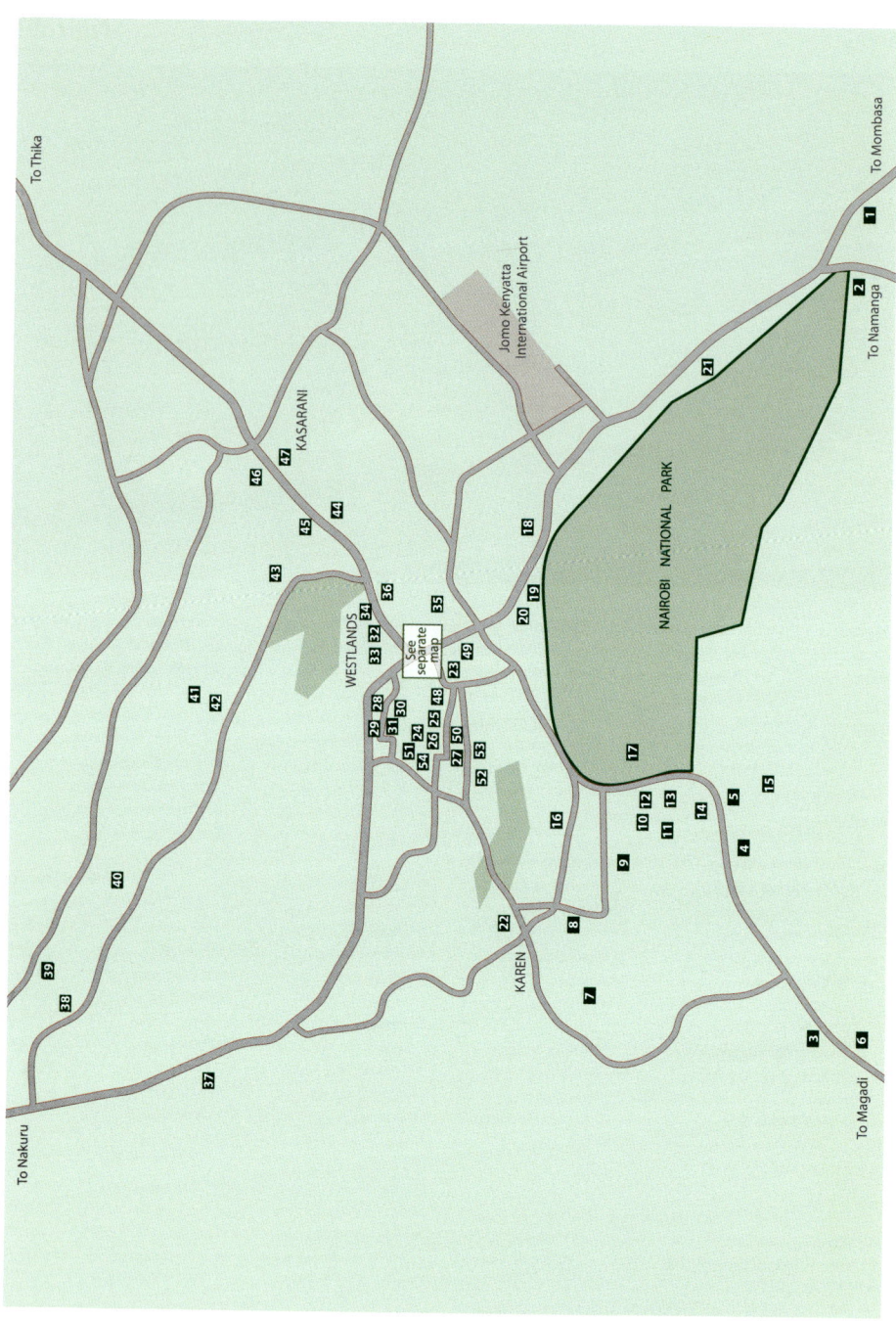

Index to all lodges and hotels in the greater Nairobi area

#	Name	#	Name
1	Acacia Camp	40	Kentmere Club
2	Maasai Ostrich Resort	41	Boni House
3	Osoita Lodge	42	Tribe
4	Gray's Oak Hotel	43	Windsor Golf and Country Club
5	Sandalwood	44	Utalii Hotel
6	Whistling Thorns	45	Hotel La Mada
7	Ngong Bounty Hotel	46	Safari Park Hotel
8	Karen Blixen Coffee Garden	47	Sportsview Hotel
9	House of Waine	48	Hill Park Hotel
10	Giraffe Manor	49	Crowne Plaza
11	Macushla House	50	Gemina Court
12	Rock House	51	Woodmere
13	Ngong House	52	Wildebeest Camp
14	Hogmead	53	Ngong Hills Hotel
15	Silole Sanctuary	54	Trisan Hotel
16	Nairobi Mamba Village		
17	Nairobi Tented Camp		
18	Panari Hotel		
19	Ole Sereni		
20	RedCourt Hotel		
21	African Heritage House		
22	Country House Inn		
23	Silver Springs Hotel		
24	Palacina Suites		
25	Olive Gardens Hotel		
26	The Methodist Guest House & Conference Centre		
27	Sandavy Guest House		
28	New HillCrest Hotel		
29	The King Post		
30	The Gables		
31	PrideInn Hotel Nairobi		
32	Sankara		
33	Jacaranda Hotel		
34	Southern Sun Mayfair		
35	Milele Hotel		
36	Hennessis Hotel		
37	Wida Highway Motel		
38	Jumuia Conference and Country Home, Nairobi		
39	Brackenhurst Conference Centre		

KaribuKenya Accommodation Guide

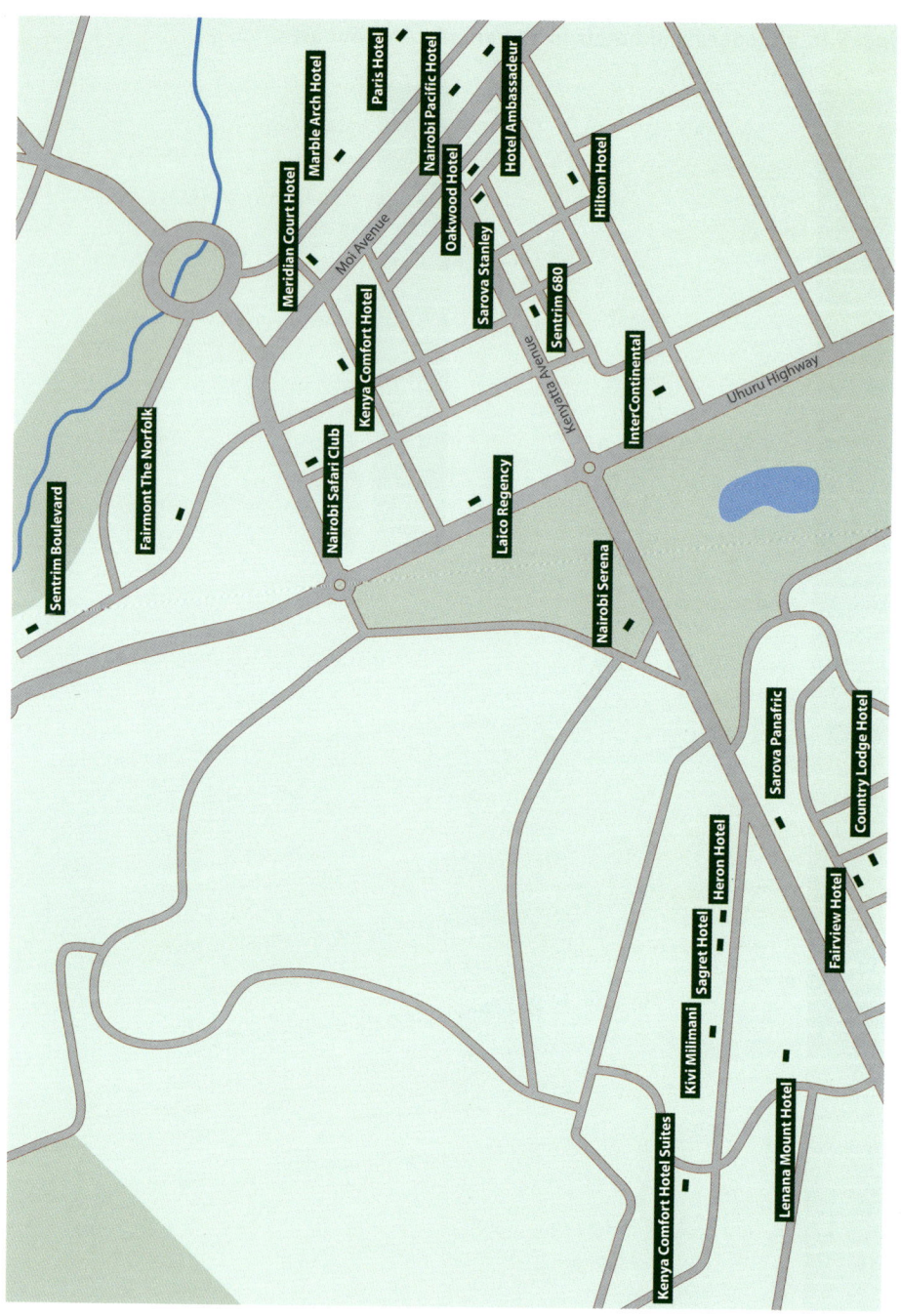

Acacia Camp

Swara Plains

Acacia Camp, Swara Plains Wildlife Sanctuary, nr Nairobi, Kenya
PO Box 47272, Nairobi 00100, Kenya

Tel	+254 20 529500
Mobile	+254 733 812556; +254 733 912994
Fax	
E-mail	acaciacamp@yahoo.com / raine@swiftkenya.com
Web	www.swaraplains.com

   JKIA, LS & CH & Intl., 40 mins
Wilson Airport, LS & CH, 1 hr

A rustic little camp, Acacia Camp is situated on Swara Plains Wildlife Sanctuary, a 20,000-acre private ranch on the Kapiti Plains. Opposite Lukenya Hill, the ranch has gently rolling terrain with the immense views that are so much a part of the high savannah.

Both Mt Kenya to the north and Mt Kilimanjaro to the south are visible from the ranch. Fully fenced, the ranch boasts a resident population of over 3,000 game animals. Giraffe, wildebeest, eland, oryx, zebra, kongoni and impala are plentiful while night drives can reveal other more elusive animals such as the Verreaux eagle owl, honey badger, aardvark, porcupine and spring hare. Birdlife is plentiful with over 270 species identified on the ranch.

Acacia Camp has rustic but comfortable accommodation. There are 13 bandas, all en-suite. The main mess area is open with views of the garden. The conservationist David Hopcraft began experiments on Swara Plains, with the support of Cornell University and the National Science Foundation, to understand the relationship between wildlife and healthy rangelands. Duma, a Warner Bros feature film, is based on Hopcraft's story. Swara Plains is also the home of the award winning children's bestseller, How It Was With Dooms.

Maasai Ostrich Resort

Kitengela

Maasai Ostrich Resort, Kitengela, nr Nairobi, Kenya
Merica Group Hotels, PO Box 72693, Nairobi 00200, Kenya

Tel	+254 20 2502128; +254 20 2502129
Mobile	
Fax	+254 20 3540014
E-mail	maasaiostrich@mericagrouphotels.com
Web	www.mericagrouphotels.com

VISA, travellers cheques JKIA, LS & CH & Intl., 30 mins
Wilson Airport, LS & CH, 1 hr

The Ostrich Farm has been supplying Kenya and other countries with meat, feathers, skins and livestock since 1991. Set in 200 acres of rolling grasslands, the Maasai Ostrich Resort is located at the farm, near Athi River and the Kitengela Plains.

The resort has 40 rooms, made up of singles, doubles and family cottages, surrounded by gardens. The restaurant serves an international buffet for breakfast, lunch and dinner. Guests can choose from the a la carte menu of Italian, Indian, Chinese and African dishes if they prefer. The Mbuna Choma Ranch serves grilled meats in the garden around the pool. The speciality is, of course, char-grilled ostrich, famous for its low cholesterol.

The bar has a TV showing sports and news. The 4 conference rooms can accommodate between 15 and 150 people and are ideal for seminars, workshops, weddings, conventions and social and cultural events. The conference rooms are equipped with state of the art audio visual equipment, including PA systems, projectors and WiFi.

Activities include a tour of the ostrich farm, and riding ostriches. A resident naturalist is available to take guests on game walks and bird walks. Game drives in Nairobi National Park can also be arranged.

Osoita Lodge

Langata

Osoita Lodge, Nazarene University Road, off Magadi Road, Langata
PO Box 407, Nairobi 00517, Kenya
Tel
Mobile +254 722 527476; +254 721 294607; +254 751 527476
Fax
E-mail osoitalodge@yahoo.com / osoitalodge@gmail.com
Web www.osoitalodge.com

 VISA, MasterCard   JKIA, LS & CH & Intl., 45 mins
Wilson Airport, LS & CH, 20 mins

In a tranquil, lush environment, Osoita Lodge has lovely views of the surrounding countryside. The lodge welcomes conferences, family lunches, exhibitions, seminars, weddings, private parties and teambuilding activities. There are 16 en-suite rooms, with balconies overlooking the swimming pool. The restaurant has an international menu, including barbecues, Indian and continental cuisine. It serves both buffet and a la carte. The terrace, adjoining the restaurant, has outdoor seating and overlooks a seasonal river that borders the lodge. There is also a Choma Hut, serving nyama choma grilled meats, and 4 spacious bandas available for karoga self-catering.

The large lounge area next to the swimming pool is ideal for pool parties. There is also a spa that offers facials and other treatments. The playground provides entertainment for children. The conference hall seats 100 pax. The lodge is located near the deep gorges of Mbagathi River, and adjoins Nairobi National Park. Places of interest in Nairobi include the Nairobi National Museum and Railway Museum in the centre of town, and the Giraffe Centre, Sheldrick Elephant Orphanage, Karen Blixen Museum and Nairobi National Park in Karen and Langata.

Gray's Oak Hotel

Kitengela

Gray's Oak Hotel, Namanga Road, Kitengela, nr Nairobi, Kenya
PO Box 104, Kitengela 00242, Kenya
Tel
Mobile +254 722 331514; +254 733 633702; +254 728 008016
Fax
E-mail info@graysoak.com / sales@graysoak.com
Web www.graysoak.com

 VISA, MasterCard    JKIA, LS & CH & Intl., 45 mins
Wilson Airport, LS & CH, 45 mins

Established in 2010, Gray's Oak Hotel offers modern accommodation and conferencing facilities in the heart of Kitengela. The hotel is not far from Nairobi, and within easy reach of Nairobi National Park and Swara Conservancy. There are 37 en-suite rooms, made up of standard, superior and deluxe. The rooms are equipped with satellite TV, cupboard, table and mosquito net. The restaurant serves an international a la carte menu, including spicy chicken wings, fish fillet with tartar sauce, T-bone steak, spaghetti bolognaise and nyama choma grilled meats. There are 2 bars, a pool bar beside the swimming pool and a lounge bar on the 3rd floor. Both serve a selection of soft drinks, beers, wines and spirits.

The barista, an open air terrace café, serves breakfast, light snacks and coffee. The spacious gardens are ideal for weddings, teambuilding and private functions. There are 4 conference halls, with a seating capacity ranging from 5 pax to 150 pax. All halls are equipped with conference equipment including projector and PA system. A full range of business services including photocopy and typing are available at reception. WiFi is available throughout the hotel.
The hotel can arrange airport transfers and taxis. Game drives in Nairobi National Park and game walks in Swara Conservancy are also available.

Sandalwood

Kitengela

Sandalwood, Namanga Road, Kitengela, nr Nairobi, Kenya
PO Box 156, Athi River 00204, Kenya

Tel	+254 20 2693303
Mobile	+254 713 737294
Fax	
E-mail	sandalwoodkitengela@gmail.com
Web	www.sandalwoodhotels.net

 VISA, MasterCard   JKIA, LS & CH & Intl., 45 mins
Wilson Airport, LS & CH, 45 mins

Sandalwood was established in 2008. The hotel offers a selection of accommodation, dining and conferencing facilities in attractive gardens. There are 26 en-suite rooms, made up of doubles and twins. All rooms are equipped with satellite TV, kettle, table, chairs and mosquito net. There are 2 restaurants; 1 restaurant serves a rodizio menu, with a selection of Brazilian style grilled meats, and the other serves an international a la carte menu. There are 2 bars, 1 at the poolside and the other adjoining the restaurant. Both bars serve soft drinks, beers, wines and spirits. The swimming pool is surrounded by sunbathing terrace furnished with sunbeds and shade umbrellas.

There are 3 conference halls. The largest hall seats 150 pax, the next seats 50 and the boardroom seats 20. All halls are equipped with conference equipment including projector and PA system. The large garden is suitable for weddings and functions.

The hotel can arrange airport transfers and taxis on request. Game drives in Nairobi National Park can also be arranged. The hotel is affiliated to Paradise Hotel in Kikambala on the north coast.

Whistling Thorns

Kiserian

Whistling Thorns, Pipeline Road, off Magadi Road, Kiserian, Kenya
PO Box 517, Kiserian 00206, Kenya

Tel	+254 20 3540720
Mobile	+254 722 721933; +254 733 703637
Fax	
E-mail	scs@iconnect.co.ke
Web	www.whistlingthorn.com

     JKIA, LS & CH & Intl., 1.5 hrs
Wilson Airport, LS & CH, 1 hr

Whistling Thorns is in attractive and peaceful gardens, with views of the Ngong Hills. The hotel offers cottages and camping, and has a variety of activities. There are 3 en-suite cottages, each with a veranda overlooking the garden. All cottages have a king size double and single bed. There are 7 en-suite standard twin rooms. All rooms overlook the Ngong Hills. There are 3 luxury en-suite tents in a private, secluded location. There is also a campsite with designated fireplaces. The compound has a swimming pool, golf driving range and a playground with tree house, bouncy castle and swings. The restaurant has a Kenyan and international menu. Specialities include homemade pizzas and nyama choma grilled meats. Other dishes include balsamic mushroom bruschetta, Swahili coconut chicken with basmati rice, oven baked red snapper, vegetable moussaka and T-bone steak with herb butter. The bar serves soft drinks, beers, wines and spirits. Activities include horse riding and guided game walks. Bird watching is recommended. Massage, manicure and pedicure are on offer. Cultural visits to a local Maasai village are available. Birthday parties, staff parties, teambuilding and retreats can all be arranged, with a choice of nyama choma grilled meats or buffet. Special Camping Safaris Ltd can arrange camping safaris around Kenya.

Ngong Bounty Hotel

Ngong

Ngong Bounty Hotel, opp Ngong Stadium, Ngong, Nairobi, Kenya
PO Box 613, Ngong 02008, Kenya

Tel	+254 45 41571; +254 20 2069599
Mobile	+254 715 069547
Fax	+254 45 41572
E-mail	ngongbountyhotel@gmail.com
Web	

   JKIA, LS & CH & Intl, 1 hr
Wilson Airport, LS & CH, 45 mins

At the foot of the Ngong Hills, Ngong Bounty Hotel is ideally situated for anyone wanting to hike the seven peaks of the hills. It is also convenient for attractions in the Karen district of Nairobi, such as the Sheldrick Elephant Orphanage, the Giraffe Centre, Karen Blixen Museum and Nairobi National Park.

There are 30 en-suite rooms, made up of singles, doubles and executive rooms. All rooms are equipped with satellite TV and telephone.

The restaurant serves local and international dishes including beef stroganoff, chicken curry, fresh fish and nyama choma grilled meats. Buffet is available on request and outside catering is also on offer. The bar is fully stocked with soft drinks, beers, wines, spirits and liqueurs, and is equipped with satellite TV.

The soundproof conference hall seats 200 pax, and is available for meetings, seminars, training programmes, product launches and cocktail parties. The hotel also has a health club with a fully equipped gym, a cyber café and a secure car park. A safety deposit box at reception is available for guests to deposit their valuables.

Karen Blixen Coffee Garden

Karen

Karen Blixen Coffee Garden, 336 Karen Road, Karen, Nairobi, Kenya
PO Box 163, Nairobi 00502, Kenya

Tel	+254 20 3517804; +254 20 2130464
Mobile	+254 733 616206
Fax	+254 20 882508
E-mail	info@karenblixencoffeegarden.com
Web	www.karenblixencoffeegarden.com

 VISA, MasterCard    JKIA, LS & CH & Intl, 40 mins
Wilson Airport, LS & CH, 20 mins

On the original estate of the Swedo African Coffee Company, the Karen Blixen Coffee Garden is a lush, manicured garden with a history stretching back to the early days of last century. The Swedo House, built in about 1908, was the farm manager's house for the Blixen Coffee Plantation, owned by Bror Blixen and his wife Karen Blixen of Out of Africa fame. The Grogan / McMillan Manor House was built in 1905 by Ewart Grogan, famed for walking from Cape to Cairo to win a lady's hand, and sold in 1910 to Northrup McMillan whose wife built the first library in Kenya. Both houses have been fully restored, and are adorned with photos of early settlers. The 16 en-suite rooms are in cottages with fireplaces and verandas overlooking the gardens. A gym and spa are also on site.

Meals can be served alfresco in the gardens, on the veranda or by the pool. For those who prefer to eat indoors, there are the Lion's Den Bistro Restaurant and the Sports Bar. More formal events can be arranged in the Swedo House or the Grogan / McMillan House. The Grand Sultan Marquee Tent is ideal for weddings, functions or fund raising events.

 Accommodation Guide

House of Waine

Karen

House of Waine, Masai Lane, off Bogani Road, Karen, Nairobi, Kenya
PO Box 25035, Nairobi 00603, Kenya

Tel	+254 20 2601455-7
Mobile	+254 734 699973
Fax	+254 20 892091
E-mail	reservations@houseofwaine.co.ke
Web	www.houseofwaine.com

 VISA, MasterCard, Amex   JKIA, LS & CH & Intl., 40 mins
Wilson Airport, LS & CH, 20 mins

The boutique hotel, House of Waine, is in Karen, the leafy suburb of Nairobi that takes its name from Karen Blixen of Out of Africa fame, who lived here from 1913 to 1931. A large colonial mansion set in sculptured gardens, House of Waine is less than 2km from Karen Blixen's house, which is now a museum.

There are 11 en-suite rooms on 2 floors, each elegantly furnished to reflect their individual themes. All the rooms have direct dial telephones, internet, minibars and satellite TV, and 9 have separate bath and shower, request on booking if required.

Breakfast, lunch and afternoon tea are served on the terrace or in the garden, while dinner is served in the dining room to the accompaniment of Afro Jazz. The cuisine is all made from the freshest ingredients, and meals are treated as a culinary experience. The lounge and the pool bar serve drinks throughout.

Guests can relax in the gardens, or do a variety of activities and excursions. House of Waine is near the Nairobi National Park, the Giraffe Centre, the Sheldrick Elephant Orphanage, Karen Blixen Museum and Karen Country Club. Trips elsewhere in Nairobi can also be arranged.

Giraffe Manor

Langata

Giraffe Manor, Langata, Nairobi, Kenya
The Safari Collection, PO Box 15565, Nairobi 00503, Kenya

Tel	+254 20 5020888
Mobile	+254 731 914732; +254 725 675830
Fax	
E-mail	info@giraffemanor.com / info@thesafaricollection.com
Web	www.giraffemanor.com / www.thesafaricollection.com

JKIA, LS & CH & Intl.
Wilson Airport, LS & CH

Famous for its resident herd of Rothschild giraffe, Giraffe Manor is the only place in the world where guests can enjoy the experience of feeding and photographing giraffes over the breakfast table and at the front door. An elegant, personally hosted hotel, Giraffe Manor is situated in the Nairobi suburb of Langata.

Giraffe Manor was built in 1932 by David Duncan of the Macintosh Toffee family and is modelled on a Scottish hunting lodge. In 1974, 2 highly endangered Rothschild giraffes were moved onto the estate and became the founders of today's herd. Giraffe Manor was opened to the public in 1984 and in 2009 became part of the Tamimi portfolio of camps and lodges.

Set in 140 acres of indigenous forest, the manor has views of Mt Kilimanjaro and the Ngong Hills. The site also includes the Giraffe Centre where visitors can climb to the level of a giraffe's head and feed him eye to eye. Profits from the centre go to various projects in Kenya. There are 2 double rooms, 3 twin rooms and a family suite. All rooms are en-suite, and elegantly furnished. The rooms are equipped with torch, hairdryer, nail kit and WiFi. Excursions to sites in and around Nairobi can be arranged.

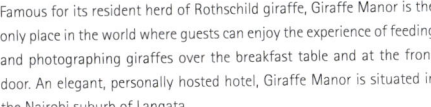 Accommodation Guide

Macushla House Langata

Macushla House, nr Giraffe Centre, Langata, Nairobi, Kenya
PO Box 42510, Nairobi 00100, Kenya

Tel	+254 20 891987
Mobile	+254 733 706178; +254 722 329863
Fax	+254 20 891971
E-mail	macushla@africaonline.co.ke
Web	www.macushla.biz

 VISA   JKIA, LS & CH & Intl., 40 mins
Wilson Airport, LS & CH, 20 mins

Macushla, Gaelic for my beloved, was the name chosen by the founder of Macushla House, whose desire was to welcome those seeking the natural joys of life. Charmed by the warmth and hospitality of the Irish on a visit to the Emerald Isle in the last century, he wanted to recreate this spirit of openness in Nairobi.

Macushla House has been described as a country inn close to Nairobi. It can comfortably accommodate 12 guests in 6 en-suite bedrooms. There are 2 lounges with covered verandas and fireplaces, furnished with an eclectic mix of artifacts from countries as far afield as Yemen and Australia. The house also has a small bar and a restaurant. The swimming pool, set in lush indigenous bush, is home to a water fountain dragon and rings to the tune of wind chimes and bird song. The garden and its immediate surroundings have been left to nature.

Macushla House, in the suburb of Langata, is within easy reach of Nairobi National Park, the Giraffe Centre, the Sheldrick Elephant Orphanage, the Karen Blixen Museum and Karen shops. Excursions to these and other destinations can all be organised on request.

Rock House Langata

Rock House, Ndovu Road, Langata, Nairobi, Kenya
PO Box 15796, Nairobi 00100, Kenya

Tel	+254 20 2242133
Mobile	+254 722 511752
Tel/ Fax	+254 20 2210051
E-mail	info@mountainrockkenya.com
Web	www.mountainrockkenya.com

 VISA, MasterCard    JKIA, LS & CH & Intl., 40 mins
Wilson Airport, LS & CH, 20 mins

Rock House was designed by a local architect to reflect its link with its sister hotel, Mountain Rock Lodge, on the rocky slopes of Mt Kenya. The landscaped gardens have been designed to replicate a mountain environment. A large-scale model of Mt Kenya has been built into the grounds, with climbing routes etched into it. Guests intending to climb the mountain can use this to plan their route, and can book mountain treks here.

There are 6 en-suite rooms, made up of 1 single and 5 doubles. All rooms are furnished with natural wood furniture. There is also a campsite. WiFi is available throughout the house and grounds. The garden, filled with lush vegetation, tropical flowers and a waterfall, attracts a wide variety of birdlife.

Meals are hosted by the owners. Dishes are created from fresh local ingredients, and guests are welcome to visit the kitchen to learn how to prepare Kenyan cuisine.

Rock House is in the Nairobi suburb of Langata. Nearby attractions within walking distance include the Giraffe Centre, Hardy horse stud farm and Karen health club and swimming pool. Attractions a short drive away include Karen Blixen Museum, Sheldrick Elephant Orphanage and Nairobi National Park. Vehicles and bicycles can be hired here.

Ngong House Karen

Ngong House, Karen, Nairobi, Kenya
PO Box 24963, Nairobi 00502, Kenya

Tel	+254 20 891856; +254 20 890140; +254 20 891296
Mobile	+254 722 434965; +254 733 600184
Fax	+254 20 890674
E-mail	reservations@ngonghouse.co.ke
Web	www.ngonghouse.com

VISA, MasterCard   JKIA, LS & CH & Intl., 40 mins
                    Wilson Airport, LS & CH, 20 mins

Ngong House is an exclusive homestay in 10 acres of gardens. The house was established in 1994, and offers luxury, privacy and personal service. There are 6 tree houses, 2-floor stilt houses of indigenous materials, each with private balcony. These are individually designed, with furniture from Lamu, batiks from Ivory Coast, Kuba cloth from Congo, lace from Belgium and ornaments in the coastal Swahili style. The private cottage, facing the swimming pool, has 2 double bedrooms and spacious seating area with fireplace. The log cabin has 2 double bedrooms, large loft, living room, bar, dining room and fireplace. There is also 1 double room in the main house, with 4-poster bed, seating area, fireplace and veranda. All rooms are equipped with mosquito net, minibar, safe, telephone and hairdryer. Children are welcome; babysitting can be arranged. The business centre has internet.

Sundowners are served around the campfire. Breakfast and lunch are served in the gardens. Dinners can be served in the dining rondavel, main house dining room, main house veranda or private rooms. Ngong House has a range of Penny Winter's fashion and jewellery for sale, designed by Penny on site. Excursions to the Giraffe Centre, Sheldrick Elephant Orphanage, Nairobi National Museum and Karen Blixen Museum are all on offer.

Hogmead Langata

Hogmead, Hog Ranch, nr Giraffe Centre, Langata, Nairobi, Kenya
The Safari and Conservation Company, PO Box 24576, Nairobi 00502, Kenya

Tel	+254 20 6006759; +254 20 2115453
Mobile	+254 712 579999; + 254 735 579999
Fax	+254 20 2194995
E-mail	reservations@scckenya.com
Web	www.hogmead.com

 VISA, MasterCard   JKIA, LS & CH & Intl., 45 mins
                                        Wilson Airport, LS & CH, 25 mins

A boutique hotel, Hogmead is located on the border of the Hog Ranch, part of the Giraffe Centre. Hogmead has luxury accommodation in beautiful gardens, which are home to several families of warthogs. The house is fully hosted and offers personal service.

There are 6 en-suite double rooms, 2 on the ground floor and 4 on the 1st floor. The rooms are elegantly furnished. The house has 3 large sitting areas with lovely views over the grounds into the Giraffe Sanctuary and the Ngong Hills beyond. Food is grown in the kitchen garden or sourced from local farm produce. Lunch is usually a buffet, while dinner is a 3-course meal. The freshly prepared meals can be served in the dining room or under the stars. All dietary requirements can be catered for with advance notice. There is WiFi throughout. The gift shop has a selection of art. Massage, manicures and pedicures can be arranged.

Excursions to sites of interest in Nairobi can be arranged. Game drives in Nairobi National Park, and visits to the Sheldrick Elephant Orphanage and Giraffe Centre are all on offer. Shopping trips and spa visits can also be arranged. Hogmead attained a place in Conde Nast Traveller's Hot List of New Hotels in 2012.

Silole Sanctuary Embakasi

Silole Sanctuary, Embakasi, Nairobi, Kenya
PO Box 938, Nairobi 00502, Kenya

Tel	+254 20 2673686
Mobile	+254 721 646588; +254 723 160888
Fax	
E-mail	info@silolesanctuary.com
Web	www.silolesanctuary.com

  JKIA, LS & CH & Intl., 1.5 hrs
Wilson Airport, LS & CH, 30 mins

Silole Sanctuary, 400 acres of private land adjoining Nairobi National Park, lies between the gorges of the Embakasi and the Kiserian Rivers. The combination of riverine forest, grassland plains and valley thickets here ensures that it is rich in birdlife and flora, and is home to 60 species of mammal.

Masai Lodge, on a cliff overlooking the Embakasi River, has 32 en-suite rooms and cottages. It also has a swimming pool, an a la carte restaurant and conference facilities.

Silole Villa, a 3-bedroom house with views over Nairobi National Park, is set In 6 acres of the sanctuary including Kingfisher Gorge which runs into the Embakasi River. The villa has a well equipped kitchen and a large studio space for children. A chef can be provided on request. Silole Cottage, a 2-bedroom thatched self-catering cottage, is in the middle of the sanctuary. The cottage has loft spaces for children and a veranda overlooking the park.

Activities include walking with or without guides, rock climbing in the gorges, bird watching and game drives in Nairobi National Park. The sanctuary is a community project dedicated to ecotourism. A 2-week field studies course teaches participants about wildlife, conservation and bio-diversity.

Nairobi Mamba Village   Langata

Nairobi Mamba Village, Langata Road, Langata, Nairobi, Kenya
PO Box 74760, Nairobi 00200, Kenya

Tel	+254 20 2486201
Mobile	+254 720 987183; +254 722 521185
Fax	
E-mail	info@nairobimambavillage.com
Web	www.nairobimambavillage.com

VISA, MasterCard, Amex JKIA, LS & CH & Intl., 40 mins
Wilson Airport, LS & CH, 20 mins

Nairobi Mamba Village is a family resort that merges fun, culture, business and wildlife. It is the only location in the city where visitors can go for dining and conferencing and at the same time enjoy the sight of giant Nile crocodiles.

There are 22 en-suite standard rooms, 15 en-suite safari tents and 1 luxury suite. The Main Restaurant and the Island Restaurant serve an a la carte menu, including the mamba barbecue which started in the early 1990s. Bandas, dotted about the lawns, provide private dining places, and are equipped with open fires. Mokoyeti Bar is furnished with comfortable sofas and tables. The 2nd floor bar opens late in the night. The Pool Bar, in the shape of a natural cave, has a manmade waterfall and plentiful greenery. The conference hall seats 60 pax, and is available for meetings, seminars or banquets. It is equipped with PA system, WiFi and wired internet access. Nairobi Mamba Village's most famous attraction is its crocodile farm. The pens are home to about 70 Nile crocodiles. Other wildlife includes reticulated giraffe and ostrich and a wide array of birdlife. Boat rides on the lake are on offer. There is also a playground, souvenir shop and exhibition of traditional crafts.

Nairobi Tented Camp

Nairobi Ntl. Park

Nairobi Tented Camp, Nairobi National Park, Kenya
PO Box 15097, Nairobi 00100, Kenya

Tel	+254 20 2603337
Mobile	+254 733 884298; +254 711 977404
Fax	
E-mail	reservations@nairobitentedcamp.com
Web	www.nairobitentedcamp.com

 VISA, MasterCard

 JKIA, LS & CH & Intl., 30 mins
Wilson Airport, LS & CH, 20 mins

Established in November 2010, Nairobi Tented Camp is the first and only safari camp in Nairobi National Park. Deep in a riverine forest, in the speckled shade of an olive grove, this authentic tented camp offers a true wilderness experience on the doorstep of Nairobi.

There are 8 en-suite tents, made up of twins and doubles. The tents are furnished with writing desks, chairs and sheepskin rugs, and their verandas have chairs and tables. Gourmet candlelit dinners are served in the central mess tent, and include freshly baked bread, poached whole salmon, soufflé and Kenyan roast beef. The bar is fully stocked with soft drinks, beers, wines and spirits. A tent can be set up for team meetings or small corporate events.

Activities include game drives in the park and game walks in Kisembe Valley. Trips to nearby attractions are also on offer, such as the Sheldrick Elephant Orphanage, the Giraffe Centre, Karen Blixen Museum and National Museum, as well as local craft designers Marula Studios, Kazuri Beads and Utamaduni.

The camp embraces the latest eco-technology, deals with its water and waste responsibly and is lit by solar power. It is truly mobile; only tent pegs are stuck in the ground.

Panari Hotel

Mombasa Road

Panari Hotel, Mombasa Road, Nairobi, Kenya
PO Box 4372, Nairobi 00506, Kenya

Tel	+254 20 3946000; +254 3574601-2
Mobile	+254 725 694600-2; +254 733 694600-2
Fax	+254 20 828985
E-mail	info@panarihotels.com
Web	www.panarihotels.com

 VISA, MasterCard, Amex

 JKIA, LS & CH & Intl., 15 mins
Wilson Airport, LS & CH, 30 mins

The Panari Sky Centre houses cinemas, restaurants, food court, shops, beauty salon, bank and an ice rink. The Panari Hotel, situated in the Panari Sky Tower, has access to all these facilities within the building. The centre is located on Mombasa Road, not far from Jomo Kenyatta International Airport.

There are 137 en-suite rooms, made up of standard, superior and deluxe, and the Royal Jade Suite. All rooms have aircon, satellite TV, telephone, internet connection, minibar and hairdryer. The Red Garnett serves a 5-course buffet. The Amber Coffee Shop has freshly brewed coffee and a snack menu, and is equipped with WiFi. Crystal Bar has an extensive list of soft drinks, juices, beers, wines, spirits and cocktails.

There are 8 conference rooms, available for conferences, seminars, exhibitions, receptions, banquets and weddings. Palm Court seats 500 pax; Hibiscus, Jasmine and Orchid each seat 100 and Tulip seats 40. There are 3 Walnut halls, each seating 220, that can be joined to form 1 large hall. Palm Atrium, with high curved glass roof and water feature, is available for functions. Dolphin Health and Fitness Club has professional equipment supplied by Cybex and Life Fitness of USA, as well as swimming pool, steam bath and sauna.

Ole Sereni

Mombasa Road

Ole Sereni, Mombasa Road, Nairobi, Kenya
PO Box 18187, Nairobi 00500, Kenya
Tel	+254 20 3901000; +254 20 5036000
Mobile	
Fax	+254 20 828563
E-mail	info@ole-serenihotel.com / sales@ole-serenihotel.com
Web	www.ole-serenihotel.com

VISA, MasterCard   JKIA, LS & CH & Intl., 15 mins
Wilson Airport, LS & CH, 25 mins

Nairobi is the only city in the world with a game park within its precincts. Ole Sereni epitomises this juxtaposition, offering the comforts and services of a city hotel and the atmosphere of a safari lodge. Meaning place of tranquility in Maasai, Ole Sereni is the name given to this part of Nairobi that lies between the airport, Nairobi National Park and the city centre. There are 134 en-suite rooms on 3 floors, made up of 58 superior rooms, 48 deluxe rooms with park view, 26 club rooms with either park or city view and 2 executive suites each with Jacuzzi on the veranda facing the park overlooking the waterhole. All rooms have direct dial telephone, high speed internet, minibar, kettle, hairdryer, safe, satellite TV and aircon. The

Big Five Restaurant and Bar overlooks the waterhole, and has an open kitchen serving Mongolian, Grills, Indian, Italian and Chinese cuisine. Other restaurants include the Waterhole Snack Bar, Ngong Pool Bar and the Eagles Grill and Bar.
The main conference hall seats 500 pax, and can be divided into 5 rooms. There are also 3 large meeting rooms, a boardroom and 4 small meeting rooms. All rooms are fully equipped including PA system, LCD projector, WiFi and video and audio conferencing facilities.

RedCourt Hotel

Mombasa Road

RedCourt Hotel, Mombasa Road, Nairobi, Kenya
PO Box 26601, Nairobi 00100, Kenya
Tel	+254 20 3904000
Mobile	+254 728 606476; +254 734 973513
Fax	+254 20 6004520
E-mail	info@redcourt.co.ke
Web	www.redcourt.co.ke

VISA, MasterCard   JKIA, LS & CH & Intl., 15 mins
Wilson Airport, LS & CH, 30 mins

RedCourt Hotel is owned by the Kenya Red Cross Society and proceeds from the hotel sustain the society. The hotel is situated in the Red Cross compound on Mombasa Road, making it convenient for both Jomo Kenyatta International Airport and Wilson Airport.
There are 60 en-suite rooms. Standard rooms are equipped with hairdryer, electronic safe, kettle, satellite TV, electronic lock and wake up service. The suites are equipped with living area with sofa, extra bathroom, work desk, minibar and high speed internet.
Restaurant Mundial, overlooking the garden and health club, serves both buffet and a la carte international dishes. Mbugani Restaurant serves

buffet lunch and is available for private functions of up to 300 pax. Afya Garden Bar serves snacks, juices and cocktails. Makutano Lounge Bar, next to the hotel's main foyer, has several satellite TVs and shows international sports matches.
The conference centre has 7 conference halls, 2 boardrooms and a fully equipped business secretariat room. 3 of the conference halls are adjoining and can form 1 large hall. All are fully equipped, including high definition LCD screens and Dolby surround sound. The Red fitness parlour has a health club and gym and is staffed by expert training assistants. There is also a sauna and steam room.

African Heritage House   Mombasa Road

African Heritage House, nr Nairobi National Park, Athi River, Kenya
PO Box 17871, Nairobi 00100, Kenya
Tel
Mobile   +254 721 518389
Fax
E-mail   ahalan@africaonline.co.ke
Web   www.africanheritagebook.com

    JKIA, LS & CH & Intl., 15 mins
                Wilson Airport, LS & CH, 40 mins

Overlooking Nairobi National Park, African Heritage House has been described as rising from the parched plains of Nairobi's outskirts like an architectural mirage. The house is inspired by the mud mosque tradition of Nigeria and Mali, the architecture of coastal Kenya and the sculptural house styles of Morocco.

There are 4 en-suite rooms, made up of 3 doubles and 1 single. All rooms are adorned with African art and ornaments, and equipped with modern facilities. The public rooms house an impressive collection of African textiles, masonry, wood, weaponry, pottery, jewellery and art. Breakfast, lunch and dinner are served on the rooftop or by the swimming pool.

Traditional African food is served; Japanese, Italian and international a la carte menus can be served on request. The bar serves soft drinks, beers, wines and spirits.

The house is available for conferences and functions, as well as for larger events of up to 600 pax, such as weddings and parties. Visitors not staying at the house can book tours of the house, with or without rooftop lunch, dinner or sundowner.

The house is said to be the most photographed house in Africa, and has been the setting for fashion shoots, architecture features and television programmes. The house funds the Nairobi National Park lion project.

Country House Inn   Karen

Country House Inn, Ngong Road, Karen, Nairobi, Kenya
PO Box 79080, Nairobi 00400, Kenya
Tel   +254 20 3882047; +254 20 3882048
Mobile   +254 714 637777; +254 738 637777
Fax
E-mail   info@countryhouse-inn.com
Web   www.countryhouse-inn.com

    VISA    JKIA, LS & CH & Intl., 40 mins
                                                Wilson Airport, LS & CH, 20 mins

Country House Inn offers a selection of accommodation, dining and conferencing. The hotel is located on Ngong Road, not far from Karen Shopping Centre, and is convenient for all the facilities of the Karen and Langata suburbs of Nairobi.

There are 15 en-suite rooms, made up of 2 economy, 8 standard and 5 deluxe. All rooms are adorned with Kenyan handmade artefacts, including woven rugs and bedspreads. The rooms are equipped with internet access and satellite TV. The restaurant has an a la carte menu of international dishes such as chicken cordon bleu, and has a selection of tapas. Guests are also welcome to dine in the garden. The bar serves soft drinks, hot drinks, beers, wines and spirits. Outside catering is available.

The conference hall seats 40 pax. The hall is equipped with PA system and projector. The garden makes a lovely location for weddings. Photo shoots and teambuilding can be arranged. The hotel is convenient for Nairobi National Park, the Giraffe Centre, the Sheldrick Elephant Orphanage, Karen Blixen Museum and Karen Blixen Coffee Garden. Taxis to other parts of Nairobi can be arranged.

Silver Springs Hotel Hurlingham

Silver Springs Hotel, Junction of Argwings Kodhek and Valley Road
PO Box 61362, Nairobi 00200, Kenya

Tel	+254 20 2722451-4; +254 20 2722456-7
Mobile	+254 722204870; +254 733616217
Fax	+254 20 2720545; +254 20 2728061
E-mail	info@silversprings-hotel.com
Web	www.silversprings-hotel.com

VISA, MasterCard, Amex

JKIA, LS & CH & Intl., 45 mins
Wilson Airport, LS & CH, 30 mins

Silver Springs Hotel offers a wide variety of services and facilities at a convenient location between the city centre and the airport.

There are 160 en-suite rooms, made up of standard, superior, deluxe and executive. Standard rooms have aircon, telephone, satellite TV, safe, electronic door lock, kettle and WiFi. Superior rooms are more spacious and have bay window with seats. Deluxe rooms include a dining area and Jacuzzi. Executive rooms include a living room and kitchenette. There is also a 2-bedroom penthouse suite. Flagship Restaurant offers international buffet, and has an a la carte menu. There is also a live Chinese cooking station and an Indian corner. Haven Bar has an extensive drinks list, including cocktails, and serves snacks. Amigo Coffee Shop has gourmet coffee, smoothies and freshly squeezed juices. There are 10 meeting rooms, with seating capacities ranging from 20 to 200 pax. All rooms are equipped with audio visual equipment and WiFi. The meetings and events team provides technical, administrative and practical support. The business centre is fully equipped.

Silver Spa Gym has modern equipment and a range of classes such as yoga, salsa and step. Silver Spa Health Club has an extensive list of treatments, including aromatherapy and Indian head massage, and offers hen weekend and bridal packages.

Palacina Suites State House

Palacina Suites, Kitale Lane, off Dennis Pritt Road, nr State House
PO Box 48728, Nairobi 00100, Kenya

Tel	+254 20 2715517
Mobile	+254 720 493747
Fax	+254 20 2715519
E-mail	info@palacina.com
Web	www.palacina.com

VISA, MasterCard, Amex

JKIA, LS & CH & Intl., 40 mins
Wilson Airport, LS & CH, 30 mins

A boutique hotel conveniently located near the centre of Nairobi, Palacina Suites combines understated elegance with warm hospitality.

There are 14 luxury suites, including 2 penthouses, each with its own living room and private furnished balcony. The suites are decorated in natural shades, with teak wood, crisp cottons and African crafts. Their state of the art features include flat screen satellite TV, digital safe, microwave, fully stocked bar and Jacuzzi. The Residence consists of 1, 2 and 3-bedroom serviced apartments, each tastefully designed, and furnished with a fully equipped kitchen.

Moonflower Restaurant serves a fusion of Mediterranean and Swahili cuisines in a stylish ambience, to the rhythm of live jazz music. Moonflower Bar has a wide range of local and imported beers, wines, spirits and liqueurs. The Lobby serves as a reading room and bar.

The meeting room, on the riverbanks of the State House Valley, is available for meetings, seminars, press releases, gala dinners, birthday parties and cocktail parties. Each event is tailor-made. The fitness room has the latest aerobic and anaerobic equipment; the spa offers treatments and massage. Palacina also has a business centre, swimming pool and a 24-hour reception willing to book taxis, reserve restaurants, give directions or arrange airport shuttles.

Olive Gardens Hotel Hurlingham

Olive Gardens Hotel, Argwings Kodhek Road, Hurlingham, Nairobi
PO Box 3049, Nairobi 00506, Kenya

Tel	+254 20 2737854; +254 20 2727777
Mobile	+254 714 680745
Fax	+254 20 2737924
E-mail	info@theolivegardens.com
Web	www.theolivegardens.com

 JKIA, LS & CH & Intl., 50 mins
Wilson Airport, LS & CH, 40 mins

In the Nairobi district of Hurlingham, Olive Gardens Hotel is ideally situated for many shops, restaurants and bars, is a short distance from Nairobi Women's Hospital and not far from Nairobi Hospital.

There are 62 en-suite rooms and 1 serviced apartment, all equipped with satellite TV and telephone. Standard rooms have twin beds; deluxe rooms are carpeted and have fridges; suites have sitting rooms. The serviced apartment has a kitchen and a sitting room. The ground floor rooms are suitable for guests with disabilities.

The Dining and Terrace Restaurant serves international food, including seafood, steaks and grilled chicken. Lunch can be buffet or a la carte.

Breakfast can be served as early as 5am if required. The bar is well stocked with soft drinks, beers and spirits.

The conference centre houses 3 halls: Flamingo seats 70 pax, Malibu seats 30 and Kiwi seats 20. Other facilities include a gym, a sauna and a secure car park. The executive guest lounge has a satellite TV and a selection of books. Reception is happy to assist with international telephone calls and faxes.

The Methodist Guest House and Conference Centre Lavington

Methodist Guest House, Loitokitok Road, Lavington, Nairobi, Kenya
PO Box 25086, Nairobi 00603, Kenya

Tel	+254 20 3871080; +254 20 3867225
Mobile	+254 722 205784; +254 733 699994
Fax	+254 20 3862385
E-mail	reservations@methodistguesthouse.org
Web	www.methodistguesthouse.org

VISA, MasterCard   JKIA, LS & CH & Intl., 1 hr 15 mins
Wilson Airport, LS & CH, 50 mins

The Methodist Guest House and Conference Centre offers accommodation and conferencing in a serene environment. The guesthouse is located in Lavington, within easy reach of Lavington Green Shopping Centre.

There are 84 en-suite rooms, including 5 Bishop Suites. All rooms are equipped with telephone, TV and internet. The suites have a private lounge and veranda. 2 rooms are equipped for guests with disabilities. There are 2 dining rooms, serving local, African and international dishes. Alcohol is not served.

The conference centre has 15 rooms, all of which are equipped with conference facilities. The largest conference room, the Bishop Lawi Imathiu Hall, seats 300 pax. Conferences, workshops and seminars can all be catered for. The business centre has WiFi, wired internet access, photocopy, fax and telephone. Laptops and computers are available for hire. Typing and printing services are offered. There is also a ½ Olympic size swimming pool; swimming lessons can be booked with resident swimming instructors. The music centre offers recreation and music. The gift shop has an assortment of Kenyan curios and artefacts, and stocks a selection of Christian literature. The hair salon has a range of beauty treatments.

Sandavy Guest House Kilimani

Sandavy Guest House, Ndemi Close, off Ndemi Road, Kilimani, Nairobi
PO Box 15006, Nairobi 00100, Kenya

Tel	+254 20 3002543
Mobile	+254 726 600210
Fax	+254 20 3867540
E-mail	sandavyguesthouse@gmail.com
Web	www.nairobiguesthouse.com

JKIA, LS & CH & Intl., 50 mins
Wilson Airport, LS & CH, 40 mins

Sandavy Guest House fuses the comfort of a private house with the advantages of a guesthouse. It is located in Kilimani district of Nairobi, next to the Language Centre and close to many shops and restaurants. The guesthouse welcomes long stay volunteer and intern students, charity and religious groups, and offers these groups subsidised rates. The rooms are named after local birds, echoing the owners' love of birdlife. Greater Flamingo has a king size double bed and en-suite bathroom. Lesser Flamingo has a queen size double bed and private bathroom. Violet Backed Starling has 3 single beds and private bathroom. Cordon-bleu has twin beds and shared bathroom. Little Bee Eater and Bronze Sunbird both have bunk beds and shared bathroom.

Breakfast is included. Lunch and dinner can be served on request. Local drinks and snacks are available throughout the day. The common room has TV and DVD; there is also a quiet sunroom, a large garden, a car park and a luggage store.

The guesthouse is smoke free and welcomes children. There is WiFi throughout and a selection of books. Sandavy Tours can book tours in and around Nairobi, as well as trips to national parks and other destinations.

New HillCrest Hotel Westlands

New HillCrest Hotel, Waiyaki Way, Westlands, Nairobi, Kenya
PO Box 53598, Nairobi 00200, Kenya

Tel	+254 20 4448046; +254 20 4444883
Mobile	+254 737 967643; +254 715 936817
Fax	+254 20 4444208
E-mail	hillcrest@africaonline.co.ke / info@newhillcresthotel.com
Web	www.newhillcresthotel.com

 VISA, MasterCard

JKIA, LS & CH & Intl., 1 hr 15 mins
Wilson Airport, LS & CH, 1 hr

New HillCrest Hotel was established in 1972, and was completely refurbished in 2009. The hotel is located in Westlands, and is convenient for all the shops, businesses, restaurants and bars of this bustling hub. There are 26 en-suite rooms, made up of singles, doubles and superiors. All rooms have TV with local channels, telephone and mosquito net. The restaurant has an a la carte menu, and serves Kenyan and international dishes. The lounge has daily newspapers and magazines, and a TV with local channels. The peaceful garden has tables and chairs shaded by umbrellas. There is plentiful secure parking. The conference hall seats 30 pax. There is WiFi at reception.

Laundry and dry cleaning services are available. Services include airport pick up and assistance with booking spa, gym and other appointments in Nairobi. The 24-hour reception can also assist with booking tours, excursions and safaris to destinations in Kenya. A 24-hour taxi service is available. The hotel is located on the slip road parallel to Waiyaki Way, the highway that passes through Westlands.

The King Post

Westlands

The King Post, Rhapta Road, Westlands, Nairobi, Kenya
The Gables Group, PO Box 13606, Nairobi 00800, Kenya

Tel	+254 20 4454130-1
Mobile	+254 734 261182; +254 722 261182
Fax	+254 20 4448697
E-mail	thekingpost@the-gables.org
Web	www.the-gables.org

 VISA, MasterCard   JKIA, LS & CH & Intl., 1 hr 15 mins
Wilson Airport, LS & CH, 1 hr

Instantly recognisable by its castle façade, The King Post offers luxury, serviced, self-catering apartments. Established in 2007, the apartments blend traditional design with modern facilities. The King Post is owned and managed by The Gables Group, together with the nearby The Gables. There are 53 apartments, made up of 12 studios, 24 1-bedroom, 15 2-bedroom and 2 3-bedroom apartments. All apartments have living room, fully equipped kitchen and utility room. The furniture is created from exotic solid mahogany, cedar and oak, by a family that has been in the business for a century. The décor is Oriental, with exotic wall hangings and lamps. The apartments also have satellite TV, WiFi, international direct dial telephone and security including CCTV. Housekeeping services are included; laundry and dry cleaning services are available for a charge. Minimum stay is 1 day.

There is a swimming pool, with sunbathing terrace and barbecue area. There is also a fully equipped gym. The car park is secure. A selection of restaurants and a health club with a gym is within walking distance of the apartments. Taxis are easily available.

The Gables

Westlands

The Gables, Rhapta Road, Westlands, Nairobi, Kenya
The Gables Group, PO Box 13606, Nairobi 00800, Kenya

Tel	+254 20 4444630-1
Mobile	+254 735 258131; +254 722 258131
Fax	+254 20 4448697
E-mail	info@the-gables.org
Web	www.the-gables.org

 VISA, MasterCard    JKIA, LS & CH & Intl., 1 hr 15 mins
Wilson Airport, LS & CH, 1 hr

The Gables has luxury, serviced, self-catering apartments in the Westlands area of Nairobi. Established in 1997, the apartments are designed to replicate English pub style. The name comes from the gables that are used to support the roof in traditional English buildings. The Gables is owned and managed by The Gables Group, together with the nearby The King Post. There are 16 apartments, made up of 1 and 2-bedroom apartments. All apartments have living room, fully equipped kitchen and balcony with pot plants. The furniture is created from exotic solid mahogany, cedar and oak, by a family that has been in the business for a century. The apartments also have satellite TV, WiFi, international direct dial telephone and security including CCTV. Housekeeping services are included; laundry and dry cleaning services are available for a charge. Minimum stay is 1 month.

The Gables has a swimming pool surrounded by terrace with barbecue. There is also a sauna. The car park is secure. A selection of restaurants and a health club with a gym is within walking distance of the apartments. Taxis are easily available. The Gables received the International Arch of Europe Award Frankfurt 2002, in recognition of commitment to quality, leadership, technology and innovation.

PrideInn Hotel Nairobi Westlands

PrideInn Hotel Nairobi, Rhapta Road, Westlands, Nairobi, Kenya
PO Box 66969, Nairobi 00200, Kenya

Tel	+254 20 8155399
Mobile	+254 701 454556; +254 734 348999; +254 770 1333438
Fax	
E-mail	stay@prideinn.co.ke
Web	www.prideinn.co.ke

VISA, MasterCard, Amex   JKIA, LS & CH & Intl., 1 hr 15 mins
Wilson Airport, LS & CH, 1 hr

PrideInn Hotel Nairobi is conveniently located in Westlands, near the shopping centres, restaurants and bars of this bustling part of Nairobi. The hotel offers accommodation, dining and conferencing.
There are 27 en-suite rooms, made up of singles and doubles. All rooms have aircon, satellite TV, DVD, telephone, WiFi, safe and kettle. Royal Kitchen styles itself as a multi cuisine restaurant. It has an extensive menu, and serves Indian, Chinese, Italian and continental cuisine. A private dining room can be taken on request. The restaurant also offers outside catering, wedding receptions and birthday parties.
The conference room seats 100 pax. Conference equipment includes video, PA system, WiFi and projector. The gardens can be used for functions, teambuilding or training sessions. The business centre has internet, printing, scanning, photocopy, telephone and fax. There is also a car park.
PrideInn Hotel Nairobi is affiliated to PrideInn Hotel Mombasa, PrideInn Hotel Nyali and PrideInn Hotel Diani, all part of the Glory Safaris group. Glory Safaris also offers car hire on a short or long-term basis, and runs a driving school. Glory Safaris books tours and safaris and has a selection of activity packages in Kenya and Tanzania.

Sankara Westlands

Sankara, Woodvale Grove, Westlands, Nairobi, Kenya
PO Box 1638, Nairobi 00606, Kenya

Tel	+254 20 2490210-3; +254 20 4208000
Mobile	
Fax	+254 20 4208888
E-mail	connect@nairobi.sankara.com
Web	www.sankara.com

VISA, MasterCard   JKIA, LS & CH & Intl., 1 hr 15 mins
Wilson Airport, LS & CH, 1 hr

Established in September 2010, Sankara is a sleek, contemporary hotel in the heart of Westlands, Nairobi's commercial and entertainment centre.
There are 156 en-suite rooms on 7 floors, made up of 82 superior, 65 deluxe, 7 junior suites and 2 executive suites. All rooms are equipped with interactive LCD flat screen TV with plug and play panel, internet access, 3 telephones, aircon, digital safe, minibar and marble bathrooms with bathtub and rain shower.
The Artesan serves global cuisine, including Watamu fresh oysters, salmon and tuna cerviche and paneer Makhani. Muhibbah serves East Asian food, including laksa noodles, roasted duck Singapore style and Thai tom-yam-gung. The bar is fully stocked with wines, champagnes and cocktails. On the roof top, there is a heated swimming pool, sunbathing deck with panoramic views, sauna, steam room, pool bar and restaurant. There is wheelchair access throughout the hotel.
Angsana Spa, affiliated to Thailand's famous Banyan Tree, has water features, mood lighting and relaxation scents, and offers a fusion of treatments from East and West. The gym has touch screen equipment, and is staffed by personal trainers. The Business Centre has 3 fully equipped meeting rooms that interlink to form 1 conference hall seating 220 pax.

Jacaranda Hotel

Westlands

Jacaranda Hotel, off Waiyaki Way, Westlands, Nairobi, Kenya
Jacaranda Group of Hotels, PO Box 14287, Nairobi 00800, Kenya

Tel	+254 20 4448713-7
Mobile	+254 733 601613-4; +254 722 205486-7
Fax	+254 20 4445818; +254 20 4448977
E-mail	bookings@jacarandahotels.com
Web	www.jacarandahotels.com

VISA, MasterCard, Amex   JKIA, LS & CH & Intl., 1 hr 15 mins
                          Wilson Airport, LS & CH, 1 hr

Surrounded by the Jacaranda trees that give it its name, the Jacaranda Hotel is in Westlands, the commercial centre of Nairobi. The hotel started in the 1960s as Agip Motel, joined the Block Group of hotels in the 1970s, and was finally refurbished and rebranded in 2003 under Jacaranda Hotels, Kenya.

There are 125 en-suite rooms. All rooms are equipped with ceiling fans, telephones, satellite TV, minibar, electronic safe and hairdryers.

Safari Café is a pavilion style restaurant that serves buffet breakfast and a la carte lunch and dinner to the accompaniment of piped music. Safari Bar, a lounge bar, overlooks the swimming pool. The Pool Bar and Restaurant, in a collection of Kenyan style bandas dotted around the gardens, has a snack menu and shows satellite TV sports and news. The Wariara Conference Centre houses the Palm Room and the Jacaranda Room. The Jacaranda Conference Centre houses Conference Room 201 and a boardroom. Conference facilities include an overhead projector, TV and video. The Gazebo Banda is equipped to host product launches, cocktail parties and wedding ceremonies. The gym has state of the art facilities. There is also a fully equipped business centre, a hair salon and a gift shop.

Southern Sun Mayfair

Westlands

Southern Sun Mayfair, Parklands Road, Westlands, Nairobi, Kenya
PO Box 66807, Nairobi 00100, Kenya

Tel	+254 20 3740920; +254 20 3740921; +254 20 3688000
Mobile	+254 722 204599
Fax	+254 20 3748823
E-mail	admin@southernsun.co.ke
Web	www.southernsun.co.ke

VISA, MasterCard   JKIA, LS & CH & Intl., 1 hr 15 mins
                    Wilson Airport, LS & CH, 1 hr

Built in 1945 as the Mayfair Court Hotel, the hotel is set in 12 acres of lush landscaped gardens and retains the charming architecture of the colonial days. The hotel became Southern Sun Mayfair in 2010, and has a selection of conferencing and recreational facilities.

There are 171 en-suite rooms. All rooms are equipped with satellite TV, radio, telephone, kettle and WiFi. Executive rooms have a private patio overlooking the gardens, minibar, trouser press and modem point access. Some rooms are designed for guests with disabilities.

Oasis Restaurant, next to the pool, serves breakfast, lunch and buffet dinner. The Golden Spur Steak Ranch offers specialty steaks, burgers, pizzas, salads and snacks. Oasis Poolside Bar and Golden Spur Cocktail Bar have extensive drinks lists. There are 2 swimming pools, both surrounded by sunbathing terraces. The Health Club has a fitness centre, aerobics studio, sauna and steam room. There is also a casino, gift shop and hair salon. The conference centre houses 8 conference halls; 3 halls each seat 100 pax, 1 hall seats 50 and 4 halls each seat 30. Conference equipment including LCD projector, TV, video, PA system and microphones is available for hire. The business centre is fully equipped. Weddings, functions, conferences, product launches and workshops can be arranged.

Karibu Kenya Accommodation Guide

Sentrim 680

Central Business District

Sentrim 680, Kenyatta Avenue, Nairobi, Kenya
Sentrim Hotels and Lodges, PO Box 43826, Nairobi 00100, Kenya

Tel	+254 20 315680; +254 20 315371
Mobile	+254 722 207361; +254 733 852083; +254 733 680680
Fax	+254 20 343875; +254 20 2218314
E-mail	reservations680@sentrim-hotels.com
Web	www.sentrim-hotels.net

JKIA, LS & CH & Intl., 50 mins
Wilson Airport, LS & CH, 40 mins

Sentrim 680, located in the heart of Nairobi on the busy Kenyatta Avenue, offers easy access to the Central Business District institutions, city shops, cinemas, restaurants and bars. City tours and even leisurely strolls within the city are also possible from here.

There are 253 rooms on 10 floors, made up of 111 doubles, 124 twins, 8 triples and 2 suites. All rooms are en-suite and have fans. Mosquito nets and minibars are available on request.

The main guest area consists of the reception, lounge area and coffee shop. The Mezzanine floor houses the conference facilities, the restaurant and the bar. The hotel also has a casino and a band that plays every Friday night.

The selection of conference and banqueting facilities is extensive. Mkutano hall holds 250 pax, Sherehe holds 350, Exhibition holds 800, Taj Mar holds 100 and Taj Palace holds 100. Boardroom 1 seats 20 and Boardroom 2 seats 15.

The hotel can arrange visits to major sites of attraction in and around Nairobi. It can also book transfers to the airports, JKIA and Wilson.

Fairmont The Norfolk

Central Business District

Fairmont The Norfolk, Harry Thuku Road, nr Nairobi University
PO Box 58581, Nairobi 00200, Kenya

Tel	+254 20 2265000
Mobile	+254 711 081000
Fax	+254 20 2216796
E-mail	kenya.reservations@fairmont.com
Web	www.fairmont.com/norfolkhotel

All major cards
JKIA, LS & CH & Intl., 50 mins
Wilson Airport, LS & CH, 40 mins

The signature hotel of Nairobi, Fairmont The Norfolk has a long, rich history dating back to the very first days of colonial settlement. Centred on a courtyard garden adorned with vintage cars and carriages, the Norfolk is a sweeping Tudor-style building. Corridors decorated with period photos of Nairobi and a traditional English tea room lined with books compliment the ambiance.

The 165 en-suite rooms are made up of 52 Fairmont rooms, 41 Fairmont courtyard rooms and 31 deluxe rooms all luxuriously furnished with plush carpets, dressing tables and TVs. There are also 15 junior suites, 2 karura suites, 7 duplex suites, 8 signature suites and 9 acacia suites. The suites each include a sumptuous dining and living area with flat screen TV and a balcony overlooking the garden.

Lord Delamere Terrace has a fresh grill and international a la carte menu. The poolside terrace serves lunch and snacks. Tatu is a chic restaurant serving creative and innovative lunches and dinners. The wine bar has canapés and a large selection of wines. Recently renovated by Fairmont, the Norfolk now has 3 fully equipped conference rooms and 4 boardrooms. The heated pool, health suite and aerobic studio are all state of the art and the spa offers massage and treatments.

Nairobi Safari Club Central Business District

Nairobi Safari Club, University Way, Nairobi, Kenya
PO Box 43564, Nairobi 00100, Kenya

Tel	+254 20 2821000
Mobile	+254 722 209842; +254 734 251333
Fax	+254 20 2215137; +254 20 2224625
E-mail	reservations@nairobisafariclub.com
Web	www.nairobisafariclub.com

VISA, MasterCard, Amex, Diners Club

JKIA, LS & CH & Intl., 50 mins
Wilson Airport, LS & CH, 40 mins

Established in 1984 as a private members club, Nairobi Safari Club reopened in 2001 as Kenya's only all suite hotel. The hotel is located in the Central Business District close to Nairobi University.

There are 146 suites, made up of 100 panoramas, 40 executives and 6 presidential suites. All suites have en-suite bedroom and lounge, and are equipped with high speed internet, safe, minibar, hairdryer, satellite TV and 3 telephones. The presidential suites are more spacious and have a Jacuzzi. The Safari Restaurant, complete with resident pianist, serves local and international dishes. The Safari Terrace Bar serves snacks and cocktails. The Pool Deck serves snacks, lunch and dinner. The Sundeck, overlooking University Way, offers a wide selection of pizzas and grills.

Mawingo conference room seats 300 pax; Kirinyaga and Nyambene halls each seat 150; Elgon, Kilimambogo and Longonot each seat 25; Ngong seats 10. The halls are equipped with audio visual equipment and can be used for conferences or banquets. The business centre has internet, fax and photocopy, and offers secretarial service. The health centre has a modern gym, steam bath, sauna, massage parlour and swimming pool. The hotel also has an airport shuttle service, gift shop and secure car park.

Kenya Comfort Hotel Suites Milimani

Kenya Comfort Hotel Suites, Junction of Milimani and Ralph Bunche Roads
PO Box 30425, Nairobi 00100, Kenya

Tel	+254 20 2719060-1; +254 20 2723414
Mobile	+254 733 608867
Fax	+254 20 2723078
E-mail	sales@kenyacomfort.com
Web	www.kenyacomfort.com

VISA, MasterCard

JKIA, LS & CH & Intl., 50 mins
Wilson Airport, LS & CH, 40 mins

Having started life in 1983 as Eagle Star Apartments, the property was rebranded as Kenya Comfort Hotel Suites in 2005. In the Milimani district of Nairobi, the hotel is close to State House, Nairobi Hospital and a number of businesses, bars and restaurants.

There are 64 suites, made up of studios and 1, 2 and 3-bedroom suites. The ground floor suites are designed for guests with disabilities. All suites have kitchens equipped with basic crockery and cutlery, and TVs. The suites can be taken on a daily, weekly or monthly basis.

Sokoni Restaurant, meaning market place in Swahili, uses fresh market food to create local dishes such as soups, stews, curries and grilled meats. The bar serves soft drinks and beers.

The ground floor conference room, overlooking the swimming pool, seats 60 and is suitable for guests with disabilities. The 6th floor executive suite can be used for meetings of up to 30 pax. Conference equipment, including LCD projector, PA system and computers, is available for hire. The hotel also has a swimming pool, spa, lounge, safety deposit boxes, small internet café and car park. Kenya Comfort Hotel Suites is affiliated to Kenya Comfort Hotel, in the Central Business District of Nairobi.

KaribuKenya Accommodation Guide

Meridian Court Hotel

Central Business District

Meridian Court Hotel, Muranga Road, off Moi Avenue, Nairobi, Kenya
PO Box 30278, Nairobi 00100, Kenya

Tel	+254 20 313991; +254 20 317481; +254 20 313135
Mobile	+254 722 509826; +254 734 313997/8
Fax	+254 20 2230700
E-mail	info@meridianhotelkenya.com
Web	www.meridianhotelkenya.com

VISA, MasterCard, Amex

 JKIA, LS & CH & Intl., 50 mins
Wilson Airport, LS & CH, 40 mins

Meridian Court Hotel is a combination of Oriental architecture, African style and modern facilities. It is aimed at both business travellers and holiday makers. Its central location makes it convenient for all businesses, shops, bars and restaurants of Nairobi's Central Business District. There are 85 en-suite rooms, made up of singles, doubles and triples. There are also maisonette style rooms, with an upstairs sleeping area. Some rooms are interconnecting, suitable for families. All rooms are equipped with telephone, satellite TV and balcony. Rendezvous Restaurant, adjacent to the lobby, serves continental, Indian and Chinese cuisine. Meridian Sports Bar serves soft drinks, beers and spirits, and is equipped with 5 pool tables and satellite TV.

The rooftop swimming pool has sunbathing terrace and poolside snack bar. There is also a sauna and massage parlour. The gym is fully equipped with modern equipment and has a resident instructor. There are 2 conference halls. The 5th floor hall seats 70 pax and the ground hall seats 250. Conference equipment is available for hire. Secretarial services are available. The business centre has internet, photocopying, fax and courier services; it also has a list of business information and useful contact numbers. The hotel has secure parking, room service and a safety deposit box at reception.

Marble Arch Hotel

Central Business District

Marble Arch Hotel, Lagos Road, off Tom Mboya Street, Nairobi, Kenya
PO Box 12224, Nairobi 00400, Kenya

Tel	+254 20 2677989; +254 20 2245623; +254 20 2245725
Mobile	+254 722 209633; +254 735 337660
Fax	+254 20 2677990
E-mail	info@marblearchotelnairobi.com
Web	www.marblearchotelnairobi.com

VISA, MasterCard

 JKIA, LS & CH & Intl., 50 mins
Wilson Airport, LS & CH, 40 mins

Marble Arch Hotel is located in the centre of Nairobi, next to Akamba Bus Services. Affiliated to Kibubuti Coffee Farm, the hotel's coffee shop serves its own Kentmere coffee with homemade cakes and pastries.
There are 40 en-suite rooms, made up of singles, doubles and triples. There is also a deluxe suite. All rooms are fully tiled, and have telephone, TV, video and piped music. The restaurant, on the mezzanine floor, has an international menu for breakfast, lunch and dinner. The bar, next to the restaurant, has a selection of soft drinks, beers, wines and spirits. The hotel offers outside catering, and specialises in cakes and pastries. There are 4 conference halls; the largest hall seats 200 pax and the smallest seats 20. The business centre is equipped with telephone, fax and internet, and also offers secretarial services. There is a car park with space for 100 vehicles. The hotel also offers a shuttle service and can book taxis 24hrs. The hotel's location in the centre of Nairobi's Central Business District makes it convenient for all the shops, businesses, restaurants and bars of the area. Nearby sites of interest include the Kenya National Archives and McMillan Library.

Paris Hotel

Central Business District

Paris Hotel, 12 Mfangano Street, Nairobi, Kenya
PO Box 72632, Nairobi 00200, Kenya

Tel	+254 20 2229615; +254 20 2722451-4
Mobile	+254 721 539427; +254 728 607597; +254 733 616217
Fax	+254 20 2223195; +254 20 2720545; +254 20 2728061
E-mail	info@silversprings-hotel.com
Web	www.silversprings-hotel.com

JKIA, LS & CH & Intl., 1 hr
Wilson Airport, LS & CH, 50 mins

In the centre of Nairobi, Paris Hotel offers budget accommodation and conferencing conveniently close to the restaurants, bars, shops and businesses of the Central Business District. It is also close to the commercial bus stage, and not far from Nairobi Railway Station. The hotel was established in the 1980s and was renovated in 2010. The hotel is adorned with original photographs of Nairobi and the people of Kenya, dating back to the early 1900s.

There are 40 en-suite rooms, made up of standard, superior, deluxe and twin. All rooms are equipped with telephone, safe and satellite TV, and their doors have electronic locks. Superior rooms have, in addition, kettles, and duluxe rooms have fridges. WiFi is available throughout the hotel. A computer is available for the use of guests in the office.

Diamond Restaurant serves international cuisine, both buffet and a la carte. Dishes include beef stroganoff, fricassee of chicken, pan fried tilapia fillet, mushroom and pea risotto, penne arabiata and classic beef and chicken burgers. The bar serves soft drinks, beers, wines and spirits. The conference hall seats 70 pax, and is equipped with projector and PA system. The car park, behind the hotel, is securely enclosed.

Nairobi Pacific Hotel

Central Business District

Nairobi Pacific Hotel, Tom Mboya St, Nairobi, Kenya
PO Box 21113, Nairobi 00505, Kenya

Tel	+254 20 2222562
Mobile	+254 711 463266
Fax	
E-mail	pacific@nairobipacifichotels.com
Web	www.nairobipacifichotels.com

JKIA, LS & CH & Intl., 1 hr
Wilson Airport, LS & CH, 50 mins

In the bustling centre of town, the Nairobi Pacific Hotel is situated next to the commercial bus stage and the Kenya National Archives, and not far from Nairobi Railway Station. The hotel offers budget accommodation and easy access to all businesses, shops and amenities of the Central Business District.

There are 30 en-suite rooms, made up of singles, doubles and executives. All rooms contain satellite TV.

Nyama Choma Hippo Point serves grilled meats, and is happy to host birthday and graduation parties. Simba Restaurant, with red check table clothes, serves local dishes such as barbecue and stews, and has a snack menu including samosas and pastries. The coffee shop serves a selection of hot and cold drinks. No alcohol is served. Outside catering is also on offer. The meeting room seats 20 pax, and is available for conferences, seminars and workshops. Audio visual equipment is not provided, and should be brought by groups if required. Nairobi Pacific Hotel is affiliated to Three Steers Hotel in Meru.

KaribuKenya Accommodation Guide

Oakwood Hotel Central Business District

Oakwood Hotel, Kimathi Street, Nairobi, Kenya
Mada Hotels, PO Box 40683, Nairobi 00100, Kenya
Tel	+254 20 2220593
Mobile	+254 722 208905; +254 735 478924
Fax	+254 20 6003595
E-mail	oakwood@madahotels.com
Web	www.madahotels.com/oakwood

JKIA, LS & CH & Intl., 1 hr
Wilson Airport, LS & CH, 50 mins

Named after the traditional wood that decorates the interiors of its rooms and reception areas, Oakwood Hotel is a small hotel in the very centre of the city of Nairobi. The hotel, located on Kimathi Street, is close to all the amenities of the Central Business District. It is also within easy walking distance of the Kenya National Archives and McMillan Library. The 20 en-suite rooms are equipped with telephone, satellite TV, safe, kettle and in-house video. The hotel has a bar and a restaurant with an a la carte menu, including chef's salad, beef stew, pepper steak, grilled fish, chicken curry and layered club sandwich. Full English breakfast is included for all guests. Group bookings should be made through the Mada Hotels central reservations office.

The central location makes this hotel accessible to all business institutions, city shops, markets, restaurants, bars and cinemas.
The business centre has computers and internet. WiFi is available in the bar and the rooms. Reception can book accommodation at all affiliated Mada Hotels.

Sarova Stanley Central Business District

Sarova Stanley, Kenyatta Avenue, Nairobi, Kenya
Sarova Hotels, PO Box 30680, Nairobi 00100, Kenya
Tel	+254 20 316377; +254 20 2767000; +254 20 2716688
Mobile	+254 727 531953; +254 734 333233
Fax	+254 20 2229388; +254 20 2249757
E-mail	thestanley@sarovahotels.com
Web	www.sarovahotels.com

VISA, MasterCard, Diners Club
Amex, JCB

JKIA, LS & CH & Intl., 50 mins
Wilson Airport, LS & CH, 40 mins

The Sarova Stanley has been making history since the day it opened its doors in 1902, and has hosted a long line of legendary personalities such as Edward, Prince of Wales, Ernest Hemingway and Ava Gardner. The Exchange Bar, overlooking Kenyatta Avenue Boulevard, was the home of the Kenya Stock Exchange for over 50 years. The hotel continues to provide services and facilities for business and leisure travellers including health and fitness facilities, beauty treatments and a shopping boulevard. The Sarova Stanley has 217 en-suite aircon rooms on 8 floors made up of 90 deluxe double, 64 deluxe twins, 6 deluxe triple; 2 courier single, with single beds; 32 club rooms; 16 executive suites, 3 junior suites, 2 state suites, 1 presidential suite and 1 penthouse.
Dining options are varied and eclectic. The Thai Chi serves authentic Thai food; the Thorn Tree Café, a historic landmark in Nairobi, serves bistro-style food with daily entertainment and the Pool Deck Restaurant is an alfresco restaurant serving healthy buffets and salads, specialising in tandoori and grill.
Centrally located in the Central Business District of Nairobi, the Sarova Stanley has 9 meeting and conference rooms and a fully equipped business centre, with state of the art audio visual equipment and WiFi.

Hotel Ambassadeur Central Business District

Hotel Ambassadeur, Moi Avenue, Nairobi, Kenya
PO Box 30399, Nairobi 00100, Kenya

Tel	+254 20 2246615-6; +254 20 2246203; +254 20 2242833
Mobile	+254 724 259829
Fax	+254 20 2245517
E-mail	reserve@hotelambassadeurkenya.com
Web	www.hotelambassadeurkenya.com

    JKIA, LS & CH & Intl., 1 hr
Wilson Airport, LS & CH, 50 mins

The Hotel Ambassadeur opened in 1961, on the eve of Kenya's independence, and immediately became an important hub in East African politics. As the only adequate African peoples' hotel, it entertained East African presidents, senior government officials and civil servants and hosted significant conferences and meetings of state. Jomo Kenyatta, Kenya's 1st president, was a regular visitor.

There are 84 en-suite rooms, made up of 14 singles, 20 twins, 45 doubles and 5 triples. All rooms have satellite TV. Safety deposit boxes are available at reception. Other facilities include a bureau de change, room service, dry cleaning and valet service.

The restaurant, on the mezzanine floor, serves local and international dishes. African buffet, or private dining, can be arranged. The Lounge Bar, open from 11am to 11pm, has a selection of soft drinks, beers, wines and spirits. A live band plays on Wednesdays and Fridays; live jazz plays on Mondays and Thursdays.

The hotel is centrally located near the Kenya National Archives and not far from the Railway Station. All the businesses, shops, restaurants and amenities of Nairobi's Central Business District are easily accessible.

Laico Regency Central Business District

Laico Regency, Loita St, Uhuru Highway, Nairobi, Kenya
PO Box 57549, Nairobi 00200, Kenya

Tel	+254 20 2211199; +254 20 2887000
Mobile	
Fax	+254 20 2217120
E-mail	reservations@laico.regency.com
Web	www.laicohotels.com

 VISA, MasterCard, Amex   JKIA, LS & CH & Intl., 50 mins
Wilson Airport, LS & CH, 40 mins

An imposing 12-floor white and glass structure, the Laico Regency towers over the centre of Nairobi. The hotel is a member of Laico Hotels and Resorts. There are 196 en-suite rooms, made up of 160 deluxe, 33 executive suites, 2 deluxe suites and a presidential suite. All rooms are equipped with aircon, satellite TV, telephone, internet, play station and safe, and have additional services such as shoe shine.

The Royal Terrace Coffee Shop serves snacks, pastries, cakes, coffees and teas. Atrium Garden Restaurant has a la carte and buffet, with dishes from the Middle East, India, China and Italy. There is live entertainment during Sunday brunch. Panorama Pool Deck serves snacks and salads, with a barbecue for Sunday lunch. Roberto's serves Italian food, including pizzas and ice cream. Summit, on the top floor, serves French cuisine. Outside catering is available. There are 3 bars, including a jazz bar.

There are 7 conference halls. The Crystal Ballroom seats 900 pax, and is available for conference or banquet. The Marsabit, Shaba and Ol Donyo meeting rooms are ideal for smaller groups. The Regency Centre has 5 executive boardrooms equipped with audio visual equipment. Other facilities include a swimming pool, gym, Jacuzzi, sauna, steam bath, beauty salon, travel agent and casino.

Sentrim Boulevard

Museum Hill

Sentrim Boulevard, Museum Hill, Nairobi, Kenya
Sentrim Hotels and Lodges, PO Box 42831, Nairobi 00100, Kenya

Tel	+254 20 2227567; +254 20 218806; +254 20 315680
Mobile	+254 733 623727; +254 722 200755; +254 722 207361
Fax	+254 20 317825; +254 20 2218314
E-mail	info@sentrim-hotels.com
Web	www.sentrim-hotels.net

JKIA, LS & CH & Intl., 1 hr
Wilson Airport, LS & CH, 50 mins

At the foot of Museum Hill, the Sentrim Boulevard is set in 4.5 acres of lush gardens that slope gently to Nairobi River. Conveniently located between Nairobi National Museum, Nairobi University and the National Theatre, this hotel is within easy reach of both the commercial district of Westlands and the Central Business District.

There are 70 en-suite rooms, 40 in the garden wing and 30 in the pool wing. Every room has a safe, satellite TV, radio, internet facilities, a direct dial telephone and a balcony overlooking the garden or the pool. The restaurant offers a comprehensive a la carte menu to cater for local and international tastes, while the terraces surrounding the dining room provide a peaceful venue for guests to enjoy their sundowners. There are 3 bars, including the garden bar and the pool bar. There are 3 fully equipped conference rooms with PA system and projector, and a well equipped business centre. The hotel's proximity to the city centre and its serene scenic location makes it a good choice for conferences and seminars.

Hilton Hotel

Central Business District

Hilton Hotel, Mama Ngina St, Nairobi, Kenya
PO Box 30624, Nairobi 00100, Kenya

Tel	+254 20 2790000
Mobile	
Fax	+254 20 2226477
E-mail	reservations.nairobi@hilton.com
Web	www.hilton.com

VISA, MasterCard, Amex
Diners Club

JKIA, LS & CH & Intl., 1 hr
Wilson Airport, LS & CH, 50 mins

In the heart of Nairobi's Central Business District stands the circular tower of the Hilton Hotel, a landmark in the centre of Nairobi.

There are 287 en-suite rooms, made up of doubles, twins, suites and deluxe executive rooms. All rooms are equipped with aircon, satellite TV with movie channel, clock radio with MP3, high speed internet, iron, safe, kettle, work desk and security alarm. In addition, the suites have 2nd bedroom, 2nd bathroom, living room and working and dining areas. Travellers' Restaurant, decorated like an old fashioned train with leather suitcases and other travelling paraphernalia, serves themed buffets and has an international a la carte menu. Sale E Pepe, with the décor of a taverna, serves Italian cuisine. Pool Garden Restaurant serves nyama choma grilled meats, sandwiches, salads and pizzas. Café American has a selection of homemade breads and cakes. Jockey Pub, a British-style pub adorned with pictures of horses, serves snacks and has a fully stocked bar. The hotel also boasts a fully equipped business centre with meeting rooms and secretarial service, a swimming pool, health club, gym, airline desk, car rental desk, beauty salon, gift shop, currency exchange, florist and valet service.

InterContinental

Central Business District

InterContinental, City Hall Way, off Uhuru Highway, Nairobi
PO Box 30353, Nairobi 00200, Kenya

Tel	+254 20 3200000
Mobile	
Fax	+254 20 3200030
E-mail	sales@icnairobi.com
Web	www.ichotelsgroup.com

VISA, MasterCard, Amex Diners Club

JKIA, LS & CH & Intl., 45 mins
Wilson Airport, LS & CH, 30 mins

A graceful whitewashed building, the InterContinental has for many years been a prominent hotel in Nairobi. The hotel combines classic style with modern facilities. It is centrally located, and is within walking distance of the parliament buildings and the Kenyatta International Conference Centre. There are 376 en-suite rooms, including 16 suites. All rooms are equipped with aircon, satellite TV, whirlpool, trouser press, iron, kettle, hairdryer and minibar. In addition, the rooms on the club floor have a private check-in area and exclusive lounge. The suites include adjoining rooms and dining area.

The Terrace is an informal restaurant with a mixture of international and local cuisine. La Prugna D'oro serves Italian cuisine and Bhandini serves Indian cuisine. Plantation Lobby Café and Safari Bar serve drinks and snacks.

The ballroom, with 5 adjoining rooms, seats 800 pax, and can be divided into 2 soundproof sections if required. There is also a meeting room that seats 100. The Health Club has a swimming pool, sauna, Jacuzzi, Turkish bath and a fully equipped gym with qualified fitness instructors. The hotel also has a business centre with secretarial services, a travel desk and a large, secure car park.

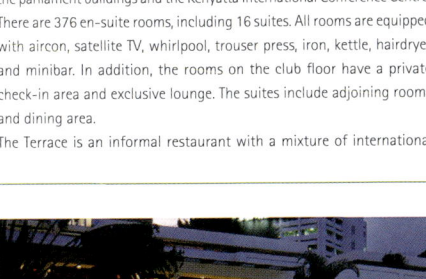

Nairobi Serena

Milimani

Nairobi Serena, Nyerere Road, off Processional Way, Nairobi, Kenya
Serena Hotels, PO Box 48690, Nairobi 00100, Kenya

Tel	+254 20 2822000; +254 20 2842000; +254 20 2842333
Mobile	+254 733 282200; +254 733 282283; +254 733 282292
Fax	+254 20 2725184; +254 20 2718102-3
E-mail	cro@serena.co.ke
Web	www.serenahotels.com

VISA, MasterCard, Amex

JKIA, LS & CH & Intl., 50 mins
Wilson Airport, LS & CH, 40 mins

Nairobi Serena is a member of the Leading Hotels of the World group. The hotel offers a selection of dining, conferencing and recreational facilities. There are 183 en-suite rooms, made up of standard, superior and deluxe rooms, and a selection of suites. Interconnecting rooms, suitable for families, are available. All rooms have aircon, 2 telephones, WiFi, minibar, digital safe, kettle and satellite TV. The 6 executive suites have extended seating areas and verandas; the 3 garden suites have open plan sitting room and garden patio; the bateleur suite has separate sitting room and integrated work space.

The Bambara Lounge is a residents' lounge, with café and newspapers.

The Mandhari Restaurant serves an a la carte international menu. The ballroom suite, including the Allamanda and Frangipani function rooms, is available for conferences and functions. The conference centre houses the Amani room, the Hibiscus room, the Canna room and the Lantana room. The rooms are equipped with PA system, microphones, TV, video, DVD, projector and WiFi. Maisha Health Club and Spa has a 25-meter heated outdoor swimming pool, Jacuzzi, steam room, sauna, state of the art gym and aerobic studio with classes and sessions including kick boxing, step aerobics, Astanga yoga, spinning and Tai Chi. The Hazina Gift Shop stocks local handicrafts, glassware and pottery.

Kenya Comfort Hotel

Central Business District

Kenya Comfort Hotel, Junction of Muindi Mbingu and Monrovia Street
PO Box 30425, Nairobi 00100, Kenya

Tel	+254 20 317605-9; +254 20 2727991
Mobile	+254 733 511438
Fax	+254 20 317610
E-mail	sales@kenyacomfort.com
Web	www.kenyacomfort.com

 VISA, MasterCard   JKIA, LS & CH & Intl., 50 mins
Wilson Airport, LS & CH, 40 mins

Originally known as Mombasa House, this family owned property was constructed in the 1950s and has housed government offices, banks and TV stations. In 2002, it became Kenya Comfort Hotel. Its location in the Central Business District makes it convenient for Nairobi University, the National Theatre, Jeevanjee Gardens and all other businesses and facilities of the city.

There are 91 en-suite rooms, made up of budget, standard and superior. The rooms can be single, double, twin or triple. All rooms have telephone and mosquito net. Superior rooms also have cupboard and TV with local channels.

Sokoni Restaurant, meaning market place in Swahili, uses fresh market food to create local dishes such as soups, stews, curries and grilled meats. Drinks are served at the Coffee Bar and the Blue Spirits Bar.

There are 2 meeting rooms that each seat 20 pax. The rooftop guests' lounge, with a view over the city, can be used for conferences of up to 80 pax. Conference equipment including PA system and LCD projector are available. The hotel also has a small enclosed car park and an internet café. Kenya Comfort Hotel is affiliated to Kenya Comfort Hotel Suites, in the Milimani district of Nairobi.

Kivi Milimani

Milimani

Kivi Milimani, Milimani Road, Milimani, Nairobi, Kenya
PO Box 20681, Nairobi 00100, Kenya

Tel	+254 20 2722358; +254 20 2711245
Mobile	+254 735 491064; +254 723 491064
Fax	
E-mail	info@kivimilimanihotel.com
Web	www.kivimilimanihotel.com

 VISA   JKIA, LS & CH & Intl., 50 mins
Wilson Airport, LS & CH, 40 mins

Set in mature gardens in the Milimani district of Nairobi, Kivi Milimani offers rooms, apartments and conference facilities. Its location makes it convenient for many shops, businesses and facilities of Nairobi.

There are 73 en-suite rooms, with garden and pool views. All rooms have telephone, TV and veranda. There are also 56 furnished apartments. Each apartment has 1 en-suite bedroom, fully equipped kitchen, balcony and private parking space. Full housekeeping and laundry services, as well as all other facilities of the hotel, are offered to residents of the apartments. WiFi is available throughout the hotel.

The restaurant, with an African and continental menu, serves buffet, table d'hote and a la carte. The Kivi Sunday poolside barbecue has an assortment of grilled meats. The conference centre houses several rooms, and is staffed by a team of conference coordinators. The hotel is able to cater for conferences for up to 300 pax and has smaller rooms for board meetings and smaller conferences. Motivational breaks and teambuilding exercises can also be arranged. The business centre offers a range of secretarial services and facilities. The garden and swimming pool provide a quiet environment in which guests can relax.

Sagret Hotel

Milimani

Sagret Hotel, Milimani Road, Milimani, Nairobi, Kenya
PO Box 18324, Nairobi 00500, Kenya

Tel	+254 20 2720933; +254 20 2720934
Mobile	
Fax	
E-mail	sagret@sagrethotels.co.ke
Web	

   JKIA, LS & CH & Intl., 50 mins
       Wilson Airport, LS & CH, 40 mins

Sagret Hotel offers budget accommodation, dining and conferencing in the Milimani district of Nairobi. The hotel is particularly popular for its nyama choma grilled meats.

There are 40 en-suite rooms, made up of singles, doubles and triples. Some of the rooms have balconies. The restaurant, in a thatched building across the car park from the hotel, serves a selection of local Kenyan dishes, including its speciality nyama choma grilled meats. It surrounds a central circular bar stocked with soft drinks, beers and spirits, and is equipped with satellite TV. Dining booths around the restaurant are named after animals in Swahili, such as Ndovu and Kiboko.

The conference centre has 3 conference halls. The halls are divided by partitions, and can be joined to form 1 large hall with a seating capacity of 100 pax. The business centre offers printing, internet, scanning, photocopy, lamination, binding and international telephone calls. There is a safe at reception and a secure car park. The hotel is conveniently located for all the government offices in the Milimani area of Nairobi, and is not far from all the shops, businesses and restaurants of the Central Business District.

Heron Hotel

Milimani

Heron Hotel, Milimani Road, off Kenyatta Avenue, Nairobi, Kenya
PO Box 41848, Nairobi 00100, Kenya

Tel	+254 20 2720740-3
Mobile	
Fax	+254 20 2721698
E-mail	reservations@heronhotel.com
Web	www.heronhotel.com

 VISA, MasterCard    JKIA, LS & CH & Intl., 50 mins
                                                    Wilson Airport, LS & CH, 40 mins

Established in 1975, Heron Hotel is situated in the Milimani district of Nairobi. The hotel was extensively refurbished in 2005. This friendly hotel is conveniently located for government offices and Nairobi Hospital, and not far from all the businesses, shops and facilities of the Central Business District.

There are 103 en-suite rooms, made up of superior, superior deluxe and suites. The suites sleep up to 4 pax. Services such as wake up call, daily newspaper delivery and safety deposit are available.

TJ's Steak-out serves local and international dishes such as chilli garlic calamari, chicken wings pilipili, chicken masala, beef fajitas, traditional fish and chips and Lamu prawns. The grill serves a selection of steaks, spare ribs and lamb chops. TJ's Bar serves snacks, soft drinks, beers and cocktails, and is equipped with a large satellite TV. The Bistro serves sandwiches, pizzas and pastries.

The conference centre has 6 halls; the largest seats 80 pax, another seats 60 and the remaining 4 each seat 40. The business centre offers internet, fax, scanning, photocopying and CD writing, and has secretarial and courier services. The hotel can book tours and airport transfers, as well as trips to Nairobi National Park and further afield. There is also a swimming pool, sauna, residents' lounge and gift shop.

Sarova Panafric Milimani

Sarova Panafric, Kenyatta Avenue, Nairobi, Kenya
Sarova Hotels, PO Box 72493, Nairobi 00200, Kenya

Tel	+254 20 720822; +254 20 2716688; +254 20 2767000
Mobile	+254 20 722 200945/6; +254 734 699751/2
Fax	+254 20 2715566
E-mail	panafric@sarovahotels.com
Web	www.sarovahotels.com

 VISA, MasterCard, Diners Card Amex, JCB   JKIA, LS & CH & Intl, 50 mins / Wilson Airport, LS & CH, 40 mins

Named in honour of the Pan African movement, Sarova Panafric was inaugurated in 1965 by the first president of Kenya, Jomo Kenyatta and truly represents Neo Africa. Throughout the 1960s, the Panafric was a centre for liberalism and hosted many of Africa's nationalists and future statesmen.

The Sarova Panafric has 153 en-suite rooms on 6 floors, made up of 4 suites, 3 club twins, 10 club doubles, 17 superior twins, 48 superior doubles, 65 standard twins and 6 standard doubles. It also has 2 rooms for guests with diabilities and 42 serviced apartments with fully equipped kitchens, made up of 28 1-bedroom and 14 2-bedroom.

The Flame Tree brasserie and bar has a terrace with a panoramic view of the city and serves buffet breakfast and a la carte lunch and dinner, with a weekly entertainment programme. The Poolside Garden Restaurant offers snacks and a la carte, and is an ideal place for barbecues, parties and wedding receptions. Local bands play in the poolside gardens every weekend. Tulia Wellness offers massage and other treatments.

The Sarova Panafric is set in lush, landscaped gardens. The hotel has 9 conference and banqueting rooms, modern conferencing equipment and a fully equipped business centre.

Lenana Mount Hotel Milimani

Lenana Mount Hotel, Ralph Bunche Road, Milimani, Nairobi, Kenya
PO Box 40943, Nairobi 00100, Kenya

Tel	+254 20 2717048; +254 20 2710426
Mobile	+254 723 970165
Fax	+254 20 2719394
E-mail	lenanamounthotel@iconnect.co.ke
Web	www.lenanamouthotel.com

  VISA    JKIA, LS & CH & Intl, 50 mins / Wilson Airport, LS & CH, 40 mins

The Lenana Mount Hotel was established in the 1970s. The hotel, in the style of a country house hotel, is set in attractive gardens in Milimani. There are 50 en-suite rooms. All rooms are equipped with telephone and satellite TV. The restaurant serves local and international dishes; both buffet and a la carte are on offer. The bar serves soft drinks, beers and spirits. There are 3 conference halls; the largest seats 50 pax, and the others seat 30 and 25 pax. All conference halls are equipped with projector, clipboard and clip chart. Conference packages include morning and afternoon tea, and buffet lunch. The cyber café has high speed internet, scanning and printing. WiFi is available in the reception, restaurant and bar. The health club has a sauna and swimming pool with sundeck, and is staffed by a swimming instructor. Massage is also on offer.

There are both indoor and outdoor car parks. A 24-hour taxi service operates from the hotel. Laundry and dry cleaning services are available. The hotel is conveniently located for Nairobi's Central Business District, and all the businesses, shops, restaurants and bars in that area. Other highlights of Nairobi include the National Museum, Kenya National Archives and the Railway Museum.

Fairview Hotel   Upper Hill

Fairview Hotel, Bishops Road, off 2nd Ngong Avenue, Upper Hill, Nairobi
PO Box 40842, Nairobi 00100, Kenya
Tel   +254 20 2881000; +254 20 2881419; +254 20 2710090
Mobile
Fax   +254 20 2721320
E-mail book@fairviewkenya.com
Web   www.fairviewkenya.com

VISA, MasterCard, Amex   JKIA, LS & CH & Intl., 45 mins
                              Wilson Airport, LS & CH, 30 mins

Set in 5 acres of lush gardens, Fairview Hotel is a country hotel near the centre of the city. The hotel combines comfort with modern facilities and a state of the art security system.

The hotel has over 100 rooms, categorised as economy, economy plus, business and first. The economy rooms have desks and showers, and are cooled by fans. The first class rooms have eco-friendly air coolers, fridges, desks with stationery, and trouser presses. There are also executive suites, with high speed broadband. And for those staying a minimum of 3 months, there are serviced apartments with 1, 2 or 3 bedrooms, with voice mail, satellite TV and WiFi.

There are 4 restaurants. Pango Brasserie, a member of Chaîne des Rôtisseurs, is a fine dining restaurant with an underground wine cellar. Mukutan Garden Café serves coffees and light meals such as sandwiches, pizzas, quesadillas and sushi. Pwani Pool Restaurant serves international cuisine. And Mitende Atrium, in an airy greenhouse, provides breakfasts, buffet lunches and a la carte dinners.

The 4 conference rooms are fully equipped with modern equipment, including high speed internet and LCD projectors. Functions can be catered for in the gardens, the wine cellar, the Aquarist room or the Atrium.

Country Lodge Hotel   Upper Hill

Country Lodge Hotel, 2nd Ngong Avenue, Upper Hill, Nairobi, Kenya
PO Box 40842, Nairobi 00100, Kenya
Tel   +254 20 2881600
Mobile
Fax   +254 20 2881599
E-mail stay@countrylodge.co.ke
Web   www.countrylodge.co.ke

VISA, MasterCard, Amex   JKIA, LS & CH & Intl., 45 mins
                              Wilson Airport, LS & CH, 30 mins

Country Lodge Hotel opened in 2006 as an affordable hotel for business travellers. The hotel is owned by the Fairview Hotel and shares its 5-acre garden. It has modern facilities and comfortable rooms.

There are 31 singles, 3 twins, 10 doubles and a family room. The rooms are all en-suite and sound proof, and are equipped with satellite TVs, desks, electronic safes, WiFi and voice mail. All rooms also have Swedish duvets, an automated wake up service, tea and coffee makers, and are mosquito proof. The family room consists of two interlinked rooms, one double and one with bunk beds for children under the age of 12.

Breakfast is included in the rate, and served in the hotel. Lunch and dinner can be eaten at any of the 4 restaurants at the Fairview, or at any other restaurant in Nairobi.

The hotel has a business centre with an internet service, and a gym with modern fitness equipment. There is an extensive security system, including CCTV and guards trained by an international security firm. Backup generators, 94,000 gallons of water storage and a fire alarm system support the hotel.

Milele Hotel

South C

Milele Hotel, Muhoho Road, South C, off Mombasa Road, Nairobi
PO Box 27573, Nairobi 00506, Kenya

Tel	+254 20 6007144; +254 20 6003971
Mobile	+254 725 253777
Fax	+254 20 6004371
E-mail	reservations.nairobi@milelehotels.com
Web	www.milelehotels.com

VISA, MasterCard

JKIA, LS & CH & Intl., 20 mins
Wilson Airport, LS & CH, 40 mins

Milele Hotels are managed by the Presbyterian Church of East Africa Foundation, PCEA. The hotels offer the family-friendly concept of holidaying in an unpolluted environment, complimented by the hotel's slogan The Heavenly Experience. Milele means forever in Swahili.

Milele Hotel, Nairobi, was established in 2005. Located just off the Nairobi-Mombasa Highway, the hotel is convenient for Jomo Kenyatta International Airport, JKIA. There are 84 en-suite rooms, made up of singles, doubles, triples and superior rooms. There is also a 3-bedroom apartment that can accommodate a family of 6. The restaurant has an a la carte menu of international cuisine, and also serves buffet. The hotel is an alcohol and smoking free zone. Soft drinks, juices and non-alcoholic wines are served.

The conference centre has 5 halls; the largest seats 180 pax, 2 seat 40, 1 seats 30 and 1 seats 20. There are also 3 boardrooms, each seating 10 pax. All halls are equipped with PA system and projector. WiFi is available throughout the hotel. The spacious grounds are suitable for wedding receptions, teambuilding activities and parties. The hotel can arrange taxi service, laundry and airport transfers. Milele Hotel is affiliated to Milele Beach Hotel in Bamburu and Milele Resort Presbyterian Guest House in Nakuru.

Hennessis Hotel

Museum Hill

Hennessis Hotel, Limuru Road, next to Stima Plaza, Nairobi, Kenya
PO Box 6859, Nairobi 00100, Kenya

Tel	+254 20 2654970; +254 20 2654972
Mobile	+254 737 111844; +254 701 111844
Fax	
E-mail	margaret@hotelhennessis.com
Web	www.hennessis.com

VISA, MasterCard

JKIA, LS & CH & Intl., 1 hr
Wilson Airport, LS & CH, 50 mins

Hennessis Hotel opened in 2010. The hotel, located on Limuru Road next to Stima Plaza, offers modern accommodation and conference facilities. There are 103 en-suite rooms, made up of singles, doubles, twins and executive rooms. All rooms are equipped with satellite TV and telephone. The restaurant has an international a la carte menu and a selection of drinks including a wine list. Buffet can be served for large groups on request. Dishes include southern fried chicken, beef stroganoff, vegetable ratatouille, palak paneer and butter chicken. Sir Joseph's Lounge is stocked with soft drinks, beers, wines and spirits. A DJ or live band plays every night. There are 2 conference halls; the larger hall seats 50 pax and the smaller seats 35. PA system and projector are available for hire, advance notice required. WiFi is available throughout the hotel. There is also a secure car park. The hotel is conveniently located for the National Museum of Kenya. It is situated between the Central Business District and Westlands, making it convenient for the restaurants, bars, shops and businesses of both the Central Business District and Westlands. Sites of interest within Nairobi include Kenya National Archives, the Railway Museum and Nairobi National Park.

Wida Highway Motel
Nairobi-Nakuru Highway

Wida Highway Motel, nr Sigona Golf Club, Nairobi-Nakuru Highway
PO Box 55196, Nairobi 00200, Kenya

Tel	+254 20 2240853
Mobile	+254 719 444993
Fax	
E-mail	info@hotelwida.com
Web	www.hotelwida.com

VISA, MasterCard

 JKIA, LS & CH & Intl., 1 hr 15 mins
Wilson Airport, LS & CH, 1 hr

On the highway heading out of Nairobi towards Naivasha and Nakuru, Wida Highway Motel is well set up for conferences. It is ideally located for breaking a long drive, and offers food and entertainment.

There are 43 en-suite standard rooms and 67 en-suite deluxe rooms. All rooms have telephone and room heater. Some rooms have satellite TV. The restaurant serves a buffet of local and international dishes, and also has an a la carte menu. There is also a nyama choma grill, and seating booths in the garden. The main bar and the garden bar serve soft drinks, beers and spirits. A takeaway kiosk on the highway serves food and snacks. The garden has a children's play area, with climbing frame and slide. Entertainment such as live bands, acrobatic shows and magic shows are provided at the weekend.

Mangrove Hall seats 600 pax; Hebron Hall seats 200; Judah and Bamboo Shoot each seat 100; Bethel seats 40 and the computer annex seats 25. Conference equipment such as overhead projector, TV and video are available. Conference packages with full board accommodation, tea breaks and stationery are on offer. The motel is located next to Sigona Golf Club, about 16km from Nairobi.

Jumuia Conference and Country Home, Nairobi
Limuru

Jumuia Conference and Country Home, Limuru Road, Limuru, Nairobi
PO Box 212, Limuru 00217, Kenya

Tel	+254 20 2048881; +254 20 2060964-7
Mobile	
Fax	+254 20 2048929
E-mail	reservations.limuru@resortjumuia.com
Web	www.resortjumuia.com

JKIA, LS & CH & Intl., 1 hr 45 mins
Wilson Airport, LS & CH, 1 hr 30 mins

Jumuia Resorts aim to be the leading Christian resort chain in Kenya. Jumuia, Swahili for community or federation, refers to the National Council of Churches of Kenya. Jumuia ya makanisa ya Kenya. There are 5 Jumuia Resorts, in Kisumu, Nakuru, Limuru, Mombasa and Nairobi. Formerly known as the Limuru Conference and Training Centre, Jumuia Conference and Country Home has been a centre of Christian leadership training for over 50 years. The centre was fully renovated in 2003. There are 116 en-suite rooms, made up of standard and executive. There are also 4 cottages, with 2, 3 or 4 bedrooms. Maple Restaurant serves an international a la carte menu, including Victoria whole tilapia, chicken kiev and Jumuia mixed grill for 2. Kids' Corner includes fish nuggets and chicken in a basket. The bakery serves chocolate donuts, flaky croissants and Swahili mandazi. No alcohol is served.

The conference centre houses 3 conference halls and 6 boardrooms. Acacia room seats 400 pax, Cyprus room seats 70 and Dove seats 35. The boardrooms seat 15 to 20. All halls are fully equipped, including LCD projector, PA system, TV and video. A selection of conference packages is available. The large gardens are ideal for weddings, teambuilding and functions. Secretarial and transport services are also available.

Brackenhurst Conference Centre Limuru

Brackenhurst Conference Centre, Limuru-Tigoni-Banana Rd., Limuru, Kenya
PO Box 32, Limuru 00217, Kenya

Tel	+254 20 2014092; +254 20 2056528; +254 20 2013162
Mobile	+254 736 424242; +254 724 256721
Fax	+254 20 2045785
E-mail	bookings@brackenhurst.com
Web	www.brackenhurst.com / www.africanencounter.org

 VISA, MasterCard   JKIA, LS & CH & Intl., 1 hr 45 mins
Wilson Airport, LS & CH, 1 hr 30 mins

Brackenhurst Conference Centre, set amongst the green tea fields of Limuru, is part of the African Encounter group of companies. The hotel started life in 1914 as a farm called Three Tree Farm because of the 3 tall muna trees that stood on the ridge. It became a hotel in 1927 and was renamed Brackenhurst. Shortly after Kenya's independence in 1963, Brackenhurst became a conference centre.

There are 30 single rooms, 10 double rooms with 2 double beds, 10 double rooms with double and single beds, and 25 family rooms with double bed, single bed and bunk beds. The 4 dining rooms serve Kenyan and international buffet. Dining A seats 150 pax; Dining B, C and D each seat 30. The Coffee Shop has an a la carte menu. No alcohol is served. The conference centre has 5 fully equipped conference halls: Clarke Chaple, seating 250 pax, Saunders Auditorium, Muturi Hall, Tea Room and Lion's Den.

Brackenhurst has basketball, tennis and volleyball courts. Nearby forest trails are ideal for walking, jogging or bird watching. The activity centre for children is also available for Sunday school. The centre also has a clinic which serves the local community. African Encounter, a tour operator affiliated to Brackenhurst, can arrange excursions and safaris.

Kentmere Club Limuru

Kentmere Club, Limuru-Tigoni-Banana Road, Limuru, Kenya
PO Box 39508, Nairobi 00623, Kenya

Tel	+254 20 2021369; +254 20 3585511
Mobile	+254 722 276357
Fax	+254 20 2020076
E-mail	reservations@kentmereclub.com
Web	www.kentmereclub.com

     JKIA, LS & CH & Intl., 1 hr 45 mins
Wilson Airport, LS & CH, 1 hr 30 mins

Kentmere Club opened its doors in the 1920s, when it was particularly popular with the members who used the nearby shooting range. Since then the club has changed management several times; the current team took over in 1986. The club is set in extensive, manicured gardens, filled with trees, plants and shrubs named in Latin and English.

There are 16 en-suite rooms. The rooms are decorated in traditional English style, with chintz wallpaper, heavy curtains and open fireplaces. The Club is still a members club, but non-members are most welcome. Members receive a 20% discount on accommodation; new members must be proposed and seconded by current members. The restaurant serves local and international cuisine. Meals are served in the dining room or on the terrace overlooking the garden. Outside catering is available on request. The bar is fully stocked with soft drinks, beers, wines, spirits and cocktails. The club's proximity to Nairobi makes it an excellent place to stop for lunch, dinner or accommodation en route to or from Nairobi. It is also convenient for company parties and functions; transfers from Nairobi are available. Activities include visits to the local coffee plantations and tea farms. Weddings, banquets, conferences and teambuilding can be arranged.

Boni House

Runda

Boni House, 16 Acacia Drive, off UN Avenue, Runda, Nairobi, Kenya
PO Box 112, Nairobi 00621, Kenya
Tel
Mobile +254 722 553794; +254 732 246761
Fax
E-mail house.boni@gmail.com
Web www.bonihouse.com

   JKIA, LS & CH & Intl., 1 hr
Wilson Airport, LS & CH, 1 hr

Boni House is an elegantly furnished private house in manicured gardens, in a quiet area of Nairobi. Situated within easy reach of the UN complex and a number of embassies, the house is conveniently located for both business and holiday travellers.

There are 8 en-suite rooms, made up of 6 doubles, 1 triple and 1 triple with kitchenette equipped with microwave and cooker. Each room is individually decorated, and is equipped with TV, kettle and minibar. The downstairs lounge is furnished with gilt armchairs and plush curtains, and has polished wooden floors. The bar is stocked with soft drinks, beers, wines and spirits. The standard arrangement is bed and breakfast, but other meals can be arranged on request. The a la carte menu includes fillet steak, grilled tilapia and lamb chops, as well as snacks such as burgers, sandwiches and salads. The business room has a computer and printer. WiFi is available upstairs; satellite TV is available in the upstairs lounge. Boni House is within easy distance of the Village Market shopping centre, a number of craft markets and Westlands, where many of Nairobi's best restaurants, bars, casinos, health clubs, spas and shops are located. Boni House can arrange tours to places of interest in Nairobi and safaris to destinations in Kenya.

Tribe

Gigiri

Tribe, the Village Market, Limuru Road, Gigiri, Nairobi
PO Box 1333, Nairobi 00621, Kenya
Tel +254 20 7200000
Mobile
Fax +254 20 7200110
E-mail reservations@tribehotel-kenya.com
Web www.tribe-hotel.com

 VISA, MasterCard, Amex   JKIA, LS & CH & Intl., 1 hr 15 mins
Wilson Airport, LS & CH, 1 hr

Tribe has been designed to meld New York Chic with the warmth of Africa. It blends rich earth colours with stainless steel and gleaming glass, rustic metal with natural stone and handmade wooden furniture. The hotel has 20 standard rooms, 80 delux rooms, 14 delux spa rooms, more spacious than deluxe, and 5 superior king rooms. There are 5 junior suites, 5 lofted business suites, 1 Ambassadorial suite complete with 2 flat screen TVs and an open plan sitting room and 1 Presidential suite with 2 flat screen TVs, a large open plan sitting and dining room and a balcony overlooking the pool. All the rooms have WiFi, direct dial telephones, electronic safes, TVs and personal aircon systems. Their open plan bathrooms have power showers, baths on request, and are equipped with Eartherapy amenities.

The executive chef at EPIC Restaurant creates dishes with exotic flavours. The poolside dining has a snack menu and serves an extensive buffet brunch. A private dining room is available on request. From the landscaped gardens to the fantasy heated pool, from the 24-hour business centre to the executive boardrooms, from the sound room to the KAYA spa, this is a hotel that relishes modern elegance.

Tribe was selected by Conde Nast Traveller for the Hot List 2010 and was awarded a WOW Pick by Kiwi Collection.

Windsor Golf and Country Club
Thika Road

Windsor Golf and Country Club, Thika Road, Nairobi, Kenya
PO Box 45587, Nairobi 00100, Kenya

Tel	+254 20 8562300; +254 20 8562500; +254 20 8647000
Mobile	
Fax	+254 20 8563322
E-mail	admin@windsor.co.ke
Web	www.windsorgolfresort.com

 VISA, MasterCard, Amex    JKIA, LS & CH & Intl., 1 hr
Wilson Airport, LS & CH, 1 hr

Set around a lovely 18-hole golf course, the Windsor Golf and Country Club is an attractive country house hotel. The hotel combines Victorian style buildings with modern amenities and facilities.
There are 130 en-suite rooms, made up of 80 deluxe, 20 studio suites and 15 2-bedroom cottages. All rooms have satellite TV, safe and telephone. The studio suites have an open plan lounge. The cottages have living room with minibar. The Country Room Restaurant serves international cuisine for breakfast, lunch and dinner, including homemade bread and fresh salads. The Conservatory Restaurant, by the swimming pool, has a coffee shop style menu, with coffee, tea, pastries and savouries. The

Windsor Room Restaurant is open for dinner, and serves an international a la carte menu. Library Bar, Kingfisher Bar and Club House Bar all serve a range of soft drinks, beers, wines and spirits.
The Oak Room is available for conferences. Conference equipment including overhead projector, TV and video is available. Conference packages, including buffet lunch, can be arranged. There is also a fully equipped business centre. The Health Club offers massage and hair and beauty treatments. The hotel also has tennis courts, squash courts, gym and spacious secure car park. The golf course has a driving range and offers a life membership package.

Utalii Hotel
Thika Road

Utalii Hotel, Thika Road, opp national youth service institute, Nairobi
PO Box 31067, Nairobi 00600, Kenya

Tel	+254 20 8563540; +254 20 8561201
Mobile	+254 722 205891/2
Fax	+254 20 2686759
E-mail	utaliihotel@utalii.co.ke
Web	www.utalii.co.ke

 VISA    JKIA, LS & CH & Intl., 1 hr
Wilson Airport, LS & CH, 1 hr

In spacious grounds and lovely gardens, Utalii Hotel provides a peaceful country environment. The hotel offers conferences, functions and catering in a serene location in the outskirts of Nairobi.
There are 57 en-suite rooms. All rooms have aircon, electronic safe, telephone, mosquito net and satellite TV. Wataalamu Restaurant serves an international menu with both a la carte and table d'hote. Buffet lunches are served every Tuesday; poolside barbecue is served every Saturday night; international buffet lunch is served every Sunday. Ukarimu Coffee Shop serves coffee, tea and patisseries daily. The poolside terrace serves snacks. Outside catering can be provided for up to 2000 pax.

Sebule Bar serves soft drinks, beers and spirits. Shangwe Bar offers happy hours, live entertainment and nyama choma grilled meats. There are 4 function rooms, available for conferences, seminars and banquets for over 250 pax, as well as a business centre and a souvenir shop. The hotel also has an Olympic size swimming pool and tennis courts. The children's club has bouncy castle, animations, face painting and treasure hunts. The hotel is located opposite the national youth service institute. A shuttle bus runs regularly between the hotel and Nairobi city centre. The hotel is a practical school for the hotel and catering students of Utalii College.

Hotel La Mada

Thika Road

Hotel La Mada, Karura Forest, off Thika Road, Nairobi, Kenya
PO Box 40683, Nairobi 00100, Kenya

Tel	+254 20 8561460
Mobile	+254 722 208906
Fax	+254 20 8561194
E-mail	lamada@madahotels.com
Web	www.madahotels/lamada

 VISA, MasterCard, Amex, JCB   JKIA, LS & CH & Intl., 1 hr
Wilson Airport, LS & CH, 1 hr

Set on a 7-acre property on the edge of Karura Forest, Hotel La Mada is surrounded by woodland. The hotel's garden, with a stream flowing through it, attracts a variety of birdlife and several species of monkey. Located 10km from Nairobi city centre, just off the Thika Road, the hotel is ideally situated for those who want access to the city without being submerged in its hustle and bustle.

There are 35 en-suite rooms, made up of 25 double rooms, 6 twin rooms and 4 executive suites.

The hotel has an a la carte restaurant, a coffee shop and a guest lounge. There are 3 conference halls, one that holds up to 50 pax, another that holds up to 150 pax and the last that holds up to 300 pax. An executive boardroom and a business centre are also available for the guests' use. There is a swimming pool, with nearby pool bar, and a curio shop. Transfers to Jomo Kenyatta International Airport and Wilson Airport are available.

Safari Park Hotel

Thika Road

Safari Park Hotel, Thika Road, Nairobi, Kenya
PO Box 45038, Nairobi 00100, Kenya

Tel	+254 20 3633000; +254 20 3568644/8
Mobile	+254 734 333175/6; +254 722 205683
Fax	+254 20 3633919/8
E-mail	sales@safariparkhotel.co.ke
Web	www.safaripark-hotel.com

 VISA, MasterCard, Amex   JKIA, LS & CH & Intl., 1 hr
Wilson Airport, LS & CH, 1 hr

The Safari Park Hotel stands in 50 acres of scenic grounds incorporating a wide variety of indigenous trees and offering sanctuary to a startling array of birds and butterflies. The hotel's elegant architecture is centred around landscaped gardens and water features. There are 204 en-suite rooms, made up of 168 deluxe rooms, 21 junior suites, 8 business suites, 6 executive suites and 1 presidential suite. All are furnished with an African flavour and have modern facilities like an electronic safe and internet connectivity and private balconies overlooking the gardens. The hotel also offers luxurious housing units for long stay guests. The hotel has 5 specialty restaurants. Cafe Kigwa, open 24 hours, serves international food, Nyama Choma Ranch serves African, Winners' Pavilion serves Chinese, La Piazzetta serves Italian and Chiyo serves Japanese and Korean. Nightlife is varied, with the Cats Club disco, the famous Safari Cats dancers, the contemporary Piano Bar, Hemingways lounge and bar, the Casino Paradise and King Solomon's Mines. The Paradise Business Centre offers 24-hour global connectivity and equipment hire and a professional business support team offering secretarial services and on site management support. The hotel also includes the Jambo Conference Centre with a range of boardrooms and banqueting facilities, and a fully equipped fitness centre.

Sportsview Hotel

Kasarani

Sportsview Hotel, Mwiki Road, Kasarani, Nairobi, Kenya
PO Box 74194, Nairobi 00200, Kenya

Tel	+254 20 3000409; +254 20 3008516; +254 20 8561648/9
Mobile	+254 722 881101
Fax	+254 20 3002611; +254 20 8562811
E-mail	info@sportsviewhotel.com
Web	www.sportsviewhotel.com

VISA

JKIA, LS & CH & Intl., 1 hr
Wilson Airport, LS & CH, 1 hr

Located 12km north of Nairobi, Sportsview Hotel combines the atmosphere of a country inn with the amenities of a city hotel.

There are 200 en-suite rooms, made up of singles, doubles and mini-homes. The 20 mini-homes offer more privacy, and each has a garage attached. The restaurant serves local and international dishes, including barbecue, and also offers a children's menu. Outside catering is available for birthdays, weddings and other functions. The bar serves soft drinks, beers and spirits. Sportie Health Club is equipped with swimming pool, sauna and steam room. Water aerobics and other fitness classes are on offer, and nutrition advice is given if required. The professional masseuse offers deep tissue sports massage, relaxation massage and aromatherapy massage designed to detox and energise the body. The beauty salon has a selection of hair, skin, nail, hand and feet treatments.

There are 6 modern conference halls, seating from 20 to 200 pax. Conference packages can be tailored to the requirements of each group. The business centre has internet, photocopy and fax, and offers secretarial services. Wedding and honeymoon packages are available. Children's activities range from face painting to pony riding. The hotel also offers bouncy castle, magic and acrobatic shows, play station and playground.

Hill Park Hotel

Lower Hill

Hill Park Hotel, Lower Hill, Nairobi, Kenya
PO Box 46037, Nairobi 00100, Kenya

Tel	+254 20 2724313; +254 20 2724315
Mobile	+254 724 256201; +254 735 337522
Fax	+254 20 2716768
E-mail	reservations@hillparkhotel.com
Web	www.hillparkhotel.com

VISA

JKIA, LS & CH & Intl., 45 mins
Wilson Airport, LS & CH, 30 mins

Hill Park Hotel is located in Lower Hill, next to Upper Hill. The hotel offers personal service in a peaceful area.

There are 80 suites, made up of 16 standard, 56 premium, 4 executive and 4 deluxe. The suites are all equipped with satellite TV, minibar, kettle, safe and WiFi. There are also 30 serviced apartments, made up of 23 1-bedroom apartments, 2 3-bedroom apartments and 5 penthouses. All apartments have a sitting room and a fully equipped kitchen.

The Hill Park Restaurant, in a garden pavilion with outdoor seating area, offers an international a la carte menu; buffet can be provided for large groups. The Poolside Grill serves barbecues and salads, as well as smoothies and other drinks. The Bar, with open fireplace, serves soft drinks, beers, wines and spirits. The hotel has a swimming pool with sunbathing terrace, gym with modern equipment, steam room, sauna and massage parlour. There are 3 conference rooms and 3 boardrooms, each named after a Kenyan hill. Cherangani, the largest, seats 60 pax; Loita seats 30 and Tugen seats 20. Chyulu boardroom seats 15, Nyambeni seats 9 and Legetet 7. Conference equipment including projector and PA system are available for hire. All rooms have WiFi, telephone, reception area and balcony.

Hill Park Hotel is affiliated to Hill Park Tiwi Beach on the South Coast.

Crowne Plaza

Upper Hill

Crowne Plaza, Kenya Road, Upper Hill, Nairobi, Kenya
PO Box 25574, Nairobi 00100, Kenya

Tel	+254 20 2746000
Mobile	+254 732 166000; +254 734 766000; +254 719 096000
Fax	+254 20 2746100
E-mail	info@cpnairobi.com
Web	www.ichotelsgroup.com

VISA, MasterCard, Amex

JKIA, LS & CH & Intl., 40 mins
Wilson Airport, LS & CH, 30 mins

Crowne Plaza, which opened in 2010, is a modern hotel offering quality business and leisure facilities.

There are 162 en-suite rooms on 5 floors, made up of 48 standard, 68 superior, 4 deluxe, 29 club and 13 suites. All rooms are equipped with aircon, satellite TV, work area with data port, universal sockets, high speed WiFi, iron, kettle, hairdryer, safe and minibar. In addition, the rooms on the club floor have a private check-in area and exclusive lounge. The suites include adjoining rooms and dining area.

Baraza Restaurant serves buffets, while Sikia Restaurant serves a la carte, specialising in grills, steaks and seafood. Alabaster Lounge serves light meals and pastries; Babalu's Bar is stocked with everything from single malt whisky to rare cognac. The Health Club and Fitness Suite has a swimming pool, sauna, steam room, beauty salon and a state of the art gym with personal trainers.

The pillarless ballroom seats up to 500 pax. With an adjoining kitchen, it is equipped for either banqueting or conferencing. There are 6 boardrooms, seating 14 pax each, that are fully equipped with audio visual equipment. The hotel also has a business centre with internet, printer, fax and photocopy, a travel desk and a large, secure car park.

Gemina Court

Kilimani

Gemina Court, George Padmore Road, Kilimani, Nairobi, Kenya
PO Box 44491, Nairobi 00100, Kenya

Tel	+254 20 2021200; +254 20 2020565
Mobile	+254 721 931119
Fax	
E-mail	enquiry@geminacourt.co.ke
Web	www.geminacourt.co.ke

JKIA, LS & CH & Intl., 1 hr
Wilson Airport, LS & CH, 45 mins

Gemina Court offers a selection of self-catering serviced apartments available for short and long-term lease. The apartments are in a quiet compound, with a variety of facilities.

There are 55 apartments, made up of 1, 2 and 3-bedroom apartments, and a penthouse. All apartments have a kitchen equipped with fridge, electric cooker, glassware, cutlery, crockery and utensils. All are fully furnished, including dining table, lounge furniture, TV and bed linen. All apartments have a balcony, some of which overlook the swimming pool. Satellite TV channels are available for a surcharge. The deluxe apartments are more spacious and include a walk-in wardrobe. The penthouse has a master bedroom, 2nd bedroom, kitchen, dining area, lounge and balcony. WiFi and wired internet connection is available in all apartments. A safe is available at reception. Laundry and dry cleaning services are available for a surcharge. A backup generator ensures 24-hour electricity; a borehole ensures 24-hour water.

There is a gym, sauna and steam bath. The swimming pool is surrounded by a sunbathing terrace. A personal trainer is available. Classes include Chinese martial arts and kick boxing. On site offices provide fax, email and internet services. There is no restaurant. There is a large, enclosed car park.

Woodmere

Hurlingham

Woodmere, Rose Avenue, off Lenana Road, Nairobi, Kenya
PO Box 74381, Nairobi 00200, Kenya

Tel	+254 20 2712511; +254 20 2715170; +254 20 2715113
Mobile	+254 722 344778; +254 733 939730
Fax	+254 20 2713720
E-mail	woodmere@woodmerenairobi.com
Web	www.woodmerenairobi.com

 VISA, Amex   JKIA, LS & CH & Intl, 40 mins
Wilson Airport, LS & CH, 30 mins

Woodmere offers serviced apartments and studios in an attractive garden in Nairobi. The hotel is located just off Lenana Road, making it convenient for the Yaya Centre and all the shops and businesses of Hurlingham, as well as for the Central Business District. The striking building was designed by an award-winning architect.

There are 14 studios, made up of 10 budget and 4 deluxe. There are also 30 apartments, made up of standard 1 and 2-bedroom apartments, super 1 and 2-bedroom apartments, 2-bedroom conservatories and 4-bedroom vistas. The apartments are equipped with a small kitchen, built in kitchen appliances, dining utensils, microwave, toaster, coffeemaker and kettle.

They are furnished with hardwood, custom-made furniture, bed linen and satellite TV. Foreign language TV, including French, Japanese, German and Italian channels, are available on request. Services include daily maid service, 24-hour telephone switchboard and free internet access in the business centre. WiFi is available throughout for a surcharge. A borehole ensures 24-hour water and a generator ensures 24-hour electricity.

The swimming pool is surrounded by a sun terrace, and furnished with tables, chairs, sunbeds and umbrellas. Barbecue is available. There is also a gym, Jacuzzi and sauna. The compound has a secure car park.

Wildebeest Camp

Kilimani

Wildebeest Camp and Travels, Kibera Road, off Ngong Road, Nairobi
PO Box 18209, Nairobi 00100, Kenya

Tel	+254 20 2103505
Mobile	+254 734 770733
Fax	
E-mail	info@wildebeesttravels.com
Web	www.wildebeesttravels.com

 VISA, MasterCard, Amex    JKIA, LS & CH & Intl, 45 mins
Wilson Airport, LS & CH, 30 mins

The only tented camp in the city of Nairobi, Wildebeest Camp offers a safari experience from visitors' 1st night in Kenya. Within attractive gardens, the camp has a campsite, budget accommodation, safari tents and a travel agent.

There are 8 en-suite safari tents, made up of doubles, triples and quads. They have mosquito nets on windows and doors, lights, power sockets and verandas furnished with table and chairs. There are 6 garden tents, made up of doubles and twins, with lights and power sockets. There are 4 budget rooms, made up of 2 doubles and 2 twins. There is a dorm with 6 beds, and a campsite. Shared bathroom facilities are available for guests in the garden tents, budget rooms and campsite.

The friendly house has a lounge, restaurant and bar, complete with games, TV and DVDs. The menu includes sandwiches, burgers, salads and full English breakfast. A useful noticeboard gives information on local buses, trains and flights, as well as local supermarkets, shops, events and community projects. There is a luggage storeroom, safe, gift shop and secure car park.

Wildebeest Camp is the base for Wildebeest Travels, which offers a plethora of tours and safaris, including trips to Hell's Gate, the Maasai Mara and Lake Nakuru, kayaking expeditions and Nile cruises.

Ngong Hills Hotel

Kilimani

Ngong Hills Hotel, nr Uchumi Hyper, Ngong Road, Kilimani, Nairobi
PO Box 40585, Nairobi 00100, Kenya

Tel	+254 20 3860894-5; +254 20 3876745
Mobile	+254 729 476072
Fax	+254 20 3871750
E-mail	info@ngonghillshotel.com
Web	www.ngonghillshotel.com

VISA, MasterCard, Diners Club

 JKIA, LS & CH & Intl., 45 mins
Wilson Airport, LS & CH, 30 mins

The Ngong Hills Hotel was established in 1978, and has remained in the hands of the same family since then.

There are 35 en-suite rooms, made up of doubles and singles. The rooms are all equipped with satellite TV, telephone and WiFi. Lenana Restaurant serves African cuisine, and offers both buffet and a la carte. The Choma Centre serves nyama choma grilled meats. The bar serves soft drinks, beers and spirits, and is equipped with a pool table. There is also a disco. There are 2 conference halls and a meeting room. The larger hall seats 250 pax and the smaller seats 100. The meeting room seats 20 pax. All halls are equipped with LCD projector. The business centre has high speed internet, printing, scanning, photocopy and fax. The centre manager is available to assist with any queries. The hotel can book taxis and arrange car hire. Tours and excursions to places in Nairobi can be arranged. Places of interest in Nairobi include the National Museum and Railway Museum in the centre of town, and the Giraffe Centre, Sheldrick Elephant Orphanage, Karen Blixen Museum and Nairobi National Park in Karen and Langata.

Trisan Hotel

Hurlingham

Trisan Hotel, Turbo Road, off Lenana Road, Nairobi, Kenya
PO Box 43630, Nairobi 00100, Kenya

Tel	+254 20 2713046
Mobile	+254 722 530440
Fax	
E-mail	info@trisan.co.ke
Web	

 JKIA, LS & CH & Intl., 45 mins
Wilson Airport, LS & CH, 30 mins

Set in attractive gardens, Trisan Hotel is a peaceful retreat in the Hurlingham area of Nairobi. The hotel is conveniently located for the Yaya Centre and is not far from the shops, restaurants, businesses and offices of the Central Business District.

There are 32 en-suite rooms, made up of doubles and triples. All rooms are equipped with TV with local channels. The restaurant has an a la carte menu, and also serves buffet. The cuisine is international, and includes a selection of Indian and Kenyan dishes such as Trisan chicken tikka, fish masala, grilled prawns, chicken dhania and mutton curry. Snacks include fish fingers, chicken wings and potato bhajias. Conferencing and banqueting menus are available. The bar, with dark red velvet seats, has a large selection of soft drinks, beers, wines, spirits and liqueurs. The conference centre has 3 conference halls. The largest seats 50 pax, the next seats 30 and the smallest seats 25. Internet and printing facilities are on offer. WiFi is available throughout the hotel. There is a secure, enclosed car park. The reception can book taxis, city tours and airport transfers.

EXPLORE CREATIVITY

Shop
Discover unique, ethically-made creations crafted by local artisans who are working to make a difference.

Moniko's Café
Relax with friends and family as you enjoy an organic food experience in our garden café.

Workshops
Explore our recycling and production hub and see how the artisans masterfully transform cast away flipflops into imaginative, usable products.

Bliss Beauty Clinic
Indulge in relaxing spa treatments at Bliss's tranquil salon.

Kids' Haven
Bring the kids out for a fun-filled day of arts and crafts as they learn about eco-friendly ways of conserving and sustaining the environment.

40 Marula Lane (off Karen Rd), Karen Nairobi
Website: www.marulastudios.com

Cleaning Beaches, Creating Masterpieces.

A story of logic and magic; the logic of recycling our rubbish using the magic of imagination and creativity.

The FFRC is a social enterprise that up-cycles discarded flipflops into a bouquet of colourful, well designed sculptures, household items, fashion accessories and bespoke pieces. We tailor our orders to suit any market and supply to shops, hotels, tour groups, corporate companies, conservation groups, individuals and more.

YOUR TRAVEL MANAGEMENT PARTNER

OUR SERVICES
- AIR TICKETING
- HOTEL ACCOMMODATION
- SAFARI & HOLIDAY PACKAGES
- CAR RENTALS
- AIRPORT TRANSFERS
- VISA SERVICES
- TRAVEL INSURANCE
- MEET & ASSIST SERVICE
- CONFERENCES & EXHIBITIONS
- INCENTIVE TOURS

"A 2012 WORLD TRAVEL AWARD NOMINEE"

RICKSHAW TRAVELS (K) LTD
Ukay Center, 3rd Floor, Mwanzi Road,
Westlands, Nairobi - Kenya
Tel: + 254 20 3750007 / 3750069 / 3750079
Email: admin@rickshawtravels.com

www.rickshawtravels.com

• TANZANIA • KENYA • RWANDA • SOUTH AFRICA • ZIMBABWE • UNITED KINGDOM • CANADA • INDIA

Lion in Nairobi National Park – Photo © Marie-Claire Webner

The Central Highlands

Mt Kenya – Photo © Andrew Nightingale, kembu.com

Mt Kenya rises spectacularly in the centre of the highlands, its icy peaks glinting white. Mountain ranges, bustling towns, fertile farms and rushing waterfalls garnish its shoulders. Highlights include the Aberdare Range, Meru National Park, Thomson's Falls, Mwea National Reserve and Ol Donyo Sabuk National Park.

The major towns are Thika, Muranga, Nyeri, Nyahururu, Nanyuki, Meru and Embu. Made famous by Elspeth Huxley's Flame Trees of Thika, Thika is now known for pineapples and coffee. Muranga, called Fort Hall in colonial times, is now a lively provincial capital. Nyeri is the gateway to the Aberdare National Park, Nanyuki to Laikipia, Meru to Meru National Park and Embu to Mwea National Reserve. Nyahururu, called Thomson's Falls by the British, is Kenya's highest town.

Nanyuki has a busy domestic airport. Airstrips suitable for charter flights are dotted around the region. A good road system links the towns; 4WD vehicles are required in the national parks. Kikuyu, Meru and Embu are the traditional inhabitants of the region, now home to a diverse mix of tribal groups.

At just over 5,100m, Mt Kenya is the highest mountain in Kenya, and the second highest in Africa after Mt Kilimanjaro. According to Kikuyu tradition, the mountain is the throne of the god Ngai who bestowed the surrounding highlands on the Kikuyu people. The mountain's original name, Kirinyaga, has been condensed to Kenya, giving the country its name. The three peaks of Mt Kenya are Batian, Nelion and Point Lenana. Batian and Nelion require professional climbing equipment. Point Lenana can be climbed along the Naro Moru, Sirimon, Chogoria, Burguret and Timau routes. Guides and porters can be booked through adventure tourism companies, or hired privately in towns around the mountain.

Aberdare National Park comprises a range of lush mountains adorned with forest, ravines and waterfalls. In 1952, the young Princess Elizabeth was staying at Treetops in the Aberdare National Park when she learned she was now Queen of England. Wildlife includes rhino, leopard, colobus monkey and the elusive bongo; 250 species of birds have been recorded. Park gates are at Ark, Treetops, Ruhuruini, Kiandagoro, Mutubio, Wandare, Shamata and Rhino. There is an airstrip at Mweiga. Activities include game viewing, bird watching, camping and trekking.

Meru National Park has wooded grasslands, thorny bush and dense riverine forest. It was the former home of Joy and George Adamson, and Elsa the lioness of Born Free fame. Wildlife includes rhino, cheetah, leopard, Grevy's zebra, reticulated giraffe and bush pig; over 300 species of birds have been recorded. Park gates are at Murera and Ura. Airstrips are at Kinna, Mulika and Elsa's Kopje. There is a public campsite at Bwatherongi.

Thomson's Falls was named for Joseph Thomson, a naturalist and geologist from Scotland who, in 1887, was the first white man to see the spectacular waterfalls. The viewpoint, at which viewing fees are charged, is cluttered with curio stalls and traditional dancers. Mwea National Reserve and Ol Donyo Sabuk National Park are small, little-visited gems. Mwea is known for its dam and abundance of rare water birds; Ol Donyo Sabuk is known for its mountain and the Fourteen Falls. Both offer game viewing, bird watching, trekking and camping.

KaribuKenya Accommodation Guide

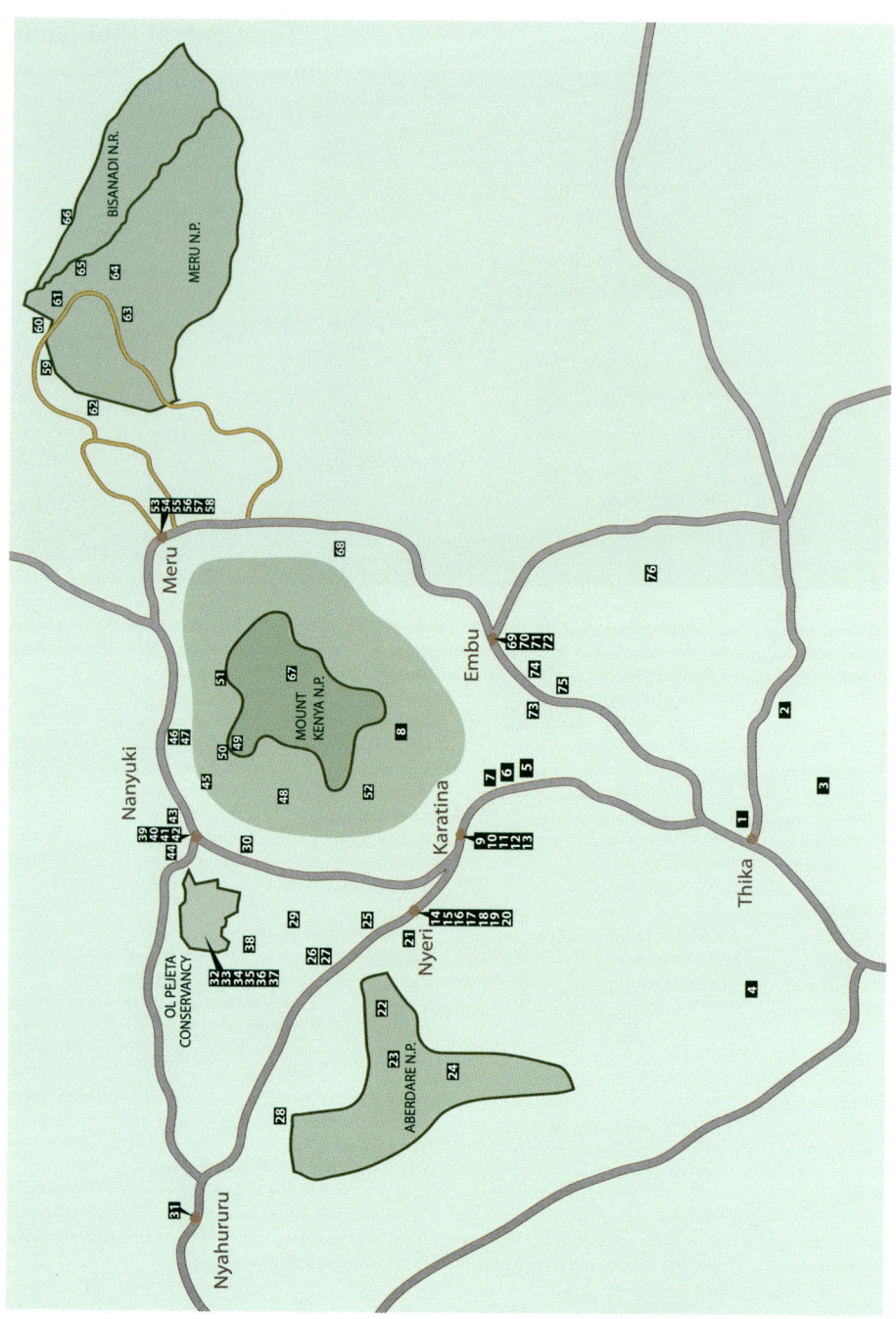

Index to all camps, lodges and hotels in the greater Central area

#	Name	#	Name
1	Blue Post Hotel	40	Ibis Hotel Nanyuki
2	Fourteen Falls Lodge	41	The Sportsman's Arms
3	KWS, Sabuk Guest House	42	Kongoni Camp
4	Ruiki Cultural Centre	43	Nanyuki River Camel Camp
5	Buffalo Bay Motel	44	Mukima House
6	Camp Malta	45	Fairmont Mount Kenya Safari Club
7	Rapids Camp	46	Timau River Lodge
8	Castle Forest Lodge	47	Ken Trout
9	Msafiri House	48	KWS, Batian Guest House
10	Ibis Hotel Karatina 1	49	Old Moses and Shipton
11	Hotel Starbucks	50	KWS, Sirimon Bandas
12	Ibis Hotel Karatina 2	51	Rutundu Log Cabins
13	Elephant Castle Hotel	52	Serena Mountain Lodge
14	Banana Leaf Hotel	53	Hotel Incredible
15	Batian Grand Hotel	54	Hotel Three Steers
16	Green Hills Hotel	55	Meru County Hotel
17	Ibis Hotel Nyeri	56	Meru Safari Hotel
18	Ivory Resort Hotel	57	Pig and Whistle Resort
19	Outspan Hotel	58	White Star Hotel
20	Westwood Hotel	59	Jungle Green Bar and Grill
21	Sandai Homestay and Cottages	60	Murera Springs Eco Lodge
22	Treetops	61	KWS, Murera Bandas
23	The Ark	62	Rhino River Camp
24	KWS, Fishing Lodge & Tusk Camp	63	Elsa's Kopje
25	Aberdare Country Club	64	KWS, Kinna Bandas
26	Rhino Watch Camp and Lodge	65	Leopard Rock Lodge
27	Solio Lodge	66	Offbeat Meru Camp
28	Sangare Tented Camp	67	Meru Mt Kenya Lodge
29	Naro Moru River Lodge	68	Transit Motel
30	Mountain Rock Lodge	69	Izaak Walton Inn
31	Thomson's Falls Lodge	70	Slopes Villa Hotel
32	Sweetwaters Tented Camp	71	Maina Highway Hotel
33	Ol Pejeta House	72	Panesic Hotel
34	Ol Pejeta Bush Camp	73	Owoods Lodge and Annex
35	Porini Rhino Camp	74	Stopover Hotel
36	Kicheche Laikipia Camp	75	Philadelphia Retreat
37	Pelican House	76	Masinga Dam Lodge
38	Ngobit River Lodge		
39	Equator Chalet		

 Accommodation Guide

Blue Post Hotel Thika

BLue Post Hotel, Muranga Road, Thika, Kenya
PO Box 42, Thika 01000, Kenya
Tel   +254 20 2529332-4; +254 20 2080606
Mobile   +254 721 578245 ; +254 733 426300
Fax   +254 20 2529330
E-mail   bluepost007@africaonline.co.ke
Web

                              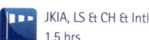 JKIA, LS & CH & Intl.
                                          1.5 hrs

Built in Thika in 1908, the Blue Post Hotel was one of the early stops for settlers travelling from Nairobi to their plantations in the central highlands. The area was made famous by Elspeth Huxley's memories of her childhood, The Flame Trees of Thika. The name Thika might have come from the Kikuyu word guthika, to bury, after a battle for water during a drought between the Kikuyu and Maasai left many dead, buried under a mound near the Blue Post Hotel.

On a promontory at the convergence of the Chania and Thika Rivers, the Blue Post Hotel has extensive grounds with viewpoints over the Chania and Thika waterfalls. A long flight of steps leads from the grounds down to the base of the Thika waterfall. The grounds are home to a variety of bird species, and to a number of indigenous trees found only in this area. The 32 en-suite rooms, in the Chania wing and the Thika wing, all have digital TV. The restaurant serves both buffet and a la carte. The bar has a selection of soft drinks, beers and spirits. The hotel also has a cyber café, wedding tents, a salon and entertainment including discos and children's playground. The 4 conference rooms can seat 20, 40, 60 and 300 pax. Activities include horse riding, nature walks and rafting.

Fourteen Falls Lodge   Ol Donyo Sabuk

Fourteen Falls Lodge, Thika-Garissa Highway, 10km from Thika, Kenya
PO Box 5142, Thika 01002, Kenya
Tel
Mobile   +254 715 894898
Fax
E-mail   fourteenfallslodge@yahoo.com
Web   www.fourteenfallslodge.com

                                JKIA, LS & CH & Intl.
                                1.5 hrs

Overlooking waterfalls known as the Fourteen Falls, Fourteen Falls Lodge offers budget accommodation and lovely views. It is set in 30 acres of gardens on the banks of the Chania River.

There are 9 traditional African rondavels, made up of 7 standard and 2 family. The family cottages have a bedroom, lounge and kitchenette. All rondavels have en-suite bathroom, satellite TV and mosquito net. There is also a campsite and a picnic site. Goat meat can be provided for campers who want to have a barbecue. The open sided restaurant serves an a la carte menu of African and continental dishes. Outside catering is available. No alcohol is served. The lodge has 24-hour security.

The conference hall seats 20 pax. Large tents can also be used for meetings, seminars or conferences. Weddings and wedding receptions can be arranged in the gardens or on the riverbanks. Tents, chairs, decorations and PA system are all available for hire. The playground has swings, slides and trampoline; the grounds have volleyball, basketball and football pitches. Boat rides and fishing for tilapia are available on the fishpond. As well as the Fourteen Falls, nearby sites of interest include Ol Doinyo Sabuk National Park, Masinga Dam, Ndakaini Dam, Sagana Fish Farms and Mwea Irrigation Scheme.

KWS, Sabuk Guest House Ol Donyo Sabuk National Park

KWS, Sabuk Guest House, Ol Donyo Sabuk National Park, Kenya
Kenya Wildlife Service, PO Box 40241, Nairobi 00100, Kenya

Tel	+254 20 6000800 ; +254 20 6002345; +254 20 3991000
Mobile	+254 726 610508; +254 726 610509; +254 736 663421
Fax	+254 20 6003792
E-mail	kws@kws.go.ke / reservations@kws.go.ke
Web	www.kws.go.ke

   JKIA, LS & CH & Intl.
2 hrs

Sabuk Guest House is owned and managed by Kenya Wildlife Service, KWS. It is situated in Ol Donyo Sabuk National Park.
There are 5 bedrooms and 4 bathrooms. The master bedroom has a double and single bed. There are also 2 doubles, a triple and a twin. There is a spacious sitting room with open fireplace, an open plan dining room, a kitchen equipped with gas cooker, fridge and cutlery and a long veranda. The house is attractively furnished in hand-carved wooden furniture, with woven rugs and wall hangings. There is also a conference room that seats 14 pax. The resident caretaker provides bed linen, towels, soap and mosquito nets.

Ol Donyo Sabuk National Park constitutes a mountain entirely covered with dense montane forest but for a small clearing at the top. Lookout Point, on the mountain, has panoramic views. Wildlife includes buffalo, leopard, bushbuck, colobus monkey, Sykes monkey, bush pig, rock hyrax, bushbaby, python and monitor lizard. The park is home to 45 species of birds including African pied wagtail, mourning dove, augur buzzard and purple-breasted sunbird. The Fourteen Falls can be seen from the park. Sabuk Guest House is 2km from the Main Gate; the gate is open from 8.30am to 6pm. 4WD is required. Park fees should be paid in cash at the gate.

Riuki Cultural Centre Githunguri

Riuki Cultural Centre, Karia Village, Githunguri, Kenya
Dr. Kinuthia Njoroge, PO Box 42458, Nairobi 00100, Kenya

Tel	
Mobile	+254 722 944441; +254 738 422670
Fax	
E-mail	info@riokiculture.org
Web	www.riokiculture.org

  JKIA, LS & CH & Intl.
1.5 hrs

Riuki means hearth, the centre of a Kikuyu homestead. Riuki Cultural Centre is a traditional Kikuyu village that aims to provide awareness of the practices of the Kikuyu people. In an interactive and inspiring way, the centre provides information on traditional lifestyle, architecture, food, drink, culture and dance. Accommodation is in traditional Kikuyu clay huts, with open fires. Food served includes Kikuyu dishes such as grilled goat, rukuri, marinated steak, sweet potato mash, sukuma wiki, irio, salads, fruits and traditional wine.
A typical day at the cultural centre starts with a guided tour of the village. Visitors are introduced to the layout of the homestead, and invited into the huts. Artifacts, weapons and crafts are displayed.
The remainder of the day can be spent on the activities, lectures and performances that interest the guests. Traditional plays are performed, based on Kikuyu ceremonies, themes, myths and rituals, as well as modern African life and modern literature. Authentic Kikuyu songs and dances are performed, and visitors are welcome to join in. Lectures on Kikuyu poetry, folklore, riddles, proverbs and tongue twisters are also on offer. Dr Kinuthia Njoroge established the centre in 1988 as a focal point for research and cultural preservation.

Buffalo Bay Motel Kagio

Buffalo Bay Motel, Samson Corner–Karatina Road, Kagio, nr Kerugoya, PO Box 1185, Kerugoya 10300, Kenya
Tel
Mobile +254 723 406593 ; +254 722 710102
Fax
E-mail buffalobaymotel@gmail.co.ke
Web

  JKIA, LS & CH & Intl.
2 hrs

Centred on an open air bar filled with plants and dotted with tables, Buffalo Bay Motel offers budget accommodation and nightly entertainment.
There are 12 en-suite rooms, made up of 6 singles and 6 doubles. All rooms have basin, table, chair and satellite TV. The rooms are on the 1st floor and look down on the garden bar. There is also a balcony at the front of the hotel overlooking the road, where food and drink can be served. The restaurant serves predominantly Kenyan dishes, such as nyama choma grilled meats, including chicken, goat, beef and fish, served with roast potatoes, ugali or rice. The weekend seafood special includes prawns, tewa, taffy fish, octopus and squid.
The circular thatched bar in the centre of the motel serves a selection of local and international soft drinks, beers and spirits. There is also a pool table, and a dance floor. Live bands play every Friday, Saturday and Sunday. The 2 seminar halls seat 150 pax each. Equipment is not provided and groups should bring their own if required. The car park beside the hotel is enclosed, and guarded during the night.
Buffalo Bay Motel is a convenient place to stop between Nairobi and the Mt Kenya region.

Camp Malta Sagana

Camp Malta, nr Sagana, Kenya
PO Box 2095, Nairobi 00200, Kenya
Tel +254 20 2730807; +254 20 2734852
Mobile +254 724 175037; +254 720 681066; +254 735 435192
Fax +254 20 2713677
E-mail info@tanari.org
Web www.tanari.org

 JKIA, LS & CH & Intl.
2 hrs

Camp Malta is a church-initiated adventure camp offering adventure holidays that, through interaction and bonding, give participants a sense of togetherness and community. The camp is a ministry of the Nairobi-based Tanari Trust, a sister organisation of Tanari International, which aims to assist local churches and institutions to become relevant in communities by providing creative programmes, materials, training and consultation in order to stimulate encounters with God, others, the environment and the self.
The camp is in an attractive area with lush foliage. There are 5 tents, each of which sleeps 10 pax. Mattresses and sleeping bags are provided. There is also a campsite; 2-man tents can be provided by the camp if required. The camp has communal bathroom facilities.
Dining options range from full board, with all meals provided, to self-catering. A chef is available for hire by self-catering groups, if required. Activities include group camping expeditions, adventure hikes and walks. Startling rock formations and cliffs provide excellent climbing sites. Teambuilding activities can be 1-day, or many days, as the group requires. Bike-athalons and treasure hunts can be arranged. The camp also offers youth or church retreats and family gatherings.

Rapids Camp Sagana

Rapids Camp, Thika-Sagana Highway, Kenya
Sagana Waterfalls Adventures, PO Box 66908, Nairobi 00200, Kenya
Tel	+254 20 2212818; +254 20 2216439
Mobile	+254 722 308026; +254 732 308026
Fax	
E-mail	meet-n-assist@wananchi.com
Web	www.raftinginkenya.com

 JKIA, LS & CH & Intl. 2 hrs

Established in 2004, Rapids Camp offers camping holidays for the adventurous, with activities such as white water rafting, bungee jumping, river boarding, mountain climbing, rock climbing, bird watching, guided safaris and teambuilding programmes. The camp supports local initiatives including conservation projects, eco concepts, environmental projects and community based help. Visitors can bring their own tents or hire tents, and place them anywhere in the 3 acres of lawns dotted with acacia trees, overlooking the Tana River. There are 5 covered eating areas, seating about 18 pax, with mobile barbeques. The chef specialises in marinated nyama choma grilled meats, and also serves buffets with a combination of local and international dishes. River Tana's grade 5 rapids not only give the camp its name, but also provide opportunity for adrenaline-filled kayaking, diving from a height of 60ft and freshwater fishing. About 100 bird species have been recorded here. Children's activities combine education and enjoyment. The teambuilding programmes have been designed to enable participants to think outside the box.

Rapids Camp's Big Five are the waterfall, the startling rocks, the grade 5 rapids, the manicured lawns and the serene habitat. The camp hosted the 1st ever African Olympic qualifier in the Kayaking Games in January 2008.

Castle Forest Lodge Kimunye

Castle Forest Lodge, Kimunye, off Kutus-Kianyaga Road, Kerugoya
PO Box 29886, Nairobi 00202, Kenya
Tel	
Mobile	+254 721 422908; +254 722 314918
Fax	
E-mail	castlelodge@wananchi.com
Web	www.castleforestlodge.com

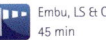 Embu, LS & CH 45 min

Castle Forest Lodge nestles in a rain and bamboo forest, listed a UNESCO World Heritage Site for its large variety of endemic species such as the lobelias, the senecios and the rock hyrax. On the slopes of Mt Kenya, the lodge is committed to maintaining the fragile ecological balance of this unique natural environment.

The main house, built in 1910 with river stones and wood from the surrounding forest, is said to have been visited by both Queen Elizabeth and President Jomo Kenyatta when they were students. The house has double, single and twin rooms. The cottages have living rooms with fireplaces. The bungalows have 2 double rooms, living rooms with fireplaces and private verandas. There is also a large campsite with bathroom facilities. A self-catering bush hut, 8km north of the lodge, is accessible only by a forest track, on foot or horseback. A resident caretaker cooks, lights the fire, guides walks and cares for the horses.

Activities include trout fishing, horse riding and hiking on the slopes of Mt Kenya. Walkers should always be accompanied by a guide. The little known, adventurous Kamweti route from the lodge to the peak takes 4 – 7 days. Experienced porters and guides can be booked at the lodge.

Msafiri House Karatina

Msafiri House, 1km from Karatina, Nairobi-Nyeri Highway, Kenya
PO Box 673, Karatina 10101, Kenya
Tel	
Mobile	+254 722 517768; +254 700 145800
Fax	+254 20 6005296
E-mail	ggnguru@yahoo.com
Web	

Nanyuki, LS & CH
1.5 hrs

An elegant stone building in manicured gardens, Msafiri House offers serviced apartments on the outskirts of Karatina. The house opened in March 2009, and the facilities are modern.

There are 6 apartments, made up of 3 suites and 3 family apartments. The suites have a double bedroom, with interconnecting living room, a kitchenette, a shower room and a WC. The family apartments have 2 double bedrooms, a living room, a shower room and a WC. All the suites are fully furnished and equipped, and have TV with local channels. The restaurant serves table d'hote, and also offers barbecue and a snack menu. The bar has soft drinks, beers and spirits, and is equipped with TV.

The garden has tables shaded by umbrellas, where food can also be served. The conference room seats 100 pax. Equipment is not provided and groups should bring their own or rent from elsewhere if required. A safe for guests' valuables is available at reception. There is also a campsite, with bathroom facilities, and a secure enclosed car park.

Msafiri House is 1km from Karatina, on the road to Sagana and Nairobi.

Ibis Hotel Karatina 1 Karatina

Ibis Hotel, Nairobi-Nyeri Highway, Karatina, Kenya
PO Box 240, Karatina 10101, Kenya
Tel	+254 61 72777
Mobile	+254 771 122855
Fax	+254 61 72132
E-mail	kihuria@ibishotels.co.ke
Web	www.ibishotel.co.ke

Equity Bank

Nanyuki, LS & CH
1.5 hrs

The Ibis chain of hotels started with 1 hotel in Nyeri, and now has 2 hotels in Karatina, 1 in Nanyuki and 1 in Nyeri.

Ibis Hotel has 45 en-suite rooms, made up of singles, twins and executive, with a double bed. All twins and executives have telephone and satellite TV; the whole hotel has WiFi.

The road front restaurant has a predominantly Kenyan menu, with a few international dishes. The traditional Ibis Special Dish is a mixed grill platter including fish, served with sweet potatoes and arrowroot. Buffets can be provided for large groups.

Nyaki Restaurant, named after the owner's wife, and Kinde Bar, named after the owner's son, are on the 1st floor. There are 3 conference halls, seating 150 pax, 40 pax and 30 pax. Conference equipment can be provided if requested in advance.

The Ibis chain also owns Kings Butchery Hotel, behind Starbucks Hotel and next to Kenya Commercial Bank, which houses 2 restaurants, 2 bars and a cyber café. Kings Choma Banda serves nyama choma grilled meats and Kings Café has an international menu including pepper steak and spaghetti bolognaise. Kings Bistro and Kings Tavern serve soft drinks, beers and spirits. Kings Cyber Café has internet, fax, laminating and spiral binding.

Hotel Starbucks

Karatina

Hotel Starbucks, Nairobi-Nyeri Highway, Karatina, Kenya
PO Box 1299, Karatina 10101, Kenya

Tel	+254 61 72829
Mobile	+254 721 466577
Fax	+254 61 72506
E-mail	info@hotelstarbucks.com
Web	www.hotelstarbucks.com

 VISA, MasterCard, Amex   Nanyuki, LS & CH 1.5 hrs

Facing the main road through Karatina, Hotel Starbucks opened in May 2003, and offers a selection of dining and conferencing facilities. There are 58 en-suite rooms, made up of singles, doubles and suites. The rooms are divided between the West Wing and the East Wing, and all include satellite TV. They are fully tiled and are painted a cheerful assortment of colours, such as orange, yellow, purple and green. The suites have a double room, a single room and a bathroom.

Stings Restaurant and Family Restaurant, both on the 1st floor, serve Kenyan and international dishes including chicken tawa, beef stroganoff, meatballs in pepper sauce and a platter of grilled meats entitled Jambo Kenya Choma Mix. Buffets can be arranged for large groups. Casper Bar and Terrace, adjoining Family Restaurant, is fully stocked with soft drinks, beers, spirits and wines. Chicken Inn, on the ground floor, serves fast food. The conference centre on the top floor consists of Jasmine Hall, with a capacity of 80 pax, and Lillian Hall, with a capacity of 50. Conference facilities such as projector and PA system are available. The car park is guarded over night.

Ibis Hotel Karatina 2

Karatina

Ibis Hotel, Kibaki St, Karatina, Kenya
PO Box 240, Karatina 10101, Kenya

Tel	+254 61 72600
Mobile	+254 771 122855
Fax	+254 61 72132
E-mail	kihuria@ibishotels.co.ke
Web	www.ibishotel.co.ke

Equity Bank   Nanyuki, LS & CH 1.5 hrs

The Ibis chain of hotels started with 1 hotel in Nyeri, and now has 2 hotels in Karatina, 1 in Nanyuki and 1 in Nyeri.

The Ibis Hotel is formed of 2 interconnecting buildings, the new wing and the old wing. There are 55 en-suite rooms, made up of singles, twins and executives. All twins and executives have telephone and satellite TV. The rooms in the new wing are larger and better equipped than those in the old wing.

The road front restaurant has a predominantly Kenyan menu; buffets can be served for large groups. The bar, with velvet cushioned chairs and polished wooden tables, serves soft drinks, beers and spirits. There are 2 large enclosed car parks, 1 in the basement and 1 at road level. There are 6 conference halls. The largest hall seats 200 pax, and interconnects with another that seats 60 pax; 2 more halls seat 60, 1 seats 55 and 1 seats 30. The boardroom, with full length windows and a large round table, seats 9.

The 2 restaurants, 2 bars and cyber café at Kings Butchery Hotel, behind Starbucks Hotel and next to Kenya Commercial Bank, are also part of the Ibis chain.

Elephant Castle Hotel Karatina

Elephant Castle Hotel, Lagati Road, Karatina, Kenya
PO Box 730, Karatina 10101, Kenya
Tel
Mobile +254 729 368413
Fax
E-mail
Web

  Nanyuki, LS & CH 1.5 hrs

The Elephant Castle Hotel, which opened in 1973, was the first hotel to be built in Karatina. The hotel consists of 2 round buildings swathed in creepers, one on either side of the reception area. One round building houses the rooms while the other houses the restaurant, bar and conference room.

There are 20 en-suite rooms on the ground floor and the 1st floor, all named after towns and states around the world such as New Delhi, Florida, Jerusalem, Rome, Tokyo and California. The rooms are quirky shapes, their outer walls round, and their bathrooms and furniture neatly slotted in. The restaurant, with bench seats and canteen-style tables, serves Kenyan and international food, such as fillet of fish, curries and stews. Snacks such as burgers, samosas and sandwiches are also on offer. The bar serves soft drinks, beers and spirits, and is equipped with satellite TV. A terrace, between the bar and the restaurant, can also be used for dining. The conference room seats 40 pax. Conference equipment is not provided. The hotel is located a few blocks behind the Total petrol station on the Karatina–Nyeri Highway.

Banana Leaf Hotel Nyeri

Banana Leaf Hotel, ½km from Nyeri, Nairobi-Nyeri Highway, Kenya
PO Box 2081, Nyeri 10109, Kenya
Tel   +254 61 2031655
Mobile   +254 723 532474
Fax   +254 61 203130
E-mail   ndizikijani@yahoo.com
Web

VISA   Nanyuki, LS & CH 1 hr

Banana Leaf Hotel is a small friendly hotel on the outskirts of Nyeri. The reception is through the restaurant, on the ground floor. There are 9 en-suite double rooms, all of which are equipped with TV with local channels.

The Sweet Banana, consisting of 3 custom-made interlinked tents in the garden, forms the dining and entertainment centre. The 1st tent is a lounge with chairs, tables, satellite TV and a pool table. The central tent has a dance floor, a fully stocked bar and a DJ booth, where a DJ plays every Friday and Saturday. The last is a restaurant, with satellite TV. The large international menu includes chicken tikka, whole grilled tilapia, Molo lamb chops, fish curry and fillet steak. There is also a wide selection of vegetarian dishes. Buffets are available for large groups. A Nyama Choma Grill, serving grilled meats and stews, is also on offer. Outside catering is available for both small groups and large parties.

The conference hall is fully equipped with projector and PA system and seats 20 pax. The Sweet Banana tents can be set up for conferences and meetings for larger groups. The car park is securely enclosed.

Batian Grand Hotel

Nyeri

Batian Grand Hotel, Gakere Road, Nyeri, Kenya
PO Box 12100, Nyeri 10109, Kenya

Tel	+254 61 2030743
Mobile	+254 722 265863
Fax	+254 61 2034513
E-mail	batianhotel@gmail.com
Web	

 VISA

Nanyuki, LS & CH
1 hr

Originally the Crested Eagle Hotel, the hotel was renovated and became the Batian Grand Hotel in 2002. The hotel is conveniently located in the centre of Nyeri.

There are 61 en-suite rooms, made up of singles, doubles and twins. The singles look into the open centre of the hotel, while the doubles and twins look outwards. On a clear day, some rooms have lovely views of Mt Kenya. All rooms have satellite TV, telephone, writing table and chair and are adorned with African artwork.

Chania Restaurant has a wide selection of Kenyan and international dishes, and can serve buffet or a la carte, as required. A coffee shop, on the ground floor, serves nyama choma grilled meats. Zebra Pub, on the ground floor, is well stocked with a selection of local and imported drinks, and is equipped with satellite TV and a pool table. Lenana Bar, on the 1st floor, is a large, dark wood panelled bar, and is also fully stocked, including wines and liqueurs, with a full list of beers including Guinness and Windhoek.

Mt Kenya conference hall seats 90 pax, and Batian Room seats 30. Conference facilities, including TV, video, overhead projector and flipchart board, are available.

Green Hills Hotel

Nyeri

Green Hills Hotel, Bishop Gatimu Road, Nyeri, Kenya
PO Box 313, Nyeri 10100, Kenya

Tel	+254 61 2030604; +254 61 2030709; +254 61 2030710
Mobile	+254 716 431988 ; +254 733 600887 ; +254 716 431969
Fax	+254 61 2032199
E-mail	reservations@greenhills.co.ke / info@greenhills.co.ke
Web	www.greenhills.co.ke

 VISA, MasterCard

 Nanyuki, LS & CH
1 hr

Set in landscaped gardens, Green Hills Hotel is a lush haven in Nyeri. The 110 en-suite rooms all have desk, telephone, TV and free WiFi. The superior rooms have king size beds, writing table and chair. The executive rooms are more spacious. The deluxe rooms have 4-poster beds and lounges.

Tetu Restaurant serves buffet breakfast and lunch and has an a la carte menu. Wazalendo Bar and Restaurant is contemporary. The Pool Terrace Restaurant serves snacks and light meals. Kieni Bar and Terrace overlooks the gardens. Rainbow Grill serves nyama choma grilled meats. Mazingira Yetu Conference Centre is a ballroom for up to 500 pax, with adjoining secretariat rooms, equipped with simultaneous translation equipment, projectors and wireless PA system. Kitmikai seminar room holds up to 35 pax and the Residents Lounge seminar room holds up to 40 pax. The gardens hold up to 1000 pax and are ideal for teambuilding, weddings or product launches.

Green Spa, beside the swimming pool, has a full range of treatments including facials, massages and scrubs, as well as a fully equipped gym, steam room, sauna and Jacuzzi. The mirrored aerobics studio has daily aerobics, step and taibo classes.

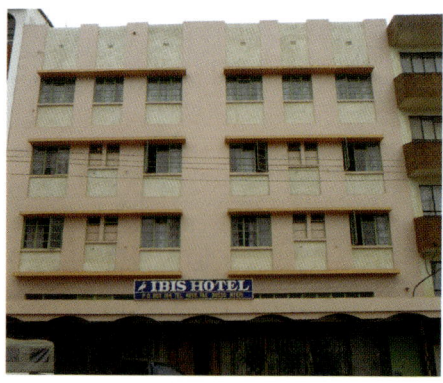

Ibis Hotel Nyeri Nyeri

Ibis Hotel, Kanisa Road, Nyeri, Kenya
PO Box 184, Nyeri 10100, Kenya
Tel	+254 61 2034858
Mobile	
Fax	+254 61 2030530
E-mail	kihuria@ibishotels.co.ke
Web	www.ibishotel.co.ke

    Nanyuki, LS & CH 1 hr

The Ibis Hotel in Nyeri was the first hotel of the Ibis chain to be built. The other Ibis hotels are located in Nanyuki and Karatina. The hotel is centrally located in Nyeri, making it convenient for all shops, restaurants and businesses of the town. The entrance to the hotel is through the restaurant; stairs lead down to the basement reception.

There are 40 en-suite rooms, made up of singles, twins and executive, containing a double bed. The rooms centre on an open stairwell that allows plentiful daylight to fall through the hotel.

The road front restaurant has a predominantly Kenyan menu, with a few international dishes such as beef curry and chicken jeera. The snack menu includes egg, sausage, toast, samosa, pancake and omelette. Buffets can be provided for large groups, and outside catering is available. The road front bar, next to the restaurant, serves soft drinks, beers and some spirits. There is also a bar on the 1st floor, opposite the staff offices, that has satellite TV.

The boardroom seats 20 pax. The main conference hall seats 100 pax and the small conference hall seats 30. The roadside parking is guarded at night.

Ivory Resort Hotel Nyeri

Ivory Resort Hotel, Nairobi-Nyeri Highway, Ruring'u, Kenya
PO Box 959, Nyeri 10100, Kenya
Tel	
Mobile	+254 722 929013
Fax	
E-mail	barujoyce@yahoo.com
Web	

     Nanyuki, LS & CH 1 hr

Established in 2007, Ivory Resort Hotel is a small colourful hotel on the outskirts of Nyeri.

There are 36 en-suite rooms, made up of singles and doubles. The rooms have tiled floors and brightly painted walls of sky blue, green and terracotta. Some rooms are equipped with TV with local channels.

The restaurant at the entrance of the hotel serves a selection of local and international dishes including stews, curries, sandwiches and steaks. Nyama choma grilled meats are also available. Outside catering can be arranged. A tall wooden building houses a bar stocked with soft drinks, beers and a few spirits. The bar is equipped with satellite TV and food can also be served here.

The conference hall seats 50 pax, and is equipped with LCD projector. The car park is enclosed and guarded.

Ivory Resort Hotel is about 2km from Nyeri on the Nairobi-Nyeri Highway, next to Caltex petrol station.

Outspan Hotel

Nyeri

Outspan Hotel, Baden Powell Road, opp Nyeri Club, Nyeri, Kenya
Aberdare Safari Hotels, PO Box 24, Nyeri 10100, Kenya

Tel	+254 61 2032424; +254 61 2032425
Mobile	+254 722 207762
Fax	+254 61 2032286
E-mail	outspan@aberdaresafarihotels.com
Web	www.aberdaresafarihotels.com

VISA, MasterCard   Nanyuki, LS & CH 1 hr

The Outspan Hotel opened in 1929. The elegant hotel is steeped in history, its guest list sprinkled with aristocracy. Paxtu Cottage, the final resting place of Lord Baden-Powell, founder of the Scouting Movement, is now a museum displaying an extraordinary collection of memorabilia. Set in manicured tropical gardens containing a massive 500-year-old Mugumo tree believed to be sacred by the Kikuyu people, the Outspan has spectacular views of Mt Kenya.

There are 45 en-suite rooms, made up of 8 stylish Chania rooms, 3 spacious Chania cottages and 34 standard rooms, 19 of which have fireplaces. Sherry Restaurant serves breakfast and lunch on the veranda overlooking the garden. Dinner is served inside or under the stars. Sherry Bar has an extensive drinks list, including wines and liqueurs, and Kirinyaga pub is an olde English tavern. The Sherbrooke-Walker Room seats 60 pax, the Kirinyaga Room seats 60 and the Chania Boardroom seats 10; all contain up-to-date conference facilities.

As well as game drives in the Aberdare National Park and Solio Ranch Rhino Sanctuary, the Outspan offers guided tours around the 70-year-old Kihuri Arabica Coffee Estate and full use of Nyeri Golf Club. Guests for Treetops check in and have lunch before departing for Treetops.

Westwood Hotel

Nyeri

Westwood Hotel, Baden Powell Road, opp. Nyeri Club, Nyeri, Kenya
PO Box 245, Nyeri 10100, Kenya

Tel	+254 20 2636448
Mobile	+254 733 184760; +254 714 588500
Fax	
E-mail	info@westwoodhotel.co.ke
Web	www.westwoodhotel.co.ke

Nanyuki, LS & CH 1 hr

Established in March 2010, Westwood Hotel has a fresh design and modern facilities. Its eye-catching green façade looks across Baden Powell Road at Nyeri Club's golf course.

There are 57 en-suite rooms, made up of standard rooms and executive rooms. All rooms are equipped with flat screen satellite TV, telephone and balcony, and their bathrooms have glass cabinet showers. The executive rooms have, in addition, tea and coffee making facilities, and their bathrooms have both bath and shower.

The restaurant serves a selection of Kenyan and international dishes, such as soups, salads, stews and mixed grill. The kitchen opens onto the restaurant, and has an active cooking station. Buffets can be provided for large groups. The bar, near the entrance on the ground floor, has a variety of soft drinks, beers and spirits, and is equipped with satellite TV. A terrace joins the bar and the restaurant, and meals and drinks can also be served here.

The conference hall seats 120 pax and is fully equipped with projector, laptop and PA system. The 1st floor lounge has comfortable sofas, coffee tables, large windows and satellite TV. The car park is enclosed and securely guarded.

Sandai Homestay & Cottages

Aberdares

Sandai Homestay & Cottages, nr Aberdare National Park, Kenya
PO Box 1518, Nyeri 10100, Kenya

Tel
Mobile +254 733 734619
Fax
E-mail petra@africaonline.co.ke / sabine-weidlich@web.de
Web www.africanfootprints.de

Nanyuki, LS & CH
1 hr

Sandai Homestay and Cottages is a farm located near the Aberdare National Park. The comfortable farmhouse is surrounded by indigenous flora and interesting animals. The homestay offers a homely and relaxing atmosphere, and a range of activities.

There are 2 double rooms with shared bathroom in the main farmhouse. There are also 4 en-suite double rooms in the 2 guesthouses. The farmhouse has a living room with open fireplace, and a dining room where all meals are served. Electricity is supplied by generator and solar power. Horse riding for beginners and advanced riders is offered on the farm. Trips can be for half a day, or for multiple days, including camping. Guided bird watching is recommended; 160 species of birds have been recorded here, including the rare spotted creeper, African grass owl and little rock thrush. For a surcharge, game drives are offered in Aberdare National Park, Solio Ranch, Ol Pejeta Conservancy and Lake Nakuru National Park. Sandai also offers shopping trips to Nyeri, with visits to Baden Powell Museum at the Outspan Hotel. Excursions to Nairobi can be arranged, with visits to National Museum, Karen Blixen Museum, Sheldrick Elephant Orphanage and Giraffe Centre. Sandai also offers personalised safaris to destinations around Kenya, and group trips for individuals travelling on their own.

Treetops

Aberdare National Park

Treetops, Aberdare National Park, Kenya
Aberadare Safari Hotels, PO Box 24, Nyeri 10100, Kenya

Tel +254 61 2032425
Mobile +254 722 207761
Fax +254 61 2032286
E-mail treetops@aberdaresafarihotels.com
www.aberdaresafarihotels.com

 VISA, MasterCard

 Mweiga, CH
10 mins

Treetops started as a 2-room tree house in 1929. It aroused international interest in February 1952 when a young British visitor climbed into the tree as Princess Elizabeth and climbed down the following morning as Queen Elizabeth II.

The lodge is now raised on stilts and has 4 decks and a rooftop viewing platform. The rooms, small ship-like cabins overlooking two floodlit waterholes, are made up of 43 standard rooms, 5 triples and 2 suites.

Guests check in at the Outspan Hotel, 17km away, where they eat lunch before transferring to Treetops for afternoon tea and dinner. Malkia Bar on the top deck is open for sundowners while the Main Bar is open until midnight.

Treetops is located at the Salient, the area with the highest concentration of wildlife in the Aberdare National Park. Rare animals include black rhino, the elusive bongo, the giant forest hog and civet and serval cats. 290 bird species have been recorded. Treetops offers a full day tour during which guests ascend through bamboo forest first to Chania falls, then Magura falls and finally the spectacular 300m Karuru falls.

Treetops is engaged in a 4-year conservation initiative Restore the Bush with KWS involving the rehabilitation of 125 hectares of the Aberdare National Park.

The Ark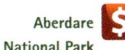

Aberdare National Park

The Ark, Aberdare National Park, Kenya
PO Box 17545, Nairobi 00500, Kenya
Tel	+254 20 2101333
Mobile	+254 737 799992
Fax	
E-Mail	reservations.ke@marasa.net
Web	www.thearkkenya.com

  VISA, MasterCard   Nanyuki, LS & CH 45 mins

The Ark, shaped like a ship with wood-panelled alleys and port holes, overlooks a waterhole in the Aberdare National Park. Passengers board the Ark on a wooden gang plank and are given a 'sailing certificate' when they leave.

The Ark operates with the Aberdare Country Club. Guests stay at the Country Club for a night, or just stop for lunch, and are transferred to the Ark at 2.30pm or at 5.30pm.

There are 63 en-suite rooms, made up of 7 singles, 39 twins, 9 triples and 8 doubles with queen beds. Each of the 4 floors has a deck that overlooks the waterhole, some enclosed in glass and others open. On the ground floor, a hide with open viewing holes is tucked into the base of the boat. Game viewing is good, with buffalo and elephant seen almost every night. Giant forest hog, bongo and suni are among the rare mammal species spotted here, while Hertlobs turaco, red-fronted parrot and Egyptian geese are among the rare bird species. The Ark operates a buzzer system so that even when sleeping guests are alerted to action at the waterhole – 1 buzz for an elephant, 2 for a rhino, 3 for a leopard and 4 for any rare species.

KWS, Fishing Lodge & Tusk Camp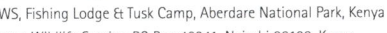

Aberdare National Park

KWS, Fishing Lodge & Tusk Camp, Aberdare National Park, Kenya
Kenya Wildlife Service, PO Box 40241, Nairobi 00100, Kenya
Tel	+254 20 6000800; +254 20 6002345; +254 20 3991000
Mobile	+254 726 610508; +254 726 610509; +254 736 663421
Fax	+254 20 6003792
E-mail	kws@kws.go.ke / reservations@kws.go.ke
Web	www.kws.go.ke

       Mweiga, CH 30 mins

The Aberdare Fishing Lodge is set in the central moorlands of the southern Aberdare National Park. The lodge is made up of 2 self-catering timber cabins. Each cabin has 3 bedrooms; 2 en-suite bedrooms have a double and single bed and a 3rd bedroom has a single bed. Each cabin has a sitting room with a log fire, an open plan dining area, a fully equipped kitchen and a veranda.

The Tusk Camp is a forest camp with 2 self-catering cabins. The 1st cabin has 4 single beds, while the second has 2 double beds. An unfurnished aluminium hut is available for staff. The sitting room, with log fire, has a dining table and chairs. The kitchen is fully equipped; the bathroom is outside.

Both the Fishing Lodge and Tusk Camp are owned and managed by Kenya Wildlife Service, KWS. At both sites, resident caretakers provide kerosene lamps. The surrounding area is notable for spectacular waterfalls, moorland scenery and colourful flora. Wildlife includes elephant, sykes and colobus monkey, leopard, lion, black rhino, giant forest hog, suni, serval, reedbuck, eland and rare bongo antelope. 250 bird species have been recorded. Activities include mountain climbing and trout fishing; fishing license is available at the park gate. Entry to the park is by SafariCard; cards may be obtained and loaded at Mweiga HQ.

 Accommodation Guide

Aberdare Country Club

Aberdares

Aberdare Country Club, Mweiga Hill, nr Nyeri, Kenya
PO Box 17545, Nairobi 00500, Kenya
Tel +254 20 2101333
Mobile +254 737 799992
Fax
E-mail reservations.ke@marasa.net
Web www.thearkkenya.com

VISA, MasterCard
Amex

Nanyuki, LS & CH
45 mins

Originally the home of the early settlers Mr and Mrs Lyons, the Aberdare Country Club was built as a farmhouse between 1930 and 1936. In 1968 it was converted into a country club. The charming house sits in gardens bursting with colour and studded with peacocks.

The club's 1,300-acre wildlife sanctuary is rich with elands, gazelles, zebras, giraffes and the more reclusive leopards.

The club holds 107 guests in 36 cottages and 12 rooms. The bedrooms are all en-suite, and are furnished in the style of an English country house. The cottages have 2 bedrooms with interconnecting doors, and most have fireplaces. All rooms and cottages have views of the plains, the Aberdare National Park and Mt Kenya.

The main building houses the dining room and lounge bar, where a selection of European, Asian and Kenyan dishes is served. The 4 conference rooms are equipped with a full range of audio visual equipment. Facilities include a swimming pool, putting green, tennis courts and 9 hole golf course. Activities include game drives in the Salient and Solio Ranch, horse riding and trout fishing.

Guests for the Ark check in and eat lunch or tea at the club before being driven to the Ark at 2.30pm or 5.30pm.

Rhino Watch
Camp & Lodge

Solio

Rhino Watch Camp & Lodge, nr Solio, Kenya
PO Box 1346, Nairobi 00618, Kenya
Tel
Mobile +254 711 585495/7
Fax
E-mail info@rhinowatchlodge.com
Web www.rhinowatchlodge.com

Solio, CH, 5 min
Mweiga, CH, 10 mins

Set in 30 hectares adjacent to Solio rhino sanctuary, Rhino Watch Camp and Lodge is committed to the protection of this endangered species. The camp's owners, with a background in animal observation projects such as whale watching in the Azores, built the camp according to strict environmental principles. The camp aims to integrate responsible tourism with conservancy projects and to increase local employment.

The lodge has 7 chalets, 5 with 1 en-suite bedroom and 2 with 2 en-suite bedrooms. The spacious Kikuyu-style chalets have balconies with views of Mt Kenya.

The camp, in the forested lower area of the resort, is made up of 5 en-suite safari tents. There is a campfire, a bush bar and a dining area. The higher camp, in natural forest, has 2 chalets, each with an en-suite bedroom, an open fireplace and a large veranda.

Game drives cover Solio Ranch, Aberdare National Park and Ol Pejeta Conservancy. Trips to climb Mt Kenya and other handmade safaris can be arranged here. Guests are also welcome to participate in the project for the protection of rhinos and the tree planting programme.

The Rhino Watch team has extensive experience of working with professional photographic and film-making groups.

Solio Lodge

Solio Ranch

Solio Lodge, Solio Ranch, Kenya
The Safari Collection, PO Box 15565, Nairobi 00503, Kenya
Tel	+254 20 2513166
Mobile	+254 731 914732; +254 732 238429
Fax	
E-mail	info@thesafaricollection.com
Web	www.thesafaricollection.com

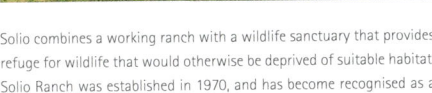

VISA, MasterCard   Solio, CH, 10 mins
Nanyuki, LS & CH, 20 mins

Solio combines a working ranch with a wildlife sanctuary that provides refuge for wildlife that would otherwise be deprived of suitable habitat. Solio Ranch was established in 1970, and has become recognised as a successful rhino breeding ground. It has translocated 100 black rhino and 60 white rhino to destinations around Kenya.

Solio Lodge was built using local materials. There are 6 en-suite cottages, each with private deck, fireplace and large plate glass windows to maximise the view. The décor combines African culture with modern elegance. All rooms have WiFi, hairdryer, fridge, kettle and ipod docking station. Fresh, light meals are served in the main dining room.

A wide variety of activities can be done on and around Solio. Game drives, game walks and horse riding are all available on the ranch, which is home to over 70 black and 150 white rhino, as well as buffalo, zebra, giraffe, eland, oryx, warthog, lion, leopard and cheetah. There is also an abundance of birdlife, especially along the Moyo River, which traverses the entire ranch. Children's activities include learning bush skills and tracking animals. External activities, for a surcharge, include trout fishing in the Aberdare National Park and helicopter flights to Mt Kenya. Solio supports projects in community, environment and wildlife conservation.

Sangare Tented Camp

Aberdares

Sangare Tented Camp, nr Aberdare National Park, Kenya
PO Box 61362, Nairobi 00200, Kenya
Tel	+254 20 2722451-4; +254 20 2722456-7
Mobile	+254 728 607597; +254 733 616217
Fax	+254 20 2720545; +254 20 2728061
E-mail	sales@silversprings-hotel.com
Web	www.sangaretentedcamp.com

   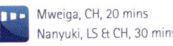

Mweiga, CH, 20 mins
Nanyuki, LS & CH, 30 mins

Sangare Tented Camp is located in a 6,500-acre private ranch in the northern foothills of the Aberdare Mountains. The ranch contains the famous Mau Mau caves where Kenya's freedom fighters were based during their battle for the independence of Kenya in the 1950s. The camp overlooks a magnificent freshwater lake against a backdrop of Sangare Hill. There are 10 spacious tents, 2 honeymoon suites and 2 cottages. All tents and cottages are en-suite and are tastefully furnished with 4-poster beds and African rustic furniture, and can be double, twin or triple as required. They have private romantic verandas and cosy lounges with views of the lake.

Meals can be served in the main dining room by the fireplace or on the terrace overlooking the lake. All meals are made from pure organic vegetables and fruits grown in the garden. The specialty dish is the Rainbow trout from the famous River Horny.

Sangare Lake is home to over 300 species of birds, as well as migratory birds. Activities range from mountain biking to boat trips and from fly fishing to horse riding. Game drives to the Aberdare National Park and Solio Ranch are also available.

Naro Moru River Lodge

Naro Moru

Naro Moru River Lodge, Nyeri–Nanyuki Road, nr Naro Moru, Kenya
PO Box 18, Naro Moru 10105, Kenya

Tel
Mobile +254 724 082754; +254 737 102955
Fax
E-mail info@naromoruriverlodge.com
Web www.naromoruriverlodge.com

 VISA, MasterCard   Nanyuki, LS & CH 20 mins

This log-cabin style lodge has been dubbed the base for climbing Mt Kenya for its tailor-made mountain climbing itineraries backed by its experienced teams of guides and porters. Naro Moru River Lodge supplies a wealth of information on the mountain, its zones of vegetation and the pros and cons of its various climbing routes.

There are 12 standard en-suite twin rooms. The 12 superior rooms, with twin, double or triple beds, are more spacious and most have a fireplace and interconnecting rooms for families. The 14 delux rooms have fireplaces and balconies with panoramic views of Mt Kenya. There are 5 self-catering cottages, with 2 or 3 bedrooms and fully equipped kitchenettes, and 5 self-catering country homes in private compounds, with 3 bedrooms, fully equipped kitchenettes and dining rooms. There are also bunkhouses and a campsite.

Kirinyaga Restaurant serves breakfast, lunch, dinner and children's food. Nelion Restaurant serves a la carte snacks, lunch and dinner. Point Lenana Bar looks out on the Naro Moru River, while Batian Pool Bar views Mt Kenya. The fully equipped Makutano meeting room seats 120 pax, Mt Kenya seats 60 and the boardroom seats 10. Sauna, squash, tennis, table tennis and pool are also available.

Mountain Rock Lodge

Naro Moru

Mountain Rock Lodge, Naro Moru, Kenya
PO Box 15796, Nairobi 00100, Kenya

Tel +254 20 2210051-2
Mobile +254 722 511752 ; +254 772 511752 : +254 722 808406
Fax +254 20 2210051
E-mail info@mountainrockkenya.com
Web www.mountainrockkenya.com

 VISA, MasterCard    Nanyuki, LS & CH 20 mins

Tucked into the woods at the foot of Mt Kenya, Mountain Rock Lodge is a natural base for climbing the mountain. The lodge is surrounded by luxuriant gardens, a lawn and its own lake. The lodge has 28 rooms, made up of 16 standard rooms and 12 superior. The standard rooms are 2 singles, 7 doubles and 7 triples or quads that are ideal for school groups or budget travellers. The superior rooms, with inbuilt fireplaces, are doubles that can comfortably be converted to triples.

The lodge also has a campsite with kitchen and bathroom facilities, and a conference hall seating 150 pax. Entertainment includes traditional dances, a pool table and disco music.

The lodge organises mountain treks for climbers of any age, group size and mountain experience. It also has 2 mountain huts on the Sirimon Trail, a sizeable stock of mountain equipment and crisis management apparatus. Other activities include horse riding, boating and fishing. Excursions to Mt Kenya and Aberdare National Parks, Ol Pejeta Conservancy and El Karama game reserve, Ken Trout Fisheries and Mkogodo Maasai village can all be organised from here. The Mau Mau caves, where freedom fighters hid from the colonials during the battle for Kenya's independence, are also nearby.

Thomson's Falls Lodge — Nyahururu

Thomson's Falls Lodge, 1km from Nakuru–Nyeri Road, Nyahururu, Kenya
PO Box 38, Nyahururu 20300, Kenya

Tel	+254 65 2022006; +254 65 32170
Mobile	+254 700 415719 ; +254 716 108833
Fax	+254 65 2032170
E-mail	tfalls@africaonline.co.ke
Web	www.thomsonsfallslodge.com

All major cards — Nanyuki, LS & CH 1 hr

Thomson's Falls, named after Joseph Thomson, a Scottish geologist and naturalist who was the first white man to see the falls in 1883, is a 73-meter sheer drop of the Ewaso Narok River over a ledge of volcanic rock. Thomson's Falls Lodge is in 10 acres of lawns dotted with indigenous trees. The lodge was built in the 1930s by settlers as a private residence, and became a hotel in the 1960s.

There are 32 en-suite rooms, made up of 2 singles, 24 doubles and 6 triples, in the original cottages in the grounds. All rooms have open fireplaces; some have TV with local channels and balcony. The triples have an interconnecting door between a double and a single with shared bathroom.

The restaurant serves African food with a few international dishes, such as curries, stews, roast chicken and spaghetti. The bar is stocked with beers and spirits and has satellite TV.

At the end of the garden, the Municipal Council of Nyahururu has erected a viewing platform. It is only possible to view the falls by paying a fee to the council. A cluster of curio shops surrounds the platform, and Kikuyu dancers are available to dance for a fee.

Sweetwaters Tented Camp — Ol Pejeta Conservancy

Sweetwaters Tented Camp, Ol Pejeta Conservancy, Kenya
Serena Hotels, PO Box 48690, Nairobi 00100, Kenya

Tel	+254 20 2842000; +254 20 2822000; +254 20 2842333
Mobile	+254 733 282200; +254 733 282283; +254 733 282292
Fax	+254 20 2725184; +254 20 2718102/3
E-mail	cro@serena.co.ke
Web	www.serenahotels.com

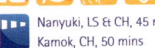

VISA, MasterCard, Amex — Nanyuki, LS & CH, 45 mins; Kamok, CH, 50 mins

The Sweetwaters Chimpanzee Sanctuary is the only place in Kenya to see this endangered and highly intelligent species. The sanctuary opened in 1993 as refuge for orphaned and abused chimpanzees from west and central Africa; the first 3 arrived that year from Bujumbura, evacuated from Burundi at the outbreak of civil war. Currently the sanctuary is home to 43 chimpanzees.

Sweetwaters Tented Camp is set around a game-rich waterhole in Ol Pejeta Conservancy. The 39 en-suite tents are made up of 13 doubles and 26 twins. Each tent has a thatched roof and a balcony overlooking the waterhole.

Built in the 1970s, the main building was the home of the ranch manager. Now Rhino Restaurant serves alfresco and table d'hote food. The Waterhole Bar has an uninterrupted view of the waterhole. And the Khashoggi Bar and Lounge provides a place to relax. There is also a swimming pool, business centre and spa.

As well as day and night game drives, activities include nature walks with a resident naturalist, bird watching, horse riding, camel trekking and lion tracking. Visits to Morani Information Centre and the rhino holding pens are also available. Sweetwaters Tented Camp has a bronze award from Ecotourism Society of Kenya.

Ol Pejeta House — Ol Pejeta Conservancy

Ol Pejeta House, Ol Pejeta Conservancy, Kenya
Serena Hotels, PO Box 48690, Nairobi 00100, Kenya
Tel +254 20 2822000; +254 20 2842333; +254 20 2842000
Mobile +254 733 282200; +254 733 282283; +254 733 282292
Fax +254 20 2725184; +254 20 2718102/3
E-mail cro@serena.co.ke
Web www.serenahotels.com

 VISA, MasterCard, Amex

 Nanyuki, LS & CH, 40 mins
Kamok, CH, 40 mins

Originally the home of Lord Tom Delamere, and subsequently the property of the infamous multi-millionaire Adnan Khashoggi, Ol Pejeta House is a private house that resonates with past events. The pictures on the walls, the secretly interlinking rooms and the grand views hark back to a bygone era. Set in Ol Pejeta Conservancy, the house looks across tropical gardens to the plains and waterhole. It has 2 superior en-suite guest rooms with dressing room and 2 standard en-suite guest rooms with terrace. One of the superior rooms houses Khashoggi's notorious immense double bed. Buffalo Cottage has 2 deluxe rooms and a fireplace. The house is staffed by room valets and private chef. Meals are served on the terrace or in the garden.

As well as day and night game drives, activities include nature walks with a resident naturalist, bird watching, camel riding and lion tracking. The house has 2 swimming pools and a selection of books and board games, and also offers beauty treatments.

From here it is possible to visit Sweetwaters Chimpanzee Sanctuary, the only place to see these endangered and highly intelligent animals in Kenya. Visits to Morani Information Centre and rhino holding pens can be arranged.

Ol Pejeta Bush Camp — Ol Pejeta Conservancy

Ol Pejeta Bush Camp, Ol Pejeta Conservancy, Kenya
Ol Pejeta Conservancy Private Bag, Nanyuki 10400, Kenya
Tel
Mobile +254 734 445253
Fax
E-mail info@insidersafrica.com
Web www.insidersafrica.com / www.olpejetaconservancy.org

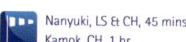 Nanyuki, LS & CH, 45 mins
Kamok, CH, 1 hr

Set on the banks of the Ewasu Nyiro River in Ol Pejeta Conservancy, Ol Pejeta Bush Camp is a traditional bush camp. The camp offers a unique safari experience, the 4-day interactive conservation safari, which gives guests an insight into modern wildlife conservation.

The camp has no permanent structures and is designed to have as little impact on the environment as possible. The 6 en-suite tents can have twin or double beds. The camp can be booked exclusively for a group of 4 or more for a surcharge. Extra tents can be added if required.

As well as day and night game drives and guided wildlife walks, visits to the Morani Information Centre and the rhino holding pens can be arranged, as can visits to the Sweetwaters Chimpanzee Sanctuary, the only place this endangered and highly intelligent species can be seen in Kenya. Highlights of this working conservancy include rhino tracking with the Ol Pejeta rangers and using radio tracking equipment to find resident lions, and to find the resident cheetah Toki, featured in the BBC documentary Toki's Tale. Guests can also spend a night in a hide, with dinner, bedroll and night-vision monocular. The camp closes in April, May and November.

Porini Rhino Camp — Ol Pejeta Conservancy

Porini Rhino Camp, Ol Pejeta Conservancy, Kenya
PO Box 388, Nairobi 00621, Kenya

Tel	+254 20 7123129; +254 20 7122504; +254 20 7121851
Mobile	+254 722 509200; +254 735 339209
Fax	Fax: +254 20 7120864
E-mail	info@porini.com / res2@gamewatchers.co.ke
Web	www.porini.com / www.olpejetaconservancy.org

VISA, MasterCard

Nanyuki, LS & CH, 45 mins
Kamok, CH, 15 mins

Set in Ol Pejeta Conservancy, the largest sanctuary in East Africa for black rhinos, Porini Rhino Camp takes its name from this endangered species. The camp is in a secluded valley, among acacia trees on the banks of a seasonal river.

The 6 en-suite tents are comfortably furnished with double and single beds, and have beautiful views. This eco-friendly camp has solar powered lighting, no generator and strict policies on water and waste disposal. Meals are served in the mess tent or can be taken out as picnics, as the guests require.

As well as day and night game drives, guided walks with local Maasai warriors are available. Expeditions on horse back are a unique and exciting way to view Ol Pejeta Conservancy. Visits to the Morani Information Centre and rhino holding pens, and to Sweetwaters Chimpanzee Sanctuary, the only place in Kenya to see this endangered and highly intelligent species, can be arranged.

For those interested in the day-to-day life of a working conservancy, lion tracking is on offer. Guests are welcome to join the research team in monitoring the lions of the area, some of whom have been collared with receivers. Sundowner drinks at scenic spots are also available.

Porini Rhino Camp holds Ecotourism Society of Kenya's silver award.

Kicheche Laikipia Camp — Ol Pejeta Conservancy

Kicheche Laikipia Camp, Ol Pejeta Conservancy, Kenya
Kicheche Camps, PO Box 15236, Nairobi 00509, Kenya

Tel	+254 20 2493569/12; +254 20 2405586
Mobile	+254 736 888055; +254 700 888055
Fax	+254 20 891379
E-mail	sales@kicheche.com
Web	www.kicheche.com

Nanyuki, LS & CH, 40 mins
Kamok, CH, 25 mins

Nestled in indigenous forest overlooking a waterhole, Kicheche Laikipia Camp is in the centre of Ol Pejeta Conservancy. The camp is small and intimate, and offers quality game viewing and an authentic experience. There are 6 en-suite tents, made up of twins and doubles and 1 triple. Meals blend African and European dishes, and are fresh and homemade. Where possible, meat and vegetables are sourced locally from the surrounding farms. Breakfast and lunch are usually served alfresco and dinner in the dining tent.

The 90,000-acre Ol Pejeta Conservancy is home to Kenya's largest population of black rhino, and rare northern species such as Grevy's zebra and Beisa oryx. Activities include both day and night game drives, as well as game viewing on horseback. Interpretative game walks focus on identifying spoor and wildlife prints. Guests are also welcome to participate in the lion tracking programme which monitors the lions of the area. From here it is possible to visit Sweetwaters Chimpanzee Sanctuary, the only place to see these endangered and highly intelligent animals in Kenya. Visits to Morani Information Centre and rhino holding pens can be arranged. The camp is closed during the rains in April and May.

Pelican House

 Ol Pejeta Conservancy

Pelican House, Ol Pejeta Conservancy, Kenya
Ol Pejeta Conservancy Private Bag, Nanyuki 10400, Kenya
Tel +254 20 2033244
Mobile +254 723 312673
Fax
E-mail info@olpejetaconservancy.org
Web www.olpejetaconservancy.org

 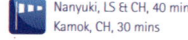 Nanyuki, LS & CH, 40 mins
Kamok, CH, 30 mins

Pelican House, a thatched upcountry cottage, is situated in the Ol Pejeta Conservancy. The self-catering house looks out across colourful gardens to the bush beyond. The house is exclusively designed to support Ol Pejeta Conservancy's community development programmes; all proceeds from renting the house go directly into the programme.

There are 3 double bedrooms, all of which open onto the shaded veranda. Extra single beds can be added if required. There are 2 bathrooms, 2 WCs and a spacious living and dining room with sofas and an open fireplace. Bed linen, towels and filtered drinking water is provided. A generator supplies power 24hr. The house is staffed by a housekeeper, assistant cook, grounds man and night guard. Children are welcome.

Activities include self drive day and night game drives around Ol Pejeta Conservancy. From here it is possible to visit Sweetwaters Chimpanzee Sanctuary, the only place to see these endangered and highly intelligent animals in Kenya. Visits to Morani Information Centre and rhino holding pens can be arranged. Other activities include lion tracking with the conservancy's research team, visiting the various community projects, camel riding and cultural visits to local villages. The house is 8km inside the conservancy from the main gate.

Ngobit River Lodge

 nr Ol Pejeta Conservancy

Ngobit River Lodge, nr Ol Pejeta Conservancy, Kenya
Ngobit Holdings Ltd, PO Box 24983, Nairobi 00502, Kenya
Tel
Mobile +254 735 099932; +254 733 613744
Fax
E-mail b@bbk.co.ke
Web

 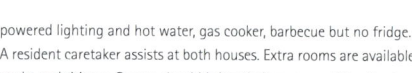 Mweiga, CH, 1 hr
Nanyuki, LS & CH, 1 hr

Ngobit River Lodge started life in the 1960s as a club, and has now been carefully restored in keeping with its original character. Set in 50 acres along the Ngobit River, the self-catering lodge is surrounded by dry forest and the relics of riverine forest, and has views of the Aberdare National Park and Mt Kenya.

The lodge consists of the original clubhouse, which now contains the sitting room, dining room and kitchen, and 6 en-suite twin cottages. The kitchen has a gas cooker, barbecue and generator, but no fridge.

Colobus House has 3 bedrooms, a triple, a double and a twin, 2 bathrooms, a kitchen and an open plan sitting and dining room. The house has solar powered lighting and hot water, gas cooker, barbecue but no fridge.

A resident caretaker assists at both houses. Extra rooms are available for cooks and drivers. Guests should bring their own eco-friendly charcoal for the barbecue, petrol for the generator, food and drinking water, and remove their own rubbish.

Ngobit River Lodge has planted a grevillea woodlot for a sustainable supply of wood and several hundred indigenous trees enjoyed by colobus, birds, bees and butterflies. Activities include hiking and bird watching. Visits to Ol Pejeta Conservancy can be arranged with advance notice.

Equator Chalet Nanyuki

Equator Chalet, Nairobi–Isiolo Road, Nanyuki, Kenya
PO Box 1147, Nanyuki 10400, Kenya
Tel   +254 62 31480
Mobile
Fax
E-mail theequatorchalet@yahoo.com
Web

Nanyuki, LS & CH
15 mins

In the heart of Nanyuki, the Equator Chalet is in a convenient location for visitors staying in Nanyuki, and for visitors wishing to climb Mt Kenya. The hotel has guides and porters for climbing the mountain, who offer a general introduction to the northern ecosystem. It also has mountain climbing equipment for hire.

A stone corridor leads between shops to the hotel's central courtyard where the reception is located. There are 27 en-suite rooms made up of 12 singles and 15 doubles. All rooms have TV with local channels, telephone, armchair and cupboard. Baby cots are also available.

The restaurant serves predominantly Kenyan food with a few international dishes such as deep fried whole tilapia and roast chicken. Buffets can be arranged for large groups. Soft drinks and wine are served in the restaurant, but the hotel stocks no beer or spirits.

The hotel has a cyber café, offering internet, printing and photocopying. The car park is securely enclosed, and a carwash service is offered. The rooftop has a sheltered sitting area, which on a clear day gives striking views of Mt Kenya.

Ibis Hotel Nanyuki Nanyuki

Ibis Hotel, Kinguku Building, Kagera Road, nr Nanyuki Municipal Park
PO Box 286, Nanyuki 10400, Kenya
Tel   +254 62 31536
Mobile
Fax   +254 62 31667
E-mail kihuria@ibishotels.co.ke
Web   www.ibishotel.co.ke

 Equity Bank

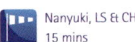 Nanyuki, LS & CH
15 mins

The Ibis chain of hotels started with 1 hotel in Nyeri, and now has 2 hotels in Karatina, 1 in Nanyuki and 1 in Nyeri.

Ibis Hotel has 38 en-suite rooms, made up of singles, twins and executive rooms. All rooms have satellite TV. The executive rooms have double beds; 15 have king size doubles and 19 have small doubles. The rooms are set around a central courtyard with skylights letting plentiful daylight into the hotel.

Nyaki Restaurant, named after the owner's wife, and Kinde Bar, named after the owner's son, are on the ground floor. The menu is predominantly Kenyan, with a few international dishes such as pepper steak, burgers, chicken platter and fillet of Nile perch. The snack menu includes sandwiches, omelettes and samosas. Buffets can be provided for large groups and outside catering is also available. The bar has satellite TV and serves soft drinks, fresh juices, beers and some spirits.

There are 3 conference halls. The large hall on the top floor seats 100 pax. The other 2 halls seat 40 and 30. Equipment can be provided on request. The basement car park is enclosed and is guarded day and night.

The Sportsman's Arms   Nanyuki

The Sportsman's Arms, off Kenyatta Avenue, Nanyuki, Kenya
PO Box 3, Nanyuki 10400, Kenya

Tel	+254 62 32347/8
Mobile	+254 724 336499; +254 734 944077
Fax	+254 62 31826
E-mail	info@sportsmansarmshotels.com
Web	www.sportsmansarmshotels.com

 VISA, MasterCard   Nanyuki, LS & CH
10 mins

The Sportsman's Arms boasts a magnificent view of Mt Kenya and has become a hub for climbers heading for the Sirimon and Burguret routes. The hotel has 172 beds, in doubles, twins and triples. Two modern wings have deluxe en-suite rooms, complete with satellite TV. Country cottages, set around an enclosed courtyard, have 1 or 2 bedrooms, a kitchenette and a lounge with a classic fireplace.

The restaurant has both a la carte and buffet menus, and serves inventive recipes using locally sourced ingredients, fresh farm vegetables and tropical fruits. Nyama choma grilled meats are also available. The hotel's 4 bars have extensive drinks lists. The Buccaneer Dance Club is equipped with pool tables and other indoor games, and showcases live bands. The fully equipped conference centre seats up to 200 pax; the boardroom seats 30. Chini kwa Chini Mega Hall and the hotel's lush gardens are perfect settings for weddings and corporate functions.

The health club offers cardio fitness sessions and sauna, Jacuzzi and steam bath. Children's activities range from riding horses and camels to playing on the playground's swings, slides and merry-go-rounds. Other activities include trout fishing, boating and climbing the spectacular mountain that towers over the hotel.

Kongoni Camp   Nanyuki

Kongoni Camp, 2km from Nanyuki, Nanyuki–Meru Road, Kenya
PO Box 1157, Nanyuki 10400, Kenya

Tel	
Mobile	+254 702 868888
Fax	
E-mail	info@kongonicamp.com
Web	www.kongonicamp.com

    Nanyuki, LS & CH
15 mins

With views of Mt Kenya, Kongoni Camp makes a good place from which to climb the mountain on the Sirimon and Burguret routes. The camp opened in 2008, and its location just outside Nanyuki makes it an ideal stop-off for visitors to the Mt Kenya and Laikipia regions.

There are 5 en-suite cottages, in the style of traditional huts. There is also a campsite with bathroom facilities, lighting and security. Camping equipment is available for hire. The bar and restaurant are in a traditional log cabin with terrace and open fire. Situated in the middle of a copse of cedar trees and shrubs, they make an attractive location from which to watch the prolific birdlife. The restaurant serves an international menu including grills and vegetarian options. The Italian-style wood fire oven produces fresh pizzas, bread and cakes. The bar is fully stocked with soft drinks, beers, wines and spirits.

Activities include mountain climbing, mountain biking, game drives, game walks, horse riding and camel riding. For the more adventurous, Kongoni Camp can arrange excursions of between 1 and 5 days in the Laikipia and Mt Kenya regions. Weddings, parties, conferences and school trips can all be arranged.

Nanyuki River Camel Camp   Nanyuki

Nanyuki River Camel Camp, 4km from Nanyuki, Kenya
PO Box 485, Nanyuki 10400, Kenya

Tel	
Mobile	+254 720 252700 ; +254 722 361642
Fax	
E-mail	nasrafield@yahoo.com / camellot@wananchi.com
Web	www.fieldoutdoor.com

    Nanyuki, LS & CH
10 mins

Nanyuki River Camel Camp was established after a 12-year project working with camel-owning nomads in the remote semi-arid regions of Kenya. The project's team lived continuously amongst the nomads and, while helping them become more self reliant in food, learned much about their remarkable bush knowledge.

The Nanyuki River Camel Camp recreates this experience for visitors. The camp host introduces guests to the fascinating lives of pastoral nomads. There are 10 traditional Somali houses made from woven palm mats attached to wooden frames. There is also a dining banda, kitchen and communal bathrooms, all based around a campfire. There are also campsites and picnic spots. Both full board and self-catering are offered. Activities and challenges are many and various. Both short and long camel rides are available. The ring quest is a series of challenges in woods and streams. Raft construction and racing are on offer. Excursions can be arranged to a cultural manyatta, wildlife reserve and animal orphanage. Trekking and mountain climbing are also recommended. Nanyuki River Camel Camp is owned and managed by Field Outdoor Enterprises, registered in 2008. The company aims to promote and develop ecotourism as an alternative livelihood for pastoralists who may no longer be able to survive on livestock alone.

Mukima House   Nanyuki

Mukima House, 6km north of Nanyuki, Kenya
PO Box 142, Nairobi 00502, Kenya

Tel	+254 20 3882755 ; +254 20 3882763
Mobile	+254 726 332399
Fax	
E-mail	info@mukimakenya.com
Web	www.mukimakenya.com

 VISA, MasterCard   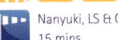 Nanyuki, LS & CH
15 mins

Set in 360 acres of rolling farmland at the foot of Mt Kenya, Mukima House is an attractive settler mansion. Built in the 1930s, the house has been painstakingly renovated, so that it retains the traditional atmosphere while including modern facilities.

There are 8 bedrooms, 6 of which are en-suite. There is also a dining room, and 1 large and 2 small reception rooms, with wood-burning fireplaces and verandas. The property also has a swimming pool, tennis court, croquet lawn, sauna and WiFi. There is a safari guide and vehicle, as well as boats on the dam. The house has a resident manager, and is fully staffed including a team of chefs and a masseuse offering massage, reflexology and beauty treatments. Mukima's food is created from home grown vegetables and eggs, and other locally sourced ingredients. The property is made up of private woods, grassland, a dam and a tree nursery, and has wonderful birdlife and a growing population of bush animals. Activities include game drives in Ol Pejeta Conservancy and Lewa Wildlife Conservancy, flights to Lake Rutundu or Samburu National Reserve, as well as horse riding on Borana Ranch and in Loldiaga Hills. The house offers a perfect setting for conferences, parties or yoga retreats.

Fairmont
Mount Kenya Safari Club

Nanyuki

Fairmont Mount Kenya Safari Club, nr Nanyuki, Kenya
Fairmont Central Reservations, PO Box 58581, Nairobi 00200, Kenya

Tel	+254 20 2265000
Mobile	+254 711 081000
Fax	+254 20 2216796
E-mail	kenya.reservations@fairmont.com
Web	www.fairmont.com

All major cards Nanyuki, LS & CH 30 mins

Founded in 1959 by the film star William Holden, Fairmont Mount Kenya Safari Club has a colourful history and a list of members that reads like a 'Who's who' of royalty, aristocracy and film stars, many of whose photos line the walls of the bar.

The club, set in manicured gardens, faces the jutting peaks of Mt Kenya, Africa's 2nd highest mountain. Straddling the equator, the club has a water feature at its centre demonstrating the clockwise - anticlockwise water movement of the northern and southern hemispheres.

There are 12 Fairmont rooms, 41 deluxe suites, 12 cottages, 8 garden suites and a lavish equator suite with lines on the floor marking the division of the hemispheres. Every room has a fireplace, en-suite bathroom with power-shower and a minibar; the suites also offer a living room and dressing room complete with chaise langue and dressing table. Golf carts are available to carry guests from cottages to the main hotel. The restaurant has an a la carte menu, the bar has a snack menu or for the utmost privacy, a group of 12 can dine in the private dining room. The hotel also boasts a swimming pool, a maze, an animal orphanage and an art gallery.

Activities include mountain climbing, horse riding, camel riding, fishing and rafting.

Timau River Lodge

Timau

Timau River Lodge, Timau Forest, 2km from Timau, nr Nanyuki, Kenya
PO Box 212, Timau 10406, Kenya

Tel	
Mobile	+254 721 331098
Fax	
E-mail	timauriverlodge@hotmail.com
Web	www.timauriverlodge.webs.com

Nanyuki, LS & CH 30 mins

Timau River Lodge is in Timau Forest, near Nanyuki. The lodge is next to a waterfall on Timau River and has lovely views of Mt Kenya. It offers budget accommodation in an attractive setting.

There are 18 rustic log cabins, accommodating a maximum of 67 pax. These cabins are made up of 10 2-person cabins, 4 4-person cabins, 1 5-person cabin, 1 6-person cabin and 2 10-person cabins. The cabins are all en-suite and self-catering. There is an external communal kitchen. There are 2 bars, 1 in the dining room and 1 on the riverside.

The lodge has a tree planting project: guests are encouraged to plant a tree, and the lodge management sends photos of their trees to those who have planted them. Activities include walks in Timau Forest, a peaceful forest with plentiful birdlife. The lodge is near Sirimon Gate, and makes a good starting point for those who wish to climb Mt Kenya using the Sirimon Route. Timau River Lodge is a 20-minute drive from Lewa Wildlife Conservancy, and a 1-hour drive from Ol Pejeta Conservancy and Samburu National Reserve. The sign to the lodge is about 1km from Timau. Telephone network is low; the manager recommends contacting him by text message and he will reply when he gets network.

Ken Trout Timau

Ken Trout, 3km from Timau, nr Nanyuki, Kenya
PO Box 14, Timau 10406, Kenya
Tel
Mobile +254 720 804751; +254 721 950691
Fax
E-mail kentrout1972@gmail.com
Web

 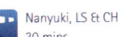 Nanyuki, LS & CH 30 mins

On the banks of Timau River, Ken Trout is an original fishing lodge. The lodge is surrounded by riverine forest, and makes an atmospheric mountain retreat.

The main house has 3 double bedrooms, 2 bathrooms, kitchen, dining room and veranda. The house can be only be taken exclusively, by a family or group of friends. The large cottage has 2 double rooms, 1 single room, 2 bathrooms, kitchen, dining room and veranda. The small cottage has 2 en-suite double rooms and a veranda. All rooms have open fireplaces. The main house and cottages all have comfortable armchairs and a selection of books. The kitchens have minimal equipment; guests choosing the self-catering option should bring utensils and food.

The restaurant serves international and local dishes, and specialises in fish. Buffets can be arranged for large groups. The bar serves soft drinks, beers and spirits. The river has plentiful fish; fishing is recommended. Walks through the forest and along the river are also on offer. Ken Trout makes a good base from which to climb Mt Kenya. If guests wish to do game drives in Ol Pejeta Conservancy or Mt Kenya National Park, the lodge can assist with hiring safari vehicles locally.

KWS, Batian Guest House Mt Kenya National Park

KWS, Batian Guest House, Mt Kenya National Park, Kenya
Kenya Wildlife Service, PO Box 40241, Nairobi 00100, Kenya
Tel +254 20 6000800; +254 20 6002345; +254 20 3991000
Mobile +254 726 610508; +254 726 610509; +243 736 663421
Fax +254 20 6003792
E-mail kws@kws.go.ke / reservations@kws.go.ke
Web www.kws.go.ke

 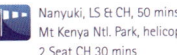 Nanyuki, LS & CH, 50 mins
Mt Kenya Ntl. Park, helicopters,
2 Seat CH 30 mins

Built in 1972 by park warden Bill Woodley, this cottage was home to the Mt Kenya National Park's wardens until 1998. The cottage is set in alpine pastures on the edge of a forested ravine, in the foothills of Mt Kenya. The rugged surrounding landscape features alpine, sub-alpine, moorland and tundra flora with many giant species flourishing above 3,800m.

The cottage is owned and managed by Kenya Wildlife Service, KWS. It has 4 bedrooms, made up of 2 doubles, 1 twin and 1 with bunk beds. The sitting room has a log fire and doors leading out to a veranda. The bathroom has hot water, and a combined bath and shower. The kitchen is fully equipped. A resident caretaker provides bed linen, towels, soap, loo paper and kerosene lamps.

Trekking and mountain climbing are highlights. Over 130 bird species have been recorded. Wildlife seen in the park includes elephant, black rhino, giant forest hog, tree hyrax, white tailed mongoose, suni, bongo, duiker, bushbuck, lion and leopard.

4WD vehicles are recommended in the dry season and essential in the rains. Naro Moru Gate is 17km beyond Naro Moru, and the cottage is ½km beyond the gate. The gate is open 6am to 7pm; park fees must be paid in cash at the gate.

Old Moses & Shipton's Mountain Huts

Mt Kenya

Old Moses and Shipton's Mountain Huts, Mt Kenya, Kenya
PO Box 15796, Nairobi 00100, Kenya

Tel	+254 20 2210051-2
Mobile	+254 772 511752 ; +254 722 511752; +254 722 808406
Fax	+254 20 2210051
E-mail	info@mountainrockkenya.com
Web	www.mountainrockkenya.com

Nanyuki, LS & CH, 15 mins
Mt Kenya Ntl. Park, helicopters,
2 Seat CH 30 mins

These 2 well-maintained huts on the Sirimon route are intended for climbers to stop for the night on their way to the peaks of Mt Kenya. Run by Mountain Rock, the huts are at strategic intervals along the way. Located at an elevation of 3,300m, the Old Moses Mountain Hut is where most hikers spend the first night of their trek. At Old Moses, climbers have the option of sleeping in bunk beds in dormitories, or camping in the large surrounding grounds. There is a kitchen and dining area, and shared bathroom facilities.

The Shipton's Camp is located at an elevation of 4,200m, just below the main peaks of Mount Kenya. As at Old Moses, guests can sleep in bunk beds in the mountain hut or pitch their tents in the grounds. The camp has a kitchen and dining area, and shared bathroom facilities. Shipton's Camp is used by most hikers on their final day before climbing to the summit of Pt. Lenana.

KWS, Sirimon Bandas

Mt Kenya

KWS, Sirimon Bandas, Mt Kenya, Kenya
Kenya Wildlife Service, PO Box 40241, Nairobi 00100, Kenya

Tel	+254 20 6000800; +254 20 6002345; +254 20 3991000
Mobile	+254 726 610508; +254 726 610509; +243 736 663421
Fax	+254 20 6003792
E-mail	kws@kws.go.ke / reservations@kws.go.ke
Web	www.kws.go.ke

Nanyuki, LS & CH, 40 mins
Sirimon KWS, CH, 2 mins

Set in lush open grassland near the foot of Mt Kenya, the Sirimon Bandas are on the edge of Mt Kenya National Park and are owned by Kenya Wildlife Service, KWS.

A stone cottage houses 2 semi-detached bandas. Each banda has 2 bedrooms, made up of 1 double and 1 twin. Each banda has a bathroom with a hot water shower. Each also has a sitting room with a log fire leading into an open plan dining room and a galley kitchen equipped with gas stove, kitchen utensils, cutlery, crockery and glassware. Doors from the sitting room open onto a veranda. A resident caretaker provides bed linen, towels, soap, loo paper and kerosene lamps.

The park is ideal for bird watching; over 130 species have been recorded. Trekking and mountain climbing are excellent in this area. Wildlife seen in the park includes elephant, black rhino, giant forest hog, tree hyrax, white tailed mongoose, suni, bongo, duiker, bushbuck, lion and leopard. The bandas are about 240km north of Nairobi and about 25km from Nanyuki, situated on the right of the road, just outside the Sirimon Gate to Mt Kenya National Park. 4WD vehicles are recommended all year round and essential in the rains.

Rutundu Log Cabins Mt Kenya

Rutundu Log Cabins, Mt Kenya, Kenya
The Safari and Conservation Company, PO Box 24576, Nairobi 00502

Tel	+254 20 2115453; +254 20 6006759; +254 20 6006769
Mobile	+254 712 579999; +254 735 579999
Fax	+254 20 2194995
E-mail	reservations@scckenya.com
Web	www.rutundu.com

    Rutundu, CH, 15 mins
Helipad, 5 mins

These rustic and atmospheric cabins on the edge of Lake Rutundu became suddenly famous in 2010 when Prince William proposed to Kate Middleton here. At an altitude of 3,060m, the cabins face the northeastern crags of Mt Kenya.

The 2 self-catering log cabins have open fires and scenic mountain views. The main cabin has a sitting and dining area, an en-suite bedroom, a kitchen with gas oven and outdoor fridge and a veranda. The smaller cabin has an en-suite bedroom. The cabins sleep 4 comfortably, but 4 more beds can be added if required. All bed linen, towels and kitchen equipment are provided. Lighting is by hurricane lamps. The resident cook and guide are available to assist guests.

The moorland around Lake Alice, with giant groundsel and heather forests, and the cedar and podo forests below, provide numerous diverse walks. Birdlife is extensive, and includes the scarlet-tufted malachite sunbird seen most mornings from the breakfast table.

For those interested in fishing, both Lake Rutundu and Lake Alice are stocked with rainbow trout, and the crystal clear waters of the Kizita River Gorge have small brown trout. From the turning off the Nanyuki-Isiolo road, 4WD vehicles are required. Guests park at Kizita Gorge where staff meet them for the final 15-minute walk across the gorge.

Serena Mountain Lodge Mt Kenya

Serena Mountain Lodge, Mt Kenya, Kenya
Serena Hotels, PO Box 48690, Nairobi 00100, Kenya

Tel	+254 20 2822000; +254 20 2842000; +254 20 2842333
Mobile	+254 733 282200; +254 733 282283; +254 733 282292
Fax	+254 20 2725184; +254 20 2718102/3
E-mail	cro@serena.co.ke
Web	www.serenahotels.com

 VISA, MasterCard, Amex, JCB Diners Club   Nanyuki, LS & CH
1 hr 15 mins

Located at an altitude of 1,950m, Serena Mountain Lodge is surrounded by a dense, ancient rainforest that comes alive at dusk with a chorus of sounds. The rocky, white-capped peaks of Mt Kenya tower over the lodge, providing a striking setting for game viewing.

The lodge is one of the earliest safari lodges built in Kenya. It overlooks a waterhole, rimmed by a diverse mixture of forest vegetation, that is visited by a wide variety of mammal and bird species. Elephant, buffalo, rhino and waterbuck are regularly sighted. A specially constructed viewing bunker, connected to the lodge by a short tunnel, gives guests the opportunity to get surprisingly close to the animals that feed at the waterhole. A spacious veranda also overlooks the waterhole.

Serena Mountain Lodge has 42 en-suite rooms, furnished with indigenous wood and African art, all brightly decorated with thick pile rugs and woven wall hangings. The traditional timbered dining room serves international cuisine.

As well as game drives, guided forest walks are on offer, giving guests a chance to view game and birdlife in the open. Hikes to the peaks of Mt Kenya can also be arranged from here.

Hotel Incredible Meru

Hotel Incredible, Kirukuri Road, off Tom Mboya St, Meru, Kenya
PO Box 2020, Meru 60200, Kenya

Tel	+254 64 30227
Mobile	+254 724 551799 ; +254 722 885511
Fax	+254 64 30107
E-mail	hotelincredible@gmail.com
Web	

   Nanyuki, LS & CH
1 hr

The distinctive yellow façade of Hotel Incredible rises from a junction in the centre of Meru town. The hotel opened in October 2008 and is equipped with modern facilities. Its central location makes it convenient for all shops, businesses and amenities of the town.

There are 35 en-suite rooms, made up of standard rooms and cottages. The standard rooms have satellite TV, telephone, safe, armchairs and coffee table. The cottages, on the top floor, have 2 double bedrooms, WC, shower room, sitting room with sofa and armchairs and a kitchenette equipped with crockery, cutlery, microwave, fridge and gas and electric cooker.

The restaurant has an extensive menu, including African dishes, Chinese dishes such as Manchurian vegetables and chicken shezwan, and Indian dishes such as chicken jalfreezi, malai kofta and paneer mattar. The hotel is owned by a Muslim family and serves no alcohol.

M Ayan conference hall seats 100 pax. When not in use for conferences, the hall is equipped with pool table, dartboard and exercise bike. Areez conference hall seats 50 pax. The guests' lounge, on the 1st floor, has satellite TV. The car park offers free carwashes.

Hotel Three Steers Meru

Hotel Three Steers, Meru–Nanyuki Road, near Makutano Junction
Nairobi Pacific Hotels, PO Box 21113, Nairobi 00505, Kenya

Tel	
Mobile	+254 728 588005
Fax	
E-mail	threesteers@nairobipacifichotels.com
Web	

   VISA, MasterCard   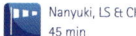 Nanyuki, LS & CH
 45 min

Set in large, well maintained gardens, Hotel Three Steers offers modern rooms and a wide variety of dining and entertainment.

There are 47 en-suite rooms, made up of single, double, superior and deluxe. All rooms, with white tiles and polished wood, have satellite flat screen TV and telephone. The superior and deluxe rooms have king size beds and spacious bathrooms. Baby cots are provided on request.

The restaurant serves international dishes such as chicken biriani and crumbed fish fillet with tartare sauce, as well as pasta, burgers and steaks. The Nyam-Chom serves grilled meats in the garden. The coffee shop serves hot and cold drinks, pastries and cakes. The bar is fully stocked with soft drinks, beers, spirits, wines and liqueurs.

A large hall in the centre of the compound has seating booths, a stage, a dance floor, a DJ booth and a bar. When set up for a conference, it seats 300 pax. There are 2 other halls, seating 100 and 50, and a boardroom seating 20. All halls are fully equipped, including projector and PA system. Hotel Three Steers offers outside catering, including wedding and birthday cakes, and can host wedding receptions, corporate functions, birthday parties and other events.

Meru County Hotel Meru

Meru County Hotel, Kenyatta Highway, opp. Municipal Council, Meru, Kenya
PO Box 3, Meru 60200, Kenya

Tel	
Mobile	+254 700 120910; +254 724 278579
Fax	
E-mail	merucountyhtl@gmail.com
Web	

     Nanyuki, LS & CH
1 hr

A whitewashed building set in well maintained gardens, Meru County Hotel faces the Municipal Council of Meru across Kenyatta Highway. There are 47 en-suite rooms, made up of standard and deluxe. All rooms have built in cupboards and balcony. The standard rooms have showers, while the deluxe have both bath and shower.

The restaurant serves Kenyan and international dishes like grilled chicken and tilapia curry. The bar serves soft drinks, beers and a few spirits, and is equipped with striking red seats and 2 flat screen satellite TVs. A beer garden, its tables shaded by thatched umbrellas, serves nyama choma grilled meats.

There are 2 conference halls, with full length windows; 1 seats 100 pax and the other seats 50. Conference equipment can be provided with advance notice. The cyber café offers internet, printing and other business services, and also has a flat screen satellite TV. The shaded rooftop provides lovely views of Meru town and the Nyambene Hills beyond. The car park behind the hotel is enclosed and securely guarded.

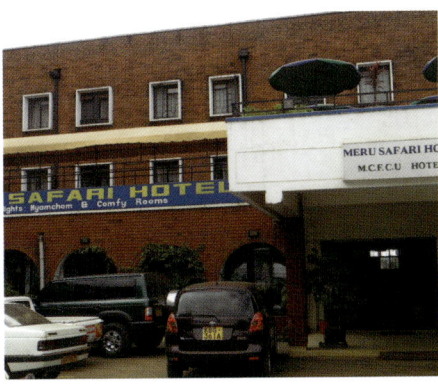

Meru Safari Hotel Meru

Meru Safari Hotel, Kenyatta Highway, opp. Police Station, Meru, Kenya
PO Box 2333, Meru 60200, Kenya

Tel	+254 64 31500
Mobile	+254 718 825844
Fax	+254 64 30511
E-mail	merusafari@yahoo.com
Web	

    Nanyuki, LS & CH
1 hr

Originally owned by Meru Central Farmers' Union, Meru Safari Hotel is now privately owned. Its central location in Meru makes it convenient for all shops, restaurants and businesses of the town.

There are 33 en-suite rooms, made up of singles, doubles, triples and superior. All rooms are equipped with TV with local channels. The superior rooms are slightly more spacious.

Safari Restaurant can serve buffet or a la carte, as required. The menu is international and includes chicken kiev, fish tikka cubes and T-bone steak. There is also a wide selection of vegetarian options such as paneer palak and egg curry. Nyamchom Ranch serves grilled meats. Safari Bar serves soft drinks, beers and a few spirits, and is equipped with satellite TV. Heritage Bar is a large hall, with a bar, pool table and dartboard. Safari Terrace, on the 1st floor, has a bar and snack menu and looks out over the car park. There are 2 conference halls, 1 seating 60 pax and the other seating 30. They are equipped with projector and PA system. The cyber café, in the basement, offers photocopy, internet, printing, faxing, scanning and laminating. The car park is enclosed and securely guarded.

Pig and Whistle Resort

 Meru

Pig and Whistle Resort, Junction of Mwenda Antu and Meru–Nairobi Road
PO Box 3160, Meru 60200, Kenya
Tel +254 64 31411
Mobile
Fax +254 64 32097
E-mail pigwhistleresort.kltd@gmail.com
Web

 VISA, MasterCard, Amex   Nanyuki, LS & CH
1 hr

The Pig and Whistle started life in the 1920s as the office of the 1st District Commissioner of Meru. In the 1930s, the DC moved to what is now Meru Museum, and the Pig and Whistle became a hotel. It came to inglorious fame when George and Joy Adamson stayed here, while Joy was married to her 1st husband, precipitating her divorce.

The reception area is adorned with posters dating from the early days of the hotel, and a display case of butterflies.

There are 20 en-suite rooms, made up of singles and doubles. All rooms have TV with local channels, cupboard and writing table. The singles are in the hotel building, while the doubles are in cottages in the garden.

The restaurant serves African and international food, including basket of chicken, stews and steaks. The healthy option offers carrot juice and muteeta soup, bone marrow soup with assorted medicinal herbs. The Choma Zone and Piggy Bar, with tables around a central bar and dance floor, serve beers and grilled meats; a live band plays every weekend. The garden, a stone pig at its centre, has tables shaded by thatched umbrellas. Maua Piggy Hotel, affiliated to Pig and Whistle Resort, opened in Maua in October 2009.

White Star Hotel

 Meru

White Star Hotel, Maua–Meru Road, near Makutano Junction, Meru
PO Box 259, Meru 60200, Kenya
Tel +254 64 31289; +254 64 32989
Mobile
Fax +254 64 32247
E-mail bluetowershotel@yahoo.com
Web

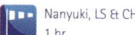 Nanyuki, LS & CH
1 hr

White Star Hotel is adorned with murals and statues of African animals, on its outer wall, in reception and along the corridors.

The rooms are named after African animals and animals from around the world, such as kangaroo, tiger and jaguar. There are 22 en-suite rooms, made up of 20 standard and 2 executive. The standard rooms can be double or twin as required, and are equipped with satellite TV and digital safe. The executive rooms are larger, are furnished with a king size bed, and have both bathroom and shower room.

Bamboo restaurant specialises in Indian food, including paneer palak, kheema, aloo jeera and tandori, and also serves international dishes such as chicken kiev and pan fried fish. The menu includes a wide selection of vegetarian options. Buffets can be served for large groups on request. The conference hall seats 100 pax. Stationery, tea and drinking water can be provided on request, but projector and PA system are not available. A central courtyard houses a pool table.

White Star Hotel is affiliated to Blue Towers Hotel, also in Meru.

Jungle Green Bar & Grill   Murera Gate

Jungle Green Bar and Grill, 7km outside Murera Gate, nr Meru Ntl. Park
PO Box 23, Maua 60600, Kenya
Tel
Mobile +254 733 413842; +254 713 534325
Fax
E-mail
Web

VISA, MasterCard   Nanyuki, LS & CH 1.5 hrs

Promising hot beats and jungle cool atmosphere, Jungle Green Bar and Grill is an attractive garden with rooms, dining and entertainment, and a well designed campsite.

There are 12 en-suite rooms, all named after African animals like giraffe, leopard, hippopotamus and rhino. In a block behind the restaurant, there are 4 singles, 2 small doubles and 2 large doubles. At the campsite, there are 4 more large doubles. All the rooms have table, chair and cupboard and the large doubles have, in addition, satellite TV.

The thatched restaurant serves nyama choma grilled meats, as well as grilled Nile perch and tilapia fresh from the fishpond. The bar has a selection of soft drinks, beers and spirits, and is equipped with satellite TV. Tables dotted around the garden provide comfortable dining areas. The campsite has a bar, sheltered dining booths and bathrooms with hot showers. There is also a table tennis table and a pool table. A borehole ensures plentiful water and a generator supplies 24hr electricity. The site also grows its own fruit including papaya and grapes. The car park is enclosed and securely guarded.

Murera Springs Eco Lodge   Murera Gate

Murera Springs Eco Lodge, outside Murera Gate, nr Meru National Park
Wilderness Getaways, PO Box 25240, Nairobi 00603, Kenya
Tel   +254 20 3876636
Mobile   +254 711 986513; +254 737 636693
Fax   +254 20 3876720
E-mail   sales@wildernessgetawaysea.com
Web   www.wildernessgetawaysea.com

    Kinna, CH 45 mins

Murera Springs Eco Lodge opened in 2010. The lodge is a stylish blend of earthy colours and modern comfort and is set in abundant woodland. It is a short drive from Meru National Park, known for its lush vegetation and rhino sanctuary.

There are 15 en-suite cabins, raised from the ground on wooden platforms. All cabins are decorated with rich fabrics in rust, ochre and brown. Each is furnished with armchair, lamps, rugs and plenty of cushions. Each cabin is set in its own lush woodland. The restaurant serves a variety of dishes, including international and African specialities. The vegetables and fruits are grown locally, in the area around the lodge. The lodge also has a bar and lounge, a gift shop and a swimming pool.

Activities include game drives in Meru National Park, local farm visits and trips to Joy and George Adamson's old base camp. Birdlife is prolific, and bird watching is recommended both during game drives and in the comfort of the lodge. The lodge minimises its environmental impact by being run entirely on solar power.

KWS, Murera Bandas Meru Ntl. Park

KWS, Murera Bandas, Meru National Park, Kenya
Kenya Wildlife Service, PO Box 40781, Nairobi 00100, Kenya

Tel	+254 20 6000800; +254 20 6002345; +254 20 3991000
Mobile	+254 726 610508; +254 726 610509; +254 736 663421
Fax	+254 20 6003792
E-mail	bookings@kws.go.ke / reservations@kws.go.ke
Web	www.kws.go.ke

Kinna, CH, 40 mins
Mulika, LS & CH, 15 mins

Murera Bandas opened in July 2007 to commemorate the branding of Meru National Park a world class tourism destination. The bandas, just inside Murera Gate, are owned by Kenya Wildlife Service, KWS.

There are 4 bandas, with 2 en-suite rooms in each. All rooms have 24hr electricity, mosquito net, fan, double and single bed. Banda No. 2, the executive banda, has armchairs, coffee table and TV with local channels. Each banda has a veranda, a barbecue and an outside dining area. A resident caretaker provides bed linen and towels.

The hostel has 4 rooms with 4 pairs of bunk beds in each and shared bathrooms. An outside classroom, with blackboard and stone seats, is available for use by students. The education centre houses the education warden's office, a library and a fully equipped conference hall with informative displays on Kenya's wildlife areas and tribal cultures.

A raised wooden walkway leads to an attractive thatched bar. The restaurant serves international dishes such as chicken pilau and sirloin steak, and has a children's menu.

The park gates are open from 6am to 7pm; park fees must be paid in cash at the gate. 4WD vehicles are recommended all year round and essential during the rains.

Rhino River Camp Meru Ntl. Park

Rhino River Camp, nr Meru National Park, Kenya
PO Box 22021, Nairobi 00100, Kenya

Tel	+254 20 2513147
Mobile	+254 732 809287
Fax	
E-mail	enquiries@rhinorivercamp.com
Web	www.rhinorivercamp.com

Kinna, CH
35 mins

Rhino River Camp, which opened in 2009, is a stylish new tented lodge near the rhino sanctuary that gives it its name. The camp is set in 80 acres of privately owned land adjacent to Meru National Park.

The 8 en-suite rooms are positioned amongst raffia palms, yellow fever trees and tamarind trees on the banks of the Kindani River. The rooms are made of canvas and local hardwood, and each has an unimpeded view of the river and riverine forest.

Meals are served in the dining and bar area, or in the bush. There is also a swimming pool surrounded by wooden decking and a spa with massage and other treatments.

Game drives cover Meru National Park and the rhino sanctuary. Other activities include mountain biking, river fishing, guided nature trail walks, bird walks and cultural visits to nearby Meru villages. Nearby places of interest include Kilimajero Caldera, an extinct volcano crater good for hiking and bicycling, and Mururi Swamps, where rhino are often spotted at dawn and dusk.

The camp implements policies to minimise its impact on the environment, such as using solar and hydro-electric power. It contributes to the sustainability of the local community by employing locals where possible.

Elsa's Kopje

Meru Ntl. Park

Elsa's Kopje, Meru National Park, Kenya
Cheli & Peacock, PO Box 743, Nairobi 00517, Kenya

Tel	+254 20 6004054/3; +254 20 6003090/1
Mobile	+254 724 255374, +254 733 490234
Fax	+254 20 6004050; +254 20 6003066
E-mail	safaris@chelipeacock.co.ke / info@chelipeacock.co.ke
Web	www.chelipeacock.com / www.elsaskopje.com

VISA, MasterCard   Mugwangho, LS & CH, 5 min
                                         Kinna, CH, 10 mins

Named after Elsa the lioness of Born Free fame, Elsa's Kopje is on the site of George Adamson's first campsite. The lodge offers stunning panoramic views over Meru's forested slopes, that combine lush springs and riverine woodland with arid areas dotted with giant baobabs and doum palms. Rare species of game include Beisa oryx, Grevy's zebra, reticulated giraffe and lesser kudu. Meru National Park incorporates a 44km² rhino sanctuary, home to over 40 white rhino and 20 black rhino.

Elsa's Kopje has 8 en-suite, open plan designer cottages, made up of 7 doubles and 1 twin. All cottages offer complete privacy and striking views. The central dining area has an award-winning infinity pool overlooking the Meru plains.

Elsa's Private House is a spacious, stylish hideaway set slightly apart from the main lodge. It has 2 en-suite bedrooms, 1 double and 1 twin, a large private living and dining area, a private garden and a swimming pool. Elsa's Honeymoon Suite is a triple level cottage, with a sitting room and en-suite double bedroom.

Ecotourism Society of Kenya has given Elsa's Kopje a silver award.
Highly qualified guides offer day and night game drives, game walks and trips to the Tana River. Elsa's Kopje was voted the Best Safari Camp in East Africa by The Good Safari Guide 2009.

KWS, Kinna Bandas

Meru Ntl. Park

KWS, Kinna Bandas, Meru National Park, Kenya
Kenya Wildlife Service, PO Box 40241, Nairobi 00100, Kenya

Tel	+254 20 6000800; +254 20 6002345; +254 20 3991000
Mobile	+254 726 610508; +254 726 610509; +243 736 663421
Fax	+254 20 6003792
E-mail	kws@kws.go.ke / reservations@kws.go.ke
Web	www.kws.go.ke

             Kinna, CH
                                         2 mins

Deep inside Meru National Park, Kinna Bandas are located at the Park HQ and are owned and managed by Kenya Wildlife Service, KWS. The bandas are 22km from Murera Gate, and are near Kinna airstrip and Bwatherongi River. This is the region of the park where game is most prolific.

There are 4 thatched bandas, containing a selection of double and twin rooms. All rooms are en-suite, and are equipped with mosquito nets. The floors are polished dark red and dotted with bright woven rugs; the furnishings are polished wood. There is no electricity and water is heated for showers by means of a kuni booster, or fire. Each banda has a veranda furnished with table and chairs, a barbecue and an outside dining area.

A resident caretaker provides bed linen, towels and kerosene lamps. A swimming pool, in the centre of the compound, has a sunbathing terrace and is surrounded by green lawns dotted with acacias and other indigenous trees. The park gates are open from 6am to 7pm; park fees must be paid in cash at the gate. 4WD vehicles are recommended all year round and essential during the rains.

Leopard Rock Lodge Meru Ntl. Park

Leopard Rock Lodge, Meru National Park, Kenya
Exclusive African Treasures, PO Box 63437, Nairobi 00619, Kenya

Tel	+254 20 7123300-2
Mobile	+254 773 777066; +254 770 289820
Fax	+254 20 7123303
E-mail	reservations@eatreasures.co.ke
Web	www.leopardmico.com / www.eatreasures.com

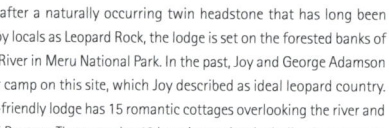

VISA, MasterCard   Kinna, CH
                       25 mins

Named after a naturally occurring twin headstone that has long been known by locals as Leopard Rock, the lodge is set on the forested banks of Murera River in Meru National Park. In the past, Joy and George Adamson set their camp on this site, which Joy described as ideal leopard country. The eco-friendly lodge has 15 romantic cottages overlooking the river and Bisanadi Reserve. There are also 10 luxurious suites including honeymoon cottages and 5 family cottages. All the cottages, with high roofs for ventilation, are built of natural materials, adorned with African artefacts and have private terraces with striking views.

The dining area, made up of 1 enclosed lounge, 1 open air lounge and 2 lounge bars, is adorned with Zanzibari mosaics.

The oasis swimming pool at the river has a fully stocked island bar at its centre and not only offers guests the chance of watching crocodiles basking on the riverbanks, but also has a glass partition at its bottom so guests can watch the crocodiles beneath them as they swim.

Game drives visit the rhino sanctuary, Meru National Park, Kora National Park and Bisanadi National Reserve. Other activities include nature walks, fishing and camel riding at the Borana village.

Offbeat Meru Camp Bisandi Ntl. Reserve

Offbeat Meru Camp, Bisanadi National Reserve, Kenya
Offbeat Safaris, PO Box 1146, Nanyuki 10400, Kenya

Tel	+254 62 2031082
Mobile	+254 704 909355; +254 704 909356; +254 725 968351
Fax	+254 62 2031082
E-mail	bookings@offbeatsafaris.com
Web	www.offbeatsafaris.com

Kinna, CH
45 mins

Offbeat Meru Camp is the only camp in the Bisanadi Reserve, adjacent to Meru National Park. The camp lies along the Bisanadi River, and looks out on the rushing water and the wildlife that come to drink from it. The area is known for Grevy's zebra, reticulated giraffe, leopard, gerenuk and lesser kudu.

There are 6 en-suite tents, made up of 3 twins and 3 doubles. The tents are furnished with iron beds, canvas safari chairs and are lit with solar powered lamps. The bathrooms have safari showers and flush loos. The mess tent is furnished with comfortable sofas, a writing table and a bar, and looks out on the campfire. The camp also has an alluring infinity pool.

There is no formal schedule and days are tailored to suit the guest's requirements. Activities include day and evening game drives, game walks, bush breakfasts, picnics and sundowners. Fly fishing in the local rivers is also on offer.

Offbeat Meru Camp is affiliated to Sosian in Laikipia, Deloraine House near Nakuru and Offbeat Mara Camp. All Offbeat camps support community projects such as clinics and schools. Offbeat Safaris can arrange guided and riding safaris around Kenya.

Meru Mt Kenya Lodge   Mt Kenya National Park

Meru Mt Kenya Lodge, Chogoria Route, Mt Kenya National Park, Kenya
Let's Go Travel ltd, PO Box 60342, Nairobi 00200, Kenya

Tel	+254 20 4441030; +254 20 4441475; +254 20 4443360
Mobile	+254 722 331899
Fax	+254 20 4441690
E-mail	info@letsgosafari.com
Web	www.uniglobeletsgotravel.com/node/945

    Nanyuki, LS & CH
2.5 hrs

On the eastern slopes of Mt Kenya at 3,000m, Meru Mt Kenya Lodge faces the jagged peaks of Batian and Nelion. The lodge perches on a ridge overlooking 2 dams frequented by elephant, buffalo and bushbuck. At this altitude, dense forest and bamboo meets windswept moors and icy lakes. There are 12 simple, self-catering bandas. Each banda has a twin bedroom, a sitting and dining area with fireplace, a kitchen equipped with gas cooker, cooking utensils, crockery and cutlery, and a bathroom. A small cottage has 2 twin rooms and a bathroom. Shower water is heated by a kuni booster, or fire. A resident caretaker provides bed linen. As well as food and drink, visitors are advised to bring dish cloths, drying cloths, washing up liquid, towels, loo paper, extra blankets and matches. A large central building houses a sitting and dining room, kitchen and bathroom. Activities include climbing to the peaks, hiking to tarns and lakes, walking along moorland trails and trout fishing in the tarns, lakes and rivers. Guides, porters and chefs should be booked in advance. The park gates are open from 6am to 7pm; park fees must be paid in cash at the gate. 4WD vehicles are essential.

Transit Motel   Chogoria

Transit Motel, Chogoria, off Meru-Embu Highway, Kenya
PO Box 190, Chogoria 60401, Kenya

Tel	
Mobile	+254 725 609151; +254 733 573494
Fax	
E-mail	transitmotelchogoria@yahoo.com
Web	www.transitmotelchogoria.com

    Nanyuki, LS & CH
2 hrs

In the foothills of Mt Kenya, Transit Motel is a good base for climbing the mountain on the Chogoria Route. The motel provides experienced mountain guides, porters and transport to the start of the Chogoria Route. Camping and climbing equipment including tents, rucksacks, sleeping bags, stoves, gas lamps and crampons are available for hire.

There are 36 simple en-suite rooms, made up of 18 singles, 15 doubles and 3 triples. The rooms all have mosquito net, cupboard, writing table and chair and small balcony. There is also a campsite, with bathroom facilities, a kitchen banda and a dining banda. Chefs can be provided on request. The restaurant serves international dishes such as beef stroganoff and fish and chips. The bar serves soft drinks, beers and spirits, and is equipped with a selection of books, scrabble, dartboard and satellite TV. The rooftop has lovely views, shaded seating areas and a pool table. Restaurant Hall, Jambo Hall and Kithima Hall are all available for conferences.

Transit Motel is 1km from the Meru-Embu Highway. From the motel to the Meru Mt Kenya Lodge is 25km, 4WD required. The start of the Chogoria Route is a further 10km beyond the lodge.

Izaak Walton Inn

Embu

Izaak Walton Inn, Meru-Embu Highway, 2km from Embu, Kenya
PO Box 1, Embu 60100, Kenya

Tel	+254 68 31129 ; +254 68 31290
Mobile	+254 712 781810
Fax	+254 68 30721
E-mail	izaakwaltoninnembu@gmail.com
Web	www.izaakwaltoninn.co.ke

VISA, MasterCard   Embu, CH 15 mins

Named after the keen angler who lived in a farmhouse on this site, the Izaak Walton Inn was established as a hotel in 1948. Set in 9-acre grounds, the inn is an eclectic mix of old colonial style, modern buildings, exotic gardens and local Kenyan customs.

There are 90 en-suite rooms, made up of standard, superior and deluxe. All rooms have satellite TV, built in cupboards, embroidered bedspreads and chintz curtains. The deluxe rooms are more spacious and have polished wooden floors, sofa and fridge.

The restaurant offers buffet and a la carte; guests can eat in the restaurant, on the terrace or in the garden. The main bar is fully stocked and overlooks the garden. The Tavern, also well stocked, is a dark wood panelled bar, with flat screen satellite TV, dance floor and DJ booth. The Observatory is a roadside bar with nyama choma grilled meats and beers. Batian Hall seats 200 pax, Lenana Hall seats 70, Teleki Hall seats 50 and Nelion Hall seats 30. The halls are fully equipped with projector, PA system and secretarial facilities. The hotel also boasts a swimming pool, squash courts, salon, cyber café and horse riding. Parties, weddings and functions can be arranged.

Slopes Villa Hotel

Embu

Slopes Villa Hotel, Meru-Embu Highway, 1½km from Embu, Kenya
PO Box 2277, Embu 60100, Kenya

Tel	+254 68 30148
Mobile	+254 721 449349; +254 728 638338; +254 722 820149
Fax	
E-mail	slopesvilla@yahoo.com
Web	

VISA, MasterCard   Embu, CH 15 mins

Slopes Villa Hotel opened in February 2009 and offers modern facilities on the outskirts of Embu town.

There are 32 en-suite rooms, made up of singles and doubles. The singles have a small double bed, and the doubles have double and single bed. The rooms are set around a central stairwell painted vivid green and adorned with puce banisters. All rooms are equipped with satellite TV, and are painted cream, with wood finishing.

The restaurant serves international dishes such as whole tilapia in tomato concase and country steak topped with an egg, as well as snacks, pastries and fruit. The bar has a selection of soft drinks, beers and spirits, and is equipped with satellite TV and a pool table.

Ngatia Rithari hall seats 70 pax, and the basement hall seats 100. Both halls have aircon and are equipped with conference facilities. Meals can be served in the halls on request. The hotel also offers free WiFi for residents, and has daily aerobic sessions.

Slopes Villa Hotel can accommodate office parties, and offers outside catering. Game drives in Mt Kenya National Park, Meru National Park and Samburu National Reserve can be arranged.

Maina Highway Hotel Embu

Maina Highway Hotel, Haile Selassie St, off Kenyatta Avenue, Embu, Kenya
PO Box 354, Embu 60100, Kenya

Tel	+254 68 31789
Mobile	+254 722 831226
Fax	+254 68 30659
E-mail	mainahighwayhotel@yahoo.com
Web	www.mainahighwayhotel.com

VISA, MasterCard, KCB   Embu, CH
                             15 mins

Established in May 2009, Maina Highway Hotel is a 7-floor hotel in Embu. Its central location makes it convenient for all businesses, shops and restaurants of the town.

There are 95 en-suite rooms, made up of standard, master and twins, all equipped with floor to ceiling mosquito nets and satellite TV. Lifts connect the rooms, restaurants and conference halls.

The 3 restaurants are all self service, and interconnect on the ground floor. The menu is predominantly Kenyan, and includes dishes such as fried chicken, githeri, njahi, irio, curries, stews and omelettes.

Jerusalem Hall seats 100 pax, and is equipped with aircon, satellite TV, LCD projector and PA system. Nazareth Hall seats 150, and is fully tiled and fully equipped. The meeting room seats 20. Additional services such as photocopying are available.

The hotel is Christian and serves no alcohol. There is a safe at reception, where guests can deposit their valuables, as well as a small reception shop selling toiletries, stationery and other necessities. The basement car park is enclosed. The hotel has a backup generator in case of power cuts. Nearby sister hotel, Highway Court Hotel, was built first and offers less modern accommodation and facilities.

Panesic Hotel Embu

Panesic Hotel, Embu-Thika Highway, 1km from Embu, Kenya
PO Box 1390, Embu 60100, Kenya

Tel	+254 68 30318/19
Mobile	+254 722 533442
Fax	
E-mail	panesichotel@yahoo.com
Web	

                             Embu, CH
                             20 mins

An elegant rose-coloured building, Panesic Hotel opened in December 2009 and offers pristine rooms and facilities. Situated on the edge of Embu town on the road to Thika and Nairobi, the hotel looks out over forested hills and lush valleys.

There are 32 en-suite rooms, made up of 25 standard, 3 twin and 4 master. All rooms have cream and terracotta tiled floors, flat screen satellite TV, floor to ceiling mosquito nets, armchairs and coffee table. The bathrooms include a glass shower cabinet. The master rooms have king size beds.

The restaurant, overlooking the shady terrace where guests are welcome to eat, serves international dishes such as chops, steaks, Nile perch, chicken masala, sandwiches and soups. There are plenty of vegetarian options. Buffets can be arranged for large groups. No alcohol is served. The conference hall seats 100 pax. Conference equipment such as projector is available for hire. A smaller hall, by the pool, seats 25. It can be used as a 2nd conference hall, or as a poolside restaurant. The swimming pool is surrounded by a sunbathing terrace with tables shaded by umbrellas and sunbeds, and includes a shallow children's section.

Owoods Lodge & Annex Embu

Owoods Lodge and Annex, Embu-Thika Highway, 2km from Embu, Kenya
PO Box 1148, Embu 60100, Kenya
Tel +254 20 3570569; +254 20 3570147
Mobile +254 722 742748
Fax
E-mail owoodsannex@ymail.com
Web

Embu, CH
25 mins

Stone elephants stand at the gate of Owoods Lodge and Annex, welcoming guests to the lodge where hospitality comes naturally.

There are 30 en-suite rooms, made up of standard, master and executive. The rooms are joined by raised walkways set with flowerbeds. All rooms are fully tiled, with plush curtains and TV with local channels. The master rooms are more spacious and include a dressing table with mirror, and their bathrooms have large corner baths and glass shower cubicles. The executive rooms have a sofa, armchair, coffee table and large flat screen TV. A circular building with a curved staircase at its centre houses the restaurant on the 1st floor and the bar on the ground floor. The restaurant has an international menu and the bar is well stocked. The conference hall seats up to 30 pax.

The large children's garden and play area includes swings, slides, seesaw and merry-go-round. The garden opens on Friday, Saturday and Sunday. During the school holidays, children's entertainment is provided.

The lodge is 2km from Embu, on the road to Thika and Nairobi.

Stopover Hotel Embu

Stopover Hotel, Embu-Thika Highway, 2km from Embu, Kenya
PO Box 2284, Embu 60100, Kenya
Tel +254 20 3544559
Mobile +254 712 842808
Fax
E-mail highlandsstopover@yahoo.com
Web

  Embu, CH
25 mins

With a sign that says Life's a journey, stopover and indulge, Stopover Hotel welcomes passing travellers for food, drinks, entertainment and accommodation.

There are 20 en-suite rooms, made up of 6 safari, 13 deluxe and 1 honeymoon suite. The safari rooms are small, and are furnished with a bed and a chair. The deluxe rooms are painted a selection of bright colours such as yellow and orange, and equipped with satellite TV. The honeymoon suite has satellite TV, sofa, coffee table, cupboard and shelves. The large restaurant and bar surrounds an open garden. There is also a dance floor with private dining booths, where a DJ plays every weekend and public holiday. The menu is predominantly Kenyan, with grilled meats, ugali, chips and rice. There is also a large meat platter that serves 8-10 people. The bar is well stocked with soft drinks, beers and spirits. Group lunches and evening parties are catered for.

Mbuni Conference Hall, on the 1st floor, is fully tiled with large windows, and equipped with projector and PA system. It seats up to 100 pax.

The hotel is 2km from Embu, on the road to Thika and Nairobi.

Philadelphia Retreat & Conference Centre

Embu

Philadelphia Retreat and Conference Centre, Embu-Thika Highway, Embu
PO Box 607, Embu 60100, Kenya

Tel	+254 20 2049927
Mobile	+254 717 430842; +254 722 756805
Fax	+254 20 2381627
E-mail	philadelphiacentre@yahoo.com / perismw@yahoo.com
Web	www.philadelphiaretreatcentre.com

  Embu, CH 40 mins

Established in April 2010, Philadelphia Retreat and Conference Centre is dedicated For the Glory of God. The retreat is owned by David Gitare, the retired Archbishop of the Anglican Church of Kenya. Its intention is to provide a good environment for the rest and relaxation of leaders and executives who need a quiet place for work and reflection.

The resort is designed with a Kikuyu thingira, or traditional homestead, in mind. A circle of 7 rondavels surrounds an attractive garden. Each rondavel contains 2 en-suite rooms, with names like love, joy, patience, hope and peace. All rooms have satellite TV, writing table and armchair. There are peace paintings on the peach-coloured walls.

The restaurant, which can also be used as a meeting room, serves Kenyan food with a few international dishes such as chicken stew, mudfish, grilled goat and sandwiches. No alcohol is served.

A large tent in the grounds can be used for conferences, and includes a lectern for the use of visiting preachers. Conference equipment is not provided. Wedding receptions and photographs can be arranged in the gardens. The garden also boasts a children's play area, with swings and slides. The Retreat is 10km from Embu, on the road to Thika and Nairobi.

Masinga Dam Resort

nr Mwea National Reserve

Masinga Dam Resort, nr Mwea National Reserve, Kenya
PO Box 47309, Nairobi 00100, Kenya

Tel	+254 20 2096288
Mobile	
Fax	
E-mail	mdresort@tarda.co.ke
Web	

  Embu, CH 1 hr

Mwea National Reserve has a savannah ecosystem, with small hills, bushy vegetation and scattered trees. Wildlife includes elephant, Rothschild giraffe, lesser kudu, aardvark, cape hare, slender mongoose, crested porcupine and tortoise. Hippos and crocodiles are found in the dams and river. Over 200 species of birds have been recorded here, most notably water birds and waders. Rare species include Pel's fishing owl, the white-backed night-heron and the Hinde's babbler which is endemic to Kenya. Masinga Dam Lodge is located outside the reserve, overlooking Masinga Dam. There are 33 en-suite rooms, made up of 22 standard and 11 executive. There are also 10 en-suite safari tents. The restaurant serves buffet to those on the full board option, and has an a la carte menu for those who have booked accommodation only or bed and breakfast. The bar serves soft drinks, beers and spirits. There is also a swimming pool. The area is good for walking and trekking. Visitors wishing to do game drives in Mwea National Reserve should come with their own vehicle. Masinga Dam produces hydroelectric power for many parts of Kenya. The dam is home to fish, hippo and crocodile.

Lewa Wildlife Conservancy – Photo © Andrew Nightingale, kembu.com

Laikipia

Rhinos and Elephants - Photo © Andrew Nightingale, kembu.com

The Laikipia plateau's magnificent escarpments, striking plains, isolated hills and cedar forests are home to ethnically diverse communities. Laikipia's conservancies combine cattle ranching, wildlife conservation and community development, and offer a plethora of activities such as camel riding, marathon running, mountain biking, trekking and fishing.

Laikipia straddles the equator, lying between the ice-capped peaks of Mt Kenya, the arid lowlands of Samburu and dazzling Lake Baringo. The region's appeal is its startling contrasts, in wildlife, landscape, people and climate. It is traversed by the Ewaso Nyiro and Ewaso Narok Rivers. The Laikipia Maasai, Kikuyu, Meru, Turkana, Samburu, Borana and Pokot all inhabit the region.

Nanyuki airport has daily scheduled flights from destinations in Kenya. Many of the ranches, sanctuaries and conservancies have airstrips suitable for charter flights. The area is accessible by road from Nanyuki, Baringo, Nyahururu, Isiolo and Maralal.

There are no national parks in Laikipia. The region is made up of private game ranches, sanctuaries and conservancies, most of whom are members of the Laikipia Wildlife Forum, LWF. The forum, established in 1992, is a broad based conservation organisation dedicated to preserving and managing wildlife populations and wilderness habitats in Laikipia. It also aims to better the lives of people in the area through supporting and generating livelihoods and expanding access to essential natural resources. Mpala Research Centre studies and monitors Laikipia's environment and wildlife, helping to ensure that its people and wildlife coexist in harmony.

The Ewaso ecosystem is home to the highest populations of endangered species in Kenya. There are eight protected rhino sanctuaries, which together hold over half of Kenya's black rhino population. The area is also a safe haven for the endangered Grevy's zebra, reticulated giraffe and Lelwel hartebeest. It has significant numbers of predators, including wild dog, and the second largest elephant population in Kenya.

Salama Ngororo Caves are called Daraja ya Mungu, or God's Bridge, by the local people because of their incredible views. Traditionally, the caves were used for religious ceremonies, and it is said that in the 1950s the Mau Mau used them as hideouts during their fight for independence from the British Colonial Government. Ngano-ini Ngororo Caves and adjacent gorge run alongside a seasonal river. During the rainy season, water flows over the caves and gorge in a frothing waterfall. Both cave sites are suitable for hiking, rock climbing, camping and picnicking.

The region offers a wealth of unusual activities. Camel safaris are an exotic way to explore the bush, and can be single-day trips, or multi-day camping safaris. Mountain biking and horse riding trips are offered in many places. Fishing in local rivers and dams is available. Game bird shooting and clay pigeon shooting are offered on some ranches. Guided game walks immerse visitors in the sheer vastness of Laikipia.

The Safaricom Lewa Marathon takes place annually in June. For the occasion, Lewa Wildlife Conservancy opens its gates and its campsites to runners and their supporters, and provides a colourful and entertaining weekend. Profits support education, health, community development and wildlife conservation projects across Kenya.

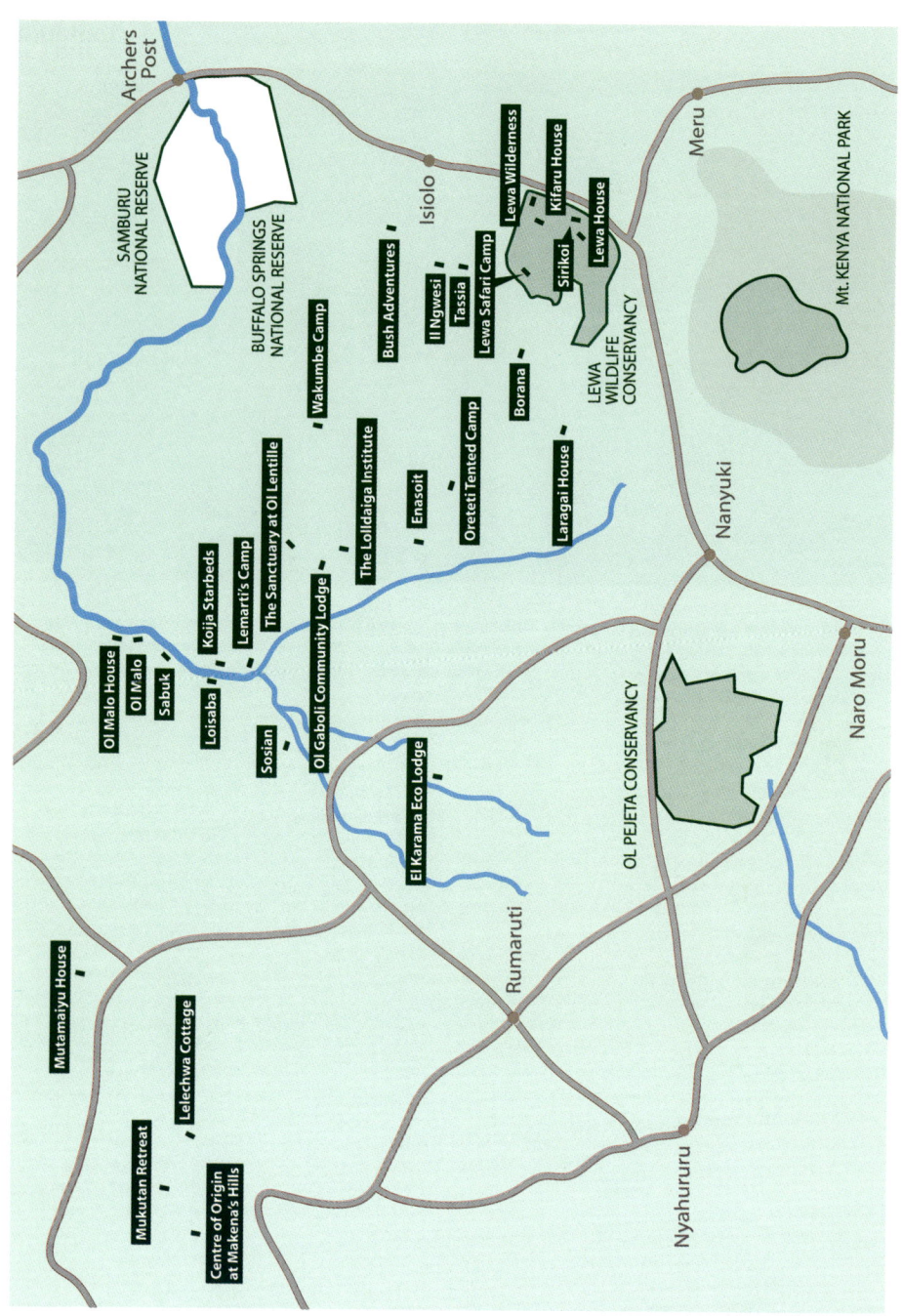

Centre of Origin at Makena's Hills
Ol ari Nyiro Wildlife Sanctuary

Makena's Hills, Ol ari Nyiro Wildlife Sanctuary, Laikipia, Kenya
PO Box 63704, Nairobi 00619, Kenya
Tel
Mobile +254 734 291710; +254 733 536324
Fax
E-mail mukutan@gallmannkenya.co.ke
Web www.gallmannkenya.org

 Laikipia Enghelesha, CH

Ol ari Nyiro, meaning place of springs, is a 100,000-acre private wildlife sanctuary on the western edge of the Laikipia plateau. The sanctuary was initiated by Kuki Gallmann, the author of I dreamed of Africa and African Nights. The Gallmann Memorial Foundation is dedicated to creative, sustainable conservation: people and wildlife developing together, through research, education and the arts. Centre of Origin at Makena's Hills is a stunning residential interfaith and meditation centre. There are 6 en-suite Arabic style tents, made up of doubles and twins. Each tent has a dressing room, veranda, massage bed and yoga mats. The central reception area has 2 fireplaces, front terrace, dining room, gift shop, swimming pool and yoga hall. The camp is adorned with antiques and African artefacts. The centre serves vegetarian cuisine. Mukutan Gorge, which plunges from 2,100 to 900 meters, slices through the sanctuary. The sanctuary has waterfalls, thermal hot springs and a diverse selection of wildlife including over 400 species of birds and some endemic flora, previously unrecorded. Activities include ethno-botanical walks, tree planting and bird watching. Picnics and sundowners can be arranged, as can cultural visits to local Pokot villages. Yoga and massage are available. Guests are also welcome to visit the conservation projects. Current projects include providing community health facilities, building schools and bursaries.

Lelechwa Cottage
Ol ari Nyiro Wildlife Sanctuary

Lelechwa Cottage, Ol ari Nyiro Wildlife Sanctuary, Laikipia, Kenya
PO Box 63704, Nairobi 00619, Kenya
Tel
Mobile +254 734 291710; +254 733 536324
Fax
E-mail mukutan@gallmannkenya.co.ke
Web www.gallmannkenya.org

    Laikipia main, CH

Ol ari Nyiro, meaning place of springs, is a 100,000-acre private wildlife sanctuary on the western edge of the Laikipia plateau. The sanctuary was initiated by Kuki Gallmann, the author of I dreamed of Africa and African Nights. The Gallmann Memorial Foundation is dedicated to creative, sustainable conservation: people and wildlife developing together, through research, education and the arts. Lelechwa was considered an invasive weed until the Gallmann Memorial Foundation proved that it can be harvested sustainably to provide a range of products including eco-charcoal, essential oils and furniture. Lelechwa Cottage is an original rustic self-catering cottage. There is an en-suite double bedroom, study with sofa bed, sitting room, fully equipped kitchen and veranda. Hurricane lamps and candles provide lighting, with solar backup. The cottage is fully furnished, equipped and serviced. Activities include bird watching and botanical walks with a resident ecologist. Mukutan Gorge, which plunges from 2,100 to 900 meters, slices through the sanctuary. The sanctuary has waterfalls, thermal hot springs and a diverse selection of wildlife including over 400 species of birds and some endemic flora, previously unrecorded. Guests are also welcome to visit the conservation projects. Current projects include providing community health facilities, building schools and bursaries. Volunteers who wish to assist with projects should apply through the website.

Mukutan Retreat
Ol ari Nyiro Wildlife Sanctuary

Mukutan Retreat, Ol ari Nyiro Wildlife Sanctuary, Laikipia, Kenya
PO Box 63704, Nairobi 00619, Kenya

Tel	
Mobile	+254 734 291710; +254 733 536324
Fax	
E-mail	mukutan@gallmannkenya.co.ke
Web	www.gallmannkenya.org

 Laikipia Main, CH

Ol ari Nyiro, meaning place of springs, is a 100,000-acre private wildlife sanctuary on the western edge of the Laikipia plateau. The sanctuary was initiated by Kuki Gallmann, the author of I dreamed of Africa and African Nights. The Gallmann Memorial Foundation is dedicated to creative, sustainable conservation: people and wildlife developing together, through research, education and the arts. Mukutan, meaning meeting, takes its name from the hills that meet here. Mukutan Retreat overlooks the spectacular Mukutan Gorge, which plunges from 2100 to 900 meters. The retreat comprises 3 individually designed traditional cottages. The cottages, built in African style using local stone, wood and thatch, each have an en-suite double room, fireplace and veranda. The central lounge and dining area is elegantly furnished with antiques and African artefacts. The infinity swimming pool overlooks the valley. Mukutan Retreat can be taken as an exclusive self-catering villa. The sanctuary has waterfalls, thermal hot springs and a diverse selection of wildlife, including over 400 species of birds and some endemic flora, previously unrecorded. Activities include game drives, game walks and cultural visits to local Pokot villages. Guests are welcome to visit the conservation projects. Current projects include providing community health facilities, building schools and bursaries. Volunteers who wish to assist with projects should apply through the website.

Mutamaiyu House
Mugie Wildlife Conservancy

Mutamaiyu House, Mugie Wildlife Conservancy, Laikipia, Kenya
Exclusive African Treasures, PO Box 63437, Nairobi 00619, Kenya

Tel	+254 20 7123300-2
Mobile	
Fax	+254 20 7123303
E-mail	info@eatreasures.co.ke
Web	www.eatreasures.com / www.mutamaiyu.com

  Loisaba, LS & CH, 45 mins
Mugie, CH, 10 mins

Mutamaiyu House is located on the 22,000-acre Mugie Wildlife Conservancy. The conservancy was formed in 2004, and has contributed to the campaign for the preservation of the endangered black rhino. It is also one of the core study areas of the Laikipia Predator Project, a project aimed at promoting coexistence between livestock and predators. There are 4 cottages, 2 with en-suite double bedroom and 2 with en-suite twin bedroom. The cottages are built to maximise the view. The cottages are equipped with charging facilities and WiFi. The family-run manor house has private lounges with fireplaces, and is adorned with family heirlooms and art collection. Meals are served in the extended dining room. There is also a heated swimming pool.

Activities include day and night game drives, lion tracking, game walks, camel trekking, fishing and daily ranch life. Visits to the Mugie Rhino Sanctuary, the weekly market in Suguta Marmar and Mugie School, supported by Mugie Wildlife Conservancy, are on offer. An introduction to the Pokot and Samburu traditional ways of life is also available. For an extra charge, clay pigeon shooting, visits to a local village and a day trip to Porro Maralal, the Roof of the World are on offer. Mutamaiyu House is closed in January and June.

Ol Malo House

Ol Malo

Ol Malo House, Laikipia, Kenya
Bush and Beyond, PO Box 56923, Nairobi 00200, Kenya

Tel	+254 20 6000457; +254 20 6005108; +254 20 6005980
Mobile	+254 733 330007; +254 723 273668
Fax	+254 20 6005008
E-mail	info@bush-and-beyond.com
Web	www.bush-and-beyond.com

 VISA, MasterCard   Loisaba, LS & CH, 40 mins
Ol Malo, CH, 10 mins

On the northern edge of the Laikipia plateau, Ol Malo House sits high on an escarpment looking down on northern Kenya. Ol Malo, or place of the greater kudu, is a wilderness area that is both remote and beautiful. Ol Malo House has 3 en-suite double bedrooms, and a large sitting and dining room. There are 2 cottages adjacent to the house, 1 with a double en-suite bedroom and 1 with 2 en-suite double bedrooms and a sitting room. There is an infinity swimming pool, with a large sunbathing terrace surrounding it, complete with barbecue and dining area. There is also a gift shop. A generator provides power morning and evening. A masseuse visits when required, reservation necessary. Internet access can be provided on request.

Activities include game drives, game walks, camel riding, mountain biking and cultural visits to local communities. Guests can also spend a night in the lookout at the waterhole. There are 15 horses, 8 of which are ride-able. Saddles, jodhpurs, riding hats and boots are all available at the house. Game seen during horse rides includes giraffe, zebra, gazelles, eland, oryx, and occasionally cat and elephant. Ol Malo House is closed in April, May and November.

Ol Malo

Ol Malo

Ol Malo, Laikipia, Kenya
Bush and Beyond, PO Box 56923, Nairobi 00200, Kenya

Tel	+254 20 6000457; +254 20 6005108; +254 20 6005980
Mobile	+254 733 330007; +254 723 273668
Fax	+254 20 6005008
E-mail	info@bush-and-beyond.com
Web	www.bush-and-beyond.com

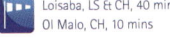 VISA, MasterCard   Loisaba, LS & CH, 40 mins
Ol Malo, CH, 10 mins

On the northern edge of the Laikipia plateau, Ol Malo sits high on an escarpment looking down on northern Kenya. Ol Malo, or place of the greater kudu, is a wilderness area that is both remote and beautiful. Ol Malo has 4 luxury cottages, each with en-suite double bedroom and veranda with a view. The lodge also has a large sitting and dining room with fireplace. There is an infinity swimming pool, with a large sunbathing terrace surrounding it, complete with barbecue and dining area. There is also a gift shop. A generator provides power morning and evening. A masseuse visits when required, reservation necessary. Internet access can be provided on request.

Activities include game drives, game walks, camel riding, mountain biking and cultural visits to local communities. Guests can also spend a night in the lookout at the waterhole. There are 15 horses, 8 of which are ride-able. Saddles, jodhpurs, riding hats and boots are all available at the lodge. Game seen during horse rides includes giraffe, zebra, gazelles, eland, oryx, and occasionally cat and elephant. Ol Malo is closed in April, May and November.

Sabuk

 Ewaso Nyiro River

Sabuk, Laikipia, Kenya
New African Territories, PO Box 76677, Nairobi 00508, Kenya
Tel +254 20 2663397, +254 20 3598871
Mobile +254 718 139359
Fax
E-mail bookings@africanterritories.co.ke
Web www.africanterritories.co.ke / www.sabuklodge.com

 Loisaba, LS & CH
1 hr

Perched on a cliff overlooking the Ewaso Nyiro River, Sabuk is an exclusive wilderness haven on the edge of the northern Laikipia Plateau. This raised location grants dramatic views of the Laikipia plains, the Karisia Hills and Matthews Mountains.

Sabuk has 6 spacious en-suite open-fronted stone cottages with thatched roofs and private verandas with stunning views. 3 have king size beds, 2 have twin beds and 1 family cottage has a king size bed and 3 singles. Eagle Cottages, a family unit, has two en-suite cottages, one with king size bed and one triple, with exclusive dining area and plunge pool. Sabuk also boasts an open mess area where guests can relax on cushions looking out over the river, an infinity pool and a church with a view for weddings. Sabuk has been operating walking and camel safaris for over 20 years, and each safari is tailor-made. The Laikipiak Maasai share their tribal and bush craft skills, such as tracking animals and explaining the medicinal uses of local plants. Guests can enjoy camel assisted walking safaris for anything between one morning and two weeks, hosted by Maasai and Samburu warriors and sleeping under the stars. Other activities include day and night game drives, game walks, horse riding, bush breakfasts and sundowners at viewpoints.

Loisaba

 Loisaba Ranch

Loisaba, Laikipia, Kenya
PO Box 1348, Nanyuki 10400, Kenya
Tel +254 62 31070-2
Mobile +254 705 202375
Fax
E-mail enquiries@loisaba.com
Web www.loisaba.com

 VISA, MasterCard

 Loisaba, LS & CH
15 mins

The vast game ranch of Loisaba combines adventure with serenity. For those with an appetite for adventure, Loisaba offers camel trekking, mountain biking, quad biking, rafting and ballooning, while for those with a love of peace, Loisaba provides pampering in the spa and the famed starbeds, raised en-suite platforms under the stars. Loisaba Lodge, with 7 en-suite double and twin rooms, is perched high on the escarpment with legendary views of Mt Kenya and the waterhole. It has a swimming pool, tennis court, croquet lawn, bocce court, fully equipped spa and gift shop. Loisaba House, with 1 double and 1 twin, is built of local materials and thatched with Mombasa palm. The ultimate getaway, the house has its own staff, game drive vehicle and cliff top swimming pool. Loisaba Cottage is set in landscaped gardens with a private swimming pool. The cottage has 3 double en-suite rooms and 1 twin room with access to a bathroom via an external staircase. Loisaba merges untamed bush with a working cattle farm. The northern species of gerenuk, Grevy's zebra and reticulated giraffe share their waterholes with domestic cows. This symbiotic relationship between ranching and tourism pays for the protection of the wider environment and its often endangered inhabitants. Loisaba was voted the best community safari property in Africa by The Good Safari Guide in 2010.

Koija Starbeds  Loisaba Ranch

Koija Starbeds, Koija Community Land, nr Loisaba, Laikipia, Kenya
PO Box 1348, Nanjuki 10400, Kenya

Tel	+254 62 31070-2
Mobile	+254 705 202375
Fax	
E-mail	enquiries@loisaba.com
Web	www.loisaba.com

VISA, MasterCard

Loisaba, LS & CH
30 mins

Koija Starbeds overlook the Ewaso Nyiro River. They are owned by the local Koija community, and managed by Loisaba. The Ecotourism Society of Kenya has awarded the Koija Starbeds a bronze level award.

There are 2 doubles and 1 twin platforms. The homemade Mukokoteni beds are on raised wooden platforms; they can be partially sheltered by a thatched roof, or wheeled out onto the open deck for a night under the stars. All platforms have en-suite bathrooms. Home cooked meals are served in the mess area. There is also a campfire and outdoor seating area, and a suspension bridge over the river. Game drives and game walks are on offer, as well as bush meals and sundowners. The community offers cultural visits to their villages, and has a selection of handmade artefacts for sale.

The starbeds can be taken as part of a stay at Loisaba, which offers a plethora of activities including camel trekking, mountain biking, quad biking, rafting and ballooning. There is also a spa with a range of treatments. Loisaba conservancy, with an area of 62,000 acres, is home to lion, leopard, elephant, buffalo, hippo, giraffe, cheetah, Grevy's zebra, Beisa oryx and wild dog. Loisaba Community Trust is dedicated to poverty alleviation and conservation. Projects include building classrooms, paying teachers and providing education supplies.

Lemarti's Camp Koija Group Ranch

Lemarti's Camp, Koija Group Ranch, Laikipia, Kenya
The Safari and Conservation Company, PO Box 24576, Nairobi 00502, Kenya

Tel	+254 20 2115453; +254 20 6006759; +254 20 6006769
Mobile	+254 712 579999; +254 735 579999
Fax	+254 20 2194995
E-mail	reservations@scckenya.com
Web	www.lemarticamp.com

Lendile, CH, 45 mins
Loisaba, LS & CH, 1.5 hrs

Lemarti's Camp, on the banks of the Ewaso Nyiro River, is a striking vision of arid wilderness. The local Samburu community own the land; the camp was built and is run by Samburu guide, Loyapan Lemarti, and his fashion designer wife, Anna Trzebinski. This chic camp opened in 2008 and has already won a Travel and Leisure Design Award.

There are 5 en-suite double tents. The tents are stylish and their bathrooms are open to the sky. They are set in a grove of palms and centenary fig trees. The Samburu chefs use fresh organic ingredients to create a fusion of Greek, Italian and French food.

Activities include game walks, mountain biking and camel trekking.

Cultural visits to local Samburu villages are recommended; guests are welcome to take part in traditional ceremonies and activities. The river provides opportunities for both swimming and fishing. For a surcharge, guests can go fly camping in the Nomadic and Stargazing Camps, or visit the Mpala Wildlife Foundation, prior reservation necessary. A beauty therapist offers a range of health and beauty treatments. The boutique features Anna Trzebinski's interior and lifestyle products, and her fashion label. Lemarti's Camp is committed to making a sustainable difference to the people of Koija, and supports projects such as local education.

Sosian

Sosian Conservancy

Sosian, Laikipia, Kenya
Offbeat Safaris, PO Box 1146, Nanyuki 10400, Kenya
Tel +254 62 2031082
Mobile +254 725 968351; +254 704 909355/6
Fax +254 62 2031082
E-mail bookings@offbeatsafaris.com
Web www.offbeatsafaris.com

VISA, MasterCard

Sosian, CH, 15 mins
Loisaba, LS & CH, 1 hr

Sosian's original ranch house was built in the 1940s by Italian artisans. After elegant restoration, it opened as Sosian Lodge. The garden, dominated by succulents, has a backdrop of Mt Kenya. Sosian is a 24,000-acre private wildlife conservancy combining tourism, conservation and traditional cattle ranching.
There are 7 en-suite double cottages, each with private veranda. Sosian's home cooking is created from fresh ingredients grown in the garden. Meals are served in the lodge, by the river, by the swimming pool or in the bush. Sosian's activities include walking, horse riding, camel safaris, day and night game drives and cultural visits to local Samburu villages. The river offers a plethora of activities including fishing, rafting and jumping off waterfalls. Archery and tennis are available. Sosian also offers specialised walking safaris: visitors explore the bush, tracking animals during the day and sleeping in a mobile tented camp in a new location each night. Sosian has a herd of over 600 Boran cattle, Kenya's zebu breed developed from the native stock, including a pedigree breeding herd and small dairy herd. A tour of the ranching side of Sosian includes assisting with dipping, weighing and vaccinating. Sosian is affiliated to Offbeat Safaris and can arrange safaris around the country and horse riding safaris.

The Sanctuary at Ol Lentille

Kijabe Group Ranch

The Sanctuary at Ol Lentille, Kijabe Group Ranch, Laikipia, Kenya
Bush and Beyond, PO Box 56923, Nairobi 00200, Kenya
Tel +254 20 6000457; +254 20 6005108; +254 20 6005980
Mobile +254 733 330007; +254 723 273668
Fax +254 20 6005008
E-mail info@bush-and-beyond.com
Web www.bush-and-beyond.com

VISA, MasterCard, Amex

Ol Lentille, CH, 15 mins
Loisaba, LS & CH, 1 hr

The Sanctuary at Ol Lentille is a collection of luxury houses in an exclusive conservancy. The 14,500-acre conservancy is a progressive conservation and tourism partnership between the Maasai community, donors and private investors.
There are 4 houses, each architecturally individual, and each representing a Voice of Africa. The Chief's House, in contemporary African style, has 3 en-suite double bedrooms. The Sultan's House, in Swahili style, has 1 en-suite double and 1 en-suite twin bedroom. The Eyrie, in African retro style, has 1 en-suite double bedroom. The Colonel's House, in campaign style, has 2 en-suite double bedrooms. The lodge has a swimming pool, spa, gift shop and library with telescope. WiFi is available throughout. Activities include day and night game drives, and game walks. Horse riding, camel riding, mountain biking and quad biking are available. Picnics, sundowners and bush dinners can be arranged. Boules and croquet are on the lawns. Activities with an extra charge include a bush skills course, kayaking and river rafting. Light aircraft and helicopter trips can be arranged. The sanctuary can also arrange safaris and excursions to other destinations in Kenya. Guests are welcome to visit the conservation projects and community work that the sanctuary supports.

Wakumbe Camp — Morupusi Group Ranch

Wakumbe Camp, Morupusi Group Ranch, Laikipia, Kenya
PO Box 1477, Nanyuki 10400, Kenya
Tel
Mobile +254 722 768071
Fax
E-mail kilwafin@yahoo.com
Web

    Nanyuki, LS & CH 2 hrs

Wakumbe Camp is located on Morupusi Group Ranch, which is a member of the 43,000-acre Naibunga Conservancy. The Naibunga Conservancy is a community initiative linking 9 group ranches in central Laikipia. A 10-year management plan guides conservation efforts and supports livelihoods. Wakumbe Camp is self-catering, and is aimed at intrepid adventurers. There are 2 twin tents, with safari-style WC and showers. There is a mess tent, with kitchen facilities. Guests cater for themselves; a guide and a camp assistant are available for a small extra charge. Visitors are also welcome to camp at a site in the Wakumbe Hills, which has stunning views across the Kipsing Stream towards northern Kenya. The campsite has scattered acacia trees and rocky outcrops with euphorbia and dracaena. There is another campsite on the sandy banks of the seasonal Sinyai River. This site is shaded by yellow fever trees and is home to many species of wildlife and birdlife.

Activities include game walks and mountain hikes. The dirt roads are good for mountain biking. Local guides must accompany visitors on all walks, because of the existence of elephant and buffalo in the area. Wakumbe Camp is 75km from Nanyuki, via Dol Dol. 4WD vehicles are essential.

Ol Gaboli Community Lodge — Il Motiok Group Ranch

Ol Gaboli Community Lodge, Il Motiok Group Ranch, Laikipia, Kenya
PO Box 764, Nanyuki 10400, Kenya
Tel
Mobile +254 725 768456
Fax
E-mail info@olgabolilodge.com
Web www.olgabolilodge.com

   Nanyuki, LS & CH 2 hrs

Ol Gaboli, meaning fig tree in Maasai, describes the location of this lodge which nestles under the branches of the largest and oldest fig tree in the area. On the banks of the Ewaso Nyiro River, the lodge is in the 15,000-acre Il Motiok Group Ranch. It is owned by an all women pastoralist group, and managed by the Il Motiok community. The self-catering lodge can only be booked on an exclusive basis.

There are 6 en-suite bandas, all built from local stone with thatched roofs. Each banda can sleep 6 pax. There is an open plan lounge and dining area and an equipped kitchen. Ol Gaboli also has a house with 2 large rooms and 2 lofts that can sleep a group of 30 pax.

The lodge is aimed at intrepid adventurers and teambuilding groups. Activities include nature walks, mountain biking, camel safari, rock climbing, abseiling and cultural visits to local Maasai villages. The river provides opportunities for swimming, fishing, rafting, canoeing, kayaking, and river tubing. Conservation projects have seen a return of wildlife such as elephants, giraffe, Grevy's zebra and wild dog.

Revenue collected from the lodge is used for community projects in primary education, drinking water, basic sanitation and health facilities. Ol Gaboli Community Lodge is 75km from Nanyuki, via Il Polei. 4WD vehicles are essential.

The Lolldaiga Institute

Lolldaiga Hills

The Lolldaiga Institute, Lolldaiga Hills Ranch, Laikipia, Kenya
PO Box 26, Nanyuki 10400, Kenya

Tel	+254 20 2665484
Mobile	+254 722 733601
Fax	
E-mail	TLI@lolldaiga.com
Web	www.lolldaiga.com

Lolldaiga, CH, 20 mins
Nanyuki, LS & CH, 50 mins

Lolldaiga Hills include the highest peak in Laikipia and provide stunning views and diverse scenery. The 50,000-acre Lolldaiga Hills Ranch has a wide variety of vegetation, including dry savannah, open woodlands and high altitude forest. The ranch is a working cattle ranch, in which people, livestock and wildlife coexist. The Lolldaiga Institute Lodge, or TLI Lodge, is a 1940s cedar log building. It has 2 en-suite double rooms and an open plan sitting and dining room with redbrick fireplace. There is a cottage with en-suite double room and fireplace, and a smaller cottage with en-suite twin room. The garden's jasmine and citrus attract plentiful birdlife. The farm also has a tennis court and a campsite. Game drives and game walks in the ranch are on offer. About 60 species of wildlife and 300 species of birdlife have been recorded here. The ridges and valleys of Lolldaiga Hills provide challenging and spectacular hikes. For a surcharge, camel riding and mountain biking are available. Nearby archaeological sites include 2 Stone Age rock shelters, rock art and ancient pottery. Guests are welcome to participate in livestock husbandry; the ranch has Merino and Dorper sheep, a pedigree herd of Boran cattle and British Red Poll cattle. The Lolldaiga Institute works towards conservation, community development and responsible livestock production.

El Karama Eco Lodge

Ewaso Nyiro River

El Karama Eco Lodge, Laikipia, Kenya
PO Box 172, Nanyuki 10400, Kenya

Tel	+254 20 2417500
Mobile	
Fax	
E-mail	elkaramalodge@gmail.com
Web	www.laikipiasafaris.com

 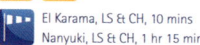

El Karama, LS & CH, 10 mins
Nanyuki, LS & CH, 1 hr 15 mins

On the banks of the Ewaso Nyiro River, El Karama Eco Lodge looks out on a riverside saltlick that attracts plentiful game. The lodge, which has been in the hands of the Grant family since the 1970s, is in 15,000 acres of private land. It was refurbished in 2010.

There are 4 en-suite bandas, made from stone, thatch and canvas, each with private veranda. There is 1 rondavel with external bathroom and 1 cottage with en-suite bathroom. Both these are suitable for families. The campsite has kitchen and bathroom facilities. The rooms are unique in design, and filled with quirky artwork such as paintings of El Karama's landscape, plaster casts of animal tracks and Stone Age hand axes found locally. The central mess area has an open fireplace, open plan dining room, bar and reading area. Guests can choose either full board or self-catering. Activities include accompanied self-drive game drives, game walks, bird walks, picnics and sundowners. Guests are also welcome to visit the ranch, see the Saihiwal cattle and attend milking, dipping and inspections. Other activities available for a surcharge include fishing for barbel and catfish, horse riding, bush meals and children's tracking adventures. El Karama Eco Lodge is committed to the preservation of wildlife habitats; a substantial portion of profit is consigned to conservation work.

Enasoit

Lolldaiga Hills

Enasoit, Lolldaiga Hills, Laikipia, Kenya
PO Box 625, Nanyuki 10400, Kenya

Tel	+254 20 2033025
Mobile	+254 722 521740; +254 722 768128
Fax	+254 20 3524477
E-mail	karen@enasoit.co.ke
Web	www.enasoit.com

  Enasoit, CH, 5 mins
Nanyuki, LS & CH, 1.5 hrs

On the edge of the Lolldaiga Hills in a private game sanctuary, Enasoit is a stylish bush camp. The camp can only be taken exclusively. Its striking location offers excellent game viewing in an important wildlife corridor between east and west Laikipia. The camp overlooks 2 saltlicks and a dam which attracts elephant, buffalo and giraffe, as well as smaller game. There are 6 en-suite double tents. All tents have stone bathrooms, fireplaces and elegant furnishings. There is also a pool house, with 2 double bedrooms and a heated swimming pool, surrounded by its own garden. The mess tent has comfortable seating areas and a dining area. Meals are provided by the team of cooks.

Activities include day and night game drives in Enasoit Ranch. The ranch has all the predators, including lion, leopard, cheetah and wild dog. Game walks and sundowners are also available. Cultural visits to local villages are on offer. Horse riding can be arranged. The camp also offers massage. Enasoit has a helicopter that can be hired for excursions to Mt Kenya and other destinations in Kenya, and a restored dhow that can be hired for cruises around Lamu. Trips to Nanyuki or elsewhere can be arranged.

Bush Adventures

nr Il Ngwesi

Bush Adventures, 30km west of Isiolo, nr Il Ngwesi, Kenya
PO Box 673, Nairobi 00606, Kenya

Tel	
Mobile	+254 724 301095; +254 723 115809
Fax	
E-mail	info@bush-adventures.com
Web	www.bush-adventures.com

 Isiolo, LS & CH
45 mins

Established in 2009, Bush Adventures combines a luxury tented camp with Maasai warrior training. The camp was built without cutting a tree or shrub, and promotes the ancient Maasai knowledge of living with nature. There are 4 en-suite tents, which can be double or twin as required. The tents are furnished with 4-poster beds, and have views over the Ngare Ndare River. Meals are served in the mess tent, in the company of the Maasai trainers. The 4-day Introductory Training familiarises guests with the Maasai culture, society and language. Maasai fighting techniques such as the use of bow and arrow, wrestling, animal tracking and the setting of an ambush are also taught. The 7-day Survivor Training teaches, in addition, the making of traditional medicines, making fire, finding drinking water and setting traps. The 12-day Full Training includes tending cows and protecting them from predators in the bush, as well as Maasai games, pastimes and beliefs. Courses can be tailor-made for children or guests with disabilities.

Bush Adventures minimises its impact on the environment by using solar powered lights, composting food waste and not using cars or fridges. It assists the local community by providing employment, increasing trade, improving security and supporting local schools.

Oreteti Tented Camp

Makurian Group Ranch

Oreteti Tented Camp, Mukogodo Forest, Laikipia, Kenya
PO Box 961, Nanyuki 10400, Kenya
Tel
Mobile +254 726 968030
Fax
E-mail eolelegei@yahoo.com
Web

Borana, CH, 30 mins
Nanyuki, LS & CH, 2 hrs

On the edge of the Mukogodo Forest in eastern Laikipia, Oreteti Tented Camp is aimed at adventurous nature lovers. The camp, which opened in 2009, is owned and operated by the Makurian Group Ranch community. There are 4 double tents, with separate safari-style WC and showers. There is a mess tent, which is also a lounge, and a large kitchen tent. Guests can choose whether to cater for themselves, or whether to have the chef cater for them.

The Mukogodo Forest is 70,000 acres of indigenous forest, dominated by podo, olive and cedar. Lichen, ferns and orchids flourish here. The area is a haven for birds, butterflies and small mammals such as aardvark, tree hyrax and bush buck. Elephant, buffalo and leopard are also found here. Activities include game walks, bird watching and visits to the caves and rock art sites. Cultural visits to local villages and engaging in traditional pastoralist activities such as milking and branding cattle are also available. All activities in the forest must be accompanied by a local guide, because of the existence of buffalo and elephant in the forest. Oreteti Tented Camp is 55km from Nanyuki. 4WD vehicles are essential.

Il Ngwesi

Il Ngwesi Group Ranch

Il Ngwesi, Il Ngwesi Group Ranch, Laikipia, Kenya
PO Box 263, Timau 10406, Kenya
Tel
Mobile +254 724 636568; +254 722 157078
Fax
E-mail info@ilngwesi.com
Web www.ilngwesi.com

Tassia, CH, 30 mins
Lewa, LS & CH, 2 hrs

On a rocky outcrop on the northeastern edge of the 16,000-acre Il Ngwesi Group Ranch, Il Ngwesi has panoramic views across northern Kenya. The lodge is managed by the Il Ngwesi Group Ranch Maasai community, and was constructed entirely from local materials.

There are 6 en-suite bandas, made up of 3 triples, 1 honeymoon suite and 2 starbeds, with raised platforms onto which beds can be rolled for a night under the stars. All bandas are open plan with sitting areas and thatched roofs. Water is heated by solar power. The timber floor of the sitting and dining area flows around tree trunks. The lodge is adorned with rustic furniture made by local Maasai and bright local fabrics. There is a swimming pool with poolside lounge.

Activities include game drives, game walks and cultural visits to local Maasai villages. Bush breakfasts, sundowners and dinners can be arranged. Il Ngwesi is affiliated to Walking Wild; camel treks should be booked in advance. Visits to Omni, the hand-reared orphan black rhino, are recommended. Profit from the lodge supports the local community and its schools, cattle dips and water supplies. Il Ngwesi received the UNDP 2002 Equator Initiative Award and was given a bronze award by the Ecotourism Society of Kenya.

Tassia

Lekurruki Community Conservation Group Ranch

Tassia, Lekurruki Community Conservation Group Ranch, Laikipia, Kenya
Tassia Lodge, Lewa Downs private bag, Isiolo 60300, Kenya

Tel	
Mobile	+254 725 972923; +254 727 049489
Fax	
E-mail	info@tassiasafaris.com
Web	www.tassiasafaris.com

Tassia, CH, 15 mins
Lewa, LS & CH, 2 hrs

Tassia, perched on the edge of the Mukogodo Escarpment, offers spectacular views across northern Kenya and the sacred Lolokwe Mountain. The lodge was built for the Mukogodo Maasai, and aims for a symbiotic relationship between community and conservation. It combines tranquil beauty with adventure and excitement.

Tassia has distinctive Maasai architecture. There are 6 en-suite rooms, all with striking views. The open plan sitting and dining area overlooks the natural rock swimming pool. Meals can be served in the dining room, by the pool or in the guests' room. No trees were cut down during the construction of the lodge, which was built using local low impact materials.

The lodge uses solar power and energy-saving hot water heaters and has been given a bronze award by Ecotourism Society of Kenya. The lodge staff are all members of the Lekurruki community.

Activities include a selection of walks, such as hiking along dry riverbeds and climbing Mt Lossos. When the rivers are flowing, attractive waterfalls and plunge pools provide opportunity for swimming. Game drives are also on offer. Mukogodo Forest has a diverse population of wildlife, butterflies, birds, plants and trees. Wild dog, giraffe, impala, gerenuk and kudu can be seeing during the day. Leopard, genet, civet and caracal can sometimes be seen in the evening.

Borana

Borana

Borana, Samangua Valley, Laikipia, Kenya
The Safari and Conservation Company, PO Box 24576, Nairobi 00502

Tel	+254 20 2115433; +254 20 6006759; +254 20 6006769
Mobile	+254 735 579999; +254 712 579999
Fax	+254 20 2194995
E-mail	reservations@scckenya.com
Web	www.borana.co.ke

 VISA, MasterCard

Borana, CH, 10 mins
Lewa, LS & CH, 1 hr

Borana, on the edge of the Samangua Valley, has panoramic views of Mt Kenya, across the Lewa Plains to the Ngare Ndare Forest. Built in 1992 by local artisans using only local building materials, the lodge is comfortable, luxurious and totally in keeping with its surroundings. Both the lodge and a game blind overlook a dam which attracts wildlife to the area.

Borana has 4 large double cottages and 4 large twin cottages. Each cottage is totally secluded from its neighbour and has its own special view. Meals are served in a central dining area with large fireplaces, decorated with local artists' and sculptors' work.

Laragai House, the private house of George and Lucilla Stephenson, is available for up to 10 guests when they are not in residence.

A stay at Borana is a unique opportunity for total immersion in the life of a working ranch where environmental and ecological considerations rank alongside responsibility to neighbouring communities. Community projects include a mobile clinic, supporting 3 women's groups, supporting 5 primary schools and working with the community on a forestry project. Borana is closed during the month of November.

Laragai House Borana

Laragai House, Borana, Laikipia, Kenya
The Safari and Conservation Company, PO Box 24876, Nairobi 00502

Tel	+254 20 2115453; +254 20 6006759; +254 20 6006769
Mobile	+254 735 579999; +254 712 579999
Fax	+254 20 2194985
E-mail	reservations@scckenya.com
Web	www.borana.co.ke/laragai

VISA, MasterCard

Lewa, LS & CH, 1 hr
Borana, CH, 10 mins

Laragai House was built by 2 brothers, Lords Valentine and Michael Cecil, on the edge of an escarpment overlooking sweeping northern Kenya. They created the most opulent house in Laikipia, and decorated it with mirrors from Ireland, fabrics from London, handmade furniture from Kenya and rugs from Rajasthan.

There are 4 en-suite doubles, 2 en-suite twins and 2 small twins with shared bathroom, suitable for children. All rooms are furnished with stylish wooden tables, carved lamps and selected artwork and sculptures. The sitting room, with large open fireplace, is adorned with paintings and medieval weapons, and equipped with a sound system and selection of CDs. There is a swimming pool and tennis court. Breakfast and lunch are served on the elevated deck, with panoramic views of Lewa Wildlife Conservancy and the peaks of Mt Kenya. Dinner is served in the dining room. The house is fully staffed, and can only be booked on an exclusive basis.

Activities include game drives, game walks, horse riding and mountain biking. For an extra charge, cultural visits to local communities are available, as are visits to Kisima floriculture project and Lewa Wildlife Conservancy. Helicopter trips to Mt Kenya and Lake Turkana can also be arranged.

Lewa Safari Camp Lewa Wildlife Conservancy

Lewa Safari Camp, Lewa Wildlife Conservancy, Laikipia, Kenya
Cheli & Peacock, PO Box 743, Nairobi 00517, Kenya

Tel	+254 20 6004054/3; +254 20 6003090/1
Mobile	+254 724 255374; +254 733 490234
Fax	+254 20 6004050; +254 20 6003066
E-mail	safaris@chelipeacock.co.ke / info@chelipeacock.co.ke
Web	www.chelipeacock.com

VISA, MasterCard

Lewa, LS & CH
40 mins

Lewa Safari Camp has a striking location in Lewa Wildlife Conservancy. Spectacular views of Mt Kenya lie to the south and of arid lowlands to the north. This private 65,000-acre wildlife conservancy is home to about 61 species of mammal and 440 species of birds, including about 10 percent of Kenya's black rhino population, and the single largest population of Grevy's zebra in the world.

There are 12 safari tents made up of 7 doubles and 5 twins, 3 of which can fit an extra bed for a child. Each tent is en-suite and has a thatched roof and a veranda. The family house has 1 double and 1 twin with a shared bathroom. The central sitting and dining area, set in lush gardens, has a large sunny veranda and swimming pool for daytime and cosy log fires for the evenings.

As well as game drives and walks, Lewa Safari Camp offers horse riding and visits to an archaeological site. Rangers give talks on the history and day-to-day operation of the conservancy. Lewa Wildlife Conservancy was the first non-profit conservation programme in East Africa. Lewa reinvests all the profits generated from tourism into its core programmes, which enhance the lives of both people and wildlife.

Lewa Safari Camp holds a bronze award from Ecotourism Society of Kenya.

Lewa Wilderness   Lewa Wildlife Conservancy

Lewa Wilderness, Lewa Wildlife Conservancy, Laikipia, Kenya
Bush and Beyond, PO Box 56923, Nairobi 00200, Kenya

Tel	+254 20 6000457; +254 20 6005108; +254 20 6005980
Mobile	+254 733 330007; +254 723 273668
Fax	+254 20 6005008
E-mail	info@bush-and-beyond.com
Web	www.bush-and-beyond.com

VISA, MasterCard, Amex   Lewa, LS & CH 30 mins

Lewa Wilderness is located on Lewa Wildlife Conservancy. Lewa Downs has been in the Craig family since 1924; Lewa Wilderness is the original home of the family, and remains in their hands today. The 65,000-acre conservancy is home to several endangered species including black rhino, Grevy's zebra and sitatunga.

There are 9 thatched cottages, each containing an en-suite double bedroom, sitting room with open fireplace and veranda with a view of the conservancy. One cottage has facilities for guests with disabilities. The generator provides electricity morning and evening. A computer with internet is available during the hours the generator is running. The main building has a sitting room with open fireplace. There is also an infinity salt water swimming pool, tennis court and gift shop. A safe is located in the office. Massage, manicure and pedicure are on offer, prior notice required. Activities include day and night game drives, game walks, horse riding and camel trekking. Visits to prehistoric sites and cultural visits to local communities are also available. The guides are happy to give educative talks on the operation of the conservancy. For an extra charge, cultural visits to Il Ngwesi villages and scenic flights over the conservancy and further afield can be arranged. Lewa Wilderness is closed in November.

Kifaru House   Lewa Wildlife Conservancy

Kifaru House, Lewa Wildlife Conservancy, Laikipia, Kenya
Bush and Beyond, PO Box 56923, Nairobi 00200, Kenya

Tel	+254 20 6000457; +254 20 6005108; +254 20 6005980
Mobile	+254 733 330007; +254 723 273668
Fax	+254 20 6005008
E-mail	info@bush-and-beyond.com
Web	www.bush-and-beyond.com

VISA, MasterCard, Amex   Lewa, LS & CH 15 mins

Named after the rhino for which Lewa Wildlife Conservancy is famed, Kifaru House is a stylish private villa located in the conservancy. The 65,000-acre conservancy is home to several endangered species including black rhino, Grevy's zebra and sitatunga. All profit from Kifaru House is directly reinvested in Lewa's conservation and community projects.

There are 6 en-suite cottages, each with 4-poster double bed, large windows with views of the conservancy and private veranda. Each cottage has solar powered electricity, and is equipped with stereo and mini-fridge. The lodge has a spacious living area with open fireplace, tastefully decorated with local lamps, rugs and artefacts. The library has internet access, DVD player and satellite TV. The swimming pool and sunbathing terrace have a view of Mt Kenya. Massage, manicure and pedicure are available with prior notice.

Activities include day and night game drives, game walks, horse riding and camel trekking. Visits to prehistoric sites and cultural visits to local communities are also available. The guides are happy to give educative talks on the operation of the conservancy. For an extra charge, cultural visits to Il Ngwesi and helicopter fishing on Lake Rutundu, Mt Kenya, can be arranged. Kifaru House is closed in April and November.

Sirikoi

Sirikoi, Lewa Wildlife Conservancy, Laikipia, Kenya
The Safari and Conservation Company, PO Box 1690, Nanyuki 10400
Tel
Mobile +254 727 232445; +254 731 325 797
Fax
E-mail bookings@sirikoi.com
Web www.sirikoi.com

VISA, MasterCard   Lewa, LS & CH 20 mins

Sirikoi is a luxury tented camp on the northern slopes of Mt Kenya. The camp, on private land surrounded by Lewa Wildlife Conservancy, looks out on a waterhole that attracts a variety of game.
There are 4 elegant en-suite tents and a private cottage with 2 en-suite bedrooms, sitting room, dining room and kitchen. All bedrooms are furnished with safari antiques, and have their own fireplaces and verandas. The spacious bathrooms have freestanding baths, shower cubicles and modern facilities. Breakfast, lunch and dinner can be served on the sweeping veranda overlooking the waterhole or in the stylish dining room. The sunbeds beside the swimming pool look across mountainous regions, open grasslands, indigenous forest and riverine valleys. As well as day and night game drives, activities include helicopter flights, lion tracking, horse riding and game walks. Sirikoi also offers sundowners at viewpoints and bush dinners under the stars.
In acquiring 7000 acres bordering the Lewa Wildlife Conservancy, Sirikoi has extended this vital wildlife corridor, crucial to increasing the populations of the endangered Grevy's zebra, black rhino and other species. Working under the umbrella of the Northern Rangelands Trust, Sirikoi also provides mobile safaris into community owned conservation areas in northern Kenya.

Lewa House

Lewa House, Lewa Wildlife Conservancy, Laikipia, Kenya
Bush and Beyond, PO Box 56923, Nairobi 00200, Kenya
Tel +254 20 6000457; +254 20 6005108; +254 20 6005980
Mobile +254 733 330007; +254 723 273668
Fax +254 20 6005008
E-mail info@bush-and-beyond.com
Web www.bush-and-beyond.com

VISA, MasterCard, Amex   Lewa, LS & CH 15 mins

Lewa House is set in Lewa Wildlife Conservancy, on a hill with views of the rolling hills and valleys of the conservancy. The 65,000-acre conservancy is home to several endangered species including black rhino, Grevy's zebra and sitatunga. All income generated by the house is directly reinvested in Lewa's conservation and community projects.
There are 3 large cottages, each with double and twin bedroom, both en-suite, and private veranda. The cottages are equipped with solar electricity. The main building has a lounge and dining area, with open fireplace, and a veranda with a view across the plains. The swimming pool and sunbathing terrace look out on the waterhole. A house computer with internet is available. Massage, manicure and pedicure are on offer, prior notice required. The house is staffed by a team of guides, staff and rangers. Activities include day and night game drives, game walks, horse riding and camel trekking. Visits to prehistoric sites and cultural visits to local communities are also available. The guides are happy to give educative talks on the operation of the conservancy. For an extra charge, cultural visits to Il Ngwesi villages can be arranged. Lewa House is closed in April and November.

Hartebeest before Mt Kenya – Photo © www.sokomoto.com

Samburu, Buffalo Springs and Shaba National Reserves

Shaba National Reserve – Photo © Andrew Nightingale, kembu.com

This trio of national reserves lies between the lush highlands of southern Kenya and the arid deserts in the north. It is a region of dramatic contrasts in which rare wildlife and diverse birdlife reside. The Ewaso Ngiro River, fringed with giant acacias, figs and doum palms, slices across the scorched land.

The three reserves can be accessed by road from Isiolo, Maralal and Marsabit. Isiolo has an airport with scheduled flights from destinations in Kenya. The tracks within the reserves are rocky and dusty in the dry season and muddy during the rains; 4WD vehicles are required throughout the year.

The area is home to the Samburu people. Cousins of the nomadic Maasai, the Samburu are semi-nomadic pastoralists. They entered Kenya from Sudan in one of the waves of Nilotic migration, and settled in northern Kenya while the Maasai continued moving south. Like the Maasai, Samburu society has traditionally been organised around cattle, used not only for food, but also for dowries, fines and ceremonies. Visits to local Samburu villages give fascinating insights into their culture and traditions and are a highlight of visiting the region.

Samburu National Reserve gates are Archers Gate and West Gate; The one airstrip is called Samburu Oryx. Lion, leopard, cheetah and crocodile all inhabit the reserve, as well as more unusual wildlife such as gerenuk, Grevy's zebra, Beisa oryx and reticulated giraffe. There are over 350 species of birds, including Somali ostrich, grey-headed kingfisher, vulturine guineafowl, lilac-breasted roller, red-billed hornbill, secretary bird and Verreaux's eagle. The harsh terrain is brightened by clusters of vivid desert roses.

The Samburu National Reserve was one of the areas in which conservationists Joy and George Adamson raised Elsa, the lioness of Born Free fame. Joy Adamson's best selling book was later made into an award winning film. Another famous lioness from Samburu is Kamunyak, who became renowned for adopting oryx calves.

On the other side of the Ewaso Ngiro River, Buffalo Springs National Reserve is less hilly and less dense than Samburu. The reserve gates are Chokaa Gate and Ngare Mare Gate; the airstrip is called Buffalo Springs. The vegetation is mainly wooded and bushy grassland, riverine forest and swamps. A sparkling oasis at the western end of the reserve gave it its name. This is one of the rare places in which reside both the Burchills zebra and the Grevy's zebra, and both the Maasai ostrich and the Somali ostrich.

Shaba National Reserve is named for a massive cone of volcanic rock that dominates the area. The solidified lava flow that streams from the rock symbolises the harsh but striking nature of the terrain. Shaba has four springs, making it less arid than Samburu or Buffalo Springs, and a scattering of small hills.

Accommodation Guide

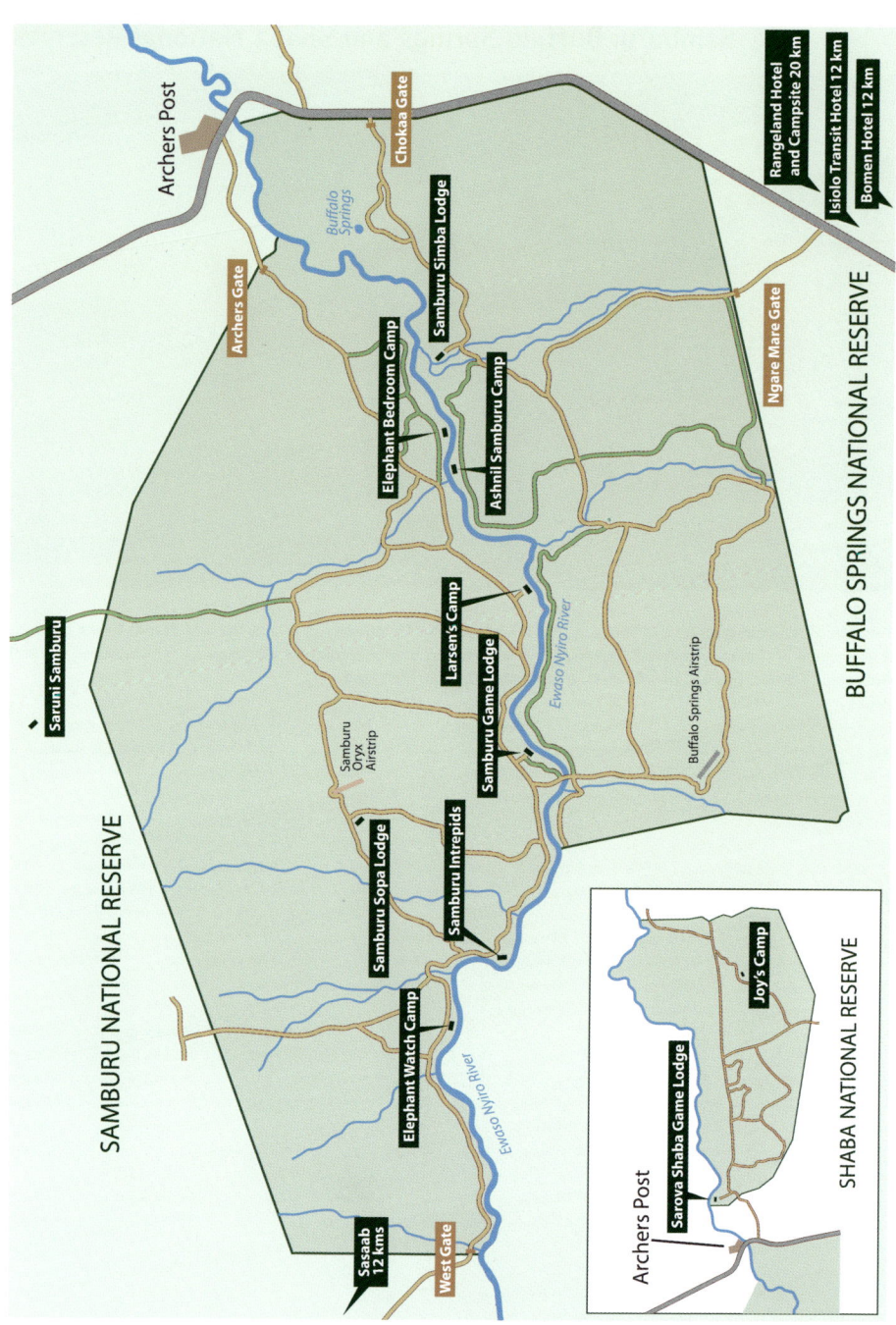

Rangeland Hotel
and Campsite

Isiolo

Rangeland Hotel and Campsite, Meru-Isiolo Road, 8km from Isiolo, Kenya
PO Box 139, Isiolo 60300, Kenya
Tel +254 64 50299
Mobile +254 721 434353; +254 711 502609; +254 726 676979
Fax
E-mail info@rangeland.co.ke
Web www.rangeland.co.ke

  Isiolo, LS & CH 25 mins

In a range area that gives the hotel its name, Rangeland Hotel and Campsite offers cottage accommodation in an attractive garden.
There are 12 en-suite rooms in a row of cottages, surrounded by bright bougainvillea hedges. The 5 modern cottages have 2 rooms in each, and the 2 original round stone cottages house individual rooms. All rooms have satellite TV, built in cupboards, white tiled floors and verandas.
The garden is dotted with tables and chairs, where guests can eat, drink and enjoy the views. Indigenous trees and herbs fit for aromatherapy grow here amongst shrubs and lawns. There is also a fishpond, with a small bridge over it. Nyama Choma Grill serves grilled meats and a bar, equipped with satellite TV, serves beers and soft drinks. The play area for children has swings, slides and merry-go-round. Rabbits and geese, kept as pets, stroll around the grounds.
The hotel has a campsite, with bathroom facilities including hot showers. It also has a fruit garden, that supplies the hotel with fresh tropical fruits. There are 2 restaurants affiliated to Rangeland Hotel and Campsite in Isiolo, the Hills Restaurant and Roots Restaurant, both serving Kenyan dishes and grilled meats.

Samburu

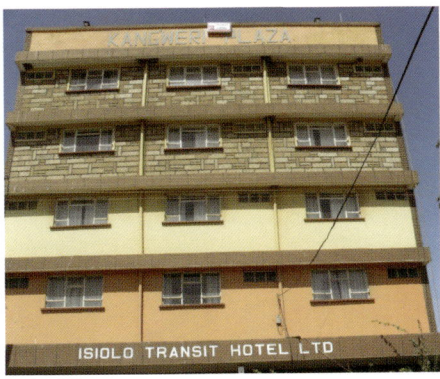

Isiolo Transit Hotel

Isiolo

Isiolo Transit Hotel, Kang'weri Plaza, nr Roots Restaurant, Isiolo, Kenya
PO Box 281, Isiolo 60300, Kenya
Tel +254 64 52083; +254 64 52122
Mobile
Fax +254 64 52207
E-mail transith@plansonline.net
Web

  Isiolo, LS & CH 15 mins

Located in the centre of town, Isiolo Transit Hotel is conveniently positioned for all the shops, restaurants and businesses of Isiolo.
The 49 en-suite rooms, made up of singles, doubles and suites, are set around a central dining area. The singles have a small double bed, and the doubles have 2 small double beds. The top floor houses 7 suites. The large suite has a bedroom, a living room with sofa, armchairs and satellite TV, and 2 bathrooms. The remaining 6 suites consist of a large bedroom with bed, sofa, cupboard and satellite TV.
The restaurant has an international menu, including chicken Maryland, beef stroganoff, spaghetti bolognaise and crepes Suzette, as well as nyama choma grilled meats. Ginseng honey ginger tea, which maintains blood pressure and prevents tiredness, and Tonkat Ali coffee, a stress reliever, are also served. Oasis Bar, furnished with maroon velvet chairs and coffee tables, is well stocked with soft drinks, beers and a wide selection of spirits, and has satellite TV.
The conference hall seats 40 pax, and conference equipment is available for hire. There is a secure enclosed car park behind the hotel. The hotel is in Kang'weri Plaza, behind Roots Restaurant.

 Accommodation Guide

Bomen Hotel

Isiolo

Bomen Hotel, behind Total St, Isiolo, Kenya
PO Box 67, Isiolo 60300, Kenya

Tel	+254 64 52389; +254 64 52272
Mobile	
Fax	+254 64 52225
E-mail	bomenhotel@yahoo.com
Web	

 VISA, MasterCard

 Isiolo, LS & CH 15 mins

Bomen Hotel is conveniently located in the centre of Isiolo.
There are 47 en-suite rooms, made up of 10 singles, 34 doubles and 3 suites. Single rooms have a small double bed, and double rooms have 2 small double beds. All rooms are equipped with satellite TV, mosquito net, chairs and a coffee table. Most rooms have a telephone. The suites, on the top floor, have a double bedroom and a sitting room. The open rooftop provides views of Isiolo town and the dusty land beyond.
Oasis Restaurant serves Kenyan and international dishes, such as soups, burgers, chicken wings, cheese plate and cakes. The terrace outside can also be used for dining. The bar is well stocked with soft drinks, beers and spirits, and also offers cocktails. The pool room, beyond the car park, has a pool table and satellite TV.
Baraza Hall can accommodate 160 pax. A projector and PA system are available for hire. The hotel also has a hair and beauty salon. There is a safe at reception where guests can deposit their valuables.
The hotel is 2 blocks behind the Total petrol station on the main road through Isiolo.

Joy's Camp

Shaba Ntl. Reserve

Joy's Camp, Shaba National Reserve, Kenya
Cheli & Peacock, PO Box 743, Nairobi 00517, Kenya

Tel	+254 20 6004054/3; +254 20 6003090/1
Mobile	+254 724 255374; +254 733 490234
Fax	+254 20 6004050; +254 20 6003066
E-mail	safaris@chelipeacock.co.ke / info@chelipeacock.co.ke
Web	www.chelipeacock.com / www.joyscamp.com

 VISA, MasterCard

Chaffa, CH, 15 mins
Buffalo Springs, LS & CH, 2.5 hrs

Joy's Camp, named after Joy Adamson, is built on the site of Joy's tented home in Shaba National Reserve. It was also the home of Penny the leopard, the heroine of Joy's last book, Queen of Shaba. In the eastern corner of the Samburu ecosystem, Shaba is a secluded idyll, an arid landscape dotted with lush springs and rocky river gorges.
The camp overlooks a large natural spring where elephant and lion share watering rights with herds of buffalo and the rare desert species of Beisa oryx, reticulated giraffe and Grevy's zebra. The nearby Ewaso Nyiro river and gorge provide striking sites for bush meals and sundowners, or scenic breaks during game drives or walks.
There are 10 spacious en-suite tents, made up of 7 doubles and 3 twins, with verandas giving views of the surrounding hills or the spring. Each tent is sumptuously decorated with Boran and Somali cloths, handmade glass and the vibrant fabrics of the local nomadic tribes. Extra beds can be added for children.
The camp has a small museum of Joy Adamson memorabilia, on loan from the Elsa Trust. Joy's Camp combines a glimpse of Kenyan history with an authentic wildlife experience. Conde Nast Traveller Magazine included Joy's Camp in their Hot List of 2007. The camp is eco-friendly and has attained Ecotourism Society of Kenya's silver award.

Sarova Shaba Game Lodge Shaba Ntl. Reserve

Sarova Shaba Game Lodge, Shaba National Reserve, Kenya
Sarova Hotels, PO Box 72493, Nairobi 00200, Kenya

Tel	+254 20 2716688; +254 64 32030/30638
Mobile	+254 728 603590; +254 722 200945/6
Fax	+254 20 2715566; +254 64 30481
E-mail	sarova.shaba@sarovahotels.com
Web	www.sarovahotels.com

VISA, MasterCard

Buffalo Springs, LS & CH
1 hr

Shaba National Reserve, where Joy Adamson spent her final years reintegrating a lion into the wild, is the untamed wilderness surrounding Sarova Shaba Game Lodge. Resident species in this arid northern reserve include Grevy's zebra, reticulated giraffe and Beisa oryx. Of the 350 species of birds found here, 5 are endemic to this area.

The lodge has 80 en-suite bedrooms on 2 floors, made up of 45 twins, 20 doubles and 15 triples. All rooms are thatched and look out over the river. There is also a presidential suite, with lounge and private Jacuzzi, and 4 executive suites with private lounge. The ground floor rooms are designed for guests with disabilities. The split-level Surpelei Restaurant overlooks the freeform pool and Ewaso Nyiro River. The restaurant serves buffet breakfast and lunch. Dinner is table d'hote with Mongolian and active cooking on alternate days. There is a lounge bar and a poolside bar. Shaba was recently the location for the popular TV show Survivor Africa and the lodge now has a Sarova Shaba Survivor Challenge. The animation team is ready to assist with teambuilding activities. The conference facilities are equipped with modern audio visual equipment. A crocodile viewing platform extends over the river. Samburu, Borana and Turkana dancers perform every night. Sarova Shaba Game Lodge has a bronze award from Ecotourism Society of Kenya.

Samburu Simba Lodge Buffalo Springs Ntl. Reserve

Samburu Simba Lodge, Buffalo Springs National Reserve, Kenya
Simba Lodges, PO Box 66601, Nairobi 00800, Kenya

Tel	+254 20 2105453-4; +254 20 2012443
Mobile	+254 722 788830; +254 734 600415
Fax	+254 20 4442218
E-mail	sales@simbalodges.com
Web	www.simbalodges.com

VISA, MasterCard, Barclaycard, JCB

Samburu Oryx, LS & CH
30 mins

Overlooking Buffalo Springs and Ewaso Nyiro River, Samburu Simba Lodge has views of both arid plains and rushing water. Rare game that is found in this area includes reticulated giraffe, Grevy's zebra, Beisa oryx and the long necked gerunuk. The area is also well known for elephants. There are 70 en-suite rooms, in 7 villas. Each villa contains 10 rooms, 6 on the ground floor and 4 on the 1st floor, including 2 interconnecting rooms suitable for families. A safe is available at reception. The restaurant serves an international menu. The Ibis Pub, overlooking the plains, has satellite TV. The Pool Bar has a selection of soft drinks, beers and spirits. The lodge has 2 swimming pools and a health club.

Game drives, picnics, sundowners and bush meals can all be arranged for an extra charge. Balloon safaris can also be arranged and paid for at the lodge. The conference centre has 4 halls, each named after a place in Kenya. Naivasha Hall holds 125 pax; Magadi Hall holds 75; Baringo Hall and Bogoria Hall hold 60 pax each. There is also a business centre which can be used as a boardroom for 12 pax.

Karibu Kenya Accommodation Guide

Elephant Bedroom Camp

Samburu Ntl. Reserve

Elephant Bedroom Camp, Samburu National Reserve, Kenya
Atua Enkop, PO Box 42475, Nairobi 00100, Kenya

Tel	+254 20 4450035-6; +254 20 4440276
Mobile	+254 715 555322
Fax	+254 20 4450037
E-mail	reservations@atua-enkop.com
Web	www.atua-enkop.com

Buffalo Springs, LS & CH
30 mins

Set on the lush banks of the Ewaso Nyiro River in Samburu National Reserve, Elephant Bedroom Camp is surrounded by doum palms and other indigenous trees and shrubs. The camp is small and intimate and was designed with simple elegance inspired by the textures and colours of African nature.

The 12 spacious en-suite tents each has a private veranda overlooking the river. The stylish lounge and dining tent is hung with original oil paintings, its large veranda offering guests a view of the tranquil surroundings. Breakfast and lunch are served alfresco on the banks of the Ewaso Nyiro River. Candlelit gourmet dinners are set either under the African sky or inside the romantic dining area. Samburu warriors provide nightly entertainment. Lectures on Samburu culture are also available. The rugged hills behind the camp provide a scenic backdrop for the herds of elephant that, true to its name, regularly visit the camp at night. Elephant Bedroom Camp is environmentally sensitive and believes in responsibly enhancing the environment on a sustainable basis. The camp employs members of the local community and also contributes to the education of this community.

Ashnil Samburu Camp

Buffalo Springs Ntl. Reserve

Ashnil Samburu Camp, Buffalo Springs National Reserve, Kenya
Ashnil Hotels Limited, PO Box 10557, Nairobi 00100, Kenya

Tel	+254 20 3566970-3; +254 20 556955
Mobile	+254 717 612499
Fax	+254 20 3566974
E-mail	info@ashnilhotels.com / sales@ashnilhotels.com
Web	www.ashnilhotels.com

VISA, MasterCard

Buffalo Springs, LS & CH
30 mins

Ashnil Samburu Camp is spread out along the shady banks of the Ewaso Nyiro River, surrounded by the doum palms and acacia trees that are a feature of the area. The camp is an ideal place from which to view the wide variety of game and birdlife that this striking river attracts.

The 24 tents, 12 on either side of the main reception and dining area, all have views of the river and the landscape around it. All the tents are en-suite and have a dressing area, sitting area and veranda. Meals can be served in the dining area, by the pool or on the banks of the river. Game drives are in both Samburu National Reserve and Buffalo Springs National Reserve, varied ecosystems that range from lava fields to jagged hills, from African savannah to forested riverbanks. This dramatic landscape is set against a backdrop of the sacred mountain Ololokwe. Samburu cultural talks and dancing in the evening give guests an insight into the traditional lifestyle of the Samburu people, which is enhanced by visits to the local villages and their local handicraft markets.

Larsen's Camp

Samburu Ntl. Reserve

Larsen's Camp, Samburu National Reserve, Kenya
Wilderness Lodges, PO Box 42788, Nairobi 00100, Kenya

Tel	+254 532329; +254 20 650392
Mobile	+254 720 626367
Fax	+254 20 650384
E-mail	info@wildernesslodges.co.ke
Web	www.wildernesslodges.co.ke

 VISA, MasterCard, Amex   Buffalo Springs, LS & CH 30 mins

Named after Erik Ole Larsen, a Dane credited with enhancing the style of luxury tented camps, Larsen's Camp is a camp that would have made him proud. On the banks of the Ewaso Nyiro River, the camp looks out across the pristine wilderness of Samburu National Reserve.

There are 20 en-suite tents, made up of doubles and twins, each named after a local Samburu bird. The spacious tents have lounge areas furnished with chairs, table, writing desk, books, minibar and kettle, and are adorned with local decorations. Each tent has its own private veranda. The bathrooms are equipped with Molton Brown amenities. Meals can be served in the dining tent, on the tree house deck, on the riverbanks or in the bush. As well as the main bar, there is a bar beside the swimming pool. Activities include game drives, game walks and cultural visits to local Samburu villages. Birdlife is abundant, and bird watching is recommended. Eseriani Spa, meaning place of peace in Samburu, offers treatments including aromatherapy massage and body scrub, and also contains a Jacuzzi. The camp is equipped with WiFi and has a postage service and a doctor on call. An electric fence surrounds the camp.

Larsen's Camp is a member of The Small Luxury Hotels of The World group.

Saruni Samburu

Samburu

Saruni Samburu, nr Samburu National Reserve, Kenya
PO Box 304, Narok 20500, Kenya

Tel	
Mobile	+254 710 842000
Fax	
E-mail	riccardo@sarunicamp.com
Web	www.sarunisamburu.com

  VISA, MasterCard   Samburu Oryx, LS & CH, 45 mins
Kalama, CH, 25 mins

Perched on a rocky outcrop, Saruni Samburu provides a spectacular view of the snowy peaks of Mt Kenya, sacred mountain Ololokwe and the vast savannah. Set in a private 95,000-hectare conservancy bordering Samburu National Reserve, Saruni is a design lodge that offers exclusivity, comfort and tailor-made service.

Saruni has two spacious en-suite houses, 1 double and 1 twin, each with its own open plan seating and dining area and veranda. It also has two spacious family houses, each with 2 en-suite bedrooms, private seating and dining area and veranda. Samburu Wellbeing Space provides massage and spa treatments. Saruni's waterhole attracts the northern reticulated giraffe, Grevy's zebra, oryx and kudu as well as the more widespread elephants, dik diks and leopards. The Samburu guides, all members of the local community, are ready to share their knowledge of indigenous species, ancient rock art and local traditions. Game drives include Samburu National Reserve, Buffalo Springs National Reserve and Westgate Conservancy. Saruni's Warrior for a Week programme gives guests the opportunity to learn the survival skills of the Samburu warriors, including tracking animals and bush craft. Drawing safaris are also offered for guests wishing to spend a few days painting in spectacular scenery with a professional artist.

Samburu Game Lodge

Samburu Ntl. Reserve

Samburu Game Lodge, Samburu National Reserve, Kenya
Wilderness Lodges, PO Box 42788, Nairobi 00100, Kenya

Tel	+254 20 532329; +254 20 650392
Mobile	+254 720 626366
Fax	+254 20 650384
E-mail	info@wildernesslodges.co.ke
Web	www.wildernesslodges.co.ke

VISA, MasterCard, Amex

Buffalo Springs, LS & CH
15 mins

Established in 1962, Samburu Game Lodge has a long history in the Samburu National Reserve. The lodge is on the banks of the Ewaso Nyiro River, and looks out on the crocodile filled river.

There are 61 en-suite rooms, made up of 42 standard, 5 riverfront, 2 junior suites and 12 cottages. The standard rooms are close to the lodge and the swimming pool, while the more spacious riverfront rooms have an exclusive front porch on the river. The junior suites have a riverfront balcony and include a dressing room. The cottages, with interconnecting rooms, suit families or groups. One cottage is equipped for guests with disabilities.

The main dining area overlooks the river. The Crocodile Bar, on the banks, views the spot where crocodiles are fed every evening. The Vulturine Bar is perched among the trees and juts out over the river. The Pool Bar serves snacks and drinks at the poolside.

Activities include game drives, game walks and cultural visits to Samburu villages. Birdlife is abundant, and bird watching is recommended. Eseriani Spa, meaning place of peace in Samburu, offers treatments including aromatherapy massage and body scrub, and also contains a Jacuzzi.

Samburu Sopa Lodge

Samburu Ntl. Reserve

Samburu Sopa Lodge, Samburu National Reserve, Kenya
Sopa Lodges, PO Box 72630, Nairobi 00200, Kenya

Tel	+254 20 3750235; +254 20 3616000
Mobile	+254 733 610060; +254 722 206328/9
Fax	+254 20 3751507
E-mail	info@sopalodges.com
Web	www.sopalodges.com

VISA, MasterCard

Samburu Oryx, LS & CH
10 mins

Samburu Sopa Lodge is built on raised ground, giving it panoramic views of the distant Samburu Hills on one side and Mt Kenya on the other. The lodge is designed in rich earth colours and decorated with local artefacts. The lodge overlooks a waterhole which attracts plentiful animal and birdlife.

There are 30 cottages, designed in a buffalo horn, converging at the public areas in the centre. Each cottage has 2 en-suite bedrooms with 2 queen size beds and private veranda. The 2 rooms nearest to the reception have been designed for guests with disabilities. The lobby, the bar and the rooms overlook the waterhole.

The dining room, also overlooking the waterhole, serves buffet breakfast, lunch and dinner. Theme dinners, such as coastal buffet, African buffet and gala dinner, are served weekly. The furniture has been uniquely carved, and the chairs have a backrest shaped like a buffalo horn. Local stones and other materials are displayed. The lodge also has a gift shop and a swimming pool surrounded by sunbathing deck.

Activities include guided nature walks and bird watching. Cultural visits to local Samburu villages and Samburu cultural talks are also on offer. Bush meals and sundowners can be arranged. Samburu Sopa Lodge has a bronze award from Ecotourism Society of Kenya.

Samburu Intrepids

Samburu Ntl. Reserve

Samburu Intrepids, Samburu National Reserve, Kenya
Heritage Hotels Ltd, PO Box 74888, Nairobi 00200, Kenya

Tel	+254 20 4446651; +254 20 4447929; +254 20 4444582
Mobile	+254 722 205894; +254 733411105
Fax	+254 20 4446533
E-mail	sales@heritage-eastafrica.com
Web	www.heritage-eastafrica.com

VISA, MasterCard, Amex

Buffalo Springs, LS & CH
20 mins

Situated on the banks of the Ewaso Nyiro River in the arid heart of Samburu National Reserve, Samburu Intrepids looks out over riverbanks on which guests have a chance of spotting the rare northern species of reticulated giraffe, Beisa oryx and gerenuk.

The 27 en-suite tents, furnished with 4-poster beds, mahogany cupboards and writing desks, have secluded verandas overlooking the river.

Meals can be served in the palm-thatched dining room, on the shady terrace, on the guests' veranda or in the bush. Lectures and slideshows on wildlife or local Samburu dances take place in the open air lounge and bar most evenings. A small conference room is equipped with TV and VCR for those who wish to watch wildlife documentaries, and the freeform oasis swimming pool is surrounded by a sunbathing garden for those who prefer to relax.

Inside the reserve, the camp offers 2 daily game drives. Outside the reserve, activities include game walks, camel safaris, visits to neighbouring Samburu communities and fly camping on sacred Mt Ololokwe. The Adventurers' and Young Rangers' clubs offer activities for children. The camp contributes a percentage of guests' fees to various development projects, including a primary school, a bee-keeping training scheme and cost-price medical services for nearby villages.

Elephant Watch Camp

Samburu Ntl. Reserve

Elephant Watch Camp, Samburu National Reserve, Kenya
Elephant Watch Safaris, PO Box 54667, Nairobi 00200, Kenya

Tel	+254 20 8891112; +254 20 8048602; +254 20 8890596
Mobile	+254 713 037886
Fax	+254 20 890596
E-mail	elephantwatch@africaonline.co.ke
Web	www.elephantsafaris.com

Buffalo Springs, LS & CH
40 mins

Perched on the banks of the Ewaso Nyiro River, Elephant Watch Camp is home to some of the largest bulls in Samburu who can often be spotted mudding in the river, resting under an acacia tree or picking pods beside the tents. The camp is owned by Oria and Iain Douglas Hamilton, who together wrote Among the Elephants and Battle for the Elephants. There are 6 en-suite tents, all adorned with bright cotton cloth and veranda; the bathrooms have safari showers. The chef provides tasty simple food, including freshly baked breads and scones, and homemade jams, preserves and fruit juices. The vegetables are home grown at the camp's farm on Lake Naivasha.

Activities include game drives which focus on elephant watching. Cultural visits to local Samburu villages, game walks and sundowners are also available. Visitors are welcome to visit the Save the Elephant's research centre. Activities available at an extra cost include climbing Mt Ololokwe, helicopter flights and Samburu dancing shows.

Elephant Watch works closely with Save the Elephants, whose projects not only work with elephants but with the local community. Their Fund for Education offers children the opportunity to get a proper secondary education combined with hands-on elephant and environmental awareness.

 Accommodation Guide

Sasaab

Westgate Community Land

Sasaab, Westgate Community Land, nr Samburu, Kenya
The Safari Collection, PO Box 15565, Nairobi 00503, Kenya
Tel +254 20 5020888
Mobile +254 731 914732; +254 725 675830
Fax
E-mail info@thesafaricollection.com
Web www.thesafaricollection.com

Buffalo Springs, LS & CH, 1.5 hrs
Sasaab, CH, 20 mins

Majestically situated high on the banks of the Ewaso Nyiro River, Sasaab commands breathtaking views across the arid landscape of northern Kenya towards the jagged peaks of Mt Kenya. Sasaab is located in Westgate Community Land, west of Samburu and Buffalo Springs National Reserves. The 9 luxury open plan rooms are designed in Moroccan style, each having an area of over 100m², with magnificent views of the surrounding land and a high level of privacy. All rooms have private plunge pools, en-suite open air bathrooms and WiFi. There are 2 connecting rooms, suitable for a family.

Sasaab's state of the art SpaSaab nestles in the rocks on the edge of the Ewaso Nyiro River. From the 2 treatment rooms and wrap-around pool guests can enjoy sweeping views across the riverbed abundant with wildlife. Liz Earle has developed a wholly organic skincare range incorporating herbs and plants from the natural environment in keeping with Sasaab's strong environmental policies.

Sasaab holds Ecotourism Society of Kenya's silver award.

Game drives take place on the conservancy, and in Samburu and Bufallo Springs National Reserves, areas renowned for their variant species. The nature trail gives children a chance to make Samburu bows and arrows as well as a traditional Samburu toothbrush. Sasaab is closed in November.

Tropic Air
explorers, adventurers & heli-safari pioneers

helicopter safaris East Africa

info@tropicairkenya.com
www.tropicairkenya.com

create connect

discover

@

KUONATRUST
CENTRE FOR VISUAL ARTS IN KENYA

Kenya's Most Vibrant Contemporary Art Space

visit us at Likoni Close, Likoni Lane, off Dennis Pritt Road, Hurlingham
Cell: +254 020 240 5960 , 0721 262326, 0733 742752
email: info@kuonatrust.org
www.kuonatrust.org

artists' studios | exhibitions | artists' talks | art library | outreach events' venue
resource centre | training & mentoring | international exchange

Northern Kenya

Cathedral Rock, Saguta Valley – Photo © www.yellowwings.com

Vast tracts of desert stretch across Kenya's remote northern region. Lake Turkana, known as the Jade Sea, slices through the desert. Jagged, forested mountains rise from this stunning yet savage terrain. The region, known as the Cradle of Mankind, is the site of some of the world's most important prehistoric discoveries.

This harsh region has dramatic scenery and spectacular vistas. The inhabitants are predominantly nomadic, and include the Turkana, Rendille, Borana, Samburu, Gabbra and Kenya's smallest tribe, the El Molo. The major towns are Maralal, Lodwar, Lokichogio, Loyangalani, Marsabit, Wajir, Garissa and Bura. Wajir and Lokichogio have airports with daily scheduled flights from destinations in Kenya. Wajir also has flights to Somalia and Lokichogio has flights to Sudan. A number of airstrips around the region are available for charter flights. Roads are limited, some barely more than a track across a lava field; 4WD vehicles are required throughout the region.

Lake Turkana, the world's largest permanent desert lake, is a spectacular slash of blue across parched desert, lava fields and craggy peaks. Central Island National Park, where camping can be arranged, has three scenic lakes called Crocodile, Flamingo and Tilapia. There is also an active volcano whose slopes are breeding colonies for water birds such as African fish eagles, ospreys, marsh harriers, pelicans, cormorants, herons and gulls. Activities include boat trips and bird watching.

Sibiloi National Park, established to protect the area's unique prehistoric and archaeological sites, lies on the northeastern shore of Lake Turkana. The Koobi Fora Museum has information on the fossil beds and other findings, some of which are linked to the origin of man. Nearby sites of interest include the Jarigole Pillor, Sibiloi Fossil Forest and Karari archaeological sites. Wildlife such as zebra, giraffe, hippo and crocodile inhabit the park, as well as numerous bird species including flamingos, pelicans and ducks.

Maralal National Reserve, amid the Ol Doinyo Lenkiyo Mountains, completely surrounds the town of Maralal. This rocky, dry reserve is home to a variety of wildlife including leopard, hyena, eland, impala, buffalo and zebra, and over 260 species of birds. Elephants pass through the area seasonally. The annual Maralal International Camel Derby, held in August, is a colourful spectacle with camel races, dancing displays and curio stalls.

Marsabit National Park comprises a densely forested mountain and three crater lakes. The park became famous in the 1970s as the home of the legendary Ahmed, a huge elephant with massive tusks. Wildlife includes elephant, Grevy's zebra, lion, leopard, kudu, buffalo and bushbuck. Activities include game viewing, bird watching and camel safaris. The Singing Wells, where local people sing while drawing water, are also an attraction.

The Matthews Range and Loroghi Hills offer scenic views and exciting trekking. Natural rock pools and mountain streams have crystal clear icy water in which the adventurous can swim.

The Northern Rangelands Trust, NRT, facilitates the development of community-led conservation initiatives in northern Kenya. The NRT has an expanding membership of community conservancies, to whom it provides technical and implementing advice. All conservancies under the umbrella of the NRT promote and develop sustainable tourism and generate income for the inhabitants of the area.

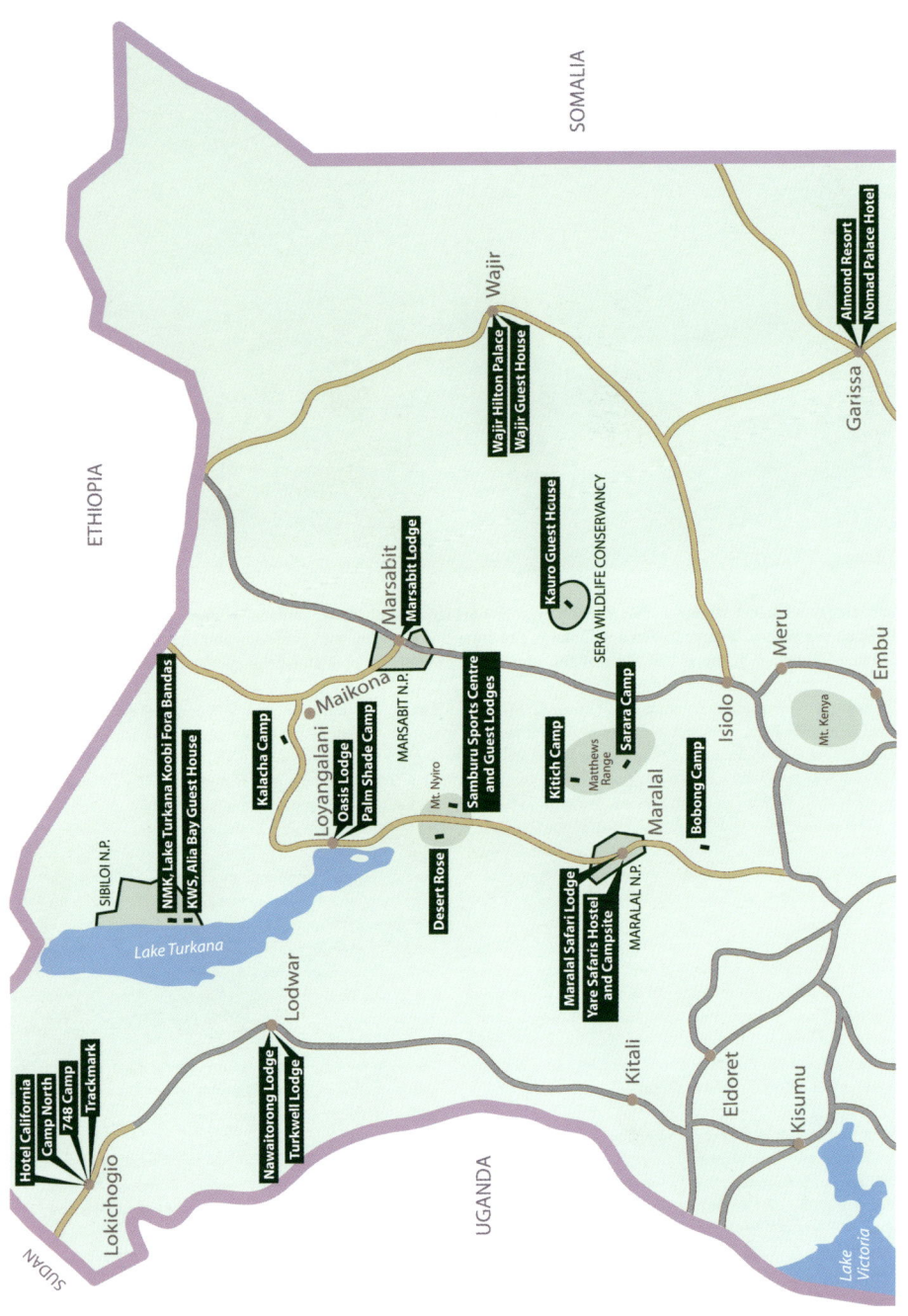

Hotel California

 Lokichogio

Hotel California, Lopiding Road, Lokichogio, Kenya
Africa Expeditions Ltd, PO Box 24598, Nairobi 00502, Kenya

Tel	+254 20 3027000
Mobile	+254 722 203115; +254 733 333543; +254 722 629143
Fax	+254 20 8019457
E-mail	lokibookings@afexgroup.com
Web	www.afexgroup.com

     Lokichogio, LS & CH
10 mins

Lokichogio, known as the gateway to South Sudan, became a bustling centre for the aid community during the 1990s. Hotel California was established to provide facilities and services to those travelling between Kenya and South Sudan. There are 8 aircon suites, 8 standard suites, 28 en-suite tents and 30 standard tents with communal, external bathroom facilities. The dining room has an active cooking station and a brick pizza oven. Specialty nights include pasta night, Mongolian night, Saturday barbecue and Sunday curry. Theme nights include carvery, Mexican, Indian, Italian and Ladies night. The bar is fully stocked, and offers cappuccino, espresso, frozen drinks and cocktails, as well as cold soft drinks, beer, wine and spirits. The recreation room has large screen TV and DVD. The conference and workshop facilities are equipped with internet. There are 9 furnished offices available for rent, and ISO containers for storage. There is a volleyball pitch and a golf driving range. The weight room has weights and machines. The Afex line of casual wear carries the Pilipili Label, endorsed by the African Wildlife Foundation. Afex Communications provides VSAT and VOIP services, including internet and email connectivity, voice over IP, and virtual private networks. AfexSecurity offers a broad range of professional security services around the world.

Camp North

 Lokichogio

Camp North, Lopiding Road, Lokichogio, Kenya
Camp North Head Office, PO Box 9168, Nairobi 00100, Kenya

Tel	+254 20 6751958; +254 20 4183610; +254 20 4183611
Mobile	+254 721 274883; +254 724 735005
Fax	+254 20 4183610
E-mail	campnorth@iconnect.co.ke
Web	

     Lokichogio, LS & CH
10 mins

Lokichogio, known as the gateway to South Sudan, became a bustling centre for the aid community during the 1990s. Camp North provides a selection of accommodation and facilities for those travelling between Kenya and South Sudan as well as for those visiting other destinations in northern Kenya.

There are 30 en-suite rooms. All rooms are fully tiled and equipped with aircon and satellite TV. There are also 18 en-suite tents, equipped with TV. The restaurant seats 60 pax, and serves an international menu. Breakfast and lunch are buffet; dinner is a la carte. The oval bar is adorned with 2 floodlit waterfalls. The recreational hall is equipped with a large screen and digital surround sound; films and international sports matches are shown. There are 10 offices available for rent. All offices are equipped with high speed internet and VSAT. The cyber café has internet, printing, scanning and photocopying; mobile phone cards are available for sale. Storage warehouses are available for rent; day and night guards provide security. Electricity is provided by 2 generators. The camp has a courtesy car for airport transfers. Taxis can be booked by the camp reception.

748 Camp Lokichogio

748 Camp, Lopiding Road, Lokichogio, Kenya
PO Box 74, Lokichogio 30503, Kenya

Tel	+254 54 32048
Mobile	+254 720 772335; +254 722 207876
Fax	+254 54 32048
E-mail	rsalim@748airservices.com
Web	www.748airservices.com

       Lokichogio, LS & CH
5 mins

748 Air Services was founded in 1994 with the aim of providing air transportation for NGOs operating in remote parts of Sudan and other East African countries. It has grown to become a major provider of transport of cargo and passengers for humanitarian, governmental and private sectors in Africa.

In 2002, 748 Air Services built a camp in Lokichogio, originally intended for the customers and staff of the company. The camp has 30 en-suite rooms, made up of doubles and twins. All rooms are equipped with ceiling and stand fans. The restaurant has an outside dining area, and serves meals at any time of day, as well as having a scheduled breakfast, lunch and dinner. It has an international a la carte menu, with a variety of dishes including seafood. Themed nights include Wednesday burrito night and Saturday night barbecue. The bar serves soft drinks, beers and spirits. The conference room seats 60 pax; conference packages including snacks, tea and coffee can be arranged. The hotel also has a gym, basketball court, volleyball court and pool table. WiFi is available throughout the hotel. Lokichogio, known as the gateway to South Sudan, became a bustling centre for the aid community during the 1990s.

Trackmark Lokichogio

Trackmark, Lopiding Road, Lokichogio, Kenya
PO Box 102409, Nairobi 00101, Kenya

Tel	
Mobile	+254 721 440967; +254 710 772626
Fax	
E-mail	nganga_rosemary@yahoo.com
Web	

       Lokichogio, LS & CH
10 mins

Trackmark was established to serve the aid community and is well equipped to accommodate holiday makers or business visitors passing through this arid region. Lokichogio, known as the gateway to South Sudan, became a bustling centre for the aid community during the 1990s.

There are 16 en-suite rooms, made up of 14 singles and 2 doubles. 4 of the rooms are equipped with aircon and 12 have table fans. There is also a suite suitable for a family, made up of a double room, single room, sitting room and bathroom. All rooms are equipped with internet cables. The restaurant has an international menu and serves buffet or a la carte as required. The bar has a selection of beers, soft drinks, hot drinks and wines. The swimming pool is surrounded by a sunbathing terrace furnished with tables, chairs and sunbeds. Trees provide plentiful shade. There is also a table tennis table and satellite TV. The meeting room seats 25 pax. Trackmark can arrange airport transfers. Local transportation and taxis can be booked by reception.

NMK, Lake Turkana Koobi Fora Bandas
Sibiloi National Park

Lake Turkana Koobi Fora Bandas, Sibiloi National Park, Kenya
National Museums of Kenya, PO Box 40658, Nairobi 00100, Kenya

Tel	+254 20 8164135; +254 20 8164136; +254 20 8164134
Mobile	
Fax	+254 20 3741424
E-mail	publicrelations@museums.or.ke
Web	www.museums.or.ke

Koobi Fora, CH
15 mins

The Koobi Fora Museum offers an introduction into the many archaeological discoveries made in this region and the research that is being done here. Lake Turkana Koobi Fora Bandas are located near the museum. They are owned and operated by National Museums of Kenya, NMK. There are 3 bandas, each with twin beds, bed linen, towels and mosquito nets. There are communal, external bathroom facilities, a communal kitchen and a dining banda. Visitors should bring all their food and drinks. A resident caretaker and 4 other staff can assist with cooking and share information about the region.

Sibiloi National Park is best known for the fossil beds and museum. Other sites of interest include the Jarigole Pillor site, a pre-Iron Age burial complex marked by pillars of basalt, and Sibiloi Fossil Forest, a fossilised forest buried by volcanic eruption. Walks in the area include the Hasuma Forest Bird Walk on the river Alia, the Koobi Fora Spit Walk, a hike with plentiful birdlife and crocodiles, and the Fish Nesting Walking Tour, which provides an introduction to the geology of the area and shows some of the sites where Maeve and Richard Leakey found hominid fossils. The Karari Archaeological Sites are located 2 hours north of the camp, and have findings between 1.9 and 1.5 million years old.

KWS, Alia Bay Guest House
Sibiloi National Park

KWS, Alia Bay Guest House, KWS HQ, Sibiloi National Park, Kenya
Kenya Wildlife Service, PO Box 40241, Nairobi 00100, Kenya

Tel	+254 20 6000800; +254 20 6002345; +254 20 3991000
Mobile	+254 726 610508; +254 726 610509; +254 736 663421
Fax	+254 20 6003792
E-mail	kws@kws.go.ke / reservations@kws.go.ke
Web	www.kws.go.ke

Koobi Fora, CH
20 mins

Alia Bay Guest House is owned and managed by Kenya Wildlife Service, KWS. It is situated near the KWS headquarters in Sibiloi National Park. The guesthouse is on the shores of Lake Turkana and has lovely views of the water. There are 3 single bedrooms, 1 bathroom, sitting room, dining room and kitchen. The kitchen is equipped with gas stove, kitchen utensils, cutlery, crockery and glassware. The resident caretaker provides electricity and mosquito nets. Visitors should bring food, water and fuel with them. Sibiloi National Park was created to protect the sites of the many remarkable hominid fossils found here. The Koobi Fora Museum offers an introduction to the many archaeological discoveries and the research that is being done here. Other sites of interest include the Jarigole Pillor site and Sibiloi Fossil Forest. Walks in the area include the Hasuma Forest Bird Walk on the river Alia, the Koobi Fora Spit Walk, a hike with plentiful birdlife and crocodiles, and the Fish Nesting Walking Tour, which provides an introduction to the geology of the area and shows some of the sites where Maeve and Richard Leakey found hominid fossils. The Karari Archaeological Sites have findings between 1.9 and 1.5 million years old.

Nawaitorong Lodge Lodwar

Nawaitorong Lodge, 2km from Kitale-Lodwar Road, Lodwar, Kenya
PO Box 192, Lodwar 30500, Kenya
Tel   +254 20 8018407
Mobile   +254 720 952399
Fax
E-mail
Web

    Lodwar, LS & CH
10 mins

Nawaitorong Lodge is conveniently located near the centre of Lodwar. The lodge offers budget accommodation, dining and conferencing.
There are 20 rooms, made up of singles, doubles and triples. The rooms all have mosquito net and fan, and share external communal bathrooms. There are also 3 cottages, 2 of which each have 1 en-suite double room, and 1 of which has 2 en-suite double rooms. The cottages all have chair, table, cupboard, mosquito net and fan. There is also a campsite; communal bathroom facilities are available at the lodge.
The restaurant has an a la carte menu, and can serve buffet for large groups on request. Dishes include marinated spicy chicken, grilled fish and a selection of curries and stews served with rice or chapatti. The list of pizzas includes Hawaiian and vegetarian. The restaurant serves soft drinks and juices; guests wishing to drink alcohol may bring their own. The conference hall seats 100 pax, and is equipped with TV. The craft shop stocks a variety of local artefacts such as beaded necklaces, bangles made from waste paper, candlesticks made from camel bone, T-shirts, earrings and pen holders. The lodge is 2km from the main Kitale Road; turn from the main road at the lodge's sign, just before the bridge.

Turkwell Lodge Lodwar

Turkwell Lodge, Kitale-Lodwar Road, Lodwar, Kenya
PO Box 14, Lodwar 30500, Kenya
Tel
Mobile   +254 735 459530
Fax
E-mail
Web

    Lodwar, LS & CH
10 mins

Turkwell Lodge is conveniently located near the centre of Lodwar. The lodge offers budget accommodation, dining and a bar.
There are 30 rooms, of which 10 share external communal bathrooms, and 20 have en-suite bathrooms. The rooms have chair, table, mosquito net and fan. Some rooms are equipped with TV with local channels. The restaurant has an a la carte menu, with local and international dishes such as beef curry, mutton stew, chicken tikka, rice, chapatti and omelette. The bar serves soft drinks, beers and spirits, and also stocks cigarettes. It is equipped with satellite TV and also has a pool table.
The conference hall seats 30 pax and is equipped with TV. A larger conference hall is available at nearby Lodwar Lodge, and can be booked through Turkwell Lodge. The lodge can book taxis when required, and also has cars for hire. Excursions to places of interest such as Lake Turkana and Eliye Springs can be arranged here.

Kalacha Camp Chalbi Desert

Kalacha Camp, Chalbi Desert, Kenya
Tropic Air, PO Box 161, Nanyuki 10400, Kenya
Tel
Mobile   +254 722 207300; +254 734 333044
Fax
E-mail   info@tropicairkenya.com
Web   www.kalacha.org / www.tropicairkenya.com

           Kalacha, CH
                                          10 mins

In the vast expanses of the Chalbi Desert, Kalacha Camp sits on the edge of an oasis. The camp was established as a community project for the Gabbra people, providing them with a source of income. The simple, attractive camp was built of local materials. It is managed by Tropic Air, and run by members of the Kalacha Camel Fund and Kalacha Self Improvement Group.

There are 4 en-suite thatched bandas, overlooking the oasis. The mess area is a circular building, housing the living and dining area. The kitchen has a charcoal oven and 2 solar fridges; the camp is self-catering and guests should bring their own food and drink. A plunge pool edged with desert roses curves appealingly around the mess area. Local Gabbra women sell their woven mats and baskets, as well as gourds, camel bells and wooden bowls.

The selection of activities is authentic and unique to the area. Visitors can watch herds of livestock drinking at the oasis while huge flights of sand grouse skim over. Nearby sites of interest include the Catholic Church with vivid biblical paintings in Kalacha town, rock art paintings and Coreli Springs in the heart of the desert. Sand grouse shooting seasons are 1st February to 31st March and 1st July to 31st October.

Oasis Lodge Loyangalani

Oasis Lodge, Loyangalani, Turkana, Kenya
PO Box 40819, Nairobi 00100, Kenya
Tel
Mobile   +254 729 954672.
Fax
E-mail   info@geosafaris.net
Web

           Loyangalani, CH
                                          20 mins

On the edge of Lake Turkana, Oasis Lodge is located at a real oasis in the arid desert of northern Kenya. The lodge has 2 fresh water swimming pools, fed by the lake, in gardens lush with doum palms. Loyangalani, the town that stands between the bleak desert and the bright blue lake, is an extraordinary and exciting site; it attracts intrepid adventurers and those who want to see a part of Kenya little visited.

There are 14 en-suite rooms, made up of twins and doubles. The restaurant has an a la carte menu of international dishes, and specialises in fresh lake fish. The bar is well stocked with soft drinks, beers and spirits. Activities, at an extra charge, include the use of a vehicle for the day, with driver and fuel. Fishing trips and boat trips on the lake can be arranged. Cultural tours of the local El Molo village and excursions to Mt Kulal are available. Light aircraft and helicopter flights over the lake can be booked from the lodge. Oasis Lodge makes an ideal starting place for trips across the Chalbi Desert and for excursions to the prehistoric sites of Koobi Fora in Sibiloi National Park.

Palm Shade Camp

Loyangalani

Palm Shade Camp, Loyangalani, Turkana, Kenya
PO Box 19, Loyangalani 60501, Kenya
Tel
Mobile +254 726 714768
Fax
E-mail
Web

   Loyangalani, CH
20 mins

Loyangalani, the town that stands between the bleak desert of northern Kenya and bright blue Lake Turkana, is an extraordinary and exciting site; it attracts intrepid adventurers and those who want to see a part of Kenya little visited. The town makes an ideal starting place for trips across the Chalbi Desert and for excursions to the prehistoric sites of Koobi Fora in Sibiloi National Park.

Palm Shade Camp offers budget accommodation and a selection of activities and facilities. There are 12 rooms, made up of 11 doubles and 1 single. The restaurant serves predominantly local food, with a few international dishes. Food is prepared to the guests' requirement. The conference hall seats 50 pax. Car hire can be arranged. Local sites of interest include the rock art paintings, the remote El Molo village and Mt Kulal. Boat trips and fishing trips on the lake can be arranged locally. Loyangalani is the meeting place for the Turkana, Rendille, Samburu and Gabbra tribes. The opportunities for expanding cultural knowledge are endless, and the street markets are filled with artefacts, tools and traditional jewellery from all the tribal groups.

Marsabit Lodge

Marsabit National Park

Marsabit Lodge, Marsabit National Park, Kenya
PO Box 76624, Nairobi 00508, Kenya
Tel +254 20 2695468; +254 20 2695260
Mobile
Fax
E-mail info@marsabitlodge.com
Web www.marsabitlodge.com

   Marsabit, CH
20 mins

Marsabit National Park was home to Ahmed, the legendary mammoth elephant who lived to a grand old age and whose remains continue to be exhibited at the National Museum of Kenya in Nairobi. The park, surrounding Mt Marsabit, is forested and lush, dotted with cliffs and waterholes. Local animal species include greater kudu, oryx, bushbuck, reticulated giraffe and warthog, as well as predators such as lion, hyena, cheetah and leopard. Prolific birdlife includes over 52 species of eagle, hawk and falcon. Marsabit Lodge overlooks Sokorte Diko, a cliff-lined waterhole that attracts game from the surrounding forest. There are 24 en-suite rooms, made up of singles, twins, doubles and triples. A communal veranda stretches along the lodge, giving views of the waterhole. There is also a campsite. Paradise Restaurant, overlooking the waterhole, serves local and international cuisine. Sokorte Bar and Lounge has an open fireplace and a selection of soft drinks, beers and spirits. The lodge also offers secretarial services and currency exchange. Childcare and babysitting can be arranged.

Game drives in the park are available. Guided walking safaris, outside the national park, can be arranged. Marsabit is a convenient place to stay during trips to the Chalbi Desert, Loyangalani, Koobi Fora and other destinations in northern Kenya.

Desert Rose Mt Nyiru

Desert Rose, Mt Nyiru, off South Horr-Loyangalani Road, Kenya
New African Territories, PO Box 76677, Nairobi 00508, Kenya

Tel	+254 20 2663397; +254 20 3598871
Mobile	+254 718 139359
Fax	
E-mail	bookings@africanterritories.co.ke
Web	www.africanterritories.co.ke / www.desertrosekenya.com

  Desert Rose, CH
10 mins

Perched on the side of Mt Nyiru, Desert Rose gives striking views across Northern Kenya. This exquisite lodge is family hosted and offers personal service and unique design.

The 5 en-suite cottages have been handcrafted, with local stone walls and peaked thatched roofs. Each is furnished with a huge wild olive bed and other aged wooden furniture. Each has an open air bathroom perfect for soaking in the starlight and a furnished deck with views of the mountains and plains. The dining room and lounge are open sided to make the most of the views, and the food is simple, fresh and tasty. The swimming pool and rocky sunbathing terrace also offer views across the forested slopes and into the valley.

This wild desert region offers itself to distinctive activities and unexploited cultural experiences. Guided walks, camel walks and water sliding are all available, as well as cultural visits to the remote northern villages of the Samburu, Turkana and El Molo peoples. Walks in the forest and bird watching are particularly of interest. Camel safaris, scenic flights, longer drives and fishing on Lake Turkana can also be arranged. The lodge is eco-friendly and uses solar power.

Samburu Sports Centre and Guest Lodges South Horr

Samburu Sports Centre and Guest Lodges, South Horr, Kenya

Tel	
Mobile	+254 720 334561; +254 720 482088
Fax	
E-mail	stakwellee@yahoo.com
Web	www.safarisportscamp.com

  Kurungu, CH
20 mins

Samburu Sports Centre and Guest Lodges was established in 2005 by a Christian ministry. It aims to bring warring tribes together in peace through the medium of sport. The lodge is surrounded by beautiful, rugged mountains and provides opportunity for hiking and rock climbing. The centre is made up of the director's house, the chief's house, 12 guest lodges, a communal kitchen, restaurant, external bathroom facilities and a tree house. A campsite is also available. Other facilities include internet, cold soft drinks, fuel kiosk and vegetable garden. The centre is an alcohol and smoking free zone.

Sports facilities include a basketball court, volleyball court, football pitch and a games room with table tennis and darts. There is also a jungle gym play area for children, including swings, trampoline, zip line, horse shoes and other games. Camel rides and donkey rides can be arranged. The centre distributes water to remote Samburu and Turkana villages, and also provides food in times of drought. It sponsors medical outreaches, and hosts children's programmes and sports camps regularly through the year. Mission teams are welcome, including youth teams, work teams, sports teams, medical teams and ecotourism teams.

Wajir Hilton Palace

Wajir

Wajir Hilton Palace, Wajir Hospital Street, Wajir, Kenya
PO Box 522, Wajir 70200, Kenya
Tel +254 46 421555
Mobile +254 722 490888; +254 733 535320
Fax
E-mail iska202@hotmail.com / abdi104@yahoo.com
Web

Wajir, LS & CH
10 mins

The Wajir Hilton Palace, which is not affiliated to the international chain of hotels of that name, is located near Wajir Airport. It is about 4km from Yahood Dam. The town makes a useful place to break the journey when travelling to the remote northern part of Kenya. It also has an airport which offers flights into Somalia and Somaliland, and to destinations in Kenya. There are 20 en-suite rooms, made up of singles and doubles. All rooms are equipped with satellite TV, aircon, smoke detector and WiFi. The restaurant serves an a la carte menu of Kenyan cuisine and local dishes, such as grilled goat, chicken stew, ugali, rice, chapatti and chips. No alcohol is served. The conference hall seats 100 pax, and is equipped with aircon, fan, projector and PA system. There is also a secure car park and a garden. The Kenya Wildlife Service, KWS, has recorded a variety of wildlife in this area, including elephant, lion, cheetah, leopard, hippo, crocodile and hartebeest. The Yahood Dam attracts wildlife that comes to drink in the heat of the day.

Wajir Guest House

Wajir

Wajir Guest House, Airport Road, Wajir, Kenya
PO Box 252, Wajir 70200, Kenya
Tel +254 46 421341
Mobile +254 717 190513
Fax
E-mail wajirguesthouse@yahoo.com
Web

Wajir, LS & CH
10 mins

Wajir Guest House offers budget accommodation, dining and conferencing in Wajir. The town makes a useful place to break the journey when travelling to the remote northern part of Kenya. It also has an airport which offers flights into Somalia and Somaliland, and to destinations in Kenya. There are 21 en-suite double rooms. All rooms are equipped with satellite TV. WiFi is available in reception. There are 2 restaurants, which have an a la carte menu of Kenyan cuisine and local dishes, such as grilled goat, chicken stew, ugali, rice, chapatti and chips. A buffet can be arranged for larger groups and conferences. No alcohol is served. Outside catering can be arranged. There are 2 conference halls, which seat 50 pax and 100 pax. The conference halls are equipped with a projector.

The Kenya Wildlife Service, KWS, has recorded a variety of wildlife in this area, including elephant, lion, cheetah, leopard, hippo, crocodile and hartebeest. The Yahood Dam attracts wildlife that comes to drink in the heat of the day.

Kauro Guest House

Sera Wildlife Conservancy

Kauro Guest House, Sera Wildlife Conservancy, off Isiolo-Marsabit Road
Northern Rangelands Trust, Private Bag, Isiolo 60300, Kenya

Tel	+254 64 31405
Mobile	+254 722 249599
Fax	+254 64 31405
E-mail	andrew.lentoijoni@nrt-kenya.org
Web	www.nrt-kenya.org/lodges/kauro

　　　　　 Sera, CH
　　　　　　　　　　　　　　　　15 mins

The Sera Wildlife Conservancy was established in 2001. Under the umbrella of the Northern Rangelands Trust, NRT, the conservancy aims to link the Samburu, Borana and Rendille with a common objective of conservation, development and sustainable uses of natural resources. Notable wildlife species include elephant, wild dog, gerenuk, Beisa oryx, buffalo, reticulated giraffe and Grevy's zebra.

The Kauro Guest House is a community conservation initiative belonging to the Samburu people. It is a self-catering house nestling in doum palms on the edge of a seasonal river. The guesthouse consists of 2 en-suite bandas, each with double bedroom, dining area and separate kitchen.

It is staffed by a cook, housekeeper and security guard. Visitors should bring their own food and drinks. The guesthouse was built from materials found in the surrounding area.

The area is ideal for walking, and for an introduction to the lives of pastoral communities. A waterhole near the guesthouse attracts wildlife and birdlife. The permanent water sources in Sera make it a critical area for wildlife, especially during the dry seasons. Local women's groups are involved in the production and sale of handicrafts through NRT Trading.

Kitich Camp

Matthew's Mountain Range

Kitich Camp, Matthew's Mountain Range, Kenya
Cheli & Peacock, PO Box 743, Nairobi 00517, Kenya

Tel	+254 20 6004053/4; +254 20 6003090/1
Mobile	+254 724 255374; +254 733 490234
Fax	+254 20 6004050; +254 20 6003066
E-mail	safaris@chelipeacock.co.ke / info@chelipeacock.co.ke
Web	www.chelipeacock.com / www.kitichcamp.com

 Ngelai, CH
　　　　　　　　　　　　　　　45 mins

The Matthew's Mountain Range, a chain of peaks covered in dense dewy forest rising out of the desert, provides a striking setting for Kitich Camp. The camp overlooks a river glade within the lush indigenous forest that is home to elephant, leopard, bushbuck, rhino, buffalo, as well as ancient cycads, spectacular butterflies, turacos and wild orchids.

The 6 traditional safari tents are all en-suite with alfresco stone bathrooms and safari showers. Kitich Camp's cosy lounge with open fire overlooks the floodlit river glade so guests can enjoy their drinks while watching animals emerging from the forest at dusk. The camp has been built with as little impact on the environment as possible, and has achieved the Ecotourism Society of Kenya's silver award.

Kitich Camp is an authentic bush camp and offers a unique and private forest wildlife experience. All activities are tailored to suit the individual preferences of the guests. Guests can walk along forest paths in the 900km² of private untouched mountain wilderness guided by the Samburu and Ndorobo people and learn their traditional methods of tracking game. Natural rock pools and mountain streams provide crystal clear icy water where guests can swim. Birdwatching and cultural visits to local Samburu families are recommended.

Sarara Camp — Matthew's Mountain Range

Sarara Camp, Matthew's Mountain Range, Kenya
PO Box 30907, Nairobi 00100, Kenya

Tel Sat	+88 216 433025; +254 20 2641190/1
Mobile	+254 722 805893; +254 721 605422
Fax	
E-mail	safaris@acaciatrails.com
Web	www.sararacamp.com

  Sarara, CH, 2 mins
Namunyak, CH, 20 mins

Sarara Camp, set in 850,000 acres of community conservation, has become known for luxury tented accommodation and exclusivity. The 6 spacious en-suite tents, all elegantly furnished, have been positioned to maximise the breathtaking views. Buffet lunch is served in the mess tent or under the trees. Dinner is served on the terrace overlooking the pool or by a campfire in the bush.

In 1995, in response to shocking poaching in the area, the Namunyak Wildlife Conservation Trust was initiated, under the umbrella of the Northern Rangelands Trust, NRT. Two years later Sarara Camp opened, with the intention of supporting and preserving this pristine wilderness and, true to its original purpose, the camp is now wholly owned by the Namunyak community.

Local Samburu guides lead game drives and walks, fly camping with camels, trekking in the Matthew's Mountain Range and game watching from a concealed hide. The area has become known for quality leopard sightings, as well as sightings of the shy lesser kudu and African wild dogs. 500 species of birds have been identified, including 5 types of hornbill and numerous birds of prey. Sarara is the only place guests can observe the magical and timeless tradition of the Samburu Singing Wells. The camp is closed in May and November.

Maralal Safari Lodge — Maralal

Maralal Safari Lodge, Maralal National Reserve, Kenya
PO Box 15020, Nairobi 00100, Kenya

Tel	+254 20 211124; +254 20 246826
Mobile	+254 722 955541
Fax	+254 20 214099
E-mail	zamaralal@fastermail.com
Web	www.angelfire.com/jazz/maralal

  Maralal, CH
15 mins

The only lodge in Maralal National Reserve, Maralal Safari Lodge overlooks a waterhole that attracts a selection of game. The reserve is set amidst the Ol Doinyo Lenkiyo Mountains. It is home to dry zone animals such as impala, eland, buffalo, baboon, warthog, giraffe, zebra, hyena and leopard, as well as over 260 species of birds. Elephants pass through the area seasonally.

There are 19 en-suite rooms, made up of doubles, twins and triples. The restaurant serves international cuisine. The bar is stocked with soft drinks, beers and spirits. The swimming pool has a sunbathing terrace and pool bar. There is also a residents' lounge and a conference room. The game viewing terraces overlook the waterhole.

The annual Maralal International Camel Derby was established in 1990, and is both a serious sport and a colourful spectacle. In addition to the camel races and fun rides, the derby includes cycling races, donkey rides, local dancing displays and stalls of local curios and handicrafts. Also of interest is the house in which Jomo Kenyatta, Kenya's 1st president, was interned by the British Colonial Government during the State of Emergency of the 1950s.

Yare Safaris
Hostel and Campsite

Maralal

Yare Safaris Hostel and Campsite, 4km from Maralal, Kenya
Yare Safaris, PO Box 63290, Nairobi 00200, Kenya

Tel	+254 20 2214099; +254 65 62295
Mobile	+254 722 895126; +723 702461
Fax	+254 20 2214099
E-mail	yare@africaonline.co.ke
Web	

  Maralal, CH
20 mins

Yare Safaris established the famous Maralal International Camel Derby in 1990 and still hosts this extraordinary event annually. The derby is both a serious sport and a colourful spectacle. In addition to the camel races and fun rides, the derby includes cycling races, donkey rides, local dancing displays and stalls of local curios and handicrafts. The derby promotes awareness of the increasing desertification of the region.

Yare Safaris Hostel and Campsite is located on a hillside 4km south of Maralal town. The hostel has 12 en-suite cottages, set in peaceful gardens. All cottages have twin beds. There is also a campsite where it is possible to view game. The hostel and campsite have a restaurant and a lounge.

Yare Safaris organises camel, walking and trekking safaris away from normal tourist routes. Local sites of interest include Maralal National Reserve, set amidst the Ol Doinyo Lenkiyo Mountains. The reserve is home to dry zone animals such as impala, eland, buffalo, baboon, warthog, giraffe, zebra, hyena and leopard, as well as over 260 species of birds. Elephants pass through the area seasonally. Also of interest is the house in which Jomo Kenyatta, Kenya's 1st president, was interned by the British Colonial Government during the State of Emergency of the 1950s.

Bobong Camp

Ol Maisor

Bobong Camp, 20km north of Rumuruti, Kenya
Bobong and Ol Maisor Camels, PO Box 5, Rumuruti 20321, Kenya

Tel	+254 62 2032718; +254 20 2033179
Mobile	+254 735 243075; +254 722 936177
Fax	
E-mail	olmaisor@africaonline.co.ke
Web	www.laikipiatourism.org

  Bobong, CH
10 mins

Bobong Camp sits on an escarpment overlooking the Ewaso Narok Swamp, the Laikipia Plains, Mt Kenya and the Aberdare range. The camp is home to an extraordinary array of birdlife, including plains species, rock species, water birds and forest birds. Bobong rated 3rd in Kenya's World Birdwatch count in 2003.

The camp makes an ideal place to start or finish a camel safari. There is 1 en-suite banda, 1 standard banda and 1 shade banda. There is also a campsite with communal bathroom facilities and 2 communal barbeques. Activities are arranged according to the visitor's interests and budget. Camel safaris with camping equipment and personal guiding are available. Shorter camel rides can also be arranged. Bird walks, nature walks and swamp visits are all on offer. Ox carting and bicycling are available. Punting on the dams and tubing on the river can be done in season. Fishing, crayfish catching, bird shooting and clay pigeon shooting are all on offer. The campsite also has an obstacle course. Cultural visits to a Turkana village can be arranged. Entertainment by traditional dancers and local drama groups is also available.

Bobong Camp supports the Wild Camel Protection Foundation which protects the critically endangered wild Bactrian camel in its pristine desert environment in the Gobi deserts of China and Mongolia.

Almond Resort

Garissa

Almond Resort, Lamu Road, Garissa, Kenya
PO Box 1054, Garissa 70100, Kenya
Tel   +254 20 2325721
Mobile   +254 711 829899
Fax
E-mail   info@almond-resort.com
Web   www.almond-resort.com

Garissa, CH
15 mins

Garissa, the largest town in northern Kenya, lies directly on the path of the Tana River, Kenya's longest river. Almond Resort is located on the banks of the river, in palm groves and leafy gardens.

There are 90 en-suite rooms, made up of doubles and twins. All rooms have balconies overlooking the gardens, swimming pool and fountains. Each room is equipped with satellite TV, desk, telephone and WiFi. The restaurant serves international food and a variety of African cuisines, as well as vegetarian dishes and seafood. No alcohol is served.

There are 3 conference halls; the largest hall seats 300 pax and the remaining 2 seat 100 pax each. All halls are equipped with projector and PA system. The resort can organise executive conferences, board meetings and international conventions, as well as creative incentive programmes, functions and weddings. The business centre has high speed internet, fax, telephone and secretarial services. The fitness centre has state of the art equipment and qualified instructors. The hotel offers a selection of children's fun programmes. It also offers a variety of excursions to local sites of interest, including cultural and historical sites. Garissa makes an ideal location to stop on the way to or from the Chalbi Desert, Loyangalani, Koobi Fora and other destinations in northern Kenya.

Nomad Palace Hotel

Garissa

Nomad Palace Hotel, Kisimayu Road, Garissa, Kenya
PO Box 126, Garissa 70100, Kenya
Tel   +254 46 2103245; +254 46 2102578; +254 46 2103514
Mobile   +254 724 294300
Fax   +254 46 2103089
E-mail   reservations@nomadpalacehotel.com
Web   www.nomadpalacehotel.com

Garissa, CH
10 mins

Garissa, the largest town in northern Kenya, lies directly on the path of the Tana River, Kenya's longest river. Nomad Palace Hotel, located not far from the banks of the Tana River, occasionally has views of giraffes strolling past its windows. The hotel offers accommodation, conferencing and workshops. It also makes an ideal location for stopping on the way to destinations in northern Kenya.

Nomad Palace Hotel is conveniently located for the shops and businesses of Garissa. There are 67 en-suite rooms, made up of standard, deluxe, superior and suites. All rooms are equipped with aircon, satellite TV, WiFi, telephone, minibar, writing table and chairs. There are 2 restaurants, 1 serving buffet and the other serving a la carte. There is also a spacious terrace. Both restaurants serve predominantly local cuisine, with a few international dishes. No alcohol is served.

There are 3 conference halls. Impala conference hall seats 200 pax, Flamingo conference hall seats 60 and Twiga conference hall seats 70. Impala hall is equipped with large screen. Laptop, LCD projector, overhead projector, TV and video are available for hire. Secretarial facilities are offered. Conferences, exhibitions, meetings, seminars, banquets and weddings can all be arranged. The hotel is stationed near the army and police, and security is good.

Road to Baragoi – Photo © www.sokomoto.com

Western Kenya

Lake Victoria - Photo © Andrew Nightingale, kembu.com

Mountainous and fertile Western Kenya is blanketed in lush green plantations of famed Kenyan tea. At its western edge, the region meets Lake Victoria, the source of the Nile. Other highlights include Mt Elgon, Kakamega Forest National Reserve, Ruma National Park, Saiwa Swamp National Park, Cherangani Hills and Kerio Valley.

Western Kenya's major towns are Eldoret, Kitale, Kakamega, Kisumu, Kisii and Kericho. Eldoret is a bustling hub at which roads linking the Rift Valley, Northern Kenya and Western Kenya meet. Kitale is the gateway to Mt Elgon, Saiwa Swamp, Cherangani Hills and Marich Pass. Kakamega has the tropical rainforest designated an Important Bird Area, IBA. Kisumu, the largest town in western Kenya and third largest in Kenya, stretches along the shores of Lake Victoria. Kisii is famed for soapstone and Kericho is renowned for producing tea. The region is home to the Luo, Luhya, Kalenjin and Gusii.

Eldoret has an international airport. Kitale and Kisumu have domestic airports. Airstrips suitable for charters are dotted around the region. The road network is well maintained and well signed. Inside the national parks, 4WD vehicles are required. Entry to national parks requires park fees be paid to Kenya Wildlife Service, KWS.

Lake Victoria lies between Kenya, Tanzania and Uganda. The lake is the largest freshwater lake in Africa and the second largest in the world. After long and treacherous exploration, the explorers of the 19th century settled on the lake as the source of the Nile. Rusinga Island houses a prehistoric excavation site whose fossils are thought to be 18-million years old. Mt Elgon, straddling the Kenya Uganda border, is famous for elephants that dig salt from its caves. The mountain offers hot springs, great hiking and several peaks to climb. Rising 4,200 meters, the mountain is the fourth highest in Africa. It is known for botanical diversity and primate and game viewing; 240 species of birds have been recorded.

Kakamega Forest is the only remnant of the once great tropical rainforest that stretched across Central Africa. The forest is home to 330 bird species, several endemic to the area. Forest walking, bird watching and game viewing are on offer. The nearby Crying Stone of Ilesi, rich in folklore, is another attraction. Kisumu Impala Sanctuary, on the shores of Lake Victoria, is a holding area for animals needing special protection and incorporates an animal orphanage. The sanctuary has nature trails and picnic sites, and is known for an abundance of birdlife.

Ruma National Park, created to protect its indigenous population of rare roan antelopes, is home to 400 species of birds. Camping, picnicking, bird watching and game viewing are all available. Saiwa Swamp National Park was created to protect the sitatunga, a rare web-footed antelope. Other indigenous species of interest include otter, genet cat, serval cat, mongoose, bushbuck and monkeys; 370 species of bird have been recorded. The park has a nature boardwalk and campsite.

Cherangani Hills, Tugan Hills and Kerio Valley offer spectacular views and interesting hiking. Long and short hikes and camping are available. Marich Pass, further north, also has wonderful hiking and mountain climbing. The highlands are famed for being the home of Kenya's marathon-winning athletes.

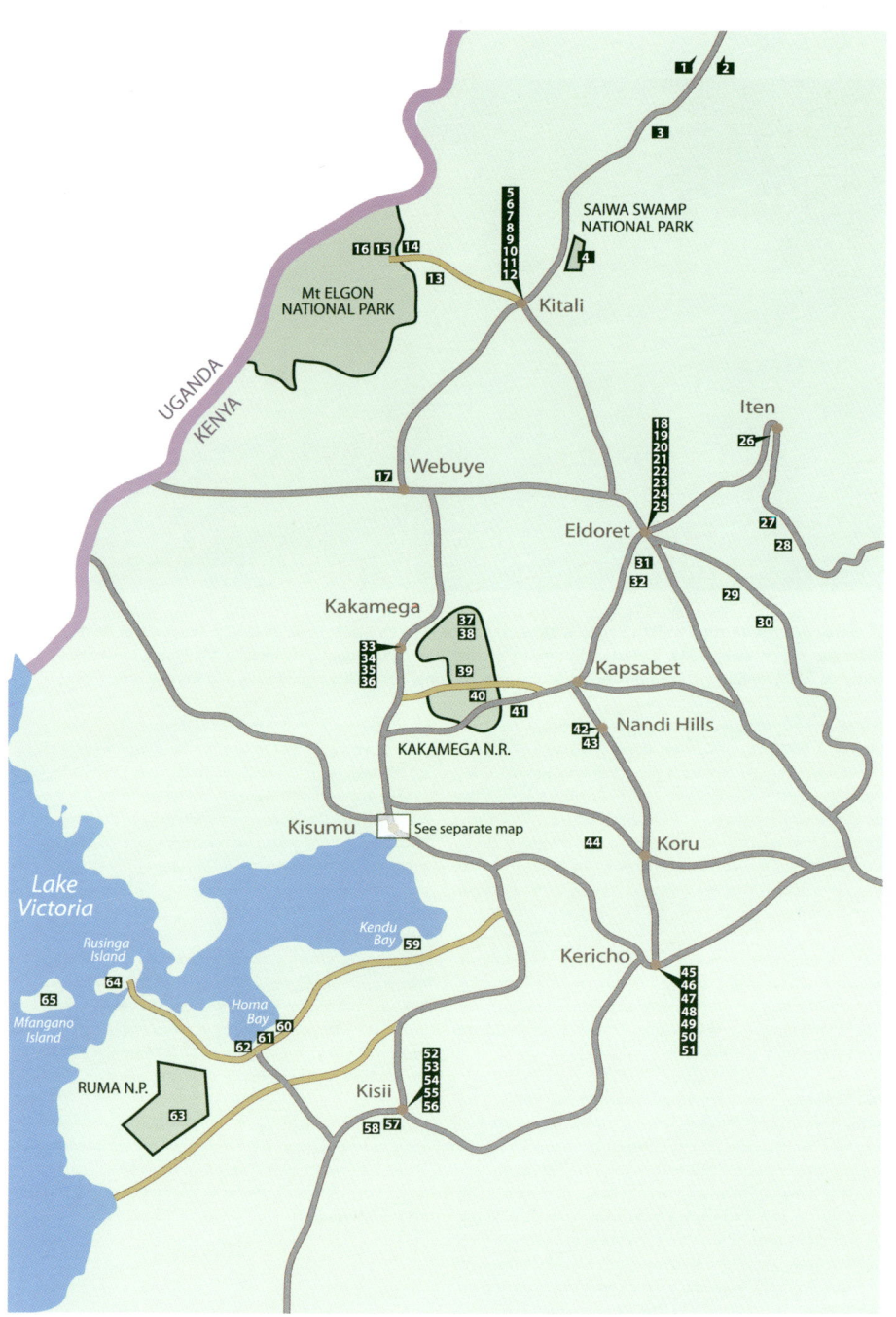

Index to all camps, lodges and hotels in the greater Western area

#	Name	#	Name
1	Mt Mtelo Cottages and Campsite	40	Rondo Retreat
2	Marich Pass Field Studies Centre	41	Mago Guest House
3	Sirikwa Safaris	42	Nandi Bears Club
4	KWS, Tree Top House	43	Tea Planters' Inn
5	Jehovah Jire Hotel	44	Kweisos House
6	Vision Gate Hotel	45	The Exotic House
7	Alakara Hotel	46	Hills Country Lodge
8	Kitale Highview Hotel	47	Kericho Club
9	Mid Africa Hotel	48	Teavale Guest Cottages
10	Pinewood	49	Tea Hotel
11	Karibuni Lodge	50	Kimugu River Lodge
12	Kitale Club	51	Ray's Place Inn
13	Delta Crescent Wildlife Sanctuary	52	Ufanisi Resort
14	Mt Elgon Lodge	53	Jazz Restaurant and Hotel
15	KWS, Koitoboss Guest House	54	Zonic Hotel
16	KWS, Kapkuro Bandas	55	Magharibi Luxury Suites
17	Park Villa Hotel	56	Hotel Dados
18	Eldoret Wagon Hotel	57	Bluu Nile Hotel
19	Hotel Sirikwa	58	Savana Executive Hotel
20	White Highlands Inn	59	Kisindi Lodge and Spa
21	White Castle Motel	60	Homa Bay Tourist Hotel
22	Klique Hotel	61	Hotel Hippo Buck
23	Poa Place Resort	62	Little Nile Guest House
24	The Nobel Conference Centre	63	KWS, Oribi Guest House
25	Eldoret Club	64	Rusinga Island Lodge
26	Kerio View	65	Mfangano Island Camp
27	Lelin Campsite and Bandas		
28	Sego Safari Lodge		
29	Naiberi River Campsite & Resort		
30	Twiga Resort		
31	Relax Inn, Simba Village		
32	Marriott Hotel		
33	Siaya Guest House		
34	Sheywe Centre		
35	Kakamega Sports Club		
36	Golf Hotel		
37	KWS, Isukuti Houses		
38	KWS, Udo Bandas		
39	KEEP, Isacheno Bandas		

KaribuKenya Accommodation Guide

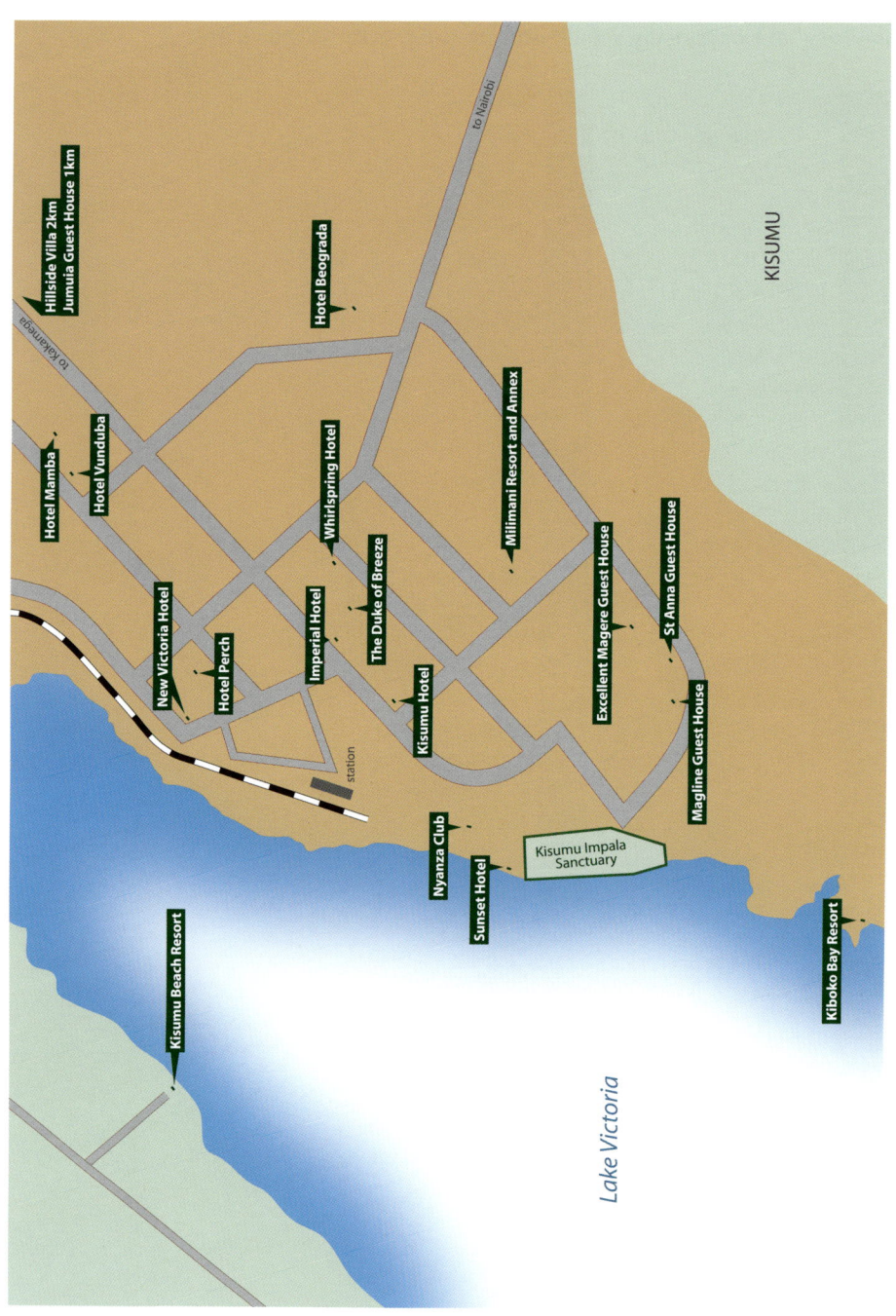

Mt Mtelo Cottages and Campsite

Mt Mtelo

Mt Mtelo Cottages and Campsite, West Pokot, Kenya
PO Box 39, Kapenguria 30600, Kenya
Tel
Mobile +254 737 941400; +254 729 449502; +254 718 281729
Fax
E-mail yoposiwa@yahoo.com
Web www.freewebs.com/mbara1

Kitale, LS & CH
3 hrs

High above the Great Rift Valley in the highlands of West Pokot, Mt Mtelo Cottages and Campsite offers spectacular views and exhilarating hiking. There are 5 thatched bandas, made up of singles, doubles and triples, equipped with bed linen, mosquito nets and lantern. There is also an executive en-suite banda with wonderful views of Mt Mtelo. The campsite has shaded seating areas and hammocks where guests can relax and appreciate the views. The restaurant serves local dishes, such as grilled beef, roast chicken, green grams and tropical fruits.
Activities include mountain climbing, hiking, bird watching, studying the unique flora and fauna and experiencing the indigenous Pokot culture.

The owner and manager, John Ywalasiwa, coordinates and assists with community projects such as the distribution of water, local education, health clinic and a tree nursery project. He gives generous discounts to volunteers assisting with these projects.
From Kitale, take the A1 road to Ortum and Marich Pass; 3km after the police checkpoint at Marich Pass, take a left at the campsite's signpost to ascend the escarpment. The cottages and campsite are a 3-hour trek or a 1½ hr drive from Marich Pass, 4WD required. Call John Ywalasiwa in advance and he will arrange transport, or guides can be obtained from Marich Pass Field Studies Centre.

Marich Pass Field Studies Centre

Marich Pass

Marich Pass Field Studies Centre, West Pokot, Kenya
PO Box 564, Kapenguria 30600, Kenya
Tel
Mobile +254 722 139151
Fax
E-mail marich.pass@gmail.com
Web www.gg.rhul.ac.uk/marichpass

Kitale, LS & CH
1.5 hrs

Marich Pass is a deep, rocky cleft carved where the Moruny River emerges from the Cherangani Hills onto the dry plains of the Lake Turkana Basin. The Marich Pass Field Studies Centre lies between these distinctive ecological zones. It welcomes student field classes, expedition groups and individual researchers as well as holidaymakers. The area is ideal for studies in environment, anthropology, linguistics, archaeology, geology and conservation. The centre is built on land leased from the Pokot County Council, using traditional materials; it donates a percentage of its takings to the local development fund and employs local Pokots. There are 19 bandas that can be doubles or triples and 4 cottages for 6 pax. There are several dormitories, with between 5 and 20 beds in each, and a campsite. An external bathroom block has cold showers; hot bucket showers can be arranged. Buffet meals, including African and international dishes, are served in the dining room, on the terrace or on the riverbank.
Activities include hiking along Moruny River, trekking in the Cherangani Hills, game driving in Nasalot National Reserve, swimming and picnicking in Weiwei Valley and climbing Mt Koh. Local sites of interest include Turkwell Gorge, Lomut market, Sigor Agricultural Project and Sokar Caves.

Western

Sirikwa Safaris

Cherangani Hills

Sirikwa Safaris, nr Saiwa Swamp National Park, Kenya
The Barnleys, PO Box 332, Kitale 30200, Kenya

Tel	
Mobile	+254 737 133170; +254 723 917953; +254 733 237932
Fax	
E-mail	sirikwabarnley@gmail.com
Web	www.sirikwasafaris.com

  Kitale, LS & CH
1 hr

Jane Barnley has lived in Kenya for over 75 years. Together with her son Richard and daughter Julia, she runs Sirikwa Safaris, welcoming guests into her farmhouse and tailor making their safaris. The Barnleys' house, with its home cooking and comfortable atmosphere, makes an ideal base from which to explore the highlands.

Guests can stay in the farmhouse, which has 2 double rooms, or pitch their tents in the campsite. Breakfast, lunch and dinner are served in the dining room; dishes are homemade, and include home baked chocolate cake.

Each safari is carefully planned to suit the wishes of the individual. Activities include trekking through the Cherangani Hills and climbing Mt Elgon with guides and porters. Ornithological tours with bird guides cover Saiwa Swamp National Park, Mt Elgon National Park, Cherangani Hills, Kongelai Escarpment and Marich Pass, or go further afield to Lake Turkana or Kakamega Forest. Cultural visits to Kapenguria, the site of Jomo Kenyatta's trial, to West Pokot villages and to Kitale can be arranged. Guided fishing excursions are on offer; local fish includes brown trout, rainbow trout, tiger perch, nile perch, barbel, tilapia and catfish. Both Kitale Club and Eldoret Club have golf courses and swimming pools. Road transfers from Kitale and Eldoret can be arranged.

KWS, Tree Top House

Saiwa Swamp National Park

KWS, Tree Top House, Saiwa Swamp National Park, Kenya
Kenya Wildlife Service, PO Box 40241, Nairobi 00100, Kenya

Tel	+254 20 6000800; +254 20 6002345; +254 20 3991000
Mobile	+254 726 610508; +254 726 610509; +254 736 663421
Fax	+254 20 6003792
E-mail	kws@kws.go.ke / reservations@kws.go.ke
Web	www.kws.go.ke

  Kitale, LS & CH
50 mins

Saiwa Swamp National Park, Kenya's smallest national park, provides the setting for this unique house. Tree Top House is named for its location in a tree inside the park. The house is owned by Kenya Wildlife Service, KWS. The house is a single unit, with twin beds and an en-suite bathroom. There is no kitchen. Cooking should be done at the Park Headquarters. No cooking utensils are provided so guests should bring whatever they require. A resident caretaker provides kerosene lamps, bed linen, towels, soap and loo paper.

Saiwa Swamp National Park is famed for its abundant birdlife, especially water birds, including the lesser jacana, grey heron and African black duck. Rare game includes the semi-aquatic sitatunga antelope, otter, giant forest squirrel and both the de brazza and colobus monkey. The park also has a wealth of flora species.

Saiwa Swamp National Park is 22km from Kitale. From Kitale, take the tarmac road towards Kapenguria. At Kipsaina junction, take the murrum road and follow it for 5km to the only park entrance, Sinverere Gate. The park gates are open from 6am to 7pm; park fees must be paid in cash at the gate.

Jehovah Jire Hotel

Kitale

Jehovah Jire Hotel, Lini Moja, past Kitale market, Kitale, Kenya
PO Box 4276, Kitale 30200, Kenya

Tel	+254 54 31752
Mobile	+254 726 508086
Fax	
E-mail	
Web	

    Kitale, LS & CH
20 mins

Jehovah Jire Hotel is a Christian hotel, whose motto 'On the Lord's Mountain, it shall be provided', Genesis 22:14, is written at reception. The whitewashed building is light and airy, with tiled floors and spacious verandas.

The 30 en-suite rooms are made up of 24 singles, 3 small doubles and 3 large doubles. The small doubles are equipped with 2 double beds and TV with local channels. The large doubles are spacious, and are equipped with 2 king size beds, desk, cupboard, TV and armchairs. All beds have mosquito nets.

The restaurant serves African dishes such as stew, fish, sweet potato, chapatti and ugali, as well as international snacks like soups and sandwiches. No smoking or alcohol is permitted.

The floors are divided by grills that let sunshine flow between the floors. Each floor has a sitting area equipped with satellite TV. The conference hall on the top floor seats 100 pax. It has a wooden floor and plentiful windows, as well as a tea and coffee bar. Conference equipment is not provided. The enclosed car park is guarded throughout the night.

A shop on the ground floor sells Christian literature and wedding decorations. Wedding cakes can be made to order.

Vision Gate Hotel

Kitale

Vision Gate Hotel, Kitale-Edibes Road, nr post office, Kitale, Kenya
PO Box 1829, Kitale 30200, Kenya

Tel	+254 54 31722
Mobile	+254 720 702779
Fax	+254 54 31250
E-mail	michaelwerunga@yahoo.co.uk
Web	

    Kitale, LS & CH
25 mins

Vision Gate Hotel, a Pentecostal hotel, has a church within its building. Guests enter through the ground floor restaurant, climb to the 1st floor restaurant, climb to the 2nd floor businesses and church to the reception on the 3rd floor.

The hotel is next to the post office, and overlooks Kitale's bustling market. It is within easy reach of Kitale Museum, and all the shops, restaurants and businesses of the town.

There are 40 en-suite rooms, made up of 22 singles, 8 doubles, 6 twins and 4 more spacious superior doubles. Some of the rooms have TV. Baby cots are available on request.

Each floor has a simple lounge area with chairs and TV. The hotel also has a balcony and a terrace. Both the ground floor restaurant and the 1st floor restaurant serve African grilled meats and stews and a few international dishes. The hotel serves no alcohol. Smoking is prohibited. There is a conference hall that seats 80 pax and another that seats 30. Conference equipment can be hired if required. A guarded basement car park provides secure parking.

Western

Alakara Hotel Kitale

Alakara Hotel, Moi Avenue, Kitale, Kenya
PO Box 1984, Kitale 30200, Kenya

Tel +254 54 31554
Mobile
Fax +254 54 30298
E-mail alakarahotel@yahoo.com
Web

 Kitale, LS & CH
20 mins

Centrally located on tree lined Moi Avenue, Alakara Hotel is a long low cream building. Its location makes it convenient for Kitale Museum, and for the shops, restaurants and businesses of the town.

There are 26 rooms, some en-suite and others with shared bathroom. There are 10 rooms, in 2 corridors of 5 rooms, with 1 shared bathroom per corridor. There are 13 en-suite standard rooms, all with telephone and some with TV. There are 3 en-suite executive rooms that include a TV and a writing desk. A safe is provided at reception for guests' valuables. The restaurant has African grilled meats and international dishes such as soups, steaks, curries and stews.

A gated car park with day and night guards ensures secure parking. The cyber café provides internet, lamination, binding and photocopy services.

Kitale Highview Hotel Kitale

Kitale Highview Hotel, corner of Moi Avenue and Kenyatta St, Kitale
PO Box 2925, Kitale 30200, Kenya

Tel +254 41 2002947
Mobile +254 723 652006
Fax
E-mail
Web

Kitale, LS & CH
20 mins

At the junction of Moi Avenue and Kenyatta Street, Kitale Highview Hotel is a corner building overlooking the 2 main streets of Kitale. It rises over a strip of shops including a bookshop and a printer. This central location makes it convenient for all businesses and restaurants in Kitale, and for Kitale Museum.

There are 30 en-suite rooms, made up of 20 doubles and 10 singles. 10 of the rooms have satellite TV. The 5 deluxe rooms each contain a double and a single bed, and have a sitting area with satellite TV.

The 1st floor restaurant has a long balcony overlooking the road, and is equipped with satellite TV. It serves African dishes such as nyama choma grilled meats and stews, served with rice, ugali or chips. There is also a small bar attached to the restaurant serving beers and soft drinks, and a larger bar stocked with spirits, beers and soft drinks. The ground floor café has the same menu as the restaurant.

Parking is available on the street outside the hotel; a security guard watches the cars throughout the night.

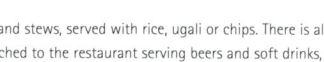

Mid Africa Hotel

Kitale

Mid Africa Hotel, Capital Plaza, Moi Avenue, Kitale, Kenya
PO Box 3339, Kitale 30200, Kenya

Tel	+25 54 31119
Mobile	+254 727 277077; +254 736 101167
Fax	+254 54 31904
E-mail	info@midafricahotel.com
Web	www.midafricahotel.com

 All major cards

 Kitale, LS & CH
20 mins

The Mid Africa Hotel is conveniently located in the centre of Kitale. The reception has a well designed information board, with details of local events, facilities and maps.

The 26 en-suite rooms are made up of singles, standard doubles, super doubles, deluxe and deluxe suites. All rooms have satellite TV, internal telephones and WiFi. The deluxe rooms are more spacious and include writing desks, while the deluxe suites have a seating area for meetings. Joyous Restaurant, decorated with local bamboo art, has a large menu with international dishes such as chicken Maryland, pork chops and spaghetti bolognaise, as well as Indian and African dishes. Joyous Bar is fully stocked, including wines, cognacs and Guinness, and serves snacks like spring rolls and chicken nuggets.

Amboseli Nyama Choma Ranch, on the rooftop, has unbroken views of Mt Elgon. It serves nyama choma grilled meats and has a wide selection of beers, wines and spirits.

The fully equipped conference facilities include small meeting rooms for between 20 and 50 pax, seminar halls for between 100 and 200 pax and a large business centre with a capacity of 300. The hotel has day and night security guards and is fitted with CCTV.

Pinewood

Kitale

Pinewood, Eldoret-Kitale Road, Kitale, Kenya
PO Box 879, Kitale 30200, Kenya

Tel	
Mobile	+254 722 310572; +254 725 429437
Fax	
E-mail	cottage@pinewoodkitale.com
Web	www.pinewoodkitale.com

Western

 Kitale, LS & CH
15 mins

Pinewood, which opened in 2002, is a large garden dotted with log cabin style cottages and a selection of restaurants and dining rondavels. There are 2 timber cottages; each has 3 en-suite bedrooms opening onto the veranda, which can be taken individually or as a whole. The rooms are furnished with TV, chairs and writing desk. There is also a campsite with bathroom facilities.

An African nyama choma restaurant serves grilled meats. There is also an Indian restaurant, a Chinese restaurant and a Pizza Garden. Pinewood Bar, a wood beamed building decorated with local art, houses a pool table, dartboard and satellite TV. International sports matches and films are shown by a projector on a wall-sized screen.

On Friday and Saturday nights, local DJs play live. On Special Supper Sundays, children's entertainment, such as face painting and games, is provided, along with affordable food and drink.

The conference centre has 2 halls that each seat 120 pax, and 3 meeting rooms that each seat 20. The centre can be taken as a whole, or in parts, and is fully equipped with conference equipment including projector and sound system. A Toyota land cruiser with driver is available for rent.

KaribuKenya Accommodation Guide

Karibuni Lodge Kitale

Karibuni Lodge, off Eldoret-Kitale Road, behind Total petrol station, Kitale
PO Box 1922, Kitale 30200, Kenya
Tel
Mobile +254 735 573798
Fax
E-mail info@karibunikitale.com
Web www.karibunikitale.com

Kitale, LS & CH
20 mins

Karibuni, meaning welcome in Swahili, is an appropriate name for this attractive and friendly lodge. In stunning raw natural landscape on the edge of Kitale, Karibuni Lodge provides comfortable accommodation and tasty home cooking. This is an ideal location for hiking, field studies, bird watching and relaxing.

The lodge has double, twin and single rooms, some with en-suite bathroom and others sharing a bathroom. There is also a dormitory and a campsite. Camping equipment and bicycles are available for hire.

Breakfast, lunch, dinner and snacks, including home baked cakes, are prepared using fresh produce from the local farms and served at a communal dining table. Meals include African and Western dishes; vegetarian, vegan and other dietary requirements can be catered for. A full selection of soft drinks, beers, wines and spirits is also available.

The lodge has a lounge with log fire, a small library, board games and a book exchange. The garden has shaded seating areas and hammocks. Excursions, ranging from a couple of hours to several days, are led by local trained guides. Visits to local homesteads, schools and markets are on offer, as well as trips to Saiwa Swamp National Park, Kakamega Forest, Marich Pass and Mt Elgon.

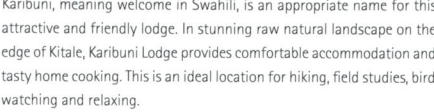

Kitale Club Kitale

Kitale Club, Eldoret-Kitale Road, Kitale, Kenya
PO Box 30, Kitale 30200, Kenya
Tel +254 54 31330; +254 54 31338
Mobile +254 726 610241; +254 733 330924
Fax +254 54 30924
E-mail ktlclub@rocketmail.com / info@kitaleclub.net
Web www.kitaleclub.net

Kitale, LS & CH
15 mins

Kitale Club, a private members' club, was established in 1924. Its 18-hole golf course was constructed in 1938. Non-members can pay a temporary membership fee to use the accommodation and facilities.

The reception has boards with the names of past chairmen, along with notices such as 'Mobile phones are strictly prohibited' and 'Firearms are not allowed'. There are 36 rooms, made up of standard and executive. The standard rooms have shared bathrooms while the executive rooms and executive cottages have en-suite bathrooms. Breakfast, lunch and dinner are served in the dining room; the food is traditional English fare, with a few Indian dishes. A dress code applies. The clubhouse's wooden panelled sitting room is decorated with maps from colonial times and glass-fronted cases of silver sporting cups. The sports bar, in dark wood, has sporting crests on the wall, next to panels inscribed with lists of past captains and championship winners. The terrace looks across the 18th hole of the golf course. Facilities, set around the lovely grounds, include a swimming pool, gym, sauna, pool table, squash courts, tennis courts and fully equipped conference centre. Reciprocal membership is offered to members of a number of local and international clubs, including the Commonwealth Trust, the Royal Bombay Yacht Club, Nairobi Club, United Kenya Club, Nanyuki Sports Club and Mombasa Club.

 Accommodation Guide

Delta Crescent
Wildlife Sanctuary

Mt Elgon

Delta Crescent Wildlife Sanctuary, Kitale-Mt Elgon Road, Kenya
PO Box 126, Endebess 30201, Kenya

Tel	
Mobile	+254 726 265306
Fax	
E-mail	nakitare@africaonline.co.ke
Web	www.deltacrescentcamps.com

Kitale, LS & CH
45 mins

This 145-acre wildlife sanctuary belongs to Captain Davis, a charismatic former pilot, who has created a fascinating, eco-friendly haven. Delta Crescent Wildlife Sanctuary has a selection of game, including white rhino, eland, Rothchild's giraffe, ostrich, antelope and colobus monkey. 254 species of birds have been recorded here.

There are 6 en-suite double rooms, each individually designed. There are 6 thatched rondavels set in lush gardens, that can be double or triple as required, with shared bathrooms. There are also 3 campsites with communal kitchen and bathroom facilities. Camping equipment, including bedding and tents, can be hired. The restaurant serves buffet or a la carte as required. The broad menu includes taste of the orient, continental cuisine, Indian, Chinese and African. The bar is well stocked with spirits, beers and soft drinks, and has a pool table and dartboard. Activities include ostrich riding, horse riding, hiking, game walks, picnics and feeding giraffe and eland. Local sites of interest include Mt Elgon and Saiwa Swamp National Parks.

The sanctuary promotes sustainable agriculture and ecotourism, and charges a small entrance fee. Lighting is powered by solar, cooking is done on bio-gas and the food served is organic. Turkeys and guinea fowl are farmed free range, and bee hives harvest honey.

Mt Elgon Lodge

Mt Elgon

Mt Elgon Lodge, 1km from Chorlim Gate, Kitale-Mt Elgon Road
PO Box 7, Endebess 30201, Kitale, Kenya

Tel	+254 20 2094643
Mobile	+254 722 875768
Fax	+254 54 30323
E-mail	mtelgonlodge@yahoo.com
Web	www.mtelgonlodge.com

Mt Elgon Ntl. Park, CH
15 mins

Chorlim House was built in 1928 by Buster and Barbara Powles, who lived in it with their family until 1969 when it was taken over by the Kenya Tourism Development Corporation and became Mt Elgon Lodge. The elegant whitewashed building, in the foothills of Mt Elgon, looks over an unkempt garden into the lush valley.

The 14 en-suite rooms are made up of doubles and triples. The rooms are sparsely furnished, and have sporadic electricity between 7pm and 10pm. Camping in the garden is permitted. The bar plays loud local music and serves warm beer. The dining room, with wooden floor, large fireplace and ornamental chandeliers, serves chicken or goat, served with rice, ugali, chapatti or potatoes.

Mt Elgon National Park is known for its botanical diversity. Over 400 species have been recorded in the area, including the rare Ardisiandra wettsteinii, Carduus afromontanus, Echinops hoehnelii, Ranunculus keniensis and Romulea keniensis.

Activities include primate and bird watching, cave exploration and hiking to Endebess Bluff and Koitoboss Peak. Vehicle circuits lead to animal viewing areas and the caves. 4WD vehicles are recommended all year, and are essential in the wet season. A guide book for the walking trails is available at the park gate.

KWS, Koitoboss Guest House Mt Elgon

KWS, Koitoboss Guest House, Chorlim Gate, Mt Elgon National Park, Kenya
Kenya Wildlife Service, PO Box 40241, Nairobi 00100, Kenya

Tel	+254 20 6000800; +254 20 6002345; +254 20 3991000
Mobile	+254 726 610508; +254 726 610509; +254 736 663421
Fax	+254 20 6003792
E-mail	kws@kws.go.ke / reservations@kws.go.ke
Web	www.kws.go.ke

      Mt Elgon Ntl. Park, CH
                         10 mins

Koitoboss Guest House is a self-catering house situated at Chorlim Gate of Mt Elgon National Park. It is owned and operated by Kenya Wildlife Service, KWS.

The house has 3 bedrooms, each furnished with 2 double beds. There are 2 bathrooms and a large sitting room adjoined to a dining room. The kitchen is equipped with gas stove, fridge, cooking utensils, cutlery, crockery and glassware. A barbeque area is outside the house. A resident caretaker provides bed linen, towels, soap and loo paper. There is electricity between 6pm and 10.30pm. Shower water is heated by a kuni booster, or fire.

Mt Elgon National Park is known for its diverse ecosystem including wet montane bamboo forests and afro-alpine moorlands. It is also famed for its bat-filled caves, where troglodyte elephants come to mine salt. Wildlife includes the rare oribi, aardvark, genet cat and leopard, as well as the more populous elephant, buffalo and waterbuck. More than 240 species of birds have been recorded here.

Activities include hiking the Kitum, Ngwarisha, Chepnyalil and Makingeni Cave Trails, as well as climbing to the peak of Mt Elgon. The park gates are open from 6am to 7pm; park fees must be paid in cash at the gate.

KWS, Kapkuro Bandas Mt Elgon

KWS, Kapkuro Bandas, 1km from Chorlim Gate, Mt Elgon National Park
Kenya Wildlife Service, PO Box 40241, Nairobi 00100, Kenya

Tel	+254 20 6000800; +254 20 6002345; +254 20 3991000
Mobile	+254 726 610508; +254 726 610509; +254 736 663421
Fax	+254 20 6003792
E-mail	kws@kws.go.ke / reservations@kws.go.ke
Web	www.kws.go.ke

      Mt Elgon Ntl. Park, CH
                         15 mins

Kapkuro Bandas are self-catering cottages located in Mt Elgon National Park, 1km from Chorlim Gate. They are owned and managed by Kenya Wildlife Service, KWS.

There are 2 cottages, with 2 self-contained bandas in each cottage. Each banda has 1 bedroom furnished with double and single bed. There is also a bathroom, a sitting room and a kitchen equipped with gas stove, kitchen utensils, cutlery, crockery and glassware. An outside dining area has table, chairs and barbeque. Shower water is heated by a kuni booster, or fire. A resident caretaker provides kerosene lamps, blankets and pillows. A small kiosk sells basic items.

Mt Elgon National Park is known for its diverse ecosystem, including wet montane bamboo forests and afro-alpine moorlands, and its bat-filled caves, where troglodyte elephants come to mine salt. Wildlife includes the rare oribi, aardvark, genet cat and leopard, as well as elephant, buffalo and waterbuck. More than 240 species of birds have been recorded here. Activities include hiking the Kitum, Ngwarisha, Chepnyalil and Makingeni Cave Trails, as well as climbing to the peak of Mt Elgon. The park gates are open from 6am to 7pm; park fees must be paid in cash at the gate.

Park Villa Hotel

Webuye

Park Villa Hotel, Webuye, Kenya
PO Box 1000, Webuye 50205, Kenya

Tel	+254 20 2036433
Mobile	+254 733 722505
Fax	
E-mail	parkvilla2009@yahoo.co.uk
Web	

Kitale, LS & CH
1 hr

Park Villa Hotel offers secluded accommodation in an attractive garden. The 18 en-suite rooms are in 2 wings overlooking the gardens. All rooms have double and single bed, built in cupboards and dressing table; most have TV. The 8 cottages are more spacious and all have TV. The 2 suites have, in addition, sitting rooms with sofa and armchairs. The 1 villa has 2 double bedrooms, 2 bathrooms with bath and shower, an extra WC, a sitting room leading into an open plan dining room and a kitchen that can be equipped with crockery, cutlery and kitchen utensils from the restaurant on request.

The restaurant, with red checked tablecloths and satellite TV, serves buffet and a selection of mixed grills, curries, salads and snacks. The main bar, the garden bar and the lounge pub are well stocked with soft drinks, spirits, wines and beers.

The small conference room seats 40 pax and the larger seats 100. Some equipment is provided, confirm on booking.

The swimming pool has a baby pool, sunbathing terrace, changing rooms and a modern sauna. Nyama choma grilled meats and barbecue are served by the poolside. Visitors not staying at the hotel can use the facilities for a small charge.

Eldoret Wagon Hotel

Eldoret

Eldoret Wagon Hotel, Elgeyo Road, off Oloo Street, Eldoret, Kenya
PO Box 2408, Eldoret 30100, Kenya

Tel	+254 53 62270-1
Mobile	+254 727 504364; +254 721 544806
Fax	+254 53 62400
E-mail	wagonhotel@africaonline.co.ke
Web	www.eldoretwagonhotel.co.ke / www.segosafarilodge.co.ke

Eldoret, LS & CH & Intl.
30 mins

The Great Trek, which took place at the end of the 19th century and in the early 20th century was an epic journey that finally ended at what is now Eldoret. The Boers left South Africa after the Boer War, sailed from the Cape to Mombasa, and trekked overland, through treacherous lands and across the Great Rift Valley, by ox wagon.

Eldoret Wagon Hotel, previously The Wagon Wheel Hotel, was the first hotel in the area. It was built as a private members' club for senior railway staff, and is adorned with memorabilia from the wagons of the Great Trek. The 102 en-suite rooms are made up of doubles and singles. All rooms are equipped with telephone, writing desk and luggage rack.

The dining room, built like a railway carriage complete with elongated arched roof, serves breakfast, lunch and dinner. The hotel also has an inside bar, an outside bar, a games room with pool tables and a casino. The fully equipped conference hall can seat 70 pax. The business centre is available for conference support. Functions including wedding receptions and cocktail parties can be organised in the garden. Trips to sister hotel, Sego Safari Lodge in Kerio Valley, can be booked here.

Hotel Sirikwa

Eldoret

Hotel Sirikwa, Elgeyo Road, off Oloo Street, Eldoret, Kenya
PO Box 3361, Eldoret 30200, Kenya

Tel	+254 53 2063614; +254 53 2062499
Mobile	+254 728 680000; +254 734 680000
Fax	+254 53 2061018
E-mail	info@hotelsirikwa.com / sirikwahotel@yahoo.com
Web	www.hotelsirikwa.com

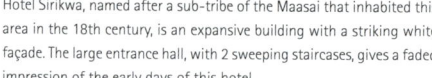

Eldoret, LS & CH & Intl.
30 mins

Hotel Sirikwa, named after a sub-tribe of the Maasai that inhabited this area in the 18th century, is an expansive building with a striking white façade. The large entrance hall, with 2 sweeping staircases, gives a faded impression of the early days of this hotel.

The 105 en-suite rooms are made up of single, double, superior and family rooms. They are set along dim corridors on 4 floors. All rooms are equipped with aircon, satellite TV, digital safe and telephone. The 6 VIP suites and the presidential suite are more spacious.

Sitatunga Restaurant serves buffet breakfast and a la carte lunch and dinner. Meals can also be served on the terrace by the pool. Theme dinners include an African dinner on Tuesday and a bush dinner on Thursday. Saturday lunch is a barbecue by the pool and Sunday lunch is curry. The fully equipped conference facilities include Kerio Lounge Bar, which seats 60 pax, and Baraza Conference Hall which seats 150.

The swimming pool, surrounded by a terracotta sunbathing terrace and whitewashed arches, has a children's section. The garden has a playground with swings. The hotel also has a gift shop, a beauty salon and a travel agent.

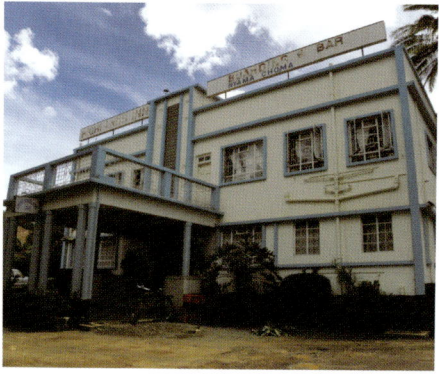

White Highlands Inn

Eldoret

White Highlands Inn, opp AP Line, Elgeyo Road, Eldoret, Kenya
PO Box 2189, Eldoret 30100, Kenya

Tel	
Mobile	+254 734 818955; +254 721 407128
Fax	
E-mail	whitehighlandsinn@gmail.com
Web	

Eldoret, LS & CH & Intl.
30 mins

In a leafy compound just outside the centre of Eldoret, White Highlands Inn is a whitewashed building with blue trimmings. This location is convenient for all shops, restaurants and businesses of Eldoret, while also being peaceful and quiet.

There are 25 en-suite double rooms and 1 en-suite twin room. All the rooms have king size beds, satellite TV, work table and chair. The bathrooms have both shower and bath.

Breakfast, lunch and dinner are served in the dining room, and include African dishes and international favourites. The inside bar is well stocked with soft drinks, beers, and spirits. The outside bar, with timber structure and rustic atmosphere, has a satellite TV for sports matches and a pool table.

The pleasant garden is suitable for business functions and wedding receptions. Marquees, tables and chairs can be hired, and outdoor buffets can be arranged. Conferences of up to 25 pax can be organised. Equipment is not provided, and should be brought be participants or hired locally. The children's playground has swings, slides, climbing frame and candy shop. Every weekend, activities and games are organised for children, including bouncy castle, inflatable slides and face painting.

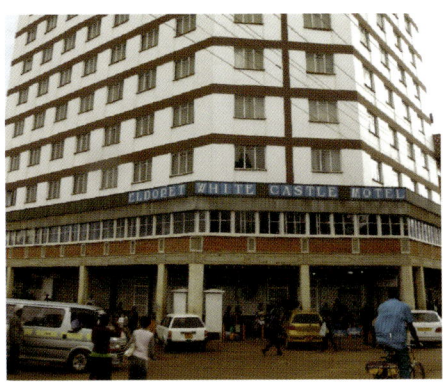

White Castle Motel Eldoret

White Castle Motel, Uganda Road, Eldoret, Kenya
PO Box 566, Eldoret 30100, Kenya

Tel	+254 53 2033095; +254 53 2062773; +254 53 2061362
Mobile	+254 711 848903; +254 720 828492
Fax	+254 53 62209
E-mail	eldoretwhitecastlemotel@yahoo.com
Web	

 VISA, MasterCard
Amex, JCB, KCB

 Eldoret, LS & CH & Intl.
30 mins

A prominent white building in the centre of town, the White Castle Motel offers accommodation within easy reach of all the shops, restaurants and businesses of Eldoret. Its higher floors have views of the town, the Sergoit Hill and the Nandi Hills.

There are 118 en-suite double and twin rooms. The rooms are simply furnished and equipped with telephones connected to reception. The bathrooms have both shower and bath.

The restaurant offers local and international dishes. The Main Bar, attached to the restaurant, is stocked with soft drinks, beers and spirits. The Pool Bar has a pool table. The Terrace Bar and Nyama Choma Ranch on the top floor serves drinks and a selection of grilled meats, and looks out over Eldoret town.

The health club provides massage. It is also equipped with a sauna and steam room. The conference hall seats up to 400 pax. Equipment is not provided and should be brought by the participants or hired locally.

Sam's Disco has bright lights, red bench seats, mirrored columns and pumping music. It is the venue for local beauty pageants and other functions.

Klique Hotel Eldoret

Klique Hotel, Oginga Odinga Street, Eldoret, Kenya
PO Box 949, Eldoret 30100, Kenya

Tel	
Mobile	+254 732 060903
Fax	
E-mail	info@kliquehotel.com
Web	www.kliquehotel.com

 Eldoret, LS & CH & Intl.
30 mins

Klique Hotel, conveniently located on Eldoret's main business street, is a tall modern building. The hotel offers a variety of styles of accommodation between its secure underground car park and its rooftop terrace.

The 30 en-suite rooms are made up of single, double and deluxe rooms. All rooms are equipped with TV and internet connection.

The restaurant, with light contemporary décor, has a wide international menu including chicken kiev, pizzas, curries, stews, steaks, seafood and platters of grilled meat. The bar, attached to the restaurant, has a full selection of beers and spirits. Guests can also choose to eat in the more private dining room.

Arorr Hall, the main conference room, seats up to 300 pax, and is equipped with TV, video, projector, PA system, internet and telephone. In addition to conferences, the hall can be used for workshops, meetings, wedding receptions, press conferences and dances.

The Orion and Chrysler rooms, next to the rooftop terrace, seat 40 and 20 respectively. They are available for meetings or for private dining.

Poa Place Resort — Eldoret

Poa Place Resort, Kaptagat Road, off Uganda Road, Eldoret, Kenya
PO Box 3273, Eldoret 30100, Kenya

Tel	+254 53 2032014; +254 53 2030685; +254 53 2032417
Mobile	+254 703 129910; +254 734 129990
Fax	+254 53 2032014
E-mail	info@poaplace.co.ke
Web	www.poaplace.co.ke

VISA, MasterCard, Amex

Eldoret, LS & CH & Intl. 30 mins

Its name, Swahili for relaxed or cool, aptly describes the atmosphere of Poa Place Resort. Attractive cottages are dotted around gardens garnished with water features and fishponds.

The 15 en-suite cottages are made up of 7 standard, 2 deluxe, 2 VIP and 4 family suites. All the cottages are thatched, with wooden floors, and open into tranquil gardens. The family suites include a spacious sitting room. Poa Bar and Restaurant serves an international menu in a dining room with tall garden-facing windows. Rock Bay Bar is set in a cavern with natural wooden furniture, chunky bar stools and satellite TV. The adjoining restaurant, reached by a small bridge over a trickling stream, serves table d'hote on a raised platform overlooking the fishpond. The fully equipped conference room seats 40 pax. The gardens make an ideal location for parties, functions and wedding receptions.

The amusement park, with nyama choma grilled meats and fully stocked bar, has a playground with merry-go-round and swings, and offers water adventures including flume rides and torpedo tubes.

The Nature and Culture Centre contains homesteads depicting the different communities of Kenya, and exhibits artefacts from the tribes. Indigenous snakes, crocodiles, birds and monkeys are also kept here.

The Nobel Conference Centre — Eldoret

The Noble Conference Centre, Kapsoya, off Nairobi Road, Eldoret, Kenya
PO Box 6516, Eldoret 30100, Kenya

Tel	
Mobile	+254 731 418309; +254 716 291815
Fax	
E-mail	info@thenoble.co.ke
Web	www.thenoble.co.ke

VISA

Eldoret, LS & CH & Intl. 30 mins

On the outskirts of Eldoret, The Nobel Conference Centre has accommodation and conference facilities in attractive gardens. The hotel and conference centre opened in 2008.

There are 30 en-suite rooms, made up of 14 standard and 16 deluxe. All rooms have silent night spring beds, writing table and cupboard. The Noble Restaurant serves both international and local dishes, and has an a la carte menu, as well as serving buffet. No alcohol is served. The Noble is Christian and is an ideal location for meetings of Christian organisations, businesses and schools.

The Noble has a range of venues suitable for corporate events, conferences, seminars, weddings, parties and functions. The business centre is fully equipped with internet and secretarial services. Mzalendo Hall, the largest conference hall, seats up to 300 pax. Marks Hall and Mathews Hall both seat 100. Zeddy Boardroom seats 30. Integrity Gardens is also available for weddings and parties. There are bandas dotted around the gardens suitable for small meetings, or private meals. There is also a swimming pool. The Noble has plentiful secure parking. There is WiFi throughout.

Eldoret Club

Eldoret

Eldoret Club, Nandi Road, off Eldoret-Nairobi Highway, opp hospice
PO Box 78, Eldoret 30100, Kenya

Tel	+254 53 2031395; +254 53 2031249; +254 53 2061127
Mobile	+254 725 736066; +254 734 330224
Fax	+254 53 2063292
E-mail	info@eldoretclub.co.ke
Web	www.eldoretclub.co.ke

Eldoret, LS & CH & Intl.
30 mins

Eldoret Club, a private members club, was established in 1924, in large manicured grounds on the edge of Eldoret. Non-members can pay a temporary membership fee to use the accommodation and facilities.

There are 24 en-suite rooms, each equipped with telephone and TV. Breakfast, lunch and dinner are served in the clubhouse's dining room, and food is traditional English fare. A snack menu is available in the bar and lounge, on the veranda and by the pool.

The clubhouse, a graceful whitewashed building, has wood panelled interiors and boards inscribed with lists of past chairmen. The library is open every evening, and contains a selection of adults' and children's books. The TV room has leather sofas and satellite TV. There is also a snooker room, a well equipped gym, a sauna and a steam room. Mobile phones are prohibited and a dress code applies.

The large grounds include a 9-hole golf course, with mature trees and flowering shrubs. There are also tennis courts, a squash court, a badminton court and a swimming pool surrounded by attractive gardens.

Reciprocal membership is offered to members of a number of local and international clubs, including the Commonwealth Trust, the Royal Bombay Yacht Club, Nairobi Club, United Kenya Club, Nanyuki Sports Club and Mombasa Club.

Kerio View

Iten

Kerio View, Eldoret-Iten Road, Iten, Kenya
PO Box 51, Iten 30700, Kenya

Tel	+254 20 2039559; +254 20 3539570
Mobile	+254 722 781916; +254 720 672939
Fax	
E-mail	info@kerioview.com / bookings@kerioview.com
Web	www.kerioview.com

VISA, MasterCard

Eldoret, LS & CH & Intl.
30 mins

Western

From this idyllic spot on the escarpment, Kerio View has panoramic views over the stunning Kerio Valley. Its glass-fronted restaurant and cottages ensure magnificent views on all sides.

There are 28 en-suite rooms, including 16 rooms built in 2009, made up of singles, doubles and triples. The rooms are dotted about the gardens and have glass fronts facing the valley. All rooms have polished wooden floors, are furnished with armchairs, coffee tables and telephones and decorated with art done by an artist from Kericho. The restaurant has a continental menu including ginger and carrot soup, honey-glazed gammon ham, chateaubriand and chocolate mousse. There are also weekly specials including an eat-all-you-can barbecue. Private dining booths in the garden overlook the valley.

The conference hall seats 65 pax. Sports matches and marathons are shown on a large screen in the hall. Because of its altitude, Kerio View is popular with the local athletes and marathon runners this area is famed for. There is a fully equipped gym. From January to March, paragliders jump from the hills; tandem jumps are available.

Excursions and safaris can be booked here, notably trips to Cheblock Gorge, Lake Baringo, Kapenguria, the Marich Pass and Lake Turkana.

 Accommodation Guide

Lelin Campsite and Bandas

Kerio Valley

Lelin Campsite and Bandas, Iten-Kabernet Road, Kerio Valley, Kenya
PO Box 589, Iten 30700, Kenya

Tel	
Mobile	+254 722 900848; +254 725 319771
Fax	
E-mail	lelincampsite@yahoo.com
Web	www.lelincampsite.com

    Eldoret, LS & CH & Intl.
1 hr

In the stunning Kerio Valley, Lelin Campsite and Bandas has a selection of rustic accommodation. The campsite offers lovely views and provides the perfect place from which to hike through the valley and up the escarpment. The area is known for prolific birdlife and striking craggy terrain. There are 5 en-suite bandas, made up of doubles and twins. The bandas all have hot water showers. There is also a campsite with bathroom and kitchen facilities. The restaurant has an a la carte menu, and offers a selection of international and Kenyan dishes. The bar is stocked with soft drinks, beers and spirits. From the bar, there is an outstanding view of the Rift Valley and Lake Kamorok. Ecotourism Society of Kenya gave

Lelin Campsite and Bandas a community based organisation award, CBO. Activities include hikes of various lengths. A nature walk through Kerio Valley takes approximately 3½ hours. A cliff walk to the top of the escarpment takes approximately 2 hours. Local sites of interest include Lake Kamorok and Cheblock Gorge. Visitors can clamber down the rocky sides of the gorge and walk along its base. Lelin Campsite is about 500 meters from the road which joins Iten to Kabernet. It is about 5km from Iten and 40km from Eldoret.

Sego Safari Lodge

Kerio Valley

Sego Safari Lodge, Emsea-Flourspar Road, Kerio Valley, Kenya
PO Box 2408, Eldoret 30100, Kenya

Tel	+254 53 21399
Mobile	+254 722 407470
Fax	+254 53 21429
E-mail	wagonhotel@africaonline.co.ke
Web	www.segosafarilodge.co.ke / www.eldoretwagonhotel.com

    Eldoret, LS & CH & Intl.
1 hr

In the lush Kerio Valley, Sego Safari Lodge offers a tranquil escape, off the beaten track. This bird watchers' paradise is within easy reach of Rimoi Game Reserve and Cheblock Gorge.
The 10 en-suite rooms are made up of 7 twin rooms, with 2 queen size beds, and 3 family rooms, with a double and a single bed.
The lodge serves fresh fruit, including oranges, paw paw, watermelon and bananas, from its own orchard. The milk, meat, eggs and grain come from nearby farms, and ensure that meals are fresh and nutritious. Mineral water is bottled locally, at a spring in Molo.

Wananchi Bar has picturesque views of the forested hills and valleys, and serves a range of soft drinks, beers, wines and spirits. The Pool Table Bar, with satellite TV, is also fully stocked. Conferences, cocktail parties and formal dinners can be arranged for groups of up to 20 pax.
Activities include bird watching, nature walks to see the crocodiles of Cheblock Gorge and visits to local homesteads, advance booking necessary. Special rates are available for guests who also stay at sister hotel, Eldoret Wagon Hotel, in Eldoret.

Naiberi River Campsite & Resort

Eldoret

Naiberi River Campsite & Resort, Kaptagat Road, nr Eldoret, Kenya
PO Box 142, Eldoret 30100, Kenya

Tel	+254 20 3550051-2
Mobile	
Fax	+254 53 2062916
E-mail	campsite@naiberi.com
Web	www.naiberi.com

VISA, MasterCard, Amex, JCB   Eldoret, LS & CH & Intl. 45 mins

Set in tropical gardens that slope down to the river, Naiberi River Campsite and Resort has an appealing variety of accommodation and facilities. Stone paths wind through the lush gardens, linking the cottages and cabins with the restaurant and swimming pool.

The 11 stone cottages, all en-suite, have thatched roofs, cedar wood floors and cool natural fabrics. The 10 en-suite log cabins are built with timber offcuts and local palms, ensuring as little impact on the environment as possible. There are 2 dormitories, 1 with 20 bunk beds and en-suite bathroom, the other with 12 bunk beds and outside bathroom. There is also a campsite with bathroom facilities.

A stone tunnel decorated with plants and hanging lanterns leads to the Cave Restaurant, adorned with waterfalls, streams and wooden bridges. The Indian chef serves Indian curries like kheema, masala and tikka, as well as international favourites. Guests can also choose to eat at the pool bar or in the shady rondavels dotted about the gardens.

A waterfall tumbles into the freeform swimming pool; indigenous trees shade the sunbathing terrace and the pool bar. Other facilities include a volleyball pitch, massage and beauty salon, gift shop and cyber café.

Twiga Resort

Eldoret

Twiga Resort, Kaptagat Road, nr Eldoret, Kenya

Tel	
Mobile	+254 731 358840
Fax	
E-mail	
Web	

                Eldoret, LS & CH & Intl. 45 mins

The highlands of Kenya, particularly the hills around Eldoret, are home to many of the most famous marathon runners of our time. The high altitude makes an ideal training ground for athletes and the area has been used by Kenyan runners during marathon training for many years. Twiga Resort, meaning Giraffe Resort in Swahili, started life as an athletes' training centre. Now owned by Albert Chepkurui, a Kenyan-born athlete who runs for Qatar, the centre has been developed into a rural resort. There are 20 en-suite rooms, in 2 blocks, facing each other across a courtyard. Originally used by athletes during training sessions, these rooms are simply furnished and are each equipped with TV.

There are 3 newly built cottages, made up of double bedroom, bathroom and living room with TV. Each cottage is self-contained, and looks out on the attractive gardens of the resort

African dishes including nyama choma grilled meats are served in the thatched rondavels in the garden. Twiga Resort is 15km from Eldoret on the Kaptagat Road, and is 1km beyond the end of the tarmac.

Western

Relax Inn, Simba Village Eldoret

Relax Inn, Simba Village, nr showground, Eldoret-Kapsabet Road, Kenya
PO Box 3592, Eldoret 30100, Kenya
Tel
Mobile   +254 724 391541; +254 724 712635; +254 720 839473
Fax
E-mail   thesimbavillage@yahoo.com / info@relaxinnhotel.org
Web   www.relaxinnhotel.org

    Eldoret, LS & CH & Intl.
15 mins

Entered beneath an arch of tusks, Relax Inn, Simba Village has a quirky collection of murals and statues set in landscaped gardens. The inn has friendly staff and budget accommodation. It is situated next to the showground between Eldoret town and Eldoret airport.

There are 70 en-suite rooms, made up of standard and executive. The rooms are single, double and twin. All rooms have aircon; room service is available. The executive rooms are more spacious, and include telephone and satellite TV. The restaurant is open 24 hours. Breakfast and lunch are buffets. For dinner, there is a selection of international and local dishes, such as chicken curry, grilled fish, kinyegi and nyama choma grilled meats. Fruit juices, soft drinks and herbal infusions are served; alcohol is not on offer.

There are 3 conference halls. The largest seats 150 pax, another seats 50 and the smallest seats 40. The halls are equipped with PA system and LCD projector. The gardens are formally designed, and dotted with brightly painted models of Kenyan animals. On a lawn, there are tables and chairs, beneath shade umbrellas. The gardens are available for weddings, functions and parties. There is plentiful secure parking and a carwash service.

Marriott Hotel Eldoret

Marriott Hotel, 5km from Eldoret, Eldoret-Kapsabet Road, Kenya
PO Box 7155, Eldoret 30100, Kenya
Tel   +254 20 2047812
Mobile   +254 720 781818; +254 727 946536
Fax
E-mail   marriothotel82@yahoo.com
Web

    Eldoret, LS & CH & Intl.
10 mins

The Marriott Hotel, which is not affiliated to the international chain of hotels of that name, opened in 2007. The hotel styles itself a country hotel in an athletics town. It is set in manicured gardens between Eldoret town and Eldoret airport.

There are 51 en-suite rooms, made up of 5 twins, 5 doubles and 41 singles. All rooms are equipped with satellite TV and mosquito net. The doubles and twins are more spacious and have both bathtub and shower. The restaurant has an international menu, including whole Lake Victoria tilapia, spaghetti bolognaise, curries, soups and sandwiches. Meals can be served in the restaurant or in the garden. Nyama choma grilled meats are served at seating booths in the garden. The bar, in the corner of the garden, serves soft drinks, beers and spirits.

The largest conference hall seats 100 pax and the other seats 70. The meeting room seats 20 pax. Conference equipment including PA system, projector, TV and video is available. The hotel welcomes business meetings, conferences and training seminars. Its location makes it convenient for groups from Eldoret, as well as for groups who are flying in.

Siaya Guest House

Kakamega

Siaya Guest House, Kakamega-Webuye Highway, Kakamega, Kenya
PO Box 1325, Kakamega 50100, Kenya

Tel	+254 56 31254
Mobile	+254 721 759820
Fax	
E-mail	info@siayaguesthouse.com
Web	www.siayaguesthouse.com

Kisumu, LS & CH
1 hr

On the Kakamega-Webuye Highway, Siaya Guest House offers modern accommodation in a convenient location. The guesthouse, overlooking Masinde Muliro Gardens, is within easy reach of the town's banks, shops and businesses, and a short drive from the Crying Stone of Ilesi and Kakamega Forest. There are 36 en-suite rooms. The 14 standard and 15 superior rooms, made up of doubles and twins, have thick duvets, bathroom amenities from the African Collection, TV and balcony. The 4 executive suites have, in addition, telephone, kettle and desk, and their bathrooms have both bath and shower. The 3 unique canvas rooms, with tent style walls and zip doors, have telephone and balcony. The restaurant, with wicker chairs and tables, serves buffets and has an international menu including nyama choma grilled meats, burgers, sandwiches, pizzas, soups and steaks, and an Indian menu including butter chicken, methi palak, kheema and dhal. The snack menu includes samosas, fish fingers and fish bhajias. The bar, with satellite TV, has a selection of teas, coffees and cocktails.

The fully tiled conference hall on the top floor seats 100 pax. Conference equipment is not provided. The guesthouse can organise retreats, seminars, teambuilding and cocktail parties. Airport transfers are also offered.

Sheywe Centre

Kakamega

Sheywe Centre, Kefinco Road, off Kakamega-Webuye Highway, Kakamega
PO Box 62, Malava 50103, Kenya

Tel	+254 56 30320
Mobile	+254 703 624620
Fax	+254 56 30320
E-mail	sheywe@yahoo.com
Web	

Kisumu, LS & CH
1 hr

Named after a species of local grass, the Sheywe Centre is on a large secure compound with plentiful parking. Conveniently located just off the main road through Kakamega, the centre is close to the shops and businesses of the town and within easy reach of Masinde Muliro University. The 35 en-suite rooms are made up of standard, deluxe and apartments. The standard rooms have a double and single bed. The deluxe rooms are more spacious and are also equipped with a TV. The apartments have 2 bedrooms, 2 bathrooms and a living area with TV that opens into a simple kitchenette.

The restaurant offers a range of international dishes such as macaroni cheese, chicken masala, goulash, roast chicken, sandwiches and nyama choma grilled meats, and can also provide buffets. Food can be served on the terrace or in the more private rondavels in the garden.

There are 3 conference halls, the largest of which seats 400 pax. A boardroom is available for meetings. Conference facilities including audio visual equipment and photocopy are provided.

The centre is ideally set up for executive meetings and corporate training. The AMREF Kakamega office is situated in this compound.

Transfers from and to Kisumu airport can be arranged.

Kakamega Sports Club

Kakamega Sports Club, Khasakhala Road, Kakamega, Kenya
PO Box 58, Kakamega 50100, Kenya

Tel	+254 56 30968
Mobile	+254 710 331377
Fax	
E-mail	kakamegasportsclub@gmail.com
Web	

 VISA from Commercial Bank Barclays Bank   Kisumu, LS & CH 1 hr

This long, low building started life as the official building of the Provincial Commissioner. In about 1932, it became the Kakamega Sports Club. The club is a private members club, but non-members are permitted to pay a temporary membership fee to use the accommodation.

The dark wood entrance hall is hung with boards inscribed with lists of past chairmen, patrons and golf captains. The well stocked bar has a display cabinet of silver sporting cups, and is furnished with leather and dark wood chairs.

There are 8 en-suite double rooms, furnished with desk and chairs. There are 2 blocks, containing 2 rooms each, with interconnecting doors suitable for families, and there is 1 block of 4 unconnected rooms.

The terrace, set with tables and chairs, overlooks the 18-hole golf course. Golf scorecards are issued to all players detailing local rules, dress code and etiquette, as well as instructions on what to do about obstacles such as animal tracks. The club also has tennis courts and dartboards. Noticeboards around the club list ongoing competitions, fixtures and prizes. Every Friday night is Mbuzi Night, when traditional nyama choma grilled meats are served.

Golf Hotel

Golf Hotel, Khasakhala Road, Kakamega, Kenya
PO Box 118, Kakamega 50100, Kenya

Tel	+254 56 30150-1; +254 56 31044
Mobile	+254 728 833974; +254 731 338705; +254 771 808094
Fax	+254 56 30155
E-mail	info@golfhotelkakamega.com
Web	www.golfhotelkakamega.com

 VISA, MasterCard, Amex, KCB   Kisumu, LS & CH 1 hr

A plaque at the entrance of the Golf Hotel states that it was opened in 1984 by His Excellency the Hon. Daniel T Arap Moi CGH, MP. The long low building looks out on smooth lawns and a swimming pool.

The 60 en-suite rooms are made up of singles, doubles and triples. The rooms are equipped with telephone, internet connection, satellite TV and mosquito nets. There are also 2 executive suites with bedroom, bathroom and living room.

Turaco Restaurant serves international dishes such as beuf bourguignon and escalope of pork. Hunter's Cave Zone serves steaks. There is also a snack menu, served by the pool or in the rondavels in the garden, which includes chicken drumsticks, omelettes, pasta, salads and sandwiches. The bar serves a selection of soft drinks, beers and spirits. The gardens are available for private parties and wedding receptions.

The conference hall seats 400 pax, and can be bisected by sliding doors. There is also a hall that seats 100 and a hall that seats 50. The conference rooms are all fully equipped. The swimming pool has a sunbathing terrace and a children's play area with swings, slide and merry-go-round. Barbecues are served at the poolside every weekend.

KWS, Isukuti Houses

Kakamega Forest Ntl. Reserve

KWS, Isukuti Houses, Kakamega Forest National Reserve, Kenya
Kenya Wildlife Service, PO Box 40241, Nairobi 00100, Kenya

Tel	+254 20 6000800; +254 20 6002345; +254 20 3991000
Mobile	+254 726 610508; +254 726 610509; +254 736 663421
Fax	+254 20 6003792
E-mail	kws@kws.go.ke / reservations@kws.go.ke
Web	www.kws.go.ke

      Kisumu, LS & CH
1.5 hrs

Isukuti Houses are self-catering cottages situated at the Park HQ in Kakamega Forest National Reserve. They are owned and managed by Kenya Wildlife Service, KWS.

There are 2 cottages, each containing 2 self-contained bandas that can be taken together or separately. Each banda has an en-suite bedroom with twin beds, a sitting room, a dining area and a small kitchen equipped with gas stove, kitchen utensils, cutlery, crockery and glassware. Shower water is heated by a kuni booster, or fire. A resident caretaker provides kerosene lamps, blankets and pillows.

Rare game in the reserve includes the clawless otter, giant water shrew, tree pangolin and bush pig. Over 300 bird species have been recorded, some of which are found nowhere else in the country, as well as 27 species of snakes. Other attractions include massive trees, scenic spots and waterfalls. Activities include forest walking, hiking and primate, bird and butterfly watching.

Kakamega Forest National Reserve is 419km from Nairobi, via Nakuru and Kapsabet. The park gates are open from 6am to 7pm; park fees must be paid in cash at the gate.

KWS, Udo Bandas

Kakamega Forest Ntl. Reserve

KWS, Udo Bandas, Kakamega Forest National Reserve, Kenya
Kenya Wildlife Service, PO Box 40241, Nairobi 00100, Kenya

Tel	+254 20 6000800; +254 20 6002345; +254 20 3991000
Mobile	+254 726 610508; +254 726 610509; +254 736 663421
Fax	+254 20 6003792
E-mail	kws@kws.go.ke / reservations@kws.go.ke
Web	www.kws.go.ke

     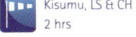 Kisumu, LS & CH
2 hrs

Udo Bandas are self-catering rondavels situated in Kakamega Forest National Reserve. They are owned and managed by Kenya Wildlife Service, KWS.

There are 5 bandas, set in a clearing in the forest. Each banda is a small, thatched rondavel containing 2 single beds with mosquito nets. A resident caretaker provides kerosene lamps, blankets and pillows. Basic bathroom facilities and kitchen facilities are external. There is also a campsite. Guests should bring their own food, firewood and drinking water.

Rare game in the reserve includes the clawless otter, giant water shrew, tree pangolin and bush pig. Over 300 bird species have been recorded, some of which are found nowhere else in the country, as well as 27 species of snakes. Other attractions include massive trees, scenic spots and waterfalls. Activities include forest walking, hiking and primate, bird and butterfly watching.

Kakamega Forest National Reserve is 419km from Nairobi, via Nakuru and Kapsabet. The park gates are open from 6am to 7pm; park fees must be paid in cash at the gate.

KEEP, Isacheno Bandas Kakamega Forest Ntl. Reserve

KEEP, Isecheno Bandas, Isecheno Station, Kakamega Forest Ntl. Reserve
PO Box 11, Shinyalu 50107, Kenya
Tel
Mobile +254 735 610095; +254 734 535600
Fax
E-mail keeporg@yahoo.com
Web www.keeporg.cjb.net

   Kisumu, LS & CH
2 hrs

Established in 1995 and registered as a Community Based Organisation, CBO, in 1999, Kakamega Environmental Education Programme aims to educate people about the fragile Kakamega Rainforest ecosystem. The forest is the only surviving remnant of the Guineo-Congolian type of forest in Kenya. It is rated as the 3rd priority area for conservation by the World Conservation Union.

KEEP owns and operates the Isecheno Bandas and Campsite. These are based at Isecheno, the KEEP HQ in the southern part of the forest. Visitors can stay in a banda, rent a tent or pitch their own tents. The campsite has bathroom facilities, a restaurant and a gift shop selling local artefacts.

KEEP offers guiding services; their guides are well trained and understand the natural history of the forest, and its biodiversity. KEEP has initiated a number of programmes designed to preserve the local environment. They have a tree nursery, a snake park, an animal farm and a butterfly farm. They run environmental education courses and health education courses. They produce briquettes, as an alternative to charcoal, and keep bees. All their programmes are designed to protect, conserve and use Kakamega Forest resources sustainably. KEEP also facilitates research on the forest's biodiversity and publicises its findings both nationally and internationally.

Rondo Retreat Kakamega Forest Ntl. Reserve

Rondo Retreat, Khayega-Shinyalu-Kapsabet Road, Kenya
PO Box 2153, Kakamega 50100, Kenya
Tel +254 56 30268
Mobile +254 733 299149; +254 735 894474
Fax +254 56 31057
E-mail rondo@trinityfellowship.or.ke
Web www.rondoretreat.com

   Kisumu, LS & CH
2 hrs

Rondo was built by a saw miller at the base of a towering Elgon Olive in 1948, and left to the Christian Council of Kenya in 1961. In 1966, the Trinity Fellowship took over and ran it as a youth centre and orphanage. Now a hospitable homestead, it has become Rondo Retreat.

The homestead consists of the main house and 5 cottages. There are 15 en-suite double rooms, and 3 double rooms with shared bathroom. The rooms are creatively decorated, with a mix of antique prints and photographs, and local paintings, crafts and fabrics. This Christian sanctuary offers hiking, bird watching, research and peaceful contemplation. Home cooked breakfast, lunch and candlelit dinner are served in the dining room. No alcohol is served.

The chapel, on the edge of the garden overlooking the forest, is ideal for individual prayer, congregational services, meetings, seminars and small conferences.

The undulating gardens are a delightful mix of lawn, flowers, streams, fishponds and forest. Birds and butterflies, flora and fauna are abundant, including several endemic species. Rondo has facilitated research by Kenya Indigenous Forest Conservation Project, KIFCON, and KWS. Future projects include Community Outreach, Environmental Education and Regenerative Agroforestry. The Kitchen Toto was filmed here.

Mago Guest House

 Mago

Mago Guest House, Mago, nr Chavakali, Kenya
PO Box 1, Mago 50325, Kenya
Tel	+254 20 2037032
Mobile	+254 723 352792; +254 729 498391
Fax	
E-mail	magoguesthouse@gmail.com
Web	www.magoguesthouse.com

Kisumu, LS & CH
1.5 hrs

Mago Guest House opened in 2007 as an income generating project of the Mago Youth Polytechnic School. It serves as a training centre for the catering and hospitality students, who assist in the kitchen, serve the food and prepare the rooms.

There are 11 en-suite rooms, made up of 6 doubles, 2 twins and 3 singles. The rooms are decorated with African art; the bathrooms are modern and tiled. The lounge is equipped with shelves of books and films for the use of visitors. The terrace overlooks the polytechnic's football field and volleyball court. The conference room seats 40 pax, and is equipped with computers, internet, LCD projector, overhead projector, flipchart and whiteboard.

Activities in the school compound include a tour of the polytechnic, cooking lessons with the catering students and playing football or volleyball with the students. Local attractions include tea factories and plantations, Kakamega Forest, Kisumu Museum, Kaimosi Waterfall and Mt Elgon. Boat trips on Lake Victoria, bird walks in Kisumu Bird Sanctuary and game drives in Kisumu Impala Sanctuary can be arranged.

In 2009, Mago Guest House was recognised for its work in the community and received Ecotourism Society of Kenya's Community Based Organisation, CBO award.

Nandi Bears Club

 Nandi Hills

Nandi Bears Club, Nandi Hills, Kenya
PO Box 20, Nandi Hills 30301, Kenya
Tel	
Mobile	+254 717 525202; +254 733 634945
Fax	
E-mail	nandibearsclub@gmail.com
Web	

 VISA, MasterCard

Kapsimbiwa, CH
20 mins

The Nandi Bears Club opened in 1954 as a private members' club. It was named for the recurring tales of the Nandi Bear who, according to legend, stood 1 metre high with a heavy mane of hair and on occasion skulked from the forest to decapitate villagers.

There are 3 cottages, each containing 2 twin rooms, bathroom, living room and kitchen equipped with gas cooker and fridge. Crockery and cutlery can be provided on request. Non-members are welcome to use the accommodation and facilities.

The entrance hall has a noticeboard with information on club events and competitions. The bar, with heavy wooden panelling and silver sports cups, is well stocked. The restaurant is adorned with boards embossed with the names of past competition winners, and serves international dishes such as grilled chicken with chips and salad, pork chops, vegetable curry and toasted sandwiches. The club also boasts a 9-hole golf course, rugby pitch, lawn tennis court, full size snooker table and squash court. Myths of the Nandi Bear have yet to be laid to rest. One claims that in 1957, the manager of Chemoni Tea Estate shot 2 bears and delivered their skeletons to the National Musuem to be identified. But the museum has no record of this.

Tea Planters' Inn

Nandi Hills

Tea Planters' Inn, just past Post Office, Nandi Hills, Kenya
PO Box 260, Nandi Hills 30301, Kenya
Tel   +254 20 8013339
Mobile
Fax
E-mail teaplantersinn@yahoo.com
Web

    Kapsimbiwa, CH
                              20 mins

Set in attractive gardens on the edge of Nandi Hills town, Tea Planters' Inn has a collection of cottages and rooms. This peaceful retreat makes an ideal place from which to explore the rolling Nandi Hills.
There are 5 en-suite rooms in the main building, made up of 4 doubles and 1 twin. There are also 3 cottages, each containing 2 en-suite double rooms and a small kitchenette. All rooms have built in cupboard, writing table, chair and TV with local channels. The kitchenettes in the cottages have sink, kettle, tea, coffee and cups.
The restaurant, adorned with a poster of the Lord's Prayer, serves a selection of local and international dishes and snacks, such as soups, sandwiches, grilled fillet steak, fish fillet stew, chicken tikka, beef curry, pasta with Napolotana sauce and kienyeji with ugali. Buffets can be arranged on request. Chinese green tea, Masala tea and fresh juices are served. The inn is Christian; no alcohol is served and no smoking is permitted.
The conference hall seats 70 pax, and is equipped with projector and PA system. A private dining room, next to the restaurant, is available for meetings. There is also a small kiosk selling toiletries and essentials. The manicured gardens are available for functions.

Hillside Villa

Kisumu

Hillside Villa, Riat Hill, nr Kisumu, Kenya
PO Box 4740, Kisumu 40100, Kenya
Tel
Mobile   +254 724 715044; +254 722 291891
Fax
E-mail   hillside.village@yahoo.com / info@hotelmamba.com
Web   www.hotelmamba.com

 VISA, MasterCard, Amex    Kisumu, LS & CH
                                                        30 mins

On Riat Hill, on the outskirts of Kisumu, Hillside Villa is a country hotel with easy access to the city. The hotel has budget accommodation with lovely views of Kisumu and the hilly Kibos strip.
There are 42 en-suite rooms, made up of singles, doubles, twins and cottages. The cottages are furnished, self-catering, 1-bedroom apartments, with personal maid. All rooms have satellite TV, internet and room service. Extra beds and baby cots are available on request. Safari Restaurant serves a combination of international and local dishes. The chef specialises in steamed, fresh vegetables, fruits, organic soups, marinated poultry and steaks. The bar stocks soft drinks, beers, wines and spirits. Thatched seating booths in the garden make pleasant places to eat and drink.
The conference centre has several halls, with a combined seating capacity of 1000 pax. Conference equipment includes TV, video, PA system, overhead projector and LCD projector. The hotel offers airport transfers, as well as guided tours of various attractions in the city, including Kibuye Market, Kisumu Impala Sanctuary, Kisumu Bird Sanctuary and Hippo Point. Trips to nearby Kit Mikayi sacred stone and Ndere Island National Park can also be arranged. The hotel has ample secure parking space, and offers a carwash service. Hillside Villa is affiliated to Hotel Mamba, in Kisumu.

Jumuia Guest House, Kisumu   Kisumu

Jumuia Guest House, Gumbi Road, Kisumu, Kenya
PO Box 770, Kisumu 40100, Kenya

Tel	+254 20 2110695-6; +254 57 2020014
Mobile	+254 713 576969; +254 738 444490
Fax	+254 57 2023712
E-mail	reservations.kisumu@resortjumuia.com
Web	www.resortjumuia.com

    Kisumu, LS & CH
20 mins

Jumuia Resorts aim to be the leading Christian resort chain in Kenya. Jumuia, Swahili for community or federation, refers to the National Council of Churches of Kenya, Jumuia ya makanisa ya Kenya. There are 5 Jumuia Resorts, in Kisumu, Nakuru, Limuru, Mombasa and Nairobi.
Jumuia Guest House was founded in 1972, and was originally called Nakuru Community Centre. In 2003, when the National Council of Churches of Kenya, NCCK, was celebrating 90 years of service to Kenya, the guesthouse was renovated and renamed. It is conveniently located in Kisumu, giving access to all businesses and services of the city.
There are 65 en-suite rooms, made up of 35 twins, 30 doubles and 5 penthouses. The restaurant serves buffet breakfast, lunch and dinner. A snack menu is also available on the terrace. No alcohol is served. The guesthouse is equipped with an Olympic size swimming pool.
Lake Victoria Hall seats 250 pax; Lake Kyoga Hall seats 80; Lake Natron Hall seats 80; Lake Nakuru Hall seats 30. Conference equipment including PA system and projector is available. The history of conferencing at Jumuia Resorts goes back to 1946, and the chain offers tailor-made conference and training packages according to the needs of each group.

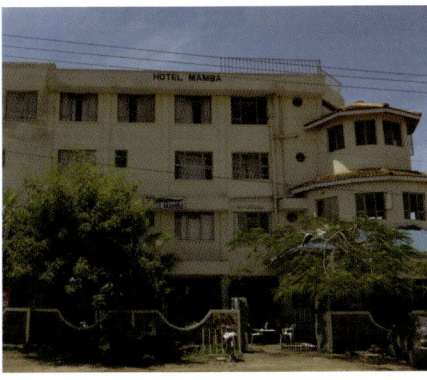

Hotel Mamba   Kisumu

Hotel Mamba, Ondiek Highway, Kisumu, Kenya
PO Box 4740, Kisumu 40100, Kenya

Tel	
Mobile	+254 722 731342; +254 720 758918
Fax	
E-mail	hillside.village@yahoo.com / info@hotelmamba.com
Web	www.hotelmamba.com

VISA, MasterCard, Amex   Kisumu, LS & CH
20 mins

Behind Mamba Filling Station and next to Mamba Nyama Choma Ranch stands Hotel Mamba. Guests enter through the restaurant and climb the stairs to the reception on the 1st floor.
There are 32 en-suite rooms, made up of doubles, twins and suites. All rooms have TV with local channels, fan, mosquito net and balcony. The suites have a double and single bed, built in cupboards and a sitting area with armchairs and coffee table.
The restaurant serves fish, chicken or goat, grilled or stewed, with ugali, chips, sukuma and kachumbari. There is also a snack menu including samosas, bhajias and kebabs. Guests are welcome to eat in the hexagonal 1st floor lounge or in the ground floor bar. The bar serves soft drinks, beers and spirits, and is equipped with satellite TV showing international sports matches, pool table and dartboard.
There are 2 conference rooms on the top floor. The larger room seats 50 pax and the smaller seats 25. A safe is available for guests' valuables at reception. The sister hotel, Hillside Villa, located between Kisumu and Kakamega, can be booked here.

Hotel Vunduba

Kisumu

Hotel Vunduba, Ondiek Highway, Kisumu, Kenya
PO Box 4852, Kisumu 40103, Kenya

Tel	+254 20 3530085; +254 57 2020043; +254 57 2511073
Mobile	+254 723 710866
Fax	+254 57 2022826
E-mail	hotelmerryland@yahoo.com
Web	

 Kisumu, LS & CH
20 mins

Hotel Vunduba, formerly Hotel Merryland, is a large hotel set around a shady courtyard.

There are 62 en-suite rooms in 2 buildings, made up of singles, doubles and apartments. All rooms have TV with local channels and overhead ceiling fan. The apartments have a double room with en-suite bathroom, an interlinking room with single bed, armchairs, coffee table and TV, and a basic kitchenette. Crockery, cutlery and kitchen utensils can be provided by the hotel restaurant if required.

The 1st floor restaurant offers fish, chicken, goat or beef, grilled or stewed, with ugali, chips, rice or chapatti. Buffet can be arranged for large groups. Guests can also eat on the 1st floor veranda, looking down on the courtyard. The ground floor restaurant and bar serves nyama choma grilled meats and soft drinks, beers and spirits. It also has a satellite TV, and an outside terrace shaded by an awning.

The conference rooms have tiled floors and whiteboards on the walls, and are equipped with LCD projector and sound system. The larger room seats 40 pax and the smaller seats 25.

There is a car park behind the hotel, with a 24-hour guard, and a safe at reception for guests' valuables.

Kisumu Beach Resort

Kisumu

Kisumu Beach Resort, off Nkrumah Road, nr Pipeline Depot, Kisumu, Kenya
PO Box 1059, Kisumu 40100, Kenya

Tel	
Mobile	+254 733 749327; +254 720 763146
Fax	
E-mail	kisumubeachresort@gmail.com
Web	www.kisumubeachresort.com

  Kisumu, LS & CH
10 mins

On the shores of Lake Victoria, Kisumu Beach Resort offers a unique experience not far from Kisumu town. The resort opened in 1997, and has budget accommodation and camping facilities in a 20-acre garden overlooking the lake. There are 10 en-suite double rooms. The restaurant has an a la carte menu of Indian and Kenyan dishes, and also serves buffet including fresh Lake Victoria fish. The bar serves soft drinks, beers and spirits. There is a campsite, with bathroom facilities. Bandas equipped with electric sockets, running water and firewood are located on the lakeshore, for guests wishing to cook. WiFi is available throughout the resort. The resort is an ideal location for canoeing, sailing and fishing.

Boat rides, including a romantic dinner cruise, are available. Trips to game reserves and local fishing villages can be arranged. Special events such as weddings, conferences and company parties can be arranged; disco facilities and sound system are available. The veranda, with wicker sofas loaded with plump cushions, is an attractive place from which to watch the hippos at sunrise and sunset. Birdlife includes fish eagles, Egyptian geese, kingfishers, black ibis and hamercop. The resort is environmentally friendly, grows its own fruits including mangos and papayas, and has an independent water supply.

New Victoria Hotel Kisumu

New Victoria Hotel, junction of Gor Maha Road and Ogada Street, Kisumu
PO Box 276, Kisumu 40100, Kenya

Tel	+254 57 2021067; +254 57 2020413
Mobile	+254 734 246615; +254 722 143910
Fax	+254 57 2022874
E-mail	newvictoriahotel@yahoo.com
Web	

    Kisumu, LS & CH 20 mins

New Victoria Hotel is a large white building not far from the centre of Kisumu.

The 19 rooms are on 2 floors, linked by open air corridors adorned with pot plants. There are 15 en-suite doubles, with a double and a single bed, 2 en-suite singles and 2 singles with shared bathroom. An extra bed can be added if required. The rooms are spacious, and have fan, armchairs, coffee table and TV with local channels and a small selection of satellite channels. The rooms have mosquito nets on both the beds and the windows, and balconies with chairs and pot plants overlooking a busy street. The café on the ground floor is open to the street. The restaurant on the 1st floor is wood panelled. Both serve African and international dishes such as masala, biriani and mixed grill platters. Daily specials include chicken pilau on Monday and fish biriani on Thursday. The snack menu includes masala chips, kebabs, omelettes and burgers. No alcohol is served. Cars parked on the street outside are guarded day and night. The 1st floor restaurant can be used as a meeting room.

Hotel Perch Kisumu

Hotel Perch, Makasembo Road, Kisumu, Kenya
PO Box 1217, Kisumu 40100, Kenya

Tel	+254 57 2026053
Mobile	+254 722 974607
Fax	+254 57 2026053
E-mail	hotelperch@yahoo.com
Web	

   Kisumu, LS & CH 20 mins

Hotel Perch has striking views over Lake Victoria, a lake filled with the Nile perch which gave the hotel its name. The hotel is a prominent orange building, with terracotta embellishments. A polished wooden staircase leads from the large stone entrance hall to the wood panelled reception on the 1st floor.

There are 70 en-suite rooms, made up of singles, doubles and twins. All rooms have armchairs, coffee table, writing desk, TV with local channels and mosquito net. The dining room has lovely views over the lake, and serves buffet breakfast and a la carte lunch and dinner. The international menu includes chicken Maryland, chicken tikka, nyama choma grilled meats and a selection of fresh lake fish dishes. The bar, with comfortable armchairs and large windows with views of the lake, serves soft drinks, beers and spirits. It has a snack menu and is equipped with TV.

There are 3 conference halls, which seat 60, 100 and 300 pax. All halls are equipped with LCD projector and PA system. There is a safe at reception and a secure basement car park. The hotel's central location in Kisumu makes it convenient for all the shops, businesses, restaurants and bars of the town.

Western

Imperial Hotel

Kisumu

Imperial Hotel, Jomo Kenyatta Highway, Kisumu, Kenya
PO Box 1866, Kisumu 40100, Kenya

Tel	+254 57 2020002; +254 57 2022661-7
Mobile	+254 734 608111; +254 721 240515
Fax	+254 57 2022685
E-mail	info@imperialhotel.co.ke
Web	www.imperialhotel.co.ke

 VISA, MasterCard, Amex, KCB   Kisumu, LS & CH 20 mins

Imperial Hotel offers luxury accommodation in the heart of Kisumu. The imposing white building surrounds a leafy central courtyard and swimming pool. There are 70 en-suite rooms. The standard rooms have twin beds, and are equipped with armchairs, coffee table, desk, electronic safe and telephone. The deluxe rooms have, in addition, minibar, kettle and bathroom amenities. The 3 spacious executive suites and 1 presidential suite include an elegant living area, and are equipped with iron, hairdryer, daily newspapers, TV, CD player and 2 telephone extensions. There are also 12 apartments with sitting room, study and fully equipped kitchenette. Florence Restaurant, in polished dark wood, has an international menu including fish goujons andalouse, Chinese noodles and pizzas fresh from the pizza oven. Victoria Terrace, at the poolside, serves snacks. Shalimar lounge bar, on the 5th floor, has WiFi and serves canapés and cocktails. Fish Eagle boardroom seats 18 pax and Lolwe Hall seats 40. Mayfair Hall seats 200 and can accommodate corporate functions and wedding receptions. All are equipped with full conference facilities. Business services such as printing, scanning and photocopying are available. Visitors not staying at the hotel can use the facilities including swimming pool, sauna and gym for a charge.

The Duke of Breeze

Kisumu

The Duke of Breeze, off Jomo Kenyatta Highway, Kisumu, Kenya
PO Box 2011, Kisumu 40100, Kenya

Tel	
Mobile	+254 717 105444
Fax	
E-mail	reservations@thedukeofbreeze.com
Web	www.thedukeofbreeze.com

 Kisumu, LS & CH 20 mins

The Duke of Breeze is conveniently located in Kisumu near the centenary arches, close to the shops, restaurants and businesses of the town centre. The 29 en-suite rooms are situated on 3 floors, and made up of singles, doubles and triples. The rooms are comfortably furnished, and most have TV with local channels. 10 spacious rooms are designed for long-term guests. The Sports Bar, on the first floor, is entered by a swinging cowboy style door, and embellished with a red Real Kisumu FC sign and a cabinet of silver sports cups. A large flat screen TV shows international sports matches. Drinks and snacks are served.
The Rooftop Bar and Restaurant, shaded by a canvas awning, has a panoramic view of the town, leafy Kenyatta Sports Grounds and Lake Victoria. It serves cocktails and a selection of international dishes such as fajitas and Mongolian stir fry. It also has a children's play area with trampoline, cushioned seats overlooking the lake and WiFi.
The 2 conference halls, with attractive wicker walls, each seat 50 pax. Conference equipment is not provided and can be brought by groups or hired locally. A cyber café on the ground floor provides internet, typesetting and printing.

Whirlspring Hotel

Kisumu

Whirlspring Hotel, Nzola Road, off Nairobi Road, nr Sai Petrol Station
PO Box 19378, Kisumu 40100, Kenya

Tel	+254 20 3530185-6
Mobile	+254 726 774304; +254 714 163314
Fax	+254 57 2020683
E-mail	reservations@whirlspringhotelkisumu.com
Web	www.whirlspringhotelkisumu.com

Kisumu, LS & CH
20 mins

Behind a grey brick façade adorned with vivid pink and purple paintwork and white grills, Whirlspring Hotel offers comfortable accommodation near the centre of Kisumu.

The 23 en-suite rooms are made up of 14 doubles, with 2 double beds in each, and 9 singles. Each room is painted a different colour and all are equipped with satellite TV, fan and WiFi. Ground floor rooms are suitable for guests with disabilities. Upper floor rooms have balconies.

The restaurant serves a wide international menu including pizzas, steaks and fish. There is also a varied African menu, including many local Luo dishes such as kamongo, local fish first smoked then stewed in lemon, tomato and onion, and obambla, dried fish. On Friday nights, an African buffet gives guests the chance to try local specialities such as aliya, atholoa, aluru, creamed dek and osuga.

The Pancho Meeting Point, an outside bar, has satellite TV and shows sports matches. The striking murals on its walls were painted by a local artist. The hotel also exhibits local artists' work, all of which is for sale. The cyber café offers services such as typesetting, printing and binding and the well equipped conference hall seats 60 pax.

Kisumu Hotel

Kisumu

Kisumu Hotel, Jomo Kenyatta Highway, Kisumu, Kenya
PO Box 3335, Kisumu 40100, Kenya

Tel	+254 57 2024157; +254 57 2022833; +254 57 2022718
Mobile	+254 733 500036
Fax	+254 57 2020508
E-mail	hotel@maseno.ac.ke
Web	www.maseno.ac.ke/hotelkisumu

 VISA, MasterCard Kisumu, LS & CH
20 mins

Kisumu Hotel, owned by Maseno University, faces the university across Jomo Kenyatta Highway. The hotel's bright and airy Terrace Restaurant and Bar lies along the front of the hotel; guests enter through it and climb the stairs to the reception on the 1st floor.

The 80 en-suite rooms, in shaded wings positioned around the colourful gardens, are made up of standard and deluxe rooms, and suites. All rooms have satellite TV, telephone and aircon, and their bathrooms have both bath and shower. The more spacious deluxe rooms have, in addition, a fridge, kettle and internet. The suites include a sitting room.

The Terrace Restaurant and the Main Restaurant serve an international menu including crispy fried chicken, grilled parrot fish and king prawns with garlic and chilli, as well as snacks like sandwiches and salads. The Terrace Bar, with satellite TV, is fully stocked with soft drinks, beers, wines and spirits; the Pool Bar serves soft drinks and beers. The Executive Bar, with leather sofas, can be used by private groups on request.

There are 10 fully equipped conference rooms; the largest conference hall seats 300 pax and the smallest seats 20. The swimming pool, surrounded by palm trees, has a sunbathing terrace and children's swimming pool.

Hotel Beograda

Kisumu

Hotel Beograda, nr matatu stage, Kisumu, Kenya
PO Box 920, Kisumu 40100, Kenya
Tel
Mobile
Fax +254 728 630527
E-mail
Web

                                           Kisumu, LS & CH
                                                                           20 mins

Near the large matatu stage, Hotel Beograda is a tall building in the centre of Kisumu, rising over a large sign Kelly's Bar and Restaurant.

The 63 en-suite rooms are made up of doubles and twins. The rooms are small and basic, and are furnished with bed, table, chair and basin. The hotel does not serve food, but there are several restaurants nearby. The top floor of the hotel houses a fully equipped sports centre, open 24 hours. The gym has modern equipment, including weights and exercise machines. The wall charts provide training advice and information on the facilities. The dance studio, with wall mirrors and large windows, offers dance, step, tai-bo and challenge classes daily. The rooftop box-

ing area has 2 punch bags and great views. Personal trainers provide instruction and assistance.

The underground nightclub is open 24 hours. The large bar is well stocked with imported beers and spirits, and has 4 flat screen TVs and 1 large TV showing sports, and a pool table. The disco has a 24-hour DJ, black light, secluded sitting areas and a rotating disco ball.

Visitors not staying at the hotel can use the facilities for a small charge.

Nyanza Club

Kisumu

Nyanza Club, Aput Road, nr State House and Braeburn Intl. School
PO Box 29, Kisumu 40100, Kenya
Tel   +254 57 2022433
Mobile   +254 724 270984
Fax   +254 57 2024058
E-mail   info@nyanzaclub.com / nyanzaclub@africaonline.co.ke
Web   www.nyanzaclub.com

VISA, MasterCard   Kisumu, LS & CH
                                     25 mins

Nyanza Club, overlooking Lake Victoria, has attractive whitewashed buildings set in manicured gardens. This private members' club permits non-members to use the accommodation and facilities for a temporary membership fee.

The 56 en-suite rooms are made up of singles, doubles, twins and triples. All rooms are equipped with satellite TV, fridge, aircon, fan and kettle. Each room also has a balcony or veranda with a view of either the gardens or the lake.

The restaurant serves international dishes, and has a selection of soft drinks, beers, wines, spirits and cocktails. A barbecue is served by the pool

every Sunday lunch, while on Friday, dinner is cooked at a live cooking station by the pool. The gardens, sloping gently to the lakefront, are ideal for functions such as wedding receptions, cocktail parties and corporate dinners. The chefs are also available for outside catering.

The club can arrange executive meetings and corporate training. The business centre offers both WiFi and landline internet.

The swimming pool, beside the lake, has a sunbathing terrace. The club also has tennis courts, squash courts, board games and snooker. Its 18-hole golf course is off the premise, about 5km away. Local activities include bird watching and boat trips.

Sunset Hotel Kisumu

Sunset Hotel, Impala Way, Kisumu, Kenya
PO Box 215, Kisumu 40100, Kenya

Tel	+254 57 2020464-6, +254 57 2022174
Mobile	+254 723 686483; +254 733 411001
Fax	+254 57 2022745
E-mail	hotelsunset1977@yahoo.co.uk
Web	

VISA, MasterCard, Amex   Kisumu, LS & CH
                                 25 mins

An imposing 5-floor orange and white building, Sunset Hotel sits on the shores of Lake Victoria. The hotel was opened by Daniel arap Moi, then vice president, in 1977. Close to Kisumu Impala Sanctuary and Kisumu Museum, the hotel is within a short drive of the shops and businesses of the town. The 50 en-suite rooms are made up of singles, doubles and triples. All rooms have satellite TV, radio, telephone, aircon and treated mosquito nets. All rooms except the top floor have balconies looking over the garden and swimming pool towards the lake. They are decorated with African art and locally made furniture.

Breakfast, lunch and dinner are served in the tiled dining area on the mezzanine floor. The menu includes African meat platters, fresh fish from Lake Victoria and Indian curries, as well as international favourites like spaghetti bolognaise, steaks and sandwiches.

The Pool Bar, on the poolside, serves soft drinks and beers. The Hippo Bar, with garden terrace, serves beers, wines and liqueurs, and has satellite TV showing sports matches.

The small conference hall seats up to 50 pax, and the large one seats up to 200. Both are equipped with LCD projector and PA system.

Milimani Resort & Annex Kisumu

Milimani Resort and Annex, Got Huma Road, nr Ring Road, Kisumu
PO Box 2652, Kisumu 40100, Kenya

Tel	+254 57 2023245; +254 57 2020148; +254 2020915
Mobile	+254 734 414466; +254 715 525233
Fax	+254 57 2023242
E-mail	info@milimaniresort.co.ke / dyonake@yahoo.com
Web	www.milimaniresort.co.ke

                    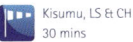 Kisumu, LS & CH
                                                        30 mins

Set in bright gardens filled with bougainvillea, Milimani Resort and Annex offers comfortable accommodation and a relaxed atmosphere. It is said that Barack Obama stayed here during his visit to Kenya in 2005. The 48 en-suite rooms have mahogany furniture and pile carpets, and are equipped with aircon, radio and satellite TV. All the bathrooms are fitted with showers and most also have baths. There is a safe at reception for guests' valuables.

The sitting room, which opens onto the reception through cream arches, has wooden beamed ceiling, carved wooden doors, comfortable leather sofas and satellite TV. The spacious tiled restaurant serves African, European and Indian cuisine including mixed grill, chicken masala and fresh fish from Lake Victoria. The resort is Christian and serves no alcohol. The large conference hall seats 200 pax; the 2 smaller conference rooms seat 40 and 30. All conference rooms are fully equipped, including projector and sound system.

The large freeform swimming pool is spanned by small bridges. It has a terrace with sunbeds and a children's pool with play area and is surrounded by manicured gardens. Visitors not staying at the resort can use the pool and other facilities for a small charge.

Excellent Magere Guest House Kisumu

Excellent Magere Guest House, off Aga Khan Walk, Milimani, Kisumu
PO Box 3834, Kisumu 40100, Kenya

Tel	+254 20 2425923
Mobile	+254 733 761482
Fax	
E-mail	
Web	

    Kisumu, LS & CH
30 mins

Excellent Magere Guest House is a quiet, modern guesthouse in the Kisumu suburb of Milimani. Not far from the town centre, the guesthouse is within easy reach of the shops, restaurants and businesses of Kisumu. This peaceful and private place suits both tourists and business travellers. The 12 en-suite rooms are made up of 5 singles, 5 doubles and 2 family rooms that each has 2 double beds. All rooms have aircon, fan and TV with local channels. Mosquito nets are on both the beds and the windows. The dining room has a polished wooden floor, and red and white furnishings. It serves an international menu including chicken Maryland, vegetable curry and fresh fish from Lake Victoria. Buffets can be provided for larger groups on request. The outside barbecue area serves grilled meats and a selection of soft drinks, beers and spirits.

Conferences and meetings of up to 40 pax can be organised in the dining area. Conference equipment is not provided, and can either be brought by the participants, or hired locally. The guesthouse has a computer with internet and a photocopier available for use by the guests.

St Anna Guest House Kisumu

St Anna Guest House, Tom Mboya St, off the ring road, Milimani, Kisumu
PO Box 19100, Kisumu 40100, Kenya

Tel	+254 57 2024792
Mobile	+254 734 600119
Fax	+254 57 2023585
E-mail	stanna_gh@yahoo.com / info@stannaguesthouse.com
Web	www.stannaguesthouse.com

    Kisumu, LS & CH
30 mins

Established in 1998 under the initiative of the Franciscan Sisters of St Anna Lwak, St Anna Guest House is a Christian guesthouse in the quiet Kisumu suburb of Milimani. Behind its grey and maroon façade, the guesthouse has wide airy corridors and modern facilities.

There are 36 en-suite rooms, made up of 23 singles, 11 doubles and 2 family rooms. The family rooms have 3 beds, 2 in a large room, and 1 in an adjoining smaller room.

Breakfast, lunch and dinner are served in the dining room, and can be buffet or a la carte. The menu includes local dishes, and dishes from West Africa, as well as international favourites such as soups, sandwiches, curries, goulash and spaghetti. No alcohol is served.

The large conference hall seats 200 pax, and the small conference hall seats 25. Equipment is not provided, but the guesthouse can arrange for PA system, projector and any other equipment to be hired locally on request. Telephone, internet and photocopy services are provided. There is a secure car park. Transport to and from the city centre and the airport can be arranged. The obliging staff are also willing to run errands for guests when required.

Magline Guest House

Kisumu

Magline Guest House, ring road, next to Milimani Hospital, Kisumu
PO Box 2424, Kisumu 40100, Kenya

Tel
Mobile +254 729 527427
Fax
E-mail maglineguesthouse@gmail.com
Web

   Kisumu, LS & CH
30 mins

In the quiet suburb of Milimani, Magline Guest House offers secure accommodation, tended by obliging staff. The guesthouse, on the ring road next to Milimani hospital, has polished wooden floors, whitewashed walls and ornately carved wooden doors.

The 6 en-suite rooms are made up of singles, doubles and twins. The rooms are spacious, with built in cupboards, tables and chairs; 3 of the rooms have satellite TV.

Breakfast, lunch and dinner are served in the dining room, or at the shaded tables in front of the guesthouse. The chef can prepare chicken, beef, vegetables or fresh lake fish in the style of the guests' choice. A selection of soft drinks is stocked, and alcoholic drinks can be provided on request. The sitting room has tables, chairs, sofas and satellite TV. Seminars and meetings can be arranged. The guesthouse offers both short and long-term accommodation, and is suitable for people holidaying or working in Kisumu.

Local attractions include Lake Victoria, Kit Mikayi sacred stone and Kisumu Impala Sanctuary. The shops, restaurants, businesses and other amenities of Kisumu are a short drive from the guesthouse.

Kiboko Bay Resort

Kisumu

Kiboko Bay Resort, Dungu Fishing Village, nr Hippo Point, Kisumu
PO Box 2111, Kisumu 40100, Kenya

Tel
Mobile +254 733 532709; +254 724 387738
Fax
E-mail info@kibokobay.com
Web www.kibokobay.com

  VISA, MasterCard   Kisumu, LS & CH
40 mins

Named after the hippos that wallow in front of the resort, Kiboko Bay Resort is a tented camp on Lake Victoria. Manicured lawns, dotted with bougainvillea and palms and humming with birdsong, slope gently to the water's edge.

The 9 tents, raised on wooden platforms and shaded by thatched roofs, are set around the garden. All are en-suite, with solid tiled bathrooms, and adorned with wooden and leather furniture and Maasai artwork. The tents have verandas, with shade netting and canvas safari chairs, overlooking the lake or the garden.

There is also a permanent suite on the lakefront. The suite has aircon throughout, and is made up of a double bedroom, a large bathroom with bath, shower and dressing table, a sitting room with attractive wicker furniture and a fully equipped open plan kitchenette.

The restaurant serves international cuisine, including fresh lake fish. Guests can also eat on the shady terrace or beside the lakefront swimming pool. There is a fully stocked bar and a peaceful library.

The resort has 3 speedboats seating between 6 and 15 pax. There is also a moored barge, ideal for functions and parties. Activities include bird watching, fishing trips, boat trips and cruises to the islands.

 Accommodation Guide

Kweisos House Koru

Kweisos House, nr Koru, Kenya
Homa Lime Co Ltd, Private Bag, Koru 40104, Kenya
Tel	+254 57 51064-5; +254 20 2333678-9
Mobile	+254 722 754664; +254 733 666606
Fax	+254 57 51419; +254 20 2333737
E-mail	info@homalime.com
Web	www.homalime.com

  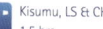

Kisumu, LS & CH
1.5 hrs

Kweisos, meaning place of palms in the Kipsigis language, implies a useful place, as palms were traditionally used to clean out calabashes. First owned by Olga Watson, of Olga in Africa, Kweisos House started life in the early 1900s as a farmhouse. It is now owned by Homa Lime, a family run business in limestone, jaggery, arable farming, livestock rearing, forestry and tourism.

There are 4 en-suite double rooms, and 2 rooms with shared bathroom. Ideal for families. The house is let to 1 group at a time. Bed linen, crockery, cutlery and cooking utensils are supplied. Staff use fresh farm produce for meals and picnics; guests can also choose to cater for themselves.

The 3000-acre estate offers a variety of activities, including walks, drives and horse riding; 4WD vehicles are required. Birdlife is prolific. Small dams, filled with tilapia, catfish and bass, provide good fishing spots. Fishing trips to Lake Victoria and the Kericho dams can be arranged. The resident guide provides trips to the waterfall, sticky dam, booze cruise and arboretum. Kweisos House has a swimming pool, and the Greenhills area of the estate has tennis courts, snooker table, badminton and table tennis. Nearby attractions include Kakamega Forest, Kerio Valley and Ruma National Park.

The Exotic House Kericho

The Exotic House, Sotik-Kericho Highway, nr Kericho, Kenya
PO Box 1122, Kericho 20200, Kenya
Tel	
Mobile	+254 725 619731; +254 722 960860
Fax	+254 52 21674
E-mail	exotic.ghse@gmail.com
Web	

Kisumu, LS & CH
1.5 hr

The Exotic House is located next to its own tea plantation and vegetable farm, both of which supply its restaurant. The attractive gardens surrounding the hotel make a peaceful place to relax and look out over the expanse of tea.

There are 25 en-suite rooms, made up of 7 standard and 18 deluxe. The standard rooms are in the main house, and are equipped with satellite TV and telephone. The deluxe wing was built in 2009; the rooms have king size bed, writing desk, handcrafted lamps and balcony with views of the garden or tea plantation. The campsite has bathroom facilities. The restaurant serves buffet and also has an international menu including

beef stroganoff and fillet steak. Outside catering is available. The large garden, with lawns, plants and water features, is available for wedding receptions, fund raisers, parties and retreats.

The conference room seats 40 pax, has its own dining room and is equipped with PA system and projector. The business centre has flat screen computers, and offers scanning, printing and photocopying as well as internet. Banda Pub, in the garden, is fully stocked including Windhoek beer, sambuca and a selection of wines. There are also 3 private booths for meetings or dining.

Hills Country Lodge

Kericho

Hills Country Lodge, Sotik-Kericho Highway, nr Kericho, Kenya
PO Box 1700, Kericho 20200, Kenya

Tel	
Mobile	+254 720 941891; +254 729 444727
Fax	
E-mail	hillscountrylodge@hotmail.com
Web	

   Kisumu LS & CH
1.5 hrs

Hills Country Lodge offers budget accommodation on the outskirts of Kericho. The lodge is about 5km from Kericho on the Sotik-Kericho Highway.

There are 7 en-suite rooms, made up of 6 doubles and 1 twin. The rooms are in an L-shape around a courtyard, the corner room being the twin. All rooms are equipped with mosquito net and satellite TV. The restaurant serves soups, stews, curries and sandwiches. Nyama choma grilled meats are served in the restaurant, the bar and the garden. The garden has tables and chairs shaded by umbrellas where visitors can relax, drink or dine. The bar has stone walls and rustic décor, and serves soft drinks, beers and spirits.

Kericho is famed for its tea plantations. Hills Country Lodge is conveniently located for trips to tea plantations, and is not far from the shops and businesses of Kericho town.

Kericho Club

Kericho

Kericho Club, James Finley Road, Kericho, Kenya
PO Box 82, Kericho 20200, Kenya

Tel	+254 52 21407
Mobile	+254 721 320606
Fax	
E-mail	kerichoclub@yahoo.com
Web	

 All major cards   Kisumu LS & CH
1.5 hrs

Kericho Club, a private members club, was established in 1927, in large manicured grounds in the centre of Kericho. Non-members can pay a temporary membership fee to use the accommodation and facilities.

There are 4 en-suite double rooms. All rooms are equipped with satellite TV. The large lounge has polished wooden floor, open fireplace, flat screen TV, sofas, armchairs and coffee tables. Its walls are adorned with wooden boards embossed with the names of past sports competition winners. The family lounge is a no smoking room. The dark wooden bar has a good selection of soft drinks, beers, wines and spirits, and is adorned with wooden boards embossed with the names of past chairmen and vice chairmen. The restaurant serves local, international and Indian food. There is a 9-hole golf course and a driving range; caddies are available for hire. The club also has a tennis court, snooker room, football pitch and squash court. There is a fully equipped gym and a presentation hall for competition winners. The huge grounds also include a children's playground. The entrance hall is full of noticeboards with information for members.

Teavale Guest Cottages Kericho

Teavale Guest Cottages, Nairobi Road, Kericho, Kenya
PO Box 1650, Kericho 20200, Kenya

Tel	+254 20 2440827; +254 20 2669740
Mobile	+254 725 843115
Fax	
E-mail	bookings@teavalecottages.com
Web	www.teavalecottages.com

 Kisumu, LS & CH
1.5 hrs

Established in 2009, Teavale Guest Cottages consists of 2 whitewashed houses facing each other across a well kept garden.

There are 15 en-suite rooms, made up of 3 doubles and 12 twins, with either 2 single beds or a double and single bed. The rooms are decorated individually and are all painted different colours. All are equipped with modern facilities including writing desk, built in cupboards, tiled bathrooms, telephone and satellite TV. The bathrooms all contain showers and some also have baths.

Breakfast, lunch and dinner are served in the dining room. Meals are often buffets. The TV lounge has large comfortable armchairs, sofas, woven rugs, a music system and a fireplace. No alcohol is served.

The conference room seats 20 pax. Equipment is not provided and can either be brought by participants or hired locally. A backup generator ensures 24-hour electricity. There is a safe at reception where guests can store their valuables. The car park is gated, and has a 24-hour security guard.

Kericho area tours and Kisumu airport transfers can be arranged.

Tea Hotel Kericho

Tea Hotel, Nairobi Road, Kericho, Kenya
PO Box 75, Kericho 20200, Kenya

Tel	+254 52 30004-5; +254 20 2050790
Mobile	+254 714 510824
Fax	+254 52 20576
E-mail	teahotel@africaonline.co.ke
Web	

VISA, MasterCard

 Kisumu, LS & CH
1.5 hrs

Tea was first cultivated in the highlands around Kericho in the 1920s. Today more than 110,000 hectares are devoted to tea, producing 215 million kilos of tea per year and bringing in 17-20% of Kenya's export revenue. The Tea Hotel started life as the guesthouse for Brooke Bond, in 1952. In the 1970s it was sold to the local community who have run it since as the Tea Hotel.

This charming hotel is made up of standard rooms in a separate wing, superior rooms and suites in the main house and cottages in the garden. All rooms are en-suite, spacious and are decorated in the English country house style, with flowery wallpaper and chintz curtains. The dining room serves a selection of international dishes. The main house also holds a large sitting room with comfortable sofas and log fires, a well stocked bar with adjoining private rooms and a terrace overlooking the grounds. The 4 conference halls seat between 25 and 200 pax. Weddings and functions can be arranged.

The luxuriant gardens attract a myriad of birds, including the joyful greenbul, the cape wagtail, the black coucal and the barn owl. The tea tour, from picking to factory, should be booked in advance.

Kimugu River Lodge

Kericho

Kimugu River Lodge, Nairobi Road, nr Tea Hotel, Kericho, Kenya
PO Box 25, Kericho 20200, Kenya
Tel
Mobile +254 720 861079; +254 733 504942
Fax
E-mail kimuguriverlodge@yahoo.com
Web

  Kisumu, LS & CH 1.5 hrs

On the banks of Kimugu River, Kimugu River Lodge overlooks lush forest and frothing water. Formerly known as Kericho Lodge and Fishing Resort, the lodge makes an ideal place from which to watch the prolific birdlife in the garden.

There are 8 en-suite double rooms and 1 en-suite triple room. Some rooms are wooden and others brick; some have local TV and 1 has a fireplace. The restaurant serves authentic Indian food, including paneer kheema, masala mushrooms, methi and mari chicken, amritsari chicken and mutton jhelum. Local and international dishes are also available. A karoga gazebo, for those who wish to cook for themselves, is in the garden, surrounded by picnic tables and chairs. The bar has a wide selection of soft drinks, beers, wines and spirits.

The conference room seats 50 pax; groups needing conference equipment should bring their own. The campsite has bathroom facilities. The gardens are home to colobus monkeys, red tailed vervets, a large variety of butterflies and 83 species of bird. Kimugu River Lodge has constructed a number of eco-friendly tools, including a hydrum pump which pumps water from the river to the rooms without electricity. The lodge also grows its own fruit and vegetables.

Ray's Place Inn

Kericho

Ray's Place Inn, Nairobi Road, Kericho, Kenya
PO Box 457, Kericho 20200, Kenya
Tel   +254 20 8017324; +254 52 30049
Mobile   +254 710 407933
Fax   +254 52 30049
E-mail   rays.place@kelunet.com
Web

  VISA, MasterCard, Amex    Kisumu, LS & CH 1.5 hrs

Formerly the home of the managing director of Brooke Bond, Ray's Place Inn is an elegant house set in spacious gardens. The house, which retains the atmosphere of a private house, is on the outskirts of Kericho. Its drive passes through the lush tea plantations for which this region is famed. There are 5 en-suite rooms, made up of 2 singles, 2 doubles and 1 triple. The rooms are decorated in traditional English style, with flowery curtains and bedspreads. The dining room serves a selection of international dishes and snacks, including samosas, chicken wings, chicken tikka, beef kofta, chicken Maryland and platters of nyama choma grilled meats. The lounge has a fireplace, and is equipped with satellite TV.

The conference room seats 50 pax, and is equipped with a PA system. The bar, in a separate building in the garden, is well stocked with soft drinks, beers, wines and spirits. This building can also be used for meetings or conferences. The garden has beautifully maintained lawns and flowerbeds, and makes a lovely setting for weddings, functions and parties. Music and entertainment can be arranged. There is also a play area for children.

Ufanisi Resort Kisii

Ufanisi Resort, Nyankongo Village, Getare Nyamira Bypass, Kisii, Kenya
PO Box 2646, Kisii 40200, Kenya

Tel	+254 20 2423157
Mobile	+254 714 966250; +254 722 920109; +254 722 245772
Fax	
E-mail	info@ufanisiresorts.com / bookings@ufanisiresorts.com
Web	www.ufanisiresorts.com

 VISA, MasterCard, Amex, JCB   Kisumu, LS & CH
1.5 hrs

Established in 2009, Ufanisi Resort is a collection of rooms, cottages and suites in a large forested compound. Lush gardens surround the restaurant, bar and rooms.

There are 16 en-suite standard rooms, 2 cottages, 1 standard suite and 4 deluxe suites. All rooms are equipped with satellite TV. The suites are spacious and furnished with leather sofas, kettle and fruit bowl. The forest paths have appropriate names like Arboretum Walk. The restaurant serves local and international dishes, including tilapia from Lake Victoria. The thatched bar has a full wine list, as well as soft drinks, beers and spirits, and is equipped with satellite TV. The conference hall seats 40 pax, and is equipped with laptop, printer, projector and PA system. There is a secure car park. WiFi is available throughout the compound. Ufanisi Resort was built without destroying trees; this natural forest is home to a wide variety of birdlife.

At the top of Manga Hills, Ufanisi Resort has a campsite with luxury safari tents and a catered mess tent. This picturesque spot is ideal for weddings and parties, or simply for relaxing and appreciating nature. The resort has Toyota vans available for trips to national parks, and can book excursions and tours.

Jazz Restaurant and Hotel Kisii

Jazz Restaurant and Hotel, Hospital Road, Hema Plaza Building, opp. KFA
PO Box 915, Kisii 40200, Kenya

Tel	+254 58 30076; +254 58 30949
Mobile	+254 733 836522; +254 720 888819
Fax	
E-mail	
Web	

      Kisumu, LS & CH
1.5 hrs

Jazz Restaurant and Hotel stands out in the centre of Kisii with its vibrant orange décor. Visitors enter through a corridor between street front shops, climb the stairs to the 1st floor bar, then continue upwards to the 2nd floor reception and restaurant.

There are 34 en-suite rooms, made up of 29 singles and 5 doubles. The walls are bright orange, the floors are tiled orange and white and the chairs in each room are orange. The curtains are printed with African animals. The restaurant serves local dishes such as liver with ugali and fish stew, as well as offering snacks and takeaways. Outside catering is available. The bar is fully stocked with soft drinks, beers, wines and spirits and has a lively atmosphere. It is equipped with a TV with local channels. Theme nights, such as Rhumba Night on Mondays, Lingala on Tuesdays and Funk on Thursdays, make the bar popular with locals.

The conference hall seats 100 pax; equipment should be brought by groups if required.

Zonic Hotel Kisii

Zonic Hotel, Kisii Hospital Road, opp. Police Station, Kisii, Kenya
PO Box 541, Kisii 40200, Kenya

Tel	+254 58 30298
Mobile	+254 735 770711
Fax	+254 58 31316
E-mail	geoffreyareri@yahoo.com / tomopenda@yahoo.com
Web	

VISA   Kisumu, LS & CH 1.5 hrs

Zonic Hotel, in the centre of Kisii, provides budget accommodation and conference facilities.

There are 62 en-suite rooms, made up of singles, doubles and 6 suites. All rooms are equipped with TV with local channels and have a balcony. The suites are larger and include a separate sitting room furnished with sofa, armchairs and writing table; their bathrooms have both bath and shower. The street front café serves fast food and snacks such as mandazi, sandwiches and chips. The restaurant has a Continental Selection including fillet of tilapia and chicken Maryland, and an Asiatic Voyage Selection including chicken jambaraya, fish fillet masala and beef curry. The Out of Africa Selection includes traditional chicken stew and ugali. The lounge, next to the restaurant, has a pool table. The bar, on the 1st floor with large windows overlooking the street, has soft drinks, beers and some spirits. The largest conference hall seats 200 pax, the 2nd seats 150 and the 3rd seats 50. Projector and PA system are available for hire. There is also a rooftop swimming pool and underground car park. The hotel can book excursions and safaris to places of interest.

Magharibi Luxury Suites Kisii

Magharibi Luxury Suites, Nairobi-Kisumu Road, opp. Uhuru Plaza, Kisii
PO Box 4361, Kisii 40200, Kenya

Tel	
Mobile	+254 724 299320
Fax	
E-mail	magharibiguesthouse@yahoo.com
Web	

Kisumu, LS & CH 1.5 hrs

Established in January 2010, Magharibi Luxury Suites offers suites with personal service in the centre of Kisii. The suites are adorned with African artefacts and equipped with modern facilities. Their central location makes the suites convenient for the shops and businesses of Kisii.

There are 6 suites, 4 en-suite and 2 with a shared bathroom. The suites are spacious and all are equipped with satellite TV, coffeemaker, fridge, Lamu bed, orthopaedic mattress, quality duvet and massaging sandals. The suites are named after Kenyan birds such as Bronze Sunbird and Bee Eater, and each is designed individually. Greater Flamingo, the largest, has sofa, armchairs, rocking chair, coffee table and a connecting dressing room with dressing table and full length mirror; its bathroom has both bath and shower.

The lounge has polished wooden floors and is decorated with traditional tools and utensils from the local area, such as the game of Bao and the instrument Nyatiti. Guests are welcome to discuss their preferred menu with the chef. Breakfast, lunch and dinner can be served in the dining room or privately, in the guests' suite. There is WiFi throughout and a secure car park.

Hotel Dados

 Kisii

Hotel Dados, Kisii-Migori Road, opp. Diocese, Kisii, Kenya
PO Box 3816, Kisii 40200, Kenya

Tel	+254 58 30841
Mobile	+254 770 670891; +254 711 929997
Fax	
E-mail	hoteldados@yahoo.com
Web	www.dadoshotelkisii.com

 Kisumu, LS & CH
1.5 hrs

Hotel Dados declares that it is in pursuit of quality. The hotel, on Kisii's hillside, looks out across the lush slopes of Western Kenya.

There are 19 en-suite rooms, made up of 11 singles, 6 doubles and 2 suites. All rooms are fully tiled, have polished wooden doors and furnishings and are equipped with satellite TV. The suites have, in addition, a living room with sofa and coffee table, a kitchen and both their bathrooms have bath and shower. The restaurant has a large terrace with views over Kisii and its environs. Its menu is both local and international, and includes Gusii chicken and chips, fish special masala and chicken wings Italian style. The speciality is the chef's special platter which serves 4, and includes grilled beef, chicken, fish, sausages, eggs and salad. Buffets can be arranged for groups. The bar serves soft drinks, beers and spirits. Amboseli Hall seats 150 pax and Masai Mara Hall seats 100. The executive lounge seats 6 pax. Conference equipment including laptop, PA system and projector are available. Beneath the hotel, there is an underground car park.

Bluu Nile Hotel

 Kisii

Bluu Nile Hotel, Kisii-Mugori Road, opp. Nyangena Hospital, Kisii, Kenya
PO Box 3041, Kisii 40200, Kenya

Tel	+254 20 2681376
Mobile	+254 731 630245
Fax	
E-mail	hotelbluunile@yahoo.com
Web	

  Kisumu, LS & CH
1.5 hrs

The Bluu Nile Hotel offers dining, accommodation and conference facilities on the outskirts of Kisii.

There are 25 en-suite rooms, made up of 15 singles, 6 doubles and 4 executive singles. The singles have 1 double bed and the doubles have 2 double beds. All rooms have mosquito nets and TV with local channels. The executive rooms have sofa, cupboard and satellite TV. The rooms are in 4 blocks, each named after a Kenyan national park such as Tsavo East and Samburu.

The restaurant has an international menu including chicken with cashew nuts, whole Tilapia, chicken pilau and vegetable ratatouille. Buffets can be arranged for large groups. Nyama choma grilled meats are also on offer. There are 4 private seating booths called Mt Kilimanjaro, Mt Elgon, Mt Kenya and Chulu Hills, as well as a terrace furnished with tables and chairs. The bar serves soft drinks, beers and some spirits. Kifaru Conference Centre has 1 room for 30 pax and another for 80. Conference equipment including projector, laptop and PA system is available. A safe is available for guests' use at reception and there is also a secure car park.

Savana Executive Hotel Kisii

Savana Executive Hotel, Kisii-Kisumu Road, near St Stephen's College
PO Box 503, Kisii 40200, Kenya
Tel
Mobile   +254 727 213158; +254 712 377747; +254 752 722435
Fax
E-mail   benterakinyi@yahoo.com
Web

   Kisumu, LS & CH
1.5 hrs

On the outskirts of Kisii, Savana Executive Hotel offers spacious rooms and suites.

There are 8 en-suite rooms and 4 suites. The rooms all have Biblical names such as Zacharia and Solomon and are furnished with sofa, armchairs, coffee table, satellite TV and fridge stocked with soft drinks. The bathrooms have both bath and shower. The suites are designed individually. David, the presidential suite, has 2 double beds, a dressing room and a small room with baby cot. Annah has, in addition, a sitting room.

The dining room has a round table that seats 8 pax. International dishes, such as fried chicken, fish in batter, stew, spaghetti and macaroni, are served. The lounge has sofas, armchairs and satellite TV, and alcoholic drinks are on offer here. The ground floor terrace has comfortable chairs, and the 1st floor balcony is available for guests wishing to work, with chairs and writing tables. There is also a secure car park.

Kisindi Lodge and Spa Kendu Bay

Kisindi Lodge and Spa, Kendu Bay, Lake Victoria, Kenya
PO Box 800, Kisumu 40123, Kenya
Tel   +254 20 2631701
Mobile   +254 736 780078; +254 721 216922
Fax   +254 50 50845
E-mail   rest@kisindi.com
Web   www.kisindi.com / www.wildernessgetawaysea.com

    Kisumu, LS & CH
1.5 hrs

On the shores of Lake Victoria, Kisindi Lodge and Spa provides a holiday of complete relaxation. Guests at this peaceful sanctuary can choose between a day full of activities or a day of exquisite pampering.

There are 6 traditional thatched cottages, made up of 5 double cottages and a family cottage that sleeps 8 pax. The cottages are all en-suite, and have verandas overlooking the lake. Each room has a double bed and a day bed which can be converted to a single if required. The restaurant serves 3-course gourmet lunches and dinners. The bar serves soft drinks, beers, wines, spirits and cocktails, and has views of the lake and the Suba Mountains. Electricity is provided by solar and wind power.

The swimming pool is surrounded by lawn and equipped with sunbeds, tables and sunshades. The spa offers a selection of health and beauty treatments, including Swedish massage, green tea bath, manicure and pedicure. Nature walks through surrounding farmland and cultural visits to local fishing villages are on offer. A hike across the Homa Hills takes 3 hours. Boat trips and sundowner cruises are also available. Transfers from Kisumu airport can be arranged. The lodge is 1½ hours by car or 2½ hours by boat from Kisumu.

Homa Bay Tourist Hotel Homa Bay

Homa Bay Tourist Hotel, Lakefront, Homa Bay, Kenya
PO Box 35, Homa Bay 40300, Kenya

Tel	+254 59 22522
Mobile	+254 727 112615; +254 720 493157
Fax	+254 59 22044
E-mail	homabaytouristhotel@yahoo.com
Web	www.homabaytouristhotel.com

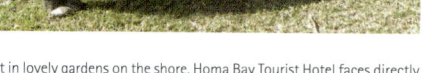

Kisumu, LS & CH
2 hrs

Set in lovely gardens on the shore, Homa Bay Tourist Hotel faces directly onto Lake Victoria. The lawns are dotted with local artwork and indigenous shrubs and plants and populated by geese, turkeys and ducks. The garden makes an attractive setting for a conference or party.

There are 23 en-suite rooms, made up of 15 standard and 8 superior. The rooms all have fan, mosquito net, writing table, satellite TV and telephone. The superior rooms have, in addition, a fridge and their bathrooms have both bath and shower. There are also 6 en-suite safari tents, all equipped with full electricity, satellite TV, table, chair and veranda overlooking the lake. The restaurant serves both buffet and a la carte, with dishes such as chicken kiev, chicken tikka, fillet mignon, vegetable cutlets and deep fried catch of the day. The bar is well stocked. Meals can be taken in the restaurant, the bar or at tables in the garden. A marquee can be put up in the garden for functions, weddings or seminars. The conference room seats 40 pax and the meeting room seats 10. The business centre, next to the lounge, offers internet, scanning and printing. There is plentiful secure parking space. Safaris and excursions can be arranged.

Activities include trips to Ruma National Park and boat rides on the lake.

Hotel Hippo Buck   Homa Bay

Hotel Hippo Buck, Rongo-Homa Bay Road, Homa Bay, Kenya
PO Box 274, Homa Bay 40300, Kenya

Tel	+254 59 22032; +254 59 22132; +254 20 8066227
Mobile	+254 723 262000; +254 733 708465
Fax	+254 59 22132
E-mail	info@hippobuck.com
Web	www.hippobuck.com

 VISA

 Kisumu, LS & CH
2 hrs

Established in 1992, Hotel Hippo Buck is situated on the outskirts of Homa Bay, in Sophia Valley. The hotel is 1km from the shores of Lake Victoria and has views of Asego Hills.

There are 40 en-suite rooms, made up of standard, deluxe and superior. All rooms have writing table, cupboard, fan and mosquito nets on all beds and windows. The deluxe and superior rooms have, in addition, satellite TV, telephone, kettle and balcony overlooking the garden. The superior rooms are in a separate wing that opened in 2008, and have more modern facilities. The Victoria Restaurant has an international menu including fresh lake fish, grilled chicken, curries and stews. The thatched circular bar is well stocked with soft drinks, beers, wines and spirits, and has a sound system. Ziwa entertainment room, next to the bar, has a pool table, satellite TV and comfortable sofas.

The executive conference room opened in 2009; it seats 200 pax, is fully tiled and has floor to ceiling windows. The club conference room seats 80. The hotel has its own well and backup generator. There is a children's playground with swings, slides and a bouncy castle. As well as Lake Victoria, local attractions include Ondago Bird Sanctuary and Homa Hills Hot Springs.

Little Nile Guest House Homa Bay

Little Nile Guest House, Rongo Road, Homa Bay, Kenya
PO Box 648, Homa Bay 40300, Kenya

Tel +254 20 8066230
Mobile
Fax
E-mail
Web

    Kisumu, LS & CH
                        2 hrs

Little Nile Guest House opened in 2005. The guesthouse is conveniently located on the main road into Homa Bay from Rongo, and offers pleasant budget accommodation.

There are 15 en-suite rooms. The rooms are painted in a variety of pastel shades, such as mint, pink and purple. All rooms have a writing table, chair, mosquito net and built in cupboard. They are also equipped with electrical mosquito devices. The guesthouse's chef is happy to discuss guests' food preferences with them in the morning, then buy ingredients fresh from the market and cook as required.

The guesthouse has a lounge on the ground floor and the 1st floor. Both lounges are furnished with comfortable sofas and armchairs, and equipped with satellite TV. Homa Bay is located directly on Lake Victoria. The lake makes an attractive edge to this little town. The town has a bustling market, a few shops and a petrol station. It is a base for UN and NGO workers in this region of Kenya. Nearby sites of interest include Ruma National Park, Rusinga Island and Mfangano Island.

KWS, Oribi Guest House Ruma Ntl. Park

KWS, Oribi Guest House, Ruma National Park, Kenya
Kenya Wildlife Service, PO Box 40241, Nairobi 00100, Kenya

Tel +254 20 6000800; +254 20 6002345; +254 20 3991000
Mobile +254 726 610508-9; +254 736 663421; +254 736 663400
Fax +254 20 6003792
E-mail kws@kws.go.ke / reservations@kws.go.ke
Web www.kws.go.ke

    Kisumu, LS & CH
                        3 hrs

Named after the rare oribi antelope which is found in Ruma National Park, Oribi Guest House is a self-catering cottage located near a waterhole at the Park HQ. It is owned and managed by Kenya Wildlife Service, KWS. The cottage has 3 bedrooms, made up of 2 doubles and 1 triple, and the annex has 2 simple bedrooms. There is also a bathroom, a sitting room with a log fire and an adjoining open plan dining room. Doors lead from the sitting room to the veranda. The kitchen is equipped with stove, kitchen utensils, cutlery, crockery and glassware. A resident caretaker provides kerosene lamps, bed linen, mosquito nets, towels, soap and loo paper. The cottage has solar electricity which powers the fridge, lights and hot water.

Ruma National Park is the last sanctuary of the endangered roan antelope. Other rare game includes oribi, bohor reedbuck, Rothschild giraffe and serval cat. The park is famed for its rare intra-African migrant, the blue swallow, and is also rich in reptiles including the African spitting cobra and eastern green mamba.

The park gates are open from 6am to 7pm; park fees must be paid in cash at the gate. 4WD vehicles are recommended.

Western

Rusinga Island Lodge — Lake Victoria

Rusinga Island Lodge, Rusinga Island, Lake Victoria, Kenya
PO Box 171, Mbita 40305, Kenya

Tel	+254 20 2531314-5
Mobile	+254 733 552845; + 254 716 055924; + 254 734 402932
Fax	
E-mail	info@rusinga.com / reservations@rusinga.com
Web	www.rusingaislandtrust.com / www.rusinga.com

VISA, Amex

Rusinga Island, CH, 2 mins
Kisumu, LS & CH, 3 hrs

Rusinga Island was catapulted into the news in 1948 when Louis and Mary Leakey announced the discovery of the Proconsul skull and other 18-million-year-old fossils. Rusinga regularly hosts a team from the American Museum of Natural History who continue this work and give personal guided tours of the sites. The two most rewarding prehistoric sites are located a short walk from Rusinga Island Lodge.

The lodge is a secluded retreat in grounds of exotic trees, a haven for a myriad of bird species. There are 6 en-suite cottages and a family cottage with interconnecting twin room and double room. All cottages are crafted from local materials, and have dressing room, living area, high thatched roof and spacious veranda. Meals are created from home grown vegetables and fruits. Breakfast and lunch are served alfresco; dinner can be served in the mess, candlelit on the jetty, at the gazebo or around the floodlit swimming pool.

Rusinga's Wellness Spa offers a selection of treatments including African Awakening, Kenyan Caress and Mogambo Massage. Activities include fishing, bird watching, biking, hiking and boat trips. Water sports include water-skiing, donutting and knee boarding. Rusinga Island Lodge supports local community projects such as Eddie Thackray Memorial School, Kageno Trust and Kibisom Women's Group.

Mfangano Island Camp — Lake Victoria

Mfangano Island Camp, Mfangano Island, Lake Victoria, Kenya
Musiara Limited, PO Box 48217, Nairobi 00100, Kenya

Tel	+254 20 2734000; +254 20 2734005
Mobile	+254 722 717529 +254 722 715306 +254 733 616204-5
Fax	+254 20 2734023; +254 20 2734024
E-mail	reservations@governorscamp.com
Web	www.governorscamp.com

VISA, MasterCard, Eurocard
Amex, Travellers Cheques

Mfangano, CH, 15 mins
Kisumu LS & CH, 3 hrs

In the late 19th century, explorers such as Speke and Burton trekked through treacherous and unmapped lands in search of the source of the Nile, and finally settled on Lake Victoria. The traditional villages and bright fishing boats on the lake have changed little since this time. On a secluded bay in Mfangano Island, Mfangano Island Camp is an ideal spot from which to view this lake with such a colourful history.

The 6 thatched en-suite rondavels are made up of 4 doubles and 2 twins, all with verandas overlooking the lake.

From the open sitting room and dining room, guests can watch dhows traversing the water, cormorants diving for fish and fish eagles perching on the treetops. Fresh salads, the daily catch and homemade bread are served. The wide variety of birdlife includes the black headed gonolek and the double toothed barbet. Birdwatchers can walk through the lush vegetation of the hills, stroll along the shore or take a trip in a boat.

Other activities include fishing, water-skiing and visiting local Luo villages. Sipping sundowners in a traditional longboat while watching the sun set over the lake makes a perfect end to the day. The camp is closed in April and May.

Lake Victoria – Photo © Andrew Nightingale, kembu.com

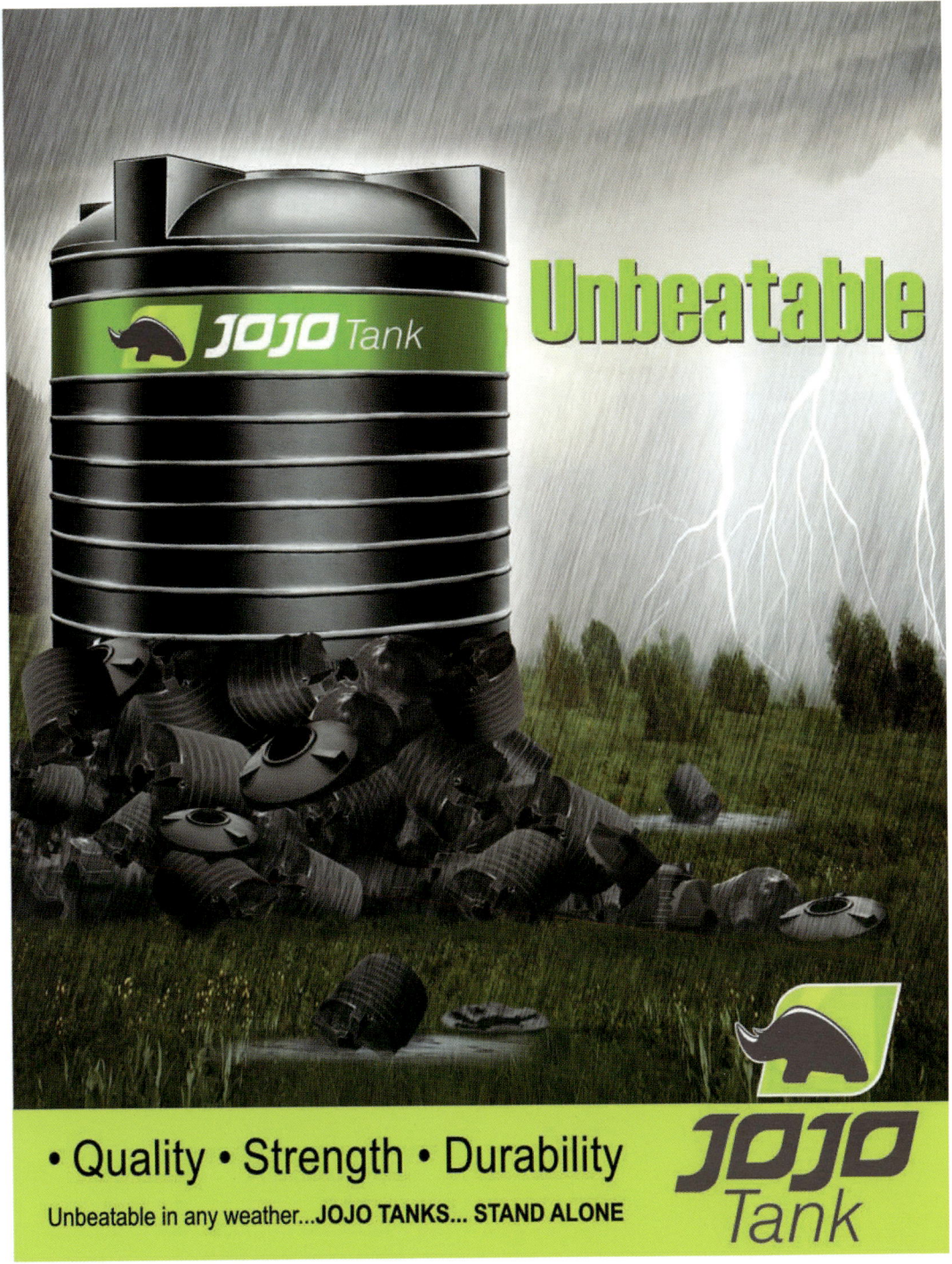

Maasai Mara National Reserve

The Great Migration – Photo © Andrew Nightingale, kembu.com

Famous around the world for its exceptional, abundant wildlife, the Maasai Mara National Reserve has become known as the Seventh Wonder of the World. Not only are all the members of safari's Big Five found here, but over 100 other mammal species and over 450 bird species live within the reserve.

The Maasai Mara was designated a National Reserve in 1974 and is under the authority of Narok County Council to whom park fees are paid. The Maasai Mara is part of the greater Serengeti-Mara ecosystem whose area of about 8,000km² is home to the largest terrestrial conglomeration of wildlife in the world, conservatively estimated at over 6 million animals.

The park gates are at Talek, Sekenani, Ololaimutiek, Sand River, Musiara, Oloololo and Mara Bridge. Scheduled flights from destinations in Kenya land at Musiara, Mara North, Mara Serena, Ol Kiombo, Kichwa Tembo, Ngerende, Siana and Keekorok. There are also a number of private airstrips where charter flights can land. The Mara River, the Talak River and the Sand River, with their various tributaries, springs and hippo pools, traverse the region.

Surrounding the reserve are conservancies and group ranches that provide a buffer zone for the reserve's wildlife. The major conservancies are Olare Orok, Ol Kinyei, Mara North, Maji Moto Olarro, Naboisho and Ol Chorro Oirouwa; privately managed, they collect their own park fees and initiate their own conservation and community development projects. The Mara Triangle, to the west of the reserve, is managed by the Mara Conservancy, a private, non-profit organisation.

The Maasai Mara takes its name from the Maasai people, a nomadic, Nilotic people famed for their prowess as warriors. Cattle represent wealth to the Maasai, and are used not only for food but also for dowries, fines and sacrifices. During their lives, the Maasai pass through a series of rites of passage, ceremonies and celebrations that take them from initiation through the levels of warriors to the highly respected position of elder.

Mara means mottled in the language of the Maasai, a reference to the savannah plains speckled with riverine forests, mountain ridges and natural springs. It is this naturally varied ecosystem, dotted with distinctive ecotones, that provides the diversity of food types needed to support the proliferation of species of mammals, birds, reptiles, plants and insects found here.

The Maasai Mara is perhaps best known for Africa's most spectacular wildlife event, the Great Migration. Hundreds of thousands of wildebeest, together with zebra, Thompson's and Grant's gazelle, impala, eland, topi and nomadic carnivores, flood north into the Mara in June, July and August, then sweep back into the Serengeti in September and October. The frenzied attacks of lions on the plains and of crocodiles in the rivers are gifts to photographers.

Game drives are the most popular activity in the reserve. Balloon safaris can be arranged at specific sites; most camps and lodges will assist with booking these. Game walks are not permitted in the reserve, but are on offer in the surrounding conservancies and group ranches. It is also possible to visit Maasai villages outside the reserve, to gain an insight into the culture and traditions of the local people.

 Accommodation Guide

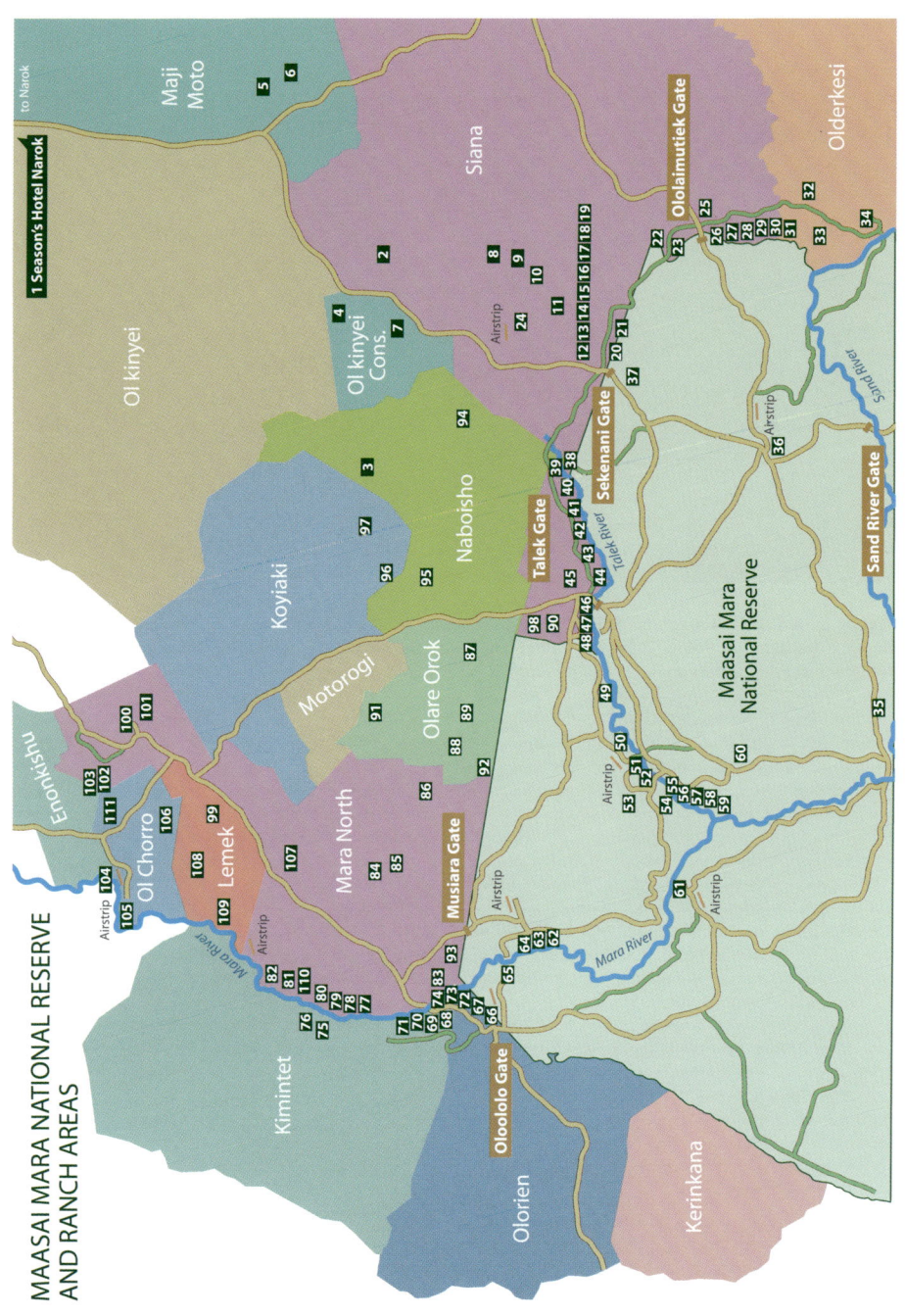

Index to all camps, lodges and hotels in the greater Maasai Mara area

1	Seasons Hotel	40	Mara Leisure Camp	79	Serian
2	Maji Moto Eco Camp	41	Tipilikwani Camp	80	Ngare Serian
3	Basecamp Wilderness	42	Ilkeliani Camp	81	Cheetah Tented Camp
4	Mara Porini Camp	43	Camp Oloshaiki	82	Royal Mara Safari Lodge
5	Olarro	44	Basecamp	83	Jacqueline's House
6	Little Olarro	45	JK Mara Camp	84	Elephant Pepper Camp
7	Ol Seki Hemingways Mara	46	Mara Kima Camp	85	Offbeat Mara Camp
8	Mara Under Canvas	47	Riverside Camp	86	Olumara Tented Camp
9	Leleshwa Camp	48	Fig Tree Camp	87	Kicheche Bush Camp
10	Siana Springs Tented Camp	49	Kichakani Camp	88	Amani Mara
11	Mara Bushtops Camp	50	Mara Explorer	89	Porini Lion Camp
12	Mara Bush House	51	Mara Intrepids	90	Topi House
13	Spurwing Camp	52	Matira Bush Camp	91	Richard's Private Camp
14	Kimana Mara Camp	53	Mara Bush Camp	92	Mara Plains Camp
15	Mara Springs Safari Camp	54	Rekero	93	Acaluma Camp
16	Semadep Safari Camp	55	Naibor	94	Kicheche Valley Camp
17	Enkolong Tented Camp	56	Little Naibor	95	Naboisho Camp
18	Oldarpoi Mara Community Camp	57	Entim	96	Encounter Mara
19	Ol Tome Mara Magic	58	Private Mara Camp	97	Basecamp Dorobo Bush Camp
20	Sentrim Mara	59	Mara Ngenche	98	Nyumbu Camp
21	Sekenani Camp	60	Ashnil Mara Camp	99	Bush Buck Camp
22	Entumoto	61	Mara Serena Safari Lodge	100	Saruni
23	Masai Mara Sopa Lodge	62	Governors' Private Camp	101	Saruni Wild
24	Mara Sokonoi	63	Governors' Camp	102	Acacia House
25	Losho Mara Camp	64	Governors' Il Moran Camp	103	Mara House
26	Masai Mara Manyatta Camp	65	Little Governors' Camp	104	Fairmont Mara Safari Club
27	Big Time Safari Camp	66	Bateleur Camp	105	Ngerende Island Lodge
28	Enchoro Wildlife Camp	67	Kichwa Tembo	106	Richard's Camp
29	Impala Wildlife Lodge	68	Kensington Mara West	107	Kicheche Mara Camp
30	Ol Moran	69	Kilima Camp	108	Duma Camp
31	Elangata Olerai Luxury Camp	70	Mara Siria	109	David Livingstone Safari Resort
32	Enkewa Mara Camp	71	Mpata Safari Club	110	Exploreans Mara Rianta Camp
33	Black Leopard Retreat	72	Salt Springs Mara Camp	111	Kileleoni Mara Guest House
34	Cottars 1920s Camp	73	Olonana		
35	Sala's Camp	74	Mara Enkipai Safari Camp		
36	Keekorok Lodge	75	Mara Timbo Camp		
37	Sarova Mara Game Camp	76	Nkorombo Mobile Camp		
38	Mara Simba Lodge	77	Karen Blixen Camp		
39	Mara Eden Safari Camp	78	Suguroi Hill Tree House		

Seasons Hotel

Narok

Seasons Hotel, Mai Mahui-Narok Highway, Narok, Kenya
PO Box 766, Narok 20500, Kenya

Tel	+254 50 22821
Mobile	+254 727 437203; +254 710 786132
Fax	+254 50 23176
E-mail	seasonshotels@gmail.com / info@seasonshotelskenya.com
Web	www.seasonshotelskenya.com

JKIA, LS & CH & Intl.
3 hrs

A structure of pink tiles and white balconies, Seasons Hotel is located in Narok, the gateway to the Maasai Mara National Reserve. The hotel opened in 2009, has modern facilities and offers local information and excursions. There are 53 en-suite rooms, made up of standard, deluxe, family and executive. The standard rooms are double or twin, and have satellite TV, telephone, writing desk and built in cupboards. The deluxe rooms are more spacious and have a double and a single bed. The family rooms consist of a deluxe room with an interlinking single room. The executive rooms are carpeted.

The restaurant serves an authentic African buffet, and also has an international a la carte menu including steaks, fish and curries. The bar, with wicker chairs and comfortable sofas, has a good selection of soft drinks, beers, spirits and wines, and is equipped with satellite TV. There is also a swimming pool, a pool bar, a residents' lounge, a beauty salon and a row of curio shops. The conference centre consists of 2 conference halls seating 200 pax each and 2 meeting rooms.

The hotel offers Maasai dancing, talks on Maasai culture and slideshows on wildlife and the Mara ecosystem, and can arrange excursions to the nearby Maasai Mara National Reserve.

Maji Moto Eco Camp

Maji Moto

Maji Moto Eco Camp, 45km from Narok, Kenya
PO Box 5750, Diani 80401, Kenya

Tel	+254 41 2006479
Mobile	+254 716 430722; +254 724 735418
Fax	
E-mail	info@majimotocamp.com
Web	www.majimotocamp.com

Siana, LS & CH
40 mins

Run by the Maasai people, this simple camp offers its guests the opportunity to experience the life of the Maasai. The camp's team welcomes guests into their culture, shows them their traditions and introduces them to local flora, fauna and wildlife.

The 6 igloo-style tents have mattresses and bedding, and sleep 2 people each. Showers and WCs are separate. All the tents are positioned to create privacy and make the most of the breathtaking views. The camp also has a Maasai-style dining area.

Designed to be part of the environment, this eco-sensitive camp blends in naturally. There is no generator and the camp is lit by candles, lanterns and campfires. Fresh food is brought each day from the nearest town and all meals are prepared by the camp's Maasai cook who combines traditional Kenyan food with international dishes.

As well as learning and participating in Maasai culture, guests can relax at camp, exchange stories around the campfire and enjoy the location. Activities offered include guided nature walks, school visits and evening baths in the hot springs that give the camp its name. For an additional charge, night game drives and mountain bike trips can also be arranged.

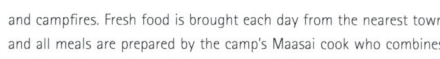

Basecamp Wilderness

Naboisho Conservancy

Basecamp Wilderness, Naboisho Conservancy, nr Mara Reserve, Kenya
PO Box 43369, Nairobi 00100, Kenya

Tel	+254 20 3877490-2
Mobile	+254 733 333909
Fax	+254 20 3877489
E-mail	bookings@basecampexplorer.co.ke
Web	www.basecampexplorer.com

 VISA, MasterCard   Ol Kiombo, LS & CH 40 mins

Perched on a ridge amongst indigenous euclea and croton bushes, Basecamp Wilderness gives stunning views over the plains of the Naboisho Conservancy. Basecamp Wilderness is owned and managed by Basecamp, a luxury eco-friendly camp near Talek Gate. Basecamp Foundation supports and cooperates with local communities, as well as developing and promoting Basecamp's sustainable tourism concept.

There are 5 en-suite safari cottages, 2 facing west towards the sunset and 3 facing east towards the sunrise. The cottages have kitchenette, canvas doors, net windows, internet connection and large verandas with sofas and sunbeds from which to enjoy the views. They are elegantly designed in cream and ochre, and adorned with natural fabrics and Maasai ornaments. 2 of the cottages are suitable for guests with disabilities. The open sided restaurant serves international dishes. The lounge has a fully stocked bar and lovely views. Activities include day and night game drives, game walks and cultural visits to local Maasai villages. Bush meals and sundowners can be arranged. Cultural talks from local Maasai on their traditions and lifestyle are available. Basecamp holds a gold award from Ecotourism Society of Kenya, and has won the WTM First Choice Responsible Tourism Award, SKAL International Ecotourism Award and TIES Ecotourism Innovation Award.

Mara Porini Camp

Ol Kinyei Conservancy

Mara Porini Camp, Ol Kinyei Conservancy, nr Mara Reserve, Kenya
Porini Camps, PO Box 388, Nairobi 00621 Kenya

Tel	+254 20 7123129; +254 20 7122504; +254 20 7121851
Mobile	+254 722 509200; +254 735 339209; +254 774 136523
Fax	+254 20 7120864
E-mail	info@porini.com / info@gamewatchers.co.ke
Web	www.porini.com

           Ol Kinyei, CH, 10 mins
Siana, LS & CH, 30 mins

Mara Porini Camp is located in the exclusive wildlife conservancy of Ol Kinyei, a beautiful wilderness area of savannah plains, riverine forest and fresh springs. The conservancy belongs to a Maasai community who recently allocated the area a sanctuary for wildlife, and contains a wide variety of animal and bird species, including a resident pride of lion. There are 6 en-suite tents, shaded by yellow-barked acacia trees on the banks of the Laetoli, a permanent spring within Ol Kinyei. The tents are furnished in traditional safari style, have double and single beds, and the bathrooms contain safari showers. The food is freshly prepared, and includes homemade bread and crisp salad.

Game drives cover both the Ol Kinyei Conservancy and the Maasai Mara National Reserve. Night drives in the conservancy give guests the chance to see the more elusive nocturnal game. Maasai warriors lead walks in the conservancy, and speak about how the various indigenous animals and plants are used by their community.

Mara Porini Camp has been granted a silver ecotourism award from Ecotourism Society of Kenya. The local Maasai community receive income for each guest in the conservancy, and employment for their members. Eco-sensitive policies cover land use, water, sewage, energy and waste disposal.

Olarro

Loita Hills

Olarro, Loita Hills, nr Maasai Mara National Reserve, Kenya
PO Box 1379, Nairobi 00502, Kenya

Tel	+254 20 2048610/21
Mobile	+254 721 921966; +254 771 574483
Fax	+254 20 2491857
E-mail	info@olarrokenya.com
Web	www.olarrokenya.com

VISA, MasterCard   Siana, LS & CH 45 mins

Nestling in the contours of an ancient hillside, Olarro is exclusive, intimate and stylish. The lodge is on a large group ranch, formed in order to secure an intrinsic part of the greater Maasai Mara for wildlife habitat. It aims to preserve the environment and wildlife and strengthen the traditional heritage of the Maasai.

There are 7 cottages, made up of 3 twins and 4 doubles. The interiors are cool white, enhanced by earth tone décor. All cottages are equipped with WiFi and hairdryer. Each cottage has its own veranda; 6 of the cottages use a common sitting area, suitable for groups or families. Meals are served in the Northern Lounge, overlooking the Loita plains. Fresh natural ingredients are used to create unique dishes. There is also a sundeck, lounge, bar and open fireplace. Bush dinners, picnics and meals beside the swimming pool are also available.

Olarro Spa has a range of therapies and treatments, designed for relaxation or energising. The swimming pool is a series of small interlinked pools. Activities include game drives, night drives with night vision goggles, game walks, mountain biking and trekking. The lodge uses solar power and has a backup generator. Olarro supports the local community with projects in education, health, water, sanitation, agriculture and alternate energy.

Little Olarro

Loita Hills

Little Olarro, Loita Hills, nr Maasai Mara National Reserve, Kenya
PO Box 1379, Nairobi 00502, Kenya

Tel	+254 20 2048610/21
Mobile	+254 721 921966; +254 771 574483
Fax	+254 20 2491857
E-mail	info@olarrokenya.com
Web	www.olarrokenya.com

VISA, MasterCard    Siana, LS & CH 45 mins

Little Olarro is a private house located a short distance from Olarro's main lodge. High on the hillside, Little Olarro offers stunning panoramic views of the Loita plains. The lodge is on a large group ranch, formed in order to secure an intrinsic part of the greater Maasai Mara for wildlife habitat. It aims to preserve the environment and wildlife and strengthen the traditional heritage of the Maasai.

There is a luxury suite with spacious master bedroom, and a smaller twin bedroom. The house also has a lounge, dining area and veranda. The Upper Deck Lounge is a 2-floor structure, with fully equipped kitchen and massage room on the ground floor and spacious lounge with fireplace and dining area on the 1st floor. Fresh natural ingredients are used to create unique dishes. Bush dinners, picnics and meals beside the series of interlinked swimming pools are also available.

Little Olarro has its own private massage room on the Upper Deck. All the therapies and treatments from the Olarro Spa are available. Activities include game drives, night drives with night vision goggles, game walks, mountain biking and trekking. The lodge uses solar power and has a backup generator. Olarro supports the local community with projects in education, health, water, sanitation, agriculture and alternate energy.

Ol Seki Hemingways Mara
Naboisho Conservancy

Ol Seki Hemingways Mara, Naboisho Conservancy, nr Mara Reserve, Kenya
Hemingways Collection, PO Box 146, Nairobi 00502, Kenya

Tel	+254 20 2295020; +254 20 2295030
Mobile	+254 729 147686; +254 771 147686; +254 735 147686
Fax	+254 20 2627373
E-mail	info@olseki.com / olseki@h-ways.com
Web	www.hemingways-collection.com / www.olseki.com

VISA, MasterCard

Siana, LS & CH
40 mins

In the unspoiled Naboisho Conservancy, Ol Seki Hemingways Mara is well positioned to see prolific game.

There are 6 en-suite tents and 2 suites. The tents are uniquely rounded, and each has 6 opening panels giving panoramic views. Each tent is completely hidden from the others, and furnished in traditional safari style. The suites, called Simba, lion, and Chui, leopard, were created in 2010 with low environmental impact. Each suite has a spacious private living and dining tent flanked by two bedroom tents, with en-suite bathroom, shower and changing area, and a private kitchen with a dedicated team of staff.

The library tent has an extensive selection of African and international books. Meals can be served in the traditional mess tent, on the veranda of the guests' tent, in the nearby caves or out in the bush.

Game drives cover both Naboisho Conservancy and the Maasai Mara National Reserve. Night drives and game walks take place in Naboisho Conservancy. Cultural visits to local Maasai villages give an insight into traditional customs. The camp works closely with the local community and supports Oleseri Primary School and Koiyaki Guiding School. Its eco initiatives have earned the camp the Ecotourism Society of Kenya's prestigious silver award.

Mara Under Canvas
Siana Conservancy

Mara Under Canvas, Siana Conservancy, nr Maasai Mara National Reserve

Tel	
Mobile	+254 723 261688
Fax	
E-mail	mara@maraundercanvas.com
Web	www.maraundercanvas.com

Siana, LS & CH
40 mins

Mara Under Canvas offers the experience of a fly camp, or traditional mobile camp. This simple private camp is seasonal, and is based in Siana Conservancy, adjoining the Maasai Mara National Reserve.

There are 4 en-suite tents. All tents have a veranda furnished with safari chairs. Maasai guards escort guests to and from their tents at night. Breakfast, lunch and dinner are served in the mess tent. Special dietary requirements can be accommodated with advance notice. The bar serves soft drinks, beers, wines and spirits.

Activities include game drives in Siana Conservancy. Other activities include game walks and cultural visits to local Maasai villages. Breakfast and lunch picnics can be provided. Sundowners in the bush can also be arranged. The Siana Conservancy is home to a resident population of wildebeest, zebra, elephant, buffalo, lion, leopard and cheetah, as well as to a variety of birdlife.

Mara Under Canvas supports the Wildland Conservation Trust and the projects that the trust has initiated. This includes Predator Aware. Guests at the camp have the opportunity to go on walking patrols with the Predator Aware wildlife scouts and to see the Wildland Conservation Trust's ongoing projects.

Leleshwa Camp Siana Conservancy

Leleshwa Camp, Siana Conservancy, nr Maasai Mara Ntl. Reserve, Kenya
The Leleshwa Safari Company Ltd, PO Box 143, Nairobi 00200, Kenya

Tel	+254 20 2413166
Mobile	+254 723 560070
Fax	
E-mail	reservations@leleshwacamp.com
Web	www.leleshwacamp.com

 VISA, MasterCard, Amex   Siana, LS & CH 20 mins

Leleshwa Camp is an intimate tented camp situated on the Siana Conservancy on the northeastern edge of the Maasai Mara National Reserve. Resting along a stream, overlooking picturesque hills and rolling plains dotted with resident game, Leleshwa Camp is a peaceful haven. The 6 en-suite tents have private verandas with striking views. The suite has an adjoining lounge, making it ideal for honeymooners or families. The tents are furnished with a simple elegance and are situated to give guests the utmost privacy. Meals can be served in the open mess tent or under the stars, surrounded by candles and hurricane lamps. The camp has no permanent structures and is entirely removable, in keeping with its philosophy of environmental sustainability. The camp recycles, reuses and composts where possible. The guests' conservation fees contribute to local development projects including infrastructure, health, education and the environment

As well as game drives and walks, the camp offers hiking in the Loita Hills in areas inaccessible to vehicles. Local Maasai guides lead guests through the 200km² Sacred Forest, introducing them to cedar, podo and strangler fig trees, breathtaking waterfalls and spectacular birdlife and wildlife. The camp also runs photography workshops and has 6 computers fully equipped with the latest photography software.

Siana Springs Tented Camp Siana Conservancy

Siana Springs Tented Camp, Siana Conservancy, nr Mara Reserve, Kenya
PO Box 41163, Nairobi 00100, Kenya

Tel	+254 20 2710542; +254 20 2383085
Mobile	+254 722 994088; +254 722 756200
Fax	+254 20 2710544
E-mail	info@siana-springs.co.ke
Web	www.siana-springs.co.ke

    Siana, LS & CH 10 mins

Siana Springs, meaning plentiful springs in the Maasai language, is set in a lush indigenous forest beneath the Ngama Hills, and is watered by the largest natural springs in the Mara ecosystem. The camp has a rich history dating back to 1920 when the 1st game warden selected its current site for his camp. Siana Group Ranch, the community-run conservancy surrounding the camp, has game-rich plains and seasonal streams.

The 38 en-suite tents are in 3 secluded wings. The Bamboo Wing, near the main camp, is surrounded by bamboo groves and ornamental trees. The Palm Wing overlooks springs, lily-filled ponds and indigenous forest. The Acacia Wing, on the camp boundary, is in open acacia woodland rich with birdlife. Meals are served in the large dining area or on the open air terrace, where local Maasai perform traditional dances. Lectures and slideshows on culture and wildlife are also available. The camp has a bar and lounge area, a conference tent with modern business facilities and a freeform swimming pool in the forest.

Strict eco-principles govern the camp's heating system, compost and waste disposal. The camp supports the development of the conservancy and assists 2 local primary schools. More than 60% of the staff are local Maasai. Siana Springs Tented Camp has a bronze award from Ecotourism Society of Kenya.

Mara Bushtops Camp

Siana Conservancy

Mara Bushtops Camp, Siana Conservancy, nr Mara Reserve, Kenya
Orion Hotels, PO Box 10283, Bamburi 80101, Kenya

Tel	+254 20 2137862
Mobile	+254 733 490209; +254 727 695 452
Fax	
E-mail	orion@orion-hotels.net
Web	www.orion-hotels.net

VISA, MasterCard, Amex
Siana, LS & CH
10 mins

Mara Bushtops Camp is perched on a hillside, with spectacular views into the valley. The camp is located in Siana Conservancy, which borders the Maasai Mara National Reserve.

There are 12 en-suite tents. The tents have been designed in modern African style, with wooden decks and sunken hot tubs from which to appreciate the view. The reception, lounge area and swimming pool are raised over the valley and are equipped with a telescope for game viewing. The restaurant, overlooking a waterhole, has an international a la carte menu and an extensive wine cellar. Fresh vegetables are home grown in the camp's garden. The lounge has an open fire, selection of books and large TV for viewing photos.

Activities include game drives in Siana Conservancy and the Maasai Mara National Reserve. Game walks, bird watching, cultural visits to local Maasai villages and hiking in the nearby Sekenani Hills are also on offer. The camp was built to be eco sustainable. It uses solar power, with a backup generator, and purifies and recycles grey water. The camp supports the Nkoilale School; current projects include a borehole near the school and practical training for the children. Mara Bushtops Camp was voted the Best Luxury Camp in Kenya by Twende Magazine in 2007 and 2008.

Mara Bush House

Sekenani Gate

Mara Bush House, 3km from Sekenani Gate, nr Maasai Mara Ntl. Reserve
PO Box 139, Mombasa 80100, Kenya

Tel	+254 20 2067264
Mobile	+254 724 093280; +254 722 413005
Fax	
E-mail	sales@elephanttrailsafaris.com
Web	www.elephanttrailsafaris.com

Siana, LS & CH
30 mins

Established in 2010, Mara Bush House is a private house on a hilltop overlooking the Maasai Mara National Reserve. The house offers personal service and spectacular views.

There are 4 en-suite rooms, made up of 2 doubles, 1 twin and 1 single. Sunrise and Sunset rooms, upstairs, give views appropriate to their names. Elephant and Rhino rooms are located downstairs. All rooms are fully tiled, decorated with a Maasai theme and have private balcony. The house has a sitting room, dining room, bar, kitchen, veranda and garden. The rooms can be taken individually, or the house can be taken as a whole. There is also a campsite with communal bathroom and kitchen facilities, and external dining areas. Tents and gas cookers are available for hire; firewood and charcoal are for sale.

The qualified chef creates African, international or French dishes, and is happy to discuss food preferences with the guests. Activities include game drives and game walks. 4WD vehicles are available for hire by those wishing to do self-drive game drives. Cultural visits to local Maasai villages are also on offer. Bush dinners and sundowners on the hilltop overlooking the Maasai Mara National Reserve can be arranged. Lights and hot water are provided by solar power; there is also a backup generator.

Spurwing Camp

Sekenani Gate

Spurwing Camp, 2km from Sekenani Gate, nr Mara Reserve, Kenya
Spurwing Travel and Tours, PO Box 390, Nairobi 00502, Kenya

Tel	+254 20 3882321; +254 20 3882306; +254 20 3884412
Mobile	+254 722 521702; +254 720 491700; +254 772 166626
Fax	+254 20 3883418
E-mail	safari@spurwingkenya.com
Web	www.spurwingsafaris.com / www.spurwingkenya.com

          Siana, LS & CH
30 mins

Spurwing Camp is located 2km from Sekenani Gate, just outside the Maasai Mara National Reserve. It is a tented camp aimed at the intrepid adventurer, and offers budget accommodation and an authentic bush safari experience.

There are 10 tents, all with twin beds. Bed linen is not provided and guests should bring their own sleeping bags and towels. There are communal external bathroom facilities. There is also a central kitchen with jiko barbecue and utensils, and a communal dining tent. Guests can choose the self-catering option or the full board option. There is also a large campsite which can accommodate up to 200 pax. The camp has no electricity or fridge. Provisions are not sold at the camp; guests should bring food, drinks, cooler box, cooking gas, kerosene for lamps and charcoal for barbecue.

Spurwing Camp is affiliated to Spurwing Travel and Tours. Packages starting and ending in Nairobi can be arranged. Driver guides in either safari minivans or 4WD land rovers collect guests from their hotel, drive to Spurwing Camp, provide game drives during the guests' stay and return them to Nairobi at the end. Safaris, excursions and trips to destinations in Kenya, Tanzania, Uganda and Rwanda can be arranged.

Kimana Mara Camp

Sekenani Gate

Kimana Mara Camp, 2km from Sekenani Gate, nr Mara Reserve, Kenya
PO Box 423, Narok 20500, Kenya

Tel	+254 20 2362863
Mobile	+254 726 757618
Fax	
E-mail	info@kimanamara.com / kimanamara@yahoo.com
Web	www.kimanamara.com

           Siana, LS & CH
30 mins

On the banks of the Sekenani River, Kimana Mara Camp is surrounded by indigenous woodland. The camp aims to provide simplicity, serenity and intimacy with nature. It is located 2km from Sekenani Gate, just outside the Maasai Mara National Reserve.

There are 37 en-suite tents, made up of singles, doubles and triples. The tents are linked by walkways through the trees. Guests can choose the full board or self-catering option. There is also a campsite, with dining area, kitchen and communal bathroom facilities. Guests can bring their own tents, or hire tents on site. The camp has a generator and charging facilities, and a secure car park.

Game drives in the Maasai Mara National Reserve can be booked at the camp, or guests can do self-drive game drives; 4WD vehicles are available for hire. The camp offers nature walks outside the reserve and hiking trails with local guides further afield. Cultural visits to local Maasai villages are on offer. Bush breakfast, dinner and sundowners can be arranged. Maasai dances at the campfire during the evening are available. The camp is open to special interest groups such as students, workshops and filming crews. Teambuilding activities can be arranged.

Mara Springs
Safari Camp

Sekenani Gate

Mara Springs Safari Camp, 3km from Sekenani Gate, nr Mara Reserve
Mountain Rock, PO Box 15796, Nairobi 00100, Kenya

Tel	+254 20 2242133
Mobile	+254 722 511752; +254 736 511752 .
Tel/ Fax	+254 20 2210051
E-mail	info@mountainrockkenya.com
Web	www.mountainrockkenya.com

          Siana, LS & CH
                                                30 mins

The underground springs that supply flowing water to the site give this camp its name. Strategically positioned at the foot of Naunare Hills in a prime game viewing area, Mara Springs Safari Camp is set in lush landscape alongside the forested banks of Sekenani River.

The camp has 3 levels of tents. The 20 en-suite tents can be singles, doubles or triples. The 15 basic tents have shared bathroom facilities. The campsite offers bathroom and kitchen facilities for those who wish to use their own tents.

The resident camp cooks prepare well-balanced meals for those on full board option and can be hired to assist those taking the self-catering option. A separate dining mess is reserved for residents staying in the en-suite tents. A shop with bar is open for guests and campers. Postcards, maps, toiletries and souvenirs are sold, along with an assortment of beers, red and white wine, cigarettes and soft drinks. Evening fires and traditional dancing can be organised on request.

Activities include nature walks to the surrounding scenic hills, sundowners from the horizons of the reserve, bike treks, educational folklore, Maasai dances and night drives outside the reserve in search of nocturnal hunters. The camp is 3km from Sekenani Gate, just outside the Maasai Mara National Reserve.

Semadep Safari Camp

Sekenani Gate

Semadep Safari Camp, 2km from Sekenani Gate, nr Mara Reserve, Kenya
PO Box 353, Narok 20500, Kenya

Tel	
Mobile	+254 721 817757
Fax	
E-mail	jplsemadep@yahoo.com
Web	www.semadepcamp.com

          Siana, LS & CH
                                                30 mins

Semadep Safari Camp was established in 2006 and is run by Semadep Maasai community organisation. The camp is located on a hillside near Sekenani Gate, just outside the Maasai Mara National Reserve. It offers budget accommodation and camping, as well as an introduction to the Maasai way of life.

There are 3 en-suite tents, that can be doubles or singles as required. The tents are located in solid structures with thatched roofs and stone floors. There is also a campsite, and 2 standard tents for hire. Locally sourced and traditionally prepared Maasai dishes are served in the dining area. Drinks are served around the campfire in the evenings. A kitchen with basic facilities is available for guests who prefer the self-catering option. Guests can do self-drive game drives into the Maasai Mara National Reserve. Vehicles and drivers can be arranged if requested in advance. Other activities include walking in the hills overlooking the Maasai Mara National Reserve, visiting Ewangan cultural village, traditional Maasai dancing and Maasai cultural talks around the campfire at night.

Semadep community project was established in 1997. It supports community welfare projects that benefit the entire community in areas like health, education and tourism.

Mara

 Accommodation Guide

Enkolong Tented Camp Sekenani Gate

Enkolong Tented Camp, 2km from Sekenani Gate, nr Mara Reserve, Kenya

Tel
Mobile
Fax
E-mail   admin@megatraveloffers.com
Web   www.megatraveloffers.com

 Siana, LS & CH
30 mins

Enkolong Tented Camp is located 2km from Sekenani Gate, just outside the Maasai Mara National Reserve. The camp offers budget accommodation and a campsite. The camp operates in partnership with the local Maasai community, and aims to enhance the living standards of the local people. There are 22 tents, made up of 8 standard and 14 basic. The standard tents have an en-suite WC and adjacent shower. The basic tents have an adjacent WC and shower. The tents can be single, double, twin or triple as required. The tents are furnished with safari chairs. Lighting and water heating are powered by solar and generator. Guests can choose the full board or self-catering option. There is also a campsite. The camp is located on the banks of Sekenani River, and has views of the water and the wildlife that comes to drink at its edges.

Game drives organised by the camp, and self-drive game drives, are available. Activities available for an extra charge include escorted nature walks, sundowners, bush breakfasts and cultural visits to local Maasai villages.

Oldarpoi Mara Community Camp Sekenani Gate

Oldarpoi Mara Community Camp, 4km from Sekenani Gate, nr Mara Reserve
PO Box 20213, Nairobi 00100, Kenya

Tel
Mobile   +254 713 547984; +254 721 731927
Fax
E-mail   info@oldarpoimaracamp.com
Web   www.oldarpoimaracamp.com

 Siana, LS & CH
30 mins

Oldarpoi Mara Community Camp is owned and managed by the local Maasai community. It aims to bring transformational development, both socially and economically, to local Maasai communities, turning them into self-reliant and self-sustaining communities through profitable ecotourism activities. The camp is located 4km from Sekenani Gate just outside the Maasai Mara National Reserve. There are 10 tents, 5 with en-suite bathrooms and 5 with communal external bathrooms. The tents have verandas furnished with safari chairs. There is also a campsite. The camp can arrange game drives into the Maasai Mara National Reserve, as well as picnic breakfasts, bush lunches and bush dinners. The camp offers a selection of interactive activities with local Maasai. Game walks through the nearby hills are led by Maasai guides who introduce guests to the application of natural resources, such as herbal medicine made from indigenous plants. The camp organises homestays in local villages, during which guests experience the traditional lifestyle of the Maasai. Evening entertainment includes traditional dancing and storytelling by Maasai moran. The camp offers volunteer opportunities for guests who would like to give their services and skills to the community's social and economic projects. Current projects include medical outreach, teaching in rural primary schools, constructing water dams, digging boreholes, leadership and business training, sports coaching and environmental conservation.

Ol Tome Mara Magic

Sekenani Gate

Ol Tome Mara Magic, 2km from Sekenani Gate, nr Mara Reserve, Kenya
PO Box 32611, Nairobi 00600, Kenya

Tel	+254 20 2498512
Mobile	+254 771 580935
Fax	
E-mail	reservations@oltomemaramagic.com
Web	www.oltomemaramagic.webs.com

   Siana, LS & CH
30 mins

Ol Tome Mara Magic is located 2km from Sekenani Gate, just outside the Maasai Mara National Reserve. The camp is owned and managed by 2 companies: Kentainers, a supplier of plastic water tanks, and Safari Seeker, a safari operator which started in 1986.

There are 7 en-suite tents, made up of 3 twins and 4 doubles. The tents are raised on concrete decks, and furnished with dressing table, writing table and safari chairs. All tents are equipped with hairdryer, kettle and mosquito net. The dining room, with bar and lounge, offers a blend of continental and Indian cuisine. Food allergies and preferences can be catered for, advance notice required.

Various packages, with or without flights into the Maasai Mara National Reserve, are offered. Activities include game drives, both inside and outside the Maasai Mara National Reserve.

Sentrim Mara

Maasai Mara Ntl. Reserve

Sentrim Mara, Ngama Hills, nr Sekenani Gate, Maasai Mara Ntl. Reserve
Sentrim Hotels and Lodges, PO Box 43436, Nairobi 00100, Kenya

Tel	+254 20 315680; +254 20 315371; +254 20 341442
Mobile	+254 722 207361; +254 733 852083; +254 733 680680
Fax	+254 20 2218314; +254 20 343875
E-mail	info@sentrim-hotels.com
Web	www.sentrim-hotels.com

 VISA, MasterCard    Siana, LS & CH
30 mins

Sentrim Mara is shaded by the cluster of acacia trees that surround it. The camp is located in the Ngama Hills, 3km from Sekenani Gate, in the Maasai Mara National Reserve.

There are 44 en-suite tents, made up of singles, doubles, twins and triples. All tents are shaded by thatched roofs, and have elevated private balconies. The tents are equipped with mosquito nets, sockets for battery charging and electric lights. The dining area serves an international menu. Activities include game walks outside the reserve. Bush breakfast, dinner and sundowners can be arranged. Picnic lunches are available for those who wish to do a full day game drive.

A masseuse is on site for those who wish to relax after a game drive or game walk.

Packages inclusive of game drives with or without flights into the Maasai Mara National Reserve can be booked from Nairobi.

 Accommodation Guide

Sekenani Camp

Maasai Mara Ntl. Reserve

Sekenani Camp, Maasai Mara National Reserve, Kenya
PO Box 15010, Nairobi 00509, Kenya

Tel	+254 20 2056423; +254 20 2700781
Mobile	+254 722 147810; +254 735 484207
Tel/ Fax	+254 20 891169
E-mail	reservations@sekenani-camp.com
Web	www.sekenani-camp.com

VISA, MasterCard

 Keekorok, LS & CH 45 mins

At the source of the Sekenani River, Sekenani Camp stretches along a stream flowing from a natural rock pool. This exotic combination of forest and river, on the edge of the Maasai Mara National Reserve, is home to plentiful game; over 200 species of birds have been recorded within 1km of the camp.

The 15 large en-suite tents are raised off the ground on platforms. Each tent is set into the bush to ensure privacy, and has a wooden veranda overlooking the forest. The well-appointed tents are adorned with woven rugs and crafted wooden furniture.

A suspension bridge connects the guest tents with the dining room, campfire and bar area, where freshly prepared meals and a wide selection of drinks are served.

As well as day and night game drives, game walks with Maasai guides in the hills surrounding the camp are a speciality here. Bush picnics and sundowners are also available.

This eco-friendly camp is operated in conjunction with 26 Maasai families. It hosts a community project that aims to improve the quality of life of the Maasai people by developing healthcare, veterinary services, education and clean water around the reserve. Interested guests are welcome to visit local community projects.

Entumoto

Ololaimutiek Gate

Entumoto, nr Ololaimutiek Gate, nr Maasai Mara National Reserve, Kenya
PO Box 24756, Nairobi 00502, Kenya

Tel	+254 20 2694189/92
Mobile	+254 713 400903
Fax	
E-mail	reservations@entumoto.com
Web	www.entumoto.com

 Keekorok, LS & CH 45 mins

Entumoto, meaning meeting place in the language of the Maasai, was established in 2010. The camp was founded by Karl von Heland, the grandson of Karen Blixen's farm manager, and is part owned by the local Maasai community.

There are 5 en-suite double tents and 4 family tents. The tents, made from multi-layered canvas, are attractively furnished with daybeds and have verandas with views of the plains. The family tents have a double room, twin room and living room with open fireplace. Meals are created from produce from the camp's own garden. The camp has a swimming pool; snacks and drinks are served at the poolside. The lounge has a library; the bar is well stocked with soft drinks, beers, wines and spirits. Activities include game drives and game walks. Maasai guides are happy to introduce guests to the indigenous plants that make their traditional medicine, and to show them how to track animals. Cultural visits to local Maasai villages are on offer. Guests are also welcome to visit the environmental projects that the camp supports. Weddings and functions can be arranged. The camp can be taken exclusively. Holistic yoga retreats, artistic programmes and creative writing workshops can all be arranged.

Masai Mara Sopa Lodge

Maasai Mara Ntl.Reserve

Masai Mara Sopa Lodge, Maasai Mara National Reserve, Kenya
Sopa Lodges, PO Box 72630, Nairobi 00200, Kenya

Tel	+254 20 3750235; +254 20 3616000; +254 20 2416485
Mobile	+254 722 206328; +254 733 610060
Fax	+254 20 3751507; +254 20 3740069
E-mail	info@sopalodges.co.ke / reservations@sopalodges.co.ke
Web	www.sopalodges.com

 VISA, MasterCard   Siana, LS & CH 40 mins

On the slopes of the Ololaimutiek Hills, Masai Mara Sopa Lodge has sweeping views across the eastern edge of the Maasai Mara National Reserve. The lodge is designed in the style of the Maasai; its guest rooms and public areas are traditional round buildings with thatched roofs. There are 88 en-suite double rooms and 12 suites. All rooms have 2 queen size beds, mosquito nets on their windows and a veranda with a view. The central dining area, adorned with polished wood and Maasai fabrics, serves buffet breakfast, lunch and dinner. Meals can be served outside on request. The 3 bars are well stocked with soft drinks, beers and spirits, and equipped with TV. Board games are available at reception. There is also a swimming pool with a children's section. The lodge is powered by generators, which run 24hrs.

Activities include game drives, game walks, cultural visits to nearby Maasai villages and nightly wildlife feeding. For an extra charge, balloon safaris can be booked here. Conferences and weddings can be arranged. Masai Mara Sopa Lodge has a bronze award from Ecotourism Society of Kenya.

Mara Sokonoi

Siana Conservancy

Mara Sokonoi, Siana Conservancy, nr Maasai Mara National Reserve
PO Box 546, Nairobi 00502, Kenya

Tel	+254 20 2734095
Mobile	+254 720 315974; +254 722 363181
Fax	
E-mail	info@marasokonoi.com
Web	www.marasokonoi.com

  Siana, LS & CH 10 mins

Established in 2011, Mara Sokonoi is a small and exclusive tented camp in the Siana Conservancy, on the banks of the seasonal Oloipili River. The camp is named for the Sokonoi, a medicinal tree used by the Maasai to treat a range of ailments.

There are 5 en-suite tents, adorned with linen drapes and safari furnishings. All tents have private verandas facing the riverine vegetation. The water is heated by briquette fuel boosters and lighting is by solar power. There are also 2 traditional Maasai huts, each containing 2 bedrooms and a small sitting area. The mess tent is raised on a platform, and has a dining area, bar, lounge with library and large terrace with a view of the sunset.

Game drives can be taken in the early morning and evening. Game walks led by Maasai moran focus on tracking and bush navigation. Other activities include night drives, bush dinners, sundowners and cultural visits to Maasai villages.

The camp is committed to collaboration with the local Maasai. Young Maasai moran are employed by the camp to learn skills such as masonry, carpentry, housekeeping and cookery through apprenticeship. The women earn income through building guest manyattas in traditional Maasai style, while simultaneously learning new methods of building maintenance.

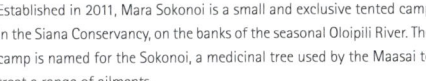
 Accommodation Guide

Losho Mara Camp Ololaimutiek Gate

Losho Mara Camp, nr Ololaimutiek Gate, nr Mara Reserve, Kenya
PO Box 867, Nairobi 00200, Kenya

Tel	+254 20 2025342
Mobile	+254 722 819084; +254 722 522083
Fax	+254 20 3546061
E-mail	info@loshomaracamp.com / milton@loitasafaris.com
Web	www.loshomaracamp.com

       Keekorok, LS & CH
                                 45 mins

Losho, meaning a high place in the language of the Maasai, aptly describes the location of Losho Mara Camp in the high altitude Mara region. The camp offers budget accommodation a short drive outside the Maasai Mara National Reserve. It was established in 2010.

There are 7 tents, 2 of which have en-suite bathrooms and the remainder of which have external bathrooms. All tents are set on wooden floors, with verandas furnished with safari chairs. The simple tents are decorated in traditional Maasai style, and give visitors an authentic bush experience. The camp has been designed to blend in with the natural environment. The camp offers game walks with a Maasai guide, which can end with a sundowner in the bush or a drink by the fireside. Activities also include game drives and night drives. Picnics can be provided. Cultural visits to local Maasai villages can be arranged, and give an insight into the culture and traditions of the Maasai. The camp is located about half an hour from the Ololaimutiek Gate of the Maasai Mara National Reserve.

Masai Mara Manyatta Camp Ololaimutiek Gate

Masai Mara Manyatta Camp, nr Ololaimutiek Gate, nr Mara Reserve, Kenya
Safe Ride Tours & Safaris Ltd, PO Box 57662, Nairobi 00200, Kenya

Tel	+254 20 2229484; +254 20 2246739; +254 20 2101162
Mobile	+254 721 714760; +254 722 496558
Fax	+254 20 2246739.
E-mail	camp@masaimaramanyattacamp.com
Web	www.masaimaramanyattacamp.com

       Keekorok, LS & CH
                                 45 mins

Masai Mara Manyatta Camp is located near the Ololaimutiek Gate of the Maasai Mara National Reserve. The camp, just outside the reserve, offers budget accommodation, camping and activities.

There are 20 en-suite tents. All tents stand on compacted surface, and are shaded by thatched roofs. The tents can be single, double or twin as required. All tents are equipped with mosquito net and power sockets. The restaurant serves plated breakfast, lunch and dinner to visitors on the full board package. Guests who take the self-catering option are welcome to bring their own food and have it prepared by the resident chef at no additional cost. The bar serves soft drinks, beers and spirits. There is a campfire at which to enjoy sundowners and after dinner conversation. The campsite has communal bathroom facilities, a communal kitchen and a barbecue area.

Activities include game drives and guided nature walks. Cultural visits to local Maasai villages can be arranged. Visitors with their own vehicle and guide are welcome to arrange their own game drives. There is also a bush volleyball court.

Big Time Safari Camp — Ololaimutiek Gate

Big Time Safari Camp, nr Ololaimutiek Gate, nr Mara Reserve, Kenya
PO Box 7014, Nairobi 00300, Kenya

Tel	+254 20 2218841; +254 20 2218837
Mobile	+254 729 780769; +254 735 867454
Fax	+254 20 2218837
E-mail	info@bigtimesafaricamp.com / info@bigtimesafaris.co.ke
Web	www.bigtimesafaricamp.com / www.bigtimesafaris.co.ke

 VISA, MasterCard   Keekorok, LS & CH 45 mins

Big Time Safari Camp is on the slopes of the Oloongams Hills, near Ololaimutiek Gate. It offers an introduction to Maasai culture, as well as to wildlife. The camp has budget accommodation just outside the Maasai Mara National Reserve. It is affiliated to Big Time Safaris, which offers camping, trekking, bird watching and beach holidays in East Africa. There are 27 en-suite tents, with twin beds and outdoor showers. The dining room serves traditional Kenyan breakfast, lunch and dinner. Meals can also be served alfresco. The bar, around a stone fireplace, has soft drinks, beers and spirits. Activities include game drives in either 4WD vehicles or safari vans.

For a surcharge, vehicles can be booked on an exclusive basis. Game walks introduce visitors to the tracks and signs that animals and birds leave in the bush. Cultural visits to local Maasai villages can be arranged; local dancers provide entertainment and traditional souvenirs are on sale. The camp also offers warrior training. The resident naturalist gives lectures and slide presentations on the Maasai Mara National Reserve. For a surcharge, a night game drive followed by bush dinner can be arranged on request. The camp can book balloon safaris with a nearby operator.

Enchoro Wildlife Camp — Ololaimutiek Gate

Enchoro Wildlife Camp, nr Ololaimutiek Gate, nr Mara Reserve, Kenya
PO Box 4473, Nairobi 00200, Kenya

Tel	+254 20 2711217; +254 20 2723012; +254 20 2726011
Mobile	+254 710 322787; +254 732 739483
Fax	+254 20 2726011
E-mail	info@enchorowildlifecamp.com
Web	www.enchorowildlifecamp.com

     Keekorok, LS & CH 45 mins

Meaning natural spring water in the language of the Maasai, Enchoro Wildlife Camp offers the chance to get close to nature. The camp is owned by the local community and run with the assistance of volunteers, ensuring that guests gain local knowledge directly from the Maasai people and the community benefits economically from the camp. Enchoro Wildlife Camp is a member of the Kenya Youth Hostels Association and offers comfortable budget accommodation. The camp can accommodate up to 30 pax. There are 11 en-suite tents, made up of doubles, twins and family tents. The tents are set in a grassy clearing in the shade of indigenous trees. The open dining area serves affordable meals and snacks throughout the day. The reception area has an activity desk that can assist with booking activities such as game drives, balloon safaris, walking, trekking and cultural visits to Maasai communities.

The camp is located just outside the Ololaimutiek Gate of the Maasai Mara National Reserve. The nearby warden's office provides security for the camp, and has a safe where guests are welcome to store their valuables. Guests wishing to volunteer at the camp or assist with community development projects should contact the Kenya Voluntary and Community Development Project at www.kvcdp.org

Impala Wildlife Lodge Ololaimutiek Gate

Impala Wildlife Lodge, nr Ololaimutiek Gate, nr Mara Reserve, Kenya
PO Box 69513, Nairobi 00100, Kenya

Tel	+254 20 2226189; +254 20 2213186
Mobile	+254 733 784505; +254 721 149919
Fax	+254 20 2213254
E-mail	info@impalawildlifelodge.com
Web	www.impalawildlifelodge.com

    Keekorok, LS & CH
45 mins

Styled on a traditional local village, Impala Wildlife Lodge offers African ambiance in a natural setting. The buildings, of clay brick with thatched roofs, are round. Dotted around a manicured garden, they are linked by stone paths. The lodge was previously called Mara Hippo Safari Lodge. There are 69 en-suite rooms, made up of singles, doubles and triples. Some rooms are solid cabins and others are tents. All rooms have verandas with views of the surrounding plains. The central lounge has terracotta walls, comfortable sofas and coffee tables. The restaurant serves international table d'hote, with African specialities. The bar has a selection of soft drinks, beers, wines and spirits, and is equipped with satellite TV. Maasai moran entertain with traditional songs and dances, around an open campfire, during the evenings.

The camp has a swimming pool, surrounded by sunbathing terrace with sunbeds and shade umbrellas. Activities include game drives in the Maasai Mara National Reserve. The lodge is not fenced, to allow the wild animals to pass through; Maasai guards are stationed throughout the camp.

Ol Moran Ololaimutiek Gate

Ol Moran, 2km from Ololaimutiek Gate, nr Mara Reserve, Kenya
PO Box 1655, Nairobi 00502, Kenya

Tel	+254 20 3882923; +254 20 3882924
Mobile	+254 722 523372; +254 254 722 774907
Fax	+254 20 3882924
E-mail	olmorantentedcamp08@gmail.com
Web	www.olmorantentedcamp.com

    Keekorok, LS & CH
45 mins

Ol Moran is a tented camp on the banks of the Ololaimutiek River. From the thatched veranda of each tent, the animals that come to drink at the river can be seen.

There are 15 en-suite tents, made up of 5 doubles, 8 twins and 2 honeymoon tents. Power is provided by a generator; charging facilities are available. Buffet breakfast, lunch and dinner are served in the dining tent or under the stars. Special food requests can be catered for with advance notice. Bush dinners can also be arranged. Maasai moran offer cultural evenings of dancing and singing around the campfire.
Activities include game drives in the Maasai Mara National Reserve.

The resident naturalist also guides nature walks, and explains the flora and fauna of the surrounding ecosystem and the culture of the Maasai community. He can also guide climbs up the nearby Lenganishu Hills; from the peak, visitors have views over the Serengeti plains. The walk takes about 3 hours at an average walking speed. Cultural visits to local Maasai villages are available. Balloon safaris can be booked with a nearby balloon operator.

Elangata Olerai Luxury Camp

Ololaimutiek Gate

Elangata Olerai, 10km from Ololaimutiek Gate, nr Mara Reserve, Kenya
PO Box 66416, Nairobi 00800, Kenya

Tel	+254 20 2047137; +254 20 2047138
Mobile	+254 720 729130; +254 725 442047; +254 705 218067-8
Fax	+254 20 2248931
E-mail	info@elangataoleraicamp.com
Web	www.elangataoleraicamp.com

 VISA, MasterCard   Keekorok, LS & CH 45 mins

Elangata Olerai Luxury Camp was established in 2011. The camp is an intimate tented camp just outside the Maasai Mara National Reserve. There are 10 en-suite tents. All tents are designed with African wood in Swahili style. A paved walkway links the tents, 5 of which have 2 double beds and 5 of which have Swahili double beds. There is also a bar, lounge and deck for sundowners. African and international cuisine is served, and the camp offers a weekly barbeque which includes local and international dishes.

The camp offers community guiding, using the expertise of local community members to introduce visitors to landscapes and animals that they understand. Activities, available for a surcharge, include nature walks, visits to a nearby hippo pool, sundowners, bush meals and night game drives. Also available are cultural visits to a local Maasai village and Maasai dancing.

Packages including flights to and from the Maasai Mara National Reserve can be arranged from destinations in Kenya and Tanzania.

Enkewa Mara Camp

Olderkesi

Enkewa Mara Camp, Olderkesi, nr Maasai Mara National Reserve, Kenya
PO Box 684, Narok 20500, Kenya

Tel	
Mobile	+254 717 779780; Spain: +34 669462451
Fax	
E-mail	infocamp@enkewamaracamp.com
Web	www.enkewamaracamp.com

    Keekorok, LS & CH 2 hrs

Established in 2010, Enkewa Mara Camp is located near the Tanzania border, southeast of the Maasai Mara National Reserve. The camp offers privacy and wilderness.

There are 5 en-suite tents, which can be double or triple as required. The tents are designed in traditional safari style and have private verandas. The camp has a living area, library and bar service. The chef serves Mediterranean and international cuisine. There is also a central open area with hammocks for relaxing and reading, surrounded by a variety of trees and birdlife. Guests are welcome to gather around the campfire in the evening.

Activities include day and night game drives. Cultural visits to local Maasai villages are available. Transfers from local airstrips, reserve gates and Nairobi can be arranged. Bush breakfast and lunch can be arranged. The camp is eco sustainable. It uses solar power, manages waste and uses no pumps or generators. An ecological vegetable patch supplies the camp with fresh fruit and vegetables.

Black Leopard Retreat

Olderkesi

Black Leopard Retreat, Olderkesi, nr Maasai Mara National Reserve, Kenya
PO Box 8910, Nairobi 00200, Kenya

Tel	
Mobile	+254 721 421918; +254 734 838828
Fax	
E-mail	bookings@blackleopardretreat.com
Web	www.blackleopardretreat.com

 VISA, MasterCard   Cottars, CH, 20 mins
Keekorok, LS & CH, 2 hrs

Set in a private concession southeast of the Maasai Mara National Reserve, Black Leopard Retreat offers an exclusive game viewing experience. Over 100 species of mammals and over 400 species of birds have been recorded here, many only a short distance from the camp. The camp was previously called Muthaiga Safari Camp, and before that was called Impiripiri Camp. The 7 en-suite tents are decorated in the rich colours of Africa and furnished with large double beds, hand-woven rugs, safari chests and writing desks. Each has a wooden veranda overlooking the savannah. The 2 villas, served by a private butler, have 2 en-suite bedrooms and a large living room adorned with local fabrics and craftwork. Their large wooden decks overlook lush woodland. The living and dining tent, elegantly furnished with traditional safari equipment and Swahili ornaments, opens onto savannah and a waterhole often visited by wildlife. This eco-friendly camp uses solar and wind energy and has initiated many wildlife and community preservation projects.

The camp is built on land leased from the Maasai and its local staff are happy to introduce guests to their culture and traditions. Guests are welcome to visit local villages and schools, and to attend the weekly Maasai market. As well as game drives and game walks, activities include night drives, bush meals and sundowners at stunning viewpoints.

Cottars 1920s Camp

Olderkesi

Cottars 1920s Camp, Olderkesi, nr Maasai Mara National Reserve, Kenya
Cheli & Peacock, PO Box 743, Nairobi 00517, Kenya

Tel	+254 20 6004053/4; +254 20 6003090/1
Mobile	+254 724 255374; +254 733 490234
Fax	+254 20 6004050; +254 20 6003066
E-mail	safaris@chelipeacock.co.ke / info@chelipeacock.co.ke
Web	www.chelipeacock.com / www.cottars.com

VISA, MasterCard   Cottars, CH, 20 mins
Keekorok, LS & CH, 2 hrs

Cottars 1920s Camp is located between the Maasai Mara National Reserve and the Tanzania border. The camp is surrounded by forested hills. There are 10 en-suite tents, made up of 6 standard and 4 family tents. All tents have mosquito net, chair, table, cupboard, luggage rack and veranda with a view of the valley. The standard tents can have double or twin beds as required. The family tents have an en-suite double bedroom, en-suite twin bedroom and living room. An extra bed can be added if required. Breakfast, lunch and dinner are served in the mess tent. Meals can also be taken in the bush or in the privacy of the guests' tent. The bar serves soft drinks, beers, wines and spirits.

Activities include day and night game drives. Game walks in the hills and cultural visits to Maasai villages are also available. Sundowners can be arranged. The gift shop sells gift items, T-shirts, fleeces, books and Maasai artefacts. The spa offers massage, manicure and pedicure.

Sala's Camp

Maasai Mara Ntl. Reserve

Sala's Camp, nr Sand River Gate, Maasai Mara National Reserve, Kenya
The Safari Collection, PO Box 15565, Nairobi 00503, Kenya

Tel	+254 20 5020888; +254 20 2513166
Mobile	+254 731 914732; +254 725 675830
Fax	
E-mail	info@thesafaricollection.com
Web	www.thesafaricollection.com

Keekorok, LS & CH
20 mins

At the convergence of the Sand River and the Keekorok River, Sala's Camp looks directly into the Serengeti of northern Tanzania. The camp nestles in indigenous forest, and has views of the northern route, which millions of wildebeest take during the annual migration.

There are 7 luxury en-suite tents, the largest of which includes a double room with central sitting area, suitable for a family or honeymoon couple. Tents are either twin or double, and contain traditional safari furniture that evokes the pioneering days of safari.

Camp food is cooked in the traditional safari way, using a campfire, and assisted with a gas cooker. Home baked pastries, breads and biscuits are a speciality. Produce is farm sourced and free from artificial pesticides. This remote wilderness area of the Maasai Mara National Reserve offers exceptional game viewing; over 450 species of birds have been recorded. Many of the staff at Sala's Camp are local Maasai, who are proud of their heritage and keen to share their knowledge. Visits to traditional Maasai manyattas can be arranged.

The camp is personally owner-managed and hosted. It is seasonal, and is closed from 15th March - 14th June and 15th October to 14th December.

Keekorok Lodge

Maasai Mara Ntl. Reserve

Keekorok Lodge, Maasai Mara National Reserve, Kenya
Sun Africa Hotels, PO Box 102124, Nairobi 00101, Kenya

Tel	+254 20 4450636; +254 20 4450639; +254 20 4450712
Mobile	+254 737 107266; +254 711 107266
Fax	+254 20 4450735
E-mail	info@sunafricahotels.com
Web	www.sunafricahotels.com

VISA, MasterCard

Keekorok, LS & CH
10 mins

Keekorok, meaning motley abundance in the Maasai language, was constructed in 1962 on an 80-acre site in an area of permanent springs and lush grassland. One of the first lodges in the Maasai Mara National Reserve, Keekorok is located in the centre of this famous reserve.

The lodge has 89 double rooms, 8 superior rooms and 4 suites, all of which are en-suite. Accommodation is in stone bungalows with private balconies. Most rooms overlook the reserve and the remainder look into a large garden. The lodge was fully refurbished in 2006.

The restaurant looks out on manicured lawns and a rock garden, and serves a variety of traditional African, Asian and Western food. The Discovery Bar reflects Keekorok's long history and features photos of its illustrious clientele. The Swimming Pool Bar serves refreshments throughout the day. The Hippo Pool Bar, connected to the lodge by a 1km wooden walkway, looks over a waterhole that is home to about 20 hippos.

Game drives can be booked in advance or on arrival at the lodge. They leave the lodge at 6.30am, 9.30am and 4.30pm. Bird walks start at 10am every day. Evening entertainment alternates between Maasai dancing and wildlife videos. The conference hall seats up to 100 pax.

Keekorok Lodge holds Ecotourism Society of Kenya's bronze award.

Sarova Mara Game Camp

Maasai Mara Ntl. Reserve

Sarova Mara Game Camp, nr Sekenani Gate, Mara Reserve, Kenya
Sarova Hotels, PO Box 72493, Nairobi 00200, Kenya

Tel	+254 20 2767000; +254 20 2714444; +254 50 22386
Mobile	+254 773 610405; +254 722 200945/6; +254 734 699751/2
Fax	+254 20 2715566; +254 50 22371
E-mail	centralreservations@sarovahotels.com
Web	www.sarovahotels.com

VISA, MasterCard

Keekorok, LS & CH
40 mins

Sarova Mara Game Camp is 5 minutes' drive from Sekenani Gate in the Maasai Mara National Reserve. Set in landscaped gardens of exotic trees and indigenous shrubs, the camp is surrounded by a 24hr electric fence. The camp has 53 en-suite standard tents with permanent roof and bathroom and canvas front, 2 family tents and 20 club tents with glass panel doors and tent deck for private dining, equipped with minibar, hairdryer and safe. Isokon Restaurant, on the ground floor, has 2 sections, 1 indoor and 1 outdoor covered by a canopy. The restaurant serves buffet breakfast and lunch and a la carte dinner with specialty live cooking. Oloip Bar and Ewaso Pool Bar, also on the ground floor, provide an opportunity for guests to gather around the log fire in the evenings. Sarova Mara Game Camp offers game drives, nature walks and cultural visits to Isokon Maasai Culture Village. It also offers balloon rides followed by a champagne breakfast. In the camp, there is a mini golf putting area, archery, table tennis and darts, as well as massage therapy at the Tulia Spa tent. Maasai dancers are also available.

Mara Simba Lodge

Maasai Mara Ntl. Reserve

Mara Simba Lodge, nr Talek River, Maasai Mara National Reserve, Kenya
Simba Lodges, PO Box 66601, Nairobi 00800, Kenya

Tel	+254 20 2105454; +254 20 2105453
Mobile	+254 722 788830; +254 734 600415
Fax	+254 20 4343963; +254 20 4444403
E-mail	sales@simbalodges.com
Web	www.simbalodges.com

Keekorok, LS & CH
45 mins

Mara Simba Lodge overlooks a dramatic bend of the Talek River. The lodge's grounds stretch along the river, and its landscaped gardens are filled with indigenous trees that are home to a variety of birds and butterflies. The lodge was designed to complement its surroundings and is decorated in traditional Maasai style.

There are 84 en-suite rooms, 6 rooms in each stone banda. They are made up of 60 twins, 12 doubles, 4 double and single and 8 triples. Each room has a private veranda with a view of the river. The public area, overlooking the Talek River, has floors of cedar wood decking elevated on timber posts, and thatched roofs. The dining area and the bar each have stone fireplaces; the terrace offers floodlit viewing at night. The gift shop stocks personal, photographic and souvenir items. There is also a swimming pool surrounded by sunbeds.

Activities are charged extra and include game drives and game walks. Bush meals and sundowners are available. The lodge's naturalist gives talks on the wildlife and ecology of the Maasai Mara National Reserve, as well as offering slideshows and Maasai cultural lectures. Mara Simba Lodge is keen to conserve the environment, and has installed a sewage treatment plant that provides water for irrigation.

Mara Eden Safari Camp   Talek River

Mara Eden Safari Camp, Talek River, nr Maasai Mara Ntl. Reserve, Kenya
Eden Luxury Camps, PO Box 26334, Nairobi 00504, Kenya

Tel	
Mobile	+254 716 059138; +254 732 785001; +254 772 729201
Fax	
E-mail	info@edenluxurycamps.com / edenluxurycamps@gmail.com
Web	www.edenluxurycamps.com

 Ol Kiombo, LS & CH, 40 mins
Keekorok, LS & CH, 40 mins

On the banks of the Talek River, Mara Eden Safari Camp overlooks both the river and the Maasai Mara National Reserve. The camp, established in 2011, is a small and intimate tented camp with an emphasis on culture-based safaris.

There are 8 en-suite tents, made up of singles and doubles. All tents are raised on wooden decks and have 24-hour solar lighting and unique wooden showers. The lounge, with dining area and bar, is in the centre of the camp, and is raised on a wooden deck overlooking the river. Lunch is served on the riverbank; dinner is served under the stars or in the dining area. A campfire in front of the deck makes a lovely place for a sundowner. WiFi and charging facilities are available in the lounge. The camp is mostly built from natural materials and aims to leave as small a footprint on the land as possible.

Activities include game drives and guided bush walks. Maasai cultural storytelling takes place around the fire in the evening and an astronomy talk is offered after dinner. Children's activities include local pottery and Maasai archery. The camp supports local Maasai women in making charcoal from cow dung, which reduces deforestation while providing fuel and income to the community.

Mara Leisure Camp   Talek Gate

Mara Leisure Camp, nr Talek Gate, nr Maasai Mara Ntl. Reserve, Kenya
PO Box 17545, Nairobi 00500, Kenya

Tel	+254 20 557009; +254 20 2101333
Mobile	+254 737 799992; +254 737 799990
Fax	+254 20 556126
E-mail	info@maraleisurecamp.co.ke
Web	www.maraleisurecamp.co.ke

  Ol Kiombo, LS & CH 40 mins

On the banks of the Talek River, Mara Leisure Camp offers views of the river and the animals that come to it to drink. The camp is located near Talek Gate, just outside the Maasai Mara National Reserve.

There are 25 en-suite tents, made up of 17 nyati tents, 6 jumbo tents and 2 family jumbo tents. The nyati tents have twin beds, wooden floor, mosquito net and veranda with a view of the river. The jumbo tents are more spacious and have, in addition, minibar and bathtub. The family jumbo tents are interconnecting and have a common meeting area for meals or relaxation. There are also 3 jamil cottages which are interconnecting, suitable for families.

The camp offers game drives in the Maasai Mara National Reserve, as well as game walks outside the reserve. Cultural visits to local Maasai villages are also available. The resident naturalist gives lectures and slideshows on the Maasai Mara National Reserve. Bush breakfasts and dinners can be arranged for an extra charge. The masseuse offers Swedish massage. The conference hall seats 60 pax, and is equipped with overhead projector and PA system. Teambuilding such as treasure hunts can be arranged. The camp also has a swimming pool, lounge, curio shop and medical clinic.

Tipilikwani Camp

Talek Gate

Tipilikwani Camp, nr Talek Gate, nr Maasai Mara National Reserve, Kenya
Atua Enkop, PO Box 42475, Nairobi 00100, Kenya

Tel	+254 20 4450035-6; +254 20 4440276
Mobile	+254 715 555322
Fax	+254 20 4450037
E-mail	reservations@atua-enkop.com
Web	www.atua-enkop.com

     Ol Kiombo, LS & CH
40 mins

Situated on the banks of the Talek River, Tipilikwani Camp overlooks the Maasai Mara National Reserve.

There are 20 luxury en-suite tents, with veranda and dressing area. Of these, 6 have a king size double bed, and 14 have queen size twin beds. Two large adjoining tents share a veranda and provide ideal accommodation for a family.

The dining and lounge area has the ambience of a tented camp with the comfort and protection of a permanent building. Being open sided, the building provides a view across the river to rolling plains dotted with game. Dinner is served in the dining area, on the veranda of the guests' tent or under the stars. Local Maasai warriors provide entertainment on request. Lectures on Maasai culture are also available.

Tipilikwani Camp is environmentally sensitive and believes in responsible and sustainable tourism. The camp provides access to free, clean water from its borehole to the neighbouring community, which has resulted in the elimination of typhoid fever in this area.

Ilkeliani Camp

Talek Gate

Ilkeliani Camp, nr Talek Gate, nr Maasai Mara National Reserve, Kenya
Africa Eco-Camps Ltd, PO Box 64196, Nairobi 00620, Kenya

Tel	+254 20 2027125/6
Mobile	+254 733 258120; +254 704 084444; +254 750 873876
Fax	+254 20 3002891; +254 20 3752848
E-mail	ilkeliani@accesskenya.co.ke
Web	www.ilkeliani.com

     Ol Kiombo, LS & CH
40 mins

Ilkeliani is the name given to young Maasai warriors, before they become Il Moran. To the Maasai, warriors represent strength, courage, wisdom and comradeship, and this name seems almost to convey magical powers. Ilkeliani Camp, an eco-friendly camp on the banks of the Talek River, aims to preserve the environment and to stay as close as possible to nature.

The 17 en-suite tents are spaced out along the Talek River, with views across the plains. All tents have solar lighting and use a sustainable hot water system. Lunch is served alfresco, while candlelit dinner is served in the mess tent. Picnics are available for any guests who wish to take an extended game drive.

The Maasai guides share their local knowledge and assist guests with the planning of each game drive. Game walks are available, outside the reserve, with an emphasis on tracking and birdlife. Visits to local Maasai communities are encouraged, to enrich the guests' appreciation of the Maasai culture.

Ilkeliani Camp assists and involves the local Maasai communities in conserving their wildlife and environment, and is dedicated to social development projects in the community. The camp employs as many staff from the local communities as possible.

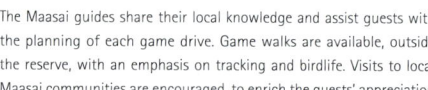

Camp Oloshaiki

Talek Gate

Camp Oloshaiki, nr Talek Gate, nr Maasai Mara National Reserve, Kenya
PO Box 1645, Nairobi 00621, Kenya

Tel	+254 20 2167230; +254 20 2167231
Mobile	+254 734 757944; +254 733 651553
Fax	
E-mail	info@camp-oloshaiki-kenya.com
Web	www.camp-oloshaiki-kenya.com

   Ol Kiombo, LS & CH
                       40 mins

Nestled in the riverine woodlands on the banks of the Talek River, Camp Oloshaiki overlooks the Posee plains. The camp is a small tented camp. There are 8 spacious en-suite tents. All tents have a king size and a queen size 4-poster bed, as well as wicker armchairs; furniture is handcrafted from local timber and other materials. The bathrooms are constructed from local Talek stone, and have a dressing area with large cupboard. The camp has a comfortable sitting room with fireplace. Meals can be served in the dining area or alfresco under the stars. The bar is well stocked, including an extensive wine list. Bush breakfasts and picnic lunches can be arranged.

Activities include game drives both inside and outside the Maasai Mara National Reserve.

Basecamp

Talek Gate

Basecamp, nr Talek Gate, nr Maasai Mara National Reserve, Kenya
Basecamp Explorer, PO Box 43369, Nairobi 00100, Kenya

Tel	+254 20 3877490-2
Mobile	+254 733 333909
Fax	+254 20 3877489
E-mail	bookings@basecampexplorer.co.ke
Web	www.basecampexplorer.com

 VISA, MasterCard   Ol Kiombo, LS & CH
                                                              40 mins

Basecamp is a luxury, eco-friendly camp that aims to have negative impact on the environment. Basecamp Foundation supports and cooperates with local communities, as well as developing and promoting Basecamp's sustainable tourism concept. The camp has 12 en-suite tents, including 1 family tent. The spacious tents are furnished with heavy wooden furniture and adorned with natural fabrics and local beadwork. Their bathrooms are alfresco; water is heated by solar power. The tents are shaded by thatched roofs and have verandas with views of the Talek River or lush garden. The open sided restaurant serves international dishes, created from fresh ingredients grown in Basecamp's garden. The restaurant has a sunset viewing platform, fully stocked bar and a selection of books and games. As well as game drives, game walks and cultural visits to local Maasai villages, Basecamp has a unique selection of activities including beading with Maasai women, visiting Talek primary school and cultural adventures with the Maasai moran. Dorobo Club offers children's activities. Basecamp's eco policies include rain catchment, tree planting, recycling grey water and a complex, efficient compost system. Basecamp holds a gold award from Ecotourism Society of Kenya, and has won the WTM First Choice Responsible Tourism Award, SKAL International Ecotourism Award and TIES Ecotourism Innovation Award.

JK Mara Camp

Talek Gate

JK Mara Camp, nr Talek Gate, nr Maasai Mara National Reserve, Kenya
Wilderness Getaways, PO Box 25240, Nairobi 00603, Kenya

Tel	+254 20 3876636
Mobile	+254 711 986513; +254 737 636693
Fax	+254 20 3876720
E-mail	info@wildernessgetawaysea.com
Web	www.wildernessgetawaysea.com

Ol Kiombo, LS & CH
40 mins

JK Mara Camp is a tented camp near Talek Gate, just outside the Maasai Mara National Reserve. The camp works with the local Maasai community, and aims to provide both satisfaction to visitors and benefit to the community.

There are 12 en-suite tents, made up of doubles and twins. The tents are in the style of traditional mobile camps, adorned with Maasai blankets and beaded artefacts. The bathrooms have safari showers. All tents have verandas with tables and chairs looking into the forest, where hammocks are slung from trees. The dining tent, decorated with Maasai shields, serves buffet breakfast, lunch and dinner. The bar has a lounge area with a selection of books. There is also a gift shop which stocks local Maasai women's beadwork and a viewing platform ideal for sundowners. The camp uses solar power and disposes of its waste responsibly.

Activities include game drives both in and out of the Maasai Mara National Reserve. Game walks, night drives and cultural visits are also on offer. This friendly camp also offers beading with Maasai women and a range of exciting activities for children. The Maasai sing and dance around the campfire before dinner; clear explanations of each dance are given by local Maasai. The camp is affiliated to JK Safaris.

Mara Kima Camp

Talek Gate

Mara Kima Camp, nr Talek Gate, nr Maasai Mara National Reserve, Kenya
Wild Routes of Kenya, PO Box 120, Subukia 20109, Kenya

Tel	
Mobile	+254 735 469925; +254 725 938344
Fax	
E-mail	muringafarm@yahoo.com / infos@wild-routes-of-kenya.com
Web	www.wild-routes-of-kenya.com

Ol Kiombo, LS & CH
40 mins

Located near Talek Gate, Mara Kima Camp is a small friendly camp. Owned and managed by Wild Routes of Kenya, the camp is eco-friendly and promotes sustainable tourism. There are 6 en-suite twin tents. All tents have simple safari furniture, a veranda and a thatched roof. Breakfast, lunch and dinner, prepared from local produce, are served in the open sided dining room. The bar has a selection of soft drinks, beers and wines. Electricity is provided by solar power. The camp has implemented strict policies on waste disposal, water use and energy saving devises. The camp is often visited by monkeys, mongooses and a variety of birds; elephant and hippos sometimes make an appearance. Game drives are on offer. Cultural visits to local Maasai villages, to Talek town and to the local school are also available.

Mara Kima Camp is affiliated to Subukia Bandas, on Muringa Farm, the former home of Mama Daktari, Kenya's most famous flying doctor. Muringa Farm offers activities such as paragliding, horse riding, camel riding, mountain biking and trekking, and also has an eco-volunteering programme. Programmes include assisting with a local orphanage, helping people with disabilities, treating domestic and wild animals and environmental conservation. Holidays combining stays at Mara Kima Camp and Subukia Bandas can be arranged.

Riverside Camp

Talek Gate

Riverside Camp, nr Talek Gate, nr Maasai Mara National Reserve, Kenya
PO Box 671, Narok 20500, Kenya

Tel	
Mobile	+254 720 218319; +254 735 700902; +254 725 848536
Fax	
E-mail	riversidecampmara@yahoo.com / leintoi@gmail.com
Web	www.riversidecampmara.com

    Ol Kiombo, LS & CH
40 mins

Riverside Camp offers a unique Maasai experience. The camp is owned and managed by Kipeen and Everlyne Saiyalel. Kipeen is the ex-chief of the Nurko Maasai. He was one of the initiators of the Koiyaki Guiding School which trains Maasai secondary school leavers as professional safari guides and is now the chairman of the Olare Orok Conservancy. Everlyne is the daughter of the late paramount chief Lorionka ole Ntutu. The couple, with their children, host the camp and introduce guests to Maasai hierarchy and culture.

Riverside Camp is situated on the banks of the Talek River, not far from Talek Gate into the Maasai Mara National Reserve. There are 10 en-suite bandas. Each banda has a view of the Talek River. There is also a campsite, with bathroom facilities; open fires are permitted.

The camp has a dining area and kitchen. Guests can take full board or self-catering options. The camp also has a bar and lounge, and a lookout tower over the Talek River. For a surcharge, the camp can provide a guide and a vehicle; activities include day and night game drives and game walks. Cultural visits to a local Maasai village are also on offer. Maasai traditional dances and lectures on Maasai customs are also available.

Fig Tree Camp

Maasai Mara
Ntl. Reserve

Fig Tree Camp, Talek River, Maasai Mara National Reserve, Kenya
Mada Hotels, PO Box 40683, Nairobi 00100, Kenya

Tel	+254 50 22163; +254 50 22131; +254 20 6005328
Mobile	+254 722 202564; +254 722 202563; +254 731 964011
Fax	+254 20 2651890; +254 20 6003595
E-mail	figtree@madahotels.com / sales@madahotels.com
Web	www.madahotels.com/figtree

   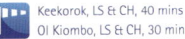 Keekorok, LS & CH, 40 mins
Ol Kiombo, LS & CH, 30 mins

Situated on the banks of the Talek River, Fig Tree Camp is inside the Maasai Mara National Reserve. This central location makes all areas of the reserve accessible during game drives.

The 70 rooms are made up of 38 tents with double and single beds, 22 garden chalets with double and single beds and 10 Ngamboli tents, in a private wing of the camp, offering more privacy and striking views. All rooms are en-suite and have private balconies overlooking the Talek River or the Maasai Mara National Reserve.

The camp's facilities include 2 bars, a main dining room, an open air dining area and a tree house coffee deck. Also available is a video room, guest lecture facilities, a swimming pool and a curio shop. There are 2 conference rooms in a private area of the camp, with PA systems, LCD projectors and computers. Secretarial and photocopying services are available. The camp has a resident nurse and medical clinic.

A local naturalist is available to give guests free lectures and slide presentations on the Maasai Mara ecosystem. Local Maasai dancers entertain clients in the evening. For a surcharge, game walks with Maasai moran, night game drives and bush barbecue dinners are available.

Kichakani Camp

Maasai Mara Ntl. Reserve

Kichakani Camp, Talek River, Maasai Mara National Reserve, Kenya
PO Box 5533, Nairobi 00200, Kenya

Tel	+254 20 2610714/5
Mobile	+254 711 300030
Fax	+254 20 2610714/5
E-mail	sales@kichakanicamp.co.ke
Web	www.kichakanicamp.co.ke

 VISA, MasterCard

 Ol Kiombo, LS & CH
25 mins

Sheltered by towering fig trees, Kichakani Camp is situated on the banks of the Talek River. The camp has views of the Burrungat and Posee plains. There are 15 en-suite tents, made up of doubles and twins. All tents have mosquito net, woven rug, luggage rack, table, chair and verandas with views of the plains. Maasai guards escort guests to and from their tents after dark. The lounge has a selection of books. Breakfast, lunch and dinner are buffet, with a combination of African and international cuisine. Meals are served in the dining area or at the open bandas overlooking the river. The bar serves soft drinks, beers and spirits. The gift shop stocks a selection of souvenirs and artefacts. Electricity is supplied by solar power and generator. The swimming pool is surrounded by sunbathing terrace furnished with sunbeds, tables, chairs and shade umbrellas.

Game drives are conducted daily and can be booked at reception. For a surcharge, game walks and bird watching are also available. Cultural visits to local Maasai villages are on offer. Sundowners and bush dinners can be arranged. Balloon safaris can be booked at a local operator.

Mara Explorer

Maasai Mara Ntl. Reserve

Mara Explorer, Talek River, Maasai Mara National Reserve, Kenya
Heritage Hotels Ltd, PO Box 74888, Nairobi 00200, Kenya

Tel	+254 20 4446651; +254 20 4447929; +254 20 4444582
Mobile	+254 722 205894; +254 733 411105
Fax	+254 20 4446600; +254 20 4446533
E-mail	sales@heritage-eastafrica.com
Web	www.heritage-eastafrica.com

 VISA, Amex

 Ol Kiombo, LS & CH
10 mins

On a forested curve of the Talek River, Mara Explorer has sweeping views along the riverbanks. This central location in the Maasai Mara National Reserve is rich in wildlife, not only during the annual migration but all year round.

The 10 luxury en-suite tents, 7 doubles and 3 twins, look out on the river, and have radios for communication with their private butlers. Furnished in the style of traditional safaris, the tents have hand-carved furniture, antique chests and prints of early explorers. The piece de resistance is a Victorian claw-foot bath on a deck overlooking the African bush, beside each tent. Meals are served in the riverside dining area, on the guests' veranda or in the bush, and are created from fresh vegetables and herbs from the camp's garden.

Activities include personalised game drives, game walks in the Mara Conservation Area and visits to Maasai communities supported by the camp. Bush meals, sundowners and private parties can be arranged. Local Maasai give lectures and slideshows on their culture and wildlife. Guests are welcome to use the swimming pool at nearby Mara Intrepids. Mara Explorer uses eco-friendly systems for heating water and disposing of waste, and supports local primary schools and medical clinics.

Mara Explorer holds Ecotourism Society of Kenya's silver award.

Mara Intrepids

Maasai Mara Ntl. Reserve

Mara Intrepids, Talek River, Maasai Mara National Reserve, Kenya
Heritage Hotels Ltd, PO Box 74888, Nairobi 00200, Kenya

Tel	+254 20 4446651; +254 20 4447929; +254 20 4444582
Mobile	+254 722 205894; +254 733 411105
Fax	+254 20 4446600; +254 20 4446533
E-mail	sales@heritage-eastafrica.com
Web	www.heritage-eastafrica.com

 VISA, Amex   Ol Kiombo, LS & CH
2 mins

Overlooking the Talek River, and only a short drive from the Mara River, Mara Intrepids is in a prime game viewing area in the Maasai Mara National Reserve. The area was used in the 2004 BBC documentary Big Cat Diary. The 30 en-suite tents, on raised platforms, are furnished with 4-poster beds and polished wooden furniture and have shady verandas looking out over the river. The camp is divided into 4 areas, each with its own open air dining area and mess tent for private functions. Breakfast and lunch are usually served alfresco, while dinner is served in the thatched dining room. There is also a freeform, riverside swimming pool with a sunbathing terrace, a game viewing platform with bar service and a fully equipped conference room.

Activities include 3 daily game drives, game walks outside the reserve and visits to local Maasai communities. Maasai naturalists give evening slideshows on local culture and wildlife. Romantic sundowners and bush meals can be arranged. The Adventurers' and the Young Rangers' clubs organise activities for children.

Mara Intrepids donates part of its fees to local community initiatives, such as medical clinics, primary schools and environmental awareness training. Environmentally aware principles govern the camp's waste disposal, hot water heating and compost.

Matira Bush Camp

Maasai Mara Ntl. Reserve

Matira Bush Camp, Ol Kiombo, Maasai Mara National Reserve, Kenya
Wilderness Getaways, PO Box 25240, Nairobi 00603, Kenya

Tel	+254 20 3876636
Mobile	+254 711 986513; +254 737 636693
Fax	
E-mail	info@wildernessgetawaysea.com
Web	www.wildernessgetawaysea.com

      Ol Kiombo, LS & CH
5 mins

Matira Bush Camp is located in the heart of the Maasai Mara National Reserve, near the junction of the Mara River and the Talek River. The camp is managed and operated by a team of local Maasai, with years of experience in tourism and guiding. This friendly camp gives the experience of an authentic bush camp.

There are 10 tents, made up of doubles and twins. The tents are decorated with Maasai blankets. External safari shower tents and WC tents are nearby. The dining tent has a bar at one end, with a good selection of soft drinks, beers, wines and spirits. Buffet breakfast, lunch and dinner are served. The camp is in a copse, at the corner of an attractive stream dotted with water-lilies. Nothing in the camp is permanent, and no trees were cut to put it up. The camp disposes of its waste responsibly. A small generator runs when necessary. Charging facilities are in the dining tent. Game drives are offered in the Maasai Mara National Reserve. Game walks and cultural visits to Maasai villages are offered just outside the reserve. Sundowners, bush breakfasts and bush dinners can all be arranged. The camp usually closes during April and May, although it can open on request.

Mara Bush Camp

Maasai Mara Ntl. Reserve

Mara Bush Camp, Olare Orok River, Maasai Mara National Reserve, Kenya
Sunworld Safaris, PO Box 39094, Nairobi, Kenya

Tel	+254 20 4445669; +254 20 4445680; +254 20 4445850
Mobile	+254 722 525400; +254 733 614055
Fax	+254 20 4445673
E-mail	info@sunworldsafaris.com
Web	www.sunworld-safari.com / www.marabushcamp.com

 VISA, MasterCard   Ol Kiombo, LS & CH
5 mins

In a riverine forest on the banks of the seasonal Olare Orok River, Mara Bush Camp is tucked discreetly into the heart of the Maasai Mara National Reserve. This eco-friendly camp has no permanent structures, and remains small and simple for private, authentic safaris. It is seasonal, and opens mid-December to early January, mid-February to mid-March and mid-July to mid-November. The 12 en-suite tents are furnished with clothes racks, storage chests and writing desks. Their private verandas overlook the river. The camp's chef serves freshly prepared buffet lunches and dinners under the stars or in the mess tent. The adjoining lounge tent, with bar and library, is a space where guests can meet and exchange highlights of the day. There is also a photo lounge with workstations and recharging facilities, and a small gift shop with Maasai artifacts.
For an additional cost, game drives can be arranged. Mara Bush Camp also offers night drives that leave camp after dinner in camp vehicles fitted with spotlights and an additional spotter. Resident naturalists teach tracking and animal identification on game walks. Cultural visits to Maasai villages can be arranged. Children's activities include animal print identification, learning about the environment and Maasai bush skills. The camp has environmental policies on responsible water and power usage and waste disposal.

Rekero

Maasai Mara Ntl. Reserve

Rekero, Talek River, Maasai Mara National Reserve, Kenya
Asilia Africa, PO Box 25150, Nairobi 00603, Kenya

Tel	+254 20 2324904; +254 20 2324906
Mobile	+254 702 964904
Fax	+254 20 2324902
E-mail	marketing@asiliaafrica.com
Web	www.asiliaafrica.com/rekero

     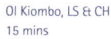 Ol Kiombo, LS & CH
15 mins

Rekero nestles in riverine forest on the banks of the Talek River. This seasonal eco-camp is owned and managed by 2 families. The Beaton family came to Kenya in 1889, and was involved in the suppression of the slave trade and the establishment of protected national parks. The Looseyia family lived here for generations, and has long experience of wildlife and the bush. Their camp offers a charming combination of luxury and proximity to nature.
There are 8 en-suite tents, made up of 7 doubles or twins, and 1 family tent. The tents are furnished in traditional safari style, and the bathrooms have safari showers. Meals, blending flavours from east and west, are served in the mess tent or in the bush.
The area is a vital wildlife corridor. The experienced Dorobo and Maasai guides offer an insight into animal behaviour, flora, fauna and local cultures. Activities include game drives, game walks and cultural visits to local Maasai villages.
The camp supports community conservation, and implements projects focusing on education and the environment. It is committed to the preservation of the Maasai Mara National Reserve. The camp is closed during the rains, in April, May and November.

Naibor

 Maasai Mara Ntl. Reserve

Naibor, Talek River, Maasai Mara National Reserve, Kenya
PO Box 15676, Nairobi 00503, Kenya

Tel	+254 20 2513147
Mobile	+254 729 406582
Fax	
E-mail	enquiries@naibor.com
Web	www.naibor.com

VISA, MasterCard

Ol Kiombo, LS & CH
20 mins

Tucked into a grove of riverine woodland on the banks of the Talek River, Naibor is a luxury tented camp in a contemporary style. The camp is strategically placed to view game all year round, and particularly during the wildebeest migration.

There are 7 en-suite tents, constructed of pale canvas and furnished with large fig wood beds, wide sofas and woven rugs. The bathrooms have safari showers and the shady verandas have private views of the surrounding vegetation. Meals are served in the graceful mess tent or beneath the trees overlooking the hippos in the river. Sundowners are served around the campfire or in the bush.

Activities include game drives in open sided 4WD vehicles, which are equipped with fridges to ensure fresh picnics and ice cold drinks. Cultural visits to local Maasai villages are also on offer, and balloon safaris can be booked from here. Naibor Spa offers massage, reflexology, manicure and pedicure.

Naibor's boutique has launched a stunning range of handcrafted jewellery, and also showcases striking items designed by local Maasai women. The camp supports the local community by providing employment, and by contributing to projects that improve the health and education of the local people.

Little Naibor

Maasai Mara Ntl. Reserve

Little Naibor, Talek River, Maasai Mara National Reserve, Kenya
PO Box 15676, Nairobi 00503, Kenya

Tel	+254 20 2513147
Mobile	+254 729 406582
Fax	
E-mail	enquiries@naibor.com
Web	www.naibor.com/little-naibor

VISA, MasterCard

Ol Kiombo, LS & CH
20 mins

Little Naibor is an exclusive luxury camp in the immediate vicinity of its sister camp, Naibor. It overlooks the Talek River, and has superb views of the river and its resident hippo population. The area is known for prolific game and easy access to the crossing points used by the wildebeest during their annual migration.

There are 2 spacious suites. Each suite has 2 en-suite bedrooms, a double and a twin, with lounge and veranda. Each suite has its own fireplace, private dining area overlooking the river and team of staff.

Little Naibor can be booked exclusively, or used in conjunction with main Naibor. The facilities at Naibor include a spa offering massage, reflexology, manicure and pedicure, and a boutique with a stunning range of handcrafted jewellery and striking items designed by local Maasai women. Activities include game drives in open sided 4WD vehicles, which are equipped with fridges to ensure fresh picnics and ice cold drinks, and cultural visits to local Maasai villages. Balloon safaris can be booked from here. The camp supports the local community by providing employment, and by contributing to projects that improve the health and education of the local people.

KaribuKenya Accommodation Guide

Entim

Maasai Mara Ntl. Reserve

Entim, Maasai Mara National Reserve, Kenya
Africa Eco Adventures, PO Box 64196, Nairobi 00620, Kenya

Tel	+254 20 2027125/6
Mobile	+254 733 258120; +254 704 084444; +254 750 873876
Fax	+254 20 3002891; +254 20 3752848
E-mail	info@entim-mara.com
Web	www.entim-mara.com

  Ol Kiombo, LS & CH
25 mins

Entim, meaning forest in the Maasai language, is tucked into riverine woodlands. The camp opened in 2008. It has been designed as a traditional safari camp, and has an atmosphere of being in the wilderness. The camp, in the heart of the Maasai Mara National Reserve, is well placed for game viewing.

There are 7 en-suite tents. The tents are adorned with bright rugs and safari chairs, and have views across the Mara River and the plains. Meals, including homemade bread, cakes and pastries, can be served in the dining area or on the veranda of the guests' tent. The lounge area has a bar and a selection of books, and is open sided to maximise the views.

The camp was built from local materials; hot water and electricity are provided by solar power.

Game drives in the Maasai Mara National Reserve are available morning and evening. Bush meals and sundowners are also on offer. The camp employs local Maasai driver guides, who are familiar with the area and the wildlife. For an extra charge, game walks and cultural visits to Maasai villages can be arranged outside the reserve. Entim assists the local Maasai community by providing employment and supporting their projects.

Private Mara Camp

Olare Orok Conservancy

Gogar Farm, off Nakuru-Kericho Highway, Rongai, Kenya
Grant and Cameron Safaris, PO Box 60, Rongai 20108, Kenya

Tel	+254 20 2045944
Mobile	+254 720 441819; +254 722 990823; +254 722 327718
Fax	+254 51 343110
E-mail	info@classicafricansafaris.com
Web	www.classicafricansafaris.com

  Ol Kiombo, LS & CH
25 mins

Private Mara Camp is operated by Grant and Cameron Safaris, which is based at Gogar Farm in Rongai. The camp is fully mobile and is sited along either the Olare Orok River or the Ntiakntiak River. Far from other camps, these locations offer excellent game viewing.

The camp has 6 en-suite tents, which can be double or twin as required. All tents are furnished with bedside tables, lamps, rugs and cupboards, and have verandas equipped with safari chairs and tables. Each tent is attended by a room steward. The mess tent, with a view of the river or the plains, has sitting and dining areas, and is equipped with power sockets, international adaptors, WiFi and a computer for downloading, viewing

and editing photos. Breakfast and lunch can be served in the mess tent or in the bush. Activities include game drives both inside and outside the Maasai Mara National Reserve, and game walks outside the reserve. Safaris can start or end at Gogar Farm, a 4,000-acre working farm that provides an opportunity to experience real Kenyan farm life. The farm combines respect for the environment with appropriate farming techniques. The NGO Friends of the Mau Watershed Area and the Vanessa Grant School for children with special needs are both based at Gogar Farm.

Mara Ngenche

Maasai Mara Ntl. Reserve

Mara Ngenche, Maasai Mara National Reserve, Kenya
Atua Enkop, PO Box 42475, Nairobi 00100, Kenya

Tel	+254 20 4450035-6; +254 20 4440276
Mobile	+254 715 555322
Fax	+254 20 4450037
E-mail	reservations@atua-enkop.com
Web	www.atua-enkop.com

  Ol Kiombo, LS & CH
25 mins

At the confluence of the Mara River and the Talek River, Mara Ngenche is an intimate, exclusive tented camp. The camp combines luxury and elegance with true bush experience, and is unfenced to allow the free movement of animals.

There are 6 spacious en-suite tents. Each tent is decorated with modern African décor, and has a 4-poster king size bed, bathtub and outside shower with a view. The dining and lounge area is open sided, with a view of the hippo pools in the river. Breakfast is served alfresco; sundowners are served around an open fire. Meals are a blend of local and international flavours. Dinner can be served in the dining area, on the veranda of the guests' tent or under the stars.

Game drives in open sided vehicles take place in the Maasai Mara National Reserve. Cultural visits to local Maasai villages are also on offer. Bush meals, picnics and sundowners are all available. The resident naturalist gives lectures on Maasai culture, and Maasai moran entertain guests with traditional singing and dancing. Mara Ngenche is environmentally sensitive and takes responsibility to conserve the environment on a sustainable basis. The camp employs members of the local community.

Ashnil Mara Camp

Maasai Mara Ntl. Reserve

Ashnil Mara Camp, Maasai Mara National Reserve, Kenya
Ashnil Hotels Limited, PO Box 10757, Nairobi 00100, Kenya

Tel	+254 20 3566970-3; +254 20 556955/46/47
Mobile	+254 717 612499
Fax	+254 20 3566974
E-mail	sales@ashnilhotels.com / info@ashnilhotels.com
Web	www.ashnilhotels.com

 VISA, MasterCard   Ol Kiombo, LS & CH, 30 mins
Keekorok, LS & CH, 45 mins

At the confluence of the Mara River and Olkeju River, Ashnil Mara Camp overlooks the Mara plains.

There are 40 en-suite tents. All tents have mosquito net, cupboard, minibar, fan, safe and veranda furnished with safari chairs and table. The restaurant serves buffets of Oriental and African cuisine. The bar serves soft drinks, beers and spirits. The main guest area has reception, lounge, dining area, bar, ice cream parlour and deck with a view of the dam. The lounge is furnished in African style, and adorned with local artefacts. The camp also has a gift shop.

Activities include game drives and sundowners. A nearby hippo pool makes an attractive place to stop for breakfast or a sundowner. There is a resident naturalist. Cultural activities take place in the camp. Bush and riverside dinners can be arranged, and picnics are provided on request. Massage is also on offer. Internet is available.

Mara Serena Safari Lodge

Maasai Mara Ntl. Reserve

Mara Serena Safari Lodge, Maasai Mara National Reserve, Kenya
Serena Hotels, PO Box 48690, Nairobi 00100, Kenya

Tel	+254 20 2842333; +254 20 2822000; +254 20 2842000
Mobile	+254 733 282200; +254 727 284200; +254 733 282283/92
Fax	+254 20 2718102-3; +254 20 2725184
E-mail	cro@serena.co.ke
Web	www.serenahotels.com

 VISA, MasterCard, Amex   Mara Serena, LS & CH 10 mins

Perched on the saddle of a hill, the Mara Serena Safari Lodge has a spectacular view across the vast plains, forests and rivers of the Maasai Mara National Reserve. The lodge has been designed within a circular cluster of brushwood, to mirror a Maasai village or Boma, and all the guest rooms are located in individual domed huts like Maasai manyattas. The lodge's furnishings have been inspired by local Maasai art giving the impression of a traditional bush encampment, while also providing Serena's modern touches.

The lodge has 1 presidential suite, 20 double rooms with king size beds, 53 twin rooms and 8 interconnecting rooms. All the rooms are en-suite, and have a private balcony with a view across the plains, and their interiors are styled in exuberant African colours reminiscent of Maasai art. A traditional safari style dining room serves international cuisine, and Riverside Bar provides local and international drinks. Guests are also welcome to eat at the Hippo swimming pool if they choose. Nightly entertainment includes local musicians, Maasai dances, wildlife films and talks. As well as game drives and bird walks, activities include dawn balloon safaris followed by a champagne breakfast. Mara Serena Safari Lodge has a bronze award from Ecotourism Society of Kenya.

Governors' Private Camp

Maasai Mara Ntl. Reserve

Governors' Private Camp, Mara River, Maasai Mara National Reserve
Musiara Limited, PO Box 48217, Nairobi 00100, Kenya

Tel	+254 20 2734000; +254 20 2734005
Mobile	+254 722 717529; +254 722 715306; +254 733 616204-5
Fax	+254 20 2734023; +254 20 2734024
E-mail	reservations@governorscamp.com
Web	www.governorscamp.com

 VISA, MasterCard, Eurocard Amex, travellers cheques   Musiara, LS & CH 10 mins

As its name suggests, Governors' Private Camp is available for the exclusive use of small private groups. The camp provides individually-tailored mobile safaris, with the added bonus of the backup of the professional and well established infrastructure of Governors' Camp. The camp is situated on the shady banks of the Mara River.

The 8 en-suite tents can have twin or double beds as required. The tents retain the traditional safari atmosphere, with a few added comforts, and are lit with gas and paraffin lamps. Each has a private veranda with a view of the river.

The executive chef plans the menus, and serves breakfast, lunch and dinner in the open bar and restaurant, overlooking the Mara River.

The camp's guides provide 3 game drives daily, and game walks. Also available, at an additional cost, are visits to local Maasai villages and balloon safaris. Trips to Mfangano Island in Lake Victoria for fishing, bird watching and boat rides can also be arranged, advance booking recommended.

Governors' Private Camp can be booked by individuals, families or small groups who want the exclusivity of a mobile camp, with completely personal service.

Governors' Camp

Maasai Mara Ntl. Reserve

Governors' Camp, Mara River, Maasai Mara National Reserve, Kenya
Musiara Limited, PO Box 48217, Nairobi 00100, Kenya

Tel	+254 20 2734000; +254 20 2734005
Mobile	+254 722 717529; +254 722 715306; +254 733 616204-5
Fax	+254 20 2734023; +254 20 2734024
E-mail	reservations@governorscamp.com
Web	www.governorscamp.com

VISA, MasterCard, Eurocard
Amex, travellers cheques

Musiara, LS & CH
10 mins

On the banks of the Mara River in the northwest of the Maasai Mara National Reserve, Governors' Camp looks straight across the plains. This location, where lush riverine forest meets the open plains, attracts a wide variety of game. Created in 1972, the camp has become known for comfort, service and good food.

The 37 en-suite tents are made up of 24 twins, 12 doubles and 1 suite. All the tents retain the authentic safari feeling, are lit with gas and paraffin lamps, and have private verandas with views over the river or the plains. The Justus Suite, set apart from the others, is perfect for honeymoon couples or those requiring a little extra luxury.

Alfresco buffets are served for breakfast and lunch. The 4-course dinner is served in the mess tent. Guests can meet at the campfire or in the bar for sundowners before dinner. A small gallery near the curio shop showcases local art.

Activities include 3 daily game drives. The camp can also arrange game walks, visits to Maasai villages and balloon safaris for an extra charge. Advance booking is recommended for trips by light aircraft to Mfangano Island on Lake Victoria for fishing, bird watching and boat rides.

Ecotourism Society of Kenya has given Governors' Camp a silver award.

Governors' Il Moran Camp

Maasai Mara Ntl. Reserve

Governors' Il Moran Camp, Mara River, Maasai Mara National Reserve
Musiara Limited, PO Box 48217, Nairobi 00100, Kenya

Tel	+254 20 2734000; +254 20 2734005
Mobile	+254 722 717529; +254 722 715306; +254 733 616204-5
Fax	+254 20 2734023; +254 20 2734024
E-mail	reservations@governorscamp.com
Web	www.governorscamp.com

VISA, MasterCard, Eurocard
Amex, travellers cheques

Musiara, LS & CH
10 mins

On the banks of the Mara River, Governors' Il Moran Camp recreates the atmosphere of the original hunting camps. Tucked into a copse of ancient trees, this exclusive camp is home to a wide variety of butterflies and birds. Nightly visits from elephants and other animals are common. The 10 en-suite luxury tents are furnished with beds hand-carved from specially selected wood from fallen, ancient olive trees and Victorian-style baths, and lit with gas and paraffin lamps. The tents' extended verandas are spacious enough for private dinners.

Lavish alfresco buffets, with live cooking stations, are served for breakfast and lunch. Candlelit dinners are served in the dining tent, with a view over the Mara River.

Activities include 3 daily game drives as well as game walks. Also available, for an extra charge, are visits to local Maasai villages and balloon safaris. Trips to Mfangano Island in Lake Victoria for fishing, bird watching and boat rides can also be arranged, advance booking recommended.

Wishing to reduce the impact of tourism on the ecosystem, Governors' Il Moran Camp, formerly Paradise Camp, has decreased the number of its tents from 20 to 10. This is probably the only time this has happened in the Maasai Mara National Reserve.

Little Governors' Camp Maasai Mara Ntl. Reserve

Little Governors' Camp, Mara River, Maasai Mara National Reserve
Musiara Limited, PO Box 48217, Nairobi 00100, Kenya

Tel	+254 20 2734000; +254 20 2734005
Mobile	+254 722 717529; +254 722 715306; +254 733 616204-5
Fax	+254 20 2734023; +254 20 2734024
E-mail	reservations@governorscamp.com
Web	www.governorscamp.com

VISA, MasterCard, Eurocard
Amex, travellers cheques

Musiara, LS & CH
30 mins

Set around a small waterhole near the Mara River, Little Governors' Camp has a perfect view of the constant flow of mammals and birds attracted to the water. The camp is on the opposite side of the river from the other Governors properties, and is reached by boat. This charming journey enhances the romantic and secluded atmosphere of the camp. The 17 en-suite tents are made up of 12 twins and 5 doubles. Tent 17 is recommended for honeymooners. The tents are furnished in traditional safari style, and lit with gas and kerosene lanterns. Their verandas overlook the waterhole, and the animals that come to drink or graze at its edge. Breakfast and lunch are served alfresco, in the shade of the trees. Candlelit dinner is served in the dining tent. The camp also has a campfire where guests can meet for sundowners, and share stories of their day. Activities include 3 daily game drives. Game walks, visits to a local Maasai village and balloon safaris are available for an additional charge. Trips by light aircraft to Mfangano Island in Lake Victoria for fishing, bird watching and boat rides are also on offer, advance booking recommended. Little Governors' Camp has a bronze award from Ecotourism Society of Kenya.

Bateleur Camp Oloololo Escarpment

Sales & Reservations for &Beyond Lodges. Southern & East Africa preferred partners, Private Bag X 27, Benmore, Johannesburg, 2010, SA

Tel	
Mobile	+27 11 8094447
Fax	
E-mail	safaris@andbeyond.com
Web	www.andbeyondafrica.com

VISA, MasterCard

Kichwa Tembo, LS & CH
30 mins

In the style of classic safaris, Bateleur Camp blends adventurous game viewing with the ambience of the Kenyan explorers of the '20s and '30s. The glamour of vintage Africa is evoked by hardwood floors, polished silver and sparkling crystal overlooking the game-studded plains of the Maasai Mara National Reserve.

The 18 en-suite tents each has a secluded private veranda furnished with leather armchairs from which to view the surrounding vegetation. A butler waits on each tent. The main dining area is adorned with safari antiques, handcrafted artefacts and keepsakes of bygone times such as brass compasses, leather trunks and framed maps. As well as day and night game drives, the camp offers interpretative bush walks both around the camp grounds and along the Oloololo Escarpment or the lush banks of the Mara River. Lectures on Maasai culture and visits to local communities are available. Sundowners at nearby viewpoints and bush meals are also on offer. Bateleur Camp is designed according to the principles of ecotourism and promotes the use of renewable energy, waste management and recycling. The camp supports the conservation of wildlife and contributes to many development projects designed to raise the standard of living of the neighbouring communities. Bateleur Camp has a bronze award from Ecotourism Society of Kenya.

Kichwa Tembo

Oloblolo Gate

Sales & Reservations for &Beyond Lodges. Southern & East Africa preferred partners, Private Bag X 27, Benmore, Johannesburg, 2010, SA

Tel
Mobile +27 11 8094447
Fax
E-mail safaris@andbeyond.com
Web www.andbeyondafrica.com

VISA, MasterCard   Kichwa Tembo, LS & CH 30 mins

Kichwa Tembo, meaning head of the elephant in Swahili, lies between the Oloololo Escarpment and the Sabaringo River, on a private concession northwest of the Maasai Mara National Reserve. The camp is set where riverine forest meets the sweeping plains of the Mara, near where the famous final scene of Out of Africa was filmed.

The 40 en-suite tents, including 12 luxury suites, each has a private outdoor deck shaded by dense forest canopy. Both twins and doubles have stone floored bathrooms and are decorated in traditional Maasai colours. Meals can be served outdoors, weather permitting, or in the thatched restaurant. Bush meals are also available. The main lodge has a curio shop, reception and a bar and lounge area. A palm-fringed swimming pool overlooks the savannah.

Activities include twice daily game drives and interpretative bush walks. For an additional price, hiking the Mara Hippo Trail or the Oloololo Escarpment can be arranged.

Kichwa Tembo supports many conservation and development projects including collaboration with the Mara Conservancy, replanting the Sabaringo Riverbanks and providing logistical support for the anti-poaching and animal rescue teams. The Green Team controls invasive alien plants and makes fuel bricks to reduce the use of firewood.

Kensington Mara West

Oloololo Escarpment

Kensington Mara West, nr Oloololo Gate, nr Maasai Mara National Reserve
PO Box 35553, Nairobi 00200, Kenya

Tel +254 20 2722251
Mobile
Fax +254 20 2722059
E-mail bookings@kensingtoncamps.com
Web www.kensingtoncamps.com

 VISA, MasterCard    Kichwa Tembo, LS & CH 15 mins

Perched elegantly on the Oloololo Escarpment, Kensington Mara West has panoramic views of the savannah below. The escarpment forms the western boundary of the Maasai Mara National Reserve.

There are 3 en-suite tents, and 8 chalets. The tents are set amongst fig trees on the ridge. All have 2 queen size beds, dressing room, hand cut stone bathroom and veranda with a view. They are decorated with lamps, local art and traditional carvings, and equipped with electricity and charging facilities. The chef serves Pan-African and traditional bush cuisine, as well as international dishes. Dietary preferences can be catered for, advance notice required. Meals can be served in the dining tent, on the guests' private veranda or in the bush. The bar serves soft drinks, beers, wines and spirits.

Game drives can be morning, evening or full day. Maasai guides can take visitors to local villages, a hippo pool or a viewpoint for sunset. Longer hikes, picnics and sundowners are also on offer. The escarpment is home to a wide diversity of birdlife, including birds of prey. At night, guides meet guests at the campfire and give information about Maasai culture and wildlife. Adjacent to the camp, Africa Mission Services provides its development program to the local Maasai community.

Kilima Camp

Olooolo Escarpment

Kilima Camp, Olooolo Escarpment, nr Maasai Mara National Reserve, Kenya
Escapades Ltd, PO Box 1206, Nairobi 00502, Kenya

Tel	+254 20 2081747
Mobile	+254 733 625399
Fax	
E-mail	info@kilimacamp.com
Web	www.kilimacamp.com

Kichwa Tembo, LS & CH
15 mins

True to its name, Swahili for mountain, Kilima Camp sits high on the Olooolo Escarpment and has a sweeping view of the plains of the Maasai Mara National Reserve and the Mara River. The camp opened in 2007 and offers an authentic camp experience.

The 12 en-suite tents can be either twin or double, and have solar powered lighting, safari showers and views across the plains. There are also 2 spacious deluxe tents. The camp has minimal permanent structures, and has made as little impact as possible on the environment. Lunch is served in the mess tent, and can be either a la carte or buffet. Dinner is served under the stars, weather permitting, and is a traditional African buffet, with grilled meats, ugali and chapatti.

Activities include 2 game drives per day, and game walks. Other activities, for an additional charge, include night game drives, visits to a local Maasai village and market, archery with a Maasai instructor, bush dinners and massages.

Rated bronze by Ecotourism Society of Kenya, the camp is committed to sustainable policies. Over 800 indigenous trees have been planted here since the camp was created, and the camp is self-sufficient in water and has an efficient waste management scheme. The camp also supports local communities and Il Toshi primary school.

Mara Siria

Olooolo Escarpment

Mara Siria, Olooolo Escarpment, nr Maasai Mara National Reserve
Phoenix Safaris, PO Box 1141, Nairobi 00621, Kenya

Tel	+254 20 7122254
Mobile	+254 721 650889; +254 733 261846
Fax	+254 20 7122254
E-mail	info@mara-siria-camp.com / info@phoenix-safaris.de
Web	www.mara-siria-camp.com / www.phoenix-safaris.de

 VISA, MasterCard

 Kichwa Tembo, LS & CH
15 mins

On top of the Siria Escarpment, Mara Siria has stunning views of the plains of the Mara Triangle. The camp is an eco-friendly tented camp. There are 8 en-suite luxury tents, 2 en-suite deluxe tents, 2 Maasai luxury cottages and 2 family tents. All tents have verandas furnished with safari chairs, and their bathrooms have safari showers. The camp is powered by solar power, and has a backup generator linked to charging facilities. Buffet breakfast, lunch and dinner can be served in the dining area or in the bush.

Activities include game drives in the Maasai Mara National Reserve, and game walks to the Mara River and hippo pools. Maasai archery and mountain biking are available on request.

For a surcharge, scenic flights to Rusinga Island in Lake Victoria can be arranged. Balloon Safaris can also be booked at an operator nearby.

Mpata Safari Club

Olololo Escarpment

Mpata Safari Club, Olololo Escarpment, nr Maasai Mara National Reserve
Mpata Investments Ltd, PO Box 58402, Nairobi 00200, Kenya

Tel	+254 20 244773; +254 20 217015; +254 20 244987
Mobile	+254 722 402249; +254 733 674284
Fax	+254 20 310859; +254 20 229420
E-mail	mpata4@africaonline.co.ke
Web	www.mpata.com

 VISA, MasterCard, Amex   Kichwa Tembo, LS & CH 45 mins

Mpata Safari Club is named after the famed Tanzanian artist, SG Mpata, and designed by Edward Suzuki, a leading architect in Japan. Set high on Olololo Escarpment, the club has panoramic views across the Mara plains. There are 23 cottages, made up of 12 deluxe units and 11 suites, all positioned to maximise the view. The deluxe units are designed with interlocking curved walls separating the bedroom, bathroom and veranda, and have an outside barbecue. The suites are larger, and have bedroom, bathroom, lounge, kitchenette and an outside Jacuzzi.

The clubhouse houses the restaurant, library and sunken rock bar. Baboon Bar, crafted into the landscaped garden overlooking the plains, makes a perfect sundowner spot. All meals prepared at the club are nouvelle cuisine, based on inventive recipes by Kiyomi Mikuni.

Morning game drives leave at 6am and return for a full English breakfast. Evening game drives leave at 3pm. Full day game drives are also available. Other activities include game walks and cultural visits to a Maasai village. Balloon safaris and fishing trips to Lake Victoria can be booked here. Mpata Safari Club was voted the best safari lodge in Kenya by The Kenya Association of Travel Agents in 1996.

Salt Springs Mara Camp

Olololo Escarpment

Salt Springs Mara Camp, Olololo Escarpment, nr Maasai Mara Ntl. Res.
PO Box 780, Narok 20500, Kenya

Tel	
Mobile	+254 728 537465; +254 736 425022; +254 735 638084
Fax	
E-mail	info@saltspringsmaracamp.com
Web	www.saltspringsmaracamp.com

     Musiara, LS & CH, 25 mins
Kichwa Tembo, LS & CH, 30 mins

Salt Springs Mara Camp is named for the Olotulo-emurt salt lick which the camp overlooks. It is perched high on a rocky hill with expansive views of the Mara River and the Mara plains. The camp is owned and operated by the Maasai community. Its aim is to empower the community by giving local employment and providing space for the women to sell their handmade artefacts.

There are 5 en-suite tents. All tents are decorated with bright Maasai fabrics, and have verandas with views of the salt lick and the animals that are attracted to it. The dining area has a large veranda on the cliff with panoramic views. Meals can be served in the dining area or in the guests' tent. Continental style cuisine is served. The bar serves soft drinks, beers, wines and spirits.

Game drives in the Maasai Mara National Reserve are on offer. Bush breakfast and bush dinner can also be arranged. Game walks with Maasai moran and cultural visits to local Maasai villages are also available. Sundowners and picnics can be provided. For a surcharge, a balloon safari can be arranged at a location not far from the camp. The camp is located on the Olololo Escarpment, not far from the Mara Rianta Bridge.

Olonana   Mara River

Olonana, Mara River, nr Maasai Mara National Reserve, Kenya
PO Box 41789, Nairobi 00100, Kenya

Tel	+254 20 6950002; +254 20 2487374
Mobile	+254 728 888418; +254 733 638043
Fax	+254 20 6950320
E-mail	kenya@sanctuaryretreats.com
Web	www.sanctuaryretreats.com/lodges

VISA, MasterCard, Amex

Kichwa Tembo, LS & CH
20 mins

Olonana is a luxury tented camp on a private stretch of the Mara River at the foot of the impressive Siria Escarpment. The camp has initiated a number of eco projects, and is known for good game viewing as well as for its Sanctuary Spa.

There are 14 spacious en-suite tents. The tents have polished wooden floors, Oriental rugs and comfortable armchairs. Their large verandas have views of the river, and of the hippos often found wallowing in its water. The main dining room and veranda stretches along a striking section of the Mara River, providing a scenic setting for breakfast, lunch and dinner. The camp also has a swimming pool and a gift shop.

Activities include game drives and cultural visits to local Maasai villages. Bush meals and sundowners can be arranged. The Sanctuary Spa offers a range of treatments, including facials and massages, and uses the world-wide recognised Africology and French marine-based Thaigo products. Olonana works closely with a local Maasai village, offering employment and donations to community projects. Olonana received the prodigious silver award from Ecotourism Society of Kenya, for its eco policies which include solar power, a wetlands which cleanses wastewater before returning it to the natural environment and a tree planting initiative.

Mara Enkipai Safari Camp   Mara River

Mara Enkipai Safari Camp, Mara River, nr Maasai Mara Ntl. Reserve, Kenya
PO Box 726, Nairobi 00502, Kenya

Tel	
Mobile	+254 729 987742
Fax	
E-mail	info@mara-enkipai.com
Web	www.mara-enkipai.com

Kichwa Tembo, LS & CH
20 mins

On the banks of the Mara River, Mara Enkipai Safari Camp is a traditional safari camp. The camp is family owned and managed, and is committed to sustainable ecotourism.

There are 8 en-suite tents. All tents have handcrafted furniture created from local materials, and their bathrooms have safari showers. Electricity is provided by solar power. There is an outdoor living area on the riverbank, where tea or sundowners can be served. The chef uses fresh produce grown in the camp's vegetable garden. Meals can be served in the dining area or on the veranda of a guest's tent. Picnics can also be provided. Game drives are done in the visitors' own car; guides are provided by the camp. Other activities include game walks and cultural visits to Maasai villages. Children's activities include learning how to use bows and arrows with the Maasai, and fishing for catfish in the Mara River.

Several films and documentaries have been filmed at Mara Enkipai Safari Camp, such as The Serengeti Symphony and The Leopard Sun. Mara Enkipai's Dawntodusk Foundation aims to empower local communities by providing clean water and alternate energy, and by providing training in conservation and tourism skills.

Mara Timbo Camp

Mara River

Mara Timbo Camp, Mara River, nr Maasai Mara National Reserve, Kenya
Safari and Style Ltd, PO Box 517, Nairobi 00621, Kenya

Tel	
Mobile	+254 737 138140
Fax	
E-mail	booking@maratimbo.com / welcome@maratimbo.com
Web	www.maratimbo.com

 VISA, MasterCard   Kichwa Tembo, LS & CH 30 mins

Below the Oloololo Escarpment, Mara Timbo Camp is located in a loop of the Mara River and looks out on hippos and crocodiles. The camp is German owned, and is named after Tim, the owners' son.

There are 7 en-suite tents, all under canvas with thatched roofs and wide verandas. Each tent is served by a trained female butler. The décor combines warm earthy colours with custom-made furniture including a king size bed. The bathrooms have bathtubs from which guests can watch the hippos in the river. All materials are natural and locally sourced. The chef specialises in Italian, Asian and African food, and every meal includes at least 3 choices. Meals are served on 3 small restaurant islands near the campfire. They can also be served alfresco or in the guests' tent. The lounge has a reference library and a cocktail bar. Safari Spa offers Swedish massage and aromatherapy massage; a 10-minute massage is complimentary.

Morning and evening game drives are on offer. Guests can also choose full day game drives with a picnic lunch or night drives. Maasai guides escort guests to local Maasai villages and lead informative game walks that focus on tracking and bush skills.

Nkorombo Mobile Camp

Mara River

Nkorombo Mobile Camp, Mara River, nr Maasai Mara Ntl. Reserve, Kenya
New African Territories, PO Box 76677, Nairobi 00508, Kenya

Tel	+254 20 2663397; +254 20 3598871
Mobile	+254 718 139359
Fax	
E-mail	bookings@africanterritories.co.ke
Web	www.africanterritories.co.ke / www.serian.net

  Musiara, LS & CH 1 hr

Designed to blend unobtrusively into the surrounding vegetation, Nkorombo Mobile Camp focuses on viewing wildlife. The camp is truly mobile, and its location varies according to the movement of the animals. It is reserved on an exclusive basis.

There are 5 en-suite tents, furnished in traditional safari style, with single cots, canvas chairs, woven rugs and tray tables. The bathrooms have long drop loos and safari showers. The mess tent is furnished with candelabras, trunks, tables, Lamu beds, soft cushions and chairs. Meals are served in different locations around the camp or in the bush; dinner is often served at the campfire.

All guests are allocated their own 4WD vehicle, with guide and spotter, and can choose the times of their game drives, night drives and game walks. Other activities include picnics, bush dinner, bush bath, river fishing and fly camping. The camp can also arrange trips to Lake Victoria, balloon safaris, scenic flights and horse riding. Walking with Warriors is a 9-day walking safari led by Maasai moran that combines bush camping with nights in Nkorombo Mobile Camp and sister camps Serian and Suguroi Hill Tree House.

All Serian camps promote eco-friendly practices such as responsible waste management, sustainably grown firewood and solar power.

Karen Blixen Camp

Mara North Conservancy

Karen Blixen Camp, Mara North Conservancy, nr Maasai Mara Ntl. Reserve
PO Box 913, Nairobi 00100, Kenya

Tel	+254 20 3883898; +254 20 3524215
Mobile	+254 773 063863
Fax	+254 20 3883899
E-mail	info@karenblixencamp.com
Web	www.karenblixencamp.com

 Mara North, LS & CH
 40 mins

Named after Karen Blixen of Out of Africa fame, Karen Blixen Camp recreates the aura of the 1920s. The camp was voted runner up for Best New Safari Property in Africa by The Good Safari Guide 2008.

The 22 luxury en-suite tents are raised on mahogany platforms, and adorned with fresh safari colours and natural fabrics. Their spacious verandas are furnished with cushioned daybeds.

The chefs use some of Karen Blixen's favourite recipes; the food served reflects her love of the cuisines of France, England, Italy and Denmark. Camp facilities include a bar, a lounge, a gift shop with WiFi and a swimming pool. A resident masseuse offers a wide range of wellness treatments.

Set on the banks of the Mara River, against the backdrop of the Oloololo Escarpment, the camp provides game drives in both Mara North Conservancy and the Maasai Mara National Reserve. Also available are game walks on Oloisuk private concession and visits to Maasai villages, markets and schools. A member of Ecotourism Society of Kenya and UN Global Compact, the camp's policies reflect its belief that responsible tourism can protect a natural wildlife area, alleviate poverty through proper conditions and contribute positively to local communities. The camp plants 10,000 indigenous trees every year.

Suguroi Hill Tree House

Mara River

Suguroi Hill Tree House, Mara River, nr Maasai Mara National Reserve
New African Territories, PO Box 76677, Nairobi 00508, Kenya

Tel	+254 20 2663397; +254 20 3598871
Mobile	+254 718 139259
Fax	
E-mail	bookings@africanterritories.co.ke
Web	www.africanterritories.co.ke / www.serian.net

 Musiara, LS & CH
 1 hr

An intimate tree house, Suguroi Hill Tree House accommodates 6 people. It is in Pusinkariak Conservancy, and is accessible only by foot. Game walks are led by Maasai moran, or warriors. Other activities include picnics, bush dinners, bush baths and river fishing.

The tree house offers a unique outdoor fly camping experience, and is lit by lanterns and moonlight. Meals are cooked on an open fire and eaten under the stars.

Suguroi Hill Tree House can be taken as part of a safari with sister camps Serian, Ngare Serian and Nkorombo Mobile Camp. Guests are welcome to keep their tents at these camps while staying at the tree house.

Walking with Warriors is a 9-day walking safari led by Maasai moran that combines bush camping with nights in Suguroi Hill Tree House, Serian and Nkorombo Mobile Camp. The camp can also arrange trips to Lake Victoria, balloon safaris, scenic flights and horse riding.

All Serian camps promote eco-friendly practices such as responsible waste management, sustainably grown firewood and solar power. The Serian Trust supports children attending secondary school and vocational training institutes. Serian is the Predator Project Research Base and works to save lions and other predators in unprotected areas.

Serian

Mara North Conservancy

Serian, Mara River, nr Maasai Mara National Reserve, Kenya
New African Territories, PO Box 76677, Nairobi 00508, Kenya

Tel	+254 20 2663397; +254 20 3598871
Mobile	+254 718 139359
Fax	
E-mail	bookings@africanterritories.co.ke
Web	www.africanterritories.co.ke / www.serian.net

Musiara, LS & CH
45 mins

Set in a secluded valley in the Mara North Conservancy, Serian fulfils the meaning of its name: peaceful. This traditional bush camp, overlooking the Mara River and the Oloololo Escarpment, combines luxury with comfort. There are 8 chic en-suite marquees, each decorated in the style of safaris of a bygone era, with woven carpets on hardwood floors, and swathes of cotton setting off the colonial furniture. The chef plans personal menus with the guests.

All guests are allocated their own 4WD vehicle, with guide and spotter, and can choose the times of their game drives, night drives and game walks. Other activities include picnics, bush dinner, bush bath, river fishing and fly camping. The camp can arrange trips to Lake Victoria, balloon safaris, scenic flights and horse riding. Walking with Warriors is a 9-day walking safari led by Maasai moran that combines bush camping with nights in Serian and sister camps Suguroi Hill Tree House and Nkorombo Mobile Camp.

Serian promotes eco-friendly practices such as responsible waste management, sustainably grown firewood and solar power. The Serian Trust supports children attending secondary school and vocational training institutes. Serian is the Predator Project Research Base and works to save lions and other predators in unprotected areas.

Ngare Serian

Mara River

Ngare Serian, Mara River, nr Maasai Mara National Reserve, Kenya
New African Territories, PO Box 76677, Nairobi 00508, Kenya

Tel	+254 20 2663397; +254 20 3598871
Mobile	+254 718 139359
Fax	
E-mail	bookings@africanterritories.co.ke
Web	www.africanterritories.co.ke / www.serian.net

Musiara, LS & CH
45 mins

Ngare Serian is located in the Pusinkariak Conservancy, and has views of the Mara River and the towering Oloololo Escarpment. This intimate camp can be taken on an exclusive basis, and provides a true safari experience. It is accessed by a rope bridge over the river and has access to a 4,000-acre walking area.

The 4 en-suite marquees are set on hardwood decks, furnished with large 4-poster beds and lit by lanterns and candlelight. Their bathtubs are raised on decks over the river. The chef plans his menus according to the guests' preferences.

All guests are allocated their own 4WD vehicle, with guide and spotter, and can choose the times of their game drives, night drives and game walks. Other activities include picnics, bush dinner, bush bath, river fishing and fly camping. The camp can also arrange trips to Lake Victoria, balloon safaris, scenic flights and horse riding.

All Serian camps promote eco-friendly practices such as responsible waste management, sustainably grown firewood and solar power. The Serian Trust supports children attending secondary school and vocational training institutes. Serian, the nearby sister camp of Ngare Serian, is the Predator Project Research Base and works to save lions and other predators in unprotected areas.

Karibu Kenya Accommodation Guide

Cheetah Tented Camp Mara River

Cheetah Tented Camp, Mara River, nr Maasai Mara National Reserve, Kenya
PO Box 66356, Nairobi 00800, Kenya

Tel
Mobile +254 770 168678; +254 771 189181
Fax
E-mail jorgesalvator@yahoo.es
Web www.cheetahtentedcamp.com

 VISA

 Mara North, LS & CH, 5 mins
Musiara, LS & CH, 1 hr

Cheetah Tented Camp is a small and exclusive tented camp, that aims to recreate the safaris of old. It offers personal service and aims to make its guests feel chaperoned throughout their stay. The camp is located on the banks of the Mara River.

There are 2 large en-suite tents and 1 treetop tent overlooking the river. The camp has been designed to welcome families. There is also a youngsters' camp, which enables children to live in their own tent right next to their parents. Meals can be served in the restaurant beside the open fire, on the terrace by the riverbanks, on the terrace of the guests' tent or out in the bush.

The camp has no set schedule. All guests have a private 4WD land cruiser at their disposal with a driver and a Maasai guide. Game drives can be taken as and when the guests wish, including during the night. Game walks with Maasai moran are also available. Cultural visits to Maasai villages can be arranged. Bush meals and sundowners are on offer. The guides in camp are all Maasai and have certificates in tour guiding, diplomas in field experience and certificates in first aid.

Royal Mara Safari Lodge   Mara North Conservancy

Royal Mara Safari Lodge, Mara North Conservancy, nr Maasai Mara Ntl. Res.
Exclusive African Treasures, PO Box 63437, Nairobi 00619, Kenya

Tel +254 20 7123300/1/2
Mobile +254 773 777066
Fax +254 20 7123303
E-mail info@eatreasures.co.ke
Web www.eatreasures.com

 Mara North, LS & CH, 15 mins
Musiara, LS & CH, 35 mins

Royal Mara Safari Lodge sits on the banks of the Mara River in Mara North Conservancy. The lodge blends the appearance of a classic tented camp with the facilities of a lodge.

The 8 en-suite tents stand on raised mahogany platforms with private verandas overlooking the river. They are furnished with hand-carved solid wood furniture including 4-poster bed, and equipped with electronic safety deposit box and minibar. Meals can be served near a hippo pool, on the open savannah, under the stars in the bush or privately on the guests' veranda. All dishes are homemade with fresh Kenyan produce and prepared in a professional kitchen.

Daily activities are tailored to the guests' wishes. Activities include day and night game drives, game walks and cultural visits to Maasai villages. Royal Mara Safari Lodge is committed to the environment. All non-biodegradable waste is transported to an urban collection point. All materials used including guest supplies, cleaning materials, waste disposal methods and landscaping are eco-friendly.

Jacqueline's House   Mara River

Mara Enkipai Safari Camp, Mara River, nr Maasai Mara Ntl. Res., Kenya
PO Box 726, Nairobi 00502, Kenya

Tel	
Mobile	+254 729 987742
Fax	
E-mail	info@mara-enkipai.com
Web	www.mara-enkipai.com

    Kichwa Tembo, LS & CH
15 mins

Jacqueline Roumeguere-Eberhardt, a French social anthropologist, is famous for her research into the culture and traditions of the Maasai. Jacqueline lived for more than 40 years amongst the Maasai people, studying, filming and photographing their traditions. She married Ole Kapusia, a Maasai moran who was her research assistant throughout her studies. Jacqueline's House has been fully renovated. It has 4 en-suite double rooms and an upstairs open plan living and dining area with views of the plains. The long veranda overlooks the Mara River. The house is elegantly rustic, and furnished with locally made furniture. It can be taken on self-catering or full board basis. The house is hosted by George and Vanessa Roumeguere, son and daughter-in-law of Jacqueline. Game drives are done in the visitors' own car; guides are provided by the camp. Other activities include game walks and cultural visits to Maasai villages. Children's activities include learning how to use bows and arrows with the Maasai, and fishing for catfish in the Mara River. Several films and documentaries have been filmed at Mara Enkipai Safari Camp, such as The Serengeti Symphony and The Leopard Sun. Mara Enkipai's Dawntodusk Foundation aims to empower local communities by providing clean water and alternate energy, and by providing training in conservation and tourism skills.

Elephant Pepper Camp   Mara North Conservancy

Elephant Pepper Camp, Mara North Conservancy, nr Maasai Mara Ntl. Res.
Cheli & Peacock, PO Box 743, Nairobi 00517, Kenya

Tel	+254 20 6004054/3; +254 20 6003090/1
Mobile	+254 724 255374; +254 733 490234
Fax	+254 20 6004050; +254 20 6003066
E-mail	safaris@chelipeacock.co.ke / info@chelipeacock.co.ke
Web	www.chelipeacock.com / www.elephantpeppercamp.com

 Travellers cheques   Mara North, LS & CH, 15 mins
Musiara, LS & CH, 25 mins

Named after the Warburgia Ugandensis, commonly known as the Elephant Pepper Tree, this bush camp maintains the atmosphere of the traditional mobile luxury safari. Nestled in a grove of Ebony and Elephant Pepper trees, the camp is situated in Mara North Conservancy. It looks out over the Mara plains which support a vast concentration of game all year round, and at certain times of year includes the annual wildebeest and zebra migration.

The camp has 7 double tents and a honeymoon or family tent, all with en-suite bathrooms and verandas. The showers are safari showers and the tents are lit by hurricane lamps. Meals are candlelit and served family style. A holder of a prestigious Ecotourism Society of Kenya gold award, the camp implements eco-friendly systems of recycling and waste disposal. It can be completely dismantled, leaving no trace on the precious ecosystem of the Mara. There are no generators or cement or permanent structures. The camp assists the local Maasai communities with a number of wildlife and conservation projects and works closely with a local school. The local Maasai community make up 80% of the camp staff. In October 2005, Elephant Pepper Camp was included in Travel Weekly Magazine's Five of the Best as an authentic camping experience. The camp is closed in April and May.

Offbeat Mara Camp

Mara North Conservancy

Offbeat Mara Camp, Mara North Conservancy, nr Mara Reserve, Kenya
Offbeat Safaris, PO Box 1146, Nanyuki 10400, Kenya

Tel	+254 62 2031082
Mobile	+254 725 968351; +254 704 909355-6
Fax	+254 62 2031082
E-mail	bookings@offbeatsafaris.com
Web	www.offbeatsafaris.com

            Musiara, LS & CH
                                 1 hr

Situated in Mara North Conservancy, Offbeat Mara Camp is a small, tented camp on the Olare Orok River. The camp is one of the founding members of Mara North Conservancy, a prime wildlife viewing area bordering the Maasai Mara National Reserve. The camp practises sustainable tourism and is a member of Eco Hotels of the World.

There are 6 en-suite tents. The tents are traditional safari tents, with large handmade cedar beds, 24-hour solar lighting and safari showers. The mess tent has comfortable sofas, writing desk, library with wildlife books and a well stocked bar. English breakfasts, light lunches and 3-course dinners are served in the mess tent, around the campfire or in the bush. Activities include day and night game drives and game walks in the conservancy. Game drives in the Maasai Mara National Reserve, cultural visits to a local Maasai village and excursions to the nearby rhino sanctuary are also available. Offbeat Mara Camp works closely with the local Maasai community, many of whom helped build the camp. All guides are local Maasai and are qualified by Kenya Professional Safari Guide Association, KPSGA. The camp supports Koiyaki Guiding School and employs graduates from the school

Offbeat Mara Camp is affiliated to Offbeat Safaris and can arrange safaris around the country and horse riding safaris.

Olumara Tented Camp

Olare Orok River

Olumara Tented Camp, Olare Orok River, nr Maasai Mara Ntl. Res.
PO Box 16550, Nairobi 00100, Kenya

Tel	+254 20 2363741; +254 20 2018105
Mobile	
Fax	+254 20 4180318
E-mail	info@olumara.com
Web	www.olumaracamp.com

 VISA, MasterCard    Ol Kiombo, LS & CH, 30 mins
                                                      Musiara, LS & CH, 30 mins

Olumara Tented Camp sits on the banks of the Olare Orok River, deep within lush riverine forest. A rope and wood suspension bridge over the gorge makes an arresting entrance to the camp.

The 11 en-suite tents all have wooden deck verandas with canvas chairs on which to relax and enjoy the surroundings. They are decorated with natural fabrics of earthy browns and ochres. The dining area, with its open kitchen where chefs cook before the guests' eyes, is fitted out with canvas chairs surrounding a long dining table and adorned with bright Maasai cloths.

The lounge is a rustic open sided building with a thatched roof, furnished with natural wood tables and wicker chairs from where guests can view the camp. There is also a bush bar, at the riverbank, serving wines, beers and spirits.

Game drives cover the Maasai Mara National Reserve as well as Mara North Conservancy. Local species include lion, cheetah, elephant and zebra as well as the rarer honey badger, lesser kudu and leopard. At the end of the day, sundowners are served by the guides at scenic spots.

Kicheche Bush Camp

Olare Orok Conservancy

Kicheche Bush Camp, Olare Orok Conservancy, nr Mara Reserve, Kenya
Kicheche Camps, PO Box 15236, Nairobi 00509, Kenya

Tel	+254 20 8890541; +254 20 2493569/12; +254 20 2405586
Mobile	+254 736 888055; +254 700 888055
Fax	+254 20 891379
E-mail	sales@kicheche.com
Web	www.kicheche.com

Ol Kiombo, LS & CH
40 mins

A classic tented camp, Kicheche Bush Camp offers a luxury experience with an intimate atmosphere. The camp is located in the Olare Orok Conservancy bordering the Maasai Mara National Reserve. Through strict limit on bed numbers, the Olare Orok Conservancy offers quality game viewing without crowds.

There are 6 en-suite tents, made up of doubles, twins and 1 triple. The tents are equipped with luggage racks and woven rugs, and the bathrooms have safari showers. Meals, which are a blend of African and European dishes including homemade bread and pastries, are served alfresco or in the dining tent. The lounge area has a selection of reference books and sells curios designed by the families of the staff.

Kicheche's guides are highly qualified and experienced, and take regular training courses. Activities include game drives, game walks and cultural visits to Maasai villages, as well as local schools supported by the camp. The Kicheche Community Project, established in 2004, encourages the preservation of the environment and improves the welfare of the community. Kicheche was applauded by Chris Haslam, AITO travel writer of the year, for its passionate commitment to the community. The camp is seasonal, and closes in March, April, May and November.

Amani Mara

Olare Orok Conservancy

Amani Mara, Olare Orok Conservancy, nr Maasai Mara Ntl. Reserve, Kenya
PO Box 61394, Nairobi 00200, Kenya

Tel	+254 20 4347583
Mobile	
Fax	+254 20 4343306
E-mail	sales@amanimara.com
Web	www.amanimara.com

Ol Kiombo, LS & CH
40 mins

The Swahili word Amani derives from the Arabic, meaning peace, desires, wishes and aspirations. The name represents the atmosphere of the camp and its eco-friendly nature. Set on a hillside, Amani Mara has wonderful views across the Mara plains. Prior to refurbishment, the camp was called Oloiren.

There are 5 en-suite double rooms and 4 en-suite twin rooms. There is also a family suite, with double room, twin room, lounge and fireplace. All rooms are built of stone, canvas and hessian, in an eco-friendly construction. The double rooms have outside baths with views. The lounge has a deck with sweeping views, a collection of books and a fireplace.

The chef provides both local and international dishes. The swimming pool is surrounded by wilderness.

Activities include game drives and guided walks. Amani Mara works with local communities to minimise the impact of tourism on the environment and improve the facilities and resources available. Current projects include providing water filters to Maasai villages and assisting the set up of a medical dispensary. Environmental projects include a waste water management project. Amani Mara is located in Olare Orok Conservancy on the banks of the Ntiakntiak River, 5km northeast of the Maasai Mara National Reserve.

Porini Lion Camp

Olare Orok Conservancy

Porini Lion Camp, Olare Orok Conservancy, nr Maasai Mara Ntl. Reserve
Porini Camps, PO Box 388, Nairobi 00621, Kenya

Tel	+254 20 7123129; +254 20 7122504; +254 20 7121851
Mobile	+254 722 509200; +254 735 339209
Fax	+254 20 7120864
E-mail	info@porini.com / info@gamewatchers.co.ke
Web	www.porini.com

 Ol Kiombo, LS & CH
25 mins

Named for the big cats for which the Mara is famed, Porini Lion Camp is ideally positioned to see these and other big game. The camp is situated on the banks of the Ntiakntiak River in the Olare Orok Conservancy, an exclusive 20,000-acre conservancy that borders the Maasai Mara National Reserve.

The camp has no permanent structures. The 10 en-suite tents each have a double and a single bed, solar powered lighting and a private veranda. The camp chef prepares all meals with fresh produce and home baked bread. Picnics are available for guests who enjoy extended game drives. Game drives cover both the Olare Orok Conservancy and the Maasai Mara National Reserve. Night drives in the conservancy give guests the chance to see the more elusive nocturnal game. Maasai moran are also available to escort guests on walks in the conservancy, and to speak about how the various indigenous animals and plants are used by their community and how their way of life is entwined with their surroundings.

Porini Lion Camp has been granted a silver award from Ecotourism Society of Kenya. The local Maasai community receive income for each guest in the conservancy, and employment for their members. Strict policies cover landuse, water, sewage, energy and waste disposal.

Topi House

Talek Gate

Topi House, nr Talek Gate, nr Maasai Mara National Reserve, Kenya
Bush and Beyond, PO Box 56923, Nairobi 00200, Kenya

Tel	+254 20 6000457; +254 20 6005108; +254 20 6005980
Mobile	+254 733 330007; +254 723 273668
Fax	+254 20 6005008
E-mail	info@bush-and-beyond.com
Web	www.bush-and-beyond.com

 Ol Kiombo, LS & CH
40 mins

Topi House is a private house located between the the Olare Orok Conservancy and the Maasai Mara National Reserve. The house, set amongst acacia trees, has views of the conservancy and the reserve. The area has rolling hills with attractive viewpoints, which make lovely spots for bush picnics and sundowners.

There are 3 en-suite double bedrooms, linked by a veranda that runs the length of the house. There is also an open plan living and dining area, with open log fire. The kitchen is fully equipped. Electricity is provided by solar power, and a backup generator. The house is fully staffed, including chef, safari guide, night guard and house manager. The chef is happy to adapt his menus according to the preferences of the guests. A fully stocked drinks fridge is on site. WiFi is available throughout the house. Game drives are done in the visitors' vehicle; a guide is provided. A 4WD vehicle is available for hire if required. Game walks in the conservancy can be arranged. Cultural visits to local Maasai villages, schools and trading centres are all on offer. Picnics and sundowners are available. The house collects rainwater and takes care to minimise its water usage. The house is affiliated to Rekero, and is managed by Nomadic Encounters.

Richard's Private Camp

 Olare Orok Conservancy

Richard's Private Camp, Olare Orok Conservancy, nr Maasai Mara Ntl. Res.
The Safari and Conservation Company, PO Box 24576, Nairobi 00502

Tel	+254 6006759/69; +254 20 2115453
Mobile	+254 712 579999; +254 735 579999
Fax	+254 20 2194995
E-mail	reservations@scckenya.com
Web	www.richardscamp.com/private-camp

VISA, MasterCard

Richard's Private Camp, CH, 5 mins
Musiara, LS & CH, 50 mins

Richard's Private Camp is on the banks of the Njageteck River just below Klipspringer Gorge and next to Ngoyanai Springs. This permanent water around the camp ensures that there is plenty of game, including a pride of lions often seen on the hill in front of the camp.

There are 5 custom-designed tents with outdoor en-suite bathrooms. The camp is always booked on a fully exclusive basis and groups are never mixed. A minimum of 5 guests is required, and the camp can accommodate a maximum of 10. The camp was elegantly refurbished in 2011. The camp retains the charm of a bush camp, while also providing comfortable accommodation, modern plumbing and elegant decor. Lighting is by candles and lamps. Breakfast, lunch and dinner are served safari style at the dining table in the oval mess tent with a striking view.

The camp's owner, Richard Roberts, personally guides guests at this camp. Brought up in the Mara from the age of 3, Richard has a broad knowledge of the indigenous mammals and birds and the Mara ecosystem. The camp is in the Olare Orok Conservancy, a short distance from the Maasai Mara National Reserve, and supports the projects of this conservancy as well as other Mara conservation projects.

Mara Plains Camp

 Olare Orok Conservancy

Mara Plains Camp, Olare Orok Conservancy, nr Maasai Mara Ntl. Reserve
Bush and Beyond, PO Box 56923, Nairobi 00200, Kenya

Tel	+254 20 6000457; +254 20 6005108; +254 20 6005980
Mobile	+254 733 330007; +254 723 273668
Fax	+254 20 6005008
E-mail	info@bush-and-beyond.com
Web	www.bush-and-beyond.com

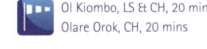

Ol Kiombo, LS & CH, 20 mins
Olare Orok, CH, 20 mins

Mara Plains Camp is in Olare Orok Conservancy, a new 20,000-acre initiative created with the aim of developing a sustainable future for both local Maasai and the wildlife. Established in 2008, the camp has been designed to have as little impact as possible on the environment while still providing a luxury safari experience; not even a teaspoon of cement can be found on site.

The 6 en-suite octagonal tents, set in riverine forest along the Ntiakntiak River, are raised on decks with sweeping views. The 3 open air interconnected marquis tents house 2 lounges, 1 with a small library and writing area, and a main dining room with a grand wood table and magnificent chandelier, tastefully decorated in rich earthy browns, coppers and reds. Mara Plains Camp is the only camp to offer game drives in the Maasai Mara National Reserve, and in both Olare Orok Conservancy and Mara North Conservancy, a conservation area of over 100,000 acres. Schedules are flexible; the highly qualified guides are available for night drives, game walks and cultural visits to local Maasai villages at any time.

The camp has committed 150,000 USD per year to the local Maasai to maintain and preserve the conservancies and their wildlife.

Acaluma Camp

Musiara Gate

Acaluma Camp, nr Musiara Gate, nr Maasai Mara National Reserve, Kenya
PO Box 40286, Nairobi 00100, Kenya
Tel
Mobile +27 715 130 529
Fax
E-mail adrianpintos@gmail.com / carolinacerdal@gmail.com
Web

                                             Musiara, LS & CH
                                                                  20 mins

A private tented camp, Acaluma Camp offers self-catering tents in attractive surroundings. The camp styles itself as immersion in the natural world, with no external distractions. It is 2km outside the Musiara Gate to the Maasai Mara National Reserve.

There are 4 tents, made up of 2 en-suite doubles and 2 doubles with shared bathroom. There is also a sitting and dining tent. The kitchen is equipped with gas cooker, gas fridge and hot and cold running water. There is no electricity. Kerosene lanterns are provided. The camp is staffed by a guide, a cook, a room assistant and 2 night guards. Guests should bring food, drinks and torches. There are no charging facilities; cameras and mobile telephones should be fully charged on arrival.

Guests can do game drives in their own vehicle; 4WD vehicles are recommended in the dry season and essential during the rains. Guided game walks in the conservancy are also available. Visitors should take the Narok Mulot Road, turn left at Ngorengore and left again at Ngorengore Junction. Continue through Lemek and Aitong, and lastly drive 4km in the direction of Leopard Gorge.

Kicheche Valley Camp

Naboisho Conservancy

Kicheche Valley Camp, Naboisho Conservancy, nr Maasai Mara Ntl. Res.
Kicheche Camps, PO Box 15236, Nairobi 00509, Kenya
Tel +254 20 8890541; +254 20 2405586; +254 20 2493569/12
Mobile +254 736 888055; +254 700 888055
Fax +254 20 891379
E-mail sales@kicheche.com
Web www.kicheche.com

                                                                  Siana, LS & CH
                                                                  40 mins

Kicheche Valley Camp is a founding tourist partner in Naboisho Conservancy which was established in 2010. Naboisho, meaning coming together in the language of the Maasai, is a community-driven initiative. The conservancy, dedicated to empowering local communities, supporting a healthy ecosystem and promoting wildlife conservation, has opened up a striking new region. Kicheche Valley Camp, which was established in 2011, is an intimate, luxury bush camp. There are 6 en-suite tents, which can be double, twin or triple as required. Each spacious tent is fully insect-proof, and equipped with large beds, bedside tables, luggage racks, lounge chair, desk and rugs. The camp is personally hosted, and run by experienced staff. The cuisine is a blend of African and European dishes; meals are served alfresco or in the spacious dining tent. Activities include game drives, game walks and cultural visits to local Maasai villages. Bush meals and sundowners can be arranged. The area is home to a wide variety of wildlife such as lion, leopard, cheetah, elephant, topi and hartebeest. The highest population of giraffe in the greater Maasai Mara area is found in Naboisho Conservancy. Rare bird species include white headed buffalo weaver, northern white-crowned shrike, pigmy falcon and Von der Deckens hornbill. Kicheche Valley Camp has attained a place in Conde Nast Traveller's Hot List of New Hotels in 2012.

Naboisho Camp — Naboisho Conservancy

Naboisho Camp, Naboisho Conservancy, nr Maasai Mara Ntl. Reserve
Asilia Africa, PO Box 25150, Nairobi 00603, Kenya

Tel	+254 20 2324904; +254 20 2324906
Mobile	+254 702 964904
Fax	+254 20 2324902
E-mail	marketing@asiliaafrica.com
Web	www.asiliaafrica.com/naboisho

Koiyaki Guide School, CH, 20 mins
Ol Kiombo, LS & CH, 1.5 hrs

Established in 2011, Naboisho Camp is a small and exclusive tented camp. The camp is situated in Naboisho Conservancy, a community-driven initiative created in 2010. The conservancy is a wildlife conservation and tourism area that supports the livelihoods of the surrounding communities; the camp provides access to this fresh region with plentiful game. There are 8 en-suite tents, set in an acacia forest looking out over a glade. The tents are the latest in traditional design, and include a spacious veranda and an outdoor shower. The experienced staff provide personal service; the certified guides deliver informed game drives; the award-winning chef creates innovative bush cuisine. The camp is eco-friendly; electricity is provided by solar power, with a backup generator. The tents are suitable for guests with disabilities, advance notice required.

Activities are tailored according to the guests' wishes, and include game drives, night drives, game walks and cultural visits to local Maasai villages. The conservancy is characterised by sweeping open plains that roll into forested seasonal streams. It is rich in plains game and predators. Naboisho Camp is affiliated to Rekero in the Maasai Mara National Reserve.

Encounter Mara — Naboisho Conservancy

Encounter Mara, Naboisho Conservancy, nr Maasai Mara Ntl. Res, Kenya
PO Box 541, Limuru 00217, Kenya

Tel	+254 20 2034197
Mobile	+254 720 016546
Fax	+254 20 2034197
E-mail	encountermara@africanencounter.org
Web	www.encountermara.com

 VISA, MasterCard    Ol Kiombo, LS & CH 1.5 hrs

Established in 2011, Encounter Mara is a luxury tented camp located in the Naboisho Conservancy. The camp is on the Olmorijo, a seasonal river, in an attractive valley which attracts plentiful game. Naboisho Conservancy, established in 2010, aims to conserve wildlife while providing direct benefit to local Maasai communities.

There are 12 en-suite tents, whose design combines natural simplicity with elegance. Each tent has a spacious veranda and a bathroom with a view. The dining and lounge areas, constructed of canvas and including reading areas and rustic lounge chairs, face the salt lick which attracts a variety of plains game. The cuisine is fresh and healthy, and includes freshly baked muffins, quiches and tropical fruits. The bar serves wines and cocktails, as well as fruit drinks, iced teas and homemade cordials. Activities include day and night game drives and game walks. Cultural visits to local Maasai villages and visits to nearby villages where African Impact volunteers are working afford genuine connection with the Maasai culture. Sundowners and guided stargazing are also available. The camp is eco-friendly, and strict policies govern its waste disposal, power, cooking methods and water conservation. Guests interested in learning more about sister project African Impact, or volunteering with them, should see www.africanimpact.com

Basecamp Dorobo Bush Camp

Naboisho Conservancy

Basecamp Dorobo Bush Camp, Naboisho Conservancy, nr Mara Reserve
Basecamp Explorer, PO Box 43369, Nairobi 00100, Kenya

Tel	+254 20 3877490-2
Mobile	+254 733 333909
Fax	+254 20 3877489
E-mail	bookings@basecampexplorer.co.ke
Web	www.basecampexplorer.com

VISA, MasterCard

Ol Kiombo, LS & CH
40 mins

Named after the Dorobo people of this area, Basecamp Dorobo Bush Camp is an eco-friendly camp. Basecamp Dorobo Bush Camp is owned and managed by Basecamp, a luxury eco-friendly camp near Talek Gate. Basecamp Foundation supports and cooperates with local communities, as well as developing and promoting Basecamp's sustainable tourism concept. There are 5 tents. Each tent has twin safari beds and shared eco bathrooms with safari showers. Mobile solar lights light the tents. Kerosene lanterns light the paths. Meals are served in the dining tent or under the stars. International dishes are prepared using, as much as possible, fresh ingredients from Basecamp's vegetable garden. The bar is well stocked with soft drinks, beers, wines and spirits.

Activities include day and night game drives, game walks and cultural visits to local Maasai villages. Bush meals and sundowners can be arranged. Full day game walks in the Naboisho Conservancy are available, and include lunch at Basecamp Wilderness. Dorobo Club offers children's activities. Cultural talks from local Maasai on their traditions and lifestyle are available. Basecamp holds a gold award from Ecotourism Society of Kenya, and has won the WTM First Choice Responsible Tourism Award, SKAL International Ecotourism Award and TIES Ecotourism Innovation Award.

Nyumbu Camp

Talek Gate

Nyumbu Camp, nr Talek Gate, nr Maasai Mara National Reserve, Kenya
PO Box 30506, Nairobi 00100, Kenya

Tel	+254 20 2662452; +254 20 2662450; +254 20 4347508
Mobile	+254 772 342487; +254 703 943127
Fax	+254 20 2662447; +254 20 25062
E-mail	info@maasaimara-nyumbu.com
Web	www.maasaimara-nyumbu.com

Ol Kiombo, LS & CH
45 mins

Nyumbu Camp is located in the Ngila Plains, just outside Talek Gate. The camp is unfenced, giving guests the chance to experience living close to nature. In keeping with its objective to provide local employment, the camp is hosted by trained professionals from the local community. There are 16 en-suite tents, made up of doubles and twins. All tents have verandas with views. Meals are served in the mess tent; Maasai guards are on hand to escort guests to and from the mess tent during the hours of darkness.

Activities include game drives in the prime game viewing areas of the Maasai Mara National Reserve. Cultural visits to the nearby Olepolos Maasai village, which the camp supports with contributions to the community's chosen projects, are recommended.

The camp works closely with the local community, providing employment and donating water from the camp's borehole. The Nyumbu Trust Conservancy is a Maasai owned concession of about 1,000 acres; the camp's conservation fees are paid to the landowners. The camp is eco conscious; lighting is provided by solar power and the fridges run off both solar and gas.

Bush Buck Camp Lemek Conservancy

Bush Buck Camp, Lemek Conservancy, nr Maasai Mara National Reserve
Bush Buck Adventures, PO Box 67449, Nairobi 00200, Kenya

Tel	+254 20 7123090; +254 20 7121554; +254 20 7121505
Mobile	
Fax	+254 20 7121505
E-mail	bushbuck@wananchi.com
Web	www.bushbuckadventures.com

  Mara North, LS & CH, 40 mins
Ngerende, LS & CH, 1 hr

In a forest grove not far from a river, Bush Buck Camp has views of the Aitong Hills. The camp is a rustic bush camp aimed at the adventure safari market. The camp is affiliated to Bush Buck Adventures, a company that offers adventure travel and safaris.

There are 6 en-suite tents, with verandas. Each tent contains washstand, chair, table, water jug and glasses, baggage stand and torch. Meals are served in the dining tent; international dishes are prepared by the camp's chef. Dietary requirements can be catered for, with advance notice. The camp is hosted by conservationists and safari guides, who join the guests around the campfire after dinner and share stories of their experiences.

Activities include game drives in Lemek Group Ranch and in the Maasai Mara National Reserve. Zebra, impala, gazelle, wildebeest, elephant, hippo and baboon are often seen around camp during the day. The camp specialises in game walks, during which local Maasai guides introduce guests to bush skills such as reading animal spoor and learning the uses of indigenous flora. Longer walking safaris can be arranged, advance booking required. Guests, with a Maasai guide, spend 1 or 2 nights away from the camp using lightweight camping equipment and dining under the stars.

Saruni Mara North Conservancy

Saruni, Mara North Conservancy, nr Maasai Mara National Reserve, Kenya
PO Box 304, Narok 20500, Kenya

Tel	+254 20 2694338
Mobile	+254 710 842000; +254 735 950903
Fax	
E-mail	riccardo@sarunicamp.com
Web	www.saruni.com

VISA, MasterCard   Ngerende, LS & CH 1 hr

Set in Mara North Conservancy bordering the Maasai Mara National Reserve, Saruni is a deluxe, design lodge. Based on a close partnership with the local community and built to ecological standards, Saruni entwines old traditions of classic safaris with modern technology.

The 6 uniquely styled cottages are furnished with colonial antiques, Persian carpets and African art, while the en-suite bathrooms include eco-loos and beautifully crafted basins and showers. The verandas have sunbeds and hammocks overlooking the plains and the passing game. Food is served at the main table in Kuro House or in the privacy of the guests' cottage. The Maasai Well-Being Space is a private treatment cottage where guests can enjoy massages and treatments while watching bushbuck and elephant stroll past. Run in collaboration with Grand Hotel des Iles Borromees, the space combines sophisticated methods with ancient Maasai wisdom.

Activities include game drives in both Mara North Conservancy and the Maasai Mara National Reserve. The camp also offers game walks that introduce guests to bush skills.

Saruni also offers drawing safaris for guests wishing to spend a few days painting in spectacular scenery with a professional artist, and Warrior for a Week programmes for guests interested in animal tracking and bush craft.

Saruni Wild — Mara North Conservancy

Saruni Wild, Mara North Conservancy, Maasai Mara National Reserve
PO Box 304, Narok 20500, Kenya

Tel	+254 20 2694338
Mobile	+254 710 842000; +254 735 950903
Fax	
E-mail	riccardo@sarunicamp.com
Web	www.saruniwild.com

VISA, MasterCard   Ngerende, LS & CH 1 hr

Saruni Wild is a private tented camp, owned and managed by Saruni, 10km from Saruni Wild. The camp was previously known as Campi ya Tembo. It is located in a wild scenic valley, familiarly known as secret valley, near the Maasai Mara National Reserve. The valley is rich in wildlife, with a large resident population of elephant, giraffe, zebra, buffalo and impala. It is also ideal for bird watching. There are 3 en-suite double tents. The tents are Oriental in design, and have large verandas with views of the Yaile Mountains. The chef specialises in Italian cuisine, and uses fresh local ingredients.

Saruni Wild offers game drives both inside and outside the Maasai Mara National Reserve. The camp is an ideal base for those interested in watching, tracking and studying elephants. The camp also offers game walks, with specialised guides who introduce guests to bush skills. Walks are individually tailored and can pass through valley, forests, springs and mountains, according to the preference of the guests. Saruni Wild also offers drawing safaris for guests wishing to spend a few days painting in spectacular scenery with a professional artist. Warrior for a Week is a special interactive wildlife safari, designed for families or small groups. The programme is ideal for guests interested in animal tracking and bush craft.

Acacia House — Mara North Conservancy

Acacia House, Mara North Conservancy, nr Maasai Mara Ntl. Reserve
Bush and Beyond, PO Box 56923, Nairobi 00200, Kenya

Tel	+254 20 6000457; +254 20 6005108; +254 20 6005980
Mobile	+254 733 330007; +254 723 273668
Fax	+254 20 6005008
E-mail	info@bush-and-beyond.com
Web	www.bush-and-beyond.com

Ngerende, LS & CH 45 mins

Located in a secluded valley in the north of Mara North Conservancy, Acacia House overlooks Ol Chorro waterhole. The house is a fully staffed private house from which guests can watch an array of wildlife and birdlife at close range. There are 2 spacious en-suite bedrooms, and an attic bedroom suitable for children. There is also a large sitting and dining room and a den that can be used as an office. Breakfast, lunch and dinner are served in the main house, by the open fireplace. Special dietary requirements can be accommodated with prior notice. Guests can choose the self-catering option if they prefer. The house has a swimming pool, TV and DVD, and is equipped with WiFi. A solar power inverter gives 24-hour electricity.

Activities include day and night game drives, and game walks, in the conservancy. Picnics in the bush and sundowners can be arranged. For an extra charge, game drives in the Maasai Mara National Reserve can be arranged. Visits to local Maasai villages, schools and markets are also on offer. The house is affiliated to Rekero, and is managed by Nomadic Encounters.

Guests interested in community conservation are welcome to participate in the Rekero Trust projects, including daily computer training for local communities at the Rekero Trust classroom.

Mara House — Mara North Conservancy

Mara House, Mara North Conservancy, nr Maasai Mara Ntl. Res., Kenya
Bush and Beyond, PO Box 56923, Nairobi 00200, Kenya

Tel	+254 20 6000457; +254 20 6005108; +254 20 6005980
Mobile	+254 733 330007; +254 723 273668
Fax	+254 20 6005008
E-mail	info@bush-and-beyond.com
Web	www.bush-and-beyond.com

Ngerende, LS & CH
45 mins

Located in a secluded valley in the north of Mara North Conservancy, Mara House overlooks the Ol Chorro waterhole. The house is a fully staffed private house from which guests can watch an array of wildlife and birdlife at close range.

There are 3 en-suite bedrooms. The house also has an open plan sitting and dining room, a den equipped with TV and DVD and a fully equipped kitchen. The swimming pool is shared with nearby Acacia House. WiFi is available throughout the house. Electricity is provided by solar power. The house is fully staffed, including chef, safari guide and night guard. The chef is happy to adapt his menus according to the preferences of the guests.

Safari itineraries are flexible. Activities include day and night game drives, and game walks, in the conservancy. Picnics in the bush and sundowners can be arranged. For an extra charge, game drives in the Maasai Mara National Reserve can be arranged. Visits to local Maasai villages, schools and markets are also on offer. Acacia House is affiliated to Rekero, and managed by Nomadic Encounters. Guests interested in community conservation are welcome to participate in the Rekero Trust projects, including daily computer training for local communities at the Rekero Trust classroom.

Fairmont Mara Safari Club — Ol Chorro Conservancy

Fairmont Mara Safari Club, Ol Chorro Conservancy, nr Maasai Mara Ntl. Res.
PO Box 58581, Nairobi 00200, Kenya

Tel	+254 20 2265000; +254 20 2265555
Mobile	+254 717 969610
Fax	+254 20 2216796
E-mail	kenya.reservations@fairmont.com
Web	www.fairmont.com/marasafariclub

All major cards

Ngerende, LS & CH
10 mins

Framed by a curve of the Mara River, the Fairmont Mara Safari Club is a tented sanctuary on the edge of the Maasai Mara National Reserve. The club opened in 1989 on the site of an old hunting camp that had been converted to photo safari after the hunting ban. It stands on 100 acres of land, leased from the late Senior Chief Lerionka Ole Ntutu.

The 51 luxury tents are made up of 35 Fairmont tents with queen beds, 9 Fairmont deluxe tents with 2 queen beds and 6 Signature tents with an additional outdoor shower and a more removed location for privacy. All the tents have en-suite bathrooms with porcelain features and walk-in shower, Mazara stone floors and a private deck with a unique view of the hippos in the Mara River below. 1 tent is equipped for guests with disabilities. The main lodge at the center of camp has an indoor restaurant and bar. A library and information centre with internet access can also be used for conferences. A spacious outside deck overhangs the river and leads to a heated pool, complete with bar and private massage tents.

The boma, a structure influenced by traditional homesteads, gives guests the opportunity to enjoy a cultural dinner reflecting African cuisine and accompanied by rich musical accompaniment.

Activities include game drives, game walks, bird watching and cultural visits to Maasai villages.

Ngerende Island Lodge   Ol Chorro Conservancy

Ngerende Island Lodge, Ol Chorro Conservancy, nr Maasai Mara Ntl. Res.
PO Box 1274, Nairobi 00502, Kenya
Tel +254 20 2103244
Mobile +254 736 391078; +254 722 861224; +254 725 943030
Fax +254 20 3883457
E-mail marketing@ngerende.com
Web www.ngerende.com

VISA, MasterCard

Ngerende, LS & CH
5 mins

The water of the Mara River laps on all sides of Ngerende Island Lodge, linked by a causeway to the riverbank. Set in the Ol Chorro Conservancy, the lodge has access to savannah plains as well as the wooded banks of the Mara River.
There are 7 en-suite canvas and wood suites. All suites are on raised mahogany platforms and have panoramic views of the river and its environs. All suites are equipped with fireplace, open air bath and spacious veranda, and are served by a personal room steward.
Activities include morning and evening game drives and visits to the nearby rhino sanctuary. Full day game drives and night drives are also offered. Birdlife is prolific and game walks are recommended. Weddings are individually planned to the specifications of the couple. Ngerende's holistic spa offers its own big five: safari soother, sensual Africa, Ngerende restorer, indulgent Mara and Ngerende teaser.
Ngerende Island Lodge is committed to empowering the local communities by providing employment, purchasing supplies locally, marketing local crafts and supporting a local school. The lodge minimises its environmental impact by using solar power, harvesting rain water and instigating a tree planting project.

Richard's Camp   Ol Chorro Conservancy

Richard's Camp, Ol Chorro Conservancy, nr Maasai Mara Ntl. Reserve, Kenya
The Safari and Conservation Company, PO Box 24576, Nairobi 00502, Kenya
Tel +254 6006759; +254 20 2115343; +254 20 6006769
Mobile +254 712 579999; +254 735 579999
Fax +254 20 2194995
E-mail reservations@scckenya.com
Web www.richardscamp.com

VISA, MasterCard

Kulolo, CH, 5 mins
Ngerende, LS & CH, 30 mins

Originally built as the Roberts' home while they were carrying out conservation work in the greater Maasai Mara region, Richard's Camp is an exclusive tented camp. A small forest fringes the camp, ensuring that elephant and plains game are regular visitors to the camp's perimeter, and birdlife is plentiful. There are 6 en-suite tents, with 24-hour solar lighting, furnished in the style of traditional safaris and adorned with local fabrics. These can be doubles or twins as required, and an extra bed can be added for a child. Breakfast, lunch and dinner are served at a long table either in the mess tent or under the stars. The camp also boasts a Victorian bath tucked away in the forest where guests can soak in comfort surrounded by flickering candles and the sounds of the bush. Located to the northwest of the Maasai Mara National Reserve, the camp is in a conservation area that is owned and managed by the Maasai people under the name of The Ol Chorro Oirouwa Wildlife Management and Conservation Association. Richard Roberts and his family continue to be very active in ongoing Mara conservation projects as well as spearheading initiatives in other parts of Kenya. Activities include day and night game drives, game walks, cultural visits to local Maasai villages, bush breakfasts and sundowners. Scenic flights can be arranged for a surcharge. The camp is closed in May and November.

Kicheche Mara Camp

Mara North Conservancy

Kicheche Mara Camp, Mara North Conservancy, nr Maasai Mara Ntl. Res.
Kicheche Camps, PO Box 15236, Nairobi 00509, Kenya

Tel	+254 20 2493569/12; +254 20 2405586
Mobile	+254 736 888055; +254 700 888055
Fax	+254 20 891379
E-mail	sales@kicheche.com
Web	www.kicheche.com

  VISA, MasterCard, Amex   Ngerende, LS & CH 30 mins

In the picturesque Acacia Valley, Kicheche Mara Camp looks out on a prime wildlife viewing area of Mara North Conservancy. The tents look out over the Olare Orok stream and the western escarpment of the valley. There are 8 en-suite tents, which can be double or twin as required. Triple tents and family tents are available on request. All tents are furnished with cedar beds, and adorned with woven rugs. Deck chairs are on the verandas and hammocks slung between nearby trees. The cuisine is a blend of African and European dishes; meals are served alfresco or in the spacious dining tent. The Nyati Tent, furnished with comfortable seating, a library of reference books, board games and local artefacts, makes a pleasant place to relax.

Kicheche's guides are highly qualified and experienced, and take regular training courses. Activities include game drives, game walks and cultural visits to Maasai villages, as well as visits to local schools supported by the camp.

The Kicheche Community Project, established in 2004, encourages the preservation of the environment and improves the welfare of the community. Kicheche was applauded by Chris Haslam, AITO travel writer of the year, for its passionate commitment to the community. The camp is closed during the rains, in April and May.

Duma Camp

Lemek Conservancy

Duma Camp, Lemek Conservancy, nr Maasai Mara National Reserve
JMAR Safaris, PO Box 25326, Nairobi 00603, Kenya

Tel	+254 20 2691607
Mobile	+254 733 614362; +254 770 425008; +254 736 554911
Fax	+254 20 3875798
E-mail	jenn@africaonline.co.ke / info@jmarsafaris.com
Web	www.jmarsafaris.com

        Mara North, LS & CH 30 mins

With a name meaning cheetah in Swahili, Duma Camp is a small camp in Lemek Conservancy near the Maasai Mara National Reserve. The camp is set in a grassy clearing and looks out across the plains.

The 6 en-suite tents are furnished with twin beds, wooden tables and canvas chairs. There is no generator in camp. Solar powered lights are in each tent, and paraffin lamps light the paths outside. Hot water for the safari showers is available whenever guests require. Meals are served alfresco when the weather permits, or in the open sided dining tent.

The camp is rented exclusively to one group at a time, and activities are planned according to the wishes of that group. Game drives in the Maasai Mara National Reserve with picnics near the Mara River are on offer, as are night drives around the camp's area. For an extra charge, game walks with Maasai moran and cultural visits to local Maasai villages can be arranged. Trips further afield, such as day trips to Rusinga Island in Lake Victoria, and balloon safaris over the Maasai Mara National Reserve, can also be factored into guests' itineraries for a surcharge.

David Livingstone Safari Resort

Lemek Conservancy

David Livingstone Safari Resort, Lemek Conservancy, Kenya
PO Box 11136, Nairobi 00400, Kenya

Tel	+254 20 8034437/9; +254 20 8034439; +254 20 3748355
Mobile	+254 738 905225
Fax	+254 20 3748355
E-mail	info@davidlivingstone.co.ke
Web	www.davidlivingstone.co.ke

 VISA, MasterCard, Amex   Mara North, LS & CH
                                                                              15 mins

Set in a bend in the Mara River, David Livingstone Safari Resort looks out on pools filled with hippos. The resort, which was formerly known as Mara Shikar, is located in Lemek Conservancy. The resort is painted Maasai red, and adorned with Maasai fabrics and artefacts.
There are 80 en-suite rooms, made up of doubles and twins. Some rooms are interconnecting, suitable for families. There are also 2 suites, each with 2 bedrooms and a living room equipped with TV and DVD. The restaurant has a long terrace that overlooks the hippo pools, and serves table d'hote lunch and dinner. The Susi Bar and Chuma Bar both overlook the river, and are stocked with soft drinks, beers, wines and spirits.

The resort offers day and night game drives. The David Livingstone Safari Walk introduces visitors to the medicinal and cosmetic uses of indigenous plants. Specialist bird safaris are available with advance reservation. Teambuilding activities include obstacle runs, treasure hunts and cookery classes. Maasai moran entertain visitors with traditional dances and songs some evenings. Bush breakfasts, dinners and sundowners are also on offer. David Livingstone Safari Resort is committed to ensuring the local community benefits in terms of employment and welfare.

Exploreans Mara Rianta Camp

Mara North Conservancy

Exploreans Mara Rianta Camp, Mara North Conservancy, Kenya
Plan Hotel Group, PO Box 741, Narok 20500, Kenya

Tel	+254 42 2120444; +254 42 2131673
Mobile	+254 778 262626
Fax	+254 42 2131872
E-mail	info.mara@exploreans.com
Web	www.marariantacamp.exploreans.com

VISA, MasterCard, Amex   Mara North, LS & CH
                             20 mins

Nestled in a curve of the Mara River, Exploreans Mara Rianta Camp overlooks the hippos that wallow in the water. The camp is a tented camp with a selection of activities.
There are 20 en-suite tents, made up of doubles and twins. The tents are built on elevated wooden platforms with private viewing decks, and have armchairs, writing desk, safe and call button for butler. All tents have a shower and some also have a Jacuzzi; water is heated by solar power. The Acacia Dining Room serves buffet breakfast and lunch and a la carte dinner. The Zebra Bar and Lounge serves soft drinks, beers, wines and cocktails. There is a library equipped with WiFi. The Mvua Spa offers a range of massages and face and body treatments, and uses nourishing natural ingredients.

Activities include morning game drives, evening game drives, guided nature walks, bird watching and cultural visits to local Maasai villages. Night game drives can be arranged on request. Bush breakfasts, lunches and sundowners are also available. Exploreans Mara Rianta Camp is a member of the Plan Hotel Group; holidays combining a stay at the camp with a stay at the affiliated resorts in Malindi can be arranged.

Kileleoni Mara Guest House

Ngerende

Kileleoni Mara Guest House, Ngerende, nr Maasai Mara Ntl. Reserve
PO Box 23011, Nairobi 00100, Kenya

Tel
Mobile +254 725 404440; +254 720 454612
Fax
E-mail info@kileleonimasaimara.com
Web www.kileleonimasaimara.com

    All major cards   Ngerende, LS & CH
                                                    10 mins

Kileleoni Mara Guest House offers budget accommodation and camping just outside the Maasai Mara National Reserve. The guesthouse is affiliated to African Safaris and Adventures, which creates personalised safari itineraries for a range of budgets.

The guesthouse has 9 rooms. The campsite has bathroom facilities, and a selection of en-suite or standard tents for hire. Meals can be taken in the dining room or alfresco. Full English breakfast and buffet lunch and dinner are served. Dishes include a selection of salads and vegetarian options. There is also a small bar and a lounge with comfortable sofas, Maasai ornaments and TV.

Activities should be booked in advance. These can include game drives, game walks, sundowners, bush breakfasts and cultural visits to local Maasai villages. Packages including transport from Nairobi and guided game drives can be arranged. Guests who wish to do game drives in their own vehicles are also welcome. The guesthouse aims to protect the wildlife, cultural heritage and environment, and to give clients a true insight into the flora and fauna of East Africa.

Kileleoni Mara Guest House can be incorporated into a variety of safari experiences and unique adventures, including living with a local Maasai family, staying at a homestay or participating in a walking safari.

How to Feel at Home in Africa.
A showcase of African art and culture: Beautifully blended with African hospitality.
Kenya | Tanzania | Zanzibar | Uganda | Rwanda | Mozambique

For reservations and more information call +254 20 2842000/2842333,
email cro@serena.co.ke or visit www.serenahotels.com

SERENA HOTELS
SAFARI LODGES • HOTELS • RESORTS

The Lakes

Pelicans and Rhino at Lake Nakuru – Photo © Tamara Britten

The Great Rift Valley carves through Kenya, its path strewn with striking escarpments, glassy lakes, dormant volcanoes and bubbling geysers. Startling views unfold from its peaks and crests. Highlights include Lake Baringo, Lake Bogoria, Lake Nakuru, Lake Naivasha, Mt Longonot, Hell's Gate and Lake Magadi.

The East African Rift System is one of the geologic wonders of the world. The exact cause of rift formation is still debated, but it is generally accepted that shifts in Teutonic plates caused fractures on the earth's crust, volcanic eruptions and the formation of inland seas. These huge changes in environment and climate may explain why early man was forced to walk upright in this region, and why the world's oldest hominid fossils have been found in the Rift Valley.

Lake Baringo lies between the Tugen Hills, an uplifted fault block of volcanic and metamorphic rocks, and the Laikipia Escarpment. The region is inhabited by several tribal groups, most notably Njemps and Pokot. Baringo airstrip is on the mainland; boats connect it to the islands. Seven freshwater fish species inhabit the lake, of which one is endemic. This attractive lake is also home to hippos and crocodiles, and is a critical habitat for significant numbers of migratory water birds.

Lake Bogoria, a saline, alkaline lake, is famous for its therapeutic geysers and resident population of lesser flamingos. The lake was designated a national reserve in 1973.

Lake Nakuru is a soda lake at which 450 species of birds have been recorded, including flamingo, pelican, African fish eagle, goliath heron, hamerkop and Verreaux eagle. The national park comprises the lake and the surrounding forested escarpments and bushy grasslands. The park gates are Main Gate, Lanet Gate and Nderit Gate. Naishi airstrip, inside the park, is suitable for charter flights. The park is a sanctuary for black and white rhino, and is inhabited by 56 other species of mammal. Nearby attractions include Menengai Crater and the prehistoric archaeological sites at Hyrax Hill and Kariandusi.

Lake Naivasha, called Nai'posha, or rough water, in the language of the Maasai, is a freshwater lake. It was used in the 1930s as a landing place for Imperial Airways flying boats between London and Durban. Activities include boat trips, bird watching and game viewing.

Mt Longonot National Park, based around a volcano, is a haven for birdlife, especially birds of prey; 103 species have been recorded. The mountain has lovely hikes and climbs; the 3-hour walk around the rim of the crater affords spectacular views.

Hell's Gate National Park is best known for its jagged cliffs and striking gorge. The park gates are Elsa and Olkaria. There are campsites at Oldubai, Nairburta and Endchata. Buffalo, zebra, eland, hartebeest, giraffe, gazelles and antelopes are resident. Activities include hiking, rock climbing, biking, bird watching, game viewing and camping.

Lake Magadi, near the Kenya Tanzania border, is a saline, alkaline lake best known for its hot springs and shimmering white expanses of salt. A single species of fish inhabits the hot, salty water. Wading birds, including flamingos, reside here.

Lake Baringo
Lake Bogoria
Deloraine House
Rongai
Kembu Cottages Campsite and Farmstay
Subukia Bandas
Mugunda House
Nakuru
Gogar Farm
Njoro
Lake Nakuru
Lake Elementaita
Gilgil
Lake Naivasha
Naivasha
Lake Naivasha Panorama Park
NMK, Olorgesailie Bandas
Lake Magadi
Oloika Guest House
Loisiijo Lodge
Enkare
N

Soi Safari Lodge
Samatian Island Lodge
Roberts' Camp
Lake Baringo Club
Island Camp
Tamarind Garden
Lake Baringo

Lake Bogoria
Lake Bogoria Spa Resort

Lake Elmenteita Luxury Camp
Sunbird Lodge
Elementaita Country Lodge
Flamingo Camp and Cottages
Lake Elementaita
View Point Lodge
Sleeping Warrior Camp
Lake Elementaita Lodge
Oasis Eco Camp
Sleeping Warrior Lodge

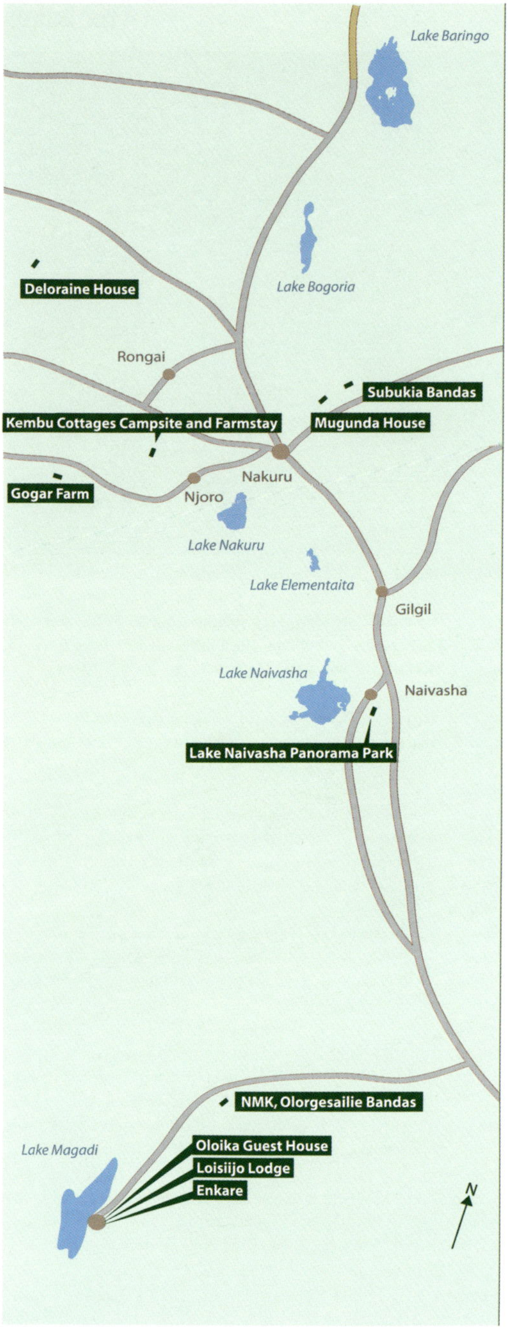

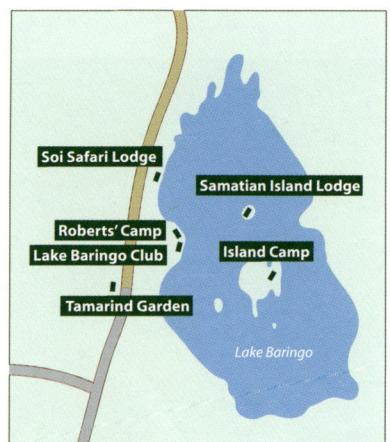

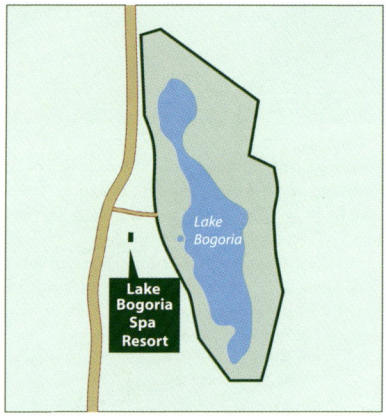

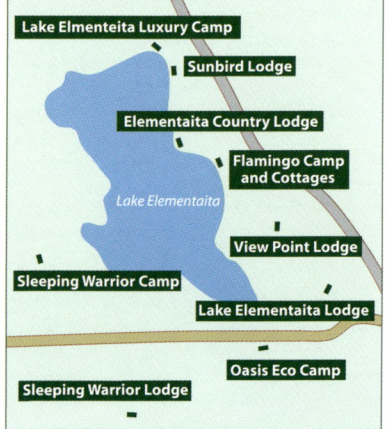

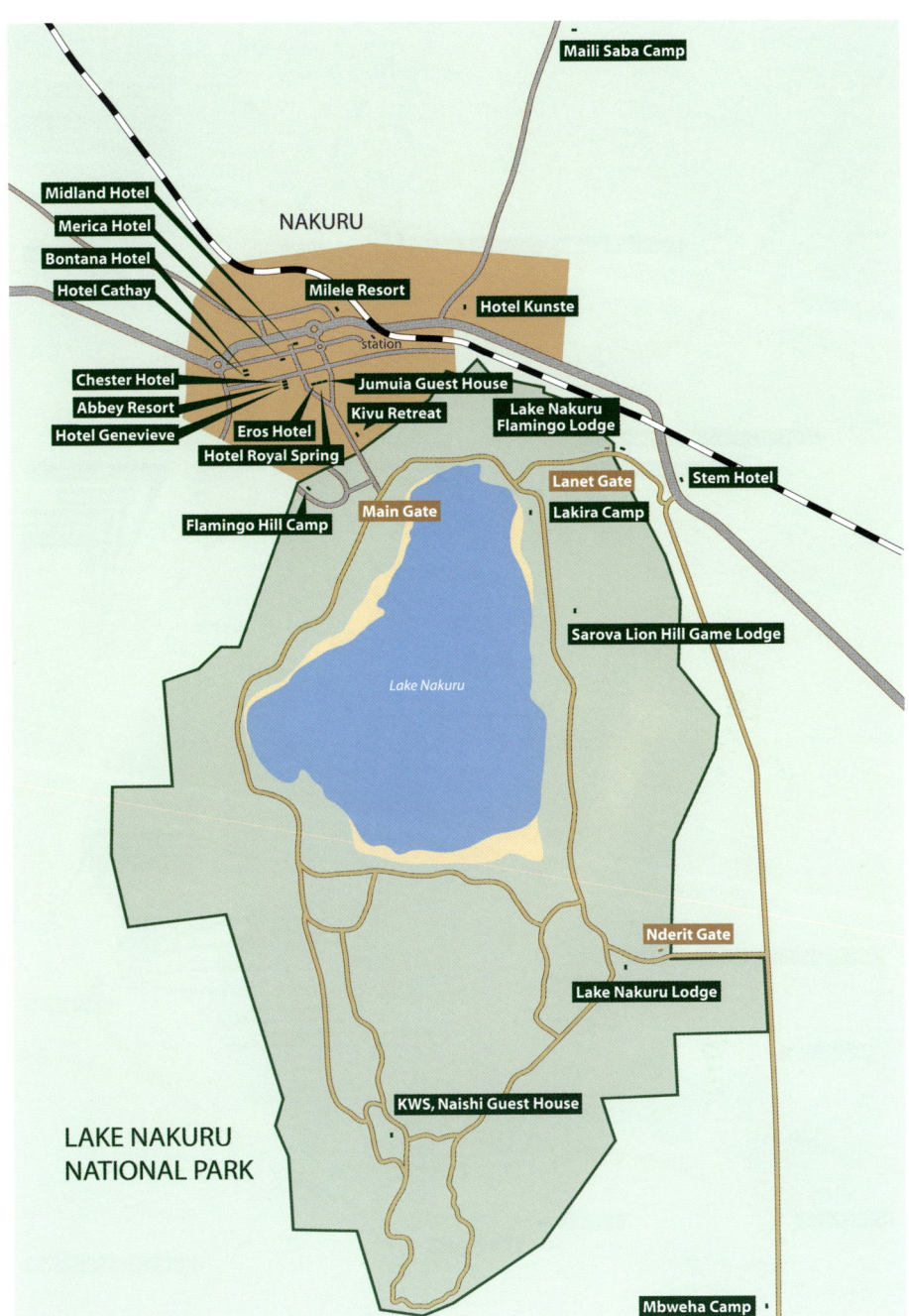

Karibu Kenya Accommodation Guide

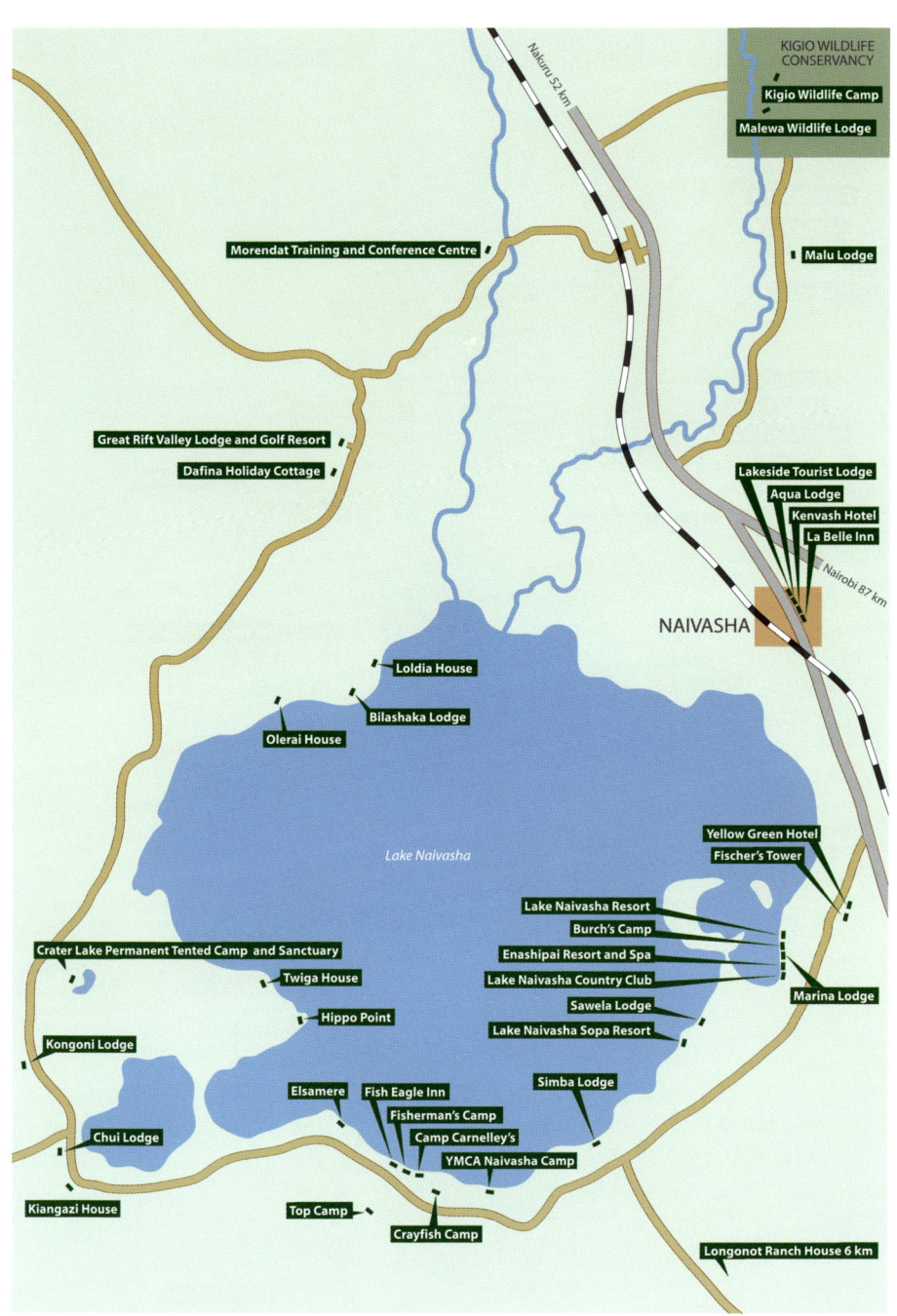

Samatian Island Lodge Lake Baringo

Samatian Island Lodge, Lake Baringo, Kenya
The Safari and Conservation Company, PO Box 1690, Nanyuki 10400
Tel
Mobile +254 727 232445; +254 731 325 797
Fax
E-mail bookings@samatianislandlodge.com
Web www.samatianislandlodge.com

VISA, MasterCard   Baringo, CH
                     20 mins by boat

On a private island in Lake Baringo, Samatian Island Lodge looks across the bronze waters of the lake to the Laikipia Escarpment. Lake Baringo is famed for sunsets that light up its waters, a dazzling array of birdlife and Njemps fishermen continuing a trade little changed for over 200 years. The exclusive lodge has 3 attractive cottages with en-suite double bedrooms, 1 family cottage with 2 en-suite bedrooms and 1 2-bedroom family cottage with a shared bathroom. All cottages are open plan, with thatched roofs and stunning views. The dining area, overlooking the infinity swimming pool, has a panoramic view of the lake. There is no fixed schedule. Activities include boat rides to visit Baringo's hot springs, and to view the resident hippos, crocodiles and giant monitor lizards. Canoeing, fishing, jogging, wakeboarding, bicycling and bird walks are all on offer. Visits to the traditional villages of the Pokot and Njemps are recommended. For a surcharge, day trips to Lake Bogoria and scenic flights over the Rift Valley can be arranged. Samatian Island Lodge is environmentally sustainable, powered by a complex solar system. This creates enough power to pump water from the lake, through a filtration system, and into the swimming pool, making it the 1st entirely eco pool in Kenya. Samatian Island Lodge supports a number of community and conservation projects, including Ruko Community Wildlife Trust.

Island Camp Lake Baringo

Island Camp, Ol Kokwe Island, Lake Baringo, Kenya
PO Box 1141, Nakuru 20100, Kenya
Tel
Mobile +254 728 478638; +254 735 919878
Fax
E-mail admin@islandcamp.co.ke
Web www.islandcamp.co.ke

VISA, MasterCard   Baringo, CH
                     20 mins by boat

Island Camp was established in 1975, making it one of the original tented camps in Kenya. The camp, on Ol Kokwe Island in Lake Baringo, offers both relaxation and activities; the area is particularly known for its prolific birdlife. The island is owned by the Njemps tribe, and a percentage of the camp's income goes to the local community.
There are 23 en-suite tents, made up of twins, doubles and triples. The tents are shaded by thatched roofs, and have verandas with views of the lake. The secluded honeymoon suite is more spacious. The swimming pool is surrounded by a sunbathing terrace. The open sided restaurant serves international cuisine and local specialities. Twice a week, barbecue dinner is served at the poolside. The main bar and pool bar have extensive drink lists. Cultural walks across the island give visitors the chance to meet the local community, visit the school and learn about the Njemps' traditions. Lakeshore cruises, including champagne breakfast on a secluded beach, view the lake's inhabitants, such as hippos, crocodiles and fish eagles. Ol Kokwe island cruises visit a Njemps village and nearby hot springs. Bird walks and sundowners are also available. Water sports include waterskiing, ski bob, paddle boards and knee boards.

Lakes

 Accommodation Guide

Soi Safari Lodge

Lake Baringo

Soi Safari Lodge, Lake Baringo, Kenya
PO Box 3170, Nairobi 00506, Kenya

Tel	+254 20 318774
Mobile	+254 723 865772
Fax	+254 20 2220303; +254 51 2210898
E-mail	managersoi@yahoo.com / info@rvath.com
Web	www.soisafarilodge_lkbaringo.com / www.rvath.com

Baringo, CH
20 mins

On the shores of Lake Baringo, Soi Safari Lodge consists of 2 large rondavels set in gardens dotted with ostriches and peacocks. The hotel opened in 2001, and added a new wing in 2007.

There are 51 en-suite rooms, made up of singles, doubles and twins. The 20 rooms with lake view have showers, and the 31 rooms with garden and pool view have bathtubs. All rooms are equipped with mosquito net, aircon, satellite TV and balcony.

The large restaurant and bar are on the 1st floor of the main building, and have lovely views across the lake to the islands. Both international buffet and a la carte are served. Dishes include fish stew, soups, steaks and curries.

There are 2 conference halls: 1 seats 200 pax and the other seats 60. Both halls are equipped with PA system and projector. The swimming pool is surrounded by sunbathing terrace. The massage and beauty parlour offers a selection of treatments. The gift shop stocks souvenirs and curios. Boat trips across the lake and to the islands can be arranged, as can cultural visits to Njemps, Turkana, Pokot and Tugen villages. Trips to the nearby community reptile park are also available.

Roberts' Camp

Lake Baringo

Roberts' Camp, Lake Baringo, Kenya
The Safari and Conservation Company, PO Box 24576, Nairobi 00502

Tel	+254 20 2115453; +254 20 6006759; +254 20 6006769
Mobile	+254 735 579999; +254 712 579999
Fax	+254 20 2194995
E-mail	info@robertscamp.com / reservations@scckenya.com
Web	www.robertscamp.com

VISA, MasterCard

Baringo, CH
10 mins

Roberts' Camp is set in beautiful gardens on the lake, with views of the dramatic cliffs and plateaus that surround it. This friendly camp offers cottages, bandas, tents and a campsite, and an abundance of activities. The area is home to 450 species of birds, as well as hippos and crocodiles.

Coots Cottage, in its own private garden, has 3 double rooms. Hammerkop's Roost, on the lakefront, has 2 double rooms. Little Egret, on the lakefront, has 2 double rooms. Heron House, on the lakefront, has 1 double room, 2 twin rooms and 1 triple room. All cottages have attractive décor, fully equipped kitchen, furnished sitting room and large veranda.

Weaver, Spoonbill and Stork bandas each have a twin room. They share bathroom facilities, fully equipped kitchen and dining area with barbecue. Coots banda, adjacent to Coots Cottage, has double and single bed. There are also 4 safari tents, made up of 1 en-suite and 3 with communal bathroom facilities. The Thirsty Goat serves local and international cuisine, and has an extensive drinks list. Dik Dik Duka stocks gift items. Activities include nature walks, bird walks, day trips to Tugen Hills, cultural visits to Pokot villages, boat trips and island cruises. Ornathologists and guides are resident at the camp. Vehicles are available for hire. Roberts' Camp supports a number of community and conservation projects, including Ruko Community Wildlife Trust.

Lake Baringo Club

Lake Baringo

Lake Baringo Club, Lake Baringo, Kenya
Sun Africa Hotels, PO Box 102124, Nairobi 00101, Kenya

Tel	+254 20 4450636; +254 20 4450639; +254 20 4450712
Mobile	+254 737 107266; +254 711 107266
Fax	+254 20 4450735
E-mail	info@sunafricahotels.com
Web	www.sunafricahotels.com

 VISA, MasterCard   Baringo, CH 10 mins

In lakeside lawns, Lake Baringo Club is surrounded by vivid bougainvillea and plentiful birdlife. The club opened in the 1960s as a private members club, and has been operating as a hotel since the 1980s.

There are 48 en-suite double rooms, overlooking the garden and the lake. The rooms are equipped with cupboard, dressing table, mosquito net and fan. The club has a wheelchair, and several rooms have wheelchair ramps. The restaurant serves a buffet, and has a daily table d'hote menu, with dishes like pan seared blue Nile perch with lemon and garlic, grilled best end of rump steak and chocolate mousse. The bar is well stocked with soft drinks, beers, wines, spirits and liqueurs. The games room has pool table, table tennis table, dartboard and badminton. Cards, draughts, backgammon and snakes and ladders are also available.

Activities include horse riding and boat rides to see the hippos and crocodiles of Lake Baringo. Trips can be arranged to the 2 nearby hot springs, as well as to Lake Bagoria and its hot springs. The conference hall seats 60 pax; conferences can be arranged either in the hall or in the gardens. The swimming pool is surrounded by sunbathing deck furnished with sunbeds.

Tamarind Garden

Lake Baringo

Tamarind Garden, Lake Baringo, Kenya
PO Box 61, Kampi ya Samaki 30406, Kenya

Tel	
Mobile	+254 722 649446; +254 723 531807
Fax	
E-mail	tamarindgarden@hotmail.com
Web	www.riftvalleytourism.org

      Baringo, CH 10 mins

Tamarind Garden is set in verdant gardens not far from Lake Baringo. The hotel offers budget accommodation and friendly service.

There are 12 en-suite rooms, made up of 8 singles and 4 doubles. The rooms are named after birds that can be seen locally, such as kingfisher, starling and ibis. All rooms are equipped with mosquito net, table, chair and cupboard. The showers are not heated.

The thatched restaurant has a seating area and a bar. It serves local and international dishes, such as beef steak, pork chops, spaghetti bolognaise, whole Tilapia fresh from the lake and nyama choma grilled meats. The bar is stocked with soft drinks, beers, wines and spirits, and equipped with satellite TV. There is a small garden with outdoor seating area. The Tamarind Garden is located just after the barrier to Kampi ya Samaki, on the left side of the road. Nearby attractions include Lake Baringo, famous for its hippos and crocodiles, and Lake Bagoria, famous for its hot springs. Boat rides can be arranged with local boat captains.

 Accommodation Guide

Lake Bogoria Spa Resort

Lake Bogoria

Lake Bogoria Spa Resort, Lake Bogoria, Kenya
PO Box 208, Menengai 20104, Kenya

Tel	+254 20 2249055
Mobile	+254 710 445627
Fax	+254 20 2249066
E-mail	info@lakebogoria-hotel.com
Web	www.lakebogoria-hotel.com

 VISA, MasterCard
 Eldoret, LS & CH & Intl. 2 hrs

Channelling the therapeutic hot spring geysers of Bogoria through its natural swimming pool, Lake Bogoria Spa Resort has been referred to as the healing place.

There are 21 en-suite standard rooms in the main hotel, 23 cottages in the garden with private parking and 2 spacious VIP suites. Ground floor rooms and suites have wheelchair access. The restaurant serves buffet and a la carte, the international menu includes weight watchers salad, fillet steak with mushroom sauce, vegetable korma and crepe Suzette. Meals are served in the restaurant, by the swimming pool or in the garden. The Bogoria Choma Ranch serves nyama choma grilled meats in thatched seating booths. The pool bar and main bar are fully stocked with soft drinks, beers, wines and spirits. Tugen dancers entertain nightly. The conference hall seats 200 pax; the boardroom seats 20.

The area is home to 380 species of birds. Guides are provided for guests wishing to do game drives in Bogoria National Park. Visits to the villages of the diverse cultures of the region, Njemps, Tugen, Turkana and Pokot, are available. Other facilities include pool table, table tennis table and ½ Olympic-sized swimming pool. Day trips to Lake Bogoria, Tugen Hills and Kapsaram historic site can be arranged.

Deloraine House

Rongai

Deloraine House, Rongai, nr Nakuru, Kenya
Offbeat Safaris, PO Box 1146, Nanyuki 10400, Kenya

Tel	+254 62 2031082
Mobile	+254 725 968351; +254 704 909355/6
Fax	+254 62 2031082
E-mail	bookings@offbeatsafaris.com
Web	www.offbeatsafaris.com

 Gogar, CH 15 mins

Deloraine House was built in 1920 by Lord Francis Scott, a prominent early settler who was instrumental in developing farms throughout Kenya. A fine example of colonial architecture, the house was visited by Queen Elizabeth, the Queen Mother, on a number of occasions. It is set in a 3,500-acre farm and surrounded by gardens with crocket lawn, tennis court and swimming pool.

There are 4 en-suite double rooms in the main house and another 3 en-suite double rooms in the cottage adjacent to the house. All rooms are decorated in English country house style, with a mixture of family heirlooms and modern amenities. The house has a large drawing room, dining room and veranda overlooking the gardens. Meals are created from fresh produce from the vegetable garden.

Deloraine is the headquarters of Offbeat Safaris' Mobile Riding Safari operation. The stables hold about 80 horses, some trained for safari and others for polo. There is a cross country course and a polo ground. Game drives in Lake Nakuru National Park, famed for its flamingo-filled lake and abundance of rhino, and trips to Lake Bogoria, famed for its hot springs, can be arranged. Deloraine House is in the foothills of Mt Londiani, about 10 mins from the Nakuru-Kericho highway.

Kembu Cottages
Campsite and Farmstay

Njoro

Kembu Cottages Campsite and Farmstay, nr Njoro, Njoro-Molo Road
PO Box 23, Njoro 20107, Kenya

Tel	
Mobile	+254 722 361102; +254 722 725003; +254 722 355705
Fax	
E-mail	kembu@africaonline.co.ke
Web	www.kembu.com

 Eldoret, LS & CH & Intl.
1.5 hrs

In the lovely grounds of a 900-acre farm, Kembu offers a collection of characterful cottages. With a wide variety of activities, dining options and facilities, Kembu has something for everyone. The romantic Acacia Cottage has an en-suite double room and an attractive conservatory. The Yellow Room has an en-suite twin room. Kenana Cottage has 2 en-suite twin rooms, living room, kitchen, veranda and private garden. Albizia Cottage has an en-suite double room, en-suite twin room, living room, kitchen, veranda and private garden. Mutati Cottage has a double room, twin room, living room, kitchen, bathroom and balcony. All these cottages are hosted for meals at the farmhouse, or can dine privately.

In the campsite, the Tree House, in a huge bougainvillea, has a double room with balcony, while Cobb's Carriage, a renovated 1920s Mvuli caravan, has a double room and living room. Both these use the bathroom facilities in the campsite. Camping and bedding equipment is available for hire. Kembu has a lively bar, barbecue, splash tank, badminton, volleyball, dartboard, pool table, postal, fax and email services. Local attractions include Lake Nakuru National Park, Lake Bogoria, Menengai Crater, Mau Forest and Kiplombe Valley. Walks on the farm are also recommended. Kembu is environmentally conscious and invests in tree planting and rain catchment.

Gogar Farm

Rongai

Gogar Farm, off Nakuru-Kericho Highway, Rongai, Kenya
Grant and Cameron Safaris, PO Box 60, Rongai 20108, Kenya

Tel	+254 20 2045944
Mobile	+254 720 441819; +254 772 441920; +254 722 327718
Fax	+254 51 343110
E-mail	info@classicafricansafaris.com
Web	www.classicafricansafaris.com

 Gogar, CH
5 mins

Gogar Farm is a 4,000-acre working farm that provides an opportunity to experience real Kenyan farm life. The farmhouse was built by the current owner's grandfather in about 1920; part of it was originally owned by Denys Finch Hatton of Out of Africa fame. The original part of the farmhouse still stands today.

There are 6 original thatched houses dating back to the 1930s, positioned around the lawn and gardens. Each house has a double or twin en-suite bedroom; some also have a living room. The main house has a large open plan sitting and dining room with a selection of books, WiFi, a children's room with TV and a long veranda overlooking the garden. There is also a 20-meter swimming pool.

Guests are welcome to have a tour of the farm, which has dairy, beef and crops. The farm combines respect for the environment with appropriate farming techniques. The NGO Friends of the Mau Watershed Area and the Vanessa Grant School for children with special needs are both based on the farm. A land rover with driver or certified safari guide is available for hire. Grant and Cameron Safaris also offer private mobile camps at exclusive destinations around Kenya, including sites in the Maasai Mara National Reserve, Meru National Park and Samburu National Reserve.

Maili Saba Camp

Menengai Crater

Maili Saba Camp, Menengai Crater, nr Nakuru, Kenya
Wilderness Getaways, PO Box 25280, Nairobi 00603, Kenya
Tel +254 20 3876636; +254 50 50845
Mobile +254 711 986513; +254 737 636693
Fax
E-mail info@wildernessgetawaysea.com
Web www.wildernessgetawaysea.com

VISA, MasterCard

JKIA, LS & CH & Intl.
3 hrs

On the edge of the stunning, dormant Menengai Crater, Maili Saba Camp is a tranquil retreat. Guests can do game drives in the nearby Lake Nakuru National Park or can simply relax and enjoy the views from the camp. There are 10 en-suite tents, made up of 8 doubles and 2 family tents. The tents have stone floors and are shaded by thatched roofs. They are adorned with attractive artefacts and kerosene-style lanterns, and have verandas overlooking the crater. There is also a cottage that can accommodate 6 pax, with stone walls and thatched roof. The cottage has 1 master en-suite double bedroom, 2 twins, bathroom, sitting room, kitchen and veranda. The main building houses the restaurant, bar and lounge with open fireplace. Meals are table d'hote; live cooking can be arranged for groups. Guests are welcome to use the internet in the manager's office. The swimming pool is surrounded by a lovely garden, furnished with sunbeds.

Activities include game drives in Lake Nakuru National Park; morning drives, evening drives or full day game drives with bush lunches are all on offer. Nature walks into Menengai Crater take about 2½ hours. Horse riding can be arranged with advance notice. Transfers to and from Nairobi can be arranged.

Subukia Bandas

Subukia

Subukia Bandas, Muringa Farm, Subukia, Kenya
Wild Routes of Kenya, PO Box 120, Subukia 20109, Kenya
Tel
Mobile +254 735 469925; +254 725 938344
Fax
E-mail infos@wild-routes-of-kenya.com
Web www.wild-routes-of-kenya.com

JKIA, LS & CH & Intl.
3.5 hrs

Dr Anne Spoerry, known locally as Mama Daktari, was Kenya's most famous flying doctor. She came to Kenya from France after World War II, learned to fly, and carried the Medicine by Air programme into remote and inhospitable parts of the country. Her autobiography, They Call Me Mama Daktari, tells of her life and achievements.

Muringa Farm was Mama Daktari's former home. It is now a centre for eco-friendly, responsible tourism. There are 6 en-suite bandas, made up of 3 doubles and 3 twins. Electricity is provided by solar power. Breakfast, lunch and dinner are served in the restaurant banda on the lake, with views of birds and otters.

Activities include paragliding over Subukia Valley. Horse riding, camel riding and mountain biking are also available. Full day treks in Hell's Gate National Park, Mt Longonot and Menengai Crater are on offer, as are multi-day treks on Mt Kenya and the Aberdare National Park.

Muringa Farm also has an eco-volunteering programme. The programmes are adapted to the skills of the participants. Examples include assisting with a local orphanage, helping people with disabilities, treating domestic and wild animals and environmental conservation. The farm is affiliated to Mara Kima Camp; stays in the Maasai Mara National Reserve can be incorporated into a visit to Muringa Farm.

Mugunda House

Subukia

Mugunda House, Subukia Farm, Solai Road, nr Nakuru, Kenya
PO Box 7001, Nakuru 20100, Kenya

Tel	+254 20 3552030
Mobile	+254 722 728911
Fax	
E-mail	teafarm2002@yahoo.com
Web	

     Madurganda Farm, CH
20 mins

Set on a plateau in the middle of a 2000-acre tea and coffee farm, Mugunda House has views across the Great Rift Valley. The house faces west, providing unforgettable views of the sun setting over the western wall of the valley. The main house is an attractive colonial building. It has 6 en-suite double bedrooms. All rooms have large oval windows with views of the garden, and are adorned with African artefacts. Breakfast, lunch and sundowners are served on the long veranda. Dinner is served in the dining room. International and local cuisine is prepared from produce from the farm. There are 3 self-catering bandas. Each banda has 2 double bedrooms and a sitting room with a fireplace. The campsite has communal bathroom facilities. Tents, bed linen, blankets and sleeping bags are available for hire.

The tropical forest around the farm is home to over 150 species of birds, including Hartlaub's turaco, Fischer's lovebird and brown parrot. Activities include tours of the farm, guided nature walks and bird watching. Cultural visits to local villages and entertainment by Turkana dancers are available. Whole day or half day hikes in nearby Menengai Crater are recommended. Game drives in Lake Nakuru National Park, and excursions to Lake Bogoria, Lake Baringo, Solai and Lake Naivasha can be arranged.

Stem Hotel

Nakuru

Stem Hotel, Nairobi-Nakuru Highway, nr Nakuru, Kenya
PO Box 1076, Nakuru 20100, Kenya

Tel	+254 51 850135; +254 51 850216
Mobile	+254 725 870066; +254 720 750475
Fax	+254 51 851273
E-mail	thestemhotel@africaonline.co.ke
Web	www.thestemhotel.com

     JKIA, LS & CH & Intl.
3 hrs

Stem Hotel is situated on the Nairobi-Nakuru Highway. It offers accommodation and conference facilities in a 20-acre garden.

There are 106 en-suite rooms, made up of 48 singles, 57 doubles and 1 triple. The Stem Oriental Restaurant specialises in Indian cuisine. The Stem Barbecue serves African dishes and local delicacies. Both restaurants are open to passers-by, as well as hotel guests. The Stem Health Club has a swimming pool, gym, sauna, massage room, steam rooms and beauty salon. The club has a trainer who can assist with activities and facilities. There are 3 conference halls. The largest seats 200 pax, another seats 150 and the smallest seats 60. Conference facilities include audio visual equipment, PA system and secretarial services. Corporate meetings, conferences and symposiums are catered for. Weddings, birthday parties and functions can be arranged in the hotel or in the garden. There is also a secure car park. Stem Hotel is involved in a number of community projects, particularly in environmental conservation projects within Nakuru town. Stem Hotel supports Friends of Lake Nakuru Environmental Conservation and Gospel Singers, a charitable group involved in environmental conservation campaigns. Lake Nakuru National Park, famous for its flamingo-filled lake and its high numbers of white rhino, is near the hotel.

Hotel Kunste

Nakuru

Hotel Kunste, Nairobi-Nakuru Highway, nr Nakuru, Kenya
PO Box 1369, Nakuru 20100, Kenya
Tel	+254 51 2212140; +254 51 2211166
Mobile	+254 725 777677
Fax	+254 51 2217433
E-mail	info@kunstehotel.com
Web	www.kunstehotel.com

JKIA, LS & CH & Intl.
3 hrs

Hotel Kunste is located on the Nairobi-Nakuru Highway, near the junction to Menengai Crater. The hotel offers accommodation and conference facilities. Lake Nakuru National Park and Menengai Crater are accessible from the hotel.

There are 105 en-suite rooms, made up of 63 singles, 10 doubles, 20 twins, 2 triples, 4 executive and 6 junior suites. There are also 2 fully furnished apartments. The restaurant has an a la carte menu, and serves a combination of international, Kenyan and Oriental dishes. It specialises in nyama choma grilled meats.

There are 4 conference halls and 2 boardrooms. The largest conference hall seats 800 pax; the boardrooms each seat 30 pax. All the halls are equipped with audio visual equipment, laptops, PA system and LCD projector. Secretarial services including photocopy and typing are provided. The hotel can arrange capacity building workshops, conferences and corporate functions. Wedding receptions and birthday parties can be catered for. Kunste Luna Park has a wide variety of activities for children, including bouncy castles, motorbike rides, horse riding, swings and slides. Nearby sites of interest include Mt Longonot, Lake Naivasha, Lake Elementaita and the Aberdare National Park.

Milele Resort
Presbyterian Guest House

Nakuru

Milele Resort Presbyterian Guest House, Milimani Estate, Nakuru, Kenya
PO Box 7364, Nakuru 20100, Kenya
Tel	+254 51 2211914
Mobile	+254 729 223364
Fax	
E-mail	info@mileleresortnakuru.co.ke
Web	www.mileleresortnakuru.co.ke

VISA, MasterCard, KCB, Equity   JKIA, LS & CH & Intl.
3 hrs

Milele Resort Presbyterian Guest House was founded by the Presbyterian Churches of East Africa in 2009. Milele, meaning forever in Swahili, was the name chosen by the church for their group of hotels. The guesthouse is affiliated to Milele Beach Hotel in Bamburi and Milele Hotel in Nairobi. There are 56 en-suite rooms, made up of singles, doubles, triples and executive suites. All rooms are equipped with satellite TV. The restaurant serves both buffet and a la carte; local Kenyan and international dishes are served. The hotel is an alcohol and smoking free zone. Soft drinks, juices and non-alcoholic wines are available.

There are 4 conference halls; the largest hall seats 400 pax and the smallest seats 10. The halls are equipped with WiFi. The attractive gardens are well maintained, and can cater for 2000 pax. They are available for workshops, seminars and functions. Wedding receptions, garden lunches, parties and other functions can all be arranged. There is also a playground with a wide selection of games for children. Local sites of interest include Lake Nakuru National Park, famous for its flamingo-filled lake and its high numbers of white rhino. Other sites of interest include Menengai Crater, Mt Longonot, Hyrax Hill and Kariandusi prehistoric sites.

Midland Hotel

Nakuru

Midland Hotel, Geoffrey Kamau Way, off Nairobi-Nakuru Highway
PO Box 908, Nakuru 20100, Kenya

Tel	+254 51 2212125
Mobile	+254 738 900380
Fax	+254 51 2217222
E-mail	reservations@midlandhotel.co.ke
Web	www.midlandhotelnakuru.com

 VISA, MasterCard   JKIA, LS & CH & Intl. 3 hrs

Midland Hotel faces the Nairobi-Nakuru Highway. Close to Nakuru, the hotel is convenient for the shops, businesses, restaurants and bars of the town. It is also within easy reach of Lake Nakuru National Park. There are 63 en-suite double rooms, made up of budget, standard and deluxe. All rooms are equipped with mahogany furnishings, telephone and satellite TV. The deluxe rooms are more spacious and have more modern furnishings. The dining room and the restaurant have an a la carte menu, and serve international and local dishes. Buffet can be provided for groups on request. The bar serves soft drinks, beers and spirits; food can also be ordered from the bar. There are 2 conference halls; 1 seats 150 pax and the other seats 100. Projector and PA system are available for hire. There is also a business centre. WiFi is available throughout the hotel. Local sites of interest include Lake Nakuru National Park, famous for its flamingo-filled lake and its high numbers of white rhino. Other sites of interest include Menengai Crater, Mt Longonot, Hyrax Hill and Kariandusi prehistoric sites.

Merica Hotel

Nakuru

Merica Hotel, Kenyatta Avenue, Nakuru, Kenya
Merica Group, PO Box 45675, Nairobi 00100, Kenya

Tel	+254 51 2214232; +254 51 2216013; +254 20 316696
Mobile	
Fax	+254 51 2217089; +254 20 315743
E-mail	mericagroup@mericaholdings.com
Web	www.mericagrouphotels.com

 VISA, MasterCard   JKIA, LS & CH & Intl. 3 hrs

In the centre of Nakuru, the Merica Hotel is within easy reach of all the facilities and institutions of this bustling urban centre.
There are 89 en-suite standard rooms, 4 junior suites and 1 executive suite, set on 10 floors. The standard rooms are equipped with satellite TV and WiFi. The junior suites have, in addition, king size beds, fridges and desks. The executive suite also has a spacious lounge with bay windows and leather seats. Some rooms are equipped for guests with disabilities. The restaurant serves an international buffet for breakfast, lunch and dinner. There is also an a la carte menu of Italian, Indian, Chinese and African dishes. Crater Bar serves soft drinks, beers and spirits, and has a TV showing sports and news.
Olympia Health Club is equipped with modern equipment, including computerised cardiovascular machines, isotonic machines and free weights. A fitness consultation is offered to all visitors; personal trainers are also available. The club offers a wide range of classes including step aerobics, dance, body toning and conditioning, circuit training, kick boxing, salsa and yoga. The hotel also has a fully equipped beauty parlor and a swimming pool with instructor and lifeguard.

KaribuKenya Accommodation Guide

Bontana Hotel

Nakuru

Bontana Hotel, Government Road, Nakuru, Kenya
PO Box 7009, Nakuru 20100, Kenya

Tel	+254 51 2210134; +254 51 2210977; +254 51 2210680
Mobile	+254 725 145460
Fax	+254 51 2210898
E-mail	info@bontanahotel-nakuru.com
Web	www.bontanahotel-nakuru.com

  JKIA, LS & CH & Intl. 3 hrs

Bontana Hotel is situated in the centre of Nakuru, near the Nakuru District Headquarters and the Nakuru High Court Building. The hotel has accommodation and conference facilities. Lake Nakuru National Park is easily accessible from the hotel.

There are 88 en-suite standard rooms. There are also 4 suites, each with double room, kitchenette and balcony. The hotel has 2 dining rooms, which serve both international and Kenyan dishes. The coffee shop, opening onto the garden, offers freshly brewed Kenyan coffee and tea, with a selection of pastries and sandwiches. Outside catering is available. The bar stocks soft drinks, beers and spirits. There is also a swimming pool and a curio shop that sells African souvenirs.

There are 7 conference halls, which can accommodate between 20 and 600 pax. Breakaway and syndicate rooms are available for small groups. The halls are equipped with overhead projector, TV and video. There is also a business centre, with 24-hour internet service. The hotel can arrange conferences, workshops and seminars. Wedding receptions, parties and corporate functions can also be arranged. As well as Lake Nakuru National Park, nearby sites of interest include Menengai Crater and Lake Elementaita. Bontana Hotel is affiliated to Soi Safari Lodge, on the shores of Lake Baringo.

Hotel Cathay

Nakuru

Hotel Cathay, Tom Mboya St, Nakuru, Kenya
PO Box 7362, Nakuru 20100, Kenya

Tel	+254 51 2215820; +254 20 2166555
Mobile	+254 732 847440
Fax	+254 51 2215384
E-mail	info@hotelcathay.co.ke
Web	www.hotelcathay.co.ke

VISA, MasterCard  JKIA, LS & CH & Intl. 3 hrs

Situated in the centre of Nakuru, Hotel Cathay is a large 6-floor building. The hotel provides a wide variety of accommodation and facilities. There are 62 en-suite rooms, made up of 3 deluxe rooms, 19 executive 1-bedroom suites and 40 executive 2-bedroom suites. All rooms have floor to ceiling windows, telephone, WiFi and flat screen TV. The suites have, in addition, fully equipped kitchen and marble bathroom with Jacuzzi. Hotel Cathay has 2 restaurants, each offering a selection of local and international dishes, including their own signature dishes.

Trump Spa has a swimming pool, sauna and fitness centre, and offers a selection of beauty treatments. The conference centre has a flexible meeting space, and is equipped for conferences, corporate meetings, board meetings, workshops and seminars. The business centre is open 24 hours, and offers high speed internet and fax services. There is also an underground disco. Receptions and cocktail parties can be arranged. Local sites of interest include Lake Nakuru National Park, famous for its flamingo-filled lake and its high numbers of white rhino. Other sites of interest include Menengai Crater, Mt Longonot, Hyrax Hill and Kariandusi prehistoric sites. Further afield, Lake Bogoria and Lake Baringo are of interest.

Chester Hotel

Nakuru

Chester Hotel, junction of Moi Road and Kariba Road, Nakuru, Kenya
PO Box 2342, Nakuru 20100, Kenya

Tel	+254 51 2215500; +254 20 2327654
Mobile	+254 727 313792
Fax	+254 51 2215440
E-mail	info@chesterhotels.co.ke
Web	www.chesterhotels.co.ke

VISA, MasterCard   JKIA, LS & CH & Intl. 3 hrs

Chester Hotel is founded on Christian values. A plaque in reception declares: The Lord has done this, and it is marvellous in our eyes; Psalms 118:23. The hotel is conveniently located between Nakuru town centre and Lake Nakuru National Park.

There are 61 en-suite rooms, made up of singles, doubles, triples and executive suites. All rooms have satellite TV, telephone and WiFi. The executive suites are more spacious, and have armchairs, carpet, kettle and fruit bowl. The stairs all have stair gates, for the protection of children. The large restaurant has floor to ceiling windows and art deco furnishings. Both buffet and a la carte are served. Dishes include chicken wings, beef skewers, fish bhajia and mixed grill. No alcohol is served.

There are 5 conference halls, all equipped with modern conference facilities including PA system and projector. The 5 conference halls seat 20 pax, 50 pax, 80 pax, 150 pax and 300 pax. The business centre is equipped with photocopy and internet facilities. African Home Adventure, a tour operator, can arrange tours and excursions from Chester Hotel. Local sites of interest include Lake Nakuru National Park, famous for its flamingo-filled lake and its wealth of white rhinos.

Abbey Resort

Nakuru

Abbey Resort, junction of Moi Road and Kariba Road, Nakuru, Kenya
PO Box 1550, Nakuru 20100, Kenya

Tel	+254 51 2213225; +254 51 8005223
Mobile	+254 727 433785; +254 721 450597
Fax	
E-mail	info@abbeyresort.co.ke
Web	www.abbeyresort.co.ke

VISA, MasterCard   JKIA, LS & CH & Intl. 3 hrs

Abbey Resort is founded on Christian values. The notice at reception reads: When times are hard, friends are few, but Jesus never fails. The resort is conveniently located between Nakuru town centre and Lake Nakuru National Park.

There are 51 en-suite rooms, made up of 40 doubles, 9 twins and 2 executive suites. All rooms have satellite TV. The ground floor rooms have wheelchair access. The restaurant serves both buffet and a la carte. Dishes include sandwiches, burgers, pasta dishes, beef stew, pan fried fish fillet and chicken curry. The hotel does not permit smoking or drinking alcohol. There is a backup generator in case of power cuts. Toiletries and soft drinks are sold at reception.

There are 2 conference halls, which each seat 100 pax. They are equipped with TV, DVD, video, PA system and projector. Wedding receptions can be catered for; decorations are designed according to the couple's wishes. Local tour operators can arrange tours and excursions from Abbey Resort. Nearby sites of interest include Lake Nakuru National Park, famous for its flamingo-filled lake and its wealth of white rhinos. Other sites of interest include Menengai Crater, Mt Longonot, Hyrax Hill and Kariandusi prehistoric sites.

Lakes

Hotel Genevieve

Nakuru

Hotel Genevieve, off Kanu Street, Nakuru, Kenya
PO Box 127, Nakuru 20100, Kenya

Tel	+254 51 2211062
Mobile	+254 722 929267; +254 714 851036
Fax	+254 51 2216745
E-mail	info@hotelgenevieve.com / bernadate2000@yahoo.com
Web	www.hotelgenevieve.com

VISA

 JKIA, LS & CH & Intl.
3 hrs

Hotel Genevieve has a timber rondavel at its entrance, adorned with local artefacts. It is conveniently located between Nakuru town centre and Lake Nakuru National Park.

There are 80 en-suite rooms, made up of singles, doubles and twins. All rooms have satellite TV and telephone. The ground floor rooms have wheelchair access. The restaurant serves both buffet and a la carte. Its international menu includes fried chicken a la king, coated fish fillet, pepper steak and a selection of curries. The bar is decorated with pot plants, and serves soft drinks, beers and a few spirits.

There are 2 conference halls. Simba Hall seats 50 pax and Taifa Hall seats 100. Both halls are equipped with PA system and projector. Local sites of interest include Lake Nakuru National Park, famous for its flamingo-filled lake and its high numbers of white rhino. Other sites of interest include Menengai Crater, Mt Longonot, Hyrax Hill and Kariandusi prehistoric sites. Further afield, Lake Bogoria and Lake Baringo are of interest. Guests wishing to do game drives should use their own vehicles. Picnic lunches can be provided on request.

Eros Hotel

Nakuru

Eros Hotel, Kanu Street, Nakuru, Kenya
PO Box 2198, Nakuru 20100, Kenya

Tel	+254 51 2213428; +254 20 2187986
Mobile	+254 723 353810
Fax	+254 51 2213916
E-mail	eros@eroshotelnakuru.com
Web	www.eroshotelnakuru.com

VISA, MasterCard

 JKIA, LS & CH & Intl.
3 hrs

Eros Hotel is adorned both inside and out in orange and white. Its slogan is: putting Nakuru on the hospitality map of Kenya. The hotel offers budget accommodation in Nakuru.

There are 42 en-suite rooms, made up of standard, deluxe and executive. All rooms have tiled floors and flowery curtains. The deluxe and executive rooms have satellite TV and telephone. The restaurant serves a predominantly Kenyan menu, with dishes such as ugali, matoke, githeri, kienyeji and managu, as well as grilled chicken, fish and pork. There are also private eating booths. The bar serves a selection of soft drinks, beers and spirits.

There are 3 conference halls. Buffalo Hall seats 140 pax, Flamingo Hall seats 100 and Executive Hall seats 60. PA system and projector are available for hire. The business centre has computers, internet, photocopy and printer. There is a secure inside car park, and a 24-hour security guard. Local sites of interest include Lake Nakuru National Park, famous for its flamingo-filled lake and its wealth of white rhinos. Other sites of interest include Menengai Crater, Mt Longonot, Hyrax Hill and Kariandusi prehistoric sites. Eros Hotel is affiliated to Lake Nakuru Flamingo Lodge.

Hotel Royal Spring

Nakuru

Hotel Royal Spring, Kanu Street, Nakuru, Kenya
PO Box 10580, Nakuru 20100, Kenya
Tel +254 51 2212146
Mobile +254 736 123890; +254 722 798378
Fax
E-mail hroyalspring@yahoo.com
Web

  JKIA, LS & CH & Intl.
3 hrs

In the heart of Nakuru, Hotel Royal Spring offers budget accommodation and conference facilities.

There are 66 en-suite rooms, made up of singles, twins and triples. All rooms have private balcony and local TV; some rooms have armchairs. The restaurant serves both buffet and a la carte. Best of African includes mukimo, matoke, kunde and managu. International dishes include beef stroganoff, spaghetti Sicilian and steak Milanese. An African breakfast is served on Wednesdays. The pub serves soft drinks, beers and spirits and is equipped with TV with local channels.

There are 3 conference halls. Simba Hall seats 150 pax, Giraffe Hall seats 40 and Buffalo Hall seats 30. The halls are equipped with projector and PA system. There is also a secure indoor car park. Local sites of interest include Lake Nakuru National Park, famous for its flamingo-filled lake and its wealth of white rhinos. Other sites of interest include Menengai Crater, Mt Longonot, Hyrax Hill and Kariandusi prehistoric sites. Tours and excursions can be booked with tour operators in Nakuru.

Jumuia Guest House, Nakuru

Nakuru

Jumuia Guest House, Kanu Street, Nakuru, Kenya
PO Box 1691, Nakuru 20100, Kenya
Tel +254 51 2213477; +254 51 2212352
Mobile +254 725 494335
Fax
E-mail nakurugh@ncck.org / jumuiaguesthouse@yahoo.com
Web www.ncck.org / www.resortjumuia.com

 VISA, MasterCard JKIA, LS & CH & Intl.
3 hrs

Jumuia Resorts aim to be the leading Christian resort chain in Kenya. Jumuia, Swahili for community or federation, refers to the National Council of Churches of Kenya, Jumuia ya makanisa ya Kenya. There are 5 Jumuia Resorts, located in Kisumu, Nakuru, Limuru, Mombasa and Nairobi. There are 59 en-suite double rooms, made up of budget, standard, executive and suite. All rooms are equipped with TV with local channels. The restaurant serves a buffet of predominantly Kenyan dishes, with a few international dishes, such as pan fried beef steak, pork chops, chicken stew, spaghetti bolognaise, stewed goat and special platters of nyama choma grilled meats. No alcohol is served. The garden adjoining the restaurant has chairs and tables shaded by umbrellas, and a children's play area. There are 5 conference halls. The largest is glass fronted with a view of the garden and seats 250 pax. The others seat 60, 40, 40 and 20 pax. The halls are equipped with LCD projector and PA system. Conference packages can be full board, or by the day. There is a secure car park. The guesthouse can arrange trips to Lake Nakuru National Park, Menengai Crater, Lake Bogoria and Kerio Valley.

Kivu Retreat Nakuru

Kivu Retreat, Main Gate, nr Lake Nakuru National Park, Kenya
PO Box 16105, Nakuru 20100, Kenya
Tel
Mobile +254 726 026894
Fax
E-mail kivuretreat@gmail.com
Web www.kivuretreat.com

Naishi, CH, 45 mins
JKIA, LS & CH & Intl., 3 hrs

Kivu Retreat is a Christian retreat just outside the main gate to Lake Nakuru National Park. Set in spacious gardens, the retreat offers both private rooms and dormitories. A wide selection of activities for all ages is available. There are 24 en-suite rooms, named after local birds such as francolin, honeybird and ibis. The rooms can be double, twin or triple as required; 1 room has wheelchair access. There are also 10 10-bed dormitories with hunk beds, named after local lakes, rivers and mountains. The campsite has a mess tent for cooking and dining, and bathroom facilities with unheated showers. The dining hall serves African and international food; guests are welcome to discuss their preferred menus with the chef. No alcohol is served, but guests are welcome to bring their own. The dining hall can be converted to a conference room for up to 600 pax, and is equipped with TV, PA system and projector. Youth groups and religious groups are welcome; teambuilding activities and children's fun activities are available. Entertainment includes traditional dancing, bouncy castle, magic shows and acrobatics. The environmentally-aware retreat plants trees and composts food waste. Kivu Retreat can assist with booking tours to local sites of interest, including Lake Nakuru National Park, Menengai Crater and Mt Longonot.

Flamingo Hill Camp Nakuru

Flamingo Hill Camp, Main Gate, nr Lake Nakuru National Park, Kenya
PO Box 50641, Nairobi 00100, Kenya
Tel +254 20 884485
Mobile +254 727 741883; +254 729 329488
Fax +254 20 884485; +254 51 2213916
E-mail flamhillres@iconnect.co.ke
Web www.flamingohillcamp.com

VISA, MasterCard, Amex

Naishi, CH, 45 mins
JKIA, LS & CH & Intl., 3 hrs

Flamingo Hill Camp is situated just outside Lake Nakuru National Park, 2km from the main gate. This friendly camp is set in landscaped gardens, surrounded by lush natural foliage.

There are 25 en-suite tents shaded by thatched roofs, which can be doubles, twins or triples as required. All the tents have 4-poster beds, writing table, mosquito net and private veranda, and are decorated with natural wood and wrought iron. Pink Restaurant seats 80 pax and serves buffet breakfast and lunch. Dinner is table d'hote; buffet dinner or private dinner can be served on request. The bar has WiFi. It is well stocked with soft drinks, beers, wines and spirits, and serves cocktails including Flamingo Hill Cocktail. The open lounge has views of the plains, comfortable sofas, a fireplace and a selection of books. The swimming pool is surrounded by a sunbathing terrace with Jacuzzi and massage room. The reception and 1 tent have wheelchair access.

The camp has conference facilities and can arrange breakfast and lunch events, board meetings and press launches. It also offers gala dinners and cocktail parties. Game drives into Lake Nakuru National Park can be organised by the camp, or self-drive. Flamingo Hill Camp recycles grey water and supports environmental restoration and conservation of endangered species.

Lake Nakuru Flamingo Lodge

Nakuru

Lake Nakuru Flamingo Lodge, Lanet Gate, nr Lake Nakuru Ntl. Park, Kenya
PO Box 2198, Nakuru 20100, Kenya

Tel	+254 20 2187951; +254 20 2187869
Mobile	+254 722 440969
Fax	+254 51 2213916
E-mail	info@lakenakuruflamingolodge.com
Web	www.lakenakuruflamingolodge.com

VISA, MasterCard, Amex

 Naishi, CH, 45 mins
JKIA, LS & CH & Intl., 3 hrs

Lake Nakuru Flamingo Lodge offers accommodation and conferencing not far from Lake Nakuru National Park. The lodge is located just outside Lanet Gate, making it convenient for game drives in the park.

There are 25 en-suite rooms, made up of 16 standard, 6 deluxe and 3 family rooms. All rooms are equipped with satellite TV. The restaurant serves buffet, with a selection of local and international dishes. Picnic lunches can be provided on request. The bar serves soft drinks, beers, wines, spirits and cocktails.

There are 2 conference halls; the larger hall seats 300 pax and the smaller seats 50. Overhead projector, TV, DVD and video are all provided. For a surcharge, LCD projector, email and computer services can also be arranged. Conference facilities include secretary and coordinator's office. Conference packages including buffet lunch and stationery are available, or conferences can be tailored to the group's requirements.

Game drives into Lake Nakuru National Park can be arranged at the lodge. The park is famous for its flamingo-filled lake and its high numbers of white rhino. Other nearby sites of interest include Menengai Crater, Mt Longonot, Hyrax Hill and Kariandusi prehistoric sites.

Lakira Camp

Lake Nakuru Ntl. Park

Lakira Camp, Lake Nakuru National Park, Kenya
PO Box 50641, Nairobi 00100, Kenya

Tel	+254 20 884485
Mobile	+254 727 741883; +254 729 329488
Fax	+254 20 884485; +254 51 2213916
E-mail	info@flamingohillcamp.com
Web	www.flamingohillcamp.com

Naishi, CH
40 mins

On a private campsite in Lake Nakuru National Park, Lakira Camp is a charming, seasonal tented camp. The camp is adorned with safari antiques and rich coloured fabrics.

There are 6 en-suite tents, all with views of the lake. The tents have 4-poster beds, mosquito nets, Persian carpets and colonial antiques. The mess tent opens onto lush lawns, and is decorated with solid wood furniture, local artefacts, comfortable cushions and traditional woven rugs. Breakfast, lunch and dinner are served in the mess tent or on the lawn outside. The bar is well stocked with soft drinks, beers and spirits. Activities include game drives in Lake Nakuru National Park. Bush meals and sundowners are also on offer. The park is famed for its flamingo tinted lake, and for the large number of rhino that roam its shores. Lookouts on cliffs on either side of the lake give superb views of the lake and the park around it.

Lakira Camp is affiliated to Flamingo Hill Camp, just outside the main park gate, which has a swimming pool, conference facilities and WiFi. Lakira Camp is seasonal, and only operates during the high seasons. The camp is completely mobile, and has no permanent structures.

Sarova Lion Hill Game Lodge
Lake Nakuru Ntl. Park

Sarova Lion Hill Game Lodge, Lake Nakuru National Park, Kenya
Sarova Hotels, PO Box 72493, Nairobi 00200, Kenya

Tel	+254 51 850288; +254 20 2767000; +254 20 2714444
Mobile	+254 728 606584; +254 722 200945/6; +254 734 699751/2
Fax	+254 51 2210836; +254 20 2715566
E-mail	centralreservations@sarovahotels.com
Web	www.sarovahotels.com

VISA, MasterCard, Amex Eurocard

Naishi, CH
40 mins

Set on a plateau overlooking Lake Nakuru, Sarova Lion Hill Game Lodge has a striking view across the flamingo-filled lake. The lodge's beautifully landscaped gardens, with natural foliage and wide variety of flowers, are surrounded by a 24hr electrical fence.

The 67 bedrooms are made up of 64 standard rooms and 3 suites: Ziwa, Chui and Faru. All the bedrooms are en-suite ground floor chalets with private patios giving panoramic views of the lake. Flamingo Restaurant, on the ground floor, serves buffet breakfast, lunch and dinner. Adjacent to the restaurant is a terrace overlooking the pool, the lodge grounds and the lake. The Rift Valley Bar also has a view of the lake. The lodge has a swimming pool, sauna, pool table and table tennis table. Massage is on offer. Archery and tree planting can be arranged, as can conferences and teambuilding activities. Traditional dancers entertain guests at 7pm every night.

Lake Nakuru National Park has an abundance of game, from the flamingos, pelicans and other birdlife on the lake to the white and black rhino, hippos and the elusive leopard on its shores. Guides and vehicles are available for hire for game drives. Nature walks around the grounds of the lodge and the vegetable garden are also on offer.

KWS, Naishi Guest House
Lake Nakuru Ntl. Park

KWS, Naishi Guest House, Lake Nakuru National Park, Kenya
Kenya Wildlife Service, PO Box 40241, Nairobi 00100, Kenya

Tel	+254 20 6000800; +254 20 6002345; +254 20 3991000
Mobile	+254 726 610508; +254 726 610509; +254 736 663421
Fax	+254 20 6003792
E-mail	kws@kws.go.ke / reservations@kws.go.ke
Web	www.kws.go.ke

Naishi, CH
5 mins

Formerly the warden's house, Naishi Guest House is ideally situated in the centre of Lake Nakuru National Park. The house is owned by the Kenya Wildlife Service, KWS. The attractive stone cottage is shaded by acacia trees, with magnificent views across game-filled plains. Highlights of the park are the flamingo-filled lake and an abundance of white rhinos. The house has 2 bedrooms, each with a double and single bed, and a bathroom with bath and shower. It also has a sitting room furnished with attractive, locally crafted wooden furniture, bright cushions, woven wall hangings and a fireplace, and a fully equipped, open plan kitchen and dining room. The sitting room opens onto a shady veranda with views across the park. Behind the house, an annex has 2 single bedrooms and a bathroom with shower. A resident caretaker provides bed linen, towels, soap, loo paper and kerosene lamps. Electricity is provided between 6pm and 10pm.

Lake Nakuru National Park has a clearly signposted network of roads. Most roads are suitable for 2WD although the roads up to the viewpoints require 4WD vehicles. The house is 18km from the main gate, at the south end of the lake. Entrance to the park is by SafariCard or by cash; cards can be loaded at the main gate.

Lake Nakuru Lodge — Lake Nakuru Ntl. Park

Lake Nakuru Lodge, Lake Nakuru National Park, Kenya
PO Box 561, Nakuru 20100, Kenya

Tel	+254 51 850518; +254 51 850228; +254 20 2687056/7
Mobile	+254 720 404480
Fax	+254 51 216250; +254 20 2677161
E-mail	nakuru@lakenakurulodge.org
Web	www.lakenakurulodge.com

VISA, MasterCard

Naishi, CH, 45 mins
JKIA, LS & CH & Intl., 3 hrs

Set in sculptured gardens overlooking a swimming pool, Lake Nakuru Lodge is situated in Lake Nakuru National Park. The park is famed for its abundance of white rhino, and for the wide variety of birdlife, notably flamingos and pelicans, found on the striking lake that lies in the centre of the park.

The lodge has 68 family rooms, cottages and suites. All are furnished with rustic African furniture, including large 4-poster beds, and are equipped with mosquito net, aircon, telephone and safe. All rooms have private verandas, some with panoramic views of Lake Nakuru and others with views of the pool or the garden.

Matarakwa Restaurant, with broad windows overlooking the park, serves international cuisine. Guests are also welcome to dine on the terrace or by the pool. Bush barbecues are available on request. Mama Niki Bar and Rhino Paddock Cocktail Bar serve soft drinks, beers and spirits. Nightly entertainment is on offer, such as traditional dancing, performances by Lake Nakuru Choir and acrobatic shows.

The conference hall seats 70 pax, and is equipped with projector and PA system. The lodge offers internet, telephone, fax and photocopy services. Game drives, bird watching and horse riding can be arranged for a surcharge.

Mbweha Camp — Congreve Conservancy

Mbweha Camp, Congreve Conservancy, nr Lake Nakuru National Park, Kenya
Atua Enkop, PO Box 42475, Nairobi 00100, Kenya

Tel	+254 20 4450035-6; +254 20 4440276; +254 50 50739
Mobile	+254 715 555322
Fax	+254 20 4450037
E-mail	reservations@atua-enkop.com
Web	www.atua-enkop.com

Congreve, CH
10 mins

Set in the private 6,400-acre Congreve Conservancy, Mbweha Camp is located just outside the southern end of Lake Nakuru National Park. The camp has 10 en-suite cottages built of lava stone, with thatched roofs. All the cottages are designed with rich African colours and textured fabrics, and have rustic but fully equipped bathrooms. Surrounded by indigenous trees such as euphorbia candelabra and yellow barked acacia, the camp retains the feeling of the wilderness.

The spacious dining area surrounds an open fire, and is full of bright cushions and clusters of tables. Dinner can be served in the dining area, on the veranda of the guests' tent or under the stars.

The camp offers day and night game drives and guided bush walks on the conservancy. Other activities available for a surcharge include game drives in Lake Nakuru National Park and Soysambu Conservancy. Visits to Lake Elementaita hot springs, hiking at Delamere's Nose hill and trips to Kariandusi prehistoric site, Menengai Crater and Hyrax Hill can all be arranged. Bicycling is recommended in this area. Mbweha Camp is committed to the environment and uses solar power as much as possible. It also provides employment to the local community.

Lake Elmenteita
Luxury Camp

 Lake Elementaita

Lake Elmenteita Luxury Camp, Lake Elementaita, Kenya
Serena Hotels, PO Box 48690, Nairobi 00100, Kenya

Tel	+254 20 2822000; +254 20 2842333; +254 20 2842000
Mobile	+254 733 282200; +254 733 282283;+254 727 282200
Fax	+254 20 2718102-3; +254 20 2725184
E-mail	cro@serena.co.ke
Web	www.serenahotels.com

VISA, MasterCard   Elementaita, CH 5 mins

Lake Elmenteita Luxury Camp was established in 2011. The camp overlooks Lake Elmenteita and offers a selection of facilities and activities. It is owned and operated by Serena Hotels.

There are 24 en-suite tents and 1 suite. All tents are equipped with telephone, WiFi, minibar, electronic safe, kettle and hairdryer. All tents also have a private veranda. The restaurant has an international menu, and serves both buffet and a la carte. The bar serves soft drinks, beers, wines and spirits. There is also a guest lounge, gift shop and an attractive sundowner site. The business centre is fully equipped. The camp has a backup generator in case of power cuts.

The camp has a swimming pool surrounded by sunbathing terrace. Massage is available. Activities include day and night game drives. Guided game walks and bird walks are also on offer; the bird hides make an interesting spot from which to watch the birdlife. A myriad of bird species have been recorded in this area, including flamingos and pelicans. Excursions to Karianduai prehistoric site can be arranged. For a surcharge, balloon safaris can be booked at a nearby site.

Sunbird Lodge

 Lake Elementaita

Sunbird Lodge, Lake Elementaita, Kenya
PO Box 13932, Nakuru 20100, Kenya

Tel	+254 20 8000075
Mobile	+254 715 555777; +254 733 555777
Fax	+254 20 2439266
E-mail	info@sunbirdkenya.com
Web	www.sunbirdkenya.com

VISA, MasterCard    Soysambu, CH, 5 mins
JKIA, LS & CH & Intl., 2.5 hrs

Named after one of the 450 species of birds found in this area, Sunbird Lodge is set on the shores of Lake Elmentaita and looks out over the vast plains of Soysambu Conservancy.

The 10 spacious en-suite cottages are built of natural local materials and have thatched roofs. Each contains a king size double and a single bed. Their large verandas have unbroken views over the lake.

The restaurant's 2 sliding glass doors maximise the view, and the 2 fireplaces create a romantic atmosphere by night. Buffet breakfast is followed by a la carte lunch and dinner, prepared by experienced chefs. The freeform swimming pool, high on the hillside, overlooks the lake and the conservancy. Massage and other beauty treatments are available. The lodge is environmentally aware, and has been given a bronze award by Ecotourism Society of Kenya for its commitment to preserving the environment. Activities available for a surcharge include balloon safaris and horse riding, as well as game drives and game walks in Soysambu Conservancy. Trips to Lake Nakuru National Park, Lake Naivasha, Hell's Gate National Park and Crescent Island can all be arranged, as can hiking on Mt Longonot, Kilima and the Maasai Trail. The nearby Karianduai and Hyrax Hill prehistoric sites are also of interest.

Elementaita Country Lodge
Lake Elementaita

Elementaita Country Lodge, Lake Elementaita, Kenya
Seasons Hotels, PO Box 3239, Nairobi 00100, Kenya

Tel	+254 20 2220572
Mobile	+254 723 858383; +254 721 258993
Fax	+254 20 2218361
E-mail	info@seasonshotelskenya.com
Web	www.elementaitacountrylodge.com

VISA, MasterCard

JKIA, LS & CH & Intl.
2.5 hrs

Set in 50 acres of lush lawns, Elementaita Country Lodge looks out on the flamingo-fringed Lake Elementaita.

The lodge has 28 en-suite rooms. All rooms have a balcony with a view of the lake. The restaurant serves a buffet of Kenyan and international dishes. There are 2 conference halls, with a combined seating capacity of 300 pax. The halls are equipped with projector and PA system. Teambuilding programmes, business meetings and seminars can be arranged. A lounge bar has music and TV. Pool tables and table tennis tables are also available. The swimming pool and surrounding sunbathing terrace are set in attractive gardens that overlook the lake. Maasai dancing can be arranged on request.

Activities include visits to Hyrax Hill, 15km from the lodge, and tours of Kariandusi prehistoric sites, 5km from the lodge. Bird watching at Lake Elementaita and Lake Nakuru, where over 422 species of birds including flamingoes and pelicans have been recorded, is also recommended. Nature walks can be arranged.

Game drives in the nearby Soysambu Conservancy, Hell's Gate National Park, Kigio Wildlife Conservancy and Lake Nakuru National Park can be arranged for a surcharge. Elementaita Country Lodge is affiliated to Seasons Hotel in Narok.

Flamingo Camp and Cottages
Lake Elementaita

Flamingo Camp and Cottages, Lake Elementaita, Kenya
PO Box 1257, Nakuru 20100, Kenya

Tel	+254 20 312483
Mobile	+254 727 914966; +254 724 775718
Fax	+254 20 312483
E-mail	fbce2001@yahoo.com
Web	

JKIA, LS & CH & Intl.
2.5 hrs

Flamingo Camp and Cottages is located on the shores of Lake Elementaita. The camp offers budget accommodation and great views.

There are 3 bandas and 5 en-suite tents. Each banda has an en-suite double room, a twin room and a veranda. The bandas can be taken on a self-catering basis. The veranda has a sink and work surface; a jiko grill, utensils, crockery, cutlery and glassware can be provided by the camp on request. Guests should bring their own charcoal, food and drinks. Each tent has an en-suite double bedroom and veranda.

The camp has a dining area and a fully equipped kitchen. Guests on the self-catering option are welcome to use the kitchen. Guests who wish to take the full board option should advise the camp of this when booking. The bar serves soft drinks, beers, wine and spirits. The camp also has a playing field.

The camp is ideally located for hiking in the nearby hills and for walks around the lake. A guide can be provided with advance notice. The area is home to plentiful birdlife, including lake and shore birds. Hot springs, on the opposite side of the lake, make an interesting day trip; the walk from camp to the springs takes about 45 minutes.

View Point Lodge

View Point Lodge, Lake Elementaita, Kenya
PO Box 142, Gilgil 20166, Kenya
Tel	+254 50 50736
Mobile	+254 727 642851; +254 735 701709
Fax	
E-mail	viewpointlodge.lake.elementaita@gmail.com
Web	www.viewpointlodge.com

 VISA, MasterCard  JKIA, LS & CH & Intl. 2.5 hrs

On the shores of Lake Elementaita, View Point Lodge offers sweeping views of the lake and the surrounding hills. On what was formerly known as Kekopey Ranch, the lodge is sandwiched between some of the oldest plate tectonic features: the Aberdare range lies to its east, the Mau range to its west and the Eburru hills to its south.

There are 6 cottages, all with views of the lake. The lodge also has a large campsite, with bathroom facilities. The restaurant serves an international menu, and can provide both buffet and a la carte. There is a conference hall, which seats 50 pax. Conferences, meetings and seminars are arranged according to the needs of each group. Weddings are also arranged as the couple wishes. The wedding venue can be located at the lake or in the lodge. Honeymoon packages are on offer.

Birdlife is prolific, with over 450 species recorded in the area. Activities include bird walks and walks in the Raparian forest, where vervet monkeys and rare species of tree are to be found. The local hot springs, believed to have medicinal properties, make a unique place to bathe. Cultural visits to local Maasai villages are on offer. Sundowners and picnics can also be arranged.

Sleeping Warrior Camp

Sleeping Warrior Camp, Soysambu Conservancy, Lake Elementaita, Kenya
PO Box 25621, Nairobi 00603, Kenya
Tel	
Mobile	+254 735 408698; +254 727 067418
Fax	
E-mail	info@mawembili.com
Web	www.sleepingwarriorcamp.com

  JKIA, LS & CH & Intl. 2.5 hrs

An extinct volcano on the shores of Lake Elementaita overlooks the Sleeping Warrior Camp. The volcano's eroded crater suggests the profile of a massive Maasai warrior resting in peace, giving the camp its name. The camp is on the private 20,000-acre Soysambu Conservancy.

There are 4 en-suite tents, 1 cottage and 1 en-suite room. Each tent is set in its own Leleshwa grove and shaded by a thatched roof; the tents are locally made and eco-friendly. Long Hill Tent and Scout Hill Tent each sleep 3 pax, Half Hill Tent and Boma Tent each sleep 2 pax. Eagle's Nest is a lava stone honeymoon cottage, located on a secluded rocky outcrop, which features a star bed. Ututu Room is located within Ututu House, a replication of a Tuscan villa. Electricity is provided by solar power. Home cooked food is served in Ututu House.

Activities include guided walks, volcano climbs, day and night game drives and lakeshore exploration. Balloon safaris can be arranged for a surcharge. Bush lunches and sundowners around the volcanoes are also available. The camp is committed to sustainable ecotourism and shares wildlife and water management responsibilities with Soysambu Conservancy, a non-profit organisation established to protect this land. The camp is sponsoring 5 local children through school.

Lake Elementaita Lodge — Lake Elementaita

Lake Elementaita Lodge, Lake Elementaita, Kenya
Jacaranda Group of Hotels, PO Box 66, Gilgil 20116, Kenya

Tel	+254 50 50836; +254 50 50648; +254 20 4448713-7
Mobile	+254 721 355157; +254 722 208486/7
Fax	+254 50 50836; +254 20 4445818
E-mail	lakeelementaitalodge@jacarandahotels.com
Web	www.jacarandahotels.com

 VISA, MasterCard   JKIA, LS & CH & Intl. 2.5 hrs

Lake Elementaita Lodge was originally built by Lord Galbraith Cole in 1916, when it was known as Kekopey Ranch. The lodge retains the features and atmosphere of an early colonial home. The expansive landscaped gardens have lovely views of Lake Elementaita.

There are 33 en-suite rooms, made up of doubles and twins. All rooms have a fireplace and a balcony with seating area and view over the gardens. Lord Cole Restaurant serves both buffet and a la carte, and has a selection of international dishes. Its terrace looks out over the lake. Lord Cole Bar serves soft drinks, beers, spirits and cocktails.

The conference room seats 50 pax, and is fully equipped. A secretariat and conference amenities are available on request. The lodge caters for cultural and religious events, weddings, sporting activities and team-building activities. Activities include nature walks; over 450 species of birds have been recorded locally. Walks to the ostrich farm can also be arranged. The lodge can assist with booking horse riding, balloon safaris and game drives in Lake Nakuru National Park. Lake Elementaita Lodge is affiliated to Jacaranda Hotel in Nairobi and Jacaranda Indian Ocean Beach Resort in Diani.

Oasis Eco Camp — Lake Elementaita

Oasis Eco Camp, Lake Elementaita, Kenya
PO Box 204, Gilgil 20116, Kenya

Tel	
Mobile	+254 733 730908; +254 729 910410
Fax	
E-mail	dchege@oasis.co.ke / bookings@oasis.co.ke
Web	www.oasis.co.ke

      JKIA, LS & CH & Intl. 2.5 hrs

Oasis Eco Camp is a secluded retreat on the shores of Lake Elementaita, with views of the spectacular Eburru Escarpment. Set in the middle of a natural acacia forest, it is home to abundant birdlife, with over 450 species recorded in the lake area.

There are 3 en-suite bandas, made of local stone and thatch, and 3 en-suite semi-permanent tents. The bandas are all built of local materials, furnished with rustic log furniture and beds and lit by solar power. The camp has a large main building with a lounge and dining area, a conference area and an upper room which can be used for meetings or private dining on request.

The camp provides a serene, peaceful environment, ideal for families or teambuilding exercises. The camp is alcohol and smoke free and guests are expected to dispose of their own rubbish. Designed with adventurous, outdoor-loving guests in mind, this camp has basketball and volleyball courts. Children must be accompanied by adults at all times.

Nearby attractions include a hot geyser, the Eburru hills and their natural caves and the Kariandusi prehistoric site. Bird watching is recommended. Walking and cycling around the lake and farm tours are also of interest.

Sleeping Warrior Lodge — Lake Elementaita

Sleeping Warrior Lodge, Soysambu Conservancy, Elementaita, Kenya
New African Territories, PO Box 76787, Nairobi 00508, Kenya

Tel	+254 20 2663397; +254 20 3598871
Mobile	+254 718 139359
Fax	
E-mail	bookings@africanterritories.co.ke
Web	www.africanterritories.co.ke

Loldia, LS & CH
1 hr

Sleeping Warrior Lodge was established in 2011. The lodge is located on Soysambu Conservancy, and offers lovely views of Lake Elementaita and across the Rift Valley. Soysambu is home to 450 species of bird, including the great white pelican, flamingo, cormorants, waders and storks. There are 7 en-suite bungalows, made up of 6 1-bedroom bungalows and 1 2-bedroom bungalow. All bungalows have private terrace with views over Soysambu Conservancy, the Sleeping Warrior Crater and Lake Elementaita. The 2-bedroom bungalow has, in addition, a sitting room. The restaurant offers an a la carte European menu and a selection of fine wines. The Hot Springs Spa has 2 pools of natural thermal water and offers massage, aromatherapy and use of local plants for wellbeing. The well stocked bar overlooks the large heated horizon swimming pool. The conference room seats 60 pax. There is also a tennis court and gift shop. Activities include day and night game drives on Soysambu Conservancy. Guided walks, bird watching, sundowners and bush meals are also available. Visits to Lake Nakuru National Park, excursions to Eburru Forest Sanctuary and cultural visits to local Maasai villages can all be arranged. The lodge is committed to sustainable tourism and supports community projects such as funding school fees, and income generating projects.

Kigio Wildlife Camp — Kigio Wildlife Conservancy

Kigio Wildlife Camp, Kigio Wildlife Conservancy, nr Naivasha, Kenya
Vintage Africa House, PO Box 1690, Nairobi 00600, Kenya

Tel	+254 20 3748369; +254 20 3522160
Mobile	
Fax	+254 20 3742465
E-mail	res@kigio.com / info@kigio.com
Web	www.kigio.com

 VISA, MasterCard

 Loldia, LS & CH, 45 mins
JKIA, LS & CH & Intl., 2 hrs

Kigio Wildlife Conservancy is a 3,500-acre conservancy of riverine and euphorbia woodlands, short grass and leleshwa shrub. Wildlife includes the endangered Rothschild giraffe, hippo and leopard; over 250 bird species have been recorded. The conservancy is dedicated to wildlife, environment and the community, and has been recognised by Tusk Trust, Born Free Trust and Lewa Wildlife Conservancy. Kigio Wildlife Camp has been built using sustainable wood, natural thatch and traditional African building methods. It uses solar power, recycles its waste and serves food sourced from local farmers. There are 11 suites and 1 2-bedroom family suite. Each suite is built on a deck and contains a bedroom, sitting area, bathroom and balcony. The dining area overlooks a striking red cliff that is home to colonies of bee-eaters; the bar is shaded by 2 fever trees. From dining decks near the river, guests can watch hippos and buffalos. The camp's naturalists are happy to assist with nature walks, day and night game drives, biking and fishing. Kigio Wildlife Conservancy is committed to being environmentally sustainable and socially conscious. Its current projects include working with local communities on a sustainable firewood project, an organic garden and a local honey scheme. The camp's shops sell products manufactured by the community such as hand-woven rugs and home grown honey.

Malewa Wildlife Lodge

Kigio Wildlife Conservancy

Malewa Wildlife Lodge, Kigio Wildlife Conservancy, nr Naivasha
Vintage Africa House, PO Box 1690, Nairobi 00600, Kenya

Tel	+254 20 3748369; +254 20 3522160
Mobile	
Fax	+254 20 3742465
E-mail	res@kigio.com / info@kigio.com
Web	www.kigio.com

 VISA, MasterCard   Loldia, LS & CH, 45 mins
JKIA, LS & CH & Intl., 2 hrs

Kigio Wildlife Conservancy is a 3,500-acre conservancy of riverine and euphorbia woodlands, short grass and leleshwa shrub. Wildlife includes the endangered Rothschild giraffe, hippo and leopard; over 250 bird species have been recorded. The conservancy is dedicated to wildlife, environment and the community, and has been recognised internationally by Tusk Trust, Born Free Trust and Lewa Wildlife Conservancy. Malewa Wildlife Lodge has been built using sustainable wood, natural thatch and traditional African building methods. It uses solar power, recycles its waste and serves food sourced from local farmers. The lodge is set in woodland on the Malewa River. It has 4 single floor cottages, 1 2-floor cottage with 2 bedrooms and 4 glass-fronted river suites, raised on stilts, with balconies overlooking the river. The mess has several sitting areas with fireplaces, a dining room and a bar. The camp's naturalists are happy to assist with nature walks, day and night game drives, biking and fishing. Kigio Wildlife Conservancy is committed to being environmentally sustainable and socially conscious. Its current projects include working with local communities on a sustainable firewood project, an organic garden and a local honey scheme. The camp's shops only sell products manufactured by the community like hand-woven rugs and home grown honey.

Malu Lodge

Malu

Malu Lodge, off Nairobi-Nakuru Highway, nr Naivasha, Kenya
PO Box 536, Naivasha 20117, Kenya

Tel	+254 50 2030181; +254 50 2021200; +254 20 883460
Mobile	+254 720 899530; +254 734 666674; +254 720 863269
Fax	+254 20 883460
E-mail	info@malu.co.ke
Web	www.malu-kenya.com

VISA   Malu, CH
10 mins

Malu Lodge is on Malu's 1,800-acre private forest reserve. The lodge offers a selection of accommodation, and a wide range of activities. The forest is the last remaining indigenous cedar forest between Mt Longonot and Nakuru, and is home to game and birdlife.
The 2 family villas each have 2 en-suite double rooms and living room. The 4 romantic cottages have 1 en-suite room and living room. The villas and cottages are situated at the main lodge area, in the centre of Malu reserve; meals are taken at the restaurant. The timber tree house, situated at Malewa River, has 2 en-suite double rooms, a children's room and a large open plan living and dining area with kitchen. The 2 Mahindu Cottages, beside Mahindu Stream, each have 1 en-suite double room. The tree house and Mahindu Cottages are self-catering. All rooms have 4-poster beds, log fires and verandas with attractive views.
The restaurant serves Italian cuisine, prepared from home grown vegetables and herbs, and free range eggs. Guided walks, guided runs, bird watching, long hikes and donkey riding are all available. The forest plunge pool, fed by hot springs, makes a lovely destination for a walk. For a surcharge, horse riding and mountain biking can be arranged.

Morendat Training and Conference Centre

Lake Naivasha
North Lake Road

Morendat Training and Conference Centre, North Lake Road, Naivasha
Kenya Pipeline Company, PO Box 73442, Nairobi 00200, Kenya

Tel	+254 20 3936285; +254 20 2606501-4
Mobile	+254 726 738968
Fax	
E-mail	bellice.rabach@kpc.co.ke / morendat@kpc.co.ke
Web	www.kpc.co.ke

JKIA, LS & CH & Intl.
2 hrs

Morendat Training and Conference Centre was constructed by Kenya Pipeline Company and is available for conferencing, workshops, seminars and recreation. The centre is located on the north side of Lake Naivasha. Morendat, meaning a place of rivers in the language of the Maasai, refers to the many seasonal streams that meander through the area. There are 21 en-suite executive rooms and 28 deluxe rooms with balconies overlooking the swimming pool. The conference centre has 8 conference halls, with seating capacities that range from 15 pax to 300 pax. Conference facilities including PA system and projector are available for hire. There is a fully equipped business centre. The restaurant serves both international and local cuisine. The Terrace Bar serves soft drinks, beers and spirits, and is equipped with satellite TV.

The swimming pool is surrounded by sunbathing terrace. There is also a sauna, steam bath, squash court and playing ground. The gym has modern equipment and an aerobic studio. The centre is set in lush grounds dotted with acacia trees. Wildlife can occasionally be seen between the centre and the lake. Kenya Pipeline Company was established by the Government of Kenya in 1978 to provide the most economical and modern way of transporting and storing petroleum products.

Great Rift Valley Lodge & Golf Resort

Lake Naivasha
North Lake Road

Great Rift Valley Lodge & Golf Resort, North Lake Road, Naivasha
Heritage Hotels, PO Box 74888, Nairobi 00200, Kenya

Tel	+254 20 4446651; +254 20 4447929; +254 20 4444582
Mobile	+254 722 205894; +254 733 411105
Fax	+254 20 4446600; +254 20 4446533; +254 20 4448806
E-mail	grvl@riftvalley-resort.co.ke / sales@heritagehotels.co.ke
Web	www.heritage-eastafrica.com

VISA, MasterCard, Equity

Great Rift Valley Lodge, CH
5 mins

Straddling the rim of the Rift Valley, at an altitude of 2,100m, the Great Rift Valley Lodge and Golf Resort looks out over this extraordinary natural fissure that cuts through 2 continents. Built around an 18-hole golf course, the lodge boasts panoramic views.

The 12 twin and 9 double rooms all have lounges with fireplaces and private balconies. The 40 Longonot villas, viewing the extinct Longonot volcano, each has a living room, dining room, kitchen and 2, 3 or 4 en-suite bedrooms.

The clubhouse serves a buffet of fresh salads from the lodge's eco-garden, African favourites, Indian cuisine and continental dishes. The 19th Hole Bar and Restaurant offers snacks and main dishes. The main bar, with open fireplace, serves soft drinks, beers, spirits and cocktails. The 4 conference rooms seat between 20 and 200 pax, and are fully equipped with audio visual equipment.

As well as the golf for which the lodge is famed, game watching on camels or horses is on offer. The lodge's naturalist offers game walks focusing on birds and plants. Guests can drive or hike to Ol Donyo Opurru, mountain of smoke, to see the steam vents, and bathe in a natural steam bath in the forest. The Adventurers' and Young Rangers' clubs offer a wide variety of children's activities.

Dafina Holiday Cottage

Lake Naivasha
North Lake Road

Dafina Holiday Cottage, Great Rift Valley Lodge and Golf Resort
PO Box 50795, Nairobi 00200, Kenya

Tel	+254 20 4441781; +254 20 4441784; +254 20 2331312
Mobile	+254 722 982999; +254 724 922025
Fax	+254 20 4448806
E-mail	info@dafinaholidaycottage.com
Web	www.dafinaholidaycottage.com

    Great Rift Valley Lodge, CH
5 mins

Dafina Holiday Cottage overlooks the golf course of the Great Rift Valley Lodge and Golf Resort. The cottage is actually an attractive pair of cottages that can be taken separately or as a single house.

Each cottage has an en-suite double room and an en-suite twin room. Each also has a kitchen, living room decorated in vibrant Swahili colours, dining room, bar area and veranda with expansive views. Each cottage is equipped with satellite TV, DVD, ipod docking station and WiFi; the landscaped gardens have garden chairs, umbrellas and barbecue area. The kitchens are equipped with utensils, cutlery, crockery and glassware. A housekeeper is on site; a chef can be arranged for a surcharge.

A person per cottage is given free golfing for the duration of their stay. Other guests can use the course at preferential members' green fee rates. The facilities of the Great Rift Valley Lodge and Golf Resort are available for the use of guests at Dafina Holiday Cottage. The clubhouse serves a buffet of fresh salads from the lodge's eco-garden, African favourites, Indian cuisine and continental dishes. The 19th Hole Bar and Restaurant offers snacks and main dishes. The main bar, with open fireplace, serves soft drinks, beers, spirits and cocktails.

Loldia House

Lake Naivasha
North Lake Road

Loldia House, North Lake Road, nr Green Park, Naivasha, Kenya
Musiara Limited, PO Box 48717, Nairobi 00100, Kenya

Tel	+254 20 2734000; +254 20 2734005
Mobile	+254 722 717529 +254 722 715306 +254 733 616204/5
Fax	+254 20 2734023; +254 20 2734024
E-mail	reservations@governorscamp.com
Web	www.governorscamp.com

VISA, MasterCard, Eurocard
Amex

 Loldia, LS & CH
15 mins

Established by a settler who came to Kenya in an ox-wagon after the Boer War, Loldia Farm has been passed through the generations of the same family to today's owners. Loldia House was built by Italian prisoners of war during World War II with stones quarried on the property. Set around a courtyard, the house's main archway frames a stunning view of the dormant volcano Mt Longonot. Peter Njoroge, Loldia's house manager, was declared by Country Life Magazine, to be probably the world's most accomplished butler.

The house has 4 double rooms. There is also a cottage with 3 double rooms and another cottage with 2 double rooms. All but 1 of the rooms are en-suite. The bedrooms, the sitting room and the dining room are furnished in English colonial style.

The 6,500-acre farm offers plentiful opportunities for walking among herds of cattle and a flock of farmed ostriches, as well as impala, waterbuck and other plains game. Day and night game drives on the farm are also available. Visits to nearby flower farms and boat trips on Lake Naivasha for fishing and bird watching can be arranged. Game drives with picnics can be arranged to Lake Nakuru National Park, Hell's Gate National Park, Lake Bogoria and Lake Elementaita.

Bilashaka Lodge

Lake Naivasha
North Lake Road

Bilashaka Lodge, North Lake Road, nr Green Park, Naivasha, Kenya
PO Box 2040, Naivasha 20117, Kenya

Tel	
Mobile	+254 722 715495
Fax	
E-mail	info@bilashakalodge.com
Web	www.bilashakalodge.com

    JKIA, LS & CH & Intl.
3 hrs

Bilashaka Lodge is located in the grounds of Bilashaka Flowers. The rose farm, owned by a Dutch family, exports roses around the world. The area is known for prolific birdlife; 400 species have been recorded in the vicinity. The lodge is ideal for groups of 10 pax. There are 5 en-suite double rooms, each decorated in its own style, and each with a private veranda overlooking the grasslands and acacia trees. There is also a living room, dining room and fully equipped kitchen. The lodge can be taken on self-catering basis or a chef can be provided. Meals are served in the dining room or on the veranda. The living room has an open fireplace, and a selection of books. The bar serves soft drinks, beers, wines and spirits.

The lodge also has a swimming pool.
Tours of the rose farm are available, giving visitors an introduction to how roses are grown, exported and shipped. Bird walks are on offer. Other wildlife includes Thomson gazelle, impala, zebra, vervet monkeys and baboons. Hippo and buffalo graze on the lawns at night. A small hill nearby, with views of Mt Longonot and Lake Naivasha, makes an excellent spot for a sundowner. Other local sites of interest include Crater Lake, Hell's Gate National Park and Elsamere.

Olerai House

Lake Naivasha
North Lake Road

Olerai House, North Lake Road, nr Green Park, Naivasha, Kenya
PO Box 54667, Nairobi 00200, Kenya

Tel	+254 20 8048602; +254 20 8891112; +254 20 8890596
Mobile	+254 713 037886; +254 716 623921
Fax	+254 20 8890596
E-mail	oleraihouse@africaonline.co.ke
Web	www.olerai.com

    Loldia, LS & CH
25 mins

A flower-covered farmhouse shaded by yellow acacia trees, Olerai House is located in a private game sanctuary on the shores of Lake Naivasha. The house overlooks a waterhole frequented by zebra, giraffe and antelope. There are 5 en-suite double rooms. All rooms are furnished with natural materials and decorated with local art and colourful fabrics. Meals are home cooked and use organic vegetables grown in the estate's gardens, as well as farm lamb, lake fish, tropical fruits, home baked bread and specially made cheese and ice cream. There is a library, and a collection of wildlife videos. The garden is sprinkled with secluded spots such as a huge daybed under the flame tree and some cushioned logs. Nearby

Sirocco House has a swimming pool open to guests at Olerai House. Activities include a romantic cruise in an African gondola and bird walks in the game sanctuary. Mountain biking and hiking in the surrounding hills are also on offer. For a surcharge, excursions by car or light aircraft to Lake Nakuru National Park, the Maasai Mara National Reserve and the Chyulu Hills can be arranged. Olerai House is owned by Oria and Iain Douglas Hamilton and is affiliated to Elephant Watch Camp in Samburu National Reserve.

Lakeside Tourist Lodge

Naivasha

Lakeside Tourist Lodge, Moi Avenue, Naivasha, Kenya
PO Box 894, Naivasha 20117, Kenya

Tel	+254 50 2020856
Mobile	+254 724 334195; +254 722 524565
Fax	
E-mail	info@lakesidetouristlodge.com
Web	www.lakesidetouristlodge.com

     JKIA, LS & CH & Intl.
2 hrs

Lakeside Tourist Lodge is located in Naivasha town. It is entered through a front terrace shaded by tall trees. The reception, restaurant and bar are located on the ground floor.

There are 42 en-suite rooms, made up of twins and doubles. All rooms have mosquito net, telephone and satellite TV. The restaurant has an international a la carte menu. Buffet can be arranged for large groups and conferences. Dishes include oxtail soup, whole Lake Naivasha black bass, Lakeside mixed grill, keema curry, chicken a la king, vegetable curry and French salad. The bar serves soft drinks, beers, wines and spirits. A safe is available at reception. The hotel has a secure car park.

There are 3 conference halls. The largest hall seats 100 pax; the other 2 halls seat 40 and 20 pax. Conference equipment including LCD projector and PA system are available. The lodge can book boat trips on Lake Naivasha and trips to Crescent Island and Hell's Gate National Park. Nearby sites of interest include Lake Nakuru National Park, Menengai Crater, Mt Longonot, Hyrax Hill and Kariandusi prehistoric sites.

Aqua Lodge

Naivasha

Aqua Lodge, Moi Avenue, Naivasha, Kenya
PO Box 195, Naivasha 20117, Kenya

Tel	
Mobile	+254 722 765093
Fax	
E-mail	
Web	

     JKIA, LS & CH & Intl.
2 hrs

Aqua Lodge was established in 2008. The hotel is located on the main road in Naivasha town. Its bright yellow and terracotta façade makes a landmark in Naivasha.

There are 11 en-suite rooms, made up of 9 singles and 2 doubles. The single rooms contain 1 queen size bed and the double rooms contain 2 queen size beds. All rooms are equipped with mosquito net, cupboard and satellite TV. The hotel is fully tiled, and has yellow walls with terracotta adornments. The restaurant has an international a la carte menu. Dishes include fish fillet steak, chicken Masala, potato stew, Aqua lamb chops and spaghetti Napolitana. There is also a snack menu with sandwiches and burgers. The bar serves soft drinks, beers and spirits, and is equipped with flat screen satellite TV. The hotel has a secure car park.

Boat trips on Lake Naivasha can be arranged with local operators. Local sites of interest include Lake Naivasha, Crescent Island and Hell's Gate National Park. Also within reach, Lake Nakuru National Park, Menengai Crater, Mt Longonot, Hyrax Hill and Kariandusi prehistoric sites make interesting day trips.

Kenvash Hotel

Naivasha

Kenvash Hotel, Biashara Posta Lane, Naivasha, Kenya
PO Box 211, Naivasha 20117, Kenya

Tel	+254 50 2030049
Mobile	+254 720 902284; +254 710 662612
Fax	+254 50 2030084
E-mail	hotel.kenvash@gmail.com
Web	www.kenvashhotel.com / www.sawelalodges.com

 JKIA, LS & CH & Intl.
2 hrs

An imposing white building with elegant balustrades, Kenvash Hotel is located in Naivasha town. The hotel was established in 1988 and renovated in 2009.

There are 70 en-suite rooms, made up of singles, doubles, twins and family rooms. All rooms are carpeted, and are equipped with telephone and mosquito net; 30 rooms have satellite TV. The restaurant has an international a la carte menu. Buffets can be prepared for large groups and conferences. Dishes include minestrone soup, Nile perch in lemon sauce, pan fried lake tilapia, spaghetti bolognaise, curries, stews, steaks and sandwiches. The bar serves soft drinks, beers and spirits and is equipped with satellite TV. There is a residents' lounge, a terrace with a view of the lake and a secure car park.

There are 3 conference halls. The largest hall seats 100 pax. The remaining 2 halls seat 50 and 20 pax. The halls are equipped with LCD projector. PA system can be hired with advance notice. The hotel can book boat trips on Lake Naivasha, and excursions to Crescent Island and Hell's Gate National Park. It can also arrange safaris, trips and excursions to destinations in Kenya. The hotel is affiliated to Sawela Lodge on Lake Naivasha.

La Belle Inn

Naivasha

La Belle Inn, Moi Avenue, Naivasha, Kenya
PO Box 532, Naivasha 20117, Kenya

Tel	+254 20 3510404
Mobile	+254 724 991830; +254 722 683218
Fax	
E-mail	labelleinn@kenyaweb.com
Web	

 VISA, MasterCard

 JKIA, LS & CH & Intl.
2 hrs

La Belle Inn was established in 1932. The hotel, an attractive colonial building in the centre of Naivasha town, is set around a central garden. It is adorned with photos of Naivasha and the hotel dating back to the 1930s. The hotel was refurbished in 2009.

There are 13 en-suite rooms, made up of 3 triples and 10 doubles. All rooms are equipped with mosquito net, fridge and satellite TV. The restaurant has an international a la carte menu. Dishes include Lake Naivasha crayfish, T-bone steak, chicken tikka kebab, dum aloo, pork spare ribs and nyama choma platter of grilled meats. The front terrace makes a pleasant place to sit, and serves food and drinks. The inside bar has music, satellite TV and pool table. The conference hall seats 50 pax, and is equipped with projector, PA system and laptop.

La Belle Inn can book safaris, excursions and trips to destinations in East Africa. A 4WD vehicle is available for trips to local sites of interest such as Hell's Gate National Park, Menengai Crater and Lake Nakuru National Park. The hotel is affiliated to Karen La Belle, a restaurant in Nairobi. It also provides catering for AMREF at Wilson Airport, the Naivasha Yacht Club and Sherkaruturi Flower Farm in Naivasha.

Lake Naivasha Panorama Park   Naivasha

Lake Naivasha Panorama Park, Mai Mahiu-Naivasha Road, Naivasha, Kenya
PO Box 435, Naivasha 20117, Kenya

Tel	+254 50 2030128
Mobile	+254 712 091777
Fax	+254 50 2030129
E-mail	lakenaivashapanoramapark@yahoo.com
Web	www.lakenaivashapanoramapark.com

VISA, MasterCard   JKIA, LS & CH & Intl. 2 hrs

Situated on a cliff that overlooks Lake Naivasha, Lake Naivasha Panorama Park offers spectacular views of Lake Naivasha, Mt Longonot and Eburru Mountain. The resort opened in 2007. It is Christian and offers accommodation, conferencing and functions.

There are 40 en-suite rooms in 20 cottages, made up of 16 singles, 7 twins, 8 doubles, 4 triples, 2 family suites and 1 tented room. The cottages are African style with modern facilities. All rooms have treated mosquito nets, writing table, satellite TV and views of the lake; some rooms are interconnecting, suitable for families. Each family suite has 2 twin rooms. There is also a private house with 4 twin rooms and fully equipped kitchen; a cook can be provided for an extra charge. The campsite has bathroom facilities and lighting. Tents, mattresses and bed linen are available for hire. The 2 conference halls hold 80 pax and 50 pax. The halls are equipped with LCD projector, TV and video. The restaurant has 2 dining areas and 2 decks with panoramic views, and is equipped with satellite TV. The menu includes Indian, continental and Oriental dishes. No alcohol is served. Outside catering for birthday parties, weddings and functions is available. Local sites of interest include Hell's Gate National Park and Crescent Island.

Yellow Green Hotel   Lake Naivasha
South Lake Road

Yellow Green Hotel, Moi South Lake Road, Naivasha, Kenya
PO Box 561, Naivasha 20117, Kenya

Tel	
Mobile	+254 724 393775; +254 734 393775
Fax	
E-mail	yellowgreen@yahoo.com
Web	

 JKIA, LS & CH & Intl. 2 hrs

Bright yellow and green wagon wheels mark the gate of the Yellow Green Hotel. The hotel is set in tropical gardens, and offers budget accommodation, dining and entertainment.

There are 18 en-suite rooms, made up of 8 singles and 10 doubles. The restaurant has an international a la carte menu. The Choma Zone, in the garden, serves nyama choma grilled meats. Take away food such as burgers and sandwiches is also available. The bar serves soft drinks, beers and spirits. There is also a private dining room and a collection of seating booths in the garden. A safe for guests' valuables is available at reception. The garden has a play area for children, with slide, swings and climbing frame.

The conference hall seats 100 pax. Conference equipment such as projector and PA system can be hired with advance notice. Evening entertainment such as disco, show and traditional dancers can be arranged for groups. The hotel can assist with booking boat trips and excursions. Local sites of interest include Lake Naivasha, Crescent Island and Hell's Gate National Park. Also of interest are Lake Nakuru National Park, Menengai Crater, Mt Longonot, Hyrax Hill and Kariandusi prehistoric sites.

Fischer's Tower

Lake Naivasha South Lake Road

Fischer's Tower, Moi South Lake Road, Naivasha, Kenya
PO Box 436, Naivasha 20117, Kenya
Tel +254 20 2327430
Mobile
Fax
E-mail
Web

    JKIA, LS & CH & Intl. 2 hrs

At Fischer's Tower, gardens bright with bougainvillea are dotted with rustic sculptures of African animals. The hotel offers budget accommodation and vibrant night life.

There are 29 en-suite rooms, made up of 8 singles and 21 doubles. The singles have 1 queen size bed and the doubles have 2 queen size beds. Some rooms have a shower while others have a bathtub. The restaurant serves an international a la carte menu. Dishes include asparagus soup, crayfish Lousiana with ugali, whole deep fried tilapia, steaks and sandwiches. There is also a Nyama Choma grill. Seating booths are available in the garden. The bar serves soft drinks, beers and spirits. There is a safe for guests' valuables at reception.

The disco is a large circular building with a dance floor at its centre. Murals of dancing figures adorn the walls. A DJ plays every weekend and live bands entertain regularly. The conference hall seats 100 pax; a projector can be hired if required. A tent in the garden is available for parties and functions. There is also a children's play area, with swings, seesaw, slide and merry-go-round.

Lake Naivasha Resort

Lake Naivasha South Lake Road

Lake Naivasha Resort, Moi South Lake Road, Naivasha, Kenya
PO Box 1184, Nairobi 00606, Kenya
Tel +254 20 2728755; +254 20 2116379; +254 50 2030298
Mobile +254 721 700775
Fax +254 20 2723517; +254 50 2020611
E-mail info@lakenaivasharesort.co.ke
Web www.lakenaivasharesort.co.ke

 VISA, MasterCard    JKIA, LS & CH & Intl. 2 hrs

Originally an English colonial farmhouse, Lake Naivasha Resort is situated on the shores of Lake Naivasha. Significant moments in the house's history include the visit of King Edward VII in 1906 and the visit of King George V in 1935.

There are 13 en-suite rooms, some with shower and others with a bathtub. There is 1 luxury tent. The restaurant serves either buffet or table d'hote as required. There is also a campsite with bathroom facilities and a kitchen. The bar serves soft drinks, beers and spirits. The resort also has a swimming pool and a games room. The cottages at Burch's Camp can be booked at Lake Naivasha Resort.

An assortment of activities is available. Boat cruises on the lake and island cruises to Crescent Island can be arranged for a surcharge. The resort can assist with organising game drives and game walks in Hell's Gate National Park. Nature walks on the shores of Lake Naivasha provide excellent bird watching as well as sights of larger game. Local sites of interest include Menengai Crater, Mt Longonot, Hyrax Hill and Kariandusi prehistoric sites. Further afield, Lake Bogoria and Lake Baringo are of interest.

Burch's Camp

Lake Naivasha
South Lake Road

Burch's Camp, Moi South Lake Road, Naivasha, Kenya
Lake Naivasha Resort, PO Box 1184, Nairobi 00606, Kenya

Tel	+254 20 2728775; +254 20 2116379; +254 50 2030298
Mobile	+254 726 860382; +254 721 700775
Fax	+254 20 2723517; +254 50 2020611
E-mail	info@lakenaivasharesort.co.ke
Web	www.lakenaivasharesort.co.ke

 VISA, MasterCard    JKIA, LS & CH & Intl.
                                               2 hrs

Burch's Camp offers self-catering cottages in an attractive garden. The camp is managed by nearby Lake Naivasha Resort and can be booked through the resort.

There are 2 thatched bandas, with 2 cottages in each. Each cottage is entered through a simple open air kitchen and dining room. Each has an en-suite double bedroom on the ground floor, and a twin bedroom, living room and balcony on the 1st floor. The kitchens are not equipped and visitors should bring all their own utensils, crockery, cutlery and glassware. Gas cookers can be rented from Lake Naivasha Resort if required. Visitors are also welcome to use the restaurant and bar at Lake Naivasha Resort.

Boat cruises on the lake and island cruises to Crescent Island are available for a surcharge. The resort can assist with organising game drives and game walks in Hell's Gate National Park. Nature walks on the shores of Lake Naivasha provide excellent bird watching as well as sights of larger game. Local sites of interest include Menengai Crater, Mt Longonot, Hyrax Hill and Karianduси prehistoric sites. Visitors to Burch's Camp should drive through Kimwa Farm; a sign saying cottages marks the entry to Burch's Camp.

Marina Lodge

Lake Naivasha
South Lake Road

Marina Lodge, Moi South Lake Road, Naivasha, Kenya
PO Box 174, Naivasha 20117, Kenya

Tel	
Mobile	+254 722 728054
Fax	
E-mail	
Web	

 JKIA, LS & CH & Intl.
2 hrs

Set in lakefront gardens, Marina Lodge offers budget accommodation and boat trips. The lodge was refurbished in 2011, and now provides safari style tents and a campsite.

There are 16 en-suite tents, made up of doubles and twins. The campsite has communal bathroom facilities and a communal kitchen. There are also some outdoor barbecues for the use of campers. The restaurant has an international a la carte menu, and can provide buffet for large groups. Dishes include curries, stews, burgers and sandwiches. The bar serves soft drinks and beers, and is equipped with a pool table. The garden has tables and chairs with shade umbrellas. The gift shop is stocked with local curios and artefacts. There is also a secure car park.

Boat trips on the lake include a 1-hour lake cruise and a trip to Crescent Island. Nearby sites of interest include Hell's Gate National Park and Crater Lake. Lake Nakuru National Park, Menengai Crater, Mt Longonot, Hyrax Hill and Karianduси prehistoric sites all make interesting day trips from Naivasha.

 Accommodation Guide

Enashipai Resort and Spa

Lake Naivasha
South Lake Road

Enashipai Resort and Spa, Moi South Lake Road, Naivasha, Kenya
PO Box 75332, Nairobi 00200, Kenya

Tel	+254 20 3592627
Mobile	+254 713 254035; +254 728 627034
Fax	
E-mail	info@enashipai.com
Web	www.enashipai.com

VISA, MasterCard

JKIA, LS & CH & Intl.
2 hrs

Enashipai is a Maasai term meaning a state of happiness. This stylish new resort has created chic modern structures from traditional Maasai designs. Enashipai Resort and Spa opened as Lake Naivasha Holiday Inn in 2008, and was comprehensively redesigned and refurbished in 2011. There are 50 en-suite rooms, made up of 9 standard and 41 executive. The standard rooms are in the original building, and the executive rooms are grouped 4 to a modern cottage. All rooms are equipped with telephone, minibar, internet, sofa and flat screen satellite TV. The décor uses earth colours and lavish fabrics. The bathrooms have bath and shower inside, and adjoining outdoor shower. The restaurant has an international a la carte menu. The main bar and lakeside bar are well stocked, and include a wine list and cocktail list. The spa has a range of beauty treatments, including Rasul and Body of Rocks signature treatments. It contains 6 private treatment rooms, steam rooms and spa lounge. Palm Conference Centre has secretariat facilities and fully equipped business centre. The large freeform swimming pool is heated. The fitness centre has modern strength building and cardio equipment. There is also a tennis court, basketball court and volleyball court. The Kids' Club has daily entertainment and activities. Mountain climbing, hiking, rock climbing, biking and bird watching can all be arranged.

Lake Naivasha Country Club

Lake Naivasha
South Lake Road

Lake Naivasha Country Club, Moi South Lake Road, Naivasha, Kenya
Sun Africa Hotels, PO Box 102124, Nairobi 00101, Kenya

Tel	+254 20 4450636; +254 20 4450639; +254 20 4450712
Mobile	+254 737 107266; +254 711 107266
Fax	+254 20 4450735
E-mail	info@sunafricahotels.com
Web	www.sunafricahotels.com

VISA, MasterCard

JKIA, LS & CH & Intl.
2 hrs

Lake Naivasha Country Club became famous in the 1930s, when it was a staging post for the Imperial Airways' flying boat service from Durban to London. The club is situated on the shores of Lake Naivasha, in 12 hectares of lawns.

There are 39 standard rooms, 3 family rooms, 7 executive cottages and 1 presidential cottage. All rooms are en-suite and overlook either the garden or the lake. They are all equipped with cupboard, dressing table, mosquito net and fan. The residents' lounge is furnished with comfortable sofas, and serves a selection of drinks including cocktails. There is also a bar beside the swimming pool. Dinners are served in the dining room or on the lawns. The club has a volleyball court, football pitch, cricket ground and snooker room. The spa offers massage, manicure and pedicure. The conference hall seats 50 pax. Activities include boat trips on Lake Naivasha for fishing or simply relaxing. Local sites of interest include Crescent Island, Crater Lake, Mt Longonot and Hell's Gate National Park. Lake Naivasha Country Club is managed by Sun Africa Hotels, and is affiliated to Lake Baringo Club on the shores of Lake Baringo and Keekorok Lodge in the Maasai Mara National Reserve.

Sawela Lodge

**Lake Naivasha
South Lake Road**

Sawela Lodge, Moi South Lake Road, Naivasha, Kenya
Sawela Lodges, PO Box 330, Nairobi 00200, Kenya

Tel	+254 20 2214960; +254 20 2627536
Mobile	+254 723 657295
Fax	+254 20 2214961
E-mail	reservations@sawelalodges.com
Web	www.sawelalodges.com

 VISA, MasterCard   Loldia, LS & CH, 40 mins
JKIA, LS & CH & Intl., 2 hrs

Set in lush, gardens on Lake Naivasha, Sawela Lodge is made up of a collection of attractive cottages. The design concept of the lodge is the head of a bull. The central restaurant forms the bull's head, while the cottages, extending outwards through the gardens, form its horns. Sawela Lodge opened in 2009.

There are 26 en-suite rooms and 1 suite. All rooms have flat screen satellite TV, telephone, hairdryer, writing desk and balcony overlooking the garden. The suite has 2 double en-suite rooms, living room, kitchenette and 3 balconies. The restaurant, bar and conference centre have floor to ceiling windows with views of the manicured garden. The restaurant serves buffet and a la carte, with dishes such as grilled sirloin steak and braised chicken in coriander. The terrace hosts dancing and acrobatic shows. All public areas and some rooms are wheelchair accessible.

The conference hall seats 50 pax and is fully equipped, including PA system and projector. The business centre offers internet, printing and photocopying. The swimming pool is set in extensive lawns. Activities include nature walks and boat trips. Weddings, functions and teambuilding can be arranged. The lodge minimises its environmental impact: only 1 tree was felled during its construction.

Lake Naivasha Sopa Resort

**Lake Naivasha
South Lake Road**

Lake Naivasha Sopa Resort, Moi South Lake Road, Naivasha, Kenya
Sopa Lodges, PO Box 72630, Nairobi 00200, Kenya

Tel	+254 20 3750235; +254 20 3616000
Mobile	+254 733 610060; +254 722 206328/9
Fax	+254 20 3751507
E-mail	info@sopalodges.com
Web	www.sopalodges.com

VISA, MasterCard   JKIA, LS & CH & Intl.
2 hrs

Lake Naivasha Sopa Resort is situated on 120 acres of lakefront gardens. The lodge is approached by a stone path along the side of a pond surrounded by plants. The resort is decorated with wrought iron chandeliers and African artefacts.

There are 84 en-suite rooms. The rooms are located in 21 cottages, built in a crescent shape; each cottage contains 4 rooms, 2 on the ground floor and 2 on the 1st floor. All rooms have dressing table, cupboard, luggage rack, minibar and veranda. They are adorned with local art. 2 rooms are suitable for guests with disabilities; 6 rooms are interconnecting, suitable for families; 48 rooms have TV and safe.

The restaurant serves buffet breakfast, lunch and dinner. It opens onto a terrace which overlooks the garden. The main bar is in the lobby; another bar is in the restaurant. There is also a pool bar which serves a light a la carte menu, and a poolside pizzeria. Longonot Conference Hall seats 120 pax, and is adjoined to 2 secretariat rooms. Suswa Conference Hall seats 20 pax. Both halls are equipped with overhead projector, LCD projector, PA system, TV and video. There is also an area designated for teambuilding exercises. Weddings can be arranged.

Lake Naivasha Sopa Resort holds a bronze award from Ecotourism Society of Kenya.

Longonot Ranch House
Lake Naivasha
South Lake Road

Longonot Ranch House, Kedong Ranch, Naivasha, Kenya
PO Box 1449, Naivasha 20117, Kenya

Tel	
Mobile	+254 722 200516; +254 700 203039
Fax	
E-mail	longonotranchhouse@gmail.com
Web	www.longonot-ranch-house.com

  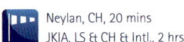
Neylan, CH, 20 mins
JKIA, LS & CH & Intl., 2 hrs

Longonot Ranch House was built by Martha Gellhorn, wife of the legendary author Ernest Hemingway. It was used by Hemingway during his East African hunting safaris immortalised in Green Hills of Africa. The colonial style house is situated on the 82,000-acre Kedong Ranch, near Lake Naivasha. It is a hosted homestay retreat, suitable for families or groups of friends.

The ranch house has 3 en-suite double rooms and the Hemingway Suite, with 2 interconnecting double rooms, suitable for a family. The cottage has 2 en-suite double rooms and an open plan dining and sitting room. The manyatta, a traditional round building, contains an en-suite double room. Breakfast, lunch and dinner are served in the ranch house, and sundowners are provided on the veranda.

Activities, for a surcharge, include horse riding and boat trips on the lake. Game drives and game walks on the ranch are also available. The area is home to prolific birdlife, as well as game including eland, giraffe, buffalo, zebra, impala, warthog, bat eared fox and spring hare. Occasionally cheetah, leopard and aardvark have been seen. Safaris and excursions to Lake Naivasha, Hell's Gate National Park, Mt Longonot, Lake Nakuru National Park and other destinations in Kenya can be arranged.

Simba Lodge
Lake Naivasha
South Lake Road

Simba Lodge, Moi South Lake Road, Naivasha, Kenya
Simba Lodges, PO Box 66601, Nairobi 00800, Kenya

Tel	+254 50 50305-7; +254 20 2105453/4; +254 20 2012443
Mobile	+254 722 207221; +254 722 603303; +254 734 600415
Fax	+254 50 50308; +254 20 4343963; +254 20 4444403
E-mail	naivasha@simbalodges.com / sales@simbalodges.com
Web	www.simbalodges.com

 VISA, MasterCard, Amex    Loldia, LS & CH, 40 mins
JKIA, LS & CH & Intl., 2 hrs

On the shores of Lake Naivasha, Simba Lodge offers a wide selection of facilities. The lodge is set in gardens with attractive water features, home to giraffe, zebra and waterbuck. The extensive conference centre hosted the Sudanese peace talks in 2003 and a plaque honours the memory of Dr John Garang.

There are 81 en-suite rooms, made up of singles, doubles, twins and triples. All rooms have satellite TV in a comfortable TV corner, telephone and balcony. A few rooms are equipped for guests with disabilities, and have wheelchair access. Gardenia Restaurant has an active cooking station and a central buffet. Kiboko Lounge Bar is fully stocked, and has an open fireplace and comfortable sofas. The gift shop stocks books, jewellery and African artefacts.

The stylish conference centre has 4 halls; 1 seats 150 pax, 1 seats 100 pax, 1 seats 25 pax and 1 seats 20 pax. All are fully equipped with flexible chairs, PA system and projector. The business centre has WiFi, and offers printing, photocopying and scanning. The Health Club has massage, steam room, sauna and fully equipped gym. There is also a tennis court, swimming pool and children's playground. Activities include nature walks and boat rides to Crater Lake and Crescent Island. The guided game walk through the grounds to the lakeshore is recommended.

YMCA Naivasha Camp

**Lake Naivasha
South Lake Road**

YMCA Naivasha Camp, Moi South Lake Road, Naivasha, Kenya
PO Box 1006, Naivasha 20117, Kenya

Tel	+254 50 50109
Mobile	
Fax	
E-mail	lakenaivashaymcacamp@yahoo.com
Web	www.kenyaymca.com

    JKIA, LS & CH & Intl.
2.5 hrs

Down a short track from Moi South Lake Road, YMCA Naivasha Camp offers bandas, dorms and camping in a large wild garden.

The bandas are circular, whitewashed buildings with thatched roofs. Each banda is named in Swahili after an animal, such as simba, kiboko and ndovu, and pictures of the animal adorn the door. There are 4 en-suite double bandas, and 2 en-suite family bandas with a partition between the double and twins beds. There are also 5 bandas with external communal bathrooms, made up of 4 doubles and 1 triple. There are 2 dorms with external communal bathrooms; 1 dorm sleeps 17 pax and the other sleeps 30.

The campsite has a bathroom block with rows of WCs and showers, a communal kitchen and a TV room with dining table. Kitchen equipment, crockery, cutlery and glassware is available for hire. The camp can prepare meals with advance notice. Campers can hire jiko barbecues if required. Small seating booths in the garden house tables and chairs. A hall is available for meetings or conferences; guests should bring equipment if required. A tree planting project offers visitors the chance to have their name on a signboard beside their tree.

Crayfish Camp

**Lake Naivasha
South Lake Road**

Crayfish Camp, Moi South Lake Road, Naivasha, Kenya
PO Box 176, Naivasha 20117, Kenya

Tel	+254 51 8002058; +254 20 4444707
Mobile	+254 720 226829; +254 717 223221; +254 720 226829
Fax	+254 50 2021361; +254 20 201733
E-mail	info@crayfishcamp.co.ke / crayfishcamp@yahoo.com
Web	www.crayfishcamp.co.ke

 VISA   Loldia, LS & CH, 30 mins
JKIA, LS & CH & Intl., 2.5 hrs

Lights on imposing statues of Maasai warriors lead visitors to Crayfish Camp. The camp is a short walk from the shores of Lake Naivasha.

There are 51 en-suite rooms, made up of singles, doubles and triples. There are also caravans, with external bathrooms, named after explorers like Livingston. There is a campsite with bathroom facilities; tents, mattresses and bedding are available for hire.

A spacious lawn dotted with tables and chairs lies between Laughter Pub and the restaurant. Buffets and a la carte are both available, including dishes like vegetable goulash, grilled Nile perch and beef stroganoff. A barbecue hut serves barbecues on request. The Lake Bar, on stilts overlooking the lake, makes an ideal place from which to bird watch. Greenhouze is a weekend disco. Suluhisha conference hall seats 30 pax, while Kirinyaga conference hall seats 75. Conference equipment including projector and PA system is available.

Mountain bike riding, horse riding and boat trips can be arranged. There is also a children's playground and GP Kart. Other facilities include a circular swimming pool surrounded by sunbathing lawns, 3 pool tables and a dartboard. Trips to Hell's Gate National Park, Crater Lake and Crescent Island can be arranged.

Camp Carnelley's

**Lake Naivasha
South Lake Road**

Camp Carnelley's, Moi South Lake Road, Naivasha, Kenya
PO Box 9, Sulmac 20151, Kenya

Tel	+254 50 50004
Mobile	+254 722 260749; +254 716 697780; +254 722 501952
Fax	
E-mail	info@campcarnelleys.com
Web	www.campcarnelleys.com

  Mirera, CH, 30 mins
JKIA, LS & CH & Intl., 2.5 hrs

Camp Carnelley's centres on a bar and restaurant with an open fireplace, bright comfortable cushions and plentiful seating. The camp offers bandas, rooms, dorms and camping in gardens that slope to the lakeshore. There are 2 en-suite bandas; 1 sleeps 6 pax and the other sleeps 4 pax. Both bandas have verandas furnished with dining table and chairs. There are 7 rooms, made up of doubles and twins, with external shared bathrooms. There is 1 dorm with bunk beds, for 8 pax. The campsite has a bathroom block, with a row of WCs and showers. The restaurant has an a la carte menu, with international dishes like spicy crayfish and steak with mushroom sauce, and also serves local dishes like ugali and sukuma. The bar is well stocked with soft drinks, beers, wines and spirits. The gardens are dotted with picnic tables and benches and shaded by tall acacia trees. Activities include nature walks and boat trips on the lake. Trips to Hell's Gate National Park, Mt Longonot and other national parks can be arranged. Boat trips to Crater Lake, water-skiing and fishing are also available. Local sites of interest include Crescent Island and Elsemere.

Top Camp

**Lake Naivasha
South Lake Road**

Top Camp, Moi South Lake Road, Naivasha, Kenya
PO Box 79, Naivasha 20117, Kenya

Tel	+254 20 2139922
Mobile	+254 729 291277; +254 728 594861
Fax	
E-mail	fishermanscamp@gmail.com
Web	www.fishermanscamp.com

 VISA, MasterCard    JKIA, LS & CH & Intl. 2.5 hrs

On a hillside with striking views of the lake below, Top Camp is just as its name implies. The camp is immediately opposite Fisherman's Camp, on the lakefront, and all the facilities and activities available at Fisherman's Camp can be accessed by visitors to Top Camp. The camp offers self-catering accommodation.

There are 3 cottages, made up of 2 1-bedroom cottages and 1 2-bedroom cottage. The cottages have a kitchenette and a veranda furnished with dining table and chairs. There are also 2 en-suite bandas and 2 bandas with a shared bathroom. All bandas have 1 bedroom and a veranda with dining table and chairs. The campsite has bathroom facilities. Campers can hire tents, mattresses, bedding and jiko barbecues. There is also a large communal barbecue.

Fisherman's Camp has a restaurant, serving homemade pizza, as well as dishes like Swahili fish, chicken tikka and a selection of burgers. The bar is well equipped with soft drinks, beers, wines and spirits, and has satellite TV and games like backgammon, chess and cards. Bird walks with a local guide and boat trips on the lake can be arranged. Waterworld, based at Fisherman's Camp, offers sundowner cruises, and trips to Crater Lake and Crescent Island. Bicycles and fishing rods are available for hire.

Fisherman's Camp

Lake Naivasha
South Lake Road

Fisherman's Camp, Moi South Lake Road, Naivasha, Kenya
PO Box 79, Naivasha 20117, Kenya

Tel	+254 20 2139922
Mobile	+254 726 870590; +254 774 142749
Fax	
E-mail	fishermanscamp@gmail.com
Web	www.fishermanscamp.com

 VISA, MasterCard    JKIA, LS & CH & Intl. 2.5 hrs

One of the original camps on Lake Naivasha, Fisherman's Camp is popular with locals and visitors alike. The circular bar and restaurant overlook large gardens sloping down to the lake's edge. The camp offers self-catering accommodation, a lively restaurant and bar and a campsite.

There are 4 bandas, each with an en-suite double room and veranda furnished with table and chairs. Kasuku Cottage has 2 bedrooms, a bathroom, a kitchenette and a large veranda furnished with table and chairs. The campsite has bathroom blocks containing rows of WCs and showers. Campers can hire tents, mattresses, bedding and jiko barbecues if required. The restaurant serves homemade pizza, as well as dishes like Swahili fish, chicken tikka and a selection of burgers. Local home delivery is available. The bar is well equipped with soft drinks, beers, wines and spirits, and has satellite TV and games like backgammon, chess and cards. Bird walks with a local guide can be arranged. Boat trips on the lake are available. Waterworld, based at Fisherman's Camp, offers sundowner cruises, and trips to Crater Lake and Crescent Island. Bicycles and fishing rods are available for hire. Curio stalls sell African artefacts and a weaver's shop sells rugs and wall hangings.

Fish Eagle Inn

Lake Naivasha
South Lake Road

Fish Eagle Inn, Moi South Lake Road, Naivasha, Kenya
PO Box 10236, Nairobi 00100, Kenya

Tel	+254 20 2067076; +254 20 2737956; +254 20 2734717
Mobile	+254 722 665800
Fax	+254 50 2021158; +254 20 2733289
E-mail	info@fisheagleinn.co.ke / fisheagleinn@gmail.com
Web	www.fisheagleinn.co.ke

 VISA, MasterCard, Amex   JKIA, LS & CH & Intl. 2.5 hrs

Fish Eagle Inn, on the shores of Lake Naivasha, offers cottages, suites, rooms and a campsite in attractive gardens.

There are 19 en-suite standard rooms, and 26 en-suite executive rooms, which are more spacious and include satellite TV and a kettle. Some rooms are accessible by wheelchair. The 5 cottages have 2 bedrooms and living room with satellite TV. The 2 suites are more spacious and include sofa, armchairs and coffee table. The campsite has bathroom facilities and communal kitchen banda.

The restaurant serves buffet and a la carte, with dishes like English fish deep fried in crispy batter, grilled marinated chicken and Maasai steak topped with bacon and cheese flakes. The children's menu includes mini burger and fish fingers. The bar has a dark wood counter and deep sofas, and is well stocked with soft drinks, beers, wines and spirits. 1 conference hall seats 30 pax and the other seats 100 pax. PA system and projector can be hired if requested in advance. There is WiFi throughout the compound. There is also a gym and sauna. Activities include boat rides and bike rides. Fish Eagle Inn is environmentally aware, and reduces power usage by boiling all water from one source.

Elsamere

Lake Naivasha
South Lake Road

Elsamere, Moi South Lake Road, Naivasha, Kenya
PO Box 1497, Naivasha 20117, Kenya

Tel	+254 50 2021055
Mobile	+254 722 648123
Fax	+254 50 2021074
E-mail	reservations@elsamere.com
Web	www.elsamere.com / www.elsatrust.org

VISA, MasterCard, Amex, JCB

Loldia, LS & CH, 30 mins
JKIA, LS & CH & Intl., 2.5 hrs

Joy Adamson said of Elsamere: It would be impossible to imagine a more attractive site for a home. The former home of Joy and George Adamson, Elsamere has a museum housing the Adamsons' collection of books and paintings, as well as memorabilia from the film Born Free.

On the shores of Lake Naivasha, Elsamere is home to a variety of wildlife and flora, and over 200 bird species, including fish eagles, pelicans, flamingos and kingfishers. Guided nature and bird walks are available, as are boat rides on the lake. Visits to Hell's Gate National Park, Mt Longonot, Crater Lake and Lake Nakuru National Park can be arranged. There are 8 cottages in the gardens, each with double or twin bedroom, en-suite bathroom and a veranda with a view of Lake Naivasha. The main house, containing the Adamsons' furniture and silverware, is decorated with Joy's paintings. Meals, prepared with fresh, local produce, are served on the veranda.

The Elsamere Field Study Centre, supported by Elsa Trust and Elsamere, educates young people about conservation and promotes environmental awareness and development education. The centre has 4 twin rooms and 4 dorms, together sleeping 62 students. Visitors are welcome to visit the centre to see conservation activities in progress.

Kiangazi House

Oserian
Wildlife Sanctuary

Kiangazi House, Oserian Wildlife Sanctuary, Lake Naivasha, Kenya
Exclusive African Treasures, PO Box 63827, Nairobi 00619, Kenya

Tel	+254 20 7123300-2
Mobile	+254 773 777066
Fax	+254 20 7123303
E-mail	info@eatreasures.co.ke
Web	www.eatreasures.com

Loldia, LS & CH, 30 mins
Oserian, CH, 10 mins

Kiangazi House, named after the hot, dry season, is situated in Oserian Wildlife Sanctuary, overlooking the shores of Lake Naivasha. The house was built of local stone and timber, with private lounges, a bar and library, all with fireplaces. It is set in a lush garden of rolling lawns.

There are 2 en-suite double rooms and 1 en-suite twin in the main house, and 2 more en-suite doubles beyond the swimming pool. The rooms are furnished with 4-poster beds and mosquito nets. The restaurant serves international cuisine.

Activities include day and night game drives, game walks, boat trips, fishing, bird walks and horse riding. Bush meals and sundowners are available, as are guided tours of Oserian flower farm. For a surcharge, game drives in Hell's Gate National Park and Lake Nakuru National Park can be arranged. Kiangazi House is committed to conservation, and contributes to the management of the 20,000-acre Oserian Wildlife Sanctuary. Over 45 different species of mammals are found here, including several non-indigenous species that were imported in order to contribute to the survival of their species such as white rhino, Grevy's zebra and cheetah. The house is closed 1st to 15th May. Children under 6 are not permitted at Kiangazi House.

Chui Lodge

Oserian
Wildlife Sanctuary

Chui Lodge, Oserian Wildlife Sanctuary, Lake Naivasha, Kenya
Exclusive African Treasures, PO Box 63437, Nairobi 00619, Kenya

Tel	+254 20 7123300-2
Mobile	+254 20 7123303; +254 773 777066
Fax	+254 20 7123303
E-mail	info@eatreasures.co.ke
Web	www.eatreasures.com

 Loldia, LS & CH, 30 mins
Oserian, CH, 10 mins

Named after the rare and imposing leopard, Chui Lodge is a private retreat on the slopes overlooking Lake Naivasha. The lodge was crafted from bush stone, and local acacia, olive and leleshwa woods. The lodge and swimming pool overlook a waterhole that attracts plentiful game. There are 8 en-suite cottages, made up of 6 doubles and 2 singles. All the cottages have a fireplace and veranda with a view; 3 of the cottages have, in addition, a living room. The cottages are adorned with handmade batiks. The dining room, lounge and bar area has ochre walls adorned with African carvings and murals.

Activities include day and night game drives, game walks, boat trips, fishing, bird walks and horse riding. Bush meals and sundowners are available, as are guided tours of Oserian flower farm. For a surcharge, game drives in Hell's Gate National Park and Lake Nakuru National Park can be arranged. Chui Lodge is committed to conservation, and contributes to the management of the 20,000-acre Oserian Wildlife Sanctuary. Over 45 species of mammals are found here, including several non-indigenous species that were imported in order to contribute to the survival of their species such as white rhino, Grevy's zebra and cheetah. The lodge is closed 15th to 31st May.

Children under 12 are not permitted at Chui Lodge.

Kongoni Lodge

Lake Naivasha
South Lake Road

Kongoni Lodge, Kongoni Game Valley, Moi South Lake Road, Naivasha
PO Box 7, Naivasha 20117, Kenya

Tel	
Mobile	+254 737 914044; +254 704 070239; +254 787 445207
Fax	
E-mail	kongonilodge@kongonilodge.com
Web	www.kgvalley.com / www.kongonilodge.com

JKIA, LS & CH & Intl.
3 hrs

Set in a private conservation area on the shores of Lake Naivasha, Kongoni Lodge is surrounded by wildlife. The house was built in the early 1900s, and has a long veranda overlooking the lake. The kongoni, or hartebeest, that gave the place its name roam freely around the area.

There are 7 en-suite double rooms and 1 single room. The house also has 2 spacious sitting rooms, a fully equipped kitchen, a dining room and 2 verandas. The furnishings are traditional English, with a touch of Arabic style from Lamu. The swimming pool is shaded by euphorbias. There are 2 cottages, each with 3 en-suite double rooms, small living room and kitchen. The 2 chefs serve predominantly Italian cuisine; guests are welcome to discuss their food preferences with them.

Activities include day and night game drives on the private conservation area, which has game such as antelope, warthog, buffalo, hippo and leopard. Boat rides around Lake Naivasha provide the opportunity to see prolific birdlife. Bush meals and sundowners overlooking the lake can be arranged. Mountain biking and horse riding are also available. Excursions to local attractions such as Hell's Gate National Park, Elsemere, Crater Lake and Lake Nakuru National Park can all be arranged.

Hippo Point

Lake Naivasha
South Lake Road

Hippo Point, Moi South Lake Road, Naivasha, Kenya
PO Box 1852, Naivasha 20117, Kenya

Tel	
Mobile	+254 733 333014; +254 733 993713
Fax	
E-mail	info@hippopointkenya.com
Web	www.hippopointkenya.com

VISA, MasterCard

Hippo Point, CH
10 mins

Hippo Point is a private wildlife sanctuary on the shores of Lake Naivasha. It aims to be a slow safari, a place where visitors relax and commune with nature. The sanctuary includes a wellness retreat and offers a selection of activities.

Dodo's Tower is an 8-floor tower, rated as 1 of the top retreats in the world. The tower has spectacular views over Oloidien Bay and the animals that graze at its shore. There are 4 en-suite double rooms and 1 en-suite single. There is also a spacious living room with balcony, fully equipped kitchen, dining room, writing room, meditation room and top view room. The Manor House, built in the 1930s and restored in 1998, is a relic of Kenya's colonial past. Surrounded by a traditional English garden of scented roses and lush lawns, the house has 8 en-suite double rooms and 1 en-suite single room, a secluded swimming pool, a gazebo for body treatments and a team of staff.

The chef serves fresh, healthy, homemade dishes. The yoga barn offers yoga sessions overlooking the lake, and week-long yoga retreats. The spa products are drawn from nature, using local knowledge of herbal medicines. Safaris, helicopter trips, cultural experiences, water sports and horse riding can all be booked from Hippo Point.

Twiga House

Lake Naivasha
South Lake Road

Twiga House, Moi South Lake Road, Naivasha, Kenya
PO Box 24335, Nairobi 00502, Kenya

Tel	
Mobile	+254 728 606193
Fax	
E-mail	info@twigahouse.com
Web	www.twigahouse.com

JKIA, LS & CH & Intl.
3 hrs

Twiga House is a private house located on the shores of Lake Naivasha. The house provides a combination of outdoor activities and comfortable living. There is a main house and a guest cottage, both elegantly furnished in European style. The main house has 3 double bedrooms, 2 bathrooms, large lounge, fully equipped kitchen and a wooden deck. The guest cottage has 2 double bedrooms, 1 bathroom and a wooden deck. The master bedroom in each house has its own fireplace; most rooms have views of the lake. The water is heated by solar power. Towels and bed linen are provided; a housekeeping service is also included.

Between the 2 houses is a swimming pool which overlooks the lake.

There is also a staff quarters with 2 bedrooms, for cook, nanny or driver. A cook can be provided on request, for an extra charge. Meals can be taken on the veranda, on the deck or around the swimming pool. The lake provides opportunities for long walks, observing the wildlife and enjoying the scenery. Local sites of interest include Hell's Gate National Park, Crescent Island and Crater Lake. Activities which can be booked locally include mountain biking, horse riding, sailing, fishing and boat rides.

314 *KaribuKenya* Accommodation Guide

Crater Lake
Permanent Tented Camp and Sanctuary

Crater Lake $

Crater Lake Permanent Tented Camp and Sanctuary, Crater Lake, Kenya
Merica Group, PO Box 45675, Nairobi 00100, Kenya

Tel	+254 20 316696; +254 20 2185147
Mobile	+254 720 950845; +254 722 203804
Fax	+254 20 315743
E-mail	mericagroup@mericaholdings.com
Web	www.mericagrouphotels.com

 VISA, MasterCard   JKIA, LS & CH & Intl. 3 hrs

Set on the shores of Green Soda Lake, Crater Lake Permanent Tented Camp and Sanctuary is a secluded retreat at the foot of Lake Naivasha. The lake and sanctuary are at the bottom of an extinct volcano, at an altitude of 1,900 meters. Lush vegetation and a wide variety of flora provide ample opportunity for bush walks, while nearby Lake Naivasha is available for sailing and boat trips.

There are 8 en-suite double tents and 2 family bandas; the bathrooms are all built from local stone. The Wedding Cloud is a beautifully decorated tent, ideal for honeymooners, that includes a deep sunken whirlpool bath overlooking the lake through a stained glass window.

Meals are served in a central dining area with a high thatched roof and an African veranda that overlooks the lake. Buffet or a la carte can be served, as required, and the dishes are simple, fresh and tasty. The menu includes Kenyan and international dishes. The bar serves soft drinks, beers and spirits.

There is also a campsite with bathroom facilities, and plentiful secure parking. Crater Lake is ideally situated for trips to Hell's Gate National Park, Mt Longonot, Crescent Island, Elsamere and the golf course at Green Park.

NMK, Olorgesailie Bandas

Oltepesi $

NMK, Olorgesailie Bandas, Oltepesi, Kenya
National Museums of Kenya, PO Box 40658, Nairobi 00100, Kenya

Tel	+254 20 8164135; +254 20 8164136; +254 20 8164134
Mobile	+254 721 308485; +254 733 296142
Fax	+254 20 3741424
E-mail	publicrelations@museums.or.ke
Web	www.museums.or.ke

      JKIA, LS & CH & Intl. 2 hrs

Olorgesailie prehistoric site is known as the factory of stone tools. The large number of human tools found here suggests that the area was a camping place for early man, and is evidence that the human species was of tropical origin. The tools were preserved by heavy falls of alkaline volcanic ash from nearby Mt Suswa and Mt Longonot. The site is in a lake basin that existed about 100,000 to 200,000 years ago. Dr and Mrs Leakey started investigations on the site in 1942; their discoveries provide information about the habits and activities of early prehistoric peoples of the Acheuleus or hand axe culture.

Olorgesailie bandas are owned and operated by National Museums of Kenya. There are 4 double bandas and 4 twin bandas. There is also a communal kitchen, dining area and bathroom facilities. A campsite and a picnic site are adjacent to the bandas.

The site has a museum with information about the discoveries made here. Mt Olorgesailie, named after a revered Maasai elder who used to meditate and hold meetings on the mountain, is a 6-hour hike, including climb and descent. The site is excellent for bird watching and has the highest number of migratory bird species in Kenya.

Oloika Guest House — Shompole Conservancy

Oloika Guest House, Shompole Conservancy, 5km from Lake Magadi
African Conservation Centre, PO Box 15298, Nairobi 00509, Kenya

Tel	+254 20 2512439
Mobile	+254 724 441677; +254 722 564059; +254 722 709514
Fax	+254 20 891741
E-mail	admin-soralo@acc.or.ke / soralo@acc.or.ke
Web	www.soralo.org

Shompole, CH, 45 mins
JKIA, LS & CH & Intl., 4 hrs

Oloika Guest House is managed by a Maasai women's self-empowerment initiative. The guesthouse is aimed at intrepid adventurers who wish to support such a group.

There are 4 twin rooms, a communal bathroom block and a communal kitchen. The guesthouse is 5km from the hot springs of Lake Magadi.

Activities are provided by nearby Enkare and Loisiijo Lodge. They include day and night game drives and guided nature walks. Bird watching, hiking and swimming are all on offer; bush breakfasts can be arranged. The nearby Laleenok resource centre offers fascinating insights into the strong links between traditional knowledge, science and conservation.

The scientists undertaking research here serve as an interface between scientists and the community. Researchers also offer the chance to walk with a troop of habituated baboons; visitors can observe the aspects of the behaviour of baboons that are similar to humans. The researchers also offer the opportunity to track night predators. Other nearby sites of interest include Lake Natron, the breeding spot of the famous flamingos.

Loisiijo Lodge — Shompole Conservancy

Loisiijo Lodge, Shompole Conservancy, nr Lake Magadi, Kenya
PO Box 24124, Nairobi 00100, Kenya

Tel	+254 20 3533338; +254 20 2463745
Mobile	+254 722 515377; +254 733 609768
Fax	
E-mail	loisiijolodge@gmail.com
Web	www.loisiijolodgeshompole.org

Shompole, CH, 45 mins
JKIA, LS & CH & Intl., 4 hrs

Loisiijo Lodge is an attractive, rustic lodge, which offers a wide selection of activities in the Lake Magadi area. The lodge nestles beneath ancient tamarind trees on the fig shaded banks of the Ewaso Ngiro River.

There are 4 airy en-suite cottages, made up of 3 cottages with a double and single bed, and 1 larger cottage with 2 double beds and a sofa that can be converted to a single bed. The lodge can be taken on self-catering or full board basis, advance notice required. There is a spacious dining area with solar lighting, and kitchen equipped with solar lighting, fridge, gas cooker, crockery, cutlery and glassware. There is a resident cook, and several staff.

Activities include day and night game drives and guided nature walks. Bird watching is recommended, with over 350 species recorded in the area. Hiking, swimming, canoeing and tubing are also available; bush breakfasts can be arranged.

The nearby Laleenok resource centre offers fascinating insights into the strong links between traditional knowledge, science and conservation. Researchers offer the chance to walk with a troop of habituated baboons, and to track night predators such as lions and striped hyenas. Other nearby sites of interest include traditional Maasai villages and the archaeological site of Olorgesailie.

Enkare

Olkiramatian Conservancy

Enkare, Olkiramatian Conservancy, nr Lake Magadi, Kenya
PO Box 114, Nairobi 00606, Kenya
Tel
Mobile   +254 701 333491
Fax
E-mail   sampucamp@gmail.com
Web   www.sampu-camp.com

Shompole, CH, 40 mins
JKIA, LS & CH & Intl., 4 hrs

Enkare is an attractive and peaceful tented camp, which offers a wide selection of activities in the Lake Magadi area. The camp, previously called Sampu Camp, was refurbished and renamed in 2012.

There are 6 en-suite tents, all furnished with queen size bed and single bed. The tents are positioned to maximise the panoramic views of the surrounding acacia woodlands and the distant peaks of Shompole Hill. The dining tent, where breakfast, lunch and dinner are served, overlooks a waterhole that attracts various species of wildlife and birdlife. Activities include day and night game drives and guided nature walks. Bird watching, hiking and swimming are all on offer; cultural visits to local Maasai villages and bush breakfasts can be arranged.

The nearby colobus monkey site makes an interesting trip from Enkare. Also nearby is Laleenok resource centre, which offers fascinating insights into the strong links between traditional knowledge, science and conservation. The scientists undertaking research here serve as an interface between scientists and the community. Researchers offer the chance to walk with a troop of habituated baboons so visitors can observe the aspects of the behaviour of baboons that are similar to humans.

The researchers also offer the opportunity to track night predators.

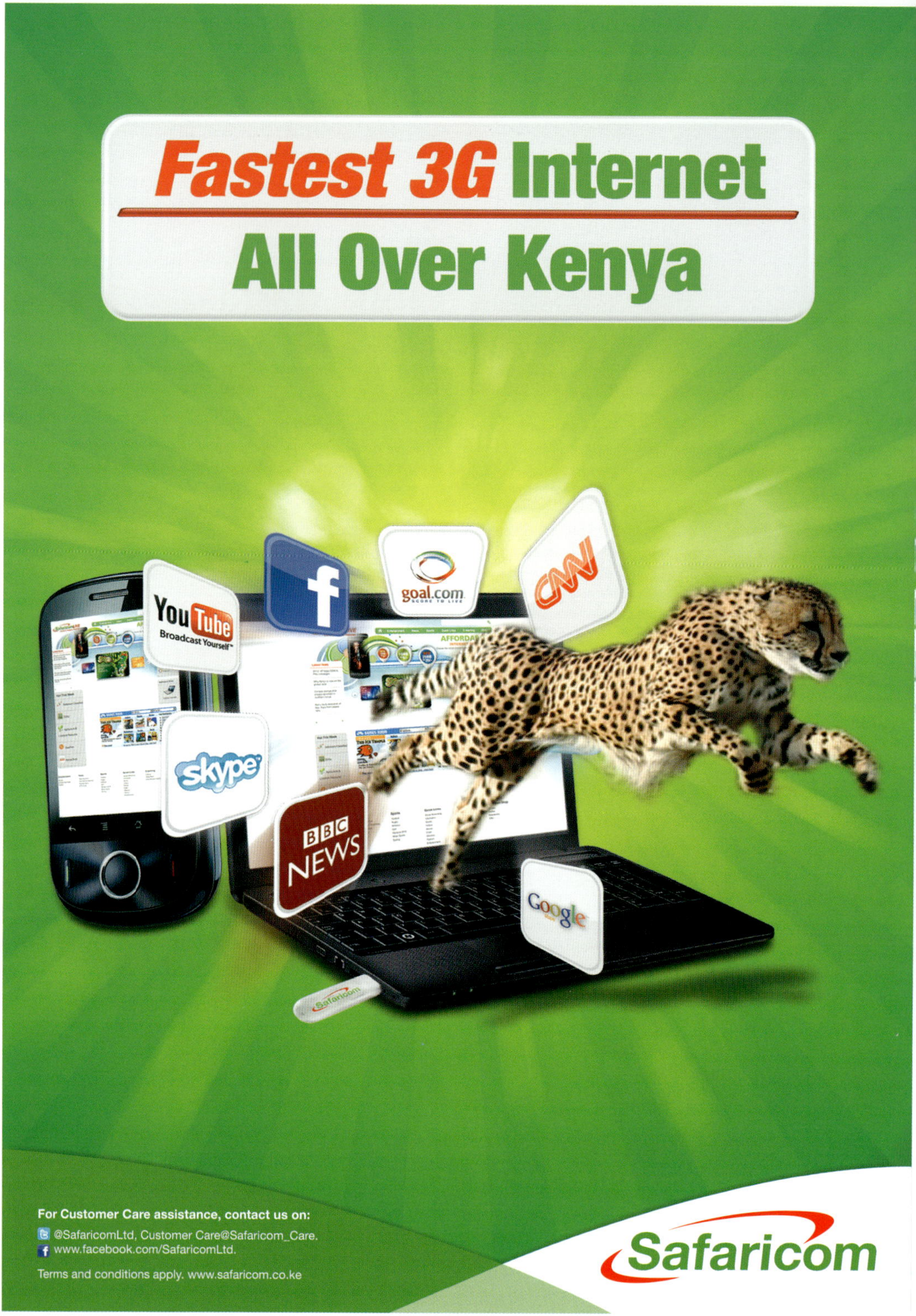
Fastest 3G Internet
All Over Kenya
For Customer Care assistance, contact us on:
@SafaricomLtd, Customer Care@Safaricom_Care.
www.facebook.com/SafaricomLtd.
Terms and conditions apply. www.safaricom.co.ke
Safaricom

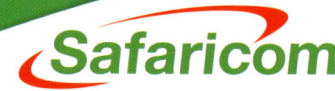

Amboseli National Park

Elephants before Mt Kilimanjaro – Photo © Marie-Claire Webner

The huge herds of elephant that roam through Amboseli National Park have made it a centre for elephant research. The park also hosts a wide variety of other wildlife and over 600 species of birds. Highlights of Amboseli include Observation Hill and spectacular views of Mt Kilimanjaro.

The region was originally known as Empusel, meaning salty, dusty place in the language of the Maasai. The park was set aside as the Southern Reserve for Maasai in 1906, but was made a Game Reserve in 1948 and, to protect its unique ecosystem, a National Park in 1974. The park has semi-arid vegetation, a dried up Pleistocene lake and several swamps. The greater Amboseli ecosystem is a critical environmental bridge that links the two Tsavo National Parks to its east with the Rift Valley and the Serengeti-Mara ecosystem to its west.

The park can be accessed by road from Nairobi through Namanga. Roads also link it to the Chyulu Hills and to Tsavo West National Park. Park gates are Olkelunyiet, Meshanani, Kitrua and Iremito. There is one airstrip inside the park. Other airstrips nearby are at Kilimanjaro Buffalo Lodge and Namanga town. As well as the world-famous elephant herds, resident wildlife includes lion, leopard, cheetah, wild dog, buffalo, rhino, giraffe, zebra, crocodile, mongoose, hyrax, lesser kudu and porcupine.

Oservation Hill gives panoramic views of the park. The swamp below Observation Hill attracts high numbers of elephants, buffalos and hippos, as well as a variety of waterfowl like pelican and Egyptian goose. Activities include game viewing, bird watching and camping.

Cynthia Moss started the Amboseli Elephant Research Project in Amboseli National Park in 1972. Since then she and her research associates have identified and recorded, often by name, more than 1,400 elephants. This research has contributed significantly to the conservation of the African elephant. Her books include Elephant Memories, Echo of the Elephants and Elephant Woman, as well as a children's picture book called Little Big Ears: The Story of Ely.

The Amboseli area is home to the Maasai people. Traditionally nomadic, the Maasai are a Nilotic people famed for their prowess as warriors. Their most prized possessions are cattle, which represent wealth to the Maasai and are used, not only for food, but also for dowries, fines and ceremonies. The Maasai pass through a series of rites of passage, ceremonies and celebrations in their lives, taking them from initiation through the levels of warriors to the highly respected position of elder. Some Maasai villages in the Amboseli region are open to visitors, and give an insight into the culture and traditions of the Maasai people.

Namanga, to the west of Amboseli, is a major border crossing between Kenya and Tanzania. Buses run frequently between Nairobi and Arusha. Tourist visas can be purchased at the border.

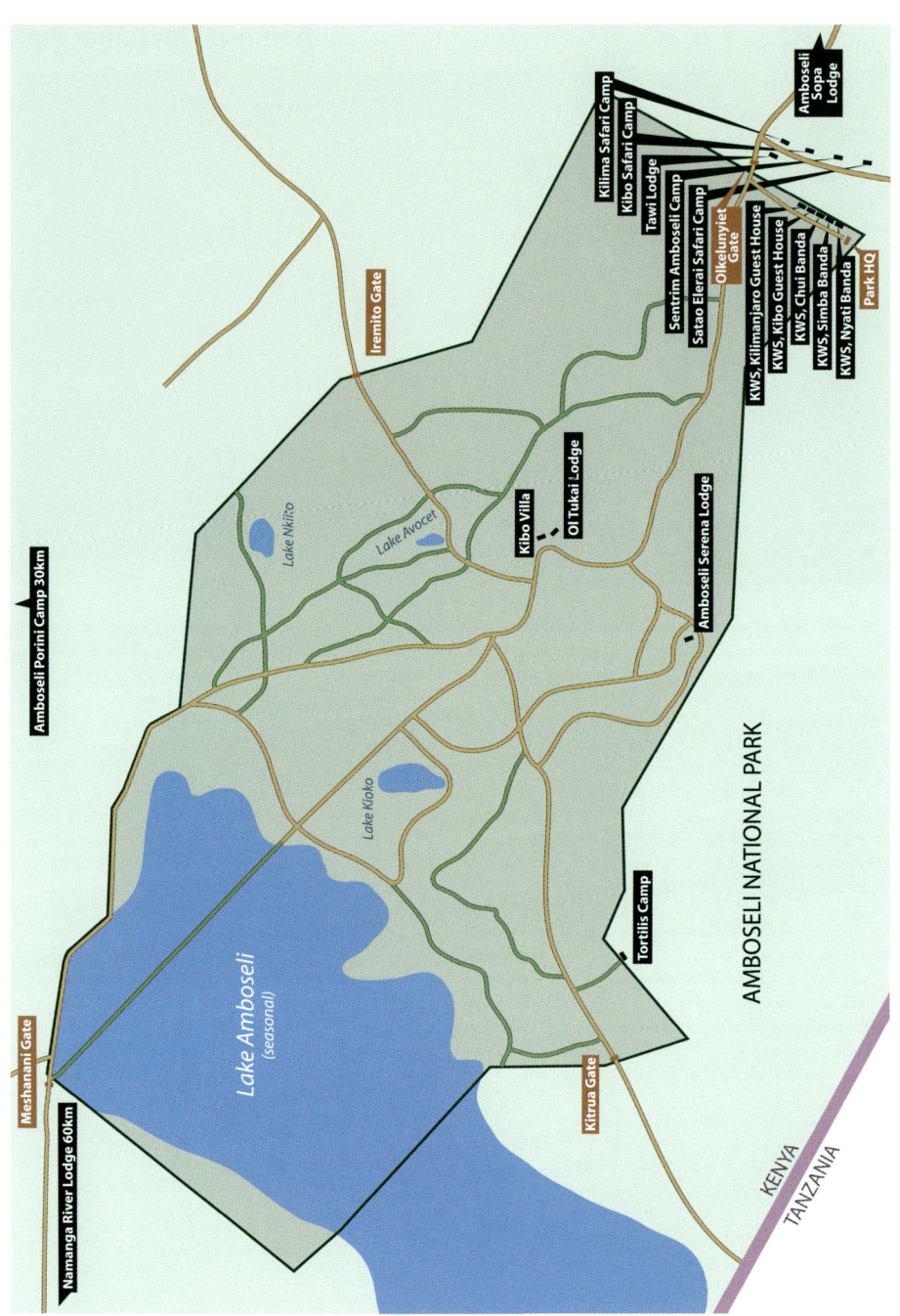

Namanga River Lodge — Olkelunyiet Gate

Namanga River Lodge, Namanga Road, Namanga, Kenya
PO Box 4, Namanga 00207, Kenya
Tel   +254 20 243245
Mobile   +254 724 041375; +254 734 591444
Fax
E-mail   info@riverlodgenamanga.com
Web   www.riverlodgenamanga.com

Lgulului, CH
15 mins

Namanga River Lodge was established in 1934, as a colonial hotel, and was refurbished in 2010. The lodge is located at Namanga, on the Kenya Tanzania border, with views of Ol Doinyo Orok mountain. It offers a variety of activities in peaceful surroundings.

There are 30 en-suite rooms, made up of 20 standard and 10 executive. The executive rooms have writing desk, chair and satellite TV. Orok Restaurant has an a la carte menu of Italian, Indian and Kenyan dishes, including a range of pizzas and nyama choma grilled meats. Buffet can be arranged for large groups. Buffalo Bar serves soft drinks, beers, wines and spirits, and is equipped with satellite TV, dartboard and pool table. The conference hall seats 70 pax, and is equipped with PA system and projector. There is also a gift shop selling curios and local artefacts. The lodge has a football pitch and volleyball court. Nearby Ol Doinyo Orok provides opportunity for hiking and climbing. The lodge assists visitors who want to cross the border, and accompanies them to the border. Camel riding to a Maasai village is also available. Trips to Amboseli National Park, including game drives in the park, can be arranged for a surcharge, for individuals or groups.

Amboseli Porini Camp — Selenkay Conservation Area

Amboseli Porini Camp, Selenkay Conservation Area, Kenya
Porini Camps, PO Box 388, Nairobi 00621, Kenya
Tel   +254 20 7123129; +254 20 7122504; +254 20 7121851
Mobile   +254 722 509200; +254 735 339209
Fax   +254 20 7120864
E-mail   info@porini.com / info@gamewatchers.co.ke
Web   www.porini.com

Amboseli, LS & CH
1 hr

Amboseli Porini Camp is located on Selenkay Conservation Area, a 15,000-acre private game reserve near the northern boundary of Amboseli National Reserve. The conservancy, owned by the Kisonko clan of the Maasai people, is an important wildlife corridor for animals moving in and out of the reserve. This area has known little tourism and in addition to the big mammals, rare game such as caracal, African wildcat, civet, gerenuk and striped hyena are seen here. Birdlife is prolific.

The camp has no permanent structures. The 9 en-suite tents are in the style of the traditional hunting bush camps. Each has a double and single bed, and is lit by solar powered lighting. Drinks are served around the campfire and meals are eaten in the shade of an acacia tortilis tree. Game drives traverse both Amboseli National Park and Selenkay Conservation Area. Other activities include game walks with Maasai trackers and visits to Maasai villages.

The camp generates an income for the community and provides employment: only the manager and head chef are not from the local Maasai community. Strict policies govern land use, water, waste disposal and energy. Ecotourism Society of Kenya has given Amboseli Porini Camp a prestigious gold level award.

Tortilis Camp

Amboseli Ntl. Park

Tortillis Camp, nr Amboseli National Park, Kenya
Cheli & Peacock, PO Box 743, Nairobi 00517, Kenya

Tel	+254 20 6004053/4; +254 20 6003090/1
Mobile	+254 724 255374; +254 733 490234
Fax	+254 20 6004050; +254 20 6003066
E-mail	safaris@chelipeacock.co.ke / info@chelipeacock.co.ke
Web	www.chelipeacock.com / www.tortilis.com

 VISA, MasterCard

 Tortilis, CH
10 mins

From a grove of the acacia tortilis trees that gave the camp its name, Tortilis Camp looks across the plains at Mt Kilimanjaro. Set in a 20,000-acre private concession bordering Amboseli National Park, Tortilis has a reputation for charm and attention to detail.

There are 17 spacious en-suite tents, made up of 9 doubles and 8 twins. The tents are raised on wooden decks and have large verandas. Meals are prepared from home recipes and are complemented by salads and herbs grown in the camp's garden.

As well as the elephants for which Amboseli is famed, the concession is home to a wide variety of mammal and bird species. Local Maasai guides share their knowledge of the indigenous species of game and of the traditions and customs of the Maasai. Tortilis is committed to the environment and actively preserves the extended Amhoseli area. For this, Tortilis has been awarded the British Airways award for ecotourism. The camp also works closely with the local communities; over 80% of the staff are employed from the local community. Tortilis was on the Conde Nast Traveller Gold List in 2005, 2006 and 2008. It was also listed in the 500 Best Hotels in the World, by Travel and Leisure Magazine in 2008. Tortilis Camp has attained Ecotourism Society of Kenya's silver award.

Kibo Villa

Amboseli Ntl. Park

Kibo Villa, Amboseli National Park, Kenya
Ol Tukai Lodge, PO Box 45203, Nairobi 00100, Kenya

Tel	+254 20 4445514; +254 20 4442473
Mobile	+254 721 363163
Fax	+254 20 4448493
E-mail	oltukai@manrikgroup.com
Web	www.oltukailodge.com

VISA, MasterCard, Amex

 Amboseli, LS & CH
15 mins

At the foot of Mt Kilimanjaro, Kibo Villa is an elegant log cabin built in stone and gum tree. The villa is sheltered by a copse of indigenous acacia tortilis trees in 5 acres of garden, and offers both peace and privacy. There are 3 en-suite bedrooms, named after Amboseli's well documented elephants, Echo, Eli and Adam. Echo, the honeymoon suite, takes up the entire 1st floor, and has a private Jacuzzi, fireplace and veranda. Eli and Adam, on the ground floor, are spacious, with large beds and sitting area. The rooms can be taken individually, or the villa taken exclusively. The lounge has a fireplace and large windows with views of Mt Kilimanjaro. Meals are served in the dining room, or can be taken privately. The villa also has a swimming pool.

Activities include game drives and guided bush walks. Bush meals and sundowners are also on offer. Massage can be arranged for an extra charge. Kibo Villa strives to protect, conserve and restore the natural environment. Committed to sustainable development, the villa operates using as few resources as possible and generates minimal waste. It has pledged to create environmental awareness among its employees, customers, suppliers and the community.

Kibo Villa is affiliated to Ol Tukai Lodge.

Ol Tukai Lodge

Amboseli Ntl. Park

Ol Tukai Lodge, Amboseli National Park, Kenya
PO Box 45403, Nairobi 00100, Kenya

Tel	+254 20 4445514; +254 20 4442473
Mobile	+254 721 363163; +254 735 350005
Fax	+254 20 4448493
E-mail	oltukai@manrikgroup.com
Web	www.oltukailodge.com

All major cards — Amboseli, LS & CH 10 mins

At the foot of Mt Kilimanjaro, Ol Tukai Lodge is in Amboseli National Park. With log cabins, raised wooden walkways and manicured lawns, the lodge makes an attractive place from which to view the famous elephants of Amboseli. The 80 en-suite rooms are chalet-style, with uninterrupted views of the wetland or Mt Kilimanjaro. All rooms have local stone floors and mosquito nets; 2 rooms are designed for guests with disabilities. Breakfast is served on the open plains, and dinner is served under the stars. Entertainment is provided by local Maasai moran. Theme dinners are offered regularly. The Elephant Bar and the Pool Bar serve a variety of cocktails. The conference hall seats 200 pax; the business centre is well equipped. Conferences, seminars and corporate functions can all be arranged. There is also a wildlife library, spa, art boutique and an attractive chapel for weddings. Activities include game drives and bird walks. Ol Tukai Lodge has been awarded a bronze level award from Ecotourism Society of Kenya. It supports a number of environmental and community welfare programmes including a primary school. The Ol Tukai medical clinic also serves the local community.

Ol Tukai Lodge is affiliated to Kibo Villa.

Amboseli Serena Lodge

Amboseli Ntl. Park

Amboseli Serena Lodge, Amboseli National Park, Kenya
Serena Hotels, PO Box 48690, Nairobi 00100, Kenya

Tel	+254 20 2842000; +254 20 2822000; +254 20 2842333
Mobile	+254 733 282200; +254 733 282283; +254 733 282292
Fax	+254 20 2725184; +254 20 2718102/3
E-mail	cro@serena.co.ke
Web	www.serenahotels.com

 VISA, MasterCard, Amex — Amboseli, LS & CH 30 mins

Framed against the stunning backdrop of Africa's highest mountain, Mt Kilimanjaro, Amboseli Serena Lodge is in Amboseli National Park. The lodge, set along the banks of a flowing natural spring and surrounded by rolling grasslands, is patrolled by the vast herds of elephant for which Amboseli is famed. A grove of giant acacias casts shade over the Maasai-styled rooms.

The lodge has 96 en-suite rooms, each with an uninterrupted view over the plains. The rooms blend an authentic nomadic aura with modern facilities and comforts. Each is designed as a traditional manyatta, adorned with Maasai beadwork and gourds, and its walls are hand-painted with murals by a local artist. The lodge's swimming pool is filled with water from a natural spring that flows from Mt Kilimanjaro. Weddings, conferences and cultural events can all be catered for by the Serena team.

As part of Serena Hotels' dedication to conserving the environment of the African Bush, guests are invited to plant a tree to help reforestation that is necessary after herds of elephants tearing up trees for food. The lodge's naturalist also gives informative talks on environmental issues relating to Amboseli National Park. Ecotourism Society of Kenya has given Amboseli Serena Lodge a silver award.

Kilima Safari Camp Olkelunyiet Gate

Kilima Safari Camp, nr Amboseli National Park, Kenya
Mada Hotels, PO Box 40683, Nairobi 00100, Kenya

Tel	+254 20 6005328; +254 20 6750938
Mobile	+254 721 701014; +254 722 202564 ; +254 733 621532
Fax	+254 20 6003595
E-mail	sales@madahotels.com
Web	www.madahotels.com

    Amboseli, LS & CH
                         20 mins

With a name that means mountain in Swahili, Kilima Safari Camp offers spectacular views of Mt Kilimanjaro. The camp is near Olkelunyiet Gate of Amboseli National Park, in an area known for the huge herds of elephants that can sometimes be seen at the waterholes in front of the camp.

The 72 tents look onto either the waterholes or Mt Kilimanjaro. The 50 en-suite classic safari tents each have a double and single bed and a private veranda. The 10 superior safari tents each have 4-poster double beds and enlarged bathrooms with lion claw bathtubs. The 12 lodge rooms each have a double and single bed and a private balcony.

Meals are served in the open dining and bar area, where Maasai dancers entertain guests nightly. A resident naturalist gives evening lectures in a nature room filled with wildlife information. The camp also has a freeform swimming pool, a spa with massage services and a clinic with a resident nurse.

Game drives take place in Amboseli National Park. A recommended activity is a night game drive that includes a moonlit bush barbecue on the Amboseli plains. For an additional charge, Maasai moran are available to take guests on nature walks.

Kibo Safari Camp Olkelunyiet Gate

Kibo Safari Camp, nr Amboseli National Park, Kenya
PO Box 49265, Nairobi 00100, Kenya

Tel	+254 20 2672834 ; +254 20 2324676
Mobile	+254 733 617977; +254 721 380539
Fax	+254 20 4450392
E-mail	info@kibosafaricamp.com
Web	www.kibosafaricamp.com

 VISA, MasterCard, Amex   Amboseli, LS & CH
                                                    25 mins

Named after the highest peak of Mt Kilimanjaro, Kibo Safari Camp is an authentic tented safari camp with striking views of the mountain. There are 71 en-suite tents, shaded by thatched roofs. They are furnished with rustic furniture including solid wood bed, mosquito net, clothes rack, writing table and chair. All the tents, and the restaurant, face Mt Kilimanjaro. Fruit and vegetables are grown at the camp's own farm; the food is fresh and tasty. The lounge, beneath acacia trees, is equipped with satellite TV. The bar serves soft drinks, beers, wines, spirits and cocktails. The camp also has a swimming pool, a massage parlour and a gift shop. Conferences and teambuilding events can be organised. Every evening after dinner, Maasai moran dance by the open fire; guests are welcome to join in. Kibo Safari Camp is approximately 5 minutes' drive from Olkelunyiet Gate of Amboseli National Park. Activities include game drives and cultural visits to local Maasai villages. While Amboseli is famed for elephants, more than 50 other mammal species are also found here, including lion, spotted hyena, buffalo and Maasai giraffe. Birdlife numbers more than 400, including Goliath heron, Cori bustard, pigmy falcon, flamingo and pelican.

Tawi Lodge

Olkelunyiet Gate

Tawi Lodge, nr Amboseli National Park, Kenya
PO Box 1206, Nairobi 00502, Kenya

Tel	+254 20 2300943; +254 20 2459708
Mobile	+254 733 625399; +254 722 745 552
Fax	
E-mail	info@tawilodge.com
Web	www.tawilodge.com

 VISA, MasterCard   Amboseli, LS & CH, 45 mins
Tawi, CH, 10 mins

Tawi Lodge is located on a private conservancy of 6,000 acres at the foot of Mt Kilimanjaro. This community-run conservancy, together with African Wildlife Foundation, promotes and maintains development and interaction between wildlife and the Maasai people along the corridor between Amboseli and the Chyulu Hills. The lodge is an eco-friendly operation, which believes in taking care of the environment and its people. Tawi Lodge has a bronze award from Ecotourism Society of Kenya.

The 12 en-suite cottages, made up of doubles and twins, combine traditional African style with the modern facilities required by visitors today. All have fabulous views of Mt Kilimanjaro from their wooden deck verandas, their beds and even their bathtubs. Fireplaces and minibars are provided, as well as a butler service.

The lodge has a unique bio-pool and a relaxing massage area. It also has a reception, bars, dining area, library, shop and a cellar with a selection of fine wines. The campfire and bush bar are ideal for enjoying the sounds of the bush at the end of the day.

Over 400 species of birds have been recorded on the conservancy. Game drives, night drives and bush meals are all on offer, and visits to Amboseli National Park, only 5 minutes from the lodge, are also available.

Sentrim Amboseli Camp

Olkelunyiet Gate

Sentrim Amboseli Camp, nr Amboseli National Park, Kenya
Sentrim Hotels and Lodges, PO Box 43436, Nairobi 00100, Kenya

Tel	+254 20 315680
Mobile	+254 722 207361; +254 733 852083
Fax	+254 20 2218314; +254 20 343875
E-mail	reservationsamboseli@sentrim-hotels.com
Web	www.sentrim-hotels.com

 VISA, MasterCard   Amboseli, LS & CH
30 mins

On the border of Amboseli National Park, Sentrim Amboseli Camp has striking views of Mt Kilimanjaro. The camp is located near Olkelunyiet Gate. There are 60 en-suite tents, made up of 34 doubles, 16 twins and 10 triples. All tents are equipped with electronic safety deposit box, minibar, fan, hairdryer and kettle, and all have views of Mt Kilimanjaro. The restaurant serves buffet breakfast, lunch and dinner. Meals can also be served on the veranda of the guests' tent, if required. The bar is well stocked with soft drinks, beers, wines and spirits. The lounge area is open sided. The freeform swimming pool and Jacuzzi are surrounded by a sunbathing terrace with sunbeds and umbrellas. There is also a spa, a souvenir gift shop and a bookshop.

Activities include game drives and cultural visits to local villages. Information on local culture and traditions is available at the camp. Game walks, sundowners and balloon safaris are available for an extra charge. Observation Hill, not far from the camp, has panoramic views of Amboseli National Park and Mt Kilimanjaro. Sentrim Hotels and Lodges are also located in Nairobi, Mombasa, Tsavo East National Park and the Maasai Mara National Reserve.

Satao Elerai Safari Camp
Elerai Conservation Area

Satao Elerai Safari Camp, Elerai Conservation Area, nr Amboseli, Kenya
Satao Camps, PO Box 99456, Mombasa 80100, Kenya
Tel	+254 20 2434600-3
Mobile	+254 720 600200; +254 721 240840; +254 733 622022
Fax	+254 20 2434610
E-mail	info@sataoelerai.com
Web	www.sataoelerai.com

 VISA, MasterCard   Tawi, CH 30 mins

Set in a 5000-acre private conservation area southeast of Amboseli National Park, Satao Elerai Safari Camp offers exclusive game viewing. The camp looks down onto Amboseli in one direction, and up towards Mt Kilimanjaro in the other, giving panoramic views.

There are 9 en-suite tents, all of which face the mountain, and 5 luxury suites, looking down on the savannah of Amboseli National Park. All rooms have sliding doors opening onto their verandas, and are furnished with large beds and luxury duvets. The bathrooms are created from natural rock and acacia wood, and have views of the plains. Dinners are a la carte, and can be served in the dining room or under the stars.

Activities include game drives in Amboseli National Park. Night drives and game walks are available in the Elerai Conservation Area. Cultural visits to the Elerai Maasai community are also on offer. The Elerai Conservation Area is located in the Kitenden Corridor, a critical wildlife corridor which links the Kilimanjaro Forest Reserve in Tanzania to Amboseli National Park and beyond. Satao Elerai Community and Wildlife Trust aims to create and support sustainable ways for Maasai communities to live in harmony with the environment and wildlife around them.

Satao Elerai Safari Camp holds a bronze award from Ecotourism Society of Kenya.

KWS, Kilimanjaro & Kibo Guest Houses
Amboseli Ntl. Park

KWS Kilimanjaro & Kibo Guest Houses, Amboseli National Park HQ
Kenya Wildlife Service, PO Box 40241, Nairobi 00100, Kenya
Tel	+254 20 6000800; +254 20 6002345; +254 20 3991000
Mobile	+254 726 610508; +254 726 610509; +254 736 663421
Fax	+254 20 6003792
E-mail	kws@kws.go.ke / reservations@kws.go.ke
Web	www.kws.go.ke

    Amboseli Park HQ, CH 5 mins

Kilimanjaro Guest House and Kibo Guest House are owned and managed by Kenya Wildlife Service, KWS. They are situated at Amboseli National Park headquarters.

Kilimanjaro Guest House has 3 bedrooms, 1 with a double and a single bed, 1 twin and 1 single. There is also a sitting room with doors leading to a veranda. Kibo Guest House has 2 bedrooms, 1 with a double and a single bed and 1 twin. The sitting room is connected to the open plan dining room. Both houses have a bathroom with bath and shower and a fully equipped kitchen. The resident caretaker provides bed linen, towels, soap and loo paper. Generator electricity is provided from 6.30pm to 10pm.

As well as magnificent views of Mt Kilimanjaro, highlights of the park include large herds of elephants in unusual swamp habitat. Other game includes lion, cheetah, leopard, black rhino, oryx and gerenuk. More than 425 bird species have been recorded.

Meshanani Gate is about 230km from Nairobi. By road, guests can drive through Namanga to Meshanani Gate or through Emali to either Iremito or Olkelunyiet Gate. 4WD vehicles are recommended. The park gates are open from 6am to 7pm. Entry is by SafariCard only, which can be loaded at Meshanani Gate.

KWS, Chui, Simba & Nyati Bandas

Amboseli Ntl. Park

KWS, Chui, Simba & Nyati Bandas, Amboseli National Park HQ, Kenya
Kenya Wildlife Service, PO Box 40241, Nairobi 00100, Kenya

Tel	+254 20 6000800; +254 20 6002345; +254 20 3991000
Mobile	+254 726 610508; +254 726 610509; +254 736 663421
Fax	+254 20 6003792
E-mail	kws@kws.go.ke / reservations@kws.go.ke
Web	www.kws.go.ke

    Amboseli Park HQ, CH
                        5 mins

Chui Banda, Simba Banda and Nyati Banda are owned and managed by Kenya Wildlife Service, KWS. They are situated at Amboseli National Park headquarters.

Chui Banda and Simba Banda each have a twin bedroom, bathroom and kitchen equipped with gas stove, fridge, kitchen utensils, crockery, cutlery and glassware. Nyati Banda has 2 units, each unit having a twin bedroom, bathroom and kitchen equipped with gas stove, fridge, kitchen utensils, crockery, cutlery and glassware. The resident caretaker provides bed linen, towels, soap and loo paper. Generator electricity is provided from 6.30pm to 10pm.

As well as magnificent views of Mt Kilimanjaro, highlights of the park include large herds of elephants in unusual swamp habitat. Other game includes lion, cheetah, leopard, black rhino, oryx and gerenuk. More than 425 bird species have been recorded.

Meshanani Gate is about 230km from Nairobi. By road, visitors can drive through Namanga to Meshanani Gate or through Emali to either Iremito or Olkelunyiet Gate. 4WD vehicles are recommended. The gates are open from 6am to 7pm. Entry is by SafariCard only, which can be loaded at Meshanani Gate.

Amboseli Sopa Lodge

Amboseli

Amboseli Sopa Lodge, nr Amboseli National Park, Kenya
Sopa Lodges, PO Box 72630, Nairobi 00200, Kenya

Tel	+254 20 3750235; +254 20 3616000
Mobile	+254 722 206328/9; +254 733 610060
Fax	+254 20 3751507; +254 02 3740069
E-mail	info@sopalodges.com
Web	www.sopalodges.com

 VISA, MasterCard   Amboseli, LS & CH
                                                1 hr

Amboseli Sopa Lodge sits in 190 acres of wooded land at the foot of Mt Kilimanjaro. The lodge is designed to reflect the style of the Maasai: its reception replicates the entrance to a Maasai hut and its ornaments are silver spear heads, beaded necklaces and wrought iron Maasai figures. There is a Maasai market on site; proceeds support the local community. There are 80 en-suite rooms, made up of 18 singles, 40 twins, 20 doubles, 1 presidential suite and 1 honeymoon suite. 6 rooms have interconnecting doors suitable for families, and 2 rooms have wheelchair access. The rooms are individual cottages, linked by shaded pathways, and are adorned with local materials like sisal and driftwood, as well as Maasai blanket fabrics.

Kibo Restaurant, named after the highest peak of Mt Kilimanjaro, serves buffet breakfast, lunch and themed dinner. Mawenzi Bar, also named after a peak of Mt Kilimanjaro, has Maasai dancers on alternate nights. Hemingway's Bar, built by Ernest Hemingway as a house, is furnished with leather armchairs and decorated with pictures of the great author. The Pool Bar, surrounded by garden, overlooks the swimming pool. Activities include game drives, game walks, cultural visits and mountain climbing. Functions, conferences and weddings can be arranged. Amboseli Sopa Lodge holds a bronze award from Ecotourism Society of Kenya.

Tsavo West National Park

Mawnzi before Mt Kilimanjaro – Photo © www.sokomoto.com

Tsavo West National Park has a diverse array of habitats, including open grasslands, rocky outcrops, isolated hills, riverine vegetation, palm thickets and mountain forests. Highlights include Mzima Springs, Ngulia Rhino Sanctuary, Lake Jipe, Shetani Caves and spectacular views of Mt Kilimanjaro. Over 600 species of birds have been recorded here.

Tsavo National Park was established in 1948 and formed one of the largest national parks in the world. The park was later split into East and West, on either side of the Nairobi Mombasa Highway, for administrative purposes. Tsavo West adjoins the Chyulu Hills National Park. Park gates are at Tsavo, Kasigau, Mtito Andei, Chyulu, Maktau and Ziwani. Airstrips are located at Kamboyo, Kilaguni, Tsavo Gate, Jipe, Kasigau, Finch Hattons, Ziwani and Maktau. Park fees should be paid to Kenya Wildlife Service, KWS; current rates can be obtained from KWS.

Wildlife in the park includes leopard, cheetah, wild dog, buffalo, rhino, elephant, giraffe, zebra, lion, lesser kudu and porcupine. Diverse bird species include the threatened corncrake and the rare Basra reed warbler.

At Mzima Springs, water filtered underground from the Chyulu Hills erupts from below a lava ridge into a series of clear pools. Lake Jipe, on the Kenya Tanzania border, is fed by runoff from Mt Kilimanjaro and attracts what is thought to be the largest variety of aquatic birdlife in Africa.

Taita Hills Wildlife Sanctuary, with wooded hills and steep winding roads, has plentiful wildlife and rare species of birds and butterflies. Lumo Community Wildlife Sanctuary is formed of three group ranches which have united to preserve this vital wildlife corridor.

Ngulia Rhino Sanctuary, at the foot of the Ngulia Hills, was established to protect the rare black rhino. Now over 50 black rhino are found in the sanctuary. The Roaring Rocks, named for the buzz of cicadas that billows around them, have panoramic views over the sanctuary and make a spectacular observation point from which to look for rhinos or enjoy a sundowner.

Shetani, meaning evil in Swahili, was the name given by locals to the vast flow of lava that spurted from the earth. The Shetani Lava Flow is 8km long; trees entwine with chunks of solid magma, and in places form caves.

The plains of Tsavo were the site of a number of World War I battles between the British, based in Kenya which was then a British protectorate, and the Germans, based in what was then Tanganika, now Tanzania. Tours of battlefields and war cemeteries are available. One of the most eccentric campaigns, immortalised in the film Shout at the Devil, featured fleets of Rolls Royces; its final surrender came three months after the rest of the world had signed an armistice.

The Chyulu Hills, made famous by Ernest Hemingway's Green Hills of Africa, are strikingly attractive extinct volcanos, blanketed in black lava and lush flora. Chyulu Hills National Park has gates at Main Gate, Mukururo and Kiboko. There are two airstrips and three public campsites. Wildlife includes eland, elephant, leopard, giant forest hog, bush pig, black mamba, puff adder and rock python. Activities include game viewing, hiking, horse riding, bird watching and camping.

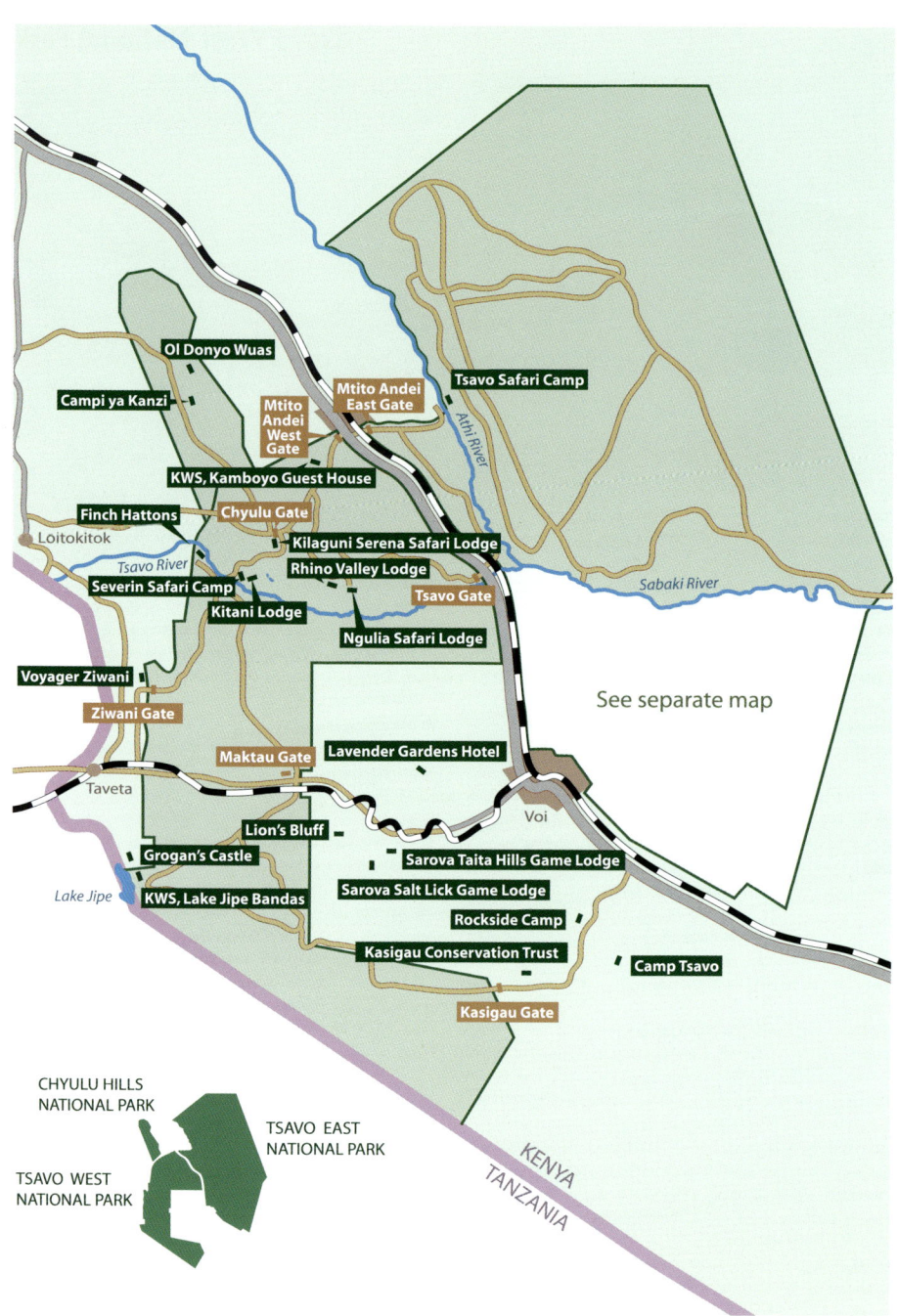

Camp Tsavo

Maungu

Camps International, Unit 1 Kingfisher Park, Headlands Business Park, Salisbury Road, Blashford, Ringwood, BH24 4HX, UK

Tel	+254 41 2007761
Mobile	+254 751 610424
Fax	
E-mail	dipesh@campsinternational.com
Web	www.campsinternational.com

     Ukunda, LS & CH
1 hr

Camp Tsavo is operated by Camps International, which supports community and wildlife projects through interaction with adventure tourism. The camp is located in Rukinga Sanctuary, part of the Tsavo Kasigau Wildlife Corridor, a vital wildlife corridor for a large population of elephant and buffalo that migrate seasonally between the parks. The camp is aimed at international volunteers and local school students and interacts closely with the local community. Camp Tsavo is set out like a traditional village. Each rondavel has 8 beds, and is equipped with mosquito nets, bed linen and shelves. The main house has 4 double bedrooms overlooking the sanctuary. There is also a campsite with dome tents and bathroom facilities. Meals are produced from fresh local produce. Camp Tsavo provides an integrated, non-touristy cultural experience. The camp has initiated long-term, sustainable development projects which fall into 3 categories: community, environment and wildlife. Current projects include reconstruction of a rural primary school, including sports facilities and teaching assistance. Other projects include habitat management, waterhole usage, wildlife recording and elephant identification. Camps International was given the Virgin Holidays Responsible Tourism Award in 2008 and won the Eco Warrior Kenya Award for the Most Sustainable Community Based Tourism Enterprise in 2010.

Rockside Camp

Maungu

Rockside Camp, Maunga, 29km from Voi, Kenya
PO Box 5, Voi 80300, Kenya

Tel	+254 20 2041443; +254 20 2041445
Mobile	
Fax	+254 20 2041446
E-mail	info@rocksidecamp.com
Web	www.rocksidecamp.com

    Voi, CH
30 mins

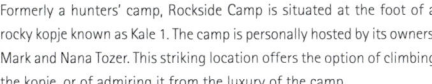

Formerly a hunters' camp, Rockside Camp is situated at the foot of a rocky kopje known as Kale 1. The camp is personally hosted by its owners, Mark and Nana Tozer. This striking location offers the option of climbing the kopje, or of admiring it from the luxury of the camp.
There are 15 en-suite bandas and 8 luxury bungalows. All meals are served in the dining room, an attractive open building centring on a large rock that supports the thatched roof. Barbecues, when the weather is clement, are served under the stars. The bar is well stocked with soft drinks, beers, wines and spirits, its speciality being the Rockside Sunset Cocktail. The swimming pool provides a welcome break from the various activities.

The area is a haven for birdlife: 84 species were spotted in a single morning. A climb up the kopje is highly recommended; from the top, there are panoramic views of the dense bush land of the Taru Desert, Sagalla Hills, Taita Hills and on, a clear day, the top of Mt Kilimanjaro. A guided hike up Mt Kasigau, which has unique flora and fauna, will take a full day. The camp minimises its environmental impact by using solar power and composting food waste.

 Accommodation Guide

Kasigau
Conservation Trust

Kasigau Conservation Trust, Mt Kasigau, nr Tsavo East and Tsavo West
PO Box 364, Voi 80200, Kenya

Tel	
Mobile	+254 710 755225; +254 726 969248; +254 718 567979
Fax	
E-mail	info@kasigauconservationtrust.org
Web	www.kasigauconservationtrust.org

  Moi Intl., LS & CH & Intl.
3 hrs

Nestled in the foothills of Mt Kasigau, Kasigau Conservation Trust is located in the vital wildlife corridor between Tsavo East National Park and Tsavo West National Park. The trust is owned by the community and all proceeds go towards the local community and community projects. The trust offers budget accommodation and cultural activities.

Kasigau Bandas consist of 5 bandas. Each banda has 2 bedrooms, a bathroom, a kitchen and a sitting room. The bandas can be taken on a self-catering basis, or local, traditional meals can be provided.

Cultural visits to the local village are on offer, as are cultural performances by local dancers and singers. Game walks in the area are rewarding; there are plentiful rare plant and birdlife species, including the globally threatened Taita White-eye Zosterops Silvanus. Visitors can also climb Mt Kasigau, which provides stunning views from its peak. Kasigau Conservation Trust's useful contribution to the local community and its local conservation work has been recognised by Ecotourism Society of Kenya. The trust is a Community Based Organisation, CBO.

Sarova Salt Lick
Game Lodge

Taita Hills

Sarova Salt Lick Game Lodge, Taita Hills, Kenya
Sarova Hotels, PO Box 72493, Nairobi 00200, Kenya

Tel	+254 20 2767000; +254 20 2714444; +254 43 30270
Mobile	+254 722 200945/6; +254 734 699751/2
Fax	+254 20 2715566
E-mail	centralreservations@sarovahotels.com
Web	www.sarovahotels.com

VISA, MasterCard, Amex JCB, Diners Club

 Sarova Taita Hills Lodge, CH
15 mins

Sarova Salt Lick Game Lodge is a unique architectural concept consisting of 96 distinctive oval-shaped rooms overlooking a waterhole and salt lick. These special constructions, elevated on stilts, give uninterrupted views of animals in close proximity. Suspended walkways, a tunnel with bunker and special windows ensure close-up viewing of game at the floodlit waterhole at night.

There are 96 rooms on 2 floors, made up of 49 twin, 32 double and 15 triple. All the rooms are en-suite, and have mosquito nets and electric fans.

Bura Restaurant serves international and local cuisine for breakfast and dinner. Vuria Bar and Lounge, a shaded terrace bar overlooking the main waterhole, is open for snacks and drinks from 10am to 11pm. Special meals and functions such as bush breakfast, barbeque lunch or Out of Africa dinner can be arranged at Kudu viewpoint or elsewhere in the sanctuary. The lodge is set in Taita Hills Wildlife Sanctuary, a privately owned conservation area adjacent to Tsavo West National Park. Day and night game drives give guests the opportunity to view the sanctuary's 50 species of mammal and over 300 species of birdlife. Wildlife talks are available on request.

Sarova Taita Hills
Game Lodge

Taita Hills

Sarova Taita Hills Game Lodge, Taita Hills, Kenya
Sarova Hotels, PO Box 72493, Nairobi 00200, Kenya

Tel	+254 20 2767000; +254 20 2714444; +254 43 30540
Mobile	+254 722 200945/6; +254 734 699751/2
Fax	+254 20 2715566
E-mail	centralreservations@sarovahotels.com
Web	www.sarovahotels.com

VISA, MasterCard, Amex, JCB Diners Club

Sarova Taita Hills Lodge, CH 10 mins

Based on the design of a German fortress, Sarova Taita Hills Game Lodge is located in an area rich in World War I history. With its 2 conference rooms and trained staff, this lodge is a good base for meetings, incentives and experiential learning.

The lodge has 62 rooms on 3 floors, made up of 20 twin rooms, 31 double rooms, 9 triple rooms and 2 suites. All the rooms are en-suite with bath and shower, and have balconies overlooking the gardens and the sanctuary. Chala Restaurant, open for breakfast, lunch and dinner, serves international and local cuisine. Taita Bar and Lounge, open from 10am to 11pm, has snacks and drinks. Special meals and functions such as bush breakfast, barbeque lunch or Out of Africa dinner can be arranged at Kudu viewpoint or elsewhere in the sanctuary. Local musicians are also available on request.

The lodge is set in Taita Hills Wildlife Sanctuary, a privately owned conservation area adjacent to Tsavo West National Park. Day and night game drives give guests the opportunity to view the sanctuary's 50 species of mammal and over 300 species of birds. Wildlife talks are available on request.

Lavender Gardens Hotel

Wundanyi

Lavender Gardens Hotel, Wundanyi, Taita Hills, Kenya
PO Box 1295, Wundanyi 80304, Kenya

Tel	+254 20 8091989
Mobile	+254 715 876473
Fax	
E-mail	info@lavendergardenhotel.com
Web	www.lavendergardenhotel.com

VISA, MasterCard

Moi Intl., LS & CH & Intl. 3 hrs

Lavender Gardens Hotel is in collaboration with Mgeno Ranch, Lumo Ranch and Kore Camp. The hotel offers both hotel rooms and homestay accommodation. Conference facilities and a selection of activities are also available. The hotel has 40 en-suite rooms, made up of singles, doubles and triples. The rooms all have balconies with views of Wesu Rock and Taita Hills. The restaurant has an international menu. The bar serves soft drinks, beers and spirits. Catering for cocktail parties and business functions is on offer. The gym has modern equipment and is staffed by a personal trainer. There are 2 fully equipped conference halls, 1 seating 40 pax and the other seating 100.

The hotel provides support, assistance and training to community based tourism in the area, and is affiliated to private homestays providing a total of 100 beds. Homestays give visitors an insight into the life of the people in the region. Transport between the homestays and Lavender Gardens Hotel is provided by the hotel.

Shomoto Nature Trail and Shomoto Caves are a 10-minute walk from the hotel. Other highlights include Mwachora Nature Trail, Taita Hills, Ngangao Forest, Chawia Forest, Mbololo Forest, Sagalla Hills and Lumo Community Wildlife Sanctuary. A 4WD jeep is available for tour packages, or for chauffeur driven private hire.

Lion's Bluff

 Lumo Community Wildlife Sanctuary

Lion's Bluff, Lumo Community Wildlife Sanctuary, Kenya
PO Box 80658, Mombasa 80100, Kenya

Tel	+254 20 3882868
Mobile	+254 733 222420 ; +254 733 222428.
Fax	+254 20 3882868
E-mail	reservations@advantage-ea.com
Web	www.lionsblufflodge.com

VISA, MasterCard   Sarova Taita Hills Lodge, CH 20 mins

Perched high on a bluff, Lion's Bluff appears suspended over Lumo Community Wildlife Sanctuary. Describing itself as the view with a lodge, Lion's Bluff has stunning views to North and South Pare Mountains, Taita Hills and, on a clear day, Mt Kilimanjaro. Lion's Bluff was conceived and built by the local Taita community; every visitor directly benefits the community and ensures the preservation of the sanctuary. There are 12 en-suite bandas, traditionally built of sustainable timber, canvas and coconut thatch. The bandas are linked by timber bridges, and each has a handmade 4-poster bed, mosquito net and balcony with a panoramic view. Fruit and vegetables come from local farmers, many of whom are shareholders in the sanctuary.

Activities are tailor-made to the wishes of the guests, and include day and night game drives. Battlefield tours of World War I sites are recommended. Ornithological walks are remarkable: 600 species of bird have been recorded here. The nature trail provides exciting adventures for children. Cheetah campsite, with kitchen and bathroom facilities, is affiliated to Lion's Bluff; guests camping here can use the facilities and activities of Lion's Bluff. The Lumo Community Wildlife Sanctuary is made up of 3 group ranches, Lualenyi, Mramba and Oza, which have united to preserve this vital wildlife corridor.

KWS, Lake Jipe Bandas

 Tsavo West Ntl. Park

KWS, Lake Jipe Bandas, Tsavo West National Park, Kenya
Kenya Wildlife Service, PO Box 40241, Nairobi 00100, Kenya

Tel	+254 20 6000800; +254 20 6002345; +254 20 3991000
Mobile	+254 726 610508; +254 726 610509; +254 736 663421
Fax	+254 20 6003792
E-mail	kws@kws.go.ke / reservations@kws.go.ke
Web	www.kws.go.ke

     Jipe, CH 15 mins

Owned by the Kenya Wildlife Service, KWS, the Lake Jipe Bandas provide budget accommodation in Tsavo West National Park. The bandas are situated on the shores of Lake Jipe, and have lovely views of the water and the game that frequents it.

There are 3 bandas, each equipped with 2 single beds. The communal bathrooms are external. Bed linen, mosquito nets and kerosene lamps are provided. Jiko barbeques, kitchen utensils and water for cooking are also provided. A resident caretaker lives on site. KWS recommends that guests bring drinking water, gas cooker, candles, torches and insect repellent. Guests will also need to bring food, drink, firewood and charcoal.

Rare species of wildlife found in the park includes wild dog, lesser kudu and nocturnal porcupine. 600 bird species have been recorded, including the threatened corncrake and Basra reed warbler. Highlights of the park are recent volcanoes, lava flows and caves, as well as Mzima Springs. Activities include game viewing, cave exploration and underwater hippo and crocodile watching. From Nairobi, enter through Mtito Andei Gate; from Amboseli enter through Chyulu Gate; from Mombasa enter through Tsavo Gate. Entry to the park is by SafariCard only. Cards may be loaded, but not obtained, at Mtito Andei Gate.

Grogan's Castle

Lake Jipe

Grogan's Castle, 20km from Taveta, nr Tsavo West National Park, Kenya
PO Box 15081, Nairobi 00509, Kenya
Tel
Mobile +254 718 810795
Fax
E-mail langata@mweb.co.za
Web www.kafafa.com/groganscastlekenya

Grogan's Castle, CH
2 mins

Ewart Scott Grogan, who lived from 1874 to 1967, was one of the founding members of the British East African Protectorate. He is remembered for his audacious walk from Cape to Cairo in the late 1890s, which he undertook to win the hand of Gertrude Coleman-Watt.
Grogan built Grogan's Castle in the 1930s, and lived there until the 1950s. The castle, described as part monastery, part Moorish fort and part hacienda, has panoramic views of the Pare Mountains, Lake Jipe, Tsavo West National Park and Mt Kilimanjaro. It remained unoccupied until 2011, when it was refurbished and opened as a hotel.
There are 5 en-suite double rooms, with décor of the early colonial era.

The spacious living room has a selection of books, TV and DVD. The dining room contains Grogan's original dining table; fresh homemade meals are served. There is also a self-catering guest cottage that sleeps 6 pax. Grogan's Castle supports nearby Lumo Community Wildlife Sanctuary. Lake Jipe is thought to have the largest variety of aquatic birdlife in Africa. Other local sites of interest include the Taita Hills with rare species of birds and butterflies. Climbing the rocks at Wesu, Vuria or Eyale gives panoramic views into the Serengeti. The steep climb into Lake Chala, a water-filled extinct volcano, is recommended.

Voyager Ziwani

Ziwani Gate

Voyager Ziwani, Ziwani Gate, nr Tsavo West National Park, Kenya
Heritage Hotels Ltd, PO Box 74888, Nairobi 00200, Kenya
Tel +254 20 4446651; +254 20 4447929; +254 20 4444582
Mobile +254 722 205894; +254 733 411105
Fax +254 20 4446600; +254 20 4446533
E-mail reservations@heritage-eastafrica.com
Web www.heritage-eastafrica.com

Voyager Ziwani, CH
10 mins

On a 30,000-acre private farm on the western edge of Tsavo West National Park, Voyager Ziwani is a tented camp. Sitting on the verge of Ziwa Dam on the Sante River, the camp looks out on the hippos that have made this their home.
There are 25 en-suite tents, 16 on the southern bank of the Sante River and 9 on the northern bank. All tents have double or twin beds, and secluded verandas overlooking the river. The main building, overlooking Ziwa Dam, houses the bar and dining room. Breakfast is served on the veranda. Dinner, which is table d'hote, can be served on the lawn beside the campfire. The camp also has a gift shop with souvenirs and safari essentials.

Activities include day and night game drives, game walks and horse riding. Boating amongst crocodiles and turtles on Ziwa Dam is also on offer. Trips to the twin volcano lakes of Chala and Jipe, and to Grogan's Castle, and tours of the World War I battlefields are available. Local experts give evening slideshows on local culture and wildlife. Romantic sundowners and bush meals can be arranged. The Adventurers' and the Young Rangers' clubs organise activities for children.

Finch Hattons   Tsavo West Ntl. Park

Finch Hattons, Tsavo West National Park, Kenya
PO Box 5623, Nairobi 00506, Kenya

Tel	+254 20 3518349; +254 20 3577500
Mobile	+254 720 444419; +254 735 832453
Fax	+254 20 553245
E-mail	finchhattons@iconnect.co.ke
Web	www.finchhattons.com

Finch Hattons, LS & CH
5 mins

Denys Finch Hatton, an English aristocrat, first travelled to East Africa in 1911 at the age of 24. His name soon became synonymous with elegance, style and adventure. His courage, his charm and his insistence on crystal and fine cuisine while on safari have been recreated in this camp named after him.

Finch Hattons, on a 35-acre concession, surrounds 3 crystal clear pools of a natural freshwater spring. The tents, spread along the water's edge and shaded by yellow barked acacia xanthophlea trees, view the surrounding plains on which a wide variety of game has been sighted.

The camp has 26 twin tents, 4 double tents and 1 Finch Hatton club tent.

All the tents are en-suite, furnished with brass fittings, Swahili chests and antique writing desks, and have large deck balconies.

The elevated pool is filled with filtered mineral water. The country house styled lounge and bar play classical music including Finch Hatton's favourite selection of Mozart. A mezzanine floor houses a cosy library and reading room. An open air terrace, where breakfast and lunch are served, gives views across the springs and hippo pools to the snow capped peak of Mt Kilimanjaro. Dinner is served in the formal dining room.

Severin Safari Camp   Tsavo West Ntl. Park

Severin Safari Camp, Tsavo West National Park, Kenya
Severin, PO Box 82169, Mombasa 80100, Kenya

Tel	+254 41 2111000; +254 41 2111803/4
Mobile	
Fax	+254 41 2111624
E-mail	sales@severinsealodge.com
Web	www.severin-kenya.com / www.severisafaricamp.com

 All major cards   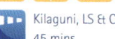 Kilaguni, LS & CH
45 mins

Set in Tsavo West National Park, Severin Safari Camp is an eco-friendly camp overlooking a floodlit waterhole. The camp received an award from TÜV Rhineland in Germany for the quality of its service and its spa. There are 27 en-suite rooms, equipped with WiFi, and spread over 25 hectares of bush land. The 21 octagon tents have private terraces. The 4 concrete-walled junior suites also have a separate lounge, a sundeck with sunbeds and a private courtyard. The 2 suites have lookout decks with views of Mt Kilimanjaro, and are equipped with a corner bathtub and connected to a 2nd tent, making them suitable for families.

The 80m² Baraza conference tent seats up to 30 pax and is equipped with modern communication and presentation technology. The Out of Africa Restaurant offers an à la carte menu, the chef's specialty being chicken and beef prepared on a hot stone or served as fondue. The Thorn Tree Bar has a wide selection of drinks.

Kenbali Spa, with its infinity ying-yang swimming pool, offers therapies in the centuries-old techniques of Southeast Asia. Its open air treatment rooms are peaceful, relaxing havens. Activities include game drives, game walks and trips to Mzima Springs.

Severin Safari Camp holds Ecotourism Society of Kenya's silver award.

Kitani Lodge Tsavo West Ntl. Park

Kitani Lodge, Tsavo West National Park, Kenya
Severin, PO Box 82169, Mombasa 80100, Kenya

Tel	+254 41 2111000; +254 41 2111803/4
Mobile	
Fax	+254 41 2111624
E-mail	sales@severinsealodge.com
Web	www.severin-kenya.com / www.severisafaricamp.com

Kilaguni, LS & CH
45 mins

Kitani Lodge is a collection of self-catering bandas managed by Severin. Guests staying at the bandas are welcome to use the facilities at nearby sister lodge, Severin Safari Camp.

There are 8 thatched bandas, each equipped with double bedroom, bathroom, kitchenette and terrace. Each banda has a private campfire, from which guests can watch passing game. The reception is located at Severin Safari Camp, about 1½km from the bandas. For a surcharge, guests at the bandas are welcome to dine at Out of Africa Restaurant, located at the camp. The restaurant offers an à la carte menu, the chef's specialty being chicken and beef prepared on a hot stone or served as fondue. The camp's Thorn Tree Bar is well stocked with soft drinks, beers, wines and spirits.

Guests at Kitani Lodge are also welcome to use Kenbali Spa, with its infinity ying-yang swimming pool. Use of the pool is complimentary, while the therapies are charged. The spa offers therapies in the centuries-old techniques of Southeast Asia. Its open air treatment rooms are peaceful, relaxing havens. Local highlights include Poachers Point, a scenic viewpoint ideal for sundowners, and Mzima Springs. Both Severin Safari Camp and Kitani Lodge were carefully constructed to minimise their impact on the environment.

Ngulia Safari Lodge Tsavo West Ntl. Park

Ngulia Safari Lodge, Tsavo West National Park, Kenya
Kenya Safari Lodges and Hotels, PO Box 42013 Nairobi 00100, Kenya.

Tel	+254 20 344201-2; +254 20 229751-2; +254 20 311474-9
Mobile	+254 722 203143-4
Fax	+254 20 2222661
E-mail	sales@kenya-safari.co.ke / info@kenya-safari.co.ke
Web	www.safari-hotels.com

Kilaguni, LS & CH
45 mins

Spectacularly situated on the edge of the Ndawe Escarpment, Ngulia Safari Lodge offers panoramic views of the sweeping plains of Tsavo West National Park. The lodge was built in 1969.

There are 52 en-suite standard rooms. All rooms have a balcony with a view of the plains and the floodlit waterholes. The restaurant is open sided to maximise the view of the waterhole and the tree where staff put food out for a resident leopard. It serves buffet breakfast, lunch and dinner. The Main Bar and the Leopard View Bar both serve soft drinks, beers and spirits. The lodge also has a swimming pool and a viewing bay from which to watch animals drinking at the waterhole. A borehole provides plentiful water for both the lodge and the garden.

Local sites of interest include Mzima Springs, inhabited with fish, hippos and crocodiles, Hippo Point, Shetani Caves, Chaimu Lava Flows and Roaring Rocks. Visitors driving from Nairobi should enter Tsavo West National Park through Mtito Andei Gate; those driving from Mombasa should enter through Manyani Gate. The lodge is affiliated to nearby Voi Safari Lodge and to Mombasa Beach Hotel. Packages which combine the 3 lodges are available from Kenya Safari Lodges and Hotels.

Rhino Valley Lodge Tsavo West Ntl. Park

Rhino Valley Lodge, Tsavo West National Park, Kenya
Tsavo Camps and Lodges, PO Box 244, Voi 80300, Kenya

Tel	+254 43 30050
Mobile	+254 721 328567; +254 733 391458
Fax	+254 43 30285
E-mail	tsavocamps@zmail.co.ke
Web	www.tsavocampsandlodges.com

    Moi Intl., LS & CH & Intl.
            2.5 hrs

Set against the backdrop of the Ngulia Hills, Rhino Valley Lodge looks out over Tsavo West National Park. The waterhole in front of the lodge attracts plentiful game. The lodge has been designed to blend in to its surroundings; from a distance it looks almost like another rocky outcrop of the Ngulia Hills.

The lodge offers a variety of levels of accommodation. There are 6 self-catering bandas, each equipped with an en-suite twin room and a well equipped kitchenette. There are 6 en-suite standard rooms, and 10 luxury rock rooms, offering a unique caveman experience. There is also a campsite, with bathroom facilities. The restaurant serves international cuisine. The Tree Bar makes an unusual place to enjoy a sundowner. The lodge also has a gift shop, selling locally made artefacts.

Activities include morning and evening game drives, and game walks. Climbing the Ngulia Hills is recommended; the climb offers enjoyable rock climbing and excellent bird watching, and the views from the top make the climb well worth it. Sundowners at local viewpoints are on offer, as are bush breakfasts and dinners. Conferences, teambuilding activities and prayer retreats can be arranged.

Kilaguni Serena Safari Lodge Tsavo West Ntl. Park

Kilaguni Serena Safari Lodge, Tsavo West National Park, Kenya
Serena Hotels, PO Box 48690, Nairobi 00100, Kenya

Tel	+254 20 2842333; +254 20 2822000; +254 20 2842000
Mobile	+254 733 282200; +254 733 282283; +254 733 2882292
Fax	+254 20 2718102-3
E-mail	cro@serena.co.ke
Web	www.serenahotels.com

            Kilaguni, LS & CH
            10 mins

Kilaguni, meaning young rhino, in the language of the Kamba, is located on a ridge with sweeping views of the Chyulu Hills at the foot of Mt Kilimanjaro. Opened in 1962, Kilaguni Lodge was the first safari lodge ever to be built in a national park. It has been under the management of Serena Hotels since December 1999.

The lodge is located in the middle of Tsavo West National Park. Overlooking a waterhole, the lodge offers the chance of good sightings of game without leaving its viewing decks. The 56 en-suite bedrooms, all with private verandas, have been elegantly renovated using the colours of the African bush: sun-gold, sky-blue and bush-green. The lodge has a broad terrace where guests can enjoy their sundowner while watching spectacular African sunsets. There is also an open air restaurant serving ethnic and international cuisine, several timbered game-viewing decks and a bar hewn out of rock, all with uninterrupted views of the legendary snows of Mt Kilimanjaro and the elephant studded plains.

Activities include game drives, excursions to Mzima Springs, with its crystal clear water welling up from volcanic rocks, the rhino sanctuary, Chaimu Lava Floor, Sheitani Lava and Roaring Rocks, a volcanic hill formation with caves and rocks. Kilaguni Serena holds Ecotourism Society of Kenya's bronze award.

KWS, Kamboyo Guest House
Tsavo West Ntl. Park

KWS, Kamboyo Guest House, Tsavo West National Park, Kenya
Kenya Wildlife Service, PO Box 40241, Nairobi 00100, Kenya

Tel	+254 20 6000800; +254 20 6002345; +254 20 3991000
Mobile	+254 726 610508; +254 726 610509; +254 736 663421
Fax	+254 20 6003792
E-mail	kws@kws.go.ke / reservations@kws.go.ke
Web	www.kws.go.ke

  KWS Park HQ, CH
5 mins

Formerly the warden's house, Kamboyo Guest House has lovely views across Tsavo West National Park. The house is owned by the Kenya Wildlife Service, KWS. It looks out over a waterhole which attracts plentiful game, both during the day and the night.

The house has 4 bedrooms. The master bedroom is en-suite, and has a double and a single bed. The other rooms are a double, a twin and a single. There is a bathroom in the house, and an outdoor shower in the courtyard. The open plan sitting and dining room opens onto the veranda, which has an outside seating area; steps lead from the veranda to the upper wildlife viewing deck. The kitchen is equipped with gas stove, fridge, utensils, cutlery, crockery and glassware. The resident caretaker provides bed linen, towels, mosquito nets, soap and loo paper. There is both electricity and kerosene lamps.

Highlights of the park are recent volcanoes, lava flows, caves and Mzima Springs. 600 bird species have been recorded. Activities include game viewing and cave exploration. Kamboyo Guest House is at the Park HQ, 8km from Mtito Andei Gate. Entry to the park is by SafariCard only. Cards may be loaded, but not obtained, at Mtito Andei Gate.

Campi ya Kanzi
Chyulu Hills National Park

Campi ya Kanzi, Chyulu Hills National Park, Kenya
PO Box 236, Mtito Andei 90128, Kenya

Tel	+254 45 622516
Mobile	+254 720 461300
Fax	+254 20 6005450
E-mail	lucasaf@africaonline.co.ke / bookings@africaunlimited.co.ke
Web	www.maasai.com

 Kanzi, CH
5 mins

The Chyulu Hills, called The Green Hills of Africa by Ernest Hemmingway, provide the setting for the 1,036km² group ranch on which Campi ya Kanzi is situated. The diverse beauty Hemmingway loved is here, from savannah grasslands to green river woodlands, from cool mountain forests to the volcanic hills themselves.

Campi ya Kanzi, Camp of the Hidden Treasure, is a community project with the local Maasai. The first camp to be awarded the Ecotourism Society of Kenya's gold award, this camp was built entirely of local materials, without felling any trees, and has instigated numerous recycling and composting programmes. Its Maasai Wilderness Conservation Trust works to preserve the culture and wildlife of the Maasai with conservation, education and health projects.

The 6 luxury tented cottages and the Hemingway and Simba suites, all set on wooden platforms with thatched roofs and large en-suite bathrooms, have solar hot water and eco-friendly flush loos. Kanzi House, a luxurious private experience, has 3 double and 2 twin rooms, a 18m swimming pool, a Jacuzzi and a swimming pool cottage. Tembo House, constructed of local materials such as lava and grass, is an open plan dining and living room serving Italian cuisine with a panoramic view of Mt Kilimanjaro and the Tsavo Hills.

Ol Donyo Wuas Chyulu Hills National Park

Ol Donyo Wuas, Chyulu Hills National Park, Kenya
Bush and Beyond, PO Box 56923, Nairobi 00200, Kenya

Tel	+254 20 6000457; +254 20 6005108; +254 20 6005980
Mobile	+254 733 330007; +254 723 273668
Fax	+254 20 6005008
E-mail	info@bush-and-beyond.com
Web	www.bush-and-beyond.com

VISA, MasterCard   Chyulus, LS & CH
                   20 mins

Ol Donyo Wuas, in 275,000-acre Mbirikani Maasai Group Ranch on the slopes of the Chyulu Hills National Park, has stunning views of Mt Kilimanjaro. In the path of traditional wildlife migration routes, the lodge is ideally situated to view the abundant wildlife.

The lodge was built in the 1980s and elegantly redesigned in 2008. There are 10 expansive guest suites in 6 villas. Each villa is unique, with opulent décor, high thatched roofs, natural stone walls and private swimming pools. Each suite has a rooftop star bed, sitting room, indoor and outdoor showers and a veranda. The 4-bed villas suit families or friends, and come complete with private vehicle, guide and chef.

As well as day and night game drives and game walks, Ol Donyo Wuas offers an exciting selection of activities. Horse safaris for advanced and novice riders, mountain biking and tracking with bloodhounds are all on offer. An open air log-jam gives guests the chance to view elephants close up. The lodge also organises sleep-outs on the Kopjes at Seduction Rock and fly camping.

The lodge's community outreach programme, managed through Maasailand Preservation Trust, initiates conservation projects including Predator Compensation Fund, Environmental Scouts, Lion Guardians, water management and reforestation.

Hippos at Mzima Springs - Photo © www.sokomoto.com

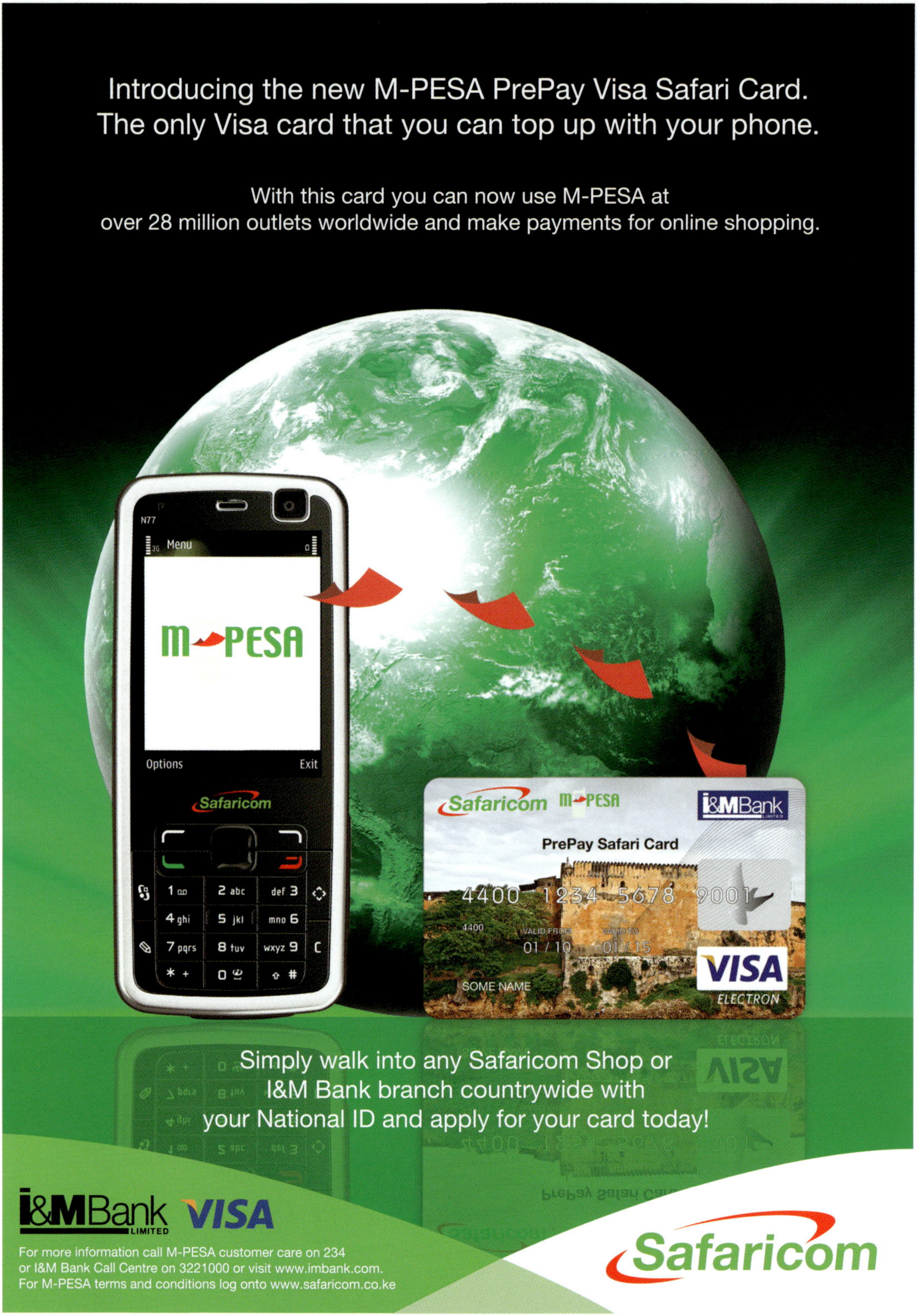
Introducing the new M-PESA PrePay Visa Safari Card.
The only Visa card that you can top up with your phone.
With this card you can now use M-PESA at over 28 million outlets worldwide and make payments for online shopping.
M-PESA
Safaricom
PrePay Safari Card
I&M Bank
VISA ELECTRON
Simply walk into any Safaricom Shop or I&M Bank branch countrywide with your National ID and apply for your card today!
I&M Bank LIMITED
VISA
For more information call M-PESA customer care on 234 or I&M Bank Call Centre on 3221000 or visit www.imbank.com.
For M-PESA terms and conditions log onto www.safaricom.co.ke
Safaricom

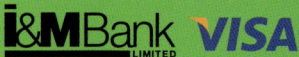

Tsavo East National Park

Mudanda Rock – Photo © www.sokomoto.com

Tsavo East National Park is a vast area of arid bush through which the emerald Galana River meanders. Attractions include dust-red elephants, Aruba Dam, Mudanda Rock, Yatta Plateau and Lugard's Falls. The park became known as the site where the infamous Man Eaters of Tsavo presided over their reign of terror.

Tsavo National Park was established in 1948 and formed one of the largest national parks in the world. The park was later split into East and West, on either side of the Nairobi Mombasa Highway, for administrative purposes. Tsavo East, the larger of the two, has park gates at Mtito Andei, Voi, Buchuma, Manyani and Sala. Park airstrips are Tsavo Gate, KWS Voi, Lugard's, Manyani, Tsavo Safari Camp and Satao. Park fees should be paid to Kenya Wildlife Service, KWS; current rates can be obtained from KWS.

As well as huge herds of dust-red elephants, most of the larger mammals are found here, including rhino, buffalo, lion, leopard, hippo, crocodile, waterbuck, lesser kudu, gerenuk and the endangered hirola. Birdlife is prolific; 500 species have been recorded here.

Aruba Dam, built in 1952, is located on the north bank of the seasonal Voi River. Visited by thousands of animals, the dam makes an appealing game viewing site. Mudanda Rock towers above a rock pool which attracts herds of elephants. At a length of 300km, Yatta Plateau is the longest lava flow in the world, and draws migrating birds from all over the world. Lugard's Falls are named after Captain Lugard, the first proconsul to East Africa. The falls plunge through bizarrely eroded rocks into foaming rapids and crocodile pools.

Activities include game viewing, bird watching, trekking and camping. There is a public campsite at Ndololo, as well as several special campsites that can be booked in advance with KWS.

In 1896, the British began building what was then known as the Uganda Railway, from Mombasa to Lake Victoria. The project, nicknamed the Lunatic Express, was led by Captain John Patterson. During the construction, two maneless male lions developed a taste for human blood, achieving the moniker the Man Eaters of Tsavo. Over a period of three months, while building the bridge over the Tsavo River, about 140 railway construction workers were killed by the lions, an episode immortalised by the film The Ghost and the Darkness. The lions were eventually shot by Patterson.

During World War I, British forces built forts along Tsavo River to counter threats from the invading German army, based in what was then Tanganyika, now Tanzania. Tours of the sites and the battlefields are available.

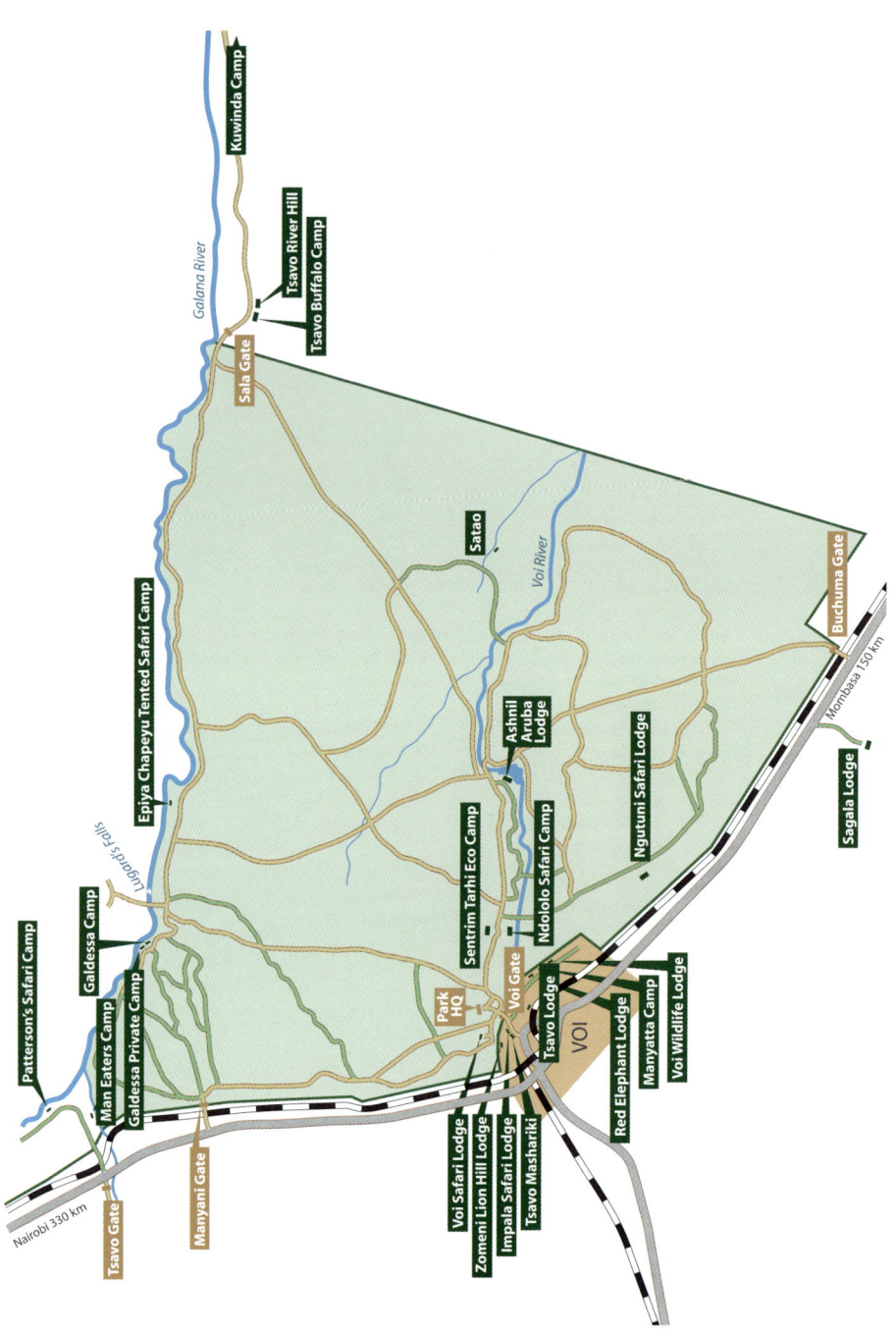

Tsavo Safari Camp Mtito Andei

Tsavo Safari Camp, Tsavo East National Park, Kenya
PO Box 20, Mtito Andei 90128, Kenya
Tel
Mobile +254 729 613210; +254 737 720863
Fax
E-mail tsavosafaricamp@gmail.com
Web www.tsavosafaricamp.com

Tsavo Safari Camp, CH
10 mins

Tsavo Safari Camp nestles between the Athi Galana River and the Yatta Plateau. The camp offers a homely and relaxed atmosphere in the wilderness of Tsavo East National Park.

There are 15 en-suite tents, which can be double or triple as required. All tents are furnished with table, chair and mosquito net, and have a veranda. The bathrooms have views of the Athi Galana River and the Yatta Plateau. The restaurant has an a la carte menu, and serves international cuisine. There is also a swimming pool with sunbathing terrace.

Day and night game drives and bush walks can be arranged with Kenya Wildlife Service rangers. Boat trips on the Athi Galana River and cultural visits to local villages are available. Bush breakfasts and dinners are on offer; sundowners on the top of the Yatta Plateau can be arranged. Tsavo East National Park has a wide variety of wildlife, and about 500 species of birds. Highlights of the park include Lugard's Falls, the Athi Galana River, Mudanda Rock and the Yatta Plateau, Africa's longest lava flow. Further afield, Taita Hills and Sagalla Hills are worth a visit, as are Mzima Springs in Tsavo West National Park.

Please see the map of Tsavo West National Park (page 330) for the location of Tsavo Safari Camp.

Patterson's Safari Camp Tsavo Gate

Patterson's Safari Camp, 9km from Tsavo Gate, Kenya
PO Box 10239, Mombasa 80101, Kenya
Tel +254 20 2021674
Mobile +254 723 752173; +254 733 390787
Fax +254 20 2024552
E-mail info@pattersonsafaricamp.com
Web www.pattersonsafaricamp.com

 VISA, MasterCard    Tsavo Gate, CH
30 mins

During the construction of what was then known as the Uganda Railway, nicknamed the Lunatic Express, two maneless male lions developed a taste for human blood. In 1898, over a period of 3 months, about 140 railway construction workers were killed by these lions while building the railway bridge over the Tsavo River, an episode immortalised by the film The Ghost and the Darkness. Patterson's Safari Camp is named for Colonel John Patterson, who finally succeeded in shooting the man eaters and ending their reign of terror. There are 20 en-suite tents, with verandas overlooking the Athi River and the wildlife that frequents its banks. All tents are furnished in traditional Swahili style and shaded by thatched roofs. The dining room serves international cuisine, with plenty of vegetarian options from locally grown produce. Sundowners are served on the banks of the Athi River. The diverse vegetation and extensive river system attract a high variety of species of wildlife and birdlife; game drives are recommended. Yatta Plateau, an idyllic spot with panoramic views, is the biggest lava flow on earth, and was created over 11 million years ago. Mudanda Rock, a 1½ km long geological spectacle, provides a lovely vantage point from which to watch numerous mammals bathing and drinking in surrounding ponds.

Man Eaters Camp

Tsavo Gate

Man Eaters Camp, nr Tsavo Gate, Kenya
PO Box 445, Nairobi 00621, Kenya

Tel	+254 20 7125741; +254 20 7125742
Mobile	+254 722 201204; +254 734 201240
Fax	+254 20 7125743
E-mail	info@voiwildlifelodge.com
Web	www.voiwildlifelodge.com / www.maneaterslodge.com

   KWS Voi, CH
1 hr

During the construction of what was then known as the Uganda Railway, nicknamed the Lunatic Express, two maneless male lions developed a taste for human blood. In 1898, over a period of 3 months, about 140 railway construction workers were killed by these lions while building the railway bridge over the Tsavo River, an episode immortalised by the film The Ghost and the Darkness.

Man Eaters Camp, which reopened in 2007, is set on the site of this chilling piece of history. The 30 spacious en-suite tents stretch along the Tsavo River, and have views of Tsavo West National Park. The tents are decorated with locally made furniture and linen, and all have balconies with sunbeds.

The names of the facilities pay homage to the story behind the camp. Man Eater's Lounge is adorned with authentic items and memorabilia from the time of the building of the railway. Simba Mbili Bar, or Two Lions Bar, makes a perfect point from which to view the river and the animals that come to it to drink. Lion's Den Boutique offers safari and gift items. The Tsavo River Restaurant serves nouvelle cuisine, including 5-course dinners. The camp also has a rock pool and massage facilities.

Galdessa Camp

Tsavo East Ntl. Park

Galdessa Camp, Tsavo East National Park, Kenya
PO Box 454, Ukunda 80400, Kenya

Tel	+254 40 3202630; +254 40 3202431; +254 40 3202217
Mobile	+254 722 870065
Fax	+254 40 3202218
E-mail	reservations@galdessa.com
Web	www.galdessa.com

      Lugard's, CH, 15 mins
Manyani, CH, 30 mins

On the southern banks of the Galana River, Galdessa Camp is in a cluster of doum palms. This riverside location gives plentiful sightings of the game that frequents the cool water in the heat of the day. The camp overlooks the Yatta Plateau, the world's longest and oldest fossilised lava flow.

There are 11 en-suite semi-tented bandas, on raised wooden platforms with white canvas walls and thatched roofs. Each banda has a bathroom with safari shower and a large veranda. The bandas are well spaced, concealed from each other by foliage, and are designed in natural wood and earthy colours.

Activities are tailored to the requirements of each guest. Game drives, game walks, sundowners and meals in the bush are all on offer. Rare local species include lesser kudu, gerenuk, fringed-eared oryx, Hirola and Peter's gazelle. Galdessa works closely with Kenya Wildlife Service's black rhino reintroduction project, and visits to the conservation project are recommended. 50 black rhino live in the vicinity of the camp, Africa's largest unfenced rhino population.

The camp has been built with as little impact on the environment as possible. It recycles its waste, uses solar power and has a water treatment plant. The camp is closed in May.

Galdessa Private Camp   Tsavo East Ntl. Park

Galdessa Private Camp, Tsavo East National Park, Kenya
PO Box 454, Ukunda 80400, Kenya

Tel	+254 40 3202630; +254 40 3202431; +254 40 3202217
Mobile	+254 722 870065
Fax	+254 40 3202218
E-mail	reservations@galdessa.com
Web	www.galdessa.com

Lugard's, CH, 15 mins
Manyani, CH, 30 mins

An exclusive private camp located a short distance from the main Galdessa Camp, Galdessa Private Camp is a peaceful retreat. The camp can be booked exclusively, giving guests their own dining room and lounge, and the freedom to plan days and meals as and when they wish. There are 3 en-suite semi-tented bandas. All bandas are on wooden platforms, with white canvas walls and thatched roofs, and their bathrooms have safari showers. 2 of the bandas have separate sitting rooms and large private verandas on stilts; these are particularly intended for honeymooners.

Activities are tailored to the requirements of each guest. Game drives, game walks, sundowners and meals in the bush are all on offer. Rare local species include lesser kudu, gerenuk, fringed-eared oryx, Hirola and Peter's gazelle. Galdessa works closely with Kenya Wildlife Service's black rhino reintroduction project, and visits to the conservation project are recommended. 50 black rhino live in the vicinity of the camp, Africa's largest unfenced rhino population.

The camp has been built with as little impact on the environment as possible. It recycles its waste, uses solar power and has a water treatment plant. The camp is closed in May.

Epiya Chapeyu Tented Safari Camp   Tsavo East Ntl. Park

Epiya Chapeyu Tented Safari Camp, Tsavo East National Park, Kenya
PO Box 63269, Nairobi 00619, Kenya

Tel	
Mobile	+254 733 743210; +254 727 869700
Fax	
E-mail	bigi@wananchi.com
Web	www.epiya-chapeyu-camp.com

Lugard's, CH, 20 mins
KWS Voi, CH, 1.5 hrs

Epiya Chapeyu Tented Safari Camp sits on the banks of the Galana River at the foot of the Yatta Plateau, amongst doum palms and acacia trees. The camp is often referred to as Bigi Camp, after the family who built it in 1998 and still manage it today.

There are 15 en-suite tents, which can be double, twin, triple or quadruple as required. The tents are fixed on local flagstone floors and shaded by thatched roofs. All tents are furnished with cupboard, safari chairs and coffee table, and have verandas overlooking the river and the animals that frequent it. Traditional Italian dishes from the Emiglia Romagna region are served. Dishes include tagliatelle, gnocchi and mini pizzas; lunch is often a barbecue served on the dining deck overlooking the river. There is an elevated game viewing platform, with bar service. The camp is keenly eco-friendly. Electricity is supplied by solar power, as well as a generator. Local attractions include Lugard's Falls, Aruba Dam and Crocodile Point. Visitors can do game drives in their own vehicles. The camp has mechanics and tyre repair facilities on site. From Nairobi, enter the park through Manyani Gate; from Malindi or Watamu, use Sala Gate; from Mombasa, use Buchuma Gate.

Voi Safari Lodge

Voi

Voi Safari Lodge, Voi, nr Tsavo East National Park, Kenya
Kenya Safari Lodges and Hotels, PO Box 42013, Nairobi 00100, Kenya
Tel   +254 20 344201-2; +254 20 229751-2
Mobile
Fax   +254 20 2222661
E-mail   sales@kenya-safari.co.ke
Web   www.safari-hotels.com

                                          KWS Voi, CH
                                                              20 mins

On a hillside overlooking Tsavo East National Park, Voi Safari Lodge makes a lovely place from which to watch the wildlife and birdlife of the park. From the lodge, 3 waterholes are visible so guests can see animals coming to drink without leaving the lodge.
There are 50 en-suite rooms, all of which have both bathtub and shower. The main restaurant, with wooden beams and large windows, serves buffet breakfast, lunch and dinner. Tembo Bar serves a selection of soft drinks, beers and spirits. The lodge also has a hide accessed by an underground tunnel, in which guests can get close to the animals without being seen by them. The swimming pool and raised sunbathing terrace have views of the waterholes.
Voi Safari Lodge is within easy reach of Tsavo East and Tsavo West National Parks. It is also an ideal location for exploring the Taita Hills, including the highlands around Wundanyi, which have lovely views all the way to the coast. The lodge is affiliated to nearby Ngulia Safari Lodge and to Mombasa Beach Hotel. Packages which combine the 3 lodges are available from Kenya Safari Lodges and Hotels.

Zomeni Lion Hill Lodge

Voi

Zomeni Lion Hill Lodge, Voi, nr Tsavo East National Park, Kenya
PO Box 249, Voi 80300, Kenya
Tel   +254 20 8030828
Mobile   +254 734 639491; +254 723 231556
Fax
E-mail   info@lionhilllodge.com
Web   www.lionhilllodge.com

                                          KWS Voi, CH
                                                              10 mins

Situated on mlima ya simba, or lion hill, Zomeni Lion Hill Lodge has expansive views across Tsavo East National Park. The lodge is set in bright tropical gardens, and is built from local timber with a thatched roof. It is located near Voi Gate, at the entrance of Tsavo East National Park.
There are 8 en-suite rooms and 4 en-suite tents. The rooms can be double, twin or triple, and are equipped with mosquito nets. The tents have verandas overlooking the park. The lodge is surrounded by an electric fence. The dining room has both indoor and outdoor seating areas. The menu is a combination of continental cuisine and local dishes. Breakfast and lunch are buffet, while dinner is a la carte.

Tsavo East National Park has a wide variety of wildlife species; 500 species of bird have been recorded here. Local highlights include Tsavo River Railway Station, made famous by the man eaters of Tsavo, the true story of man eating lions immortalised by the film The Ghost and the Darkness.

Impala Safari Lodge   Voi

Impala Safari Lodge, Voi, nr Tsavo East National Park, Kenya
PO Box 185, Voi 80300, Kenya

Tel	+254 43 2030282; +254 43 2030316; +254 20 2108174
Mobile	+254 713 817115; +254 731 669577
Fax	
E-mail	info@impalasafarilodge.com
Web	www.impalasafarilodge.com

      KWS Voi, CH
20 mins

Impala Safari Lodge merges the atmosphere of a tented camp with that of a safari lodge. It contains a selection of tents and cottages, set in manicured gardens. At the foot of the Mwakingali Hills, the lodge is located 5km from Voi Gate to Tsavo East National Park.

There are 2 safari cottages, each with 3 bedrooms, and 6 en-suite tents which can be single, double or triple as required. Bush Restaurant, a semi-tented restaurant with terrace, can seat 50 pax and serves breakfast, lunch and dinner. The bar is stocked with a selection of soft drinks, beers and spirits, and equipped with satellite TV showing international news and sports. The swimming pool is surrounded by a sunbathing terrace, with sunbeds, and has a section for children. There is also an outdoor barbecue area.

The animation team provides games and activities throughout the day. Activities include game drives in Tsavo East, Tsavo West and Amboseli National Parks. Nature walks and bird watching are also on offer. Cultural visits to local villages are available, as are sundowners at nearby viewpoints. Weddings and honeymoons are welcome.

Tsavo Mashariki   Voi

Tsavo Mashariki, Voi, nr Tsavo East National Park, Kenya
PO Box 353, Voi 80300, Kenya

Tel	+254 43 2031444; +254 43 2031444
Mobile	+254 735 842043; +254 729 179443
Fax	
E-mail	info@masharikicamp.com
Web	www.masharikicamp.com

 KWS Voi, CH
5 mins

Mashariki, meaning east, is an apt description of this camp which looks east into the sunrise, and offers views across Tsavo East National Park. The camp is operated by the Italian-based Ora Hotel Chain.

There are 3 double tents, 2 triple tents, 1 rock cottage sleeping 4 pax and 1 rock cottage sleeping 5 pax. All rooms are en-suite, have 24-hour electricity and a veranda with a view. Lunch is an international buffet; dinner combines Italian and Swahili dishes. Swahili dishes include beans and coconut soup, chicken curry, coconut rice and nyama choma grilled meats. Mashariki Camp offers a photography course, run by a selection of professional photographers who specialise in bush photography. Jeeps or minivans with drivers can be rented, or guests can drive their own vehicles. Game drives can be done in Tsavo East National Park, with its rolling scrub-covered hills and large herds of elephants, as well as in nearby Tsavo West National Park. Caving in the Lava Flows of Shetani and Chaimu and boat rides on Lake Chala and Lake Jipe are also on offer. A trip to Tsavo Mashariki can be combined with a visit to the coast; the camp is affiliated to Kivulini Beach near Malindi and Twiga Hotel in Watamu.

Tsavo Lodge

Voi

Tsavo Lodge, Voi, nr Tsavo East National Park, Kenya
Tsavo Camps and Lodges, PO Box 244, Voi 80300, Kenya

Tel	+254 43 30050
Mobile	+254 721 328567; +254 733 391458
Fax	+254 43 30285
E-mail	tsavocamps@zmail.co.ke
Web	www.tsavocampsandlodges.com

Moi Intl., LS & CH & Intl.
2.5 hrs

Situated between the centre of Voi and Voi Gate, Tsavo Lodge is ideally situated for those who want to visit Tsavo East National Park, but do not want to stay inside the park.
There are 15 en-suite tents. All tents are furnished with hand-carved wooden furniture and equipped with TV. The dining room serves International cuisine. The bar is well stocked with soft drinks, beers and spirits. Highlights of Voi include its traditional market, held on Tuesdays and Fridays. Also of interest are Voi Commonwealth War Graves Cemetery, Bura Mission and the Tsavo River Railway Station, made famous by the man eaters of Tsavo, the true story of man eating lions immortalised by the film The Ghost and the Darkness. Tsavo East National Park has a wide variety of wildlife, and about 500 species of birds. Highlights of the park include Lugard's Falls, the Athi Galana River, Mudanda Rock and the Yatta Plateau. Further afield, Taita Hills and Sagalla Hills are worth a visit, as are Mzima Springs, in Tsavo West National Park.
Tsavo Lodge is affiliated to Ndololo Safari Camp in Tsavo East National Park and Rhino Valley Lodge in Tsavo West National Park.

Red Elephant Lodge

Voi

Red Elephant Lodge, Voi, nr Tsavo East National Park, Kenya
PO Box 290, Voi 80300, Kenya

Tel	+254 20 2688985
Mobile	+254 727 112175
Fax	
E-mail	office@red-elephant-lodge.com
Web	www.red-elephant-lodge.com

Moi Intl., LS & CH & Intl.
2.5 hrs

Red Elephant Lodge is named for the elephants, red with dust, that roam through Tsavo East National Park. The lodge is located at Voi Gate, just outside the park.
The lodge has 2 wings, containing 12 en-suite double rooms, 2 en-suite triple rooms and the Mini Suite. All rooms are equipped with mosquito nets and fans. The Mini Suite has a double room, single room and sitting room. There are also Bush Houses, private bungalows dotted about the grounds. The thatched restaurant serves a combination of African and European cuisine. Breakfast and lunch are buffet, while dinner is plated. Safari Bar serves soft drinks, beers, spirits and cocktails. During lunch and dinner, a local band, the Taita Traditional Entertainers, performs music from various Kenyan tribes. The small swimming pool is surrounded by a sunbathing terrace. The gift shop sells local souvenirs.
The lodge offers game walks, during which the guides share their knowledge of the tracks and spoors of the animals. Guests are welcome to do game drives in their own vehicles or to book game drives at the lodge. Local highlights include Tsavo River Railway Station, made famous by the man eaters of Tsavo, the true story of man eating lions immortalised by the film The Ghost and the Darkness.

Manyatta Camp

Voi

Manyatta Camp, Voi, nr Tsavo East National Park, Kenya
PO Box 545, Nairobi 00621, Kenya

Tel	+254 20 7125741; +254 20 7125742
Mobile	+254 722 201204; +254 734 201240
Fax	+254 20 7125743
E-mail	info@voiwildlifelodge.com
Web	www.voiwildlifelodge.com / www.manyattacamp.com

      KWS Voi, CH
5 mins

Set on Voi River, on the boundary of Tsavo East National Park, Manyatta Camp enjoys spectacular views of the park. Just off the Nairobi-Mombasa Highway, the camp is in an ideal location for those who want a holiday that combines beach and bush. It is well situated for breaking this journey or for a weekend getaway from the coast or the capital.

There are 24 en-suite tents. Each tent is decorated with African fabrics in earthy colours, and has its own private swimming pool. The verandas, complete with sunbeds, look out on Tsavo East National Park and on Voi River. Meals are served in Twiga Restaurant; the menu combines local and international dishes. Maasai Bar serves soft drinks, beers, wines and spirits, and specialises in the famous African sundowner.

The waterfall swimming pool gives guests the chance to cool off after the arid heat of Tsavo. The Safari Spa offers relaxation and treatments. Tsavorhine Boutique has safari essentials and gift items. Tsavo East National Park is home to some of the largest elephant populations in Kenya. About 500 species of birds have been recorded in the park. Nearby attractions include Lugard's Falls, Mudanda Rock and the Yatta Plateau.

Voi Wildlife Lodge

Voi

Voi Wildlife Lodge, Voi, nr Tsavo East National Park, Kenya
PO Box 545, Nairobi 00621, Kenya

Tel	+254 20 7125741; +254 20 7125741
Mobile	+254 722 201240; +254 734 201240
Fax	+254 20 7125743
E-mail	info@voiwildlifelodge.com
Web	www.voiwildlifelodge.com

       KWS Voi, CH
5 mins

Set on the boundary of Tsavo East National Park, Voi Wildlife Lodge looks out at Kasigau, Sagalla and Mwakingali Hills and has a natural waterhole which often attracts big game.

The lodge has 72 rooms, made up of 16 standard rooms, 32 superior rooms and 24 luxury rooms. All the rooms have spacious en-suite bathrooms and are furnished with African décor. The luxury rooms have, in addition, 2 4-poster beds and balconies with views of the savannah. The rooms close to the lobby have wheelchair access. There are also 20 en-suite tents with twin beds.

Tembo Restaurant and Mandhari Bar view the waterhole and Tsavo East National Park. The Safari Spa Bar is raised on stilts overlooking the waterhole. The Safari Spa contains a steam bath, sauna, Jacuzzi, 5 treatment rooms, a gym and yoga room and a swimming pool. Sports facilities include a volleyball court, 2 badminton courts, a pool table, a table tennis table and a children's outdoor recreation area. The Chinmaya Conference Hall seats 250 pax and the boardroom seats 10. There is also a business centre, temple, church and mosque. Approximately 2 hours' drive from Mombasa, the lodge is ideally situated for those wanting a holiday that combines bush and beach.

Ashnil Aruba Lodge Tsavo East Ntl. Park

Ashnil Aruba Lodge, Tsavo East National Park, Kenya
Ashnil Hotels Limited, PO Box 10557, Nairobi 00100, Kenya
Tel	+254 20 3566970-3; +254 20 556955/46/47
Mobile	+254 717 612499; +254 722 414487
Fax	+254 20 3566974
E-mail	info@ashnilhotels.com / sales@ashnilhotels.com
Web	www.ashnilhotels.com

 VISA, MasterCard   KWS Voi, CH 30 mins

The lodge takes its name from the Aruba Dam, constructed in 1952, a watery oasis that forms an irresistible attraction to the game in the dry Tsavo East National Park. Ashnil Aruba Lodge sits in landscaped gardens on an advantageous watering site overlooking the Aruba dam, its viewing decks offering views of the striking scenery.

The 40 en-suite deluxe rooms, made up of doubles, twins and triples, all have terraces overlooking the plains or the Aruba dam. Some are interconnecting, and some have facilities for the less mobile. There are also 6 en-suite tents, each with a unique view of the dam. The dam provides a beautiful setting for a bush breakfast or sundowner, while the pool is the venue for evening barbecues.

Tsavo East National Park is noted for the rare Hirola and the pancake tortoise. Game drives are done in the visitors' own cars. Ashnil Aruba Lodge recommends trips to the Voi Commonwealth War Graves Cemetery where the caretaker is happy to guide guests through the graves and explain the history around each. Other nearby places of interest include Lugard's Falls and the Athi Galana River, the Buffalo Wallows and Tsavo River Railway Station, infamous site of the man eaters of Tsavo.

Sentrim Tarhi Eco Camp Tsavo East Ntl. Park

Sentrim Tarhi Eco Camp, Tsavo East National Park, Kenya
Sentrim Hotels and Lodges, PO Box 43436, Nairobi 00100, Kenya
Tel	+254 41 2220628; +254 41 2222682
Mobile	+254 735 339920
Fax	+254 41 2230688
E-mail	reservationscastle@sentrim-hotels.com
Web	www.sentrim-hotels.com

 All major cards    KWS Voi, CH 20 mins

In a glade of boskia trees, Sentrim Tarhi Eco Camp is a traditional tented safari camp. The camp offers a selection of activities, both inside and outside Tsavo East National Park.

There are 19 en-suite tents, made up of 4 twins, 8 doubles, 6 family tents and 1 suite. All tents are furnished with cupboard and writing desk and equipped with mosquito net, fan and electrical sockets. All tents also have a veranda with a view. The dining room serves international cuisine. The swimming pool is surrounded by a sunbathing terrace with sunbeds.

Tsavo East National Park has a wide variety of wildlife, and about 500 species of birds. Sentrim Tarhi Eco Camp offers guided game walks.

Highlights of the park include Lugard's Falls, the Athi Galana River, Mudanda Rock and the Yatta Plateau. There are also sites of interest outside the park, including Voi town and its traditional market, held on Tuesdays and Fridays. Voi Commonwealth War Graves Cemetery, Bura Mission and the Tsavo River Railway Station, made famous by the man eaters of Tsavo, are also of interest. Further afield, Taita Hills and Sagalla Hills are worth a visit, as are Mzima Springs, in Tsavo West National Park.

Ndololo Safari Camp   Tsavo East Ntl. Park

Ndololo Safari Camp, 7km from Voi Gate, Tsavo East National Park, Kenya
Tsavo Camps and Lodges, PO Box 244, Voi 80300, Kenya

Tel	+254 43 30050
Mobile	+254 721 328567; +254 733 391458
Fax	254 43 30285
E-mail	tsavocamps@zmail.co.ke
Web	www.tsavocampsandlodges.com

                                                           Moi Intl., LS & CH & Intl.
                                                           2.5 hrs

Set in dense forests on the banks of Voi River, Ndololo Safari Camp is surrounded by a concentration of diverse wildlife and birdlife. The camp has been designed to blend into its environment, and to have as little impact on the environment as possible.

There are 20 en-suite tents, which can be singles, doubles or triples as required. The tents are furnished in a combination of ancient and modern, with hand-carved olive wood furniture and modern amenities. The dining room serves breakfast, lunch and dinner. Barbecues are served in the bush on occasion. The bar has a selection of soft drinks, beers and spirits. The gift shop stocks local artefacts and books.

Activities include day and night game drives, nature walks and bird watching. The forests around the camp are home to big game such as lion, leopard and elephant, as well as a wide variety of bird species. Local specialists at the camp are happy to share their knowledge of local culture, wildlife, the history of Tsavo and the famed man eaters of Tsavo. Conferences, corporate teambuilding activities and prayer retreats can all be arranged.

Ndololo Safari Camp is affiliated to Tsavo Lodge in Voi and Rhino Valley Lodge in Tsavo West National Park.

Ngutuni Safari Lodge   Sagalla Hills

Ngutuni Safari Lodge, nr Tsavo East National Park, Kenya
Rex Resorts, PO Box 5292, Diani 80401, Kenya

Tel	+254 20 2720610; +254 20 2720611; +254 41 2225493
Mobile	+254 722 524708
Fax	+254 20 2720624
E-mail	rhinonbo@africaonline.co.ke
Web	www.rexresorts.com/_africa/_ngutuni_safari_lodge

                                                           KWS Voi, CH
                                                           30 mins

Ngutuni Safari Lodge is in a 10,000-acre private game sanctuary, surrounded on three sides by Tsavo East National Park. The lodge, overlooking a waterhole, is set against the spectacular backdrop of the Sagalla Hills. With thatched roofs, timber decking and furniture made from wood and canvas, the lodge blends traditional African design with the modern comforts of a luxury lodge.

The 48 en-suite rooms all have a double and a single bed. Many of the rooms have interconnecting doors for families. All the rooms have private balconies overlooking the floodlit waterhole. The ground floor rooms are suitable for guests with disabilities.

The restaurant and terrace have panoramic views over the savannah. Kenyan specialties and international cuisine are served. The chef uses locally sourced, fresh ingredients, and makes homemade bread and freshly ground coffee. Meals are either buffet or table d'hote.

The lodge offers morning, afternoon and night game drives. These include riverside circuits beside the Voi River and the viewpoint on Ngutuni Hill, as well as Tsavo East National Park. Visitors with their own vehicles are welcome to do self-drive game drives. The lodge also offers a romantic wedding package, including traditional dancers, game drives, registrar and legal fees.

Sagala Lodge

Sagala Game Sanctuary

Sagala Lodge, Sagala Game Sanctuary, 15km from Voi, Kenya
PO Box 754, Voi 80300, Kenya
Tel
Mobile +254 724 567700; +254 717 562232
Fax
E-mail sagalalodge@hotmail.com
Web www.kenya-sagala-lodge.com

   Voi, LS & CH
30 mins

Sagala Lodge is in Sagala Game Sanctuary, a 5000-acre private sanctuary bordering Tsavo East National Park.

There are 24 en-suite bandas in lush gardens. The bandas are double or twin, and have spacious verandas. The restaurant serves international cuisine; breakfast is buffet, lunch and dinner are a la carte. The bar has a selection of soft drinks, beers and spirits. The lodge also has a swimming pool, campsite, a conference room that seats 100 pax and a gift shop selling local souvenirs and safari essentials. The rooftop terrace has lovely views and can be used for informal meetings.

Safari vehicles can be rented at the lodge, reservations advisable, or guests can use their own vehicles. Game drives can cover the sanctuary as well as both Tsavo East and Tsavo West National Parks. Other activities include bird watching, bush trekking, motorhike safaris and climbing Mt Kilimanjaro. Local highlights include the world's largest baobab tree and the Tsavo River Railway Station, made famous by the man eaters of Tsavo, the true story of man eating lions immortalised by the film The Ghost and the Darkness. Cultural visits to local villages can be arranged. Sagala Hill, famed for the magic rock, caves, traditional prophets, myths and superstitions, offers lovely walks and attractive sundowner spots.

Satao

Tsavo East Ntl. Park

Satao, nr the seasonal Voi River, Tsavo East National Park, Kenya
Satao Camps, PO Box 99726, Mombasa 80100, Kenya
Tel +254 20 2434600-3
Mobile +254 720 600200; +254 721 240840 ; +254 733 622022
Fax +254 20 2434610
E-mail sales@sataocamp.com
Web www.sataocamp.com

 VISA, MasterCard    Satao, CH
10 mins

Built in a semicircle around a waterhole, Satao looks out on the multitude of wildlife that frequents the water. There are 20 en-suite tents, made up of 16 family tents and 4 suites. All tents are constructed of sisal and timber, with thatched roofs, to blend in with their environment. The tents are furnished with locally made beds and African fabrics; the bathrooms have safari showers. The suites have authentic antique writing desks and African style beds and cushions. Each tent has a veranda with a view of the waterhole. The camp welcomes guests with disabilities. It has been refurbished extensively to accommodate those with disabilities, and the vehicles have been redesigned to accommodate wheelchair users.

Lunch is served under a 200-year-old tamarind tree, with a view of the waterhole. Dinner is served in the restaurant. The camp also has a campfire and an observation tower. Each day, 2 game drives are offered, with local guides in well equipped vehicles. Sundowners at a scenic spot near the camp are also available. Tsavo East National Park has a wide variety of wildlife; 500 species of birds have been recorded. From Nairobi, enter the park through Voi Gate; from Mombasa, enter the park through Bachuma Gate. The camp was built using local materials with minimal impact on the environment and has attained Ecotourism Society of Kenya's bronze award.

Tsavo Buffalo Camp

Sala Gate

Tsavo Buffalo Camp, nr Tsavo East National Park, Kenya
Malindi Key Group, PO Box 556, Malindi 80200, Kenya

Tel	+254 42 2130717; +254 42 2130718; +254 20 3873597
Mobile	+254 722 207319; +254 733 368844
Fax	+254 42 2130715
E-mail	info@coralkeymalindi.com / info@malindikey.com
Web	www.coralkeymalindi.com / www.malindikey.com

   Malindi, LS & CH
2 hrs

On the banks of the Galana River, Tsavo Buffalo Camp is adjacent to sister safari camp, Tsavo River Hill. The camp looks out on the river and the wildlife that comes to it to drink.

There are 10 en-suite bungalows, surrounding the campfire. All bungalows have twin beds and mosquito nets. Breakfast, lunch and dinner are served in the restaurant. The bar is stocked with soft drinks, beers and spirits. There is also a relaxation area, overlooking the river. The campfire makes an attractive place to enjoy a sundowner before dinner, while listening to the noises of the hippos and crocodiles in the river.

The camp offers a morning and an evening game drive. Maasai guides also offer game walks that focus on identifying the tracks and spoors of the wildlife. Night game drives outside the park are also available. Tsavo East National Park has an abundance of wildlife; 500 species of birds have been recorded here. Tsavo Buffalo Camp and Tsavo River Hill are part of the Malindi Key Group, and are affiliated to 4 resorts in Malindi. The Malindi Key Group built the St Peter Hospital and donated a school building to the city of Malindi.

Tsavo River Hill

Sala Gate

Tsavo River Hill, nr Tsavo East National Park, Kenya
Malindi Key Group, PO Box 556, Malindi 80200, Kenya

Tel	+254 42 2130717; +254 42 2130718; +254 20 3873597
Mobile	+254 722 207319; +254 733 368844
Fax	+254 42 2130715
E-mail	info@coralkeymalindi.com / info@malindikey.com
Web	www.coralkeymalindi.com / www.malindikey.com

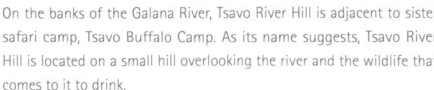   Malindi, LS & CH
2 hrs

On the banks of the Galana River, Tsavo River Hill is adjacent to sister safari camp, Tsavo Buffalo Camp. As its name suggests, Tsavo River Hill is located on a small hill overlooking the river and the wildlife that comes to it to drink.

Tsavo River Hill is a safari lodge. All rooms are en-suite, and furnished with beds and mosquito nets. Breakfast, lunch and dinner are served in the restaurant. The bar is stocked with soft drinks, beers and spirits. There is also a relaxation area, overlooking the river. The campfire makes an attractive place to enjoy a sundowner before dinner, while listening to the noises of the hippos and crocodiles in the river.

The lodge offers a morning and evening game drive. Maasai guides also offer game walks that focus on identifying the tracks and spoors of the wildlife. Night game drives outside the park are also available. Tsavo East National Park has an abundance of wildlife; 500 species of birds have been recorded here. Tsavo River Hill and Tsavo Buffalo Camp are part of the Malindi Key Group, and are affiliated to 4 resorts in Malindi. The Malindi Key Group built the St Peter Hospital and donated a school building to the city of Malindi.

Kuwinda Camp

Sala Gate

Kuwinda Camp, 10km from Tsavo East National Park, Kenya

Tel	+39 339 3425459
Mobile	
Fax	
E-mail	kuwindacamp@gmail.com / kuwindacamp@yahoo.it
Web	www.obligisviaggi.it / http://kuwindacamp.weebly.com

Malindi, LS & CH
2 hrs

Just outside Tsavo East National Park, Kuwinda Camp sits on the banks of the Galana River. This attractive location is suitable for game drives both in and out of the park.

There are 10 en-suite tents, made up of doubles, twins and triples. The tents are shaded by thatched roofs. The main building overlooks the river. Breakfast, lunch and dinner are served in the restaurant on the ground floor. The menu is a combination of Italian, international and local cuisines. There is also a well stocked Italian wine cellar. On the mezzanine level, the observatory is equipped with a powerful telescope. There is also a swimming pool surrounded by sunbathing terrace, and in the evenings, a campfire is lit.

A variety of activities are on offer. Guests are welcome to do game drives in Tsavo East National Park. Night drives and game walks outside the park are also on offer. Fishing in the Galana River is available. Kuwinda Camp is a 2-hour drive from Malindi and a visit to the camp can easily be combined with holidays at the coast.

Red Elephant of Tsavo – Photo © www.sokomoto.com

The Lamu Archipelago

Shela Village – Photo © Tamara Britten

Made up of a collection of idyllic islands at the northern end of Kenya's coastline, the Lamu Archipelago is living history. The Old Town's narrow alleys, Arabic architecture, fort and mosques speak of age old culture, while the surrounding beaches and reefs sparkle in today's sunshine.

There are four main islands: Lamu, Manda, Pate and Kiwayu. The airport is on Manda Island; dhows ferry new arrivals from the pier beside the airport to other islands. There are no vehicles on the islands. Residents and visitors walk, ride donkeys or take boats. The people of Lamu are predominantly Muslim. Activities include dhow cruises, water sports, big game fishing and bird watching. Festivals of interest include the Lamu Cultural Festival in November and the Islamic Festival of Maulidi in February.

Lamu Old Town was designated a UNESCO World Heritage Site in 2001. Stories abound of Chinese ships visiting over a thousand years ago, but the first written testimony of the island dates to 1441, when an Arab traveller met a judge from Lamu in Mecca. Waves of invasions, including the Portuguese, Omani and British, did not hinder the island from becoming a trading centre known for arts, crafts, ivory and slaves. Of interest in the Old Town are the Sultan's Fort, Lamu Museum, Shiaithna Asheri Mosque, German Postal Museum and donkey sanctuary.

Shela Village, on Lamu Island, was established in the 17th century by migrants fleeing the abandoned settlement of Takwa on Manda Island. The charming Swahili village is fringed by a white sand beach. Mnarani Mosque, one of many mosques on the island, is authentic and attractive. Matondoni, in the northwest of Lamu Island, produces the dhows seen gliding between the islands. Kipungani, at the southwest tip of Lamu Island, is a traditional village known for handicrafts and wide expanses of empty beaches.

Takwa Ruins, on Manda Island, are the well preserved remains of a Swahili trading town that flourished in the 15th and 16th centuries before being mysteriously abandoned in the 17th century. The ruins include mosques, tombs and houses, all aligned towards Mecca. Manda Toto Island, just off Manda Island, offers some of the best snorkelling in the archipelago.

Pate Island has a number of historical sites. Pate town is home to the crumbling Nabahani Ruins. Siyu, founded in the 15th century, was once a centre of Islamic scholarship, but is now a simple village dominated by a large fort. Faza was destroyed by Pate in the 13th century, and rose again only to be destroyed by the Portuguese in the 16th century. Kunjanja Mosque, on the creek, is Faza's main attraction.

Kiwayu Island is part of the Kiunga Marine National Reserve, which incorporates a chain of about 50 islands and coral reefs. The reserve provides nesting sites for migratory seabirds, and conserves coral reefs, sea grass and mangrove forests. It is a refuge for sea turtles and dugongs, and home to olive ridley, reef fish, lobsters, sea urchins and starfish. Activities include windsurfing, scuba diving, snorkelling and water-skiing.

LAMU ARCHIPELAGO

KIWAYU ISLAND
- Kiwayu Safari Village
- Champali Camp
- Munira Island Camp

PATE ISLAND

Manda Bay

MANDA ISLAND
- Southern Dream
- The Majlis
- Diamond Beach Village

LAMU ISLAND
- Kizingo
- Kizingoni Beach Villas
- Kipungani Explorer

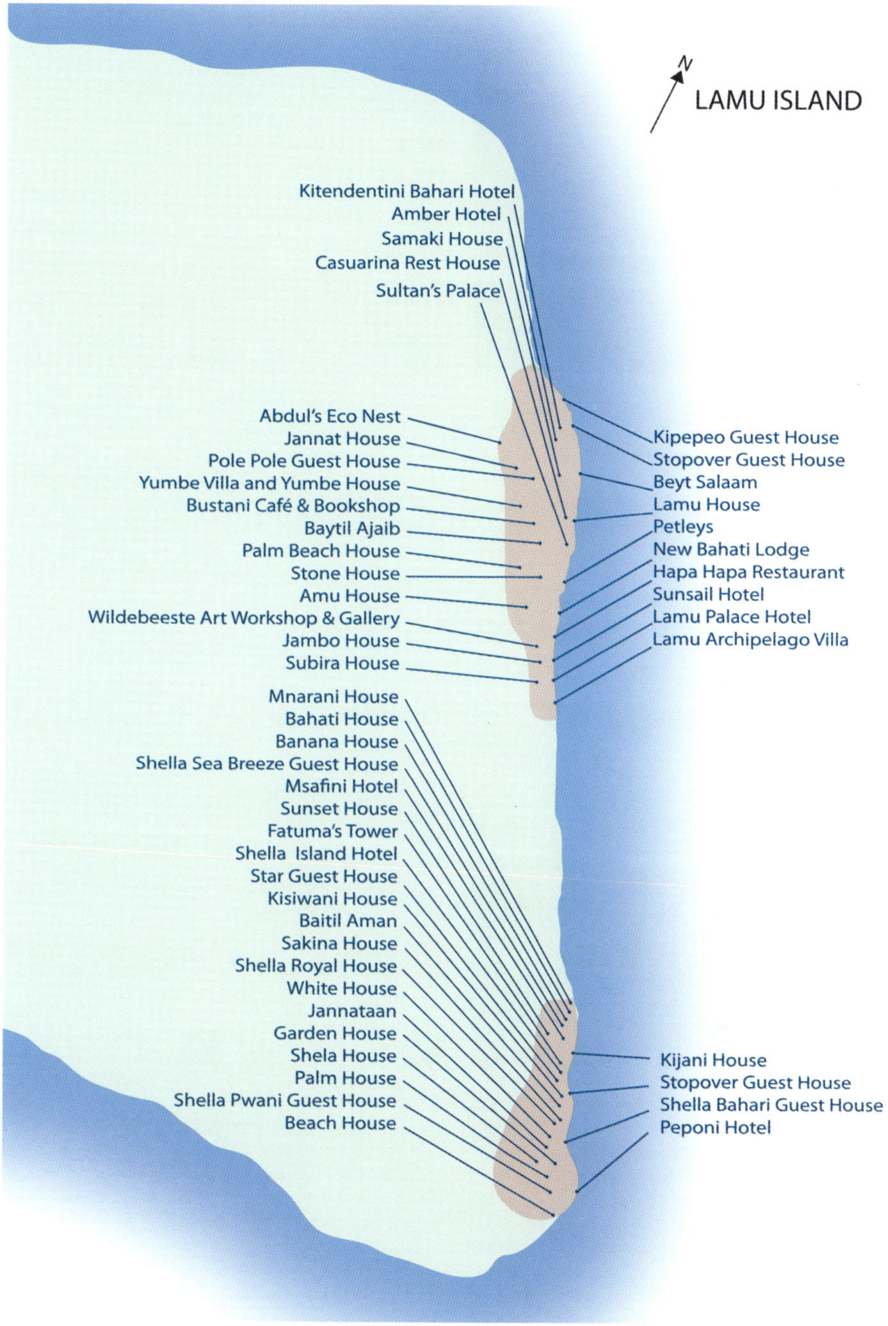

LAMU ISLAND

Map labels (north to south):

- Kitendentini Bahari Hotel
- Amber Hotel
- Samaki House
- Casuarina Rest House
- Sultan's Palace
- Abdul's Eco Nest
- Jannat House
- Pole Pole Guest House
- Yumbe Villa and Yumbe House
- Bustani Café & Bookshop
- Baytil Ajaib
- Palm Beach House
- Stone House
- Amu House
- Wildebeeste Art Workshop & Gallery
- Jambo House
- Subira House
- Kipepeo Guest House
- Stopover Guest House
- Beyt Salaam
- Lamu House
- Petleys
- New Bahati Lodge
- Hapa Hapa Restaurant
- Sunsail Hotel
- Lamu Palace Hotel
- Lamu Archipelago Villa
- Mnarani House
- Bahati House
- Banana House
- Shella Sea Breeze Guest House
- Msafini Hotel
- Sunset House
- Fatuma's Tower
- Shella Island Hotel
- Star Guest House
- Kisiwani House
- Baitil Aman
- Sakina House
- Shella Royal House
- White House
- Jannataan
- Garden House
- Shela House
- Palm House
- Shella Pwani Guest House
- Beach House
- Kijani House
- Stopover Guest House
- Shella Bahari Guest House
- Peponi Hotel

KaribuKenya Accommodation Guide

Kiwayu Safari Village Kiwayu Island

Kiwayu Safari Village, Kiwayu Island, nr Lamu, Kenya
Cheli & Peacock, PO Box 743, Nairobi 00517, Kenya

Tel	+254 20 6004054/3; +254 20 6003090/1
Mobile	+254 724 255374; +254 733 490234
Fax	+254 20 6004050; +254 20 6003066
E-mail	safaris@chelipeacock.co.ke / info@chelipeacock.co.ke
Web	www.kiwayu.com

 VISA, MasterCard   Kiwayu, CH, 10 mins
Manda, LS & CH, 2 hrs by boat

In the Lamu Archipelago, between the Kiunga Marine National Reserve and the Dodori Forest Reserve, lies a coastline rich in extraordinary marine life. Green turtles are seen daily swimming in the bay in front of the lodge, their nestlings hatching mainly in July, August and September. Humpback whales can be seen during October, and dolphins from November to March. Kiwayu Safari Village has been family owned since 1973. Through its Kibodo Trust, Kiwayu works to protect the indigenous coastal woodland, the mangrove ecosystem, the coral reef, the marine life and the local Boni people. There are 18 beachfront bandas, each with a spacious en-suite bedroom, dressing area and sheltered veranda and 1 family banda, consisting of 2 connecting bandas. Baobabs of Kitangani is an en-suite double or twin bedroom and sitting room with private seating and dining area on the beach. The spacious cottages, handcrafted from local materials, are spread out along 1km of private sandy shoreline, ensuring guests experience tranquillity and privacy.

Guests can relax and enjoy the view or they can plunge into the many activities on option. Choices range from guided bird walks to deep sea fishing, from dhow cruises to windsurfing, from mangrove canoe trips to scenic flights.

Champali Camp Kiwayu Island

Champali Camp, Kiwayu Island, nr Lamu, Kenya
PO Box 60, Lamu 80500, Kenya

Tel	
Mobile	+254 724 706928; +254 719 368033; +254 724 983147
Fax	
E-mail	info@champali.co.ke / bookings@champali.co.ke
Web	www.champali.co.ke

     Kiwayu, CH, 10 mins
Manda, LS & CH, 6 hrs dhow
2 hrs speedboat

Champali Camp is an eco-friendly bush home on Kiwayu Island. Situated on mangrove creeks, the camp is on a pristine stretch of beach. The rustic camp is built from mangrove poles and palm thatch. It is managed by Kiwayu community members; a percentage of the camp's profit supports the local community and Kiunga Marine National Reserve.

There are 3 en-suite bandas, made up of 2 family bandas and 1 double banda. The bandas are equipped with fan and mosquito net. The bathrooms have long drop loos and safari showers. The mess tent is spacious and comfortable; the kitchen is equipped with gas cooker, oven, fridge and cooler box. Electricity is provided by solar and wind power. Food is not provided; the chef prepares food brought by guests.

Champali Camp is ideally situated for exploring the mangrove creeks, the many beaches and the marine reserve. The camp has 2 kayaks; 2 fully equipped deep sea fishing boats are available for charter. Big Beach, on the eastern side of the island, suits kite surfing; windsurfers and kite surfers should bring their own equipment.

Kiwayu is 6 hours from Lamu by dhow and 2 hours from Lamu by speedboat. Visitors are advised to bring food, drinks, water sports equipment, sun protection, first aid and mobile telephone.

Munira Island Camp Kiwayu Island

Munira Island Camp, Kiwayu Island, nr Lamu, Kenya
PO Box 40088, Nairobi 00100, Kenya

Tel	+254 20 512213
Mobile	+254 718 004920
Fax	+254 20 512543
E-mail	bigblue@africaonline.co.ke
Web	www.mikescampkiwayu.com

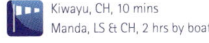
Kiwayu, CH, 10 mins
Manda, LS & CH, 2 hrs by boat

Munira Island Camp, also known as Mike's Camp, is on the beautiful and remote Kiwayu Island. It opened in 1992, and has remained since then in the hands of Mike Kennedy, who still hosts the camp personally. There are 7 en-suite thatched bandas, made up of 6 doubles and 1 family banda. 6 bandas have safari showers and 1 has running water and outside baths. The bandas are built from local materials such as palm fronds, and furnished with simple beach furniture and local fabrics. This eco-camp is powered by wind and solar, and uses water brought by donkey. The central living area is decorated with local flip flop art. Sunset Bar, overlooking the mangroves, serves cold beers and fresh fruit juices. The chef serves fresh seafood, salads, Swahili dishes and organic meats.

The island is an ideal destination for relaxation and also offers a wide selection of activities. Water sports include snorkelling, water-skiing, scuba diving, windsurfing, sand yachting, boogie boarding and kite flying. The camp has a state of the art deep sea fishing boat and 2 motorised sailing dhows; long and short-term excursions are available. Long uninhabited beaches offer private walks and bird watching. There is a 24hr rescue service. The camp is closed during May and June.

Kipepeo Guest House Lamu Town Seafront

Kipepeo Guest House, Seafront, Lamu Old Town, Kenya
PO Box 14, Lamu 80500, Kenya

Tel	+254 424 633569
Mobile	+254 722 559436; +254 720 749811
Fax	
E-mail	mamakipepeo@yahoo.com / request@kipepeo-lamu.com
Web	www.kipepeo-lamu.com

Manda, LS & CH
20 mins

On the seafront of Lamu Old Town, Kipepeo Guest House is a whitewashed building overlooking the sea. The guesthouse opened in 2005.

There are 5 rooms, 4 of which are en-suite, and 1 which has a private bathroom next to it. There are also 2 apartments, 1 on the ground floor and the other on the rooftop. All the rooms have homemade Lamu bed, table and chair, as well as fridge, kettle and a selection of books. On the 1st floor there is a communal galley kitchen equipped with a gas cooker, and a communal balcony with a sea view. The ground floor apartment has wheelchair access. It has its own kitchen, equipped with gas cooker, fridge and freezer, the beds are lower, to suit guests with disabilities, and the shower is extra large. The rooftop terrace has lovely views; barbecues can be arranged here on request.

Kipepeo Guest House has its own boats: boat trips, fishing trips and airport transfers can be arranged. It also has a garden on the mainland at Kipilana which guests are welcome to visit. The garden produces vegetables such as tomatoes and cucumber, as well as fruits including papaya and watermelon. Goats and sheep are reared here.

Stopover Guest House Lamu Town Seafront
Lamu Old Town

Stopover Guest House, Seafront, Lamu Old Town, Kenya
PO Box 59, Lamu 80500, Kenya

Tel
Mobile   +254 714 450801; +254 731 509760
Fax
E-mail   stopoverlamu@yahoo.com
Web

Manda, LS & CH
20 mins

Established in 2009, Stopover Guest House is a new house built in Lamu traditional architectural style. The house is whitewashed, and the furniture was handmade by the grandfather of the owner, the famous Abdalla whose portrait hangs in the Lamu Museum.

There are 8 en-suite rooms, including 2 suites. All the rooms have 4-poster bed, Lamu table, chair, fan and mosquito net; 3 of the rooms have private balconies with views of the sea. The bathrooms are fully tiled and have solar heated water. The ground floor room is suitable for a wheelchair. The house is adorned with local artwork and crafts such as lamps, chests and receptacles. Meals are served on the rooftop, with wonderful views across the sea towards Manda Island. It is partially shaded by a thatched roof, and furnished with Lamu sofa, sunbeds and a dining table and chairs. The menu combines traditional Swahili food, seafood and international dishes, and includes fishcakes, prawn pilau, grilled lobster and shish kebab.

Activities include boat trips with local captains and tours of Lamu Old Town. Stopover Guest House can also arrange longer excursions, such as trips to Takwa Ruins, visits to neighbouring islands, fishing and scuba diving.

Beyt Salaam Lamu Town Seafront

Beyt Salaam, Seafront, Lamu Old Town, Kenya
PO Box 41507, Mombasa 80100, Kenya

Tel   +254 41 2225471;
Mobile   +254 722 781150; +254 734 781111
Fax   +254 41 2225471
E-mail   reservations@beytsalaamlamu.com
Web   www.beytsalaamlamu.com

Manda, LS & CH
20 mins

Beyt Salaam, meaning house of peace, is an attractive house which combines traditional Arabian and Swahili styles with modern facilities. The hotel opened in 2010, and overlooks the seafront.

There are 4 en-suite double rooms. Ndau room is on the ground floor, Pate and Siyu rooms are on the 1st floor and the spacious Shela suite is on the 2nd floor. All rooms have aircon, fan, desk, telephone, terrace and sea view. The furniture has been handcrafted in traditional Lamu style; particularly of note are the heavy Lamu doors and the intricately carved dressing tables. Breakfast is served on the 3rd floor rooftop terrace, with views of the sea. Lunch and dinner can be provided with advance notice. The chef creates Swahili dishes or international cuisine, as required. Dinner can also be served on a dhow, for a surcharge. Electricity is provided by solar power.

The hotel staff can assist with booking water sports, including snorkelling, scuba diving, windsurfing and deep sea fishing. Dhow cruises to Takwa Ruins, Siyu Island and Pate Island can also be arranged. Tours of Lamu Old Town and Lamu Museum are on offer. The hotel can also book safaris, excursions and trips to destinations around Kenya.

Lamu House

Lamu Town Seafront

Lamu House, Seafront, Lamu Old Town, Kenya
PO Box 471, Lamu 80500, Kenya

Tel	+254 424 633491
Mobile	
Fax	+254 424 633492
E-mail	info@lamuhouse.com
Web	www.lamuhouse.com

VISA, MasterCard   Manda, LS & CH
                          15 mins

In charming Swahili architecture, Lamu House is an elegant fusion of traditional style and modern facilities. The house faces directly onto Lamu seafront, and is made up of 2 restored houses surrounding a central courtyard with swimming pool.

There are 10 en-suite rooms, made up of 4 singles and 6 doubles. One wing of the hotel, made up of 5 rooms including the rooftop superior suite, can be rented as a private house, and comes with private plunge pool and courtyard. The rooms are individually designed, and all are equipped with spacious bathroom, dressing room, WiFi and private terrace. Moonrise Restaurant serves international cuisine, including spicy ginger crab casserole baked in its shell, tuna carpaccio, T-bone steak, chicken and banana curry and frozen chocolate mousse with passion topping. The fully stocked bar serves cocktails such as Manda Island, Frozen Daquiri and Tequila Sunrise.

Body Wave Spa, on the rooftop, offers aromatherapy massage, reflexology, facial, manicure and pedicure. Lamu House has 2 traditional Swahili dhows, each comfortably seating 10 pax and available for short or full day excursions. Other activities include tours of the Old Town, museums and dhow shipyard. Panoramic flights, scuba diving and deep sea fishing can also be arranged.

Petleys

Lamu Town Seafront

Petleys, Seafront, Lamu Old Town, Kenya
PO Box 421, Lamu 80500, Kenya

Tel	+254 424 632260; +254 424 633164
Mobile	+254 724 251955
Fax	+254 424 633104
E-mail	lamuparadise@africaonline.co.ke
Web	www.lamuparadiseholidays.com

VISA, MasterCard   Manda, LS & CH
                          15 mins

Directly opposite the jetty, Petleys is a landmark on the Lamu seafront. The tall whitewashed building has attractive rooms, a swimming pool with terrace and a glass-fronted rooftop bar with views across the sea. There are 11 en-suite rooms and a penthouse. The rooms all have aircon, and are furnished with Lamu 4-poster beds, antique furniture and artefacts. The penthouse has a twin and a double room and a rooftop with a view over the sea. The rooftop bar has ceiling to floor windows and overlooks the sea. It serves bar snacks and full meals, such as pizza, seafood and steak. It is fully stocked with soft drinks, beers, wines and spirits. The ground floor bar, under different management, has music, satellite TV and a selection of beers and spirits. Petleys uses a combination of solar power and mains power. Lamu Palace Hotel has WiFi; guests from Petleys are welcome to use it.

Activities include a tour of Lamu Old Town, boat trips, fishing, sailing and donkey rides. A masseuse is available and a local doctor is on call. The hotel is close to Lamu Museum, the donkey sanctuary and all the seafront shops and restaurants. Petleys is affiliated to Lamu Palace Hotel and Sultan's Palace.

New Bahati Lodge — Lamu Town Seafront

New Bahati Lodge, Seafront, Lamu Old Town, Kenya
PO Box 260, Lamu 80500, Kenya
Tel
Mobile +254 714 934804
Fax
E-mail bushgardenrest@yahoo.com
Web

         Manda, LS & CH
                                                  15 mins

Previously called Tausi Guest House, New Bahati Lodge is a thatched building on the seafront of Lamu Old Town. The lodge is attached to Bush Gardens Restaurant; its reception is in the restaurant and its rooms are entered through the restaurant.
There are 5 en-suite double rooms and a rooftop honeymoon suite. All rooms have fan and mosquito net. Bush Gardens Restaurant, owned by the charismatic Bush, specialises in seafood, including deep fried squid, prawns and fish. Fresh juices and shakes are available; no alcohol is served. Outdoor catering and birthday parties can be arranged. The sister cyber café is in Lamu Old Town, a short distance from Bush Gardens Restaurant.

The Raspberry Boat is fully equipped with snorkelling gear and fishing equipment. Day trips can be arranged and lunch is served on board. Sundowner cruises and other boat trips are also available. The convenient seafront location near the jetty makes this ideal for booking boat trips, and for the shuttle boat service to the airport. It is also close to Lamu Museum, the donkey sanctuary and all the seafront shops and restaurants.

Hapa Hapa Restaurant — Lamu Town Seafront

Hapa Hapa Restaurant, Seafront, Lamu Old Town, Kenya
PO Box 213, Lamu 80500, Kenya
Tel
Mobile +254 722 773926
Fax
E-mail hapahaparestaurant@yahoo.com
Web

         Manda, LS & CH
                                                   15 mins

On the seafront of Lamu Old Town, Hapa Hapa Restaurant offers fresh seafood and budget accommodation. The reception for the rooms is in the restaurant, and the rooms are entered through the restaurant.
There are 5 en-suite double rooms. Each room has a fan and mosquito net. The restaurant serves a selection of international dishes, vegetarian options and seafood, and includes dishes such as pan fried prawns, seafood platter and seafood spaghetti. A small bar serves soft drinks; no alcohol is served. A local artist exhibits and sells his paintings in the restaurant, including pictures of Lamu scenes, traditional dancing and local customs. There is also a book swap, with a selection of books for

sale, swap or rent, and a curio stall.
Hapa Hapa Restaurant works with Ahadi Group, and through them can organise tours, fishing and boat trips. The restaurant is also connected to the Red Cross, and can assist in case of medical emergency. The convenient seafront location near the jetty makes this ideal for booking boat trips, and for the shuttle boat service to the airport. It is also close to Lamu Museum, the donkey sanctuary and all the seafront shops and restaurants.

Sunsail Hotel   Lamu Town Seafront

Sunsail Hotel, Seafront, Lamu Old Town, Kenya
PO Box 400, Lamu 80500, Kenya

Tel	+254 424 632065
Mobile	+254 722 666303
Fax	+254 424 632077
E-mail	sunsailhotel@gmail.com / sunsailhotel@yahoo.com
Web	

 VISA   Manda, LS & CH 15 mins

Sunsail Hotel, on the seafront of Lamu Old Town, is a building whose history of trading befits an island that was for many years a vital Arab trading post. The building belonged to the MacKenzie family, and was originally a sugar depot.

There are 17 en-suite double rooms. 15 rooms have fans and 2 are equipped with aircon. The 6 ground floor rooms are suitable for guests with disabilities. The 1st and 2nd floors have communal balconies overlooking the sea. The rooftop has an open sided conference hall that seats 200 pax. Conference equipment including projector, laptop and PA system are all available. The restaurant can serve buffet or a la carte, as required. The menu includes seafood platter, spaghetti bolognaise, fish kebab with lemon sauce and fried banana in hot chocolate sauce. Swahili dinners can be arranged on request. No alcohol is served. The whole hotel is equipped with WiFi.

The convenient seafront location near the jetty makes this ideal for booking boat trips, sunset cruises and excursions to other islands, as well as for the shuttle boat service to the airport. The hotel is also close to Lamu Museum, the donkey sanctuary and all the seafront shops and restaurants.

Lamu Palace Hotel   Lamu Town Seafront

Lamu Palace Hotel, Seafront, Lamu Old Town, Kenya
PO Box 421, Lamu 80500, Kenya

Tel	+254 424 633164; +254 424 633272
Mobile	+254 723 593292; +254 724 251955
Fax	+254 424 633104
E-mail	lamuparadise@africaonline.co.ke
Web	www.lamuparadiseholidays.com

 VISA, MasterCard    Manda, LS & CH 15 mins

Lamu Palace Hotel is a whitewashed building with thatched roof, located directly on the seafront in Lamu Old Town.

There are 22 en-suite rooms and 1 suite. The rooms are all furnished with Lamu 4-poster beds. They are on the 1st and 2nd floors; both floors have communal sea facing balconies. The suite has minibar, satellite TV, kettle and 24-hour room service. There is WiFi throughout the hotel. The ground floor restaurant serves a wide variety of African and international cuisine, as well as Japanese tepanyaki and Italian pizza. Dishes include tuna sashimi, calamari allegro, grilled lobster, chateaubriand and crispy soya chicken. The bar is fully stocked with soft drinks, beers, wines and spirits, furnished with comfortable sofas and adorned with local artefacts. Sheesha pipes are available.

Activities include a tour of Lamu Old Town, boat trips, fishing, sailing and donkey rides. A masseuse is available and a local doctor is on call. The hotel is close to Lamu Museum, the donkey sanctuary and all the seafront shops and restaurants. Lamu Palace Hotel is affiliated to Petleys and Sultan's Palace.

Lamu Archipelago Villa
Lamu Town Seafront

Lamu Archipelago Villa, Seafront, Lamu Old Town, Kenya
PO Box 339, Lamu 80500, Kenya

Tel	+254 424 633247
Mobile	+254 721 108650; +254 725 010578; +254 726 333331
Fax	+254 424 633247
E-mail	mohamedshariff@live.com
Web	

    Manda, LS & CH
15 mins

A whitewashed building with a thatched roof, Lamu Archipelago Villa offers budget accommodation on the seafront of Lamu Old Town. Each floor has a communal balcony with attractive views, overlooking the waterfront. There are 13 en-suite rooms, made up of 6 singles, 6 doubles and 1 triple. A single room has a small double bed, while a double room has a double and single bed. Each room has fan, mosquito net, dressing table and 4-poster bed. The bathrooms are fully tiled and have cold showers. From the entrance at street level, stairs lead to the reception on the 1st floor. The rooms are on the 1st and 2nd floors. Full English breakfast is served at 7.30am and is included in the rate. Lunch and dinner are not served. The convenient seafront location makes this ideal for booking boat trips, and for the shuttle boat service to the airport. It is also close to Lamu Museum, the donkey sanctuary and all the seafront shops and restaurants.

Kitendentini Bahari Hotel
Lamu Main Street

Kitendentini Bahari Hotel, behind Lamu County Council, Kenya
PO Box 298, Lamu 80500, Kenya

Tel	+254 424 633172
Mobile	+254 721 903835; +254 716 582521
Fax	
E-mail	
Web	

    Manda, LS & CH
20 mins

Behind Lamu County Council, Kitendentini Bahari Hotel is in a convenient location for the shops and buildings of the Main Street, and for Lamu Museum and donkey sanctuary. The hotel offers budget accommodation, around a central courtyard with pot plants and coral walls.
There are 21 en-suite rooms. The rooms are furnished with double and single beds, fridge, fan, table and chair. The shower water is not heated, but the water tank is on the roof and is kept warm by the sun. The ground floor dining room looks out on the central courtyard, and serves both buffet and a la carte. No alcohol is served. There is a safe room where guests are welcome to store their valuables. The rooftop terrace is furnished with wicker chairs, and has a view over the rooftops to the sea and the cluster of boats at the shore.
A local boat captain is affiliated to the hotel. He offers fishing, snorkelling and sunset cruises, as well as excursions to Matondoni village, Manda Toto and Takwa Ruins. Tours of Lamu Old Town are also on offer. The hotel has a noticeboard with information about local events and activities.

Amber House  Lamu Main Street

Amber House, Main Street, Lamu Old Town, Kenya
PO Box 24963, Nairobi 00502, Kenya

Tel	+254 20 891856; +254 20 890140; +254 20 891296
Mobile	+254 722 434965; +254 733 600184
Fax	+254 20 890674
E-mail	penny@pennywinter.com
Web	www.pennywinter.com

      Manda, LS & CH
20 mins

Amber House, in the heart of Lamu Old Town, is estimated to be 400 years old. The house has been fully restored in traditional style with a contemporary edge. The house is fully staffed and is taken on a self-catering basis. There are 3 en-suite rooms. The master bedroom has its own private terrace and dining area. The house is designed around a tranquil courtyard and also has a plunge pool and a rooftop terrace with views over Old Town. The rooms and sitting areas are adorned with Swahili furniture, antiques, brass and handwoven throws.

The chef creates dishes from fresh local produce. He specialises in traditional coastal Swahili dishes, such as Zanzibar fish soup, ginger crab and Swahili fish curry with fresh coconut. He is also happy to prepare western dishes and children's meals. Guests are welcome to discuss their food preferences with him. The chef will provide soft drinks and beers; guests are requested to bring their own wines and spirits.

The staff are happy to organise activities and tours in and around Lamu. A tour of Old Town, fort and museum gives an insight into Swahili and Arabic history. A dhow boat trip or speedboat trip around the islands is also available. Snorkeling at Manda Toto, lunch on a beach and sundowners on a dhow can all be arranged.

Samaki House Lamu Main Street

Samaki House, Main Street, Lamu Old Town, Kenya
PO Box 457, Lamu 80500, Kenya

Tel	+33 493 083705
Mobile	+254 724 696739; +254 710 127508
Fax	
E-mail	connect2design@gmail.com
Web	www.freewebs.com/lamu/

      Manda, LS & CH
15 mins

Originally an Arab trader's house, Samaki House is a beautifully restored traditional Lamu house. The décor includes ornate plasterwork, timber decorative screens, carved entrance doors, painted timberwork beams and polished plaster finishes. Samaki House, Swahili for fish house, is furnished with antiques and local artefacts, and looks out directly on the seafront. There are 4 en-suite double rooms, each with sitting area or terrace. The master bedroom has a dressing room and a private terrace with plunge pool. All the rooms have their own character, and are equipped with 4-poster bed, mosquito net and fan. The house is on 4 levels with terraces on each level. The main upper terrace is ideal for relaxation and entertaining, and has panoramic views of the sea and Lamu Old Town. A covered terrace within the courtyard garden is shaded by starfruit and guava trees.

The house is fully staffed and includes a chef who prepares the seafood or other dishes guests prefer. The kitchen is fully equipped, including freezer, fridge, toaster and microwave. Water is heated by solar power; there is also an electrical backup system. The house is ideally situated for strolls around Lamu Old Town and along the waterfront. Boat trips, fishing and snorkelling can be arranged with local captains.

Casuarina Rest House Lamu Main Street

Casuarina Rest House, nr Seafront, Lamu Old Town, Kenya
PO Box 10, Lamu 80500, Kenya
Tel +254 424 633123
Mobile
Fax
E-mail kaluc36@yahoo.com
Web

   Manda, LS & CH
15 mins

Casuarina Rest House offers budget accommodation on the seafront. The entrance is at the side of the house; stairs lead up to the reception on the 1st floor.
There are 10 rooms, 4 of which are en-suite and 6 with shared bathrooms. The rooms have either double bed, double and single bed, or 3 single beds. Each floor has a shared balcony overlooking the shore and boats. There is also a rooftop with attractive views, furnished with tables and benches. No food or drink is served; guests are welcome to bring their own and eat on the rooftop. There is a noticeboard with some local information on it. A local boat captain is affiliated to the rest house, and offers boat trips, fishing and sundowner cruises. A town guide is available for tours of Lamu Old Town. The convenient seafront location makes this ideal for booking boat trips, and for the shuttle boat service to the airport. It is also close to Lamu Museum, the donkey sanctuary and all the seafront shops and restaurants.

Sultan's Palace   Lamu Main Street

Sultan's Palace, Main Street, Lamu Old Town, Kenya
PO Box 421, Lamu 80500, Kenya
Tel +254 424 632260; +254 424 633272
Mobile +254 724 251955
Fax +254 424 633104
E-mail lamuparadise@africaonline.co.ke
Web www.lamuparadiseholidays.com

   Manda, LS & CH
20 mins

Sultan's Palace is a traditional Lamu house, estimated to be 100 years old. The building was renovated and converted to a hotel, and opened in 2004. It is affiliated to Petleys and Lamu Palace Hotel, both of which are on Lamu seafront.
There are 4 en-suite rooms and 2 penthouses. The rooms are furnished with Lamu 4-poster beds, table and chair. The hotel serves breakfast; room service can be ordered from Lamu Palace Hotel. Both Petleys and Lamu Palace Hotel have restaurants which can be used by guests of Sultan's Palace. Petleys has a rooftop bar with views over the sea, which can be used by guests of Sultan's Palace. A selection of books in an aged canoe bookcase is available for the use of guests. Lamu Palace Hotel has WiFi; guests from Sultan's Palace are welcome to use it.
Activities include a tour of Lamu Old Town, boat trips, fishing, sailing and donkey rides. A masseuse is available and a local doctor is on call. The hotel is close to Lamu Museum, the donkey sanctuary and all the seafront shops and restaurants. Local attractions include Manda Toto, Kipungani, Matondoni and the Takwa Ruins.

Abdul's Eco Nest

Lamu Old Town

Abdul's Eco Nest, Lamu Old Town, Kenya
PO Box 97, Lamu 80500, Kenya
Tel
Mobile +254 729 751554; +254 733 296268; +254 723 650807
Fax
E-mail abdul@abduleconest.com / info@abduleconest.com
Web www.abduleconest.com

   Manda, LS & CH
40 mins

Established in 2009, Abdul's Eco Nest is the 1st of its kind in Lamu. Abudujannah, aka Abdul, has created a self sustainable lodge which he hopes will be a door to awareness of our environment. He promotes interaction between visitors and locals to better realise this ideal. The Eco Nest grows its own fruit and vegetables, using no chemicals or fertilisers, and offers organic Swahili food. A dynamic creator and designer, Abdul experiments with alternative methods of screen printing and recycled driftwood art.

There are 4 bungalows on stilts, a bathroom block, a kitchen and a communal lounge with hammocks, chairs, tables, piles of cushions and displays of Abdul's artwork. All structures and furniture are built of local materials such as makuti palm and driftwood; there is no glass, steel or concrete at the site. The menu is flexible, and guests are welcome to discuss their preferences with the chef. Sample dishes include grilled fish with mong beans in coconut curry sauce served in a coconut husk, or Swahili octopus served with chapatti.

A tree planting and plant maintenance project ensures that the Eco Nest looks attractive and has plentiful shade. Activities include yoga sessions and creative art with Abdul. Boat trips and tours of Lamu Old Town can be arranged.

Jannat House

Lamu Old Town

Jannat House, Lamu Old Town, Kenya
PO Box 195, Lamu 80500, Kenya
Tel +254 424 633414
Mobile +254 728 353468; +254 720 289897
Fax
E-mail jannathouse@gmail.com
Web www.jannathouse.se

 Manda, LS & CH
30 mins

Jannat House is formed of 3 interlinking houses set around a central garden and swimming pool. In traditional Arabic architecture, this attractive building has been recognised by the museum which has prohibited alteration. The house is on multiple levels, a quirky collection of staircases, terraces and gardens. There are 16 rooms, 10 en-suite and 6 with shared bathrooms. The rooms have Lamu 4-poster bed, Lamu table, chair, fan and mosquito net. The budget rooms sleep between 2 and 6 pax. The restaurant has a wide international menu, including seafood such as poached fish fillet, calamari tempura and ginger crab, as well as salads, pizzas, pasta, curries and soups. There is a grill that serves dishes like charcoal grilled lobster, barbecued beef or seafood kebab, a coffee bar and a fully stocked bar. The house has WiFi throughout and the terraces have plugs for laptops.

The Jannat House dhow holds up to 20 pax. It is fully equipped for cooking, camping, fishing and relaxation. Other activities include snorkelling at Manda Toto, diving with giant turtles in Kiungu Marine National Reserve, watching crocodiles and hippos on Tana River, tracking elephants around Mpeketoni and deep sea fishing for marlins. Jannat House grows its own coconut, guava and cashew nuts, and composts its food waste.

Pole Pole Guest House Lamu Old Town

Pole Pole Guest House, Lamu Old Town, Kenya
PO Box 366, Lamu 80500, Kenya
Tel
Mobile +254 722 736768; +254 715 259139
Fax
E-mail mwagsad@yahoo.com
Web

  Manda, LS & CH
30 mins

Pole Pole means slowly or relaxed, an apt description of the island way of life found on Lamu. The guesthouse advertises itself as the tallest building in town, and can be seen from many parts of Lamu Old Town. It offers budget accommodation; the building is set around a central courtyard. There are 7 en-suite rooms. The rooms have either a double and single bed, or twin beds, and are furnished with mosquito net, fan and African print curtains. The shower water is not heated. A fridge in reception has soft drinks and drinking water for sale. There is no restaurant or bar. The rooftop, towering over the other roofs surrounding it, has good views over Lamu Old Town. There is a thatched roof shading the rooftop, but no furniture.

Activities such as boat trips and tours of Lamu Old Town and Shela Village can be booked with local boat captains at the seafront. Local sites of interest include Manda Toto, Kipungani, Takwa Ruins and Matondoni. Transfers between Lamu Old Town, Shela Village and the airport are all available, and can be booked at the seafront.

Yumbe Villa and Yumbe House Lamu Old Town

Yumbe Villa and Yumbe House, Lamu Old Town, Kenya
PO Box 81, Lamu 80500, Kenya
Tel +254 424 633101
Mobile +254 725 352117
Fax
E-mail
Web

 Manda, LS & CH
30 mins

Yumbe is a 10th century Swahili word meaning Palace or Royal House. It was the place the town elders once met to direct the affairs of ancient Lamu. The 2 Yumbe houses are traditional buildings with whitewashed walls studded with local stone.

Yumbe House has 10 en-suite rooms. All rooms have 4-poster twin beds, fridge, table, chair and mosquito net. There is a noticeboard with information about local events and activities. The rooftop lounge, furnished with daybeds, tables and chairs, has a panoramic view of Lamu Old Town. Yumbe Villa has 5 en-suite rooms, all furnished with 4-poster beds, table, chair and mosquito net. There are terraces on the 1st floor, the 2nd floor and the rooftop.

Both houses serve breakfast on the terraces. Lunch and dinner are not usually provided, although a Swahili chef can be provided on request. Local masseuses offer henna painting, braiding, manicure, pedicure and massage. Boat trips can be organised through Promise Ahadi, a company offering sailing lessons and sunset cruises, as well as trips to Manda Toto, Takwa Ruins, Matundoni and Kipungani. Tours of Lamu Old Town can be arranged, including visits to Lamu Museum and fort.

Bustani Café & Bookshop Lamu Old Town

Bustani Bookshop and Café, Lamu Old Town, Kenya
PO Box 214, Lamu 80500, Kenya
Tel
Mobile +254 722 859594; +254 724 612424
Fax
E-mail bustanicafe@gmail.com
Web

   Manda, LS & CH
30 mins

Set in a charming garden in the centre of Lamu Old Town, Bustani Café and Bookshop makes a cool and attractive place to relax during the day. There is 1 apartment on the 1st floor, with a rooftop terrace. The apartment has a Lamu bed, Lamu table and traditional wooden shutters. The rooftop terrace has table, chairs and daybed, and overlooks the garden. The bookshop and café close at 6pm, giving guests in the apartment complete privacy after that time.

The café serves a selection of shakes and smoothies, as well as Swahili chai and Kenya coffee. The food is fresh and healthy, including homemade granola with fruit and yoghurt, mango madness salad, freshly made sandwiches and island seafood soup. The bookshop has a wide selection of fiction and non-fiction. The garden is filled with bougainvillea and frangipani, coral water features and a resident tortoise.

The owners produce Chonjo Magazine, meaning alert or ready in Swahili, a local publication with up to date information about Lamu, its activities and events. Bustani Café and Bookshop minimises its impact on the environment by composting food waste and recycling water to the garden.

Baytil Ajaib Lamu Old Town

Baytil Ajaib, Lamu Old Town, Kenya
PO Box 328, Lamu 80500, Kenya
Tel +254 424 632033
Mobile
Fax
E-mail b.ajaiblamu@gmail.com
Web www.chicretreats.com/boutique-hotels-lamu/baytil-ajaib

 VISA   Manda, LS & CH
30 mins

This traditional Lamu house has been lovingly restored and embellished with genuine antiques. The house is intended for visitors who really appreciate the traditional ambience, style and culture of Lamu.

Baytil Ajaib has 2 en-suite double rooms and 2 suites. The rooms have a long sitting area with traditional chest, writing desk and intricately carved 4-poster bed. The bathrooms have original Swahili commodes and porcelain basins. The 1st floor suite is for a family, with a double room and a small double bed in the alcove of the sitting room. It also includes a private courtyard with palms and plants. The 2nd floor suite has a double room and an open sitting room with terrace. Each room and suite has complete privacy and is furnished with authentic Lamu furniture and adorned with antiques from Morocco, China and India.

The hosts offer a tour of Lamu and introductions to local residents, shops and galleries. Visitors can discuss their food preferences with the chef, who provides Swahili cuisine, seafood or international dishes as required. Meals are served in the dining room or on the rooftop terrace, on cushions, with a view over Lamu Old Town. Dhow trips and water sports can be booked locally, as can visits to ancient sites and ruins.

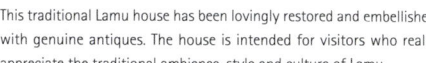 Accommodation Guide

Palm Beach House   Lamu Old Town

Palm Beach House, Lamu Old Town, Kenya
PO Box 426, Lamu 80700, Kenya
Tel
Mobile +254 725 617996
Fax
E-mail bytulkh@yahoo.com
Web www.lamuvilla.com

    Manda, LS & CH
30 mins

Palm Beach House, previously called Baytulkher House, is an attractive, traditional house. The house is built around a central courtyard with a Jacuzzi and vivid bougainvillea.

There are 6 en-suite rooms, including a large open sided penthouse with panoramic views of Lamu Old Town. The house has polished floors and walls in traditional style, and is adorned with traditional Lamu furniture and aged dhow wooden artefacts. All rooms have solid carved Lamu doors and high double beds with steps leading up to them. There are terraces on each floor furnished with Lamu daybeds and sofas. The sitting rooms are decorated with local artefacts. Guests are welcome to discuss their food preferences and plan their menus with the chef.

Palm Beach House can arrange boat trips with local captains; fishing and snorkelling can also be arranged. Local sites of interest include Manda Toto, Kipungani and the Takwa Ruins. The house also arranges massage, manicure and pedicure with local masseuses. Tours of Lamu Old Town, including Lamu Museum and the donkey sanctuary, can be arranged; tours of Shela Village, including the boat trip to the village, are also available. Boat transfers to and from the airport are included.

Stone House Lamu Old Town

Stone House, Lamu Old Town, Kenya
PO Box 315, Lamu 80500, Kenya
Tel +254 424 633544; +254 424 633149
Mobile +254 722 528377
Fax +254 424 633149
E-mail stonehouse_lamu@yahoo.com
Web www.stonehousehotellamu.com

    Manda, LS & CH
30 mins

Built as a private house in the 1960s, Stone House was converted into a hotel in 1990. The house is in traditional Swahili style, with an open central courtyard, and creepers growing up coral-studded walls.

There are 12 rooms, made up of 10 doubles and 2 triples. 8 rooms are en-suite; 2 family suites each contain 2 bedrooms, sitting room and bathroom. All rooms are furnished with Lamu bed, mosquito net and fan. The rooms are named after Swahili flowers, such as asmini and waridi. There is a backup generator, and a noticeboard containing information about local events.

The rooftop restaurant has white arches carved into coral walls, with a view over the rooftops to the sea. The menu is truly international, and includes gnocchi with tomato sauce, Somali rice with beef strips, chicken zigni Ethiopian and carrot cake. There are also seafood dishes such as lobster thermidor, grilled jumbo prawns and octopus salad. The bar serves soft drinks, beer and wine, and also has cappuccino. Stone House has a speedboat and a dhow. Snorkelling, fishing and sunset cruises are on offer, as well as trips to Manda Toto, Takwa Ruins, Matondoni and Kipungani. The house can book massage, manicure, pedicure and henna painting with local masseuses.

Amu House　　　　　　　　　Lamu Old Town

Amu House, Lamu Old Town, Kenya
PO Box 230, Lamu 80500, Kenya
Tel　　+254 424 633420
Mobile
Fax
E-mail
Web

　　　　　　　　　　　　　　　　Manda, LS & CH
　　　　　　　　　　　　　　　　30 mins

Set around a central courtyard, Amu House is formed of coral walls tinted pale ochre. The house offers budget accommodation in the centre of Lamu Old Town.

There are 7 en-suite rooms, made up of 6 doubles and a triple with a double and single bed. The rooms have fan, mosquito net and African print curtains. The bathrooms have cold showers. The rooms are on the 1st and 2nd floors; each floor has a communal terrace with comfortable chairs and sofas. The rooftop terrace, partially sheltered by a thatched roof, has views of the sea across a cluster of roofs. Amu House serves breakfast, included in the rate. Lunch and dinner are not served.

Amu House can arrange boat trips with local captains. Sunset cruises, fishing and snorkelling can all be arranged. Tours around Lamu Old Town and donkey rides are also available.

Wildebeeste Art Workshop　　Lamu
& Gallery　　　　　　　　　　Old Town

Wildebeeste Art Workshop & Gallery, Lamu Old Town, Kenya
PO Box 175, Lamu 80500, Kenya
Tel　　　+254 424 632261
Mobile　+254 712 851499; +254 733 929385
Fax
E-mail　kahindi1@hotmail.com / wildebeeste@hotmail.com
Web　　www.wildebeestelamu.com

　　　　　　　　　　　　　 Manda, LS & CH
　　　　　　　　　　　　　　　　　　　　　　　　20 mins

Wildebeeste Art Gallery exhibits local arts and crafts, including weavings, wall hangings, sketchings and paintings. Connected to the art gallery are 2 quirky buildings, with rooms and apartments for rent. The apartments are all on split levels, with unconventional furniture and local artefacts. Wildebeeste I is opposite the art gallery, and has a sign over its door: House of the Rising Sun. There are 3 apartments, 1 on the ground floor, 1 on the 1st floor and 1 on the 2nd floor. The apartments all have a double bedroom, single bedroom, living room, kitchen and bathroom. The kitchens are equipped with gas cooker, fridge and dining table. The rooftop terrace, accessible from the 2nd floor apartment, has lovely views over Lamu Old Town.

Wildebeeste II, adjoining the art gallery, has 2 wings. The original wing has 2 apartments, 2 rooms and an open plan living room and terrace. The newer wing has 2 small apartments and 1 large apartment with rooftop terrace. There is a communal kitchen on the ground floor. All apartments are taken on a self-catering basis. A chef can be provided if required. Boat trips can be organised with local boat captains. Fishing, snorkelling and sunset cruises are all available.

Jambo House Lamu Old Town

Jambo House, Mtueni area, Lamu Old Town, Kenya
PO Box 131, Lamu 80500, Kenya
Tel
Mobile　+254 713 411714
Fax
E-mail　info@jambohouse.com
Web　www.jambohouse.com

　　　 Manda, LS & CH
20 mins

Jambo House, in the centre of Lamu Old Town, offers budget accommodation and has friendly and informative staff. The house is situated in the Old Town, a short walk from the town square and Lamu Fort. It opened in 2008.

There are 5 rooms, all with either en-suite bathroom or private external bathroom. The rooms, named after local villages and islands, are called Kipungani, Manda, Matondoni, Lamu and Shela. The rooms have traditional Lamu wooden shutters and are decorated in sunny yellow and sky blue. All rooms have fan and mosquito net. Local art and photos from around the world decorate the walls. Breakfast and afternoon tea are included in the rate; lunch and dinner are not served, although lunch boxes can be provided on request. Electricity is a combination of solar and mains. The rooftop terrace, with a good view over Lamu Old Town, has sunbeds, books, games and a cool box of soft drinks. A well-designed noticeboard gives information about Lamu and local events. Guide books and maps are also available. Activities include Swahili cooking classes, henna painting, boat trips and kayaking. A local masseuse offers massage, manicure and pedicure.

Subira House Lamu Main Street

Subira House, behind the old fort, Lamu Main Street, Kenya
PO Box 341, Lamu 80500, Kenya
Tel
Mobile　+254 726 916686
Fax
E-mail　info@subirahouse.net
Web　www.subirahouse.net

　　　 Manda, LS & CH
20 mins

Formerly the house of the Liwali, or governor of the fort, Subira House is unique in style. The current owners bought the house in 1991, when it was in a state of disrepair, and restored it to its former elegance using traditional materials and methods. The house is set around a central courtyard framed by unusual arches.

There are 7 en-suite rooms, 2 on the ground floor and the remainder on the 1st and 2nd floors. Each room has a spacious balcony with a selection of books, Lamu table, sofas and views of the old fort and the sea. Karkadeh Restaurant, on the 1st floor balcony, serves fresh, homemade dishes. Subira House grows its own fruit and vegetables, including banana, papaya, custard apple, passion fruit, lime and avocado. Lunch is a selection of soups, pasta, cheeses and salads. Dinner, if required, must be booked by 9.30am, and is a 3-course set menu often including the catch of the day. Subira House has been given a silver award by Ecotourism Society of Kenya for its eco policies. Food waste is composted, grey water is recycled on the garden and the WCs are of an eco design. Captain Jelani, a boat captain and authorised guide, lives on the ground floor. He is available for boat trips, fishing, tours of the town and other excursions.

Kijani House

Shela Seafront

Kijani House, Seafront, Shela, Lamu Island, Kenya
PO Box 266, Lamu 80500, Kenya

Tel	+254 20 2435700
Mobile	+254 725 545264; +254 735 545264
Fax	
E-mail	info@kijani-lamu.com
Web	www.kijani-lamu.com

VISA, MasterCard

Manda, LS & CH
20 mins

With a name meaning green in Swahili, Kijani House is a lush retreat on the beachfront of Shela. Framed by clusters of frangipani and bougainvillea, this whitewashed Swahili house recreates the atmosphere of the early days of Lamu.

There are 9 en-suite double rooms and 2 suites which include living room and large veranda. The rooms are adorned with local antiques, lanterns and ornaments. The 2 ground floor rooms have wheelchair access. The restaurant offers a set menu that changes daily, and can include dishes such as grilled beef fillet, fish tartar, crab cakes with spicy mayonnaise and passion fruit mousse. There is also an a la carte menu including tuna kebab, saffron risotto, chef's salad and Lamu dahl. The bar has a selection of soft drinks, beers, wines, spirits and cocktails, and games such as bao, backgammon and solitaire. There is also a swimming pool and gift shop. Kijani House has its own boat and tour guide. Short and full-day boat trips can be arranged, as well as guided tours of Shela. A local masseuse offers aromatherapy massage, reflexology, manicure and pedicure. The hotel minimises its environmental impact by using solar heated water and donating food waste to local donkeys.

Stopover Guest House
Shela

Shela Seafront

Stopover Guest House, Seafront, Shela, Lamu Island, Kenya
PO Box 59, Lamu 80500, Kenya

Tel	
Mobile	+254 720 127222; +254 738 710514
Fax	
E-mail	stopoverguest_restaurant@yahoo.com
Web	www.stopoverrestaurant.com

VISA

Manda, LS & CH
20 mins

On the seafront near a cluster of boats, Stopover Guest House gleams white against the palm trees. The hotel's rooms have lovely views across the harbour and of the daily life of the fishermen and boat captains.

There are 5 en-suite rooms, all with sea views. The 1st floor has 3 rooms and a fully equipped kitchen for guests who choose the self-catering option. The 2nd floor has 2 more spacious rooms, each with 2 double beds, Lamu table and chairs. All rooms have 4-poster bed, mosquito net and fan. There is a large sea facing balcony on each floor. Stopover Restaurant has a large menu of international dishes, seafood and Asian fusion cuisine. Dishes include chicken sate, chicken laksa, crab bisque, prawns biriani, spicy coconut soup, spaghetti bolognaise, fish kebab and lobster, avocado and mango salad. Fresh fish is delivered daily by fishermen. Buffet under the stars can be arranged on request.

Boat trips around Lamu Island, to neighbouring islands, to Manda Toto and to the Takwa Ruins can all be arranged. Scuba diving and snorkelling can also be arranged. Other activities include traditional henna painting, tours of Shela Village and Lamu Old Town and donkey rides on Shela beach. Stopover Hotel is open throughout the year.

Shella Bahari Guest House

Shela Seafront

Shella Bahari Guest House, Seafront, Shela, Lamu Island, Kenya
PO Box 1234, Lamu 80500, Kenya

Tel	+254 424 632046
Mobile	+254 722 901643
Fax	
E-mail	info@shellabahari.co.ke
Web	www.shellabahari.co.ke

  Manda, LS & CH
20 mins

A whitewashed building overlooking the sea, Shella Bahari Guest House has views of the boats and their captains.

There are 5 en-suite rooms, made up of 2 singles and 3 doubles. The single rooms have a double bed; the double rooms are more spacious and have a double and single bed. All rooms contain 4-poster bed, mosquito net and fan. The sea facing rooms have a balcony. The rooms are named in Swahili, such as Safari Njema journey well, Pumzika rest and Lala Salama sleep well. There is also a kitchen for guests who choose the self-catering option.

The ground floor restaurant has open sides and looks out on the shore.

It serves an international menu including Thai som tam, soup Doria, Russian salad, Chicken Bascayola, mixed seafood soup, ginger crab and banana flambé. Food can also be served on the rooftop, which has views over the sea and a thatched shade roof. Boat trips around Lamu Island and to neighbouring islands can be arranged with local captains. Fishing trips and sunset cruises are also on offer. Local sites of interest include Manda Toto and the Takwa Ruins.

Peponi Hotel

Shela Seafront

Peponi Hotel, Seafront, Shela, Lamu Island, Kenya
PO Box 24, Lamu 80500, Kenya

Tel	+254 20 8023655; +254 20 2435033
Mobile	+254 733 203082; +254 737 203082
Fax	
E-mail	peponi@peponi-lamu.com
Web	www.peponi-lamu.com

 VISA, MasterCard, Amex    Manda, LS & CH
20 mins

With a name that means heaven in Swahili, Peponi Hotel is a beachfront paradise. The hotel opened in 1967 and has remained in the hands of the same family ever since.

There are 24 en-suite rooms, made up of 14 standard and 10 superior. Each room is individually designed and adorned with traditional artefacts. All rooms are sea facing with private balcony. Each is equipped with safe, fan, mosquito net and solar heated water. The restaurant, with seafront terrace and bar, has a selection of sushi, Swahili dishes, Italian cuisine, seafood and steaks. The bar is fully stocked with soft drinks, beers, wines, spirits and cocktails. There is a library, with books in several languages.

A local masseuse provides massage, reflexology and body scrub. The freeform swimming pool curves around ancient baobabs and overlooks the beach. The lush garden is dotted with traditional gourds and ornaments. Peponi Hotel minimises its environmental impact by disposing of waste responsibly.

Activities include deep sea fishing, water-skiing, windsurfing, scuba diving, snorkelling and boat trips. The Turtle Trust is a community project, initiated by Peponi Hotel, that protects turtles and pays fishermen to release them. The hotel also works with Lamu Marine Conservation Trust, LamCot, to protect fish and coral.

Mnarani House

Shela Village

Mnarani House, Shela, Lamu Island, Kenya
Lamu Homes & Safaris Ltd., PO Box 772, Nairobi 00606, Kenya
Tel +254 20 4446384; +254 20 4447397
Mobile
Fax
E-mail info@lamuhomes.com
Web www.lamuhomes.com

      Manda, LS & CH — 40 mins

Mnarani, meaning minaret in Swahili, is an apt name for this house that is located in Shela Village, surrounded by mosques. The house's open design invites plenty of breeze, while giving attractive views of the sea and the village. Mnarani House is a short walk from Shela Beach.

There are 4 en-suite double rooms, all equipped with mosquito net and fan. There is also a single room upstairs, without a bathroom. Several sitting areas provide pleasant places for relaxing. A rooftop sitting room has views of the sea and the village, and is equipped with a fridge. Water is heated by solar power.

A team of staff takes care of shopping, cleaning and preparation of meals. Guests are welcome to discuss their preferred menus with the chef. Local fishermen bring fresh fish and seafood to the door. Activities include strolls around Shela Village and along Shela Beach. The historic Arab trading port, Lamu Old Town, is only a short boat trip from Shela and offers museums and galleries. Dhow boat trips, fishing and snorkelling can be booked with boat captains at the seafront.

Bahati House

Shela Village

Bahati House, Shela, Lamu Island, Kenya
PO Box 24335, Nairobi 00502, Kenya
Tel
Mobile +254 728 606194
Fax
E-mail bahati@houselamu.com
Web www.houselamu.com

     Manda, LS & CH — 40 mins

Bahati House is a traditional Lamu house, built on 3 floors around an open courtyard. The house is fully staffed and is taken on a self-catering basis. There are 5 en-suite bedrooms, all furnished with king size bed. Each floor has a sitting area. The rooftop terrace overlooks the sea and the dunes; it provides plenty of lounging space and has a Moroccan corner and a swing bed. The chef uses fresh, local ingredients; guests are welcome to discuss their food preferences with him.

Both Lamu Old Town and Shela Village provide a wealth of activities. The Lamu Museum and fort make interesting day trips, and provide an introduction to Swahili and Arabic culture. Donkey rides around both villages are available. Boat trips, sunset cruises, fishing, sailing, water-skiing and snorkelling can be arranged with local boat captains. Excursions to Takwa Ruins, Manda Toto and Kipungani can also be arranged.

Banana House

Shela Village

Banana House, Shela, Lamu Island, Kenya
PO Box 119, Lamu 80500, Kenya
Tel
Mobile +254 721 275538
Fax
E-mail banana@africaonline.co.ke
Web www.bananahouse-lamu.com

  Manda, LS & CH
40 mins

This attractive retreat is formed from a collection of houses set in bright tropical gardens. It offers daily yoga sessions, treatments and courses. The main house, Banana House, has 3 interconnecting en-suite rooms opening onto the garden, 3 en-suite 1st floor rooms with shared terrace and 1 penthouse. Sweet Banana has 1 ground floor double room, 2 1st floor rooms with shared terrace and 1 penthouse. The terracotta and white rooftop has lovely views, seating area and a selection of books. Banana Wellness has 1 3-bedroom apartment and 1 2-bedroom apartment, each with living room and selection of books. Guests in the apartments discuss their food preferences with the chef; meals are served privately.

Banana Wellness also has a rooftop terrace and massage room. Courses include the Art of Wellness, Earth Painting Workshop, Reconnecting Body and Soul, Asthanga Yoga and Nutrition and Ayurvedic Food. Therapists offer reflexology, aromatherapy, shiatsu, reiki, manicure, pedicure and exfoliation. Activities include sailing, dhow dinner, henna painting, beach barbecue and deep sea fishing. Banana House supports the Banana Bursary Project, Turtle Project and Hands up for Kids. The UN Millennium Campaign acknowledged the invaluable effort of Banana House in the 'stand up and speak out' against poverty campaign in 2007.

Shella Sea Breeze Guest House

Shela Village

Shella Sea Breeze Guest House, Shela, Lamu Island, Kenya
PO Box 329, Lamu 80500, Kenya
Tel
Mobile +254 722 378730
Fax
E-mail shellaseabreeze@yahoo.com
Web

 VISA, MasterCard  Manda, LS & CH
40 mins

Shella Sea Breeze Guest House is a whitewashed building next to an attractive mosque. The guesthouse has a view of the mosque and of the sea. There are 7 en-suite double rooms. Each room is furnished with writing table, chair, mosquito net and fan; the bathrooms are fully tiled. The water is heated by solar power. The windows between the rooms and the terrace are one way, so people on the terrace cannot see into the rooms. The 2nd floor terrace and the rooftop terrace have views of the mosque and the sea. Guests are welcome to eat on either of the terraces or in the dining room on the ground floor. Lunch is not served. Dinner is an alternating daily menu. There is also a lounge, with satellite TV, on the ground floor.

The guesthouse has 2 speedboats. Activities include fishing, snorkelling, deep sea fishing and sunset cruises. Tours of Shela Village and Lamu Old Town, as well as excursions further afield can also be arranged. Local attractions include Manda Toto, Takwa Ruins, Matondoni and Kipungani.

Msafini Hotel

Shela Village

Msafini Hotel, Shela, Lamu Island, Kenya
PO Box 226, Lamu 80500, Kenya
Tel
Mobile   +254 734 627758; +254 720 223043
Fax
E-mail   msafinihotelshella@yahoo.com
Web   www.msafinihotel.com

                                    Manda, LS & CH
                                                          40 mins

 In a sea of whitewashed buildings, Msafini Hotel's bright yellow façade stands out. The hotel opened in 2009, and combines traditional style with modern architecture.

There are 14 en-suite rooms, made up of doubles, twins and triples. Each room has a private balcony. The hotel can be booked for private functions, either as a whole, or part. Mango Restaurant, on the rooftop, has panoramic views of the sea, Manda Island and the sand dunes. The chef specialises in seafood, and the menu includes snapper, barracuda, grouper, calamari, prawns, oysters and lobster. Traditional Swahili food is also available. Buffets can be arranged on request. Guests are welcome to use the internet in the manager's office. There is also a swimming pool, shaded by vivid bougainvillea.

Msafini Hotel has a boat, available for trips around Lamu and to neighbouring islands. Scuba diving and snorkelling are available. Fishing trips and sunset cruises are also on offer. Local sites of interest include Manda Toto and the Takwa Ruins. Other activities include traditional henna painting, donkey rides on Shela Beach and tours of Shela Village. Trips to Matondoni dhow building site and Lamu Museum can also be arranged. The hotel can also organise traditional weddings, with Swahili clothes and kirumbizi stick dance.

Sunset House

Shela Village

Sunset House, Shela, Lamu Island, Kenya
PO Box 301, Lamu 80500, Kenya
Tel
Mobile   +254 722 698059; +254 722 729219
Fax
E-mail   shella@africaonline.co.ke
Web   www.shelalamu.com

                                     Manda, LS & CH
                                                          40 mins

Sunset House is a new house built in traditional Lamu style, with cool neru plastered walls.

There are 5 en-suite rooms, in 3 spacious apartments. The 1st floor apartment has 3 bedrooms, a kitchen and an open plan sitting and dining room, ideal for families or groups travelling together. The 2nd floor apartment has a bedroom, large sitting room and kitchen. The penthouse, on the 3rd floor, has a rooftop sitting and dining area with sunbeds. Water is heated by solar power. There is a communal roof terrace on the 4th floor, with daybeds and dining table and chairs. A perfect place from which to watch the sunset, this terrace gave the house its name. There is also a communal kitchen on the ground floor. The chef provides breakfast, lunch and dinner; guests can discuss their food preferences with him. There is also the self-catering option.

Sunset House is affiliated to the nearby Jannataan; guests at Sunset House are welcome to use the swimming pool at Jannataan. A local chef, Ali Samosa, can be contacted at Jannataan. He creates delicious authentic Swahili food on request, booking required. Boat trips and tours of Shela Village and Lamu Old Town can be booked at Jannataan.

Fatuma's Tower

Shela Village

Fatuma's Tower, Shela, Lamu Island, Kenya
PO Box 323, Lamu 80500, Kenya
Tel
Mobile +254 722 277138
Fax
E-mail gillies@africaonline.co.ke / bookings@fatumastower.com
Web www.fatumastower.com

 VISA

 Manda, LS & CH
40 mins

Set in lush tropical gardens, Fatuma's Tower is a tranquil retreat. It is named after Fatuma Abu Bakar, a Swahili noblewoman who lived here attended by 5 female slaves during the 19th century. After her death and the abolition of slavery, the house fell into ruins. A hundred years later, this sanctuary was carefully restored and opened as a hotel in 2000. There are 10 en-suite rooms in 3 unique houses. The Tower has 5 double rooms, a yoga hall and library. The Sandcastle has a ground floor family apartment with 3 double rooms. The Garden Cottage has 2 double rooms. Sandcastle and Garden can be taken as private houses if required. The rooms recreate the atmosphere of a Swahili house, are furnished with local antiques and fabrics, and equipped with solar heated water, fan and mosquito net. Each house is staffed by a chef who specialises in Italian and Swahili cuisine. Meals are served on the balconies or in the lamp-lit gardens. There is also a plunge pool and sunbathing terrace. Beer and wine are served.

Yoga sessions take place daily at 5pm. A local masseuse offers massage, reflexology, manicure and pedicure. Boat trips and other excursions can be arranged.

Shella Island Hotel

Shela Village

Shella Island Hotel, Shela, Lamu Island, Kenya
PO Box 179, Lamu 80500, Kenya
Tel
Mobile +254 721 212786
Fax
E-mail shellaislandhotel@gmail.com
Web

 VISA

 Manda, LS & CH
40 mins

Shella Island Hotel is on the fringe of Shela Village, with views over the sand dunes. The hotel is a whitewashed building, decorated in traditional Swahili style with Lamu furniture. Pot plants are placed throughout the house.

There are 6 en-suite rooms, made up of 1 single, 3 doubles and 2 triples. The triples contain 2 small double beds and a single. The rooms are named in Swahili after flowers, such as kiluwa and waridi. All rooms are furnished with Lamu 4-poster bed, table and dressing table. Each room has its own terrace, with table, chairs, daybed and a selection of books enterprisingly set into the walls. The penthouse has its own rooftop seating and dining area. The terraces and rooftop have views across Shela Village to the sea, and in the other direction, to the sand dunes. Guests are welcome to use the internet in the manager's office.

Barracuda Restaurant has an international menu, specialising in Indian cuisine and seafood. Dishes include tamarind fish, garlic prawns, ginger and garlic crab, aubergine in coconut, bhajia, vegetable curry and chocolate pancake. Fresh seafood is delivered by fisherman daily. Shella Island Hotel uses purified water from the sand dunes. Boat trips can be booked with local fishermen at the seafront.

Star Guest House

 Shela Village

Star Guest House, Shela, Lamu Island, Kenya
PO Box 59, Lamu 80500, Kenya
Tel
Mobile +254 726 335233
Fax
E-mail jakamal@hotmail.com
Web

 VISA, MasterCard   Manda, LS & CH 40 mins

Star Guest House is a whitewashed building, with large balconies on each level. The guesthouse offers self-catering accommodation and also has a restaurant.

There are 4 en-suite rooms, each furnished with a 4-poster Lamu bed, mosquito net and fan, and decorated with kikoi curtains. Water is heated by solar power. Each floor has a large open terrace, furnished with dining table, chairs and daybeds. There is also a kitchen with cooker and fridge for those who choose the self-catering option. The rooftop, with hammocks and daybeds, has views over Shela Village to the sea. The ground floor restaurant has a selection of international dishes and seafood. Dishes include fish curry, coconut prawns, grilled lobster, spaghetti with seafood and grilled chicken with chips. Drinks include spiced tea with ginger and cinnamon, coffee, juices and fruit shakes.

Boat trips can be arranged with local boat captains at the seafront. Snorkelling, fishing and sunset cruises are all on offer. Tours of Shela Village and Lamu Old Town, as well as excursions further afield can also be arranged. Local attractions include Manda Toto, Takwa Ruins, Matondoni and Kipungani.

Kisiwani House

 Shela Village

Kisiwani House, Shela, Lamu Island, Kenya
PO Box 368, Lamu 80500, Kenya
Tel
Mobile +254 723 672388
Fax
E-mail kisiwanishella@yahoo.com
Web

 VISA    Manda, LS & CH 40 mins

Kisiwani House, meaning island, was formerly known as the Island Hotel. The house looks out on the village square where local weddings and other events are celebrated. The house showcases local artists, and has regular art exhibitions.

There are 16 en-suite rooms, made up of singles, doubles and triples. There is also a rooftop apartment, containing 3 doubles and 1 single. The house has a communal kitchen for those who choose the self-catering option. Suli Suli Restaurant, meaning sailfish, is on the rooftop. It has a daily set menu and an a la carte menu. Dishes include grilled whole red snapper, chicken tikka, shrimp curry with coconut, pilau fish, beef samosas and vegetable pancakes. Fresh juices and shakes are also served. A selection of books is available.

Kisiwani House has a wide selection of excursions, at an additional cost. Tours of Shela Village and Lamu Old Town, either walking or on a donkey, are available. Boat trips to Takwa Ruins, Kipungani, Matondoni, Kiwayu Island and Manda Toto are all on offer. Lunch can be served on a beach if requested. Fishing and sunset cruises can also be arranged, as can boat transfers between Shela Village, Lamu Old Town and the airport on Manda Island. Massage, manicure and pedicure can be arranged.

Baitil Aman

Shela Village

Baitil Aman, nr the mosque, Shela, Lamu Island, Kenya
PO Box 179, Lamu 80500, Kenya

Tel	+254 20 8084077-8
Mobile	+254 772 576669; +254 733 375380
Fax	+254 42 4633584
E-mail	contact@baitilaman.com
Web	www.baitilaman.com

 VISA  Manda, LS & CH 40 mins

According to legend, Baitil Aman was built in the 18th century by Hajj Abdalla as a gift for his bride, the beautiful Binti Luali of the Shela clan. The building collapsed, but so great was Hajj Abdalla's love for Binti Luali that he rebuilt the entire palace. Rich with the history that has been played out within its walls, Baitil Aman is an elegant retreat in the centre of Shela Village.

There are 8 en-suite rooms, made up of doubles and triples, on different levels of the house. The rooms are spacious and minimalist, with whitewashed walls, natural wood adornments and traditional Lamu doors.

The lush garden, with vivid flowers and water features, makes a serene setting for the restaurant. Meals can also be served in the dining room or on the rooftop. The menu changes daily, with dishes like fish in banana leaf, prawn masala and stir fried vegetables with coconut rice.

After a 7-year restoration project, the house opened as a guesthouse in 2006. It was renamed Baitil Aman, meaning the house of peace. It has solar heated water and WiFi throughout. Boat trips, tours of Shela Village and other excursions can be arranged.

Sakina House

Shela Village

Sakina House, Shela, Lamu Island, Kenya
PO Box 305, Lamu 80500, Kenya

Tel	
Mobile	+254 722 698059
Fax	
E-mail	shella@africaonline.co.ke
Web	

   Manda, LS & CH 40 mins

Originally a private house for the Thune family, Sakina House is built in Swahili style on the ruins of the original house. Sakina, meaning peace in Arabic, is an apt word to describe this elegant house.

There are 3 en-suite rooms, 2 of which have adjoining single rooms suitable for a child. The rooms are furnished with 4-poster bed and Lamu table, chair and cupboard. The bathrooms are adorned with Lamu lamps and ornaments, including shells as soap dishes. Each floor has terraces and balconies. Meals are served on the rooftop terrace, which has views of both sea and village, is equipped with a fridge and shaded by a thatched roof. The chef specialises in Swahili cuisine and seafood.

The lovely swimming pool extends from indoors to the outdoor courtyard. Activities include boat trips, water sports and tours of Lamu Old Town and Shela Village. Sakina Safaris, affiliated to Sakina House, has a motorised dhow which is fully equipped for excursions including deep sea fishing. Sakina Safaris can also book trips to destinations in Kenya. The house can be rented as a whole for a minimum of 3 days.

Shella Royal House   Shela Village

Shella Royal House, Shela, Lamu Island, Kenya
Wilderness Getaways, PO Box 25240, Nairobi 00603, Kenya

Tel	+254 20 3876636
Mobile	+254 711 986513; +254 737 636693
Fax	+254 20 3876720
E-mail	info@wildernessgetawaysea.com
Web	www.wildernessgetawaysea.com

                                                              Manda, LS & CH
                                                              40 mins

In Shela Village, Shella Royal House is a peaceful retreat not far from Shela Beach. The house is made up of 2 houses. Both houses are on several levels and have multi-level rooftop terraces.

There are 10 en-suite rooms and 3 penthouses. All rooms have 4-poster bed, table, chair and chest with lock available for use as a safe. Baby cots and chairs are available. Meals are served on the rooftop, which has a dining table and chairs, a selection of books and lovely views over the village towards the sea. The menu changes weekly. Examples include gaspacho soup, followed by crab in ginger sauce with coconut rice, or lobster cocktail followed by spaghetti vongole. The bar is stocked with soft drinks, beers, wines, sparkling wines and a few spirits.

Shella Royal House has its own excursion dhow. Short and long-term excursions are on offer, and food is served on board the dhow. Fishing trips give guests the opportunity to fish, then cook and eat their catch on board. All equipment is provided, including life jackets and night lanterns. The dhow and its crew are also available for airport transfers. Other activities include tours of Lamu Old Town and trips to Pate Island.

White House   Shela Village

White House, Shela, Lamu Island, Kenya
PO Box 301, Lamu 80500, Kenya

Tel	
Mobile	+254 722 698059; +254 722 729219
Fax	
E-mail	shella@africaonline.co.ke
Web	www.shelalamu.com

                                                              Manda, LS & CH
                                                              40 mins

White House is a whitewashed building whose name accurately describes it. The house is covered in vivid bougainvillea.

There are 5 double rooms, 3 en-suite and the remaining 2 sharing a bathroom. All rooms are furnished with 4-poster bed, mosquito net and fan. Each floor has its own dining terrace, equipped with a fridge for the use of guests. There is a kitchen on the 1st floor, for the use of guests who choose the self-catering option, and a sitting room on the ground floor. A chef provides food for those who prefer not to cook. The rooftop, with views of Shela Village and the sea, is furnished with daybeds and a dining table and chairs.

White House is affiliated to the nearby Jannataan; guests at White House are welcome to use the swimming pool at Jannataan. A local chef, Ali Samosa, can be contacted at Jannataan. He creates delicious authentic Swahili food on request, booking required. Boat trips and tours of Shela Village and Lamu Old Town can be booked at Jannataan. Snorkelling, fishing and sunset cruises are on offer, as well as trips to Manda Toto, Takwa Ruins, Matondoni and Kipunguni.

Jannataan

Shela Village

Jannataan, Shela, Lamu Island, Kenya
PO Box 301, Lamu 80500, Kenya
Tel
Mobile   +254 722 698059; +254 722 729219
Fax
E-mail   shella@africaonline.co.ke
Web   www.shelalamu.com

      Manda, LS & CH
                                              40 mins

Jannataan, meaning two heavens in Arabic, is located in the centre of Shela Village. It is made up of 4 blocks surrounding a swimming pool. The main house, Block A, has 8 en-suite rooms on 4 floors, made up of singles, twins, doubles and a triple. The rooftop, on the 4th floor, is a communal terrace with cushioned barazas and daybeds and a lovely view of Shela Village. Block B and Block C each have 4 en-suite rooms, a ground floor kitchen and a rooftop terrace on the 3rd floor. Blocks B and C can each be taken as a whole, as private houses. Block D has 3 en-suite single rooms overlooking the pool. All the rooms have 4-poster bed, fan and mosquito net.

The restaurant serves international food, which can be eaten in the restaurant, by the pool or on a rooftop terrace. A local chef, Ali Samosa, creates delicious authentic Swahili food on request, booking required. The hotel is owned by a Muslim family and does not serve alcohol. A generator ensures 24-hour power, regardless of power cuts. Boat trips, village tours and other excursions can be arranged.

Garden House

Shela Village

Garden House, Shela, Lamu Island, Kenya
Shela House Management Ltd, PO Box 212, Lamu 80500, Kenya
Tel   +254 20 2405808
Mobile   +254 715 577896
Fax
E-mail   info@shelahouse.com
Web   www.shelahouse.com

 All major cards   Manda, LS & CH
                                                              40 mins

Garden House is situated on the edge of Shela Village, near the sand dunes that fringe the village. At the corner of a walled garden, this graceful house is shaded by neem trees that attract plentiful birdlife. The house is furnished with traditional Lamu furniture and adorned with local artefacts. There are 2 en-suite double rooms and 1 en-suite twin. The ground floor has a dining room and seating area, and the rooftop has comfortable baraza seats and sunbeds.

A team of staff serves the house, and a resident manager is based in Shela Village. The house cook prepares all the meals at the times the visitors require. He bakes bread, suggests menus and cooks both inter-national cuisine and Swahili fish dishes. Basic foodstuffs, fresh seasonal vegetables and fruit are supplied by the local market; other supplies are flown from Nairobi. Fish, lobster, crab and oysters can be ordered from local fishermen. Wine and spirits are not included. Internet is available at Shela House management office.

Wedding receptions and large parties can be catered for on request. Boat trips, sunset cruises, fishing, sailing, water-skiing and snorkelling can be arranged, as well as excursions to Takwa Ruins, Manda Toto and Kipungani Beach.

Shela House

Shela Village

Shela House, Shela, Lamu Island, Kenya
Shela House Management Ltd, PO Box 212, Lamu 80500, Kenya

Tel	+254 20 2405808
Mobile	+254 715 577896
Fax	
E-mail	info@shelahouse.com
Web	www.shelahouse.com

 All major cards   Manda, LS & CH 30 mins

A spacious house with great character, Shela House centres on an open courtyard, the well and an ancient gardenia. The courtyard is framed by seating and dining areas. The house is furnished with traditional Lamu furniture and adorned with local artefacts.

There are 5 en-suite rooms, made up of 3 doubles, a twin and a single. There is also a nursery. The 2nd floor has a sitting room and balcony, while the 2 rooftops have comfortable seats and striking views.

A team of staff serves the house, and a resident manager is based in Shela Village. The house cook prepares all the meals at the times the visitors require. He bakes bread, suggests menus and cooks both international cuisine and Swahili fish dishes. Basic foodstuffs, fresh seasonal vegetables and fruit are supplied by the local market; other supplies are flown from Nairobi. Fish, lobster, crab and oysters can be ordered from local fishermen. Wine and spirits are not included. Internet is available at Shela House management office.

Wedding receptions and large parties can be catered for on request. Boat trips, sunset cruises, fishing, sailing, water-skiing and snorkelling can be arranged, as well as excursions to Takwa Ruins, Manda Toto and Kipungani Beach.

Palm House

Shela Village

Palm House, Shela, Lamu Island, Kenya
Shela House Management Ltd, PO Box 212, Lamu 80500, Kenya

Tel	+254 20 2405808
Mobile	+254 715 577896
Fax	
E-mail	info@shelahouse.com
Web	www.shelahouse.com

 All major cards    Manda, LS & CH 30 mins

A striking Swahili style house, Palm House centres on an open courtyard, with a side garden. The house is whitewashed, with a thatched roof, furnished with traditional Lamu furniture and adorned with local artefacts. There are 3 en-suite doubles and 1 en-suite twin. The dining and living areas, on the ground floor, open onto the terrace. The 1st floor houses 2 doubles and a twin, all with private balconies; the 2nd floor houses the master bedroom. The rooftop has a bar, sunbeds and comfortable baraza seating.

A team of staff serves the house, and a resident manager is based in Shela Village. The house cook prepares all the meals at the times the visitors require. He bakes bread, suggests menus and cooks both international cuisine and Swahili fish dishes. Basic foodstuffs, fresh seasonal vegetables and fruit are supplied by the local market; other supplies are flown from Nairobi. Fish, lobster, crab and oysters can be ordered from local fishermen. Wine and spirits are not included. Internet is available at Shela House management office.

Wedding receptions and large parties can be catered for on request. Boat trips, sunset cruises, fishing, sailing, water-skiing and snorkelling can be arranged, as well as excursions to Takwa Ruins, Manda Toto and Kipungani Beach.

Shella Pwani Guest House Shela Village

Shella Pwani Guest House, behind Peponi Hotel, Shela, Kenya
PO Box 59, Lamu 80500, Kenya
Tel   +254 20 2600501
Mobile   +254 712 506778; +254 727 409887
Fax
E-mail
Web

                                                     Manda, LS & CH
                                                                          20 mins

Conveniently located behind Peponi Hotel, Shella Pwani Guest House offers budget accommodation a stone's throw from the seafront.
There are 5 en-suite rooms, made up of 2 singles and 3 doubles. The single rooms contain a small double bed and the double rooms contain a double and a single. An extra bed can be added if required. Each room is whitewashed and has bright kikoi curtains, and is furnished with a 4-poster Lamu bed, Lamu dressing table, fan and mosquito net. All rooms are sea facing and 1 has a private balcony. Meals are served on the rooftop terrace. There is a daily set menu with dishes such as crab curry, prawns in coconut sauce, grilled fish, barbecued chicken and salad. The rooftop terrace has a thatched roof, comfortable cushions and a view of the sea. There is a backup generator in case of power cuts.
Shella Pwani Guest House can arrange boat trips with a local boat captain Snorkelling, fishing, sunset cruises and tours around Shela on donkeys are also on offer.

Beach House   Shela Seafront

Beach House, Seafront, Shela, Lamu Island, Kenya
Shela House Management Ltd, PO Box 212, Lamu 80500, Kenya
Tel   +254 20 2405808
Mobile   +254 715 577896
Fax
E-mail   info@shelahouse.com
Web   www.shelahouse.com

 All major cards   Manda, LS & CH
                                                                          20 mins

This elegant whitewashed house overlooks the seafront. Its spacious terraces and shaded rooftop provide spectacular views across the Lamu channel, and its chic interior is ideal for relaxation.
There are 5 en-suite rooms, made up of 4 doubles and 1 triple. On the 1st floor, raised above the beach, is an infinity pool, with a bar area and comfortable baraza seats. On the 2nd floor, a large dining and living room opens onto a terrace. The rooftop has panoramic views of the Lamu channel and Manda Island. A team of staff serves the house, and a resident manager is based in Shela Village. The house cook prepares all the meals at the times the visitors require. He bakes bread, suggests menus and cooks both international cuisine and Swahili fish dishes. Basic foodstuffs, fresh seasonal vegetables and fruit are supplied by the local market; other supplies are flown from Nairobi. Fish, lobster, crab and oysters can be ordered from local fishermen. Wine and spirits are not included. Internet is available at Shela House management office.
Wedding receptions and large parties can be catered for on request. Boat trips, sunset cruises, fishing, sailing, water-skiing and snorkelling can be arranged, as well as excursions to Takwa Ruins, Manda Toto and Kipungani Beach.

Manda Bay

Manda Island

Manda Bay, Manda Island, Kenya
The Safari and Conservation Company, PO Box 24576, Nairobi 00502

Tel	+254 20 2115453; +254 20 6006759; +254 20 6006769
Mobile	+254 735 579999; +254 712 579999
Fax	+254 20 2194995
E-mail	reservations@sskenya.com
Web	www.mandabay.com

 VISA, MasterCard   Manda Bay, CH
5 mins

Manda Bay is a small boutique lodge offering informal pampering and barefoot luxury. Located on the northwest tip of Manda Island, one of the many idyllic islands of the Lamu Archipelago, and surrounded by miles of soft yellow sand and acres of bush land behind the lodge, Manda Bay offers a beach and bush experience.

There are 10 double Beach Front Cottages and 6 twin Sea View Cottages. All the bedrooms overlook the Indian Ocean, and encompass an enormous drape of mosquito netting, en-suite bathrooms and overhead fans.

The buildings at Manda Bay are in keeping with the local landscape and are constructed using mainly local materials. There is a central dining room featuring locally crafted Lamu furniture and antiques, a large lounge and bar area on the waterfront and a games room encompassing a fresh water swimming pool overlooking the creek and moorings. An upstairs sitting room with comfortable chairs is ideal for reading or company meetings. Manda Bay offers a wide variety of water sports, including windsurfing, kayaking, sailing and deep sea fishing. Excursions to Lamu Old Town are available. For a surcharge, dhow trips and scenic flights can also be arranged.

Southern Dream

Manda Island

Southern Dream, Manda Island, Kenya
PO Box 433, Lamu 80500, Kenya

Tel	
Mobile	+254 713 286749
Fax	
E-mail	info@mandadream.com
Web	www.mandadream.com

     Manda, LS & CH
20 mins

Southern Dream, formerly known as Manda Dream, consists of 2 beach-front villas available for rent on a private basis. The tasteful houses are exclusive retreats, a short boat trip from Lamu Island.

Blue Empire House has 3 en-suite bedrooms and Equator House has 4 en-suite bedrooms. The bedrooms are furnished with large beds, wooden tables and chairs, and adorned with cream linens and traditional artefacts. The bathrooms are tastefully adorned with coral, driftwood, shells and anchors. Both villas have large beach facing living rooms with fountains at their centres, designed of polished wooden floors and natural fabrics. Each villa has a wide terrace with views of the sea and an outdoor dining area. They include fully equipped kitchens, complete with chest freezer and fish poacher. The living rooms are decorated with cream linen, comfortable cushions and woven rugs, and equipped with music system. The villas use solar power and desalinated water. Each villa is looked after by a team of staff. Guests are welcome to discuss their preferred menus with the chef, who provides seafood or international cuisine as required. Southern Dream has its own boats and offers fishing and snorkelling. Activities include water sports, and trips to Pate Island and Takwa Ruins.

The Majlis   Manda Island

The Majlis, Manda Island, Kenya
Exclusive African Treasures, PO Box 63437, Nairobi 00619, Kenya
Tel	+254 20 7123300-2
Mobile	+254 770 275546; +254 773 777066; +254 770 289820
Fax	+254 20 7123303
E-mail	welcome@themajlisresorts.com
Web	www.themajlisresorts.com

VISA, MasterCard, Amex   Manda, LS & CH 20 mins

An exquisite resort on Manda Island, The Majlis reflects Lamu's traditional heritage with a fusion of Swahili, Arabic and Indian architecture. The resort extends along the seafront, and offers a wide selection of facilities and activities.

There are 25 en-suite rooms, made up of superior, deluxe and family rooms, as well as 1 junior suite and 1 royal suite. All rooms are spacious and stylish, with baraza seating areas, elegant furnishings and stunning views of the gardens, swimming pools and sea. The Junior Suite has 2 double rooms and a large terrace overlooking the garden. The vast Royal Suite has 3 double rooms, living room, dressing room and balcony.

The Majlis Restaurant, created from local materials such as casuarinas, mangrove poles and thatch, is an open plan veranda with a panoramic view of the bay. It includes a sushi bar, a pizza oven, a seafood grill and an a la carte menu with a selection of international dishes. The bar, above the restaurant, overlooks the sea. The fully equipped conference centre seats 30 pax. There is also an outside Jungle Gym, an indoor state of the art gym, a boutique and a spa with ayurvedic treatments. Activities include speedboat excursions, dhow cruises and a full range of water sports.
The Majlis was designated an outstanding hotel in the 2011 Fodor's 100 Hotels.

Diamond Beach Village   Manda Island

Diamond Beach Village, Manda Island, Kenya
PO Box 348, Lamu 80500, Kenya
Tel	
Mobile	+254 720 915001
Fax	
E-mail	info@diamondbeachvillage.com
Web	www.diamondbeachvillage.com

VISA, MasterCard   Manda, LS & CH 20 mins

Diamond Beach Village is a collection of bandas on the beach. A short boat trip from Shela, Diamond Beach Village makes a relaxing place to chill out. There are 9 traditional en-suite bandas. Created from palm fronds, the attractive, rustic bandas are furnished with locally crafted furniture. There is also a tree house in a baobab. It has a double, a twin and a single, 2 bathrooms and a private garden with swing beds. The baobab grows up through the house, blending into this unique piece of architecture. The campfire on the beach makes a lovely place to watch the sunset.
The beachfront restaurant serves international dishes such as traditional fish and chips, spaghetti bolognaise and deep fried calamari. The menu changes weekly. Fresh fish is delivered daily. The bar is well stocked with soft drinks, beers, wines and cocktails. The peaceful thatched library and chill out area is furnished with swing chairs and daybeds, and has a selection of books and games. Diamond Beach Village has 2 boats, available for trips to Manda Toto and Takwa Ruins, and for fishing trips and sundowner cruises. Diamond Beach Village minimises its environmental impact by using solar powered lamps, recycling grey water and donating food waste to the Lamu donkeys.

Kizingo

Southern Lamu

Kizingo, South Lamu Island, Kenya
PO Box 138, Lamu 80500, Kenya
Tel
Mobile +254 733 954770; +254 722 901544
Fax
E-mail info@kizingo.com
Web www.kizingo.com

  Manda, LS & CH
45 mins

Set on a secluded 12km beach in the south of Lamu Island, Kizingo styles itself a no news, no shoes resort. Kizongo is committed to the conservation of the environment; the resort has been constructed from local materials. There are 8 well spaced en-suite bandas. Each banda has a high thatched roof to maximise the breeze, and is furnished with large double bed and comfortable chairs, and adorned with local fabrics. The restaurant has an international menu, and specialises in seafood including red snapper, crab and lobster. Vegetables are grown locally. The bar has a selection of wines from South Africa, Chile and Italy, as well as cocktails.

Activities include snorkelling, fishing, kayaking, dhow boat trips and swimming with dolphins when in season. Bush walks, guided bicycle rides and tours of Lamu Old Town are also on offer, and guests are welcome to visit local villages. Kizingo is committed to conservation and ecologically sound practises. The bandas use solar power and eco-loos. Food waste is composted and grey water is recycled to the garden. Kizingo has initiated a turtle conservation project, a tree planting project and Kipungani School Trust. Guests are welcome to visit and participate in all these projects.

Kizingoni Beach Villas

Southern Lamu

Kizingoni Beach Villas, South Lamu Island, Kenya
PO Box 141, Nairobi 00502, Kenya
Tel +254 20 3882763; +254 20 388 2755
Mobile +254 733 444144
Fax +254 20 3884497
E-mail info@kizingonibeach.com
Web www.kizingonibeach.com

VISA, MasterCard Manda, LS & CH
45 mins

On the southernmost tip of Lamu Island, Kizingoni Beach Villas are a collection of elegant houses set in 23 acres of secluded beach.

The luxurious Kaskazi House, formed of 4 towers in landscaped tropical gardens, has 4 doubles and 1 triple. Kusini House, built in Swahili style around its swimming pool, has 3 doubles and 1 twin. Pepo House, shaded by 2 indigenous trees, has 4 doubles. Jahazi House, built of coral block and tinted ochre yellow, has 4 doubles and 1 twin. Kuni Jogoo House, on a sand dune with a 180° view of the coast, has 3 doubles and 2 twins. Kizingoni House, whitewashed and west-facing, has 4 doubles. Wazi Dubu House, with soft yellow walls and colourful shrubs, has 4 doubles, 1 twin and 1 children's twin. All the houses have their own swimming pool, dining and living area, terrace, fully equipped kitchen, private speedboat and team of staff.

Activities include water-skiing, windsurfing, kayaking, snorkelling, dhow sailing, fishing and swimming with dolphins when in season. A game drive on the mainland is also available. Parties and weddings can be arranged. Kizingoni Beach Villas minimise their environmental impact by using solar power and wind turbines, composting food waste and growing fruit and vegetables.

Kipungani Explorer

Southern Lamu

Kipungani Explorer, South Lamu Island, Kenya
Heritage Hotels Ltd, PO Box 74888, Nairobi 00200, Kenya

Tel	+254 20 4446651; +254 20 4447929; +254 20 4444582
Mobile	+254 722 205894; +254 733 411105
Fax	+254 20 4446600; +254 20 4446533
E-mail	sales@heritage-eastafrica.com
Web	www.heritage-eastafrica.com

VISA, Amex

Manda, LS & CH
45 mins

Overlooking the sheltered Kipungani channel, Kipungani Explorer is a remote hideaway on the southern tip of Lamu Island.

There are 13 en-suite bandas at one end of Kipungani Bay. The bandas are constructed from local materials, and have mkeka palm floors and makuti thatched roofs. Their furniture is handmade of mangrove and palm wood. Each banda has a sea facing veranda furnished with comfortable sofas and bright cushions. The lounge and bar, facing the sunset, has driftwood furniture and hanging beds. The dining room is in a tropical garden; the adjoining library houses a selection of books, magazines and board games. The fresh water swimming pool has an all day bar service.

The gift shop sells local handicrafts and beach essentials. Kipungani Explorer has its own well and backup generator.

Activities include snorkelling, fishing, deep sea fishing, dhow boat trips, bird walks and swimming with dolphins when in season. Visits to Lamu's historic mosques, markets and museums, as well as day trips to the ruins of the 14th century fort on Manda Island are also available. The lodge has assisted with the building of the local primary school and health clinic. It also supports the planting of indigenous trees and the conservation of marine life and mangroves.

Dhow at Sunset – Photo © Tamara Britten

North Coast

Delta Dunes – Photo © Andrew Nightingale, kembu.com

Stretching from Nyali to Malindi, the North Coast is known for its long white beaches, its trading history and its Swahili ruins. Highlights include Tana River Delta, Malindi Marine National Park, Watamu Marine National Park, Arabuko Sokoke Forest, Mida Creek and Gede Ruins.

What is referred to as the North Coast is the northern half of Kenya's east coast. The north coast beaches are Nyali, Bamburi, Shanzu, Kikambala, Vipingo, Takaungu, Kilifi, Watamu and Malindi. Nyali, Mtwapa, Watamu and Malindi are sizeable towns. Mombasa, to the south, has an international airport called Moi International Airport. Malindi, to the north, has a domestic airport that receives scheduled flights daily from destinations in Kenya. The road from Mombasa to Malindi is generally good; the road from Malindi to Lamu requires 4WD.

Tana River Primate Reserve, on the lower Tana River, has riparian forests, dry woodlands and savannah habitats. Two endangered primates, Mangabey and red colobus monkey, are found here, as well as a variety of wildlife and over 200 species of birds. The reserve offers bird watching, primate watching, walking trails and game viewing.

Malindi Marine National Park is Africa's oldest marine park. Located to the south of Malindi town, the marine park has fringing reefs, coral gardens, mangroves and a high diversity of fish, marine mammals and shorebirds. Activities include snorkelling, scuba diving, boat rides and nature walks. There is a resource centre, a library and an education centre. Malindi town is a 12th century Swahili town, around which resorts, bars, casinos and shopping centres have grown up.

Arabuko Sokoke Forest, Mida Creek and Watamu Marine National Park form one large ecosystem supporting a huge diversity of plant, animal and birdlife. The marine park is enclosed by Malindi Marine National Park.

Marine life includes fish, turtles, dugongs and crabs. Activities include windsurfing, snorkelling, water-skiing, scuba diving and trips in glass bottomed boats. Mida Creek, bordering Watamu Marine National Park, is a large tidal inlet with productive mangrove forests. The high diversity of mangrove species provides refuge to both resident and migrant bird species. The suspended boardwalk makes an ideal place from which to bird watch or enjoy a sundowner. Arabuko Sokoke Forest, an indigenous coastal forest, is home to over 500 species of birds, mammals, reptiles and butterflies. Nature walks, bird watching and night tours are all on offer. Nyari viewpoint and the tree platform have wonderful views. It is also possible to camp in the forest or on the tree platform.

Gede Ruins are one of the most significant and attractive Swahili ruins on the coast. Established in the 13th century, Gede became a trading post. Ming Chinese porcelain and glazed earthenware from Persia have been found here. The compound, consisting of houses, palaces, mosques and tombs, was mysteriously abandoned in the 17th or 18th century. Guided tours and nature walks are recommended.

At the entrance to the Gede Ruins, Kipepeo Butterfly Project gives visitors a chance to see conservation in action. The project was started by a zoologist from the University of Nairobi, and breeds and sells butterflies taken from Arabuko Sokoke Forest. Profits support local conservation projects; butterflies are on display in the Butterfly House.

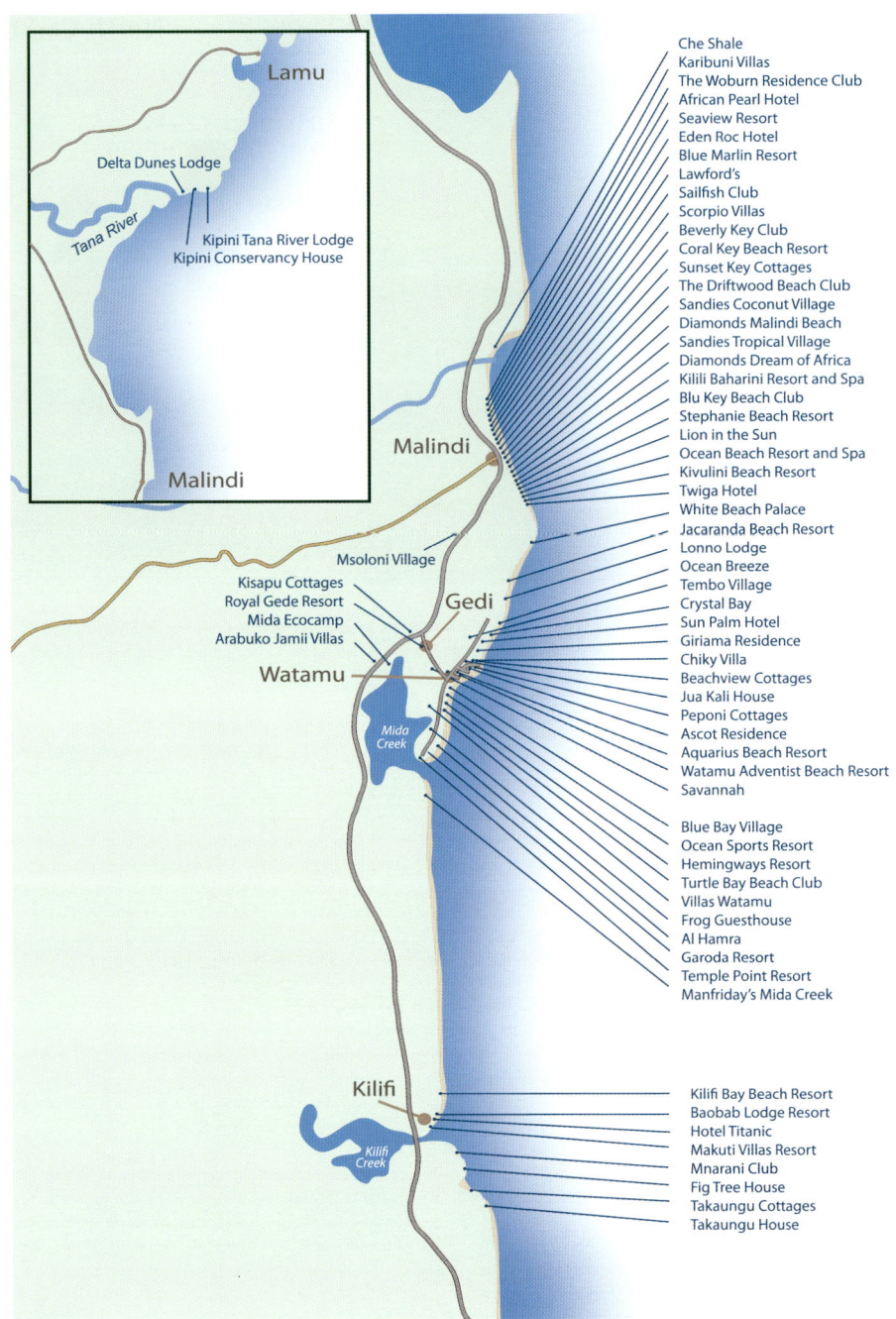

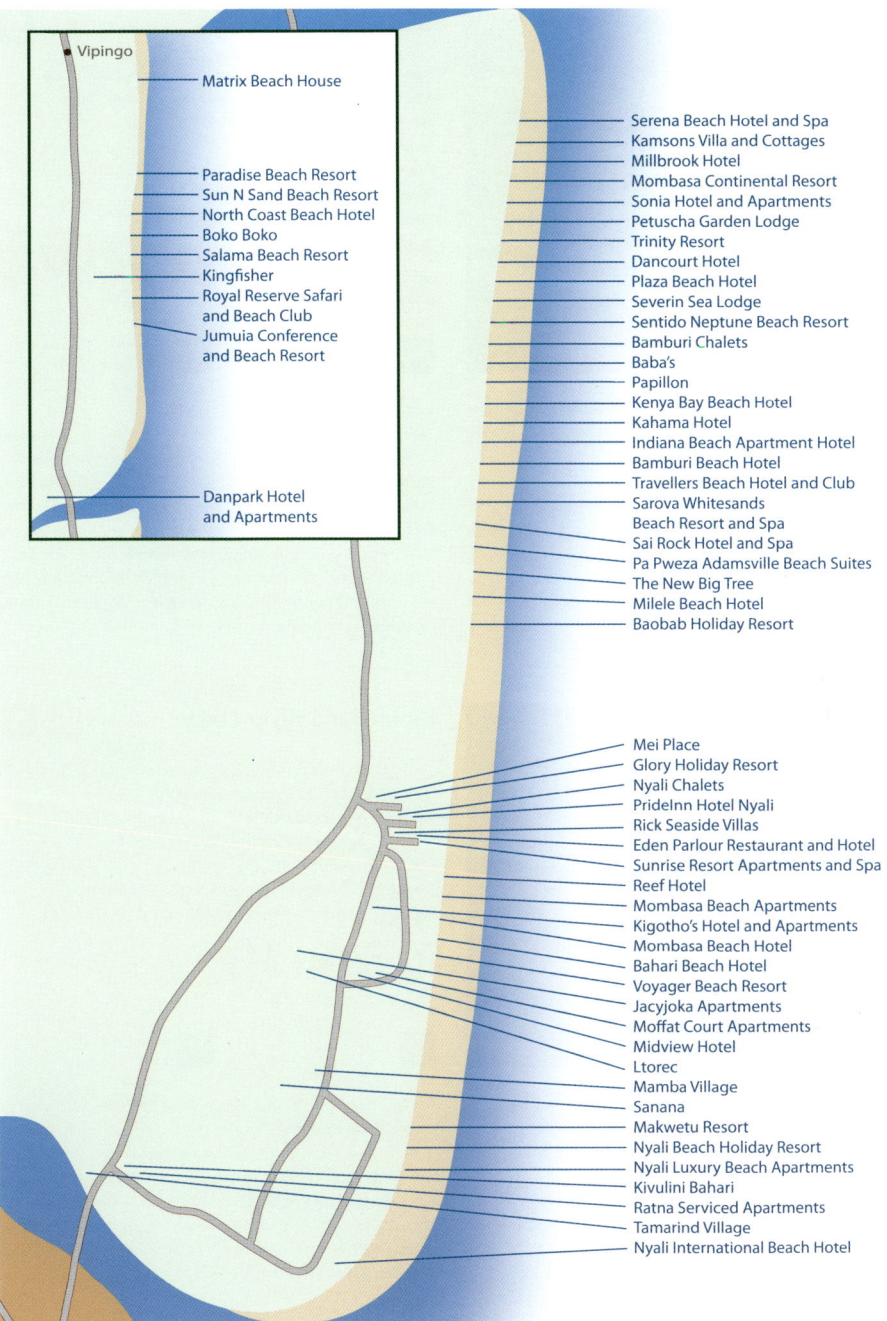

Karibu Kenya Accommodation Guide

Delta Dunes Lodge Tana River Delta

Delta Dunes Lodge, Tana River Delta, 94km from Malindi, Kenya
New African Territories, PO Box 76807, Nairobi 00508, Kenya
Tel   +254 20 2663397; +254 20 3598871
Mobile   +254 718 139759
Fax
E-mail   bookings@africanterritories.co.ke
Web   www.deltadunes.co.ke

VISA, MasterCard    Delta Dunes, CH, 15 mins
                                           Malindi, LS & CH, 2 hrs

Perched on top of rolling sand dunes, Delta Dunes Lodge has panoramic views of the Tana River Delta and the Indian Ocean. The only wetland of its type in East Africa, the area provides unique birdlife, aquatic life and wildlife.
There are 7 elegant en-suite cottages, built from driftwood, mangrove poles and thatch and shaded by doum palms, baobabs and tamarind trees. Raised on wooden platforms, the cottages are completely open, with spectacular views. The family cottage accommodates 4 people. Dining is alfresco, and includes fresh seafood, tropical fruits and other gourmet delicacies. The swimming pool lies high on the dunes; its sunbathing terrace has panoramic views.
The enticing combination of beach, river and bush provides guests with a wide selection of activities. Game and bird viewing by boat, walking safaris, creek fishing, water-skiing, surfing, river tubing, sand yachting and cultural visits to Orma villages are but a few of the activities on offer. The lodge works closely with the local community and aims to improve their standard of living, education, employment and medical facilities. A 150,000-acre conservancy is being set aside for the community, to be owned and managed by them with the support of the lodge. The lodge is closed from 1st June to 15th July.

Kipini Tana River Lodge   Tana River Delta

Kipini Tana River Lodge, Kipini, Tana River Delta, Kenya
Malindi Key Group, PO Box 556, Malindi 80200, Kenya
Tel   +254 42 2130717; +254 42 2130718
Mobile   +254 722 207319; +254 733 368944
Fax   +254 42 2130715
E-mail   info@malindikey.com / to@malindikey.com
Web   www.coralkeymalindi.com / www.malindikey.com

        Malindi, LS & CH
                                                 2.5 hrs

Kipini is a small fishing village located where the Tana River meets the sea. The Kipini Tana River Lodge, situated at this extraordinary junction of nature, overlooks a landscape where forest, river, beach, dunes and sea all merge.
The lodge has 7 bungalows and 2 suites. All rooms are en-suite, and are furnished in safari style. They are equipped with fan, mosquito net and bathtub. The bungalows have private verandas overlooking the river delta. The restaurant, on the edge of the beach, has been designed as a local Bajuni construction with a thatched roof. The restaurant serves an international menu, with a selection of meat, fish and shellfish.
The Tana River is the longest river in Kenya, stretching approximately 800km. People have settled near its banks for its full length, drawn to it for the fresh water that it provides throughout every season of the year. The Orma and Pokomo peoples live in the vicinity of Kipini, close to the mouth of the river. Over 200 species of birds have been recorded along it. Kipini Tana River Lodge is affiliated to the Malindi Key Group; holidays combining the lodge with the other properties in Malindi and Tsavo East National Park can be arranged.

Kipini Conservancy House

Tana River Delta

Kipini Conservancy House, Kipini Conservancy, Kenya
PO Box 25582, Nairobi 00603, Kenya
Tel   +254 20 4348298
Mobile +254 722 643658
Fax   +254 20 4348298
E-mail u.sherman@gmail.com
Web   www.kipiniconservancy.org

Manda, LS & CH, 20 mins by boat
Malindi, LS & CH, 2.5 hrs

Kipini Conservancy was established in 2004 and has an area of 265km². The conservancy lies between the Tana River Basin, the forest and the coast, and has a unique ecosystem of high canopy forest, low canopy forest, wetlands and sand dunes. It aims to establish itself as a centre for an unusual combination of safari and adventure sports.

The Kipini Conservancy House has 3 en-suite bedrooms, made up of 2 singles and 1 double. It also has a living room, kitchen, veranda and outdoor seating area, overlooking a lake inhabited by hippos and crocodiles. The house is taken on a self-catering basis. The resident chef prepares food according to the preferences of the guests.

Game drives and game walks are on offer. Fly camping can also be arranged. Resident species include elephant, buffalo and cheetah. The conservancy attracts migratory birds from Europe, as well as the rare Malindi barbet and the corncrake. Current conservation projects include turtle conservation.

Trips to the coast and dhow trips to Lamu can be arranged, as can water sports such as scuba diving, kite surfing, deep sea fishing and dolphin trips. Local sites of interest include an ancient mosque located inside the conservancy.

Che Shale

Malindi

Che Shale, nr Malindi, North Coast, Kenya
PO Box 2082, Malindi 80200, Kenya
Tel
Mobile +254 722 230931
Fax
E-mail cheshale@gmail.com
Web   www.cheshale.com

Malindi, LS & CH
25 mins

Che Shale is a boutique hotel situated on 5km of deserted beach, fringed by coral reef and surrounded by thousands of palm trees and lush indigenous vegetation. Che Shale is renowned for being the pioneer of kite surfing in East Africa and has conditions that are ideal for learners and experienced kite surfers alike.

There are 5 en-suite rooms, made up of 2 double rooms, 1 triple room and 2 family rooms. The rooms are adorned with unique furniture carved out of blocks of mango and cedar wood, soft natural colours and large lamps made out of palm fibre. They all have verandas furnished with daybeds, and showers that are open to the sky. The restaurant has an international a la carte menu, and specialises in seafood.

As well as kite surfing, activities include surfing and deep sea fishing. Massage is also on offer. The hotel supports community school outreach programmes and guests are welcome to visit the projects, as well as experience the culture of the local fishermen. Che Shale was built using low impact, renewable materials, such as casuarina trees, doum palm leaves, palm matting and dhow wood collected from the beach. The hotel is closed in May and June.

Karibuni Villas   Malindi

Karibuni Villas, Mambrui, nr Malindi, North Coast, Kenya
PO Box 840, Malindi 80200, Kenya
Tel	+254 20 2335957
Mobile	+254 726 863693
Fax	
E-mail	info@karibunivillas.net / direzione@karibunivillas.net
Web	www.karibunivillas.net

 VISA, MasterCard   Malindi, LS & CH
                                                                                                   20 mins

In large tropical gardens, Karibuni Villas combines Italian style with Kenyan culture. It opened in 1997, and has a collection of rooms and cottages with both self-catering and catered options.

There are 64 en-suite double rooms, in 8 buildings. All rooms have aircon, fan, telephone, safe, hairdryer, mosquito net and veranda. There are 120 thatched cottages, with either 1 or 2 bedrooms. All cottages have living room, kitchenette, aircon, fan, safe and mosquito net. Cheetah Restaurant serves buffet, with a selection of Italian and international dishes, and a list of Italian and South African wines. Once a week, Swahili dinner is served. Tembo Restaurant, at the poolside, has an a la carte menu including grilled beef and seafood. There is also an Italian pizzeria. There are 5 bars: Disco, Tembo, Sabaki, Beach and Twiga.

The villas also have 2 swimming pools, gym, Jacuzzi, spa and salon. The animation team offers a daily programme of activities, games and tournaments, as well as evening shows. Sports include horse riding, tennis, 5-aside football, beach volleyball, archery and bowling. The tour desk can arrange tours, excursions and safaris to destinations in Kenya. A nearby water sports centre has kite surfing and deep sea fishing.

The Woburn Residence Club   Malindi

The Woburn Residence Club, Lamu Road, Malindi, North Coast, Kenya
PO Box 33, Malindi 80200, Kenya
Tel	+254 42 2131085; +254 42 2130699; +254 42 2131923
Mobile	+254 710 838354; +254 738 033611
Fax	+254 42 2131183
E-mail	woburn@swiftmalindi.com
Web	www.woburnresidencemalindi.com

      Malindi, LS & CH
                                                     15 mins

The Woburn Residence Club was established in 2000. The residence is a collection of apartments, suites and luxury bedrooms, set around landscaped tropical gardens and a 3-tier swimming pool. The accommodation can be taken either short or long-term.

There are 1, 2 and 3-bedrooom apartments. All apartments are sleekly furnished, and have a modern fitted kitchen and an open plan living and dining room. The ground floor apartments have a veranda and outdoor barbecue area. There are also 14 units, made up of en-suite rooms, junior suites and superior suites. The rooms have twin beds and a veranda overlooking the gardens; the junior suites have twin beds and overlook the swimming pool; the superior suites include a bar area with fridge. The club has a restaurant with a gourmet a la carte menu including Italian, Japanese and seafood, and a bar stocked with soft drinks, beers, wines and spirits. It also has a small conference centre and offers business services. There is a fully equipped gym, health club and Jacuzzi. There is 24-hour security. The reception has a selection of recommended itineraries for trips and excursions both in Malindi and to destinations in Kenya, and can assist with booking safaris. The Woburn Residence Club received The New Millennium Award for the Tourist, Hotel and Catering Industry in 2002.

African Pearl Hotel

Malindi

African Pearl Hotel, Lamu Road, Malindi, North Coast, Kenya
PO Box 165, Malindi 80200, Kenya
Tel
Mobile +254 725 131956
Fax
E-mail reservations@africanpearlhotel.com
Web www.africanpearlhotel.com

   Malindi, LS & CH
10 mins

The African Pearl Hotel is a charming small hotel set in lush gardens. It was established in 2003 as a Bed and Breakfast, and has grown into the hotel that it is today. The hotel is located on Lamu Road, not far from Malindi Beach.

There are 15 en-suite rooms, which can be single, double or triple as required. All rooms have 4-poster bed, mosquito net and aircon. There are also 5 self-catering cottages. The restaurant serves local and international cuisine. The bar serves soft drinks, beers, wines, spirits and cocktails.

The swimming pool is surrounded by a sunbathing terrace. WiFi is available throughout the hotel. For a surcharge, water sports including scuba diving, snorkelling, fishing and windsurfing can be arranged through the hotel. Safaris, excursions and boat trips can also be booked. Local sites of interest include Arabuko Sokoke Forest, Mida Creek, Gede Ruins, Kipepeo Butterfly Project and the Snake Farm.

Seaview Resort

Malindi

Seaview Resort, Lamu Road, Malindi, North Coast, Kenya
PO Box 5799, Malindi 80200, Kenya
Tel +254 42 2130427
Mobile +254 735 432371
Fax
E-mail info@seaviewresortmalindi.com
Web www.seaviewresortmalindi.com

  Malindi, LS & CH
10 mins

Set in mature tropical gardens and natural indigenous forest, Seaview Resort is on the beachfront of Malindi. The resort offers self-catering accommodation as well as a restaurant. The Bahari Stables are home to highly trained horses that are available for rides both in the forest and on the beach.

There are 10 cottages and 11 en-suite deluxe rooms. All rooms have aircon, fan, desk, satellite TV, minibar, kettle and veranda. All cottages have fully equipped kitchenette and veranda with dining area. The restaurant, overlooking the garden and swimming pool, specialises in chargrills and seafood. Meals can also be served in the 2 poolside gazebos, which are furnished with tables and cushioned chairs. Candlelit dinners on the beach can be arranged.

Riding lessons for inexperienced riders, and longer rides for the more proficient are both available. Attractive destinations for horse rides include the pier, the Vasco da Gama Pillar and the Sabaki River Estuary. Nearby water sports centres provide scuba diving, snorkelling, windsurfing, water-skiing and deep sea fishing. Malindi town has a selection of shops, restaurants, bars and casino for those who wish to experience local culture. Nearby sites of interest include the Gede Ruins and Malindi and Watamu Marine National Parks.

Eden Roc Hotel Malindi

Eden Roc Hotel, Malindi, North Coast, Kenya
PO Box 300, Malindi 80200, Kenya

Tel	+254 42 2120480-2
Mobile	+254 720 909853; +254 732 233043
Fax	+254 42 2120333
E-mail	marketing@edenrochotel.co.ke
Web	www.edenrochotel.co.ke

VISA, MasterCard   Malindi, LS & CH 10 mins

Eden Roc Hotel is set in 22 acres of beachfront gardens. The hotel has a wide selection of facilities and activities.

There are 150 en-suite rooms, made up of standard and superior. The standard rooms have fan; the superior rooms have aircon. There are also 15 suites with ocean view. The Main Restaurant serves buffet breakfast and lunch, and theme dinners featuring cuisines like Italian and Swahili. On Saturday night, there is a Kenyan barbecue, with nyama choma grilled meats. The Dhow Grill Restaurant has an a la carte menu. There is also a lounge bar, pool bar, beach bar, open air disco and nightclub.

The animation team offers a daily programme of activities. Night time entertainment includes traditional dancers, live bands and acrobatic shows. Scuba diving instructors are on call. Other water sports available include snorkelling, sailing and fishing. Amani conference hall seats 150 pax; Sifa conference hall seats 50 pax. The boardroom seats 15 pax, and has a secretariat, bathroom and balcony. The business centre has broadband internet, fax, photocopy, scanning, laminating and secretarial services. Local sites of interest include the Vasco da Gama Pillar, Hell's Kitchen, Malindi Museum, Gede Ruins and the mangroves.

Blue Marlin Resort   Malindi

Blue Marlin Resort, Malindi, North Coast, Kenya

Tel	
Mobile	+254 711 415504
Fax	
E-mail	info@kenyaservices.com
Web	www.bluemarlinmalindi.com

Malindi, LS & CH 10 mins

Built in 1913, Blue Marlin Resort is one of the oldest hotels in Malindi. The resort hosted the explorers who were charting the interior of Africa. It is said that Ernest Hemingway and Marilyn Monroe have both visited this beachfront resort. Extensive refurbishment has recently been completed, in keeping with the original style of the resort.

There are 40 apartments. The apartments have either 1 or 2 en-suite bedrooms, living room, fully equipped kitchen and veranda. The apartments are attractively furnished with Swahili furniture. The restaurant specialises in Italian cuisine and seafood. Dishes include homemade noodles with lobster and ravioli with cuttlefish and beans. The bar has an extensive selection of soft drinks, beers, wines and spirits and offers 70 different cocktails.

The resort has 2 swimming pools. There is also a tennis court, minigolf, beach volleyball and beach football. The large gym is equipped with technogym products, and staffed by an instructor who is ready to advise and correct personal fitness routines. The beauty centre offers 12 different types of massage. The extensive tropical gardens are home to numerous birds, insects and lizards. There is a security guard on duty 24 hours a day. The resort welcomes families.

Lawford's

Malindi

Lawford's, Lamu Road, Malindi, North Coast, Kenya
PO Box 20, Malindi 80200, Kenya

Tel	+254 42 2121265-7
Mobile	
Fax	+254 42 2121268
E-mail	lawfords@swiftmalindi.com / info@malindikey.com
Web	www.lawfordsresort.com / www.malindikey.com

VISA, MasterCard   Malindi, LS & CH 10 mins

Lawford's is one of the oldest and loveliest hotels in Malindi. It was renovated in 2006, and combines old English style, African atmosphere and Italian hospitality. The resort is in a large tropical garden that extends along Malindi's beachfront.

There are 60 suites, made up of 50 junior suites and 10 executive suites. All suites have aircon, mosquito net, hairdryer, TV, DVD, minibar, dining table and large private veranda. The junior suites have 1 en-suite double room; the executive suites have 2 en-suite double rooms. Patterson Restaurant serves buffet breakfast, lunch and dinner. The cuisine is Mediterranean, and includes grilled fish and meat. Once a week, there is an African buffet and gala dinner. Victoria Queen Restaurant, open for dinner, has an a la carte menu specialising in shellfish. Lawford's Club Lounge, next to Victoria Queen Restaurant, is open nightly for drinks. The Lounge Bar, next to the pool, is open throughout the day. The Beach Bar has fresh fruit cocktails and snacks.

Lawford's Spa has a range of therapies to relax body and mind, as well as steam bath and Jacuzzi. Sports facilities include 2 swimming pools, putting green, beach tennis and beach volleyball. The resort also offers a lounge with satellite TV, internet point and boutique. The tourist office can book tours, excursions and safaris.

Sailfish Club

Malindi

Sailfish Club, Silversand Road, Malindi, North Coast, Kenya
PO Box 5200, Malindi 80200, Kenya

Tel	
Mobile	+254 733 799478; +254 722 362449
Fax	
E-mail	sailfishclubbookings@yahoo.com
Web	www.sailfishclubmalindi.com

     Malindi, LS & CH 10 mins

Sailfish Club was established in 1996 for fishermen and all those who love fishing. The club, set in landscaped gardens on Malindi Beach, is designed to be a blend of African and modern architecture.

There are 9 en-suite rooms. All rooms have a double and single bed, and are equipped with aircon, dressing table, mosquito net and balcony. The restaurant serves a buffet of international and African dishes; the African dishes include cassava leaves, goat curry, plantain, jolif rice and samosa. The dining lounge at the poolside has a snack menu. The bar offers a range of soft drinks, beers, wines, liqueurs and champagne. Parties, graduations, anniversaries and other functions can all be accommodated at the club. The club offers Malindi village walks for visitors who wish to experience the cultural diversity of the town. Safaris, trips and excursions to destinations in Kenya can be arranged here.

Big game fishing is the prime activity offered by the club. The waters off Malindi are home to sailfish, black marlin, striped marlin, swordfish, kingfish, barracuda, snapper, tuna and shark. Emiel van der Werf, the club's owner, holds 2 world records in big game fishing.

Scorpio Villas Malindi

Scorpio Villas, Mnarani Road, Malindi, North Coast, Kenya
PO Box 368, Malindi 80200, Kenya

Tel	+254 42 2120194; +254 42 2120892;
Mobile	+254 700 437680
Fax	+254 42 2121250
E-mail	bookings@scorpio-villas.com
Web	www.scorpio-villas.com

 Malindi, LS & CH
10 mins

In 3 acres of tropical gardens, Scorpio Villas offer accommodation in a collection of villas that blend Lamu style with African décor. The villas are located 2km from Malindi town centre making them convenient for visitors who want to experience the shops, restaurants, bars and casino of Malindi. There are 46 en-suite rooms, in 1 or 2-floor villas. All rooms have 4-poster bed, mosquito net, fan, aircon, satellite TV and veranda with views of the garden. The restaurant serves buffet of Italian cuisine, including meat, fish and pasta dishes. Swahili and Indian cuisine are served on occasion. There is a bar in the lounge, featuring live music, and a bar beside a swimming pool. The 3 salt water swimming pools are surrounded by sunbathing terraces furnished with sunbeds.
The resort has a small gym, a games room with billiard table, table tennis table and dartboard. There is a reading room with library, massage room, internet point and some curio shops stocked with local artefacts. The large conference hall seats 90 pax and the small hall seats 40. Malindi village walks, souvenir shopping trips and airport transfers are on offer. Safaris, tours and excursions can be arranged. Local sites of interest include the Gede Ruins and Malindi and Watamu Marine National Parks.

Beverly Key Club   Malindi

Beverly Key Club, Mama Ngina Road, Malindi, North Coast, Kenya
Malindi Key Group, PO Box 556, Malindi 80200, Kenya

Tel	+254 42 2130717/8
Mobile	+254 733 368944
Fax	+254 42 2130715
E-mail	info@malindikey.com / info@coralkeymalindi.com
Web	www.malindikey.com / www.coralkeymalindi.com

 VISA, MasterCard

 Malindi, LS & CH
10 mins

Beverly Key Club is located between Silversands Beach and Malindi town centre. The club is set in lush tropical gardens, adjacent to sister resort, Coral Key Beach Resort.
There are 35 en-suite rooms, made up of 11 deluxe rooms and 12 2-bedroom cottages. All rooms have aircon and mosquito net, and terrace overlooking the garden and swimming pool. The cottages also include a living room.
The restaurants, bars, facilities and activities at sister resort Coral Key are available to guests at Beverly Key. La Terrazza Italian Restaurant offers candlelit dinners, with refined Italian dishes and a wide variety of international wines. La Pizzeria has over 20 types of Italian pizza and an extensive barbecue of grilled meat and fish. The Buffet has themed dinners daily. The Marlin offers Italian and international buffets and barbecues. Coral Key also has 4 bars to cater to all tastes: Bogart Lounge Bar, the Main Bar, Fisherman's Cove and the Beach Bar.
Coral Key's conference centre has modern equipment and professional staff. The Italian-managed beauty centre offers personal treatments with natural products. The extensive sports facilities include 2 floodlit tennis courts, football pitch, gym, Olympic swimming pool, climbing wall, beach volleyball and a selection of water sports.

Coral Key Beach Resort   Malindi

Coral Key Beach Resort, Mama Ngina Road, Malindi, North Coast, Kenya
Malindi Key Group, PO Box 556, Malindi 80200, Kenya

Tel	+254 42 2130717/8
Mobile	+254 733 368944
Fax	+254 42 2130715
E-mail	info@coralkeymalindi.com / malindikey@gmail.com
Web	www.coralkeymalindi.com / www.malindike.com

   VISA, MasterCard   Malindi, LS & CH
                                                      10 mins

Coral Key Beach Resort provides its guests with a complete holiday without their having to leave its grounds, offering everything from conferences to beauty treatments to water sports. Harbour Key Cottages are 32 thatched bungalows set in brilliant bougainvillea gardens. Coral Key Park contains 2-floor African-style bungalows set in private grounds with 3 swimming pools. The Yachting Club has 24 finely furnished suites facing the Indian Ocean. The Sporting Club, with striking Arabic architecture, has 22 deluxe rooms. And Coral Key Hotel has 44 spacious en-suite rooms with private veranda. La Terrazza Italian Restaurant offers candlelit dinners, with refined Italian dishes and a wide variety of international wines. La Pizzeria has over 20 types of Italian pizza and an extensive barbecue of grilled meat and fish. The Buffet has themed dinners daily. The Marlin offers Italian and international buffets and barbecues. The resort also has 4 bars to cater to all tastes: Bogart Lounge Bar, the Main Bar, Fisherman's Cove and the Beach Bar.

The conference centre has modern equipment and professional staff. The Italian-managed beauty centre offers personal treatments with natural products. The extensive sports facilities include 2 floodlit tennis courts, football pitch, gym, Olympic swimming pool, climbing wall, beach volleyball and a selection of water sports.

Sunset Key Cottages   Malindi

Sunset Key Cottages, Mama Ngina Road, Malindi, North Coast, Kenya
Malindi Key Group, PO Box 556, Malindi 80200, Kenya

Tel	+254 42 2130717/8
Mobile	+254 733 368944
Fax	+254 42 2130715
E-mail	info@malindikey.com / info@coralkeymalindi.com
Web	www.malindikey.com / www.coralkeymalindi.com

   VISA, MasterCard   Malindi, LS & CH
                                                      10 mins

Sunset Key Cottages are set in tropical gardens, not far from Silversands Beach. The cottages offer peace and relaxation, adjacent to sister resort Coral Key Beach Resort. There are 12 African style thatched bungalows, and 20 rooms on the ground floor and 1st floor. All rooms are equipped with aircon, fan, mosquito net and balcony overlooking the garden or the swimming pool. There are 3 swimming pools, 1 of which is intended for children. All pools are surrounded by sunbathing terrace furnished with sunbeds and shade umbrellas. The restaurants, bars, facilities and activities at sister resort Coral Key are available to guests at Sunset Key Cottages. La Terrazza Italian Restaurant offers candlelit dinners, with refined Italian dishes and a wide variety of international wines. La Pizzeria has over 20 types of Italian pizza and an extensive barbecue of grilled meat and fish. The Buffet has themed dinners daily. The Marlin offers Italian and international buffets and barbecues. Coral Key also has 4 bars to cater to all tastes: Bogart Lounge Bar, the Main Bar, Fisherman's Cove and the Beach Bar. Coral Key's conference centre has modern equipment and professional staff. The Italian-managed beauty centre offers personal treatments with natural products. The extensive sports facilities include 2 floodlit tennis courts, football pitch, gym, Olympic swimming pool, climbing wall, beach volleyball and a selection of water sports.

The Driftwood Beach Club Malindi

The Driftwood Beach Club, Silversand Road, Malindi, North Coast, Kenya
PO Box 63, Malindi 80200, Kenya

Tel	+254 42 2120155; +254 20 2617300
Mobile	+254 721 724489
Fax	+254 42 2130712
E-mail	reservations@driftwoodclub.com
Web	www.driftwoodclub.com

VISA, MasterCard   Malindi, LS & CH
                                10 mins

The Driftwood Beach Club has long been a favourite with locals. The charming club, set in beachfront gardens, is one of the original hotels in Malindi. There are 30 thatched bandas, each containing an en-suite double room. All bandas have aircon, telephone and veranda. There are 2 luxury director's cottages, in a private walled garden with a swimming pool. Each cottage has 2 en-suite aircon rooms, living room and veranda. There are 3 villas in secluded private premises behind the club, with a swimming pool. The dining room and main bar have lovely views of the Indian Ocean. The restaurant has an international menu, including seafood and steaks. The poolside bar serves snacks. Sunday curry lunch has become a tradition.

There is a scuba diving centre on site. Other water sports include deep sea fishing, windsurfing, kite surfing, water-skiing and snorkelling. Nearby attractions include the Sabaki Delta and the Arabuko Sokoke Forest, both of which have prolific birdlife.

Malindi has a selection of restaurants and bars, as well as a casino and nightclub. Tours, excursions and safaris to destinations in Kenya can be arranged.

Sandies Coconut Village   Malindi

Sandies Coconut Village, Casuarina Road, Malindi, North Coast, Kenya
Plan Hotel Group, PO Box 868, Malindi 80200, Kenya

Tel	+254 42 2120444; +254 42 2131673
Mobile	
Fax	+254 42 2131872
E-mail	info.coconut@planhotel.com
Web	www.planhotel.com

All major cards   Malindi, LS & CH
                                 15 mins

Set on Malindi Beach overlooking the protected Malindi Marine National Park, Sandies Coconut Village is an all inclusive resort for families and young couples alike.

The 45 en-suite rooms, in 2-level bungalow blocks, are made up of 33 superior rooms with pool views and 12 superior beachfront rooms. All rooms are furnished in Swahili style with queen size canopy beds, large bathrooms with walk-in showers and private terraces with African sofas. Facilities in the rooms include aircon, mini fridge and safe. The Coconut Restaurant serves a buffet of Italian and Mediterranean dishes. Guests are welcome to eat at the Savannah a la carte restaurant at nearby Sandies Tropical Village if they prefer, reservation required. The Coconut Pool Bar serves drinks, snacks and pastries.

The water sports centre at nearby sister resort, Sandies Tropical Village, offers catamarans, windsurfing, canoeing, sailing, PADI scuba dive courses, beach volleyball and other beach entertainment. The Dream Spa at nearby Diamonds Dream of Africa has a centre of Thalassotherapy, a beauty centre, 2 salt water pools with muscle-toning water jets and a gym with a spectacular view of the ocean. Tours to the Gedi Ruins, Lamu Island, Maasai Mara National Reserve and other Kenyan destinations can be booked at Sandies Tropical Village.

Diamonds Malindi Beach

Malindi

Diamonds Malindi Beach, Casuarina Road, Malindi, North Coast, Kenya
Plan Hotel Group, PO Box 868, Malindi 80200, Kenya

Tel	+254 42 2120444; +254 42 2131673
Mobile	
Fax	+254 42 2131872
E-mail	info.malindi@planhotel.com
Web	www.planhotel.com

All major cards   Malindi, LS & CH
                         15 mins

In lush landscaped gardens, Diamonds Malindi Beach is an Arab-African styled boutique resort. The resort overlooks the protected Malindi Marine National Park and offers an all inclusive package.

The 23 deluxe rooms, made up of 6 deluxe sea view rooms and 17 deluxe garden rooms, are situated in 8 striking Arabic 2-floor villas. All rooms have international cable TV, minibar and large bathroom with walk-in shower. They also have aircon, digital safe and telephone. The Frangipane Restaurant serves a buffet of Mediterranean inspired cooking. Guests are welcome to eat at the Savannah a la carte restaurant at nearby Sandies Tropical Village if they prefer, reservation required. The Bougainvillea Bar has a selection of cocktails and other beverages. The Beach Bar serves drinks, snacks, pastries and fruit.

The water sports centre at nearby sister resort Sandies Tropical Village offers catamarans, windsurfing, canoeing, sailing, PADI scuba dive courses, beach volleyball and other beach entertainment. The Dream Spa at nearby Diamonds Dream of Africa has a centre of Thalassotherapy, a beauty centre, 2 salt water pools with muscle-toning water jets and a gym with a spectacular view of the ocean. Tours to the Gedi Ruins, Lamu Island, Maasai Mara National Reserve and other Kenyan destinations can be booked at Sandies Tropical Village.

Sandies Tropical Village

Malindi

Sandies Tropical Village, Casuarina Road, Malindi, North Coast, Kenya
Plan Hotel Group, PO Box 68, Malindi 80200, Kenya

Tel	+254 42 2120444; +254 42 2131879
Mobile	+254 735 955666; +254 720 607075
Fax	+254 42 2131872
E-mail	info.tropical@planhotel.com
Web	www.planhotel.com

VISA, MasterCard   Malindi, LS & CH
                          15 mins

Set in tropical gardens along Malindi Beach, Sandies Tropical Village offers an all inclusive package.

The 109 en-suite garden rooms are made up of 85 deluxe garden rooms, 12 of which interconnect for families with children, and 24 junior suites. The rooms are designed in Lamu or English style, and have a mini fridge, aircon and safe. In addition, the junior suites have stocked minibars, evening turn down service, free laundry and breakfast room service. The ground floor rooms have facilities for guests with disabilities.

The Tropical Restaurant serves a buffet of international and Italian cuisine. The Savannah a la carte restaurant serves a selection of seafood and fish dishes, reservation required. The Tropical Jahazi Bar serves drinks, snacks and pastries. The Tropical Beach Bar serves drinks by day and the Disco Bar serves drinks at night.

The water sports centre has catamaran, windsurfing, canoeing and sailing. The PADI scuba dive centre has dive courses and trips. The Animation Team provides daily and evening entertainment programmes such as aquagym, beach volleyball, archery and seasonal shows. The Dream Spa at nearby Diamonds Dream of Africa has a centre of Thalassotherapy, a beauty centre, 2 salt water pools with muscle-toning water jets and a gym.

Diamonds Dream of Africa Malindi

Diamonds Dream of Africa, Casuarina Road, Malindi, North Coast, Kenya
Plan Hotel Group, PO Box 68, Malindi 80200, Kenya

Tel	+254 42 2120444
Mobile	+254 735 955666; +254 720 607075
Fax	+254 42 2131872
E-mail	info.tropical@planhotel.com
Web	www.planhotel.com

All major cards   Malindi, LS & CH 15 mins

Surrounded by attractive gardens studded with palm trees, Diamonds Dream of Africa lies on Malindi Beach. This exclusive resort and spa is affiliated to Small Luxury Hotels of the World and offers an all inclusive package.

The 35 en-suite rooms are made up of 33 junior suites with garden views, and 2 suites with sea views, which also include living rooms. All the rooms have Italian designed furniture, including king size beds or twin beds, sofa beds, armchairs and dressing tables, and private terraces with Balinese sunbeds. They also have Jacuzzi, minibar, satellite TV, internet connection, digital safe and individual climate control.

The Main Restaurant serves a buffet of fresh fish and seafood with an Italian flair. The A La Carte Restaurant on the beach serves a selection of seafood and meat. The Main Bar serves local and imported beverages. The Pool Bar serves fresh fruits and snacks. The Dream Spa has a centre of Thalassotherapy, a beauty centre, 2 salt water pools with muscle-toning water jets and a gym with a spectacular view of the ocean.

The water sports centre at nearby sister resort, Sandies Tropical Village, offers catamarans, windsurfing, canoeing, sailing, PADI scuba dive courses, beach volleyball and other beach entertainment.

Kilili Baharini Resort & Spa Malindi

Kilili Baharini Resort & Spa, Casuarina Road, Malindi, North Coast, Kenya
PO Box 93, Malindi 80200, Kenya

Tel	+254 42 2120169; +254 42 2121264
Mobile	+254 770 206500
Fax	+254 42 2120634
E-mail	sales@kililibaharini.com
Web	www.kililibaharini.com

VISA, Amex   Malindi, LS & CH 15 mins

In beachfront gardens on Malindi Beach, Kilili Baharini Resort and Spa is an exclusive resort, offering luxurious relaxation.

There are 29 en-suite rooms, 4 suites and 2 junior suites. All rooms have aircon, fan, minibar, safe, telephone and mosquito net. They are tastefully furnished in Swahili style, and adorned with African artefacts and exquisite fabrics. There are 5 swimming pools; all rooms open onto 1 of the pools and have their own private veranda on which breakfast is served. An assorted lunch buffet is served in the seafront restaurant. Afternoon tea is served by the pool. Dinner is served in the resort restaurant, and is a fusion of Italian cuisine, local dishes and seafood. The snack bar, on the beach, serves snacks throughout the day. The 2 bars serve an extensive list of soft drinks, beers, wines and spirits.

Kilili Spa has a range of health and beauty treatments. It uses certified products and methods, and provides pampering and relaxation. Safaris, excursions and trips to destinations in Kenya can be booked at the resort. Local sites of interest include Arabuko Sokoke Forest, Mida Creek, Gede Ruins, Kipepeo Butterfly Project and the Snake Farm.

Blu Key Beach Club   Malindi

Blu Key Beach Club, Casuarina Road, Malindi, North Coast, Kenya
Malindi Key Group, PO Box 556, Malindi 80200, Kenya

Tel	+254 42 2131452; +254 42 2130717/8
Mobile	+254 725 091723
Fax	+254 42 2120842
E-mail	info@malindikey.com / info@coralkeymalindi.com
Web	www.malindikey.com / www.coralkeymalindi.com

VISA, MasterCard   Malindi, LS & CH
15 mins

Blu Key Beach Club is a small exclusive club located on Silversands Beach bordering Malindi Marine National Park. The club offers privacy and peace. There are 14 en-suite rooms located in 1 and 2-floor thatched cottages. There are also 12 en-suite rooms. All rooms are equipped with aircon, fan, fridge, safe and mosquito net, and all have private balcony or terrace. The restaurant serves buffet breakfast and lunch. Lunch is Mediterranean cuisine, and includes a variety of grilled fish and meat. Dinner is table d'hote; the chef specialises in seafood. The beach bar serves fresh tropical fruit shakes. The main bar serves a selection of soft drinks, beers, wines and spirits.

The club has 3 swimming pools, each of which is surrounded by a sunbathing terrace. Massage is on offer. The club also has a boutique and TV room. Nightly entertainment includes local shows and dancing. Activities include fishing, scuba diving and boat trips. For a surcharge, golf and horse riding can be arranged. The tourist office, on site, can book safaris, excursions and trips to destinations in Kenya. Local sites of interest include Arabuko Sokoke Forest, Mida Creek, Gede Ruins, Kipepeo Butterfly Project and the Snake Farm.

Stephanie Beach Resort   Malindi

Stephanie Beach Resort, Malindi, North Coast, Kenya
PO Box 583, Malindi 80200, Kenya

Tel	+39 335 8305631
Mobile	+254 723 403430
Fax	
E-mail	info@stephanieresort.com / albaclubmalindi@yahoo.it
Web	www.stephanieresort.com

Malindi, LS & CH
15 mins

On Malindi Beach, Stephanie Beach Resort is set in attractive tropical gardens.
There are 50 en-suite cottages. Each cottage has aircon, minibar, safe, fan and balcony. The swimming pool overlooks the sea. There is also a sea facing lounge and a solarium terrace. The resort has a beach volleyball court.
The resort has a team of PADI scuba diving instructors who can either guide dives or instruct those who would like to get their licence. Kite surfing is on offer. Deep sea fishing trips can be arranged. The resort also organises walks around the area, and 1-day excursions to local sites of interest such as the Maiungu atoll, the Gede Ruins and nearby beaches. Horse riding on the beaches is also available.
The resort can book safaris, tours and excursions to destinations in Kenya.

North Coast

 Accommodation Guide

Lion in the Sun

Malindi

Lion in the Sun, Marine Park Road, Malindi, North Coast, Kenya
PO Box 1056, Malindi 80200, Kenya

Tel	+254 42 2130066
Mobile	+254 725 906044; +254 733 634766
Fax	+254 42 2130735
E-mail	info@liongroup.co.ke
Web	www.lioninthesun.net

 All major cards   Malindi, LS & CH 20 mins

The sun, considered the life giver, and the lion, considered a force of nature, were chosen to give their names to this luxury resort. The resort's concept is open spaces, freedom, unique environment, complete relaxation and self discovery. Arab and Indian influences fuse in the architecture. There are 7 suites, 7 superior rooms and 2 singles in the main building and 4 annex structures. Each room is uniquely designed; each artefact and decoration has been individually chosen. The spacious suites are intended for privacy and relaxation. The superior rooms have views of the gardens and private pool. For the utmost privacy the resort can be taken exclusively.

The restaurant serves international cuisine combined with Italian dishes, created from both local and exotic ingredients. The garden contains local plants and shrubs set around 4 sea water swimming pools. The fully equipped gym has state of the art facilities and an instructor to assist with exercise regimes. The Thalaspa health centre has 6 treatment cabins, 3 sea water hydrotherapy facilities, a hair dressing salon and uses the science and technology of Henri Chenot.

Lion in the Sun was given the Life Changing Award at the 2010 Tatler Spa Awards, and the Best Spa in the World Award in 2011 by Conde Nast.

Ocean Beach
Resort and Spa

Malindi

Ocean Beach Resort and Spa, Lamu Road, Malindi, North Coast, Kenya
PO Box 5296, Malindi 80200, Kenya

Tel	+254 42 2131222; +254 42 2131951
Mobile	+254 705 204590; +254 754 333404
Fax	+254 42 2131355
E-mail	info@oceanbeachkenya.com
Web	www.oceanbeachkenya.com

 VISA, MasterCard   Malindi, LS & CH 20 mins

Ocean Beach Resort and Spa is set in attractive beachfront gardens. The resort has a wealth of facilities in an elegant setting on Malindi Beach. There are 4 standard rooms and 16 superior rooms. The 4 junior suites and 6 suites each have private deck for relaxing or dining. The 4 master suites each have en-suite double bedroom, living room and large veranda. The 1 imperial suite, directly on the beach, has private garden, massage area, double Jacuzzi and large veranda.

Tembo Court, independent from the rest of the resort, has 54 apartments suitable for families or groups. The apartments have 1 or 2 en-suite bedrooms, open plan living room and kitchen and large veranda. They are furnished in Swahili and Lamu styles. The court has a swimming pool. Victoria Restaurant, with shaded terrace, has an a la carte menu of international dishes; there is a formal dress code for dinner. Finch Hatton's Bar serves a variety of international drinks and cocktails. The Dunes Bar and Restaurant is more casual, and offers terrace dining and beach dining. The spa offers a wide range of treatments for wellness, relaxation and healing. The conference hall seats 100 pax; office services are available. There is also a library and media centre. Nearby sports centres offer a selection of sports. Safaris can be booked at the resort.

Kivulini Beach Resort Malindi

Kivulini Beach Resort, Mayungu, nr Malindi, North Coast, Kenya
Ora Hotel Group, Italy
Tel +39 521 1917481
Mobile
Fax
E-mail info@orahotels.com
Web www.kivulinibeachkenya.com / www.orahotels.com

           Malindi, LS & CH
20 mins

Kivulini Beach Resort is situated in a 4-hectare garden on the beachfront of Mayungu, not far from Malindi. The resort has panoramic views of this private beach, which is accessed by steps leading down from the resort's gardens. The camp is operated by the Italian-based Ora Hotel Group.

There are 36 en-suite rooms. All rooms have aircon, fan, telephone, minibar and satellite TV with international and Italian channels. The restaurant, with views across the bay, serves buffet breakfast, lunch and dinner. The bar has a selection of soft drinks, beers, wines and spirits, and is the venue for nightly shows and entertainment.

The resort also has a massage area with a selection of treatments and a gym. The boutique stocks a range of local curios and artefacts. There are 2 other beaches in the vicinity of the resort; a complimentary bus service transfers guests between the resort and the beaches. The bus service also provides transfers to Malindi, where guests can visit the shops, restaurants, bars and casino of the area. The resort has a dive centre, with both Italian and Kenyan staff, which offers a range of PADI scuba diving courses. The excursion centre can arrange tours, excursions and safaris to destinations in Kenya.

Twiga Hotel Malindi

Twiga Hotel, nr Malindi, North Coast, Kenya
Ora Hotel Group, Italy
Tel +39 521 1917481
Mobile
Fax
E-mail info@orahotels.com
Web www.twigahotelkenya.com / www.orahotels.com

 VISA, MasterCard   Malindi, LS & CH
20 mins

Twiga Hotel, on the beachfront, faces Sardinia Two coral atolls, which appear and disappear with the movement of the tides. The hotel is operated by the Italian-based Ora Hotel Group.

There are 64 en-suite rooms, made up of 38 standard, 24 superior and 2 ocean view. The rooms, built in Arabic style, are all within sight of the Indian ocean. Each room has a desk, cupboard and balcony, and is equipped with aircon, luggage holder, TV, safe, fridge, kettle and hairdryer. Interconnecting rooms, suitable for families, are available.

The restaurant, on the poolside, serves a buffet of Italian and local dishes, including homemade pasta, grilled fish and tropical fruits. Once a week, there is a Zanzibar theme dinner. A private, romantic lobster dinner is also available. Both the main bar and the pool bar have a wide selection of drinks. The lounge has billiards, table football and table tennis. There is also a boutique, spa and gym.

The animation team offers a daily programme of activities such as beach volleyball, 5-a-side football, lawn bowling and beach tennis. Mountain bikes are available. The water sports centre offers scuba diving, snorkelling and other sports. The information desk can book tours, excursions and safaris to destinations in Kenya.

White Beach Palace   Malindi

White Beach Palace, Mangrove Road, off Mayungu Road, Malindi, Kenya
PO Box 5797, Malindi 80200, Kenya

Tel	+254 41 2003259
Mobile	+254 773 396743; +254 722 337932; +254 775 526540
Fax	+254 41 2003259
E-mail	info@whitebeachpalace.com
Web	www.whitebeachpalace.com

   VISA, MasterCard   Malindi, LS & CH
                                                                                                                   20 mins

White Beach Palace is a boutique resort in a private bay overlooking the Mayungu Marine Park. The resort provides privacy and comfort in elegant surroundings. Designed with white furnishings and white fabrics as the name suggests, the resort exudes cool.

There are 3 deluxe beach apartments, 3 luxury suites beach apartments and 1 imperial suite. All suites are equipped with large LCD plasma satellite TV, DVD, internet connection, large bathtub and Jacuzzi, and all have private terrace with a view of the ocean. Personal butler service, babysitting and limo transfer services are all available. Pets are welcome with prior arrangements. All suites offer private dining options, including healthy diet, Italian and international. Dining is also offered in various common areas around the resort.

There is a 20-meter, 3-lane swimming pool, with a Jacuzzi, and a driving range. Last Generation Technogym has a local and international trainer, masseur, post sports trauma rehabilitator and masso physiotherapist. Beauty, hairdressing and massage services are available with prior reservations. The resort has a speedboat which goes daily to Mayungu Island for swimming and recreation. Helicopters and light aircraft can be chartered on request.

Msoloni Village   Msolini Village

Giriama Residence, Watamu, North Coast, Kenya
PO Box 576, Watamu 80202, Kenya

Tel	
Mobile	+254 738 791170; +254 711 703984
Fax	
E-mail	giriamaresidence@yahoo.com
Web	

                                                 Malindi, LS & CH
                                                                                                                                                            45 mins

Msoloni Village is a traditional Giriama village near Watamu. Accommodation on a genuine working farm can be arranged through Giriama Residence in Watamu. The trip is aimed at intrepid adventurers who are interested in a real African experience.

The accommodation is on a hill overlooking the farm. Guests can either stay in Top House, a house raised on stilts with spectacular panoramic views, or in a traditional Swahili hut. Mattresses and mosquito nets are provided. Warm water is brought to the communal bathrooms when required; showers are alfresco in shelters that have been traditionally built from palm fronds.

Meals are typical local dishes cooked with locally grown produce. Breakfast and lunch are served on the veranda of the farmhouse. Dinner is a barbecue, served under the stars on the edge of a small natural forest. Experienced guides and locals join guests around the campfire in the evening and talk about the history and culture of this area. The area has prolific birdlife and small mammals such as civet cats can also be seen here. The trip can be combined with a stay at Giriama Residence, in Watamu, or can be booked alone.

Jacaranda Beach Resort Watamu

Jacaranda Beach Resort, between Watamu & Malindi, North Coast, Kenya

Tel	+396 3218122
Mobile	
Fax	+396 32507365
E-mail	
Web	www.jacarandabeach.it

VISA, MasterCard   Malindi, LS & CH 20 mins

On a private beach between Watamu and Malindi, Jacaranda Beach Resort is surrounded by a lush garden of bougainvillea. The Sardinia Two coral atolls can be reached on foot during low tide. The resort is Italian managed. There are 118 en-suite Classic rooms, situated in 14 2-floor buildings. All classic rooms are furnished in Swahili style, and have 4-poster bed, mosquito net, aircon, telephone and veranda. Interconnecting rooms, suitable for families, are available. A wheelchair is available. There are 33 en-suite Villa Mare rooms. These beachfront rooms were refurbished in 2010, and are equipped with fridge, hairdryer and safe. The Ocean Suite is more spacious and can sleep 4 pax. The Chairman Villa has 3 en-suite bedrooms, living room and fully equipped kitchen. The villa is staffed by butler and chef, and equipped with satellite TV and music system. The restaurant serves buffet and a la carte. Jacaranda Maven Spa has a range of treatments including Thai massage. The conference hall seats 100 pax. The animation team offers a daily programme of activities. Activities include beach volleyball, tennis, table tennis, billiards, darts and petanque. There is also a library, boutique and lounge with TV and DVD. Water sports, tours, excursions and safaris can be booked at the resort.

Lonno Lodge Watamu

Lonno Lodge, nr Watamu, North Coast, Kenya
PO Box 672, Watamu 80202, Kenya

Tel	
Mobile	+254 726 226292
Fax	
E-mail	info@lonnolodge.com
Web	www.lonnolodge.com

VISA, MasterCard   Malindi, LS & CH 40 mins

Lonno Lodge opened in 2009, and offers personalised service, luxury and privacy. The lodge is conscientiously eco-friendly, and is located on a secluded section of beach, north of Watamu. The executive tower room, on the 2nd floor of the observation tower, has wide views of the ocean. The deluxe tower room, on the ground and 1st floor of the observation tower, opens onto a private terrace. The top tower room, on the 3rd floor of the observation tower, has a rooftop terrace. The grand suite has a sea view terrace and living room overlooking the swimming pool. The 2-bedroom suite has a large living room and seafront terrace. All rooms and suites are equipped with kitchenette, minibar, kettle, satellite TV, hairdryer and international electrical sockets. The restaurant serves international cuisine; personalised menus can be provided on request. The well stocked bar is beside the double swimming pool. The lodge was positioned to maximise sun on the solar panels, while using natural insulation to reduce the temperature inside. Its eco policies include desalinating water for drinking and swimming pool, rain harvesting, solar hot water and recycling grey water. The lodge can provide information on sites of interest, including Kakoneni and Sabaki Rivers, Mambrui Golden Beach, Robinson Island, Arabuko Sokoke Forest, Mida Creek and Gede Ruins.

Ocean Breeze

Watamu

Ocean Breeze, Watamu-Mayungu Road, Watamu, North Coast, Kenya
PO Box 408, Watamu 80202, Kenya
Tel
Mobile +254 736 648606
Fax
E-mail carlolnwali@yahoo.com
Web www.oceanbreezewatamu.com

  Malindi, LS & CH
40 mins

Ocean Breeze, a private house containing holiday apartments, is affiliated to the Kalumass Group. Kalumass Group is a union of firms operating in the field of tourism, based in Watamu.

Ocean Breeze has a selection of apartments. Imperial Apartment has an en-suite triple room and an en-suite double room. King's Apartment has 2 en-suite double rooms. Queen's Apartment has a double room and a single room. Prince's Apartment has a double room and 2 single rooms. There is a large ground floor lounge, a swimming pool and a restaurant serving Italian cuisine. A path leads from the garden to the beach. The house is staffed by 2 cooks, a waiter, a gardener, a driver, a handyman and 2 night guards.

Ocean Breeze staff can arrange beach picnics, dolphin watching boat trips and sundowner boat trips. The Kalumass Group companies affiliated to Ocean Breeze can assist visitors to Ocean Breeze. Kalumass Tours and Safaris arranges cultural, historical and naturalistic tours in destinations around Kenya. Happy Night Disco has African and international disco music. Kalumass Services hires cars. Kalumass Web is the online business directory connecting these companies. Kalumass is committed to social projects, including the fencing of Watamu primary school and the building of the children's Sunday School.

Tembo Village

Watamu

Tembo Village, opp Crystal Bay, Watamu, North Coast, Kenya
PO Box 504, Watamu 80202, Kenya
Tel +254 42 2332198
Mobile +254 721 980840
Fax
E-mail info@tembovillage.com
Web www.tembovillage.com

 VISA, MasterCard   Malindi, LS & CH
40 mins

Tembo Village is a lush garden dotted with a collection of cottages and thatched dining areas, and adorned with attractive local artefacts. Previously called Choma Village, the resort was extensively refurbished in 2009, and reopened as Tembo Village.

There are 5 en-suite cottages. The cottages were built in 2010. They are terracotta and white, with Lamu 4-poster beds and polished wooden cupboards. There are 6 en-suite rooms in the main building, which are more spacious. They are furnished with lovely old dhow furniture and equipped with aircon. There is 1 apartment, made up of 2 en-suite bedrooms, living room and kitchen. The main building, with coral walls and solid antique furniture, opens onto the swimming pool. It is equipped with a selection of books and games.

The restaurant has an international menu, specialising in seafood. Dishes include sashimi, prawns and mushrooms flambéed in Pernod, poached red snapper in Champagne sauce, whole pepper crab and seafood risotto. The bar, studded with coral and decorated with local artwork, stocks soft drinks, beers and spirits, and has an extensive wine list. Internet is available in the manager's office. The restaurant and bar are open to the public. Tembo Village can book safaris, water sports, tours and excursions.

Crystal Bay

Watamu

Crystal Bay, Watamu, North Coast, Kenya
PO Box 424, Watamu 80202, Kenya

Tel	+254 42 2332402; +254 42 2332150
Mobile	+254 708 565000; +254 732 630700
Fax	
E-mail	crystalbaywatamu@swiftmalindi.com
Web	www.crystalbaywatamu.com

 VISA, MasterCard

 Malindi, LS & CH
40 mins

Crystal Bay is located on the beachfront of Watamu. The resort is set in palm studded gardens and has views of the ocean.

There are 58 en-suite rooms, made up of superior and deluxe. All rooms are furnished with 4-poster beds, oriental carpets and coffee tables, and are equipped with aircon and telephone. The deluxe rooms have sea views and are equipped with fridges. The entrance lounge has comfortable sofas and satellite TV. There are 2 restaurants. The main restaurant serves buffet breakfast and lunch, and table d'hote dinner. The other restaurant, located on the beachfront, has an Italian a la carte menu.

There is a swimming pool and bar in the centre of the resort, and another swimming pool and bar at the beach. The spa offers massage and beauty treatments. The boutique has a selection of beach essentials. There is a backup generator in case of power cuts. Other facilities include volleyball pitch, football pitch and table tennis table. The animation team provides a daily programme of activities including aquagym and canoeing, and offers nightly shows in the theatre. Local sites of interest include Watamu Marine National Park, Gede Ruins, Kipepeo Butterfly Project and the Snake Farm.

Sun Palm Hotel

Watamu

Sun Palm Hotel, Watamu, North Coast, Kenya
PO Box 583, Malindi 80200, Kenya

Tel	+254 42 2332511
Mobile	
Fax	
E-mail	operation@albainternational.net
Web	www.sunpalmkenya.com

 VISA, MasterCard

 Malindi, LS & CH
40 mins

Sun Palm Hotel is a small resort with a selection of facilities and activities on the main road in Watamu.

There are 52 en-suite rooms, made up of standard and deluxe. The standard rooms are on the ground floor and the deluxe rooms are on the 1st floor. All rooms have aircon, fan, telephone and satellite TV. The deluxe rooms are more spacious and have a balcony. The main restaurant serves buffet and the beach restaurant serves a la carte. The menus are predominantly Italian, and dishes include spaghetti con gamberetti and pesce vela affumicato. There are also daily specials. The bar serves soft drinks, beers, wines and spirits.

The spa, on the 1st floor, offers massage and a selection of beauty and wellness treatments. The business centre has internet, printing and photocopying. The boutique has a range of beach items, curios and clothes. Activities include horse riding and water sports. There is also a beach volleyball court and a pool table. Kamele Tours and Safaris has an office at reception, and can book tours, excursions and safaris to destinations in Kenya. Local sites of interest include Arabuko Sokoke Forest, Gede Ruins, Mida Creek, Kipepeo Butterfly Project and the Snake Farm.

Giriama Residence Watamu

Giriama Residence, Watamu, North Coast, Kenya
PO Box 576, Watamu 80202, Kenya
Tel
Mobile +254 738 791170; +254 711 703984
Fax
E-mail giriamaresidence@yahoo.com
Web

  Malindi, LS & CH
40 mins

Giriama Residence is an attractive whitewashed house with a friendly atmosphere. The house is located near the main Watamu junction and is convenient for all the shops, restaurants and bars of Watamu.

There are 6 en-suite rooms, made up of 4 doubles and 2 family rooms. All rooms have carved 4-poster bed, table, chairs, fan and mosquito net. The spacious family rooms have 1 double and 2 single beds. A fully equipped communal kitchen is on the ground floor. There is also a self-catering apartment, with 1 bedroom, bathroom, living room and fully equipped kitchen. Children's beds can be provided, if required. The apartment has a private terrace and garden. If guests prefer not to cook for themselves, a selection of African and international dishes is available, advance booking necessary.

The 1st floor seating area has comfortable sofas and a selection of books, DVDs, CDs and games. Tea and coffee are available throughout the day. Soft drinks and beers are for sale. The garden has a barbecue and a thatched dining area. Giriama Residence operates with environmentally conscious policies: food waste is composted and vegetables are home grown, and water is stored in a large underground storage tank. Trips to Msoloni, a traditional Giriama village, which offers a real African experience, can be arranged.

Chiky Villa Watamu

Chiky Villa, Peponi Road, Watamu, North Coast, Kenya
PO Box 474, Watamu 80202, Kenya
Tel
Mobile +254 726 204340; +254 735 977603
Fax
E-mail info@chikyvilla.com
Web www.chikyvilla.com

  Malindi, LS & CH
40 mins

An attractive whitewashed house overlooking the swimming pool, Chiky Villa offers self-catering apartments and studios. The name comes from a nickname that the owner was given as a child, by her mother. The house, a short walk from Watamu Beach, is surrounded by palm trees and bougainvillea.

There are 2 apartments in the main house; each apartment has a complete floor of the house. Each apartment has 2 double bedrooms, 1 bathroom, living room, fully equipped kitchen and large balcony with dining table and chairs. There are 3 studios, in a separate building beside the swimming pool. A barbecue, by the pool, is available for the use of the guests. The compound is staffed by a housekeeper, gardener and night guard. Chefs can be provided for an extra charge, on request. Chiky Villa can assist with booking safaris, taxi transfers, car hire, bike hire and water sports. Bianca and Nero Restaurant, opposite Chiky Villa, is an attractive and friendly restaurant that serves a selection of Italian and seafood dishes, including mshakiki and fish with coconut rice. Local sites of interest include Arabuko Sokoke Forest, Gede Ruins, Mida Creek, Kipepeo Butterfly Project and the Snake Farm.

Beachview Cottages Watamu

Beachview Cottages, Peponi Road, Watamu, North Coast, Kenya
PO Box 483, Watamu 80202, Kenya

Tel	+254 42 2332383
Mobile	+254 727 954764
Fax	
E-mail	beachviewvillas@gmail.com
Web	www.beachview.co.ke

  Malindi, LS & CH
40 mins

Beachview Cottages is a collection of self-catering apartments and rooms in a large whitewashed house. The house is a short walk from the beach, and has a swimming pool surrounded by a bright blue sunbathing terrace. There are 3 apartments, 4 self-catering en-suite rooms and 5 standard en-suite rooms. The apartments have 1 bedroom, 1 bathroom, a living room and a kitchen. The self-catering rooms have an open plan kitchen. The standard rooms, on the 2nd floor, share a communal kitchen. All rooms have fan, mosquito net and built in cupboards. All kitchens are equipped with gas cooker, fridge, crockery, cutlery and glassware.

A local vendor brings fresh fish daily. Guests can cook for themselves, or a chef can be provided for an extra charge. Guests can buy their own food, or the chef can buy food for them, with advance notice.

The rooftop terrace has panoramic views of Watamu and the coast. There is a thatched open sided lounge next to the swimming pool, with satellite TV, CD player and a selection of books in various languages. There is a 4WD vehicle available for use in the local area. The friendly staff are happy to assist with booking snorkelling, bird watching, boat trips and other water sports.

Jua Kali House Watamu

Jua Kali House, Watamu Beach Road, Watamu, North Coast, Kenya
PO Box 667, Watamu 80202, Kenya

Tel	
Mobile	+254 712 792978
Fax	
E-mail	shadrack.mwanzia@yahoo.com
Web	

   Malindi, LS & CH
40 mins

Jua Kali House has coral walls with bright blue trimmings, and is decorated with striking murals of African scenes. The house offers self-catering accommodation and friendly service. It is located at the main junction in Watamu, making it conveniently positioned for all the shops, businesses, restaurants and bars of the town.

There are 6 en-suite rooms on 2 floors. Each floor has 3 double rooms, a communal kitchen and an open air lounge and dining area. All rooms are equipped with fan and mosquito net. The lounge areas are furnished with daybeds and dining table and chairs. Each floor can be taken as a whole, or the rooms can be taken separately. The swimming pool has a children's section. There is a thatched seating area by the pool suitable for dining. The gardens are filled with palm trees, papaya trees and bougainvillea. Watamu is famed for the Watamu Marine National Park. Other local attractions include the Gede Ruins, Kipepeo Butterfly Project and the Snake Farm. Nearby Mida Creek is known for mangroves and birdlife. Jua Kali House can assist with booking boat trips, water sports, safaris, tours and excursions.

Peponi Cottages Watamu

Peponi Cottages, Peponi Road, Watamu, North Coast, Kenya
PO Box 25, Watamu 80202, Kenya
Tel
Mobile +254 722 730975; +254 702 081421
Fax
E-mail
Web

    Malindi, LS & CH
40 mins

Peponi Cottages are a collection of self-catering apartments and rooms in a whitewashed house. The house overlooks the swimming pool and surrounding sunbathing terrace.

There are 4 apartments and 5 en-suite rooms. The apartments, on the 1st floor, each have 1 bedroom, 1 bathroom, a kitchen equipped with gas cooker, fridge, crockery, cutlery and glassware, and an open plan dining area. They open onto a shared balcony that overlooks the swimming pool. The rooms, on the ground floor, have 4-poster bed, fan, mosquito net and cupboard. Each has a terrace with daybed, table and chairs.

The reception can assist with booking boat trips, snorkelling and other water sports. They can also book tours, excursions and safaris to destinations in Kenya. Bianca and Nero Restaurant, next door to Peponi Cottages, is an attractive and friendly restaurant. It serves a selection of Italian and seafood dishes, including mshakiki and fish with coconut rice. Local sites of interest include Arabuko Sokoke Forest, Gede Ruins, Mida Creek, Kipepeo Butterfly Project and the Snake Farm. Watamu Beach is a short walk from Peponi Cottages. All the shops, restaurants and bars of Watamu are also within easy reach.

Ascot Residence Watamu

Ascot Residence, Watamu, North Coast, Kenya
PO Box 348, Watamu 80202, Kenya
Tel +254 42 2332326
Mobile +254 721 267761
Fax
E-mail info@ascotresidence.com
Web www.ascotresidence.com

    Malindi, LS & CH
40 mins

Ascot Residence is a collection of apartments, some of which are privately owned, and others which are available for holiday rent. The apartments face the garden and swimming pool. The compound also contains a restaurant, bar and casino.

There are 7 apartments available for holiday rent. The apartments have 1 or 2 en-suite bedrooms, living room and fully equipped kitchen. The restaurant is predominantly Italian. It has a pizza oven, with a selection of freshly baked pizzas such as capricciosa, milano, Viennese and pugliese. There are also difference pastas with a choice of sauces, as well as gnocchi and risotto. International dishes include pepper steak and grilled king prawns. The restaurant has an extensive wine list. Thatched seating areas are dotted around the gardens, for guests who prefer to dine alfresco. The bar is well stocked with soft drinks, beers, wines and spirits, and has a selection of cocktails. The casino is open nightly.

A masseuse offers massage, manicure and pedicure. The reception can book water sports, and arranges for transport to water sports centres. Safaris, fishing trips, dhow excursions and local tours can all be booked. Local sites of interest include Arabuko Sokoke Forest, Gede Ruins, Mida Creek, Kipepeo Butterfly Project and the Snake Farm.

Aquarius Beach Resort

Watamu

Aquarius Beach Resort, Watamu, North Coast, Kenya
PO Box 196, Watamu 80202, Kenya
Tel   +254 20 8032204
Mobile
Fax
E-mail   info@aquariuswatamu.com
Web   www.aquariuswatamu.com

   VISA, MasterCard, Amex   Malindi, LS & CH
                                                                        40 mins

Aquarius Beach Resort has 3 sections, each progressively closer to the beach. Aquarius, the main section, houses the reception, the boutique and the main restaurant; Lily Palm is the central section; Mapango is the beachfront section and houses the Mapango Restaurant and Bar. There are 134 en-suite rooms, made up of doubles and singles. Aquarius Restaurant serves buffet, and has a bar that stocks soft drinks, beers, wines, spirits and a selection of cocktails. Mapango Restaurant, on the beachfront, serves a la carte. Both restaurants have Italian menus, including spaghettie ai frutti de mare, patate al forno, filetto di pesce all Indiana and risotto alla zucca. The beach bar is also well stocked and has a cocktail list.

The 3 sections of the hotel are linked by overhead walkways. Each section has a swimming pool, surrounded by sunbathing terrace. There is a gym with exercise machines, but no trainer. There is also a massage parlour and a hair and beauty salon. WiFi and wired internet connection are available at reception. The animation team provides evening entertainment, including acrobatics, local musicians, singing and dancing. Cultural village walks can be arranged. Dream Safaris has a desk at reception and can book tours, excursions and safaris to destinations around Kenya.

Watamu Adventist
Beach Resort and Campsite

Watamu

Watamu Adventist Beach Resort and Campsite, nr Aquarius, Watamu
PO Box 723, Watamu 80202, Kenya
Tel   +254 20 2498725
Mobile   +254 721 766690; +254 733 928268
Fax
E-mail   watamubeach@eau.adventist.org
Web   www.watamuadventistresort.org

                                           Malindi, LS & CH
                                                                        40 mins

Managed by the Seventh Day Adventist Church, Watamu Adventist Beach Resort and Campsite offers conferences, seminars and retreats. The resort is located on Watamu Beach and many of its rooms have sea views.

There are 53 en-suite rooms. All rooms are equipped with aircon, satellite TV and telephone. Water is heated by solar power. The restaurant serves both buffet and a la carte, and offers lots of vegetarian options. WiFi is available in the reception area. There is also a communal kitchen, for guests who wish to cater for themselves. The campsite has bathroom facilities and a dining tent. The resort is an alcohol and smoking free zone. The conference hall seats 100 pax. The hall is fully equipped with conference equipment including LCD projector, large screen, TV, DVD and PA system. The swimming pool is surrounded by lawns studded with palm trees. The resort can assist with booking local activities such as boat trips and water sports. Tours, excursions and safaris can be booked with local tour operators. Local sites of interest include Arabuko Sokoke Forest, Gede Ruins, Mida Creek, Kipepeo Butterfly Project and the Snake Farm.

KaribuKenya Accommodation Guide

Savannah Watamu

Savannah, Gede-Watamu Road, Watamu, North Coast, Kenya
PO Box 570, Watamu 80202, Kenya
Tel
Mobile +254 726 287637; +254 721 845446
Fax
E-mail savannah@watamu.biz
Web

      Malindi, LS & CH
                                       40 mins

Savannah is a lush garden with an attractive restaurant and bar, and self-catering bandas.

The open sided restaurant is surrounded by flowers, succulents and driftwood art. Murals of trees stand out from whitewashed walls. The terrace is furnished with tables and chairs and shaded by umbrellas. The international menu includes chicken sate, feta and olive salad, grilled catch of the day with soy sauce and ginger, Swahili fish, prawns in creamy coconut sauce, flame grilled fillet of beef with blue cheese sauce and gammon steak with 2 fried eggs and chips. A board has daily specials. The extensive drinks list includes wines and liqueurs. There is also a pool table, satellite TV, CD player and collection of CDs. DJs visit on occasion, playing at the outdoor dance floor.

There are 2 circular bandas, with shaded verandas. Each banda is entered through an open plan living room and kitchen, equipped with gas cooker, fridge, kettle, toaster, cutlery, crockery and glassware. There is 1 en-suite double room, equipped with fan and adorned with bright print curtains. The restaurant has a noticeboard, with information on local events and activities, such as deep sea fishing, dhow trips and water sports.

Blue Bay Village Watamu

Blue Bay Village, Watamu, North Coast, Kenya
PO Box 162, Watamu 80202, Kenya
Tel +254 42 2332626
Mobile +254 733 810842
Fax +254 42 2332422
E-mail bluebay@africaonline.co.ke
Web www.igrandiviaggi.it

 VISA, MasterCard    Malindi, LS & CH
                                                                      40 mins

Blue Bay Village was taken over by the Italian IGV Club in 1986 and has been managed by the club since then. It is the only IGV Club hotel in Kenya. The hotel is designed around a freeform swimming pool, and elegantly furnished with woven rugs, bright cushions, heavy wooden chairs and crystal chandeliers.

There are 118 en-suite rooms, made up of standard, aircon, deluxe and suites. The standard rooms have fan, mosquito net and balcony. The aircon rooms have aircon as well as fan. The deluxe rooms have aircon and minibar. The suites are more spacious, and have aircon, minibar, telephone and safe, and their balconies have sea views.

Les Palmiers, named after the palm trees that surround it, serves buffet breakfast, lunch and dinner. Located between the beach and the swimming pool, the restaurant has lovely views of both. L'Oasis is an a la carte restaurant serving Italian cuisine, including carpaccio di pesce, risotto ai gamberi, misto di mare, pollo primavera alla griglia and spaghetti al sugo di Aragosta.

Activities include water sports such as windsurfing, canoeing and scuba diving. There is also a floodlit tennis court. The animation team offers a daily range of activities, as well as traditional dancing and discos at night.

Ocean Sports Resort   Watamu

Ocean Sports Resort, Mida Creek Drive, Watamu, North Coast, Kenya
PO Box 208, Watamu 80202, Kenya

Tel	+254 42 2332288; +254 42 2332008
Mobile	+254 724 389732; +254 734 195217
Fax	+254 42 2332266
E-mail	info@oceansports.net
Web	www.oceansports.net

VISA, MasterCard   Malindi, LS & CH 40 mins

In 1952, Ian Pritchard sailed into Watamu and set up a drinking hole on the beach which he named Ocean Sports. The original boat he sailed in still stands prominently in the bar, along with trophies from fishing grounds near the resort. To this day, Ocean Sports remains popular with beach lovers, anglers and sportsmen alike. There are 29 en-suite rooms, made up of doubles, twins and family rooms. All rooms have aircon, mosquito net and sea view. Ocean Cottage has 1 en-suite bedroom, 2 bedrooms with shared bathroom, a large lounge, beachfront veranda and fully equipped kitchen, and is staffed by a chef, housekeepers and babysitters. Ian's Bar, known as the Locals' Watering Hole, is the legendary bar built around the Ocean Sports boat. The main bar, serving the veranda and the deck, offers beers, wines, champagnes, cocktails and fresh juices. The restaurant, with panoramic views of the Indian Ocean, specialises in seafood. Ocean Sports has a Sunday seafood curry buffet, with live jazz band. Healing Zone has treatments and therapies such as shiatsu, aromatherapy and reflexology.

An accredited PADI scuba diving company is on site. Other activities include deep sea fishing, water-skiing, kayaking, squash and tennis. Trips to local attractions include Gede Ruins, Arabuko Sokoke Forest and Mida Creek.

Hemingways Resort   Watamu

Hemingways Resort, Mida Creek Drive, Watamu, North Coast, Kenya
PO Box 267, Watamu 80202, Kenya

Tel	+254 42 2332624; +254 42 2332076; +254 42 2332373
Mobile	+254 722 205917; +254 733 411112
Fax	+254 42 2332256
E-mail	reservations@hemingways.co.ke
Web	www.hemingways.co.ke

 VISA, MasterCard, Amex   Malindi, LS & CH 40 mins

Hemingways Resort, a luxury tropical retreat, lies along the fringe of Watamu Marine National Park. Named for Ernest Hemingway, it recreates this famous author's style and elegance. Hemingways has 2 accommodation wings, one each side of a central block which houses the bars, restaurant, reception, shops and business centre. There are 76 en-suite rooms, made up of 2 executive suites, 4 junior suites, 26 superior rooms and 44 deluxe rooms, all with sea view, aircon, fan and private balcony with panoramic views. The architecture is coastal, with whitewashed walls, traditional thatched roofs and tiled floors. The rooms are adorned with bright fabrics, hand painted lamps and handmade furniture.

The executive chef creates dishes from fresh local produce. The restaurant serves buffet or table d'hote; dishes include lobster tail soup, seafood casserole, massaman vegetable curry and cheese plate. Lunch is served at the pool or on the terrace. The main bar and the pool bar have a selection of cocktails, and serve lunch and snacks. There is also a spa, gym, boutique, jewellery shop, hair salon and bureau de change. WiFi is available throughout the hotel. Water sports include snorkelling, fishing and dhow cruises. The resort has eco-friendly policies including a recycling plant for grey water. Nearby sites of interest include Mida Creek and Arabuko Sokoke Forest.

Turtle Bay Beach Club Watamu

Turtle Bay Beach Club, Watamu, North Coast, Kenya
PO Box 457, Malindi 80200, Kenya; PO Box 10, Watamu 80202, Kenya

Tel	+254 42 2332622; +254 42 2332003; +254 42 2332226
Mobile	+254 721 830604; +254 734 601066
Fax	+254 42 2332268; +254 42 2332345
E-mail	general.manager@turtlebay.co.ke
Web	www.turtlebaykenya.com / www.turtletv.info

 VISA, MasterCard Malindi, LS & CH 40 mins

Turtle Bay Beach Club is set in 10 acres of manicured gardens on the edge of Watamu Marine National Park. Entitled the responsible resort, Turtle Bay has received a silver award from Ecotourism Society of Kenya. The 89 super club rooms have a double and single bed; some have interconnecting doors; 3 are designed for guests with disabilities. The 40 Lamu rooms are cottage style double rooms. The 14 ocean front rooms have patios with direct beach access. The 2 junior suites have sitting rooms with fridges. All rooms are en-suite and have aircon, fan, kettle and hairdryer. The main restaurant, by the pool, serves buffet breakfast and dinner. The snack bar serves buffet lunch. The Seashell Restaurant, on the beach, serves a la carte dinners, reservation required. There is also a Pizza Garden, Pool Bar, Weaver's Nest Bar and Canoe Bar. The club has theme nights and evening entertainment.

The club has tennis courts, bikes, boogie boards, paddle skis, pedalos, canoes and catamarans. The Fun Base Team organises table tennis, beach volleyball, beach Olympics, beach football, Swahili lessons, tug-of-war, water polo, snorkelling and bird watching. Children can join the supervised Mini Club and play in Tarzan's Tree House. Nearby attractions include Arabuko Sokoke Forest, Mida Creek, Kipepeo Butterfly Farm and Gede Ruins.

Villas Watamu Watamu

Villas Watamu, Villa Road, opp Turtle Bay Beach Club, Watamu, Kenya
PO Box 150, Watamu 80202, Kenya

Tel	
Mobile	+254 713 391458; +254 725 781063
Fax	
E-mail	villaswatamu@africaonline.co.ke
Web	www.villas-watamu.com

  Malindi, LS & CH 40 mins

In landscaped gardens, Villas Watamu is a collection of self-catering villas available for rent on a long or short-term basis. The villas are whitewashed, with red tiled roofs. Flower-lined paths weave between the villas. There are 11 villas, made up of 8 1-bedroom villas and 3 2-bedroom villas. All bedrooms have en-suite bathrooms, aircon and mosquito nets. All villas have kitchens equipped with gas cooker, fridge, kettle, toaster, crockery, cutlery and glassware. The large semi-circular covered verandas are furnished with dining table, chairs and pot plants. The villas have white tiled floors and hand-carved wooden furniture including 4-poster bed, bedside table, writing table and chairs. The villas have housekeeper and night guard; chef can be provided for an extra charge, on request. In the centre of the garden is a swimming pool, surrounded by sunbathing terrace. Thatched umbrellas, sunbeds and tables are provided. The reception can assist with booking tours, excursions, safaris and water sports. The villas are located on Villa Road, which is almost opposite Turtle Bay Beach Club. There is a secure car park. Local sites of interest include Watamu Beach, the Gede Ruins, Kipepeo Butterfly Project and the Snake Farm. The villas are within a short drive of the shops, restaurants and bars of Watamu.

Frog Guesthouse

Watamu

Frog Guesthouse, Temple Point Road, Watamu, North Coast, Kenya
PO Box 94, Gede 80208, Kenya

Tel	
Mobile	+254 722 374646; +254 716 620088
Fax	
E-mail	frogguesthouse@yahoo.com
Web	

   Malindi, LS & CH
40 mins

Frog Guesthouse is named for the frogs that inhabit the ponds around the house. The house, which opened in 2007, is a peaceful and friendly guesthouse surrounded by lush gardens and a swimming pool.

There are 4 en-suite rooms, including 2 which interconnect, suitable for families. All rooms have fan, mosquito net, table, chair and cupboard, and are decorated with local art. The communal sitting room is furnished with comfortable sofas and armchairs, and has a large selection of books, videos, DVDs and CDs. There is even a record player and a selection of vinyl records. Games such as trivial pursuit, pop trivia, who wants to be a millionaire, backgammon and monopoly are also available. There is a fully equipped kitchen which guests are welcome to use, or they can discuss their preferred menu with the chef who brings fresh food from the market. Meals can be taken on the veranda or at the thatched dining area in the garden. The utility room has a washing machine and a freezer for the use of guests. The swimming pool is surrounded by a sunbathing terrace, with sunbeds and hammocks. The obliging staff can book a local masseuse, as well as water sports, boat trips and safaris.

Al Hamra

Watamu

Al Hamra, Plot 38, Watamu Beach Road, Watamu, North Coast, Kenya
Advantage East Africa, PO Box 1460, Nairobi 00502, Kenya

Tel	+254 20 3882868
Mobile	+254 733 222420
Fax	+254 20 3882868
E-mail	reservations@advantage-ea.com
Web	www.alhamrakenya.com

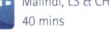 All major cards   Malindi, LS & CH
40 mins

A stylish private house, Al Hamra takes its name from the ancient Omani town of Al Hamra. The house is influenced by Omani and Swahili architecture and furnished with modern contemporary amenities. It has private access to a peaceful section of Watamu Beach.

There are 3 en-suite bedrooms. The 2 pool suites on the ground floor each have their own rooftop terrace, and the honeymoon suite on the 2nd floor has its own extensive living area. The inside plunge pool is connected to the outside swimming pool by a waterfall. Food is sourced from the local fishermen and farms, ensuring that fresh seafood, meat, vegetables and tropical fruits are served every day. The house is fully staffed. WiFi is available throughout.

Activities include dhow cruises on Mida Creek, boardwalks through the mangroves, mountain biking in Arabuko Sokoke Forest and bird watching. Water sports include kite surfing, scuba diving, snorkelling, sailing, canoeing, kayaking and sport fishing. Scenic flights up the coast to the Tana Delta sand dunes can be arranged. Local sites of interest include Watamu Marine National Park, Gede Ruins, Kipepeo Butterfly Project, Watamu Turtle Project and the Snake Farm.

Karibu Kenya Accommodation Guide

Garoda Resort

Watamu

Garoda Resort, Temple Point Road, Watamu, North Coast, Kenya
PO Box 1055, Watamu 80202, Kenya

Tel	+254 20 2692679
Mobile	+254 701 091207
Fax	
E-mail	info@blufly.it
Web	www.blufly.it / www.unaltrosole.com

VISA, MasterCard   Malindi, LS & CH 40 mins

Garoda Resort is marketed only through Un Altro Sole and Blu Fly, both based in Italy. The resort is open to visitors from Watamu who wish to use the facilities for the day for a charge.

There are 108 en-suite rooms, including 19 superior and 4 family rooms. All rooms have aircon, telephone and digital safe. There are 2 restaurants. The main restaurant serves buffet of Kenyan, Italian and international dishes. The a la carte restaurant, located on the beachfront, specialises in fish and seafood. The 2 swimming pools are surrounded by a large sunbathing terrace. The Miniclub offers daily activities for children.

Garoda Resort has beach volleyball, beach tennis, bocce and aquagym.

Yoga and meditation sessions are also on offer. Blue Fin Diving, on site, offers PADI scuba diving, kite surfing lessons and snorkelling trips in Watamu Marine National Park. The wellness centre has a range of massages and health and beauty treatments. The boutique stocks a range of beach essentials, local curios and clothes. Garoda Resort can arrange tours and excursions to local sites of interest, including Arabuko Sokoke Forest, Gede Ruins, Mida Creek, Kipepeo Butterfly Project and the Snake Farm. Blu Fly, in collaboration with Tusker Safaris, can book tours, excursions and safaris to destinations in Kenya.

Temple Point Resort

Watamu

Temple Point Resort, Temple Point Road, Watamu, North Coast, Kenya
PO Box 296, Watamu 80202, Kenya

Tel	+254 20 8009130
Mobile	+254 722 204131
Fax	+254 42 2332289
E-mail	reservations@templepointresort.com
Web	www.templepointresort.com

VISA, MasterCard   Malindi, LS & CH 40 mins

Named after an ancient temple on the headland, Temple Point Resort is an attractive resort with an extensive selection of activities and facilities. The resort, set in lush gardens, covers the whole headland and has its own private beach.

There are 106 en-suite rooms, made up of garden rooms and Mida Creek rooms. The Swahili style rooms, in thatched, whitewashed villas, are equipped with aircon, mosquito net, safe, minibar, satellite TV, hairdryer, kettle and balcony. The main restaurant serves international buffet. The poolside a la carte restaurant serves homemade pizza and seafood. There are 2 bars, 1 overlooking each of the 2 swimming pools.

A romantic candlelit dinner can be arranged in the honeymoon pavilion. The gym is fully equipped. The spa offers a range of treatments including deluxe massage and cranium sacral. The conference hall seats 200 pax, and is equipped with aircon, WiFi, projector and PA system. The animation team provides a daily programme of activities including water aerobics, beach volleyball, Latin dance and evening shows. The resort also has a water sports centre, safari desk, floodlit tennis courts, archery, football pitch, Jacuzzi, games room and bicycles. A full day trip includes snorkelling in the marine park, lunch on an island, traditional dancing and a boardwalk in the mangroves.

Kitsapu Cottages Gede

Kitsapu Cottages, Mombasa-Malindi Highway, Gede, nr Watamu, North Coast
PO Box 28, Gede 80208, Kenya
Tel
Mobile +254 716 159288; +254 771 689406
Fax
E-mail
Web

              Malindi, LS & CH
                                              30 mins

Kitsapu Cottages offers budget accommodation in a large garden dotted with statues of African animals and quirky ornaments. The garden has thatched dining areas, children's play area, swings, hammocks and a tree house. Accommodation consists of a selection of cottages, dorms and campsite.

There are 5 thatched cottages. All cottages have an open plan living room and bedroom, bathroom and veranda. They are furnished with heavy wooden double bed and sofas piled with cushions, and equipped with fan and mosquito net. Behind each cottage is an open air traditional cooking area, with a 3-stone hearth. The cottages are named after the owner's family, such as Bill, Irene and Terry. There is a dorm, intended for students, with 100 beds and bathroom facilities. Sido's Campsite has shaded camping areas; tents can be hired. There is also a traditional cooking area and a thatched dining area with table and benches.

The restaurant serves local dishes such as roast chicken, beef stew and nyama choma grilled meats. The bar serves soft drinks and beers. Bob's corner is a dining platform raised in the branches of a tree, with views over the garden. Parties and functions can be arranged. Local sites of interest include Gede Ruins, Kipepeo Butterfly Project and the Snake Farm.

Royal Gede Resort Gede

Royal Gede Resort, Gede-Watamu Road, North Coast, Kenya
PO Box 446, Watamu 80202, Kenya
Tel
Mobile +254 725 539993; +254 733 981001
Fax
E-mail royalgede@yahoo.com
Web www.royalgederesort.hotels.officelive.com

             Malindi, LS & CH
                                              30 mins

Set in attractive manicured gardens, Royal Gede Resort is a collection of cottages and hotel rooms. The hotel is located on the road between Gede and Watamu.

There are 5 cottages, made up of 3 1-bedroom cottages and 2 2-bedroom cottages. All cottages are whitewashed with red tiled roofs. Each cottage has an open plan central kitchen and living room, with bedrooms leading off it. The kitchens are equipped with gas cooker, fridge and utensils. 1 cottage has aircon and the remainder have fans. There are also 15 en-suite rooms. All rooms have fan, mosquito net, built in cupboards and veranda. The campsite has bathroom facilities.

The swimming pool has a shallow section for children. The pool bar, an open sided thatched building, serves soft drinks, beers and spirits. Mnazi Restaurant specialises in Indian cuisine, including dal tadka, butter chicken, egg curry, vegetable makhani, chilli prawns and mutton biriani. Local sites of interest include Arabuko Sokoke Forest, Gede Ruins, Mida Creek, Kipepeo Butterfly Project and the Snake Farm. Watamu Beach and all the shops, restaurants and bars in Watamu are also nearby.

Mida Ecocamp

Gede

Mida Ecocamp, Gede, off Mombasa-Malindi Highway, Kenya
PO Box 81, Gede 80208, Kenya
Tel
Mobile   +254 729 213042; +254 701 018320
Fax
E-mail   felicityfowkes@aol.com
Web   www.midaecocamp.com

Malindi, LS & CH
30 mins

Mida Ecocamp is a charming eco-friendly camp, built and operated by the Giriama community. All profit goes to community projects, such as health, education and agriculture, and to the conservation of Mida Creek, a UNESCO biosphere reserve. The camp, which opened in 2007, was entirely built from local materials such as palm leaves, casuarina poles and driftwood. The raised restaurant and bar have stunning views over the mangroves. From the restaurant, a raised walkway leads to a viewpoint. The restaurant serves Swahili cuisine, such as fish with coconut rice, chicken with banana and fresh tropical fruits. The Zanzibar hut has Zanzibar furniture and décor. The Swahili hut, decorated with shells, has a Lamu 4-poster bed. The Giriama hut is a traditional hut with walls and roof of thatched palm fronds. The campsite has bathroom facilities. The camp uses solar power and gas lanterns; strict policies govern water usage and waste disposal. Guided walks on the forest nature trail provide excellent bird watching; almost 200 species have been recorded near the camp. Activities include walking on the boardwalk over Mida Creek, canoe rides to the islands and cultural visits to Giriama villages, including drinking coconut wine. Children's activities include the Small 5 Safari, a fun introduction to strange but harmless insects and crustaceans.

Arabuko Jamii Villas

Gede

Arabuko Jamii Villas, nr Arabuko Sokoke Forest, Gede, Kenya
PO Box 58, Gede 80208, Kenya
Tel
Mobile   +254 710 241303; +254 734 535897; +254 718 194743
Fax
E-mail   arabukojamiilodge@yahoo.com
Web

Malindi, LS & CH
30 mins

Arabuko Jamii Villas is a community owned hotel managed by the umbrella organisation Arabuko Sokoke Forest Adjacent Dwellers Association, ASFADA. It was built from grants from the EU and CDTF. The profit from the project goes to the local community, for projects such as student bursaries and building health centres and classrooms.
There are 5 cottages, made up of 4 1-bedroom cottages and 1 family cottage. The cottages have coral walls and thatched roofs, are adorned with bright kanga fabric curtains and cushions. All cottages have en-suite bedroom, fan, mosquito net, table, chair and veranda. The family cottage has 2 bedrooms, bathroom, living room and veranda. There is also a campsite. The restaurant serves Swahili cuisine; the bar serves soft drinks and beers.
Arabuko Jamii Villas are close to Arabuko Sokoke Forest and make an ideal base for researchers, scientists and birdwatchers interested in the unique biodiversity of the forest. Activities include guided nature walks in the forest and along the boardwalk over Mida Creek. Canoe rides through the creek to the islands are also available. Local attractions include the Gede Ruins, Kipepeo Butterfly Project and the Snake Farm. Watamu Beach, and all the shops, restaurants and bars that surround it, is also nearby.

Manfriday's Mida Creek

Manfriday's Mida Creek, Mida Cove, nr Watamu, North Coast, Kenya
PO Box 592, Malindi 80200, Kenya

Tel	+254 20 2335387
Mobile	+254 721 388401; +254 721 734171
Fax	
E-mail	skanderson30@hotmail.com / sales@manfridays.com
Web	www.manfridays.com

Malindi, LS & CH
40 mins

Manfriday's Mida Creek is a collection of individually designed beach villas, located near the biosphere reserve Mida Creek. It combines the facilities of a hotel with the privacy of private villas.

There are 4 villas, all elegantly furnished, fully equipped and fully staffed including private chef. Stonehouse is designed in coastal Arabic Stone Town style. It has 5 bedrooms, 2 plunge pools, garden terrace, pool pavilions, games room and sundowner terrace. Jack's House, on the seafront, is constructed of local materials, and open to the sea breeze. It has 2 en-suite double bedrooms, swimming pool, living and dining area, upper observation deck and elevated sundowner deck. Mida House, with striking views of Mida Creek, has 2 double bedrooms, rooftop deck and sundowner terrace. The Guest Cottage has 1 en-suite double bedroom, living and dining area and rooftop deck.

The Boat Bar and Kite Bar have an extensive list of juices, wines and cocktails. The compound has croquet, lawn chess and a library. Stargazing and bird watching are on offer, as are lessons in arts and crafts, painting, photography and cooking. The water sports centre offers catamaran sailing, kite surfing, windsurfing, kayaking, body surfing and sport fishing. Manfriday's Mida Creek is closed in May and June.

Kilifi Bay Beach Resort

Kilifi Bay Beach Resort, Bofa Road, Kilifi, North Coast, Kenya
Mada Hotels, PO Box 537, Kilifi 80108, Kenya

Tel	+254 41 7522511; +254 41 7522264; +254 20 6005328
Mobile	+254 725 888560; +254 734 888560
Fax	+254 41 7522258
E-mail	kilifibay@madahotels.com / sales@madahotels.com
Web	www.madahotels.com/kilifi

VISA, MasterCard

Malindi, LS & CH, 1 hr
Moi Intl., LS & CH & Intl., 1.5 hrs

Set in 26,000m² of tropical gardens, Kilifi Bay Beach Resort has 130 metres of sandy beachfront. The only hotel on this stretch of beach, the resort enjoys complete privacy.

There are 49 en-suite rooms, including 9 suites intended for families, with double room, twin room, sitting room and bathroom. The main dining room serves international cuisine, including 1 barbecue and 1 theme night per week. There is also an a la carte restaurant and a teppanyaki seafood restaurant. The 3 bars are located in the lounge, beside the main pool and on the beach. The resort has 1 large swimming pool in the centre of the resort and a small pool near reception. The conference room seats 80 pax and is equipped with a PA system, LCD projector and computers. Secretarial services are also available. Parties, banquets and beach dinners can be catered for, on request.

Nightly entertainment in the outdoor amphitheatre near the small pool includes acrobatic shows, discos, live music and traditional African shows. Water sports include snorkelling, windsurfing, scuba diving, fishing and trips in a glass bottomed boat. Daily animation programmes include aquagym, beach volleyball, table tennis and bushwalks. Excursions to Mombasa, Malindi and Kilifi, and baobella boat rides can also be organised.

Baobab Lodge Resort

Kilifi

Baobab Lodge Resort, Bofa Road, Kilifi, North Coast, Kenya
Mada Hotels, PO Box 537, Kilifi 80108, Kenya

Tel	+254 41 7522511; +254 41 7522264; +254 20 6005328
Mobile	+254 725 888560; +254 734 888506
Fax	+254 41 7522258
E-mail	kilifibay@madahotels.com / sales@madahotels.com
Web	www.madahotels.com/baobab

 VISA, MasterCard

 Malindi, LS & CH, 1 hr
 Moi Intl., LS & CH & Intl., 1.5 hrs

Set in 5 acres of tropical gardens, Baobab Lodge Resort has 60 meters of sea frontage. Kilifi, a picturesque coastal town about half way between Mombasa and Malindi, grew up around a natural harbour where the creek meets the sea.

The lodge has 30 en-suite rooms. 20 rooms are in 10 thatched rondavels, each with a private veranda. 10 rooms, in a double storey block, are made up of 4 family rooms with adjacent rooms with a bunk bed and 6 twin rooms. All rooms have aircon and fan.

The restaurant serves a daily table d'hote menu to correspond with its theme nights. There are 2 bars, and a swim-up pool bar by the swimming pool. The conference room can seat up to 200 pax. The lodge can cater for banquets, dinners and beach parties. Guests receive a complimentary massage daily.

The animation team offers a daily programme of activities. Entertainment includes acrobatic shows, discos, live music and traditional African shows. A wide variety of water sports is available, including windsurfing, scuba diving, big game fishing and trips in a glass bottomed boat. Darts, table tennis, billiards, archery, tennis and beach volleyball are also on offer. Neckermann Reisen has a desk at reception, offering tours, excursions and safaris.

Hotel Titanic

Kilifi

Hotel Titanic, Biashara Street, Kilifi, North Coast, Kenya
Platinum Resorts, PO Box 85177, Mombasa 80100, Kenya

Tel	+254 41 7522370
Mobile	+254 726 363437
Fax	+254 41 7522370
E-mail	info@platinumresort.net / stanleynyachae@yahoo.com
Web	www.hoteltitanic.com / www.platinumresort.net

 Malindi, LS & CH, 1 hr
 Moi Intl., LS & CH & Intl., 1.5 hrs

In the centre of Kilifi town, Hotel Titanic offers budget accommodation and conference facilities in a location that is convenient for the shops, businesses, restaurants and bars of Kilifi. The hotel is managed by Platinum Resorts, based in Mombasa.

There are 33 en-suite double rooms. All rooms have fan and mosquito net; some rooms have satellite TV. The restaurant, on the 1st floor, has bright orange walls painted with murals of people cooking and eating. The menu is Kenyan and Italian, including penne al arobiata, risotto ortomare, spaghetti al aragosta, nyama choma grilled meats and kienyeji stew. The bar, next to the restaurant, is equipped with satellite TV. It serves soft drinks, beers and spirits, and also has keg Tusker beer on tap.

There are 2 conference halls. Utulivu Hall seats 70 pax and Jahazi Hall seats 100. The hotel can hire conference equipment, including projector and PA system, if required. There is a swimming pool and sunbathing terrace on the rooftop, shaded by a thatched roof. The hotel is located over a row of shops, including a business centre that offers photocopying, laminating, binding, printing and internet. There is also a hair salon and a boutique.

Makuti Villas Resort

Kilifi

Makuti Villas Resort, Kilifi, nr Kilifi Bridge, North Coast, Kenya
PO Box 405, Kilifi 80108, Kenya

Tel	+254 41 7522371
Mobile	+254 734 873704
Fax	
E-mail	makutivillas@yahoo.com / sales@makutivillas.com
Web	www.makutivillas.com

   Malindi, LS & CH, 1 hr
Moi Intl., LS & CH & Intl., 1.5 hrs

Makuti Villas Resort is set in attractive gardens around a swimming pool. The resort offers budget accommodation and a lively night scene. There are 35 en-suite rooms, made up of singles and doubles. All rooms are equipped with fan and mosquito net. The rooms are in whitewashed thatched cottages. There is WiFi throughout the resort. Sunday is Family Day, when children can get a special offer of chips and soda and use of the swimming pool, while adults get a special offer of chicken, chips and beer. A DJ plays every Family Day, as well as some evenings during the week. The open sided thatched restaurant has an extensive international menu, including pasta quarto formaggi, pan fried calamari, risotto ai funghi porcini, chicken tikka, cotoletta Milanese, poached red snapper in white wine sauce, prawns Masala and crepe Suzette. There is also a selection of vegetarian dishes, such as vegetable curry, stir fried vegetables on rice and pizza. The bar has a selection of soft drinks, beers, wines and spirits. At weekends, live bands play on the stage at the poolside. There are thatched seating areas around the pool. The children's play area has swings, slide and merry-go-round.

Mnarani Club

Kilifi

Mnarani Club, Kilifi-Mombasa Highway, Kilifi, North Coast, Kenya
PO Box 1008, Kilifi 80108, Kenya

Tel	+254 20 8070501-4; +254 20 8070505
Mobile	+254 727 288166; +254 733 333579
Fax	
E-mail	mnaranireservations@oaks.co.za
Web	www.mnarani.co.za

VISA, MasterCard   Malindi, LS & CH, 1 hr
Moi Intl., LS & CH & Intl., 1.5 hrs

On the opposite side of the bridge from Kilifi, Mnarani Club looks out on the creek. The name, meaning lighthouse, refers to the hotel's position at the entrance to the creek. The hotel's infinity pool appears to be tumbling into the creek.
There are 82 en-suite rooms, made up of doubles, twins and singles. They are divided between Garden Rooms and Creek Rooms. All rooms have aircon, fan and telephone. The restaurant serves buffet, with an international menu including crab cakes with chutney, chargrilled vegetables, corn and pea Masala, pork chops and hot cinnamon and carrot doughnuts. There is also a pizza oven with a selection of fresh pizzas. A snack menu is available at the poolside.
The hotel has 2 swimming pools, football pitch, squash court, crazy golf and a TV lounge with satellite TV. The spa offers facial, massage, manicure and pedicure. Neilson's Safaris has an animation team in the hotel, which offers a daily programme of activities such as water polo, water aerobics, volleyball, quiz and Swahili lessons. Other activities include sailing, windsurfing and horse riding. Trips to Arabuko Sokoke Forest, Malindi, local schools and craft markets are available. Neilson's Safaris, with a desk on site, can book tours, excursions and safaris to destinations in Kenya.

Fig Tree House Takaungu

Fig Tree House, Takaungu, North Coast, Kenya
Kenya Beachrentals, PO Box 113, Kilifi 80108, Kenya
Tel
Mobile +254 722 415447
Fax
E-mail aetkilifi@gmail.com
Web www.kenya-beachrentals.com

   Moi Intl., LS & CH & Intl.
1.5 hrs

Fig Tree House is an exclusive villa, set in 2 acres of gardens of indigenous forest and approached by an avenue of fig trees. Raised on a cliff, the house has superb views over Takaungu Creek. The house has a unique open plan design around a floodlit infinity swimming pool.

The ground floor comprises of an enclosed, pillared courtyard with carved Lamu doors and a large outdoor seating area. There is also a fully equipped fitted kitchen and an elegant dining room. The house is staffed with housekeeper, chef and security guard. Fresh fish can be bought direct from fishermen daily.

There are 4 spacious en-suite double bedrooms, situated around the 1st floor courtyard. The master bedroom has its own roof terrace with daybed, spa bath and garden. All rooms are adorned with Persian rugs and Swahili furniture, and have views over the garden and creek.

A hand-hewn tunnel through the coral cliff leads from the house to Takaungu Creek. At low tide, a beach and tide pools are revealed. At high tide, the sea is ideal for swimming, snorkelling, windsurfing and kayaking. The coastal forest beside the house is inhabited by monkeys, bushbabies, squirrels and hornbills. A nearby ferry provides transport to the village of Takaungu.

Takaungu Cottages Takaungu

Takaungu Cottages, nr Zinj, Takaungu, North Coast, Kenya
Tel
Mobile +254 710 384807
Fax
E-mail shaheen.amin@yahoo.com
Web

   Moi Intl., LS & CH & Intl.
1.5 hrs

Overlooking the attractive, twisting creek, Takaungu Cottages offer a remote location and lovely views. The simple, stone cottages are self-catering. Positioned on the creek's lush banks, the cottages face directly onto the water. Stone steps descend from the cottages to the beach.

There are 4 apartments, 2 in each of the 2 cottages. Each apartment has 2 double rooms, 1 bathroom and a balcony overlooking the creek. Bed linen and towels are provided. There is a communal kitchen, behind the cottages, which is shared by the guests in the 4 apartments. The kitchen is equipped with gas cooker, fridge, crockery, cutlery and glassware. The open air dining area, next to the kitchen, is shaded by a tall palm tree.

Guests can cook for themselves, or a chef can be provided for an extra charge. Guests can bring their own food, or the cottages can provide food on a full board basis.

The cottages are located beside Zinj, the fair trade bead and leather design workshop. Zinj employs locals to create unique leather bags and shoes, with the slogan: changing lives one bead at a time. The cottages are also close to the ferry that crosses the creek from Takaungu to Kilifi. Takaungu has a fish shop and a dispensary.

Takaungu House   Takaungu

Takaungu House, nr Zinj, Takaungu, North Coast, Kenya
PO Box 1311, Takaungu, Kenya
Tel
Mobile   +254 728 754727; +254 735 569353
Fax
E-mail
Web

Moi Intl., LS & CH & Intl.
1.5 hrs

Takaungu House, set in a stunning beachfront garden, has 3 elegant whitewashed houses available for holiday rent. The self-catering houses are stylishly furnished. The compound is on a headland and offers sea views on all sides. The gardens are bright with bougainvillea and flame trees. There is 1 3-bedroom house with a fully equipped kitchen, sitting room, dining room, veranda and private swimming pool. The house has antique wooden furniture, cream linens, traditional ornaments and a sea view. There is also a 1-bedroom house and a 2-bedroom house. These 2 houses are separated by a courtyard, and share a fully equipped kitchen and a swimming pool surrounded by sunbathing terrace. Both houses are furnished with heirlooms such as an antique writing desk, traditional wooden shutters, carved doors and books in heavy wooden bookcases. The garden has hanging seats and hammocks.

The cottages are located not far from Zinj, the fair trade bead and leather design workshop. Zinj employs locals to create unique leather bags and shoes, with the slogan: changing lives one bead at a time. The cottages are also close to the ferry that crosses the creek from Takaungu to Kalifi. Takaungu has a fish shop and a dispensary.

Matrix Beach House   Vipingo

Matrix Beach House, Vinod Dattani Road, opp Tewa Training College
Matrix Investments, PO Box 58573, Nairobi 00200, Kenya
Tel
Mobile   +254 724 966081; +254 733 600144
Fax
E-mail   matrixinvestments@yahoo.com
Web   www.matrixinvestments.com

Moi Intl., LS & CH & Intl.
1.5 hrs

In beachfront gardens, Matrix Beach House is a long white bungalow overlooking Vipingo Beach. The gardens, sloping down to the beach, are beautifully kept, and dotted with palm trees and succulents. The self-catering house is available for holiday rent, on an exclusive basis. The main house has 3 en-suite double bedrooms. There is also an open plan lounge and dining area and a sitting room furnished with wicker furniture and Maasai fabric cushions, and equipped with a CD player and satellite TV. The kitchen is fully equipped, including freezer and microwave, and has tiled work surfaces. The storeroom, adjoining the kitchen, has a washing machine. The guesthouse has 1 en-suite bedroom.

The terrace runs the full length of the house. A path leads from the terrace, through the garden, down to the beach. The house is staffed by 3 housekeepers, 1 chef, 1 gardener and 2 night guards. Guests should bring their own food; the chef will cook it for them, according to their preference. There is a stone table in the garden, for guests who prefer to eat alfresco. There is a backup generator in case of power cuts. A large cactus, in the garden, has the names of previous guests engraved on it.

Paradise Beach Resort Kikambala

Paradise Beach Resort, Kikambala, North Coast, Kenya
PO Box 78, Mtwapa 80109, Kenya

Tel	
Mobile	+254 723 110011
Fax	
E-mail	paradise@paradise.co.ke
Web	www.paradise.co.ke

   Moi Intl., LS & CH & Intl. 1 hr 15 mins

A statue of a lion greets guests at the entrance of Paradise Beach Resort, and murals of animals strut along all the walls. The reception is manned by 2 statues of Maasai moran. The hotel is set in beachfront gardens, on Kikambala Beach.

There are 64 en-suite rooms, including 8 suites. The rooms all have twin beds. They are in 3-floor buildings with coral walls that run along either side of the garden and freeform swimming pool. There are 2 restaurants; both restaurants serve buffet and also have an a la carte menu. They specialise in seafood and Kenyan food, such as grilled fish fillet, stews, curries and nyama choma grilled meats. There are 3 bars, 1 of which is in the centre of the swimming pool. The bars have thatched roofs and coral walls. A small bridge leads across the pool to the central bar. An animation team provides a daily programme of activities, such as water aerobics and team games. Water sports, like sailing, windsurfing and snorkelling, can be booked here. There is a boutique selling local curios.

Sun N Sand Beach Resort Kikambala

Sun N Sand Beach Resort, Kikambala, North Coast, Kenya
PO Box 2, Mtwapa 80109, Kenya

Tel	+254 20 2057950-3
Mobile	+254 733 644555; +254 733 611514; +254 722 204333
Fax	+254 20 2057954
E-mail	admin@sunnsand.co.ke
Web	www.sunnsand.info

 VISA, MasterCard    Moi Intl., LS & CH & Intl. 1 hr 15 mins

Sun N Sand Beach Resort, surrounded by landscaped gardens and an assortment of swimming pools, offers an activity-filled holiday. There are 300 en-suite rooms, made up of 260 standard rooms, 35 deluxe rooms with sea views, 4 executive suites and 1 royal suite with 2 bedrooms, a living room and a Jacuzzi. The rooms, in 3 wings, are equipped with aircon, fan, hairdryer, telephone, safe, TV, fridge, kettle and vape mosquito machines. Fahari Restaurant serves buffet breakfast, lunch and themed dinners. Oriental Hut serves Asian cuisine; Safari Ranch has barbecues; Safina serves snacks. La Stella serves Italian cuisine and Safina Grill is an a la carte restaurant, reservation required. There are several bars, including a swim-up bar. Water sports include kayaking, windsurfing, snorkelling, deep sea fishing, scuba diving and glass bottomed boat trips. The Sports Complex offers tennis, crazy golf, volleyball, archery, giant chess and more. Other activities include water rugby, croquet, beach Olympics, football and water aerobics. The Fun E-team organises nightly activities including bands, traditional dancing, karaoke, quizzes and cabaret shows. The Sunshine Kids' Club offers creative activities including arts and crafts, jungle tree house, talent shows, wildlife and marine discussions, African stories and face painting. The Sun and Sand Trust promotes sustainable development for the Kikambala community.

North Coast Beach Hotel

Kikambala

North Coast Beach Hotel, Kikambala, North Coast, Kenya
PO Box 89926, Mombasa 80100, Kenya

Tel	+254 20 2037784-5
Mobile	+254 722 209458; +254 733 409430
Fax	
E-mail	info@northcoastbeachhotel.co.ke
Web	www.northcoastbeachhotel.co.ke

 VISA, MasterCard   Moi Intl., LS & CH & Intl. 1 hr 15 mins

North Coast Beach Hotel is set in beachfront gardens on Kikambala Beach. Formerly known as Les Soleil Beach Club, the hotel was taken over by Kenyatta University in 2009. It now specialises in conferences, workshops and seminars.

There are 123 en-suite rooms, made up of 93 standard, 12 deluxe, 17 suites and 1 executive suite. All rooms are equipped with satellite TV, aircon, writing desk, reading lamp, hairdryer and telephone. Ground floor rooms are suitable for guests with disabilities. The suites are more spacious and include a sitting room with microwave and minibar. The restaurant serves buffet, with a predominantly Kenyan menu including nyama choma grilled meats, stews and curries, served with ugali and kachumbari. There are 3 conference halls, seating 50, 100 and 150 pax. They are all equipped with projector and PA system. The business centre has internet, printing, photocopying and secretarial services. The animation team offers teambuilding packages. There is also a gym, sauna, boutique, beauty salon and barber. The swimming pool has a swim-up bar, with seats in the water. There is also a children's playground. The hotel can assist with booking tours, excursions, safaris and water sports.

Boko Boko

Kikambala

Boko Boko, Mombasa-Malindi Highway, Kikambala, North Coast, Kenya
PO Box 10130, Bamburi 80101, Kenya

Tel	
Mobile	+254 721 375605; +254 733 728435
Fax	
E-mail	bokoboko@africaonline.co.ke
Web	www.bokoboko-kenya.de

Moi Intl., LS & CH & Intl. 1 hr 15 mins

Boko Boko started in 1975 as Porini Restaurant; the cottages were added in 2005. Boko Boko and Porini Restaurant are attractively surrounded by lush gardens, in a cool and peaceful setting.

There are 5 cottages. All cottages have clay tiled floor, 4-poster bed, heavy wooden furniture, mosquito net, window net and veranda with cushioned seating area. 3 cottages have aircon and 2 have fan. The cottages are linked by paths that wind through the dense garden. Porini Restaurant is an open sided thatched restaurant, surrounded by trees and ferns. It has an international menu, influenced predominantly by Swahili cuisine and seafood. Dishes include chargrilled Boko Boko fillet, chicken Creole, chicken in tamarind sauce, beans in coconut, banana in tomato sauce, Swahili prawns and taffy Creole. The seafood platter should be booked in advance. The bar is well stocked, and includes a wine list.

The swimming pool, in the centre of the garden, has a thatched shelter beside it. Breakfast and lunch can be served beside the pool. The Coffee House has darts and table tennis. A masseuse offers a range of massage, manicure and pedicure. There is also a pond where several crocodiles live, which can be seen from the viewing platform at the edge of the garden.

Salama Beach Resort   Kikambala

Salama Beach Resort, Kanamai Beach, Kikambala, North Coast, Kenya
PO Box 148, Mtwapa 80109, Kenya

Tel
Mobile +254 723 527145; +254 735 453253
Fax
E-mail info@salama-beach-resort.de
Web www.salama-beach-resort.com

VISA, MasterCard

 Moi Intl., LS & CH & Intl.
1 hr 15 mins

Salama Beach Resort offers beachfront bungalows and a stylish restaurant that specialises in seafood. The blue and white bungalows surround a beachfront swimming pool.

There are 10 bungalows, made up of 6 1-bedroom bungalows and 4 2-bedroom bungalows. All bungalows have an Arabic open plan living and dining room, and are equipped with aircon, fan, safe and minibar. Water is heated by solar power. The resort has installed a rain catchment system, and a tank that holds 80,000 litres. Water sports including snorkelling and scuba diving can be booked at a local water sports centre; Salama Beach Resort provides transfers to and from the centre.

Maridadi Restaurant is a thatched open sided building located on the beach. It serves an extensive selection of creative seafood dishes, such as fish fillet in pink butter, Thai bang snapper, maridadi coconut prawns, octopus in red wine sauce, prawns in Pernod and a seafood platter for 2 pax. There is also a selection of tapas including deep fried calamari, smoked fish canapés and spicy pan fried octopus. The bar is well stocked with soft drinks, juices, beers, wines, spirits and cocktails. The bar and restaurant are open to visitors not staying at Salama Beach Resort.

Kingfisher Kikambala

Kingfisher, nr Royal Reserve Safari and Beach Club, Kikambala, Kenya
PO Box 606, Mtwapa 80109, Kenya

Tel
Mobile +254 719 723338
Fax
E-mail
Web

  Moi Intl., LS & CH & Intl.
1 hr 15 mins

Centred on an attractive and quirky restaurant, Kingfisher is an oasis of green in arid Kikambala. The lush gardens create a cool and peaceful atmosphere.

The restaurant is entwined with the garden, beneath a thatched roof. The terracotta walls are studded with coral, and decorated with murals of fish, shells and kingfishers. A hat stand, holding hats of different eras and regions, stands in the corner and lanterns hang from wooden beams. The restaurant has a menu dominated by seafood and Swahili dishes, such as prawn Masala, grilled kingfish, Talitha steak, Tornado steak, Swahili fish, fish fillet Kanamai and octopus in garlic and lime. The bar is well stocked with soft drinks, beers, wines and spirits. A boutique, in the corner of the restaurant, stocks local fabrics and beachwear.

There are 4 en-suite double rooms, joined by paths through the gardens. Each room has orange walls, fan, mosquito net, table and chair. The bathrooms are fully tiled. Seating areas are in secluded parts of the garden. Kingfisher can organise and cater for staff parties and family gatherings. It is located a short walk from Kikambala Beach, and approximately 3km from the Mombasa-Malindi Highway.

Royal Reserve
Safari and Beach Club

Kikambala

Royal Reserve Safari and Beach Club, Kanamai, Kikambala, Kenya
PO Box 34190, Nyali 80118, Kenya

Tel	+254 20 2057155; +254 20 3576575
Mobile	+254 722 205220; +254 727 299998; +254 733 624320
Fax	
E-mail	info@royalreserve.com
Web	www.royalreserve.net

 VISA, MasterCard   Moi Intl., LS & CH & Intl. 1 hr 15 mins

Royal Reserve Safari and Beach Club offers exclusive apartments available for time share or holiday rental. The club is in tropical gardens on Kikambala Beach. There are 34 2-bedroom apartments and 12 1-bedrooms apartments. The apartments all have a kitchen, living room and balcony. The kitchens are equipped with fridge, microwave, gas cooker, toaster, kettle, coffeemaker and utensils. The living rooms are equipped with satellite TV, mosquito net and telephone. Baby cots are available on request, and babysitting services are offered. Daily housekeeping services are provided. Ground floor rooms are equipped for guests with disabilities. The restaurant has an exotic, extensive menu, including tuna carpaccio, fish bouillabaisse, seafood sizzler, prawn harissa, lamb fajitas, mutton rogan josh, hakka noodles, Greek salad, dhal makhani, chateaubriand and fondu. There is also a kids' menu. Baraza conference centre seats 100 pax on 2 floors, and is fully equipped. The business centre offers WiFi, photocopying and secretarial services. The club has a tennis court, volleyball court, pool table, mini golf, large swimming pool and children's swimming pool. There is also a gym, beauty salon, massage parlour, sauna and steam bath. The Kids' Club offers a range of games and activities for children. The tour desk can book tours, excursions, water sports and safaris.

Jumuia Conference
and Beach Resort, Kikambala

Kikambala

Jumuia Conference and Beach Resort, Kanamai, Kikambala, Kenya
PO Box 46, Mtwapa 80109, Kenya

Tel	+254 20 3548318
Mobile	+254 710 288043; +254 738 713444
Fax	
E-mail	reservations.kanamai@resortjumuia.com
Web	www.resortjumuia.com

      Moi Intl., LS & CH & Intl. 1 hr 15 mins

Jumuia Resorts aim to be the leading Christian resort chain in Kenya. Jumuia, Swahili for community or federation, refers to the National Council of Churches of Kenya, Jumuia ya makanisa ya Kenya. There are 5 Jumuia Resorts, in Kisumu, Nakuru, Limuru, Mombasa and Nairobi. Set on Kanamai Beach, Jumuia Conference and Beach Resort is a peaceful retreat. There are 72 en-suite rooms. All rooms have telephone and satellite TV. Water is heated by solar power. There are also 2 dormitories with bathroom facilities, intended for students or teambuilding participants. The campsite has bathroom and kitchen facilities. The large dining hall seats 400 pax; a chef is provided.

The restaurant has a glass front giving views of the beach. It serves an international menu including Kanamai caesar salad, fish and chips, deep fried taffy Jumuia style, spaghetti Napolitano, beef burger with cheese and marble cake. Non alcoholic wines and beers are served, as well as soft drinks and juices. No alcohol is served.
The swimming pool is surrounded by sunbathing terrace. Uhuru Kamili conference hall, on the beach, seats 300 pax, and is equipped with projector and PA system. Technical services are on offer; WiFi is available in reception. Weddings, functions and private parties can be arranged.

Danpark
Hotel and Apartments

Mtwapa

Danpark Hotel and Apartments, nr Total Petrol Station, Mtwapa, Kenya
PO Box 86695, Mombasa 80100, Kenya

Tel	+254 41 2000220; +254 41 2324161
Mobile	+254 715 366082
Fax	
E-mail	danpark2008@yahoo.com
Web	www.danparkhotel.com

VISA, MasterCard   Moi Intl., LS & CH & Intl. 1 hr

Danpark Hotel and Apartments is an oasis of calm in the centre of bustling Mtwapa. The hotel, in spacious palm filled gardens, opened in 2008.
There are 40 apartments, on 4 floors. Each apartment has a bedroom, bathroom, living room, fully equipped kitchen and balcony. They are equipped with fan, mosquito net and satellite TV; extra beds can be provided on request. The restaurant is open air, beneath a tented awning. The menu is predominantly Kenyan, and includes mutton curry, beef stew and grilled chicken. Buffet and a la carte are available. The bar stocks soft drinks and beers.
The main conference hall seats 100 pax, while the hall beside the pool seats 50. Conference equipment can be hired on request. The swimming pool is ½ Olympic size and is open to the public. There is also a children's pool. The large gardens make an ideal location for parties and functions. Tents can be hired on request. The boutique has a selection of clothes, and a tailor is available for adjustments. The hotel can arrange tours, excursions, dhow boat trips, fishing trips and water sports. Safaris to destinations in Kenya are also available.

Serena Beach Hotel and Spa

Shanzu

Serena Beach Hotel and Spa, Serena Beach Road, Shanzu Beach, Kenya
Serena Hotels, PO Box 48690, Nairobi 00100, Kenya

Tel	+254 20 2842333; +254 20 2842000; +254 20 2822000
Mobile	+254 727 284200-3; +254 733 282200; +254 733 282283/92
Fax	+254 20 2718102-3; +254 20 2725184
E-mail	cro@serena.co.ke
Web	www.serenahotels.com

VISA, MasterCard, Amex   Moi Intl., LS & CH & Intl. 1 hr

On peaceful Shanzu Beach, Serena Beach Hotel and Spa offers a wide selection of facilities and activities. The hotel replicates the winding lanes and colourful market places of a 13th century Swahili town. At the centre lies the coral Fortress of Tranquillity, in which is found the Maisha Mind Body and Spirit Spa. There are 66 village rooms, 48 garden rooms, 32 prime rooms and a selection of suites. All rooms have aircon, satellite TV, WiFi and telephone with voicemail. Family rooms are available and babysitting service is on offer. Central Restaurant serves pizza. Jahazi Grill, on the beach, serves seafood. There is also a selection of bars, dotted about the extensive beachfront gardens of the resort, including a swim-up bar in the freeform swimming pool. The resort also has the Arabic Coffee Terrace and an ice cream parlour.
The PADI scuba dive school offers scuba diving and an extensive range of water sports. The animation team offers a daily programme of activities. The conference centre has 3 conference halls, seating 80, 30 and 15 pax. All halls are fully equipped including aircon, WiFi, PA system, LCD projector and table microphones. The resort also has a business centre, unisex hair salon, gift shop, news stand, travel desk and taxi service. The wedding planning service works to ensure every couple gets the wedding they want.

Kamsons
Villa and Cottages
Shanzu

Kamsons Villa and Cottages, off Serena Beach Road, Shanzu, Kenya
PO Box 10593, Bamburi 80101, Kenya

Tel	+254 20 2353902
Mobile	+254 727 086936; +254 722 758093
Fax	
E-mail	kamsonvilla@rocketmail.com
Web	

  Moi Intl., LS & CH & Intl.
1 hr

Kamsons Villa and Cottages are in an attractive mature garden. The cottages can be rented separately, or the compound can be taken as a whole. The compound is also available for parties, functions or weddings. The main house has 1 en-suite master bedroom, a living room with sofas, armchairs and TV with local channels, a fully equipped kitchen and an open air dining area on the terrace. There are 2 en-suite bedrooms with kitchenettes, adjoining the main house, with separate entrances, that can be taken with the main house, or separately. There are also 2 detached cottages in the garden, with kitchenettes. Guests can choose the self-catering option, or a chef can be provided for an extra charge.

Guests can buy their own food, or the chef can buy the food they require. There is a thatched bar in the corner of the garden, stocked with soft drinks, beers, wines and spirits, and furnished with tables, comfortable sofas and CD player. The garden also has a circular stone dance floor. Cocktail tables for functions are dotted around the gardens. Tents and marquees can be hired on request, as can a DJ or live band.

Millbrook Hotel
Shanzu

Millbrook Hotel, Serena Beach Road, Shanzu, North Coast, Kenya
PO Box 10070, Bamburi 80101, Kenya

Tel	+254 20 2070585
Mobile	+254 726 708752; +254 734 067205
Fax	
E-mail	millbrookhotel@yahoo.com / info@millbrookhotel.com
Web	www.millbrookhotel.com

  Moi Intl., LS & CH & Intl.
1 hr

Tucked away behind Shanzu Beach, Millbrook Hotel offers budget accommodation, a pleasant beer garden and a swimming pool.
There are 32 en-suite rooms, made up of singles and doubles. All rooms have satellite TV, fridge and a balcony furnished with chairs. Some rooms have aircon and the remainder have fans. The hotel can provide a gas cooker for guests who wish to cater for themselves. The restaurant has a widely varied international menu, including spicy chicken wings, butter prawns, Russian egg salad, chicken Maryland, garlic crab, Indian yoghurt chicken, pepper steak, sizzling fajitas and nyama choma grilled meats. There is WiFi throughout the hotel.

The Makuti Bar is a large open sided bar with a thatched roof, opposite the car park. The Pool Bar overlooks the swimming pool, and is surrounded by a beer garden with shade umbrellas. Both bars are stocked with soft drinks, beers, wines and spirits, and play music. There is a secure car park. Shanzu Beach, a short walk from the hotel, is a peaceful beach. Water sports and boat trips can be booked with local tour operators. Millbrook Hotel is affiliated to Millbrook Safaris, which can book tours, excursions and safaris to destinations and national parks in Kenya.

Mombasa Continental Resort

Shanzu

Mombasa Continental Resort, Serena Beach Road, Shanzu, Kenya
PO Box 10649, Bamburi 80101, Kenya

Tel	+254 20 2191750-2
Mobile	+254 729 403650; +254 734 433433
Fax	+254 20 2191753
E-mail	reservations@mcr.kengahotels.co.ke
Web	www.mombasacontinentalresort.co.ke

VISA, MasterCard

 Moi Intl., LS & CH & Intl. 1 hr

Mombasa Continental Resort faces onto Shanzu Beach. Formerly part of the InterContinental chain of hotels, Mombasa Continental Resort became independent in 2000.

There are 177 en-suite rooms, all of which have views of the sea, made up of 73 doubles, 93 twins, 6 junior suites, 3 presidential suites and 2 rooms for guests with disabilities. All rooms have aircon, internet, safe, telephone and minibar. There are several restaurants to suit all tastes. The Frangipani Restaurant serves buffet breakfast and dinner, and a la carte lunch. The Governor's Lounge is an a la carte restaurant. The Dhow Terrace serves seafood. The Poolside Bar and Grill serves snacks and grilled meat and fish. The Dhow Bar, Pool Bar, Quarterdeck Bar and Madafu Bar all serve a range of drinks. Le Club Discotheque is open after dinner. The conference hall seats 300 pax, and is equipped with projector and PA system.

The gym is fully equipped and offers massage. The animation team offers a daily programme of activities including volleyball, jogging and tennis. Water sports include kite surfing, canoeing and sailing. The kids' club offers games, activities and babysitting. Weddings, functions, outdoor catering, traditional dancing and live entertainment can all be arranged.

Sonia Hotel and Apartments

Shanzu

Sonia Hotel and Apartments, Serena Beach Road, Shanzu, Kenya
PO Box 83573, Mombasa 80100, Kenya

Tel	+254 20 3501840
Mobile	+254 720 717272
Fax	
E-mail	blueedgehotels@hotmail.com
Web	www.blueedgehotels.com

Moi Intl., LS & CH & Intl. 1 hr

Sonia Hotel and Apartments offers a selection of accommodation and an attractive, quirky restaurant.

There are 27 apartments. Each apartment has an en-suite double room with aircon and fan, a kitchen and a balcony. The kitchens are not equipped, and guests should bring their own utensils if required. There is also a students' hostel, with a dormitory that sleeps 30 pax. Bathroom facilities are available. The open sided thatched restaurant serves Kenyan and international dishes, such as nyama choma grilled meats, burgers, sandwiches, pizza, pasta and seafood. The bar serves soft drinks, beers and spirits, and is equipped with satellite TV, pool table and table tennis table. Live bands and other entertainment play at the weekend.

The conference hall seats 100 pax. Conference equipment is not provided and groups should bring their own, if required. The compound also contains a massage parlour, beauty salon and chemist. A curio shop stocks local carvings and artefacts. A tour office can book tours, excursions and safaris. Sonia Hotel and Apartments is located opposite Mombasa Continental Resort, on Serena Beach Road. Water sports and other activities can be booked at local water sports centres.

Petuscha Garden Lodge

Shanzu

Petuscha Garden Lodge, Serena Beach Road, Shanzu, Kenya
PO Box 97999, Makupa 80112, Kenya
Tel
Mobile   +254 722 734755
Fax
E-mail   petuschahotel@yahoo.com
Web   www.faircons.info

                              Moi Intl., LS & CH & Intl.
                                                   1 hr

Petuscha Garden Lodge is an attractive low whitewashed building, with a red tiled roof. The small size and friendly staff give the lodge the atmosphere of a comfortable house. The rooms and suites are available on a long or short-term basis.

There are 2 standard en-suite rooms, 4 superior en-suite rooms, 2 family rooms, 2 suites and a private villa. The rooms are all equipped with aircon, fan and TV with local channels. The family rooms and suites have living room and kitchenette. The villa has 2 double bedrooms, bathroom, living room and kitchen. Outside the lounge, a terrace stretches the length of the house. Breakfast is served on the terrace, overlooking the swimming pool. A thatched lounge, at the end of the swimming pool, is also available for eating or relaxing.

Cha Cha Restaurant and Bar is an open sided restaurant, its floor a bright patchwork of tiles. The menu includes Kenyan favourites, international dishes and seafood, such as Hawaiian spicy pork chops, lobster thermidor, fish fillet meuniere, crab salad, beef stroganoff, steak Cha Cha and nyama choma grilled meats. The bar serves soft drinks, beers and spirits, and a selection of cocktails. There is a secure car park. The lodge is located a short walk from Shanzu Beach.

Trinity Resort

Shanzu

Trinity Resort, Serena Beach Road, Shanzu, North Coast, Kenya
PO Box 10066, Bamburi 80101, Kenya
Tel
Mobile   +254 726 828729; +254 712 473424; +254 727 101066
Fax
E-mail   trinityresort@yahoo.com
Web

                              Moi Intl., LS & CH & Intl.
                                                   1 hr

Trinity Resort, set in gardens studded with palm trees, offers self-catering apartments, not far from Shanzu Beach. The apartments can be taken on a long or short-term basis.

There are 29 apartments, made up of 14 1-bedroom apartments and 15 2-bedroom apartments. All apartments have a kitchen equipped with gas cooker, fridge, crockery, cutlery and glassware. Some also have an open plan living and dining room, and a balcony. There is a safe at reception where guests are welcome to deposit their valuables.

There is a swimming pool with a section for children. There is a children's playground in the garden. The outdoor lounge, by the pool, is furnished with sofas and armchairs. The bar serves soft drinks and beers. There is a secure car park. Shanzu Beach, a peaceful beach, is not far from Trinity Resort. Mtwapa town, a short drive south of Shanzu Beach, has shops, kiosks, restaurants and bars. Nearby sites of interest include Bamburi Nature Trail.

Dancourt Hotel Bamburi

Dancourt Hotel, Bamburi, North Coast, Kenya
PO Box 43240, Mombasa 80100, Kenya

Tel	+254 41 2001313; +254 41 2226278
Mobile	+254 710 846334
Fax	
E-mail	dancourt@swiftmombasa.com
Web	

     Moi Intl., LS & CH & Intl. 1 hr

Dancourt Hotel offers budget accommodation just off the Mombasa-Malindi Highway. The hotel's small size and unassuming garden restaurant make it a friendly place to stay.

There are 10 en-suite rooms, made up of 5 doubles and 5 twins. All rooms have fan, mosquito net and satellite TV. Palms Restaurant is an open sided thatched restaurant, joined to the hotel by a thatched walkway. It serves an international menu including pan fried chicken, beef skewers, pork chops, crumbed fillet of fish and fruit platter. There is also a selection of soups and burgers. The bar serves soft drinks, beers and spirits. There is a secure car park.

The hotel is within a short drive of both Bamburi and Shanzu Beaches. Local sites of interest include the Bamburi Nature Trail and Mtwapa Creek. The nearby town of Mtwapa has shops, restaurants and bars. Further up the coast, attractions include Watamu Marine National Park, Arabuko Sokoke Forest, Gede Ruins, Mida Creek, Kipepeo Butterfly Project and the Snake Farm. Dancourt Hotel can assist with booking tours, excursions and safaris to destinations in Kenya.

Plaza Beach Hotel Bamburi

Plaza Beach Hotel, Bamburi Beach, North Coast, Kenya
PO Box 88299, Mombasa 80100, Kenya

Tel	+254 41 5485321-4; +254 20 3560760
Mobile	+254 723 661008
Fax	+254 41 5485325
E-mail	info@plazabeach.co.ke
Web	www.plazabeach.co.ke

 VISA, MasterCard    Moi Intl., LS & CH & Intl. 1 hr

In terraced gardens that descend to Bamburi Beach, Plaza Beach Hotel has whitewashed buildings around a freeform swimming pool. The hotel offers the chance to relax on the beach or indulge in a wide range of activities. There are 88 en-suite rooms. All rooms have aircon, satellite TV, telephone, safe and hairdryer. Minibar and kettle are available on request. The restaurant serves a table d'hote menu that changes daily, and includes dishes such as roast leg of lamb and potato and pea curry. The pool bar has a selection of drinks and snacks. There are 2 conference halls, 1 seating 45 pax and the other seating 150. Conference equipment and secretarial services are available.

The animation team has a daily programme of activities such as beach football, beach volleyball and water aerobics. They also provide a kids' programme of games and activities. Babysitting service is available. Beach activities such as windsurfing, sailing, snorkelling, scuba diving, jet skiing and fishing can be booked at the hotel. In house activities include table tennis, billiards and massage. A doctor is on call 24 hours. Taxis and restaurants can be booked at reception. Southern Cross Safaris has a tour desk at reception and can book tours, excursions and safaris.

Severin Sea Lodge

Bamburi

Severin Sea Lodge, Malindi Road, Bamburi Beach, North Coast, Kenya
Severin, PO Box 82169, Mombasa 80100, Kenya

Tel	+254 41 5485001-5; +254 41 5487665
Mobile	+254 722 284682; +254 733 645444
Fax	+254 41 5485212
E-mail	marketing@severin-kenya.com
Web	www.severin-kenya.com

 All major cards   Moi Intl., LS & CH & Intl. 1 hr

On Bamburi Beach, Severin Sea Lodge provides a wide variety of sports, leisure and entertainment. The hotel was awarded by the TÜV Rhineland in Germany for the quality of its service.

The 200 en-suite rooms are designed in traditional Swahili style. There are standard and superior rooms in the main building, while in the bungalows, there are standard and comfort class rooms. All rooms have aircon, piped music, telephone, hairdryer, safe and balcony. In addition, the comfort class rooms have a minibar, and the superior rooms have satellite TV. The Admiral Suite has a separate living room, kitchenette, bar, changing room and sea view.

Kisima Restaurant serves buffet breakfast and themed buffet dinners. Kisima Pool Grill serves lunches by the pool. Flame Tree Bistro has Italian cuisine. Imani Dhow Restaurant, an old stranded dhow, serves a la carte seafood. Drinks are served in the Safari Bar, the Swing Bar and Johari Roof Terrace.

The hotel has the Barracuda scuba diving and water sports centre, massage centre, floodlit tennis courts and Makutano Conference Centre. After dinner entertainment includes live music, acrobatic shows, fashion shows and traditional dancing. For a special evening, guests can take the Severin dhow to Fort Jesus for dinner and son et lumiere.

Sentido Neptune Beach Resort

Bamburi

Sentido Neptune Beach Resort, Bamburi Beach, North Coast, Kenya
PO Box 83125, Mombasa 80100, Kenya

Tel	+254 41 5485701
Mobile	
Fax	+254 41 5485705
E-mail	info.neptunebeach@sentidohotels.com
Web	www.sentidohotels.com

 VISA, MasterCard    Moi Intl., LS & CH & Intl. 1 hr

North Coast

On palm fringed Bamburi Beach, Sentido Neptune Beach Resort has a family atmosphere and offers a range of activities in the water, on the beach and in the resort.

The 78 en-suite rooms are made up of doubles, superiors and deluxe. All the rooms have a telephone, satellite TV, safe, kettle, hairdryer, WiFi, aircon and a balcony. The 12 superior and deluxe rooms have sea views. The restaurant seats 100 pax and serves local and international buffets. The 2 bars serve drinks and snacks. The conference room seats up to 60 pax. The recently redesigned gardens and the terrace with a view of the sea make peaceful places to relax and enjoy the scenery.

The swimming pool has an integrated children's section. The spa offers massage and beauty treatments. Activities include aerobics, billiards, table tennis, volleyball, archery and water basketball. Windsurfing, tennis, scuba diving and deep sea fishing are available nearby for an extra charge. The kid's club, open 10am-12.30pm and 2pm-5pm, has indoor and outdoor games, bikes, TV and children's films. Childcare can also be arranged. The resort prints a daily newsletter with information on the region and the day's entertainment. A holiday concierge assists guests with the planning of their activities.

Bamburi Chalets

Bamburi

Bamburi Chalets, Bamburi Beach, North Coast, Kenya
PO Box 84114, Mombasa 80100, Kenya

Tel	
Mobile	+254 736 599271
Fax	
E-mail	bamburichalets@hotmail.com
Web	

   Moi Intl., LS & CH & Intl.
1 hr

Bamburi Chalets is a collection of self-catering cottages on Bamburi beachfront. The cottages are in manicured gardens and have been constructed in a diagonal formation that gives every cottage a view of the sea. There are 7 whitewashed cottages, in an attractive, simple design. Each cottage is open plan, and has a double and twin bedroom, living room, fully equipped kitchen, dining area and balcony. The rooms are equipped with fans and mosquito nets, and are adorned with cream linens and bright kikoy fabrics. Bed linen and towels are provided, and there is a daily housekeeping service. Sliding glass doors between the living area and balcony give guests a view of the beachfront. Each cottage is edged by flowers. There is also a swimming pool.

The cottages are between large international hotels and in close proximity of shops, restaurants and bars. A tennis club is nearby. Water sports such as snorkelling, windsurfing, sailing and deep sea fishing are all available nearby. Boat trips can also be booked with local tour operators. Bamburi Beach is about a ½hr drive from Mombasa town to the south, and not far from Nyali and Mtwapa.

Baba's

Bamburi

Baba's, Bamburi Beach, North Coast, Kenya
PO Box 85111, Mombasa 80100, Kenya

Tel	+254 41 5468000
Mobile	+254 720 958033
Fax	+254 41 5486289
E-mail	mombasasairesort@gmail.com
Web	www.mombasa-sai-resort.com

   Moi Intl., LS & CH & Intl.
1 hr

Baba's is in a beachfront location on Bamburi Beach. The resort was previously known as Mombasa Sai Resort. It is entered through a white arch, through which the Indian Ocean is visible.

There are 36 en-suite double rooms. Some have aircon and the remainder have fans. Some have TV with local channels. There are 2 restaurants, one on the ground floor and the other on the first floor. Both have glass fronts that give views of the sea. The ground floor restaurant has an international menu, including Sokoni Sunshine platter of vegetables, surf and turf, mushroom steak, spaghetti carbonara, garlic butter stir fried prawns and cheese crusted snapper. It also has a clay oven and offers a selection of freshly baked pizzas. On the 1st floor is a Chinese restaurant. There are 2 conference halls, each seating 150 pax. The garden, with bougainvillea walkway, is dotted with sunbeds. Chairs and tables are on the beachfront. Water sports can be booked with operators on the beach. Baba's can contact a local tour agent, for guests who want to book a tour, excursion or safari. Local sites of interest include Bamburi Nature Trail and Mtwapa Creek. Mtwapa town has shops, restaurants and bars.

Papillon Bamburi

Papillon, Bamburi Beach, North Coast, Kenya
PO Box 86291, Mombasa 80100, Kenya

Tel	+254 41 5487493
Mobile	+254 729 753654; +254 733 739975; +254 734 661064
Fax	
E-mail	papillongunny@yahoo.com
Web	

   Moi Intl., LS & CH & Intl. 1 hr

In gardens dotted with quirky statues of animals, Papillon is a small resort not far from Bamburi Beach. The resort has a lively night scene, with a disco, DJ and weekend live band.

There are 10 en-suite rooms, made up of 7 doubles, 2 interconnecting rooms suitable for families and 1 triple. The rooms are in whitewashed buildings with thatched roofs that run the length of the swimming pool. All rooms have fan and mosquito net. The large round restaurant has a peaked thatched roof that centres on a tall pillar. The restaurant is embellished by African statues and artefacts, and has a pool table. The extensive international menu includes fillet Madagascar, escalope Vienna, lobster thermidor, prawn pilipili, duck deluxe and fillet Rossini with brandy sauce. The grill room serves nyama choma grilled meats. The main bar, in the restaurant, has a wide selection of soft drinks, beers and spirits, and also offers a wine list. The garden bar, with thatched roof, open sides and plants, has a dance floor and a DJ booth. Friday night is reggae night while on Saturday night a live band plays. Local sites of interest include Bamburi Nature Trail and Mtwapa Creek.

Kenya Bay Beach Hotel Bamburi

Kenya Bay Beach Hotel, Bamburi Beach, North Coast, Kenya
PO Box 767, Mombasa 80100, Kenya

Tel	+254 41 5487600-2; +254 20 2408500
Mobile	+254 725 991500
Fax	+254 41 5487044
E-mail	reservations@kenyabay.com
Web	www.kenyabay.com

 VISA, MasterCard, Amex   Moi Intl., LS & CH & Intl. 1 hr

In beachfront gardens, Kenya Bay Beach Hotel has lovely views of Bamburi Beach. Formerly known as Kenya Beach Hotel, the hotel is a blend of traditional and modern architecture.

There are 106 en-suite rooms, made up of 30 standard, 60 superior and 16 deluxe. All rooms have aircon, TV with local channels, fridge, telephone and balcony. The deluxe rooms are on the beachfront. Acacia Restaurant serves buffet breakfast, lunch and dinner. Frangipani Restaurant, on the beachfront, serves an a la carte menu including chilli stir fried chicken, Bay pepper chicken, spaghetti aglio e olio, prawns pilipili and choc nut sundae, as well as snacks such as sandwiches, hot dogs and samosas. The bars are well stocked, and include a wine list.

The animation team offers a daily programme of activities such as water aerobics and volleyball. Frangipani Club has evening entertainment such as live bands and discos. Acacia conference hall seats 200 pax, and is equipped with projector and PA system. Il Covo boutique stocks designer clothing, curios and beachwear. Barracuda Scuba Dive Centre, on site, offers a selection of water sports, and a free trial dive in the swimming pool. Oger Tours, in reception, can book tours, excursions and safaris.

Kahama Hotel

Bamburi

Kahama Hotel, Bamburi Beach, North Coast, Kenya
PO Box 10626, Bamburi 80101, Kenya

Tel	+254 20 3507205; +254 41 5485395; +254 41 5485066
Mobile	+254 733 771133; +254 729 487446
Fax	+254 41 5485066
E-mail	kahamahotel@gmail.com
Web	www.kahamahotel.co.ke

  Moi Intl., LS & CH & Intl.
 1 hr

Kahama Hotel is a bright, cheerful and friendly hotel set in gardens dotted with palm trees. The hotel has a lively night scene, with regular live bands and DJs.

There are 32 en-suite double rooms and 2 apartments. All rooms are spacious, and are equipped with aircon, telephone, mosquito net and satellite TV. The rooms are fully tiled, and adorned with bright local fabrics, African batiks, traditional artefacts and attractive Lamu furniture. The suites have 2 bedrooms, fully equipped kitchen and rooftop terrace furnished with table, chairs and sunbeds. The swimming pool is surrounded by sunbathing terrace with sunbeds, and has a children's section.

The Pitcher and Butch Sports Bar and Restaurant opens onto the garden where lights adorn the trees. It serves a selection of international pub dishes including pepper steak, noodles with sweet peppers, pea and potato curry, burgers, sandwiches and nyama choma grilled meats. The extensive drinks list includes soft drinks, beers, wines, spirits and liqueurs. Local DJs and live bands provide entertainment every night. The Poolside Restaurant has the same menu. There is also a conference hall, boardroom, cyber café and carwash. Kahama Hotel is affiliated to Klub House in Nairobi.

Indiana Beach Apartment Hotel

Bamburi

Indiana Beach Apartment Hotel, Bamburi Beach, North Coast, Kenya
PO Box 82662, Mombasa 80100, Kenya

Tel	+254 41 5485895; +254 41 5485977
Mobile	
Fax	+254 41 5485861
E-mail	indiana@africaonline.co.ke
Web	www.indianabeachkenya.com

  VISA, MasterCard
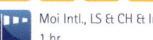 Moi Intl., LS & CH & Intl. 1 hr

Indiana Beach Apartment Hotel is located on Bamburi Beach. It offers a selection of accommodation, activities and facilities.

There are 36 en-suite deluxe rooms, made up of doubles, twins and triples. All rooms contain aircon, satellite TV, minibar, telephone and a balcony overlooking the swimming pools. There are 23 studios, with open plan bedroom and kitchenette, and a balcony. There are 10 round ovals, which have 2 bedrooms, open plan living and dining area and spacious balconies. The round ovals are 2-floor buildings, with tiled roofs in bright tropical gardens. There are 4 beach villas, which have 2 en-suite bedrooms, fully equipped kitchen and spacious living area opening onto a garden terrace.

Roberto's Pizzaria, on the beachfront, serves Italian cuisine. Sea View Deck serves international buffets. Maharajah serves Indian cuisine. Choma serves snacks and grills. Baridi Bar is well stocked with drinks, and equipped with satellite TV. The conference hall seats 250 pax, and is equipped with projector and PA system.

There are 4 swimming pools, including a children's pool. The PADI diving school offers water sports including scuba diving, windsurfing and water polo. There is a fully equipped gym, hair salon, boutique and business centre with WiFi. Car hire and excursions can be arranged.

Mombasa Beach Apartments

Nyali

Mombasa Beach Apartments, Barrack Road, Nyali, North Coast, Kenya
PO Box 89362, Nyali 80118, Kenya

Tel	+254 41 474848
Mobile	+254 722 479664
Fax	
E-mail	msabeachapts@wananchi.com
Web	www.mombasabeachapartments.com

    Moi Intl., LS & CH & Intl. 45 mins

On the beachfront in Nyali, Mombasa Beach Apartments are self-catering apartments for families or groups. The apartments are in a whitewashed building with red tiled roof; all apartments have sea facing balconies. There are 8 3-bedroom apartments. The apartments all have a double, a twin and a single room. Bed linen and toiletries are provided; extra beds are available on request. Each apartment also has a sitting room, dining room and kitchen equipped with fridge, electric cooker, microwave, crockery, cutlery and glassware. There is a bathroom, with bathtub, and a shower room. The sea facing balconies are furnished with table and chairs. The apartments are equipped with aircon, telephone and TV with local channels. A housekeeper services the apartments daily.

There is no restaurant or bar facility on site. The apartments are within easy reach of the shops, businesses, restaurants and bars of Nyali. Local sites of interest include Mamba Village, Wild Waters Amusement Park and Bamburi Nature Trail. Mombasa Old Town and Fort Jesus are also within reach, by car. Water sports can be booked with local operators on Nyali Beach. Tours, excursions and safaris can be arranged with local travel agents.

Kigotho's Hotel and Apartments

Nyali

Kigotho's Hotel and Apartments, Links Road, Nyali, North Coast, Kenya
PO Box 86178, Mombasa 80100, Kenya

Tel	
Mobile	+254 734 517026; +254 726 747050
Fax	
E-mail	kigothohotel@yahoo.com / info@kigothos.com
Web	www.kigothoshotel.com

    Moi Intl., LS & CH & Intl. 45 mins

North Coast

Known particularly for its restaurant which serves nyama choma grilled meats, Kigotho's Hotel and Apartments are popular with locals and visitors alike. The large gardens make an attractive setting for the apartments, which are conveniently located on Links Road.

There are 14 apartments, each fronted by a small private lawn and well maintained flowerbeds. There are 7 1-bedroom apartments, containing bedroom, bathroom, living room, kitchen and balcony. There are 3 deluxe 1-bedroom apartments, which are more spacious. There are 2 2-bedroom apartments, containing 2 bedrooms, bathroom, living room, kitchen and balcony. And there are 2 bedsits, with open plan bedroom and living room.

All the apartments are fully furnished, and their kitchens are equipped with crockery, cutlery and glassware.

The swimming pool has a separate section for children, and is overlooked by the thatched pool bar. The restaurant serves roast chicken, pork, goat, gizzards and chips. The bar is well stocked with soft drinks, beers and spirits, and is a lively local nightspot. There is also a children's football pitch and a pool table, as well as other games such as drafts and chess.

 Accommodation Guide

Mombasa Beach Hotel

Nyali

Mombasa Beach Hotel, Barrack Road, Nyali, North Coast, Kenya
Kenya Safari Lodges and Hotels, PO Box 42013, Nairobi 00100, Kenya.
Tel +254 20 3442012; +254 20 2297512; +254 20 3114749
Mobile
Fax +254 20 2222661
E-mail sales@kenya-safari.co.ke
Web www.safari-hotels.com

 Moi Intl., LS & CH & Intl.
45 mins

On a coral cliff overlooking Nyali Beach, Mombasa Beach Hotel offers a range of facilities and activities. The hotel was built in 1969 and refurbished in 1986, 2001 and 2006.

There are 152 en-suite rooms. All rooms have balconies with sea view. There are 5 dining areas, including Maxim's a la carte Cellar and the Cavern Beach Bistro, with its informal atmosphere and beach setting. The 2 conference halls can accommodate groups of up to 200 pax. The hotel hosted 200 athletes and media personnel to the IAAF Mombasa World Cross Country Championship in March 2007 and 250 delegates sponsored by UNDP, and has also organised retreats for a number of other corporate organisations. The hotel has a swimming pool and floodlit tennis court. WiFi is available throughout the hotel.

The animation team provide a daily and nightly programme of activities, including water aerobics, water polo, local dance and cabaret shows. Other activities include sailing, snorkelling and windsurfing. The lodge is affiliated to Ngulia Safari Lodge in Tsavo West National Park and to Voi Safari Lodge near Tsavo East National Park. Packages which combine the 3 lodges are available from Kenya Safari Lodges and Hotels.

Bahari Beach Hotel

Nyali

Bahari Beach Hotel, Barrack Road, Nyali, North Coast, Kenya
PO Box 86693, Mombasa 80100, Kenya
Tel +254 41 4472822; +254 41 4472310; +254 41 4475457-9
Mobile +254 722 206933, +254 733 477022
Fax +254 41 4472021
E-mail info@baharibeach.net / reservations@baharibeach.net
Web www.baharibeach.net

 VISA, MasterCard    Moi Intl., LS & CH & Intl.
45 mins

Beachfront on Nyali Beach, Bahari Beach Hotel offers a selection of restaurants, bars and water sports. The hotel is designed in traditional Swahili style, with coral blocks and thatched roofs in colourful gardens. There are 100 en-suite rooms. All rooms are equipped with aircon, telephone, German and international satellite TV, safe and balcony. Baby cots are available on request. The main restaurant has an international menu. Wabaharia Restaurant serves seafood, advance booking recommended. Kisiwani Restaurant, overlooking the beach, has an Italian buffet. The large main bar is inside the reception area of the hotel. Peponi Bar, on the beach, is next to Kisiwani Restaurant. Dispense Bar is next to the main restaurant. Umbrella Bar Mkokoni is raised over the beach, with views of beach and sea. Baharina Spa offers massage and a range of treatments. Peponi Divers, on site, is an accredited PADI scuba dive school and offers a range of water sports. Other activities on site include volleyball, tennis and table tennis. The hotel can also arrange golf, squash, horse riding, dhow trips and deep sea fishing. There is a split-level swimming pool, boutique and cyber café. Full board rates include meals. All inclusive rates include meals, drinks and some activities.

Voyager Beach Resort   Nyali

Voyager Beach Resort, Barrack Road, Nyali, North Coast, Kenya
Heritage Hotels, PO Box 74888, Nairobi 00200, Kenya

Tel	+254 20 4446651; +254 20 4447929; +254 20 4444582
Mobile	+254 722 205894; +254 733 411105
Fax	+254 20 4446600; +254 20 4446533
E-mail	sales@heritagehotels.co.ke
Web	www.heritage-eastafrica.com

VISA, Amex   Moi Intl., LS & CH & Intl.
              45 mins

A vibrant, ship-themed resort, Voyager Beach Resort is moored on the coast, at Nyali Beach. The resort provides family entertainment and animation programmes, including themed journeys across the seven seas. The 232 cabins are made up of 68 seaview cabins, 96 gardenview cabins, 12 superior seaview cabins, 51 superior gardenview cabins, 2 large studio cabins and 3 suites with large living areas. All cabins have secluded balconies, and are equipped with telephone, aircon and safe. The Mashua Restaurant serves themed buffets, with entertainment provided by staff at the Captain's Table. The Smugglers' Cove specialises in seafood and grilled meat. The Minestrone Restaurant serves snacks including sandwiches and pizzas. There are 4 bars: the Kaskazi bar beside the sports pool, the 24-hour Harbour Bar, the cocktail Sports Bar and the Lookout Bar, on a raised platform, that has sweeping views over the bay. Facilities include a sports pool, a beachfront pool, a fun pool, a mini gymnasium, tennis courts, volleyball court, table tennis tables and pool tables. A wide range of water sports is on offer, including scuba diving, big game fishing, canoeing, kayaking and windsurfing. Daily entertainment includes acrobatic shows, marine and conservation education and even a Beach and Pool Olympic Games. Heritage Hotels received Virgin Holidays Gold Award in 2008, 2010 and 2011.

Jacyjoka Apartments   Nyali

Jacyjoka Apartments, off Links Road, nr AAR Hospital, Nyali, Kenya
PO Box 41987, Mombasa 80100, Kenya

Tel	
Mobile	+254 720 227902; +254 770 330086
Fax	
E-mail	jacyjoka@yahoo.co.uk / info@jacyjoka.com
Web	www.jacyjoka.com

Moi Intl., LS & CH & Intl.
45 mins

Jacyjoka Apartments are spacious apartments available on a short, medium and long-term basis. The whitewashed building overlooks a freeform swimming pool, sunbathing deck and manicured lawns.

There are 4 bedsits, 1 1-bedroom, 2 2-bedroom and 1 3-bedroom apartments. All the apartments have en-suite bedrooms, large open plan sitting and dining room and a WC. The bedrooms have fans, and are furnished with 4-poster beds and built in cupboards. The sitting rooms are fully tiled, and have sofa, chaise longue, coffee table and satellite TV. The kitchens are fully equipped with gas cooker, fridge, coffeemaker, microwave, toaster and kettle, as well as crockery, cutlery and glassware.

The swimming pool has a separate children's section and a Jacuzzi. There is plentiful parking, with 24-hour security. The apartments are just off Links Road, near the AAR Hospital. They are well positioned in Nyali, with easy access to the shopping centres, cinemas, restaurants and bars, as well as being not far from the beach.

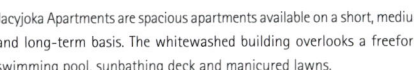

Moffat Court Apartments

Nyali

Moffat Court Apartments, Barrack Road, Nyali, North Coast, Kenya
PO Box 34126, Mombasa 80100, Kenya

Tel	+254 41 4473351
Mobile	+254 722 891781
Fax	
E-mail	moffatcourt@africaonline.co.ke
Web	www.moffatcourt.com

 VISA

Moi Intl., LS & CH & Intl.
45 mins

Moffat Court Apartments are available on a short or medium-term basis. They are known for their thatched bar and restaurant, across the garden from the apartments.

There are 1, 2 and 3-bedroom apartments. The 1 and 2-bedroom apartments have fans, while the 3-bedroom apartments have aircon. All apartments are simply furnished, and equipped with satellite TV and telephone. Their kitchens are equipped with fridge, gas cooker, crockery, cutlery and glassware. An extra bed can be supplied for the living room, if required.

The restaurant serves African cuisine, such as nyama choma grilled meats, roast chicken, stews and curries. The bar is well stocked with soft drinks, beers and spirits. Clusters of tables and chairs in the garden make a pleasant place to dine. There is also a children's sandpit, with swings and slide. The gardens are available for corporate events, wedding receptions, parties and other functions. Moffat Court Apartments are conveniently located on Barrack Road in Nyali, not far from Wild Waters Amusement Park and Mamba Village, as well as the shops and restaurants of Nyali.

Midview Hotel

Nyali

Midview Hotel, Barrack Road, Nyali, North Coast, Kenya
PO Box 34306, Nyali 80118, Kenya

Tel	+254 41 470651/3/4, +254 20 2078317/8
Mobile	+254 713 726290; +254 738 469043
Fax	+254 41 470652
E-mail	info@midviewhotels.com
Web	www.midviewhotels.com

VISA, MasterCard, Amex

 Moi Intl., LS & CH & Intl.
45 mins

Established in 2008, Midview Hotel is aimed at both business and holiday travellers. Located a short distance from Nyali Beach, the hotel has lovely views from its upper floors.

There are 68 en-suite deluxe rooms, 4 of which are family rooms. All rooms have aircon, key card access and WiFi. They are painted light coastal colours such as lime and tangerine, and have balconies overlooking the swimming pool or Nyali.

Mlaleo Restaurant has a selection of Kenyan dishes such as chicken dhania and Maasai beef stew, as well as international options like English fish and chips, pan fried whole fish, burger and chips and omelette. Msafiri Pool Bar is well stocked with soft drinks, beers and spirits. Maridadi Boutique has a selection of beach essentials, including ranges of hats, swimsuits and shoes. The lift is accessible to wheelchairs.

The conference hall seats 110 pax, and is equipped with conference equipment, including PA system and LCD panel. There is also a boardroom that seats 20. Weddings, cocktail parties and other functions can be arranged here. The business centre has secretarial services. The bright and airy reception area has sofas and coffee tables and is decorated with local art.

Ltorec
Nyali

Ltorec, off Links Road, nr AAR Hospital, Nyali, North Coast, Kenya
PO Box 89938, Mombasa 80100, Kenya

Tel	
Mobile	+254 727 300025
Fax	
E-mail	infoltorec@africaonline.co.ke
Web	

   Moi Intl., LS & CH & Intl.
45 mins

Named after the owner's grandfather, who was a comedian, Ltorec has a row of rooms opening onto the poolside deck. The rooms are let on a bed and breakfast basis.

There are 6 en-suite rooms, elegantly furnished with Lamu furniture including 4-poster bed and Swahili desk. The rooms are fully tiled, and have fans. Breakfast can be served on the veranda of the guests' room, by the pool or in the large dining room. The reception area in the main house is spacious, and opens onto the dining room. There is a fully equipped poolside kitchen, where guests can prepare their own meals if they choose to. Alternatively, they can order meals from the main house.

The thatched bar beside the pool is studded with coral, and well stocked with soft drinks, beers and spirits. There is also a secure car park. The hotel is just off Links Road, near the AAR Hospital. It is well positioned in Nyali, with easy access to the shopping centres, cinemas, restaurants and bars, as well as being not far from the beach.

Mamba Village
Nyali

Mamba Village, Links Road, Nyali, North Coast, Kenya
PO Box 85723, Mombasa 80100, Kenya

Tel	+254 20 3549303
Mobile	+254 722 415778; +254 725 702070
Fax	
E-mail	habo@africaonline.co.ke
Web	

 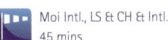 Moi Intl., LS & CH & Intl.
45 mins

Mamba Village markets itself as the largest crocodile farm in Africa, home to Big Daddy, over 5 meters long, more than 950kg and over 100 years old. Mamba Village combines wildlife farming, conservation and activities, making it popular with adults and children alike.

The daily feeding time at the crocodile farm is 5pm. The Snake Park and Spider House contain both poisonous and non-poisonous varieties including green mamba, cobra, python, tarantula and baboo spider. The Botanical Gardens has a number of rare species of plants, including carnivorous plants that feed on flesh, African orchid's cycads, ferns and succulents. The Aquarium is home to rare species of fish, including the most poisonous fish in the sea, the stone fish, as well as starfishes and seahorses. Horse riding is also available, both on the beach and in the arena. There are 5 en-suite double rooms and 2 apartments. The rooms have sofa, coffee table, armchairs, fridge, TV and aircon. The apartments have an open plan sitting and dining room, a kitchen equipped with fridge and gas cooker and a bedroom with double and single bed. Croco Restaurant serves buffet or a la carte; Arturo's Restaurant, an open air lounge with thatched roof and coral walls, serves Italian cuisine.

Sanana Nyali

Sanana, off Links Road, Nyali, North Coast, Kenya
PO Box 82596, Mombasa 80100, Kenya
Tel
Mobile +254 714 458282
Fax
E-mail sanana@africaonline.com
Web www.limuttiholdings.com/sananahotel

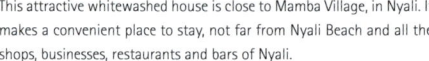

Moi Intl., LS & CH & Intl.
45 mins

This attractive whitewashed house is close to Mamba Village, in Nyali. It makes a convenient place to stay, not far from Nyali Beach and all the shops, businesses, restaurants and bars of Nyali.

There are 16 en-suite rooms, made up of 10 singles and 6 doubles. A single contains a double bed and a double contains a double and a single bed. All rooms are equipped with aircon, satellite TV, telephone and safe. The restaurant has a thatched roof and a terrace, and serves a predominantly Kenyan menu including nyama choma grilled meats. The bar has a selection of soft drinks, beers and spirits, and is equipped with satellite TV. There is a swimming pool and a children's pool in the garden, surrounded by sunbathing terrace furnished with tables and chairs. There is also a fully equipped gym, with modern machines, and a sauna and steam bath. The barber shop and hair salon offer a range of beauty treatments such as manicure, pedicure, dredlocks and nail art. The cyber café has internet and printing. Local sites of interest include Mamba Village and Bamburi Nature Trail. Water sports can be booked with local operators. Tours, excursions and safaris can be booked with local travel agents.

Makwetu Resort Nyali

Makwetu Resort, Mayonne Road, Nyali, North Coast, Kenya
PO Box 34268, Nyali 80118, Kenya
Tel +254 20 3533752
Mobile +254 720 609584
Fax +254 41 476025
E-mail info@makwetu.com / nairobisales@makwetu.com
Web www.makwetu.com

Moi Intl., LS & CH & Intl.
45 mins

Set in sweeping lawns, Makwetu Resort offers serviced apartments on a daily, weekly or monthly basis. The garden makes an ideal venue for weddings, teambuilding, cocktail parties and other functions. Makwetu Resort opened in 2008.

There are 12 apartments and 6 en-suite double rooms. The apartments have 1, 2 or 3 bedrooms. There are also studio apartments. Extra beds can be added if required. Each apartment has a lounge furnished with sofas and armchairs and equipped with flat screen satellite TV. Sliding glass doors connect the lounge to the veranda. Each apartment has an open plan kitchen, divided from the living room by a breakfast bar, which is fully equipped with crockery, cutlery and glassware, as well as kettle and microwave. Each bedroom is fitted with remote controlled aircon. The apartments are painted summer shades of orange and tangerine, and furnished in harmonious shades.

The Mnazi Mmoja conference hall has a capacity of 200 pax. The swimming pool is surrounded by a sunbathing deck furnished with sunbeds. Up to 400 pax can comfortably be catered for in the gardens. Functions are planned and designed individually to suit the needs of each group.

Nyali Beach
Holiday Resort

Nyali

Nyali Beach Holiday Resort, Mayonne Road, Nyali, North Coast, Kenya
PO Box 1874, Mombasa 80100, Kenya

Tel	+254 41 472325; +254 41 474396
Mobile	+254 725 849111; +254 733 849111
Fax	+254 41 472402; +254 41 471088
E-mail	nbhr@africaonline.co.ke
Web	www.nyalibeachresort.com

 VISA, MasterCard   Moi Intl., LS & CH & Intl.
45 mins

In beachfront gardens, Nyali Beach Holiday Resort has both hotel rooms and self-catering cottages. The hotel centres on an infinity pool, which flows into a smaller pool, suitable for children. The outside walls are decorated with murals of African animals and beach scenes.

There are 25 en-suite rooms, made up of 16 standard and 9 deluxe sea facing rooms. All rooms have clay tiled floors, minibar, satellite TV and balcony. There are 20 cottages, made up of 4 1-bedroom cottages and 16 2-bedroom cottages. The cottages have a sitting room, fully equipped kitchen, dining room and veranda. All cottages are equipped with aircon, fan, safe and satellite TV.

The restaurant has an international a la carte menu, including Chinese, Italian, Indian, Mughlai, African and seafood. The thatched, circular bar stands between the pool and the beach. It serves soft drinks, beers, wines and spirits. The games hall has a pool table, table tennis table, dartboard, cards table and table football. There is also a mini gym, with running machine and weights. The salon offers a range of massages, hair beading, manicure and pedicure. The resort can organise weddings, birthday parties and functions.

Nyali Luxury Beach
Apartments

Nyali

Nyali Luxury Beach Apartments, Mayonne Road, Nyali, North Coast, Kenya
PO Box 82843, Mombasa 80100, Kenya

Tel	+254 41 4474125
Mobile	+254 727 374826
Fax	
E-mail	nsh2@connate.co.ke
Web	

       Moi Intl., LS & CH & Intl.
45 mins

Nyali Luxury Beach Apartments are owned and operated by Nairobi Sports House. They opened in 1997, and offer self-catering apartments in a garden that opens onto the beach.

There are 4 apartments. All apartments have 3 en-suite bedrooms, living room, dining room and kitchen equipped with electric cooker, microwave, toaster, kettle, fridge, crockery, cutlery and glassware. There is also a laundry room and a balcony overlooking the beach. The bedrooms are equipped with aircon.

The apartments are in a red brick building overlooking the swimming pool on 1 side and the beach on the other. The garden has a gate that opens onto the beach. There is also a barbecue for the use of guests. There is no restaurant or bar facility on site. The apartments are within easy reach of the shops, businesses, restaurants and bars of Nyali. Local sites of interest include Mamba Village, Wild Waters Amusement Park and Bamburi Nature Trail. Mombasa Old Town and Fort Jesus are also within reach, by car. Water sports can be booked with local operators on Nyali Beach. Tours, excursions and safaris can be arranged with local travel agents.

Kivulini Bahari

Nyali

Kivulini Bahari, nr Tamarind Village, Nyali, North Coast, Kenya
PO Box 83935, Mombasa 80100, Kenya

Tel	+254 41 2491183
Mobile	+254 722 205099; +254 733 622555; +254 722 516864
Fax	+254 41 2490093
E-mail	sales@holidayvillascoast.com
Web	www.holidayvillascoast.com

Moi Intl., LS & CH & Intl.
45 mins

Kivulini Bahari has 2 self-catering villas located on a private beach near Nyali. The villas are available for holiday let. They are designed with a blend of coastal décor and modern facilities, and offer complete privacy. Shella and Pate Pate, the 2 villas, each have 3 bedrooms. The master bedroom is en-suite and the other 2 share a bathroom; each room has aircon and access to a balcony. Each villa also has an open plan lounge and dining area, a fully equipped kitchen and a terrace furnished with comfortable sofas and cushions. The villas are decorated with local art and traditional artefacts. Each villa has a minibar, safe and satellite TV. The villas are serviced daily.

Next to the swimming pool, Mkoma Banda serves snacks and has a selection of soft drinks, beers, wines and spirits. There is also a barbecue available for the use of guests. Private parties, functions and seminars can be arranged. The compound has a standby generator in case of power cuts and 24-hour security. The resort manager offers assistance whenever needed. The villas are located near Ratna Square Shopping Complex and Nyali Cinemax. They are conveniently positioned for restaurants, activities and entertainment centres, as well as shops and businesses.
Kivulini Bahari is affiliated to Ratna Serviced Apartments.

Ratna Serviced Apartments

Nyali

Ratna Serviced Apartments, Ratna Square, Nyali, North Coast, Kenya
PO Box 83935, Mombasa 80100, Kenya

Tel	+254 41 2491183
Mobile	+254 722 205099; +254 733 622555; +254 722 516864
Fax	+254 41 2490093
E-mail	sales@holidayvillascoast.com
Web	www.holidayvillascoast.com

Moi Intl., LS & CH & Intl.
45 mins

Ratna Serviced Apartments are a collection of apartments decorated in elegant Swahili style and equipped with modern facilities. The apartments are available on a short or medium-term basis.
There are 4 apartments, called Kipini, Kipepeo, Kiwayu and Kisite. Each apartment has 3 bedrooms, 1 of which is en-suite, all equipped with split unit aircon and safe. There is also a living and dining room with coastal ambience, adorned with embroidered cushions, rugs and wall hangings. The kitchen is fully equipped with fridge, cooker, crockery, cutlery and glassware, and has a breakfast bar with tall wooden stools. Each apartment also has a barbecue grill on the terrace. Facilities inside

the apartments include a water dispenser, washing machine, satellite TV and high speed internet. There is plentiful parking beneath the apartments, with 24-hour security.
The apartments are located next to Ratna Square Shopping Complex and near Nyali Cinemax. They are conveniently positioned for restaurants, activities and entertainment centres, as well as shops and businesses. The apartments are a short drive from Mombasa, and make a convenient base for visitors needing to commute to the business district.
Ratna Serviced Apartments are affiliated to Kivulini Bahari.

Tamarind Village

Nyali

Tamarind Village, Cement Silo Road, Nyali, North Coast, Kenya
PO Box 95805, Mkomani 80106, Kenya

Tel	+254 41 474600
Mobile	+254 733 623583; +254 722 205160
Fax	+254 41 473073
E-mail	reservations.village@tamarind.co.ke
Web	www.tamarind.co.ke/tamarind-village

 VISA, MasterCard, Amex   Moi Intl., LS & CH & Intl. 45 mins

Tamarind Village is a collection of luxury serviced apartments on the waterfront in Nyali. With its towering white walls, curling archways and classical turrets, the village rises from its coral ramparts like a formidable 14th century fortress. There are 48 apartments, made up of 24 1-bedroom, 9 2-bedroom and 15 3-bedroom apartments. Each apartment is individually designed with Swahili furniture, and has a lounge, fully equipped kitchen and spacious balcony. They are equipped with aircon, satellite TV and minibar. The award winning Tamarind Restaurant, which opened in the 1970s, specialises in seafood. The Harbour Restaurant, on the waterfront, serves light meals such as prawn, mango and macadamia salad, fish fillet grilled with lemon butter and pasta with a choice of sauces. The bar is well stocked. Tamarind can organise catered business meetings in private apartments. There is a fully equipped conference room that seats 40 pax. The resort also offers WiFi, fax, telephone and secretarial services. There are 2 swimming pools, Jacuzzi, squash court and the Creek Club Fitness Centre. Uzuri Wellness offers treatments including firming facial, foot treat, hopi candle, hot stone massage and de-stressing massage. Activities such as scuba diving, water-skiing, windsurfing, golf, deep sea fishing and trips to Bamburi Nature Trail and Mombasa Old Town can be arranged.

Nyali International Beach Hotel

Nyali

Nyali International Beach Hotel, Mayonne Road, Nyali, North Coast, Kenya
PO Box 90581, Mombasa 80100, Kenya

Tel	+254 41 471552; +254 41 471551; +254 41 474640
Mobile	+254 727 228344; +254 733 700533
Fax	
E-mail	sales@nyaliinternational.com
Web	www.nyaliinternational.com

 VISA, MasterCard    Moi Intl., LS & CH & Intl. 45 mins

Established in 1946, Nyali International Beach Hotel was extensively refurbished in 2010. The hotel is in lush gardens on the beachfront. There are 48 palm wing sea facing rooms, 102 garden wing rooms, 3 luxury villas, 3 presidential suites and 3 executive suites. All rooms are equipped with satellite TV, telephone, digital safe, minibar, kettle, hairdryer and WiFi. Some rooms are suitable for guests with disabilities. Bistro Mchana serves an a la carte menu and children's menu. Mvita Grill, on the beachfront, specialises in seafood. Pool Terrace serves barbecue. Pizza Place serves pizza, pasta, salad and ice cream. Parrots Terrace specialises in barbecued seafood. Aqua Bar and Restaurant serves cocktails and light snacks.

Pwani Conference Centre seats 250 pax; Malaika Room seats 150; Nyali Boardroom seats 12; Karibu Boardroom seats 15. All conference halls have internet connectivity. The business centre has a range of services including copying, printing and secretarial services. There are 2 swimming pools. The 3 bars are equipped with large screens for sports coverage; live bands and DJs play regularly. Activities include non-motorised water sports. A daily animation programme and a kids' club are available. The salon offers beauty treatments and massage.

Driftwood Beach Club, Malindi – Photo © www.sokomoto.com

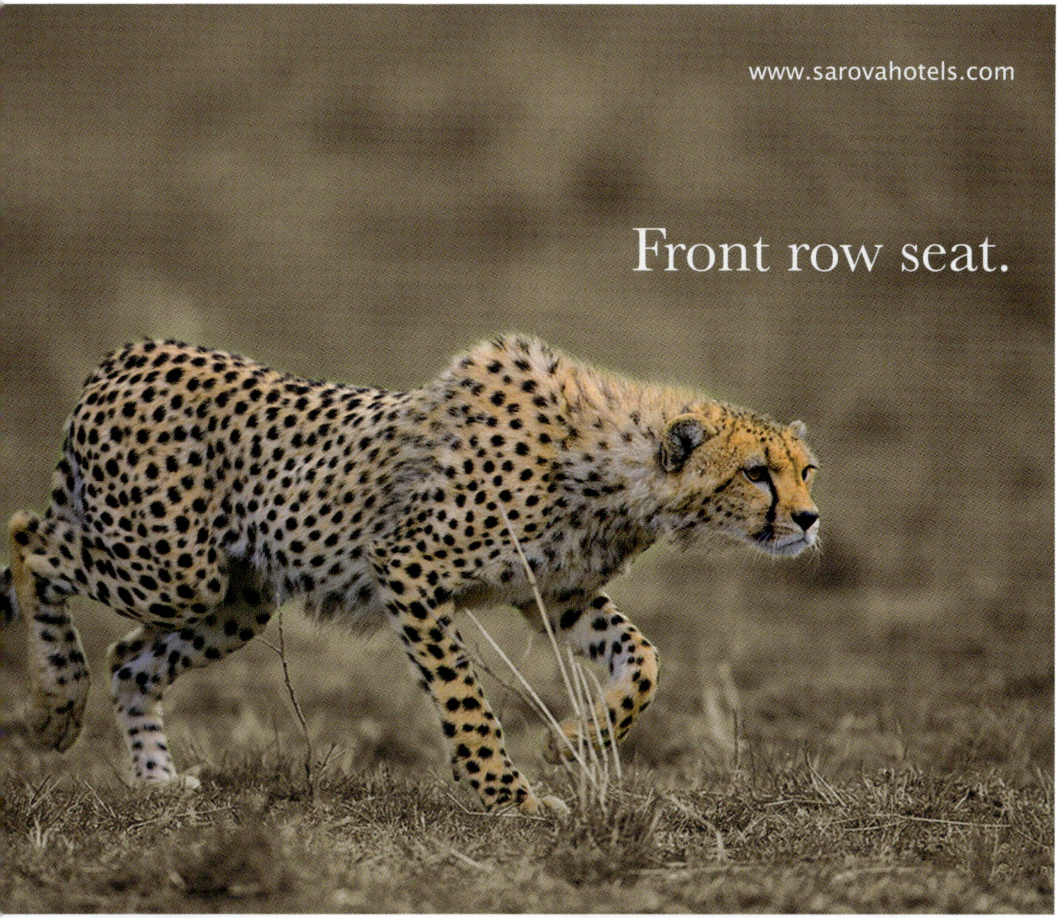

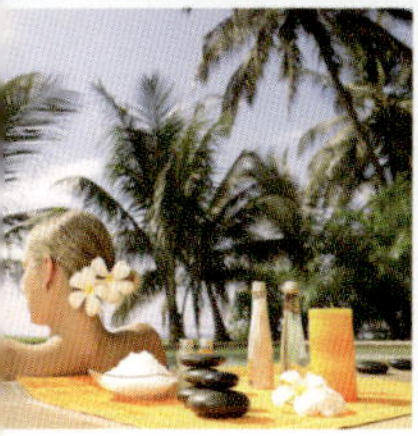

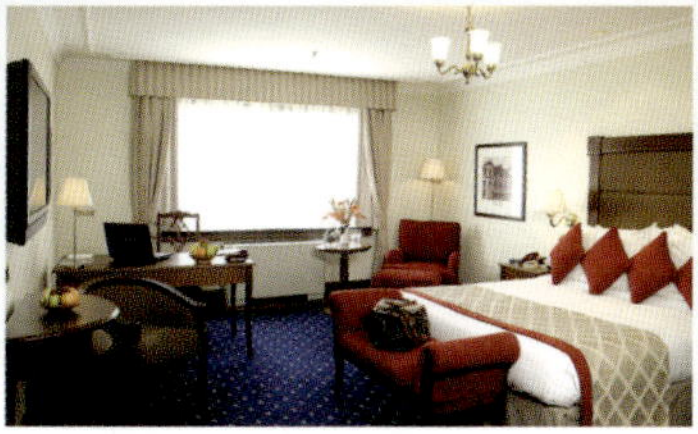

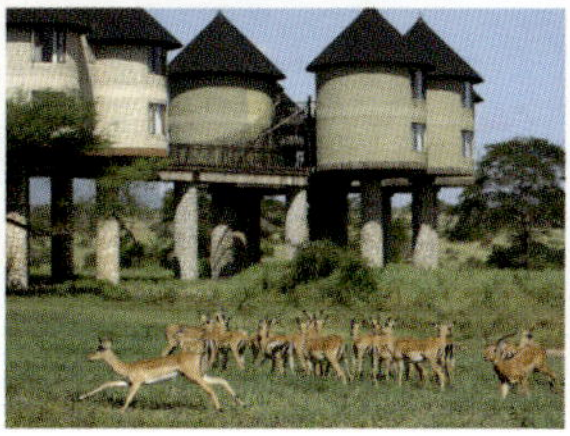

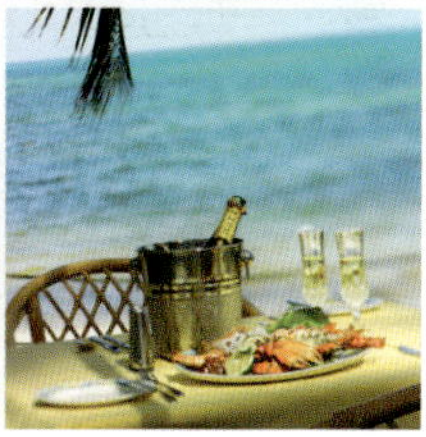

At Sarova Hotels, Kenya's premier hotel chain, unwind to the seductive beauty of the breezy beaches, explore the wild and untamed, embrace the diverse cultures and so much more. Contact your travel agent and get the best of 3 worlds.

SAROVA
HOTELS • RESORTS • GAME LODGES
KENYA • EAST AFRICA

For reservations contact our Central Reservations Office on Tel: +254 20-276 7444/ 276 7000/ 0722-200 945-6/ 0734-699 741
Fax: +254 20-271 5566 or Email: centralreservations@sarovahotels.com

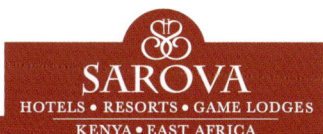

Mombasa

Mombasa Old Town – Photo © Andrew Nightingale, kembu.com

Mombasa has a colourful history stretching back a thousand years. Invasions, sieges and trade have all made their mark on the culture of this coastal island city. East Africa's largest port, Mombasa is the gateway to all the land-locked countries of central Africa, and is the second largest city in Kenya.

Mombasa Island is linked to the mainland by Makupa Causeway, to the north coast by Nyali Bridge and to the south coast by the Likoni Ferry. The Old Town is on the eastern edge of the island; the modern city has expanded to fill the whole island. Moi International Airport, in the north of Mombasa, has daily scheduled flights to destinations around Kenya, as well as to a number of cities around the world. A railway links Mombasa to Nairobi. The people of Mombasa are predominantly Swahili Muslims.

Mombasa is known in Swahili as Kisiwa ya Mvita, which means Island of War, because of its volatile strife-ridden history. In the 11th century, the town was an important trading centre between East Africa and the Indian Ocean trade routes. Its major exports were ivory and slaves. There is evidence that Ibn Battuta, Marco Polo and Zhang He all docked at Mombasa. In 1498, Vasco da Gama arrived, initiating a period of Portuguese domination. Fort Jesus, built by the Portuguese in the late 16th century, became the focus for the ongoing power struggles and changed hands nine times in the 17th and 18th centuries. After the Portuguese, the Omanis dominated in the 17th and 18th centuries, and the British in the 19th century.

Fort Jesus is now a museum, with exhibits on its history, as well as on Swahili life and culture. A Son et Lumiere Show illuminates the turrets and battlements three nights a week, while costumed actors bring the turbulent history of the fort to life.

Mombasa Old Town is an attractive labyrinth of narrow streets, liberally sprinkled with mosques and Swahili buildings. The Old Law Courts have regular exhibitions of local art. The spice market, heavy with atmosphere and enticing scents, gives an insight into the spice trade of old. Tours of the Old Town are available, as are harbour boat cruises and dinner cruises.

Mombasa Marine National Park comprises a marine area with crabs, sea urchins, sea cucumbers, starfish and jellyfish amongst mangroves, sea grass, sea weed and coral gardens. Activities include boat trips, scuba diving and snorkelling.

Haller Wildlife Park is a former disused quarry that has reopened as a small private game sanctuary. The park shot to fame in 2004 when a baby hippo, orphaned during heavy floods, was adopted by an elderly giant tortoise. The story of Owen and Mzee attracted the attention of thousands; the pair can still be visited today. The park, which has blossomed into an area of lush beauty, is home to a variety of wildlife including giraffe, eland and oryx.

Tudor Water Sports

Mombasa

Tudor Water Sports, Tom Mboya Avenue, Tudor, Mombasa, Kenya
PO Box 835, Mombasa 80100, Kenya

Tel	
Mobile	+254 722 411667; +254 726 418400
Fax	+254 41 2495598
E-mail	marinecrafts@africaonline.co.ke
Web	

  Moi Intl., LS & CH & Intl.
15 mins

Situated on the creek amongst mangroves, Tudor Water Sports is part of a marina. The complex has a restaurant overlooking the water and offers a wide selection of water sports and boat trips.

There are 18 en-suite rooms, made up of doubles and singles, and 2 family rooms. All rooms have sea view. The rooms are equipped with aircon, satellite TV and fridge. The seafront restaurant has an a la carte international menu, and specialises in barbecue, steaks, pizza and seafood. The restaurant's balcony has lovely views across the water.

The marina has boat repair facilities. Boat trips can be arranged in various kinds of boats, including glass bottomed boats, pleasure boats and fun paddle boats. Deep sea fishing is also on offer. Kayaking and rowing are available.

Tudor Water Sports, at the northern end of Mombasa Island, is conveniently located for Nyali Bridge, and the north coast beaches of Nyali, Bamburi, Shanzu and Kikambala. The island of Mombasa is known in Swahili as Kisiwa ya Mvita, which means Island of War, due to the many changes in its ownership through its long and eventful history. Local attractions include the world famous Fort Jesus and Mombasa Old Town.

Cool Breeze Hotel

Mombasa

Cool Breeze Hotel, Tom Mboya Street, Buxton, Mombasa, Kenya
PO Box 41506, Mombasa 80100, Kenya

Tel	+254 41 2492366
Mobile	+254 723 971989
Fax	+254 41 2492357
E-mail	coolbreezeinn@yahoo.com
Web	

  Moi Intl., LS & CH & Intl.
20 mins

Near Nyali Bridge, Cool Breeze Hotel offers accommodation and conference facilities. The location is convenient for visitors heading to the north coast beaches of Bamburi and Nyali.

There are 76 en-suite rooms, 24 with aircon and 52 with fan. All rooms have satellite TV; some rooms have both bath and shower, and others have shower. A baby cot is available on request. There is a safe at reception where guests are welcome to store their valuables.

The restaurant opens onto a garden terrace, where food can also be served. The menu is predominantly Kenyan, and includes nyama choma grilled meats, goat stew, grilled chicken and beef curry. There are also a few international dishes such as spaghetti bolognaise and spaghetti napolitana. The bar has a flat screen satellite TV, and serves soft drinks, beers and a few spirits. Outside catering is available. Parties and functions can be arranged. There are 2 conference halls, 1 seating 50 pax and the other seating 100. The halls are equipped with LCD projector, large screen and PA system. There is a backup generator in case of power cuts. Highlights of Mombasa include Fort Jesus and Mombasa Old Town.

Darajani Hotel Mombasa

Darajani Hotel, Ronald Ngala Street, nr JCC Buxton, Mombasa, Kenya
PO Box 43086, Mombasa 80100, Kenya

Tel	+254 41 2494692
Mobile	+254 734 796376; +254 729 045072
Fax	+254 41 2492404
E-mail	info@darajanihotel.com
Web	www.darajanihotel.com

VISA, MasterCard, Amex

Moi Intl., LS & CH & Intl.
20 mins

Darajani Hotel, meaning at the bridge in Swahili, is strategically located on Mombasa Island about 150 meters from Nyali Bridge which connects the island to the north coast. The whitewashed hotel is set around an attractive central garden and fountain.

There are 67 en-suite rooms, made up of 61 standard and 6 executive. All rooms have either aircon or fan, and are equipped with satellite TV, fridge, kettle and balcony. The executive rooms have double bedroom, bathroom and sitting room. Stair gates on all staircases make the hotel safe for children. The restaurant serves local and international dishes, such as nyama choma grilled meats, pepper steak with cream pepper sauce, kingfish with sautéed potatoes, fresh grilled tilapia and a selection of pizzas and sandwiches.

There are 2 conference halls, 1 seating 100 pax and the other seating 70. Both halls are fully equipped, including projector and PA system. Conferences, meetings and seminars can be arranged. The rooftop bar, entered by a striking bridge over the garden, is fully stocked with soft drinks, beers, wines and spirits. Both bridge and bar have bird's eye views over the garden and towards the bridge. There is a selection of toiletries for sale at reception. A safe and a secure car park are also on site.

Panaroma Gardens Hotel Mombasa

Panaroma Gardens Hotel, nr Mombasa Municipal Stadium, Mombasa
PO Box 88723, Mombasa 80100, Kenya

Tel	+254 41 2011520
Mobile	+254 719 663560
Fax	
E-mail	panaromagardenhotel@hotmail.com
Web	

 Moi Intl., LS & CH & Intl.
20 mins

Near the Mombasa Municipal Stadium, Panaroma Gardens Hotel's orange façade makes a striking landmark. The hotel is situated between the centre of the town and Moi International Airport; airport transfers can be arranged. The rooftop bar is an attractive place from which to watch the sunset.

There are 50 en-suite rooms, made up of singles, doubles and twins. The rooms on the 1st floor are painted terracotta orange, and the rooms on the 2nd floor are painted lime green. All rooms have TV with local channels, fan and mosquito net. Some have aircon and a few are equipped with a fridge. The restaurant serves a predominantly Kenyan menu with a few international dishes, including samosas, biriani, grilled tilapia and pepper steak, as well as a selection of stews and curries with ugali or rice. The bar in the corner of the restaurant stocks soft drinks, beers and a few spirits. There is also a terrace, outside the restaurant, where guests can choose to eat.

There are 2 conference rooms, 1 seating 30 pax and the other seating 50. The rooms are equipped with PA system and projector. The rooftop bar has views over Mombasa town, and shows international sports matches on a large screen.

Suhufi Palace Hotel Mombasa

Suhufi Palace Hotel, Abdul Nasser Road, Bondeni, Mombasa, Kenya
PO Box 40359, Mombasa 80100, Kenya

Tel	+254 41 2315000
Mobile	+254 722 667662; +254 731 667707; +254 733 667707
Fax	
E-mail	info@suhufihotel.co.ke
Web	www.suhufihotel.co.ke

    Moi Intl., LS & CH & Intl. 30 mins

Suhufi Palace Hotel is a quiet hotel in Mombasa town. The hotel is Muslim, and has friendly staff and serene atmosphere.

There are 36 en-suite rooms, made up of 16 doubles, 16 twins and 4 singles. All rooms have aircon, satellite TV, telephone and internet cable. Extra mattresses can be provided for children. The windows and balconies give views of the Indian Ocean, and of the roofs of Mombasa. The restaurant has an interesting menu, combining international favourites with Somali and Swahili cuisine. International dishes include spaghetti al forno, spaghetti saltate, chips Masala, fish biriani, chicken and chips and a selection of burgers. Somali dishes include chicken scolobo, chicken signig, aleso, arnosto, spesso and ansulaatoni ruusa. The hotel does not serve alcohol, or permit the consumption of alcohol at the premises. There is a lounge at reception and a mezzanine lounge. The Sweet Corner serves homemade pies and rolls. The hotel is located between the centre of Mombasa town and Nyali Bridge which links Mombasa Island to the north coast. It is conveniently located for the shops, businesses and restaurants of the town, and is ideal for guests wishing to visit the north coast beaches of Bamburi and Nyali.

Hotel Sapphire Mombasa

Hotel Sapphire, Mwembe Tayari Road, nr Railway Station, Mombasa
PO Box 1254, Mombasa 80100, Kenya

Tel	+254 41 2494893; +254 41 2494891
Mobile	+254 722 206496; +254 734 699680
Fax	+254 41 2495280
E-mail	hotelsapphire@africaonline.co.ke
Web	

 VISA, MasterCard   Moi Intl., LS & CH & Intl. 30 mins

Hotel Sapphire is a whitewashed building ornately decorated with curved balconies, with a waterfall at its entrance. The hotel offers a wide selection of facilities and activities.

There are 110 en-suite rooms, made up of singles, doubles, triples and suites. The 4 suites have en-suite bedroom and adjoining living room. All rooms have aircon, satellite TV and telephone. The terrace restaurant, on the 1st floor, overlooks the swimming pool. The menu is predominantly Indian and includes dahl machhi, palak ghosht, mutton vindaloo and purdina murgh tikka. Vegetarian options include malai kofta, aloo palak, tamatar ka bharta and bhindi do piazza. Soups, salads and snacks are also available. The bar, beneath an awning on the terrace, is fully stocked with soft drinks, beers, wines and spirits. There is also table football and a dartboard.

The gym is well equipped with fitness machines, and also has sauna and steam room. Aerobics and cardiovascular classes are on offer. The 45-minute interactive computerised screening reveals body mass index, muscular strength, cardio fitness and body fat. There are 3 conference halls: 1 seats 200 pax and 2 seat 150 pax. All halls are fully equipped, including projector and PA system. The tourist information desk at reception can book excursions, tours and safaris.

KaribuKenya Accommodation Guide

PrideInn Hotel Mombasa   Mombasa

PrideInn Hotel Mombasa, Haile Sellasie Avenue, Mombasa, Kenya
PO Box 66969, Nairobi 00200, Kenya
Tel +254 20 8000415-6
Mobile +254 725 497815
Fax
E-mail stay@prideinn.co.ke
Web www.prideinn.co.ke

Moi Intl., LS & CH & Intl.
30 mins

Originally called Kohinoor Hotel, meaning Mountain of Light, PrideInn Hotel Mombasa has been designed using ancient Indian art to enhance the light. The hotel offers serviced studios and apartments. Located on Haile Sellasie Avenue, the hotel is well situated for the shops and businesses of Mombasa.

There are studios, as well as 1 and 2-bedroom apartments. All apartments are equipped with aircon, satellite TV, DVD player, telephone, iron and ironing board. They all also have a pantry equipped with microwave, kettle, minibar and kitchen utensils. Marino's Grill offers a selection of local dishes. Pilipili Restaurant serves a selection of Chinese and Indian dishes including chicken schezwan, chilly paneer, vegetable chowmien, tandoori fish tikka, methi mutter malai, tawa jeera chicken and mutton kadai. Breakfasts are multinational. The Indian breakfast is served with chapatti and the Swahili one with mandazi and mbaazi.

PrideInn Hotel Mombasa's sister hotels are PrideInn Hotel Nairobi, PrideInn Hotel Nyali and PrideInn Hotel Diani, all part of the Glory Safaris group. Glory Safaris also offers car hire on a short or long-term basis, and runs a driving school. Glory Safaris books tours and safaris and has a selection of activity packages in Kenya and Tanzania.

Royal Court Hotel   Mombasa

Royal Court Hotel, Haile Selassie Avenue, Mombasa, Kenya
PO Box 41629, Mombasa 80100, Kenya
Tel +254 41 2223759; +254 41 2230932; +254 41 2230933
Mobile +254 722 412867; +254 733 412867
Fax +254 41 2312398
E-mail info@royalcourtmombasa.co.ke
Web www.royalcourtmombasa.co.ke

VISA, MasterCard, Amex

Moi Intl., LS & CH & Intl.
30 mins

Royal Court Hotel, located in the centre of Mombasa, is well equipped for both business and holiday visitors. The impressive 8-floor building combines coastal wood with terracotta finishing.

There are 92 en-suite rooms, made up of 59 standard, 29 executive, 2 junior suites and 2 executive suites. All rooms have aircon, digital safe, satellite TV, telephone and minibar. The junior suites are more spacious; the executive suites include a sitting room. 2 rooms are designed for guests with disabilities; a wheelchair is available. The rooftop restaurant is affiliated to Chaine des Rotisseurs. Starters include asparagus hollandaise and oysters a la maison. Main courses include risotto alla marinara, fillet mignon, satay chicken and tandori fish tikka. The plentiful vegetarian and vegan options include Grecque salad, paneer kebabs, bhindi aloo masala and dhingri shabnam. The bar is fully stocked and has an extensive wine list. The Fitness Exchange has the latest cardiovascular equipment, as well as a swimming pool, sauna and steam room. There are 4 conference halls, ranging from a boardroom for 10 pax to a function room seating 200. The halls are fully equipped with audio visual equipment. The casino features all popular games. The piano bar shows sports events on a large plasma screen. The tourist information desk can book trips, excursions and safaris.

Hotel Dorse Mombasa

Hotel Dorse, Kwa Shibu Road, off Moi Avenue, Mombasa, Kenya
PO Box 89278, Mombasa 80100, Kenya

Tel	+254 41 2312310; +254 41 2222252; +254 41 2314846
Mobile	+254 770 050116
Fax	+254 41 2224552
E-mail	hoteldorse@africaonline.co.ke
Web	

  Moi Intl., LS & CH & Intl. 30 mins

In the centre of Mombasa, Hotel Dorse offers accommodation, restaurant, bar and conference facilities. Its location makes it convenient for all shops, businesses, bars and restaurants in the centre of town.

There are 34 en-suite rooms, made up of singles, doubles and twins. All rooms have aircon, telephone and TV with local channels. The hotel is built around a central courtyard, with restaurant, bar and conference rooms opening off it.

The restaurant, equipped with satellite TV, serves both Kenyan and international dishes, including grilled whole fish, chicken stew, beef biriani and mutton curry. There is also a vegetarian corner. Snacks include soups, salads, chicken wings and fish fingers. The choma zone has a selection of nyama choma grilled meats. Sam's pub, on the road front, serves soft drinks, beers and a few spirits. There are 2 conference halls, 1 seating 60 pax and the other seating 30. The halls have both fan and aircon. Conference equipment is not provided and should be hired externally if required.

The island of Mombasa is known in Swahili as Kisiwa ya Mvita, which means Island of War, due to the many changes in its ownership through its long and eventful history. Local attractions include the world famous Fort Jesus and Mombasa Old Town.

Glory Grand Hotel Mombasa

Glory Grand Hotel, Kwa Shibu Road, off Moi Avenue, Mombasa, Kenya
PO Box 85527, Mombasa 80100, Kenya

Tel	+254 41 2313564; +254 41 2314284
Mobile	+254 722 388729; +254 733 802682
Fax	+254 41 2221196
E-mail	sales@glorykenya.com
Web	www.glorykenya.com

 Moi Intl., LS & CH & Intl. 30 mins

In the centre of Mombasa, Glory Grand Hotel offers budget accommodation and a restaurant. Its central location makes it convenient for the shops, businesses, bars and restaurants of Mombasa.

There are 43 en-suite rooms, made up of singles, doubles and triples. 25 of the rooms are equipped with aircon, TV with local channels and fridge. The remainder have fans. All rooms have telephone, writing desk, mosquito net and cupboard. Sizzling Flames Restaurant has a large selection of Indian dishes, including barbecued chicken tikka, beef mishkaki, keema chapatti, chicken jeera and egg Masala. There are plentiful vegetarian options including chana Masala, aloo palak and malai kofta. The African corner includes mutton stew with rice and grilled chicken with ugali. No alcohol is served.

Local attractions include the world famous Fort Jesus and Mombasa Old Town. Glory Grand Hotel's sister hotels are Glory Palace Hotel in Nairobi, Glory Guest House in Mombasa, Glory Ocean Villas in Diani and Glory Holiday Resort in Nyali, all part of the Glory car hire, tours and safaris group. The company has many varieties of vehicles for hire, including saloons, 4WD, pick-ups, minibuses and motorbikes. It also organises excursions and safari packages to destinations of interest around the country.

Castle Royal Hotel

Mombasa

Castle Royal Hotel, Moi Avenue, Mombasa, Kenya
Sentrim Hotels and Lodges, PO Box 43436, Nairobi 00100, Kenya

Tel	+254 41 2220628; +254 41 2222682
Mobile	+254 735 339920
Fax	+254 41 2230688
E-mail	reservationscastle@sentrim-hotels.com
Web	www.sentrim-hotels.com

 VISA, MasterCard   Moi Intl., LS & CH & Intl. 30 mins

The newly refurbished Castle Royal Hotel is situated in Mombasa town centre, only 10 minutes from the historic site of Mombasa Old Town and the world famous Fort Jesus. The island of Mombasa is known in Swahili as Kisiwa ya Mvita, which means Island of War, due to the many changes in its ownership through its long and eventful history.

There are 68 rooms on 4 floors, made up of 53 doubles, 5 twins, 4 triples and 6 singles. All rooms are en-suite and are fitted with high speed internet, electric door locks, electric safes, aircon, satellite TV, ultraviolet retardant windows and sound proofing. The hotel has a coffee bar, the long bar and a restaurant with an extensive international menu. The new veranda is a scenic place to enjoy a drink. A band plays every Friday. The conference facilities consist of Mvita which holds 40 pax, Miji Kenya which holds 120, Lamu which holds 40 and Kilindini which holds 200. The hotel can arrange visits to nearby sites such as Fort Jesus, the Gedi Ruins, Haller Park, Mamba Village and the many marine parks. It can also organise water sports and fishing expeditions on either the north coast or the south coast.

Manson Hotel

Mombasa

Manson Hotel, Mohdhar Mohd Habib Road, off Moi Avenue, Mombasa
PO Box 83565, Mombasa 80100, Kenya

Tel	+254 41 2222419; +254 2222420-1
Mobile	+254 722 610615
Fax	+254 41 2222422
E-mail	hoteladmin@mansonhotel.com
Web	www.mansonhotel.com

 VISA, MasterCard    Moi Intl., LS & CH & Intl. 30 mins

Manson Hotel is within walking distance of the giant elephant tusks, famous symbol of Mombasa.

There are 80 en-suite rooms, made up of standard, deluxe and executive. Standard rooms are equipped with fan, while deluxe and executive have aircon, telephone and satellite TV. All rooms have traditional coastal carved doors and balconies. Eden Parlour Restaurant serves Kenyan and international dishes such as chicken wings, spaghetti bolognaise, fried fish fillet, stir fried liver and mixed grill. The menu is adorned with proverbs like giving is the key to living, a stitch in time saves nine and virtue and happiness are mother and daughter. The Health Bar serves a variety of fruit and vegetable shakes such as avocado and yoghurt, beetroot, mango and spinach, and tomato, carrot and passion. The bar serves soft drinks and beers. There is a terrace, adjoining the restaurant, where food and drinks can also be served.

The large reception area contains a pool table, sofas and armchairs. The hotel also houses a cyber café. Reception staff can arrange transfers within Mombasa, and are happy to book taxis. The hotel's central location makes it convenient for all shops, businesses, restaurants and bars of Mombasa, and within easy reach of Mombasa Old Town and Fort Jesus.

Club Rio Mombasa

Club Rio, Baluchi Street, behind GPO, Mombasa, Kenya

Tel	
Mobile	+254 714 906851; +254 787 574320
Fax	
E-mail	
Web	

   Moi Intl., LS & CH & Intl. 30 mins

Club Rio is known for its vibrant nightspots, Calypso Bar and Calypso Club. The hotel rises up over a cluster of shops including a clothes shop, bookshop, stationery shop and a cyber café. Club Rio's reception is open 24 hours.

There are 52 en-suite rooms, 30 of which have satellite TV. All the rooms are equipped with fan and mosquito net. The restaurant serves a selection of international dishes, including honey chicken, sheesh kebab, grilled jumbo prawns and nyama choma grilled meats. There is also a selection of soups, salads and sandwiches.

Calypso Bar, complete with bright lights, pink chairs and disco ball, is well stocked with soft drinks, beers, wines and spirits, and also has a selection of cocktails. Every night has a theme: Monday is rhumba nite, Tuesday is karaoke and Friday is live music. The bar has a number of large screens and shows international sports matches. Upcoming matches are written on a board outside the hotel. Calypso Club, on the 2nd floor, is a nightclub with DJ and dance floor, that goes through the night. Club Rio is situated behind the GPO, and is convenient for all the shops, businesses, restaurants and bars of Mombasa.

New Palm Tree Hotel Mombasa

New Palm Tree Hotel, opp Barclays Bank, Nkrumah Road, Mombasa
PO Box 90013, Mombasa 80100, Kenya

Tel	+254 20 8025682
Mobile	+254 715 442017; +254 736 489197
Fax	
E-mail	info@newpalmtreehotel.com
Web	www.newpalmtreehotel.com

   Moi Intl., LS & CH & Intl. 30 mins

Not far from Fort Jesus, New Palm Tree Hotel evokes the history of the old part of Mombasa. This colonial building is whitewashed, with a sweeping wooden staircase and a large rooftop courtyard decorated with pot plants. There are 30 en-suite rooms. All rooms have aircon, fan, mosquito net, fridge and satellite TV. WiFi is available throughout the hotel. The rooms open onto the courtyard which has plenty of seats and makes a comfortable place to spend the evening. Room service and laundry service are provided.

The restaurant serves buffet lunch, with a selection of beef, chicken, fish and rice dishes. Dinner is a la carte, with Swahili and coastal dishes such as biriani, shwamah and a variety of fish dishes. Fresh juices and soft drinks are served; no alcohol is stocked. The central lounge, decorated with murals of African scenes and animals, has a coffee bar with cakes and ice cream.

Local sites of interest include Fort Jesus and Mombasa Old Town. The hotel is conveniently located for all the shops, businesses, restaurants and bars of Mombasa. South coast beaches such as Tiwi and Diani, and north coast beaches such as Bamburi and Nyali are all within easy reach of Mombasa town.

Lotus Hotel

Mombasa

Lotus Hotel, Cathedral Lane, off Nkurumah Road, Mombasa, Kenya
PO Box 90123, Mombasa 80100, Kenya

Tel	+254 41 2313207; +254 20 2041890
Mobile	+254 722 612517
Fax	+254 41 2311789
E-mail	lotus@lotushotelkenya.com
Web	www.lotushotelkenya.com

 VISA, MasterCard, Eurocard

 Moi Intl., LS & CH & Intl.
30 mins

Near Mombasa Old Town, Lotus Hotel is located within easy reach of the historic Fort Jesus and its surrounding picturesque alleys. The bright orange hotel is a landmark on Cathedral Lane, just off Nkurumah Road. The hotel welcomes families, and can also arrange conferences and seminars. The Lotus Hotel's aim is for visitors to feel like a Lotus-eater in the Odyssey of Homer, the Greek, full of contentment and if you wish, dreamy indolence. There are 24 en-suite rooms, made up of singles, doubles and triples. All rooms have aircon, writing table, armchair and telephone. The furnishings are a combination of Oriental and modern. Vitamu Restaurant serves Kenyan and international dishes, including grilled Kikambala chicken, grilled whole taffy, pili pili prawns, fillet steak de Paris and roasted goat meat. Kaka Bar, at the entrance of the hotel, has Oriental arches and wooden panelling. Karibu Bar, adjoining the reception, is designed with a long bar along orange walls. Both bars are well stocked with soft drinks, beers, wines and spirits.

The conference hall seats 40 pax, and is equipped with projector and PA system. The reception can book taxis if required. The hotel is within easy reach of all the shops, businesses, restaurants and bars of Mombasa.

LANTANA GALU BEACH

Beach Front Holiday Homes – Diani

added space, more privacy, more comfort

Excellent for family and groups

Two swimming pools, Le Café beachside restaurant and bar, Coffee Bar, Massage and Beauty Studio, Gym, Convenience Shop, Business Centre, Satellite TV, DVD Player, Free WiFi, Airport Transfers, Housekeeping, Cooks, Baby Cots and High Chairs, Barbeques, Reception and Concierge services, proximity to water sport activities, located on a pristine and quiet sandy beach.

For bookings and enquiries contact:
Lantana Galu Beach [Diani Beach]
+254 (20) 260 4434
+254 (0) 714 315 151
+254 (0) 738 650 828
info@lantana-galu-beach.co.ke

www.lantana-galu-beach.co.ke

South Coast

Galu Beach – Photo © Andrew Nightingale, kembu.com

The South Coast is known for its long attractive beaches, vibrant night life, marine national parks, coastal national parks and remote islands. Highlights include Diani Beach, Kisite Mpunguti Marine Park, Shimoni Caves, Shimba Hills and Mwaluganje Elephant Sanctuary.

What is referred to as the South Coast is the southern half of Kenya's east coast, linked to Mombasa Island by the Likoni car and passenger ferry. The beaches, joined by a coastal road, are Shelly, Pungu, Sand Island, Tiwi, Diani, Galu, Kinondo, Msambweni and Shimoni. The main islands are Chale, Funzi and Wasini. Ukunda Airport, near Diani Beach, has daily scheduled flights to destinations in Kenya. Moi International Airport is located on Mombasa Island. The area has traditionally been inhabited by the Wakamba, Digo and Duruma people.

Diani Beach is the longest and liveliest of the beaches. It offers a plethora of water sports including kite surfing, windsurfing, scuba diving, snorkelling and jet skiing. Golf courses, spas, restaurants, bars, nightclubs, tour operators and shops are all found here. The Colobus Trust, based in Diani, protects the rare colobus monkey; tours of the research station reveal the monkey in its natural habitat.

Kisite Mpunguti Marine Park covers a marine area with four small islands surrounded by coral reef. The islands have dense coastal equatorial forests; sea grass and marine algae cover the reef. Attractions include dolphins and coral gardens. More than 250 fish species have been recorded. Snorkelling, scuba diving, bird watching and camping are all on offer. The marine park headquarters, at which park fees should be paid, is situated on the mainland, at Shimoni.

Shimoni, meaning the place of the caves in Swahili, is a coastal fishing village south of Diani. The caves are believed to have been holding pens for slaves prior to their transportation to Zanzibar. Now a community owned project, the caves provide an income for the local people. From Shimoni, boat trips go to Wasini Island and Kisite Mpunguti Marine Park, both famed for snorkelling.

The Shimba Hills National Reserve has one of the largest coastal forests in East Africa, after Arabuko Sokoke Forest, near Watamu. Park gates are at Main Gate, Kivumoni, Kidongo and Shimba. There are four campsites, including one at the lovely Sheldrick Falls. The reserve is rich in flora and fauna, and is home to the highest density of elephant in Kenya. Other species of interest include the rare Sable antelope, leopard, genet cat, greater galago, elephant shrew, bushy tailed mongoose and fruit bat. 111 bird species have been recorded, including 22 which are coastal endemic such as African hawk-eagle, greater honeyguide, crowned hornbill and uluguru violet-backed sunbird. Activities include game viewing, bird watching, camping and trekking.

Mwaluganje Elephant Sanctuary was established in 1995. A community owned project, it covers an ancient elephant migration route between the Shimba Hills and Mwaluganje Forest. The sanctuary is also known for its rare cycad forest.

Chale Island, Funzi Island and Wasini Island are all little developed, rustic islands, with mangroves, dolphins and crocodiles. The Wasini Women's self-help group manages the boardwalk. Boat trips and water sports can be arranged.

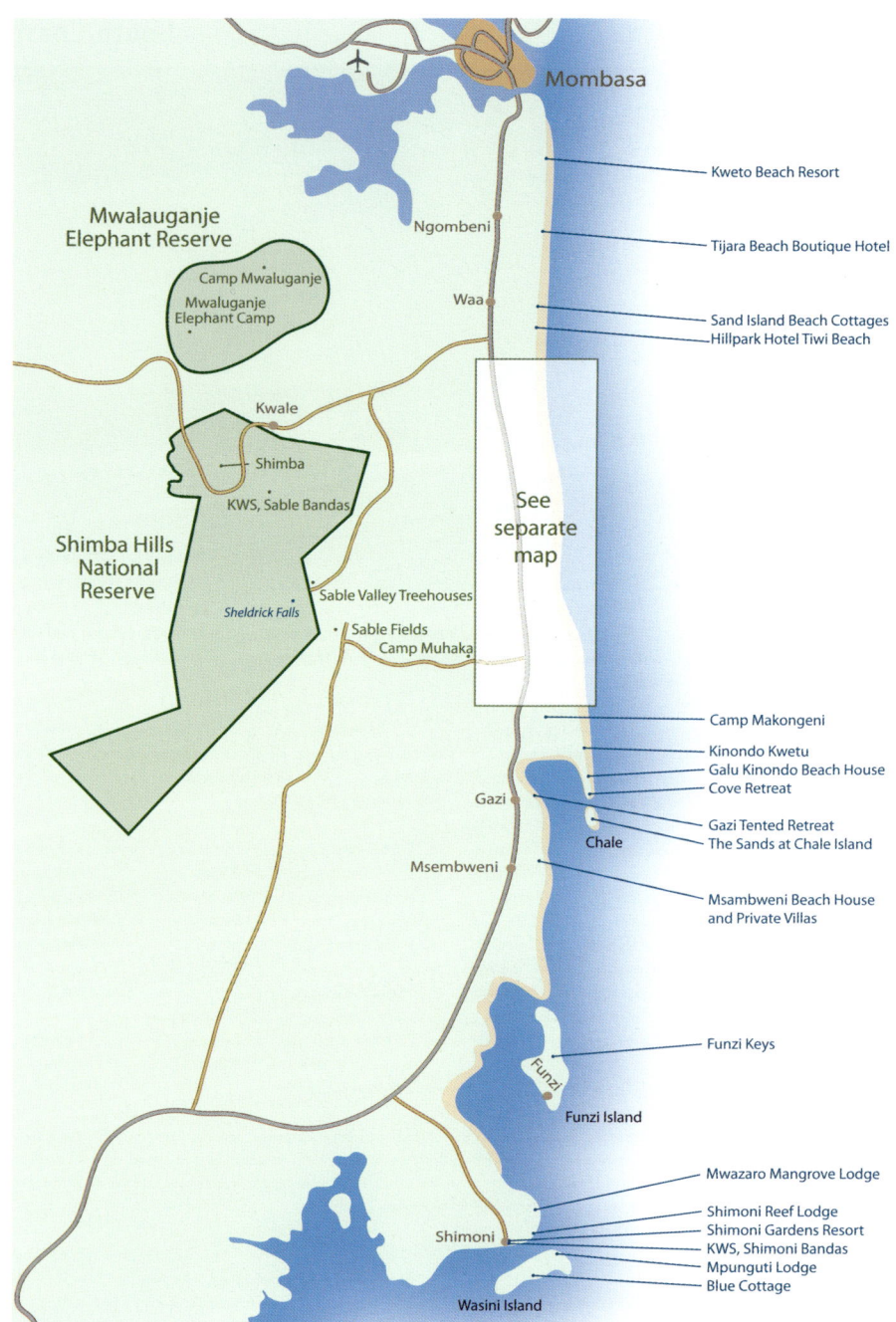

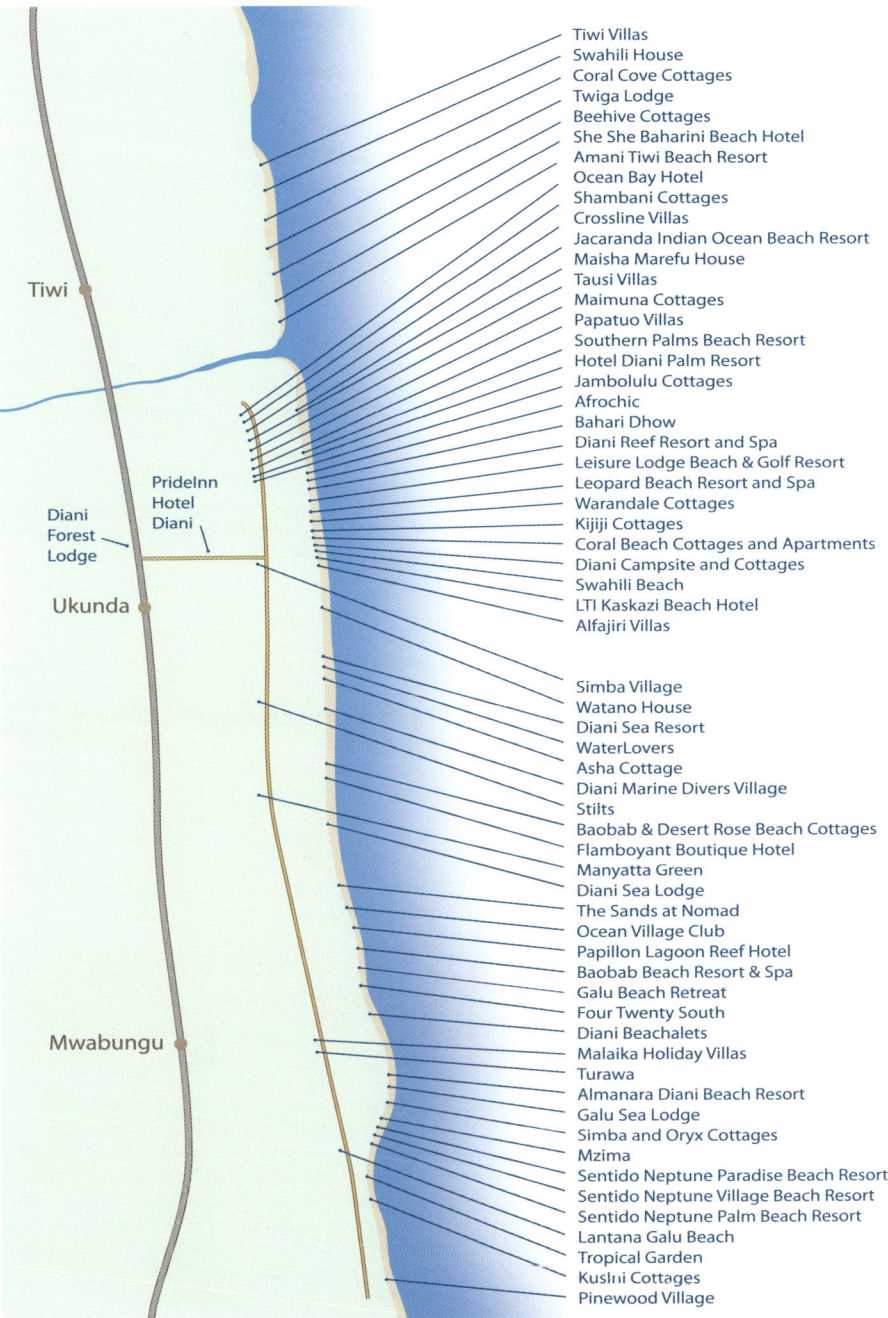

Kweto Beach Resort Shelly Beach

Kweto Beach Resort, Shelly Beach, nr Likoni, South Coast, Kenya
PO Box 4563, Likoni 80110, Kenya

Tel	
Mobile	+254 726 940895
Fax	
E-mail	
Web	

    Moi Intl., LS & CH & Intl.
                         50 mins

Kweto Beach Resort opened in 2009. The resort offers tented accommodation as well as hotel rooms, and is set in a garden fringed by Shelly Beach. The location is convenient for Likoni town and for the ferry that links the south coast beaches to Mombasa Island.

There are 10 en-suite safari tents. Each tent is shaded by a thatched roof, and has a bamboo veranda at its front and a solid bathroom at its rear. The tents are all raised on solid stone floors. There are also 4 standard en-suite rooms, made up of doubles and twins.

The restaurant, raised on stilts, overlooks the beach. It serves a predominantly Kenyan menu, including fried chicken, goat stew and beef curry, served with ugali and kachambari. The bar, beneath the restaurant, also overlooks the beach and is stocked with soft drinks, beers and a few spirits. There are 2 large screen satellite TVs in the restaurant and 2 more in the bar. International sports matches and news are shown. There is a sandwich bar in the garden, with several shaded dining areas around it. Tours, excursions and water sports can be booked in Mombasa, and at most of the south coast beaches.

Tijara Beach Boutique Hotel Pungu Beach

Tijara Beach Boutique Hotel, Pungu Beach, South Coast, Kenya
PO Box 99982, Kilindini 80107, Kenya

Tel	+254 20 2057701
Mobile	+254 722 701701; +254 734 755754
Fax	
E-mail	admin@tijarabeach.com
Web	www.tijarabeachcom

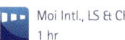   Moi Intl., LS & CH & Intl.
                          1 hr

Overlooking its own private and secluded beach, Tijara Beach Boutique Hotel is a perfect location for a peaceful, romantic holiday. Situated approximately 9km south of Mombasa Island, the house is a luxurious retreat. There are 4 cottages in 5 acres of beachfront gardens, made up of 3 standard and 1 honeymoon. Every cottage has an ocean view, thatched roof, ceiling fan, handcrafted Swahili furniture, private veranda and bathroom with a view. Meals can be taken in the open dining room, on the guests' veranda, on the cliff overlooking the beach or in any other location. The chefs specialise in fresh seafood and coastal cuisine. The freshwater swimming pool is surrounded by a sunbathing terrace. A masseuse offers massage and beauty treatments. WiFi is complimentary. Activities include snorkelling on the reef, bird watching, beach walks and cave walks. Trips to the 3 Mombasa golf courses, Shimba Hills National Reserve, Mombasa Old Town and Fort Jesus can be arranged, as can deep sea fishing, scuba diving, dolphin watching and kite surfing. Weddings, anniversaries, birthdays and meetings can be organised. Tijara's commitment to conservation includes recycling grey water, solar water heating, composting degradable waste, recycling and continuous tree planting. Tijara Beach Boutique Hotel has been nominated for the Best Beach Safari Property in the 2012 Safari Awards.

Sand Island Beach Cottages

Sand Island Beach

Sand Island Beach Cottages, Sand Island Beach, South Coast, Kenya
PO Box 5516, Diani 80401, Kenya

Tel	
Mobile	+254 733 660554; +254 722 395005
Fax	
E-mail	sandisland@africaonline.co.ke
Web	www.sandislandbeach.com

 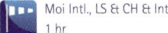 Moi Intl., LS & CH & Intl. 1 hr

On remote and peaceful Sand Island Beach, Sand Island Beach Cottages are a selection of beachfront self-catering cottages. The cottages are in indigenous gardens that attract dik dik and colobus monkeys.

There are 8 cottages, all of slightly different designs. Simu, Futa and Kasa are open plan bedsitters, with fully equipped kitchenettes and verandas. Badu, Tafi and Papa have 2 double bedrooms, 2 bathrooms, fully equipped kitchen opening onto living room and veranda. Tewa has 3 double bedrooms, 2 bathrooms, fully equipped kitchen, an open plan living and dining room and a veranda. The Campette, behind Tewa, has 3 beds and can be taken with Tewa if required. Bed linen, towels and mosquito nets are provided. A chef can be provided on request. Water is heated by solar power.

Sand Island Beach has 2 water pools which extend into caves with a wide variety of fish and coral. Local guides offer walks through the coastal forests, introducing guests to the uses of local tree species. Local boat captains offer boat trips and snorkelling. Sand Island Beach Cottages is committed to providing employment for local people, and has initiated a number of community projects. It has also started the Turtle Watch project. Bookings should be made directly, not through travel agents.

Hillpark Hotel
Tiwi Beach

Sand Island Beach

Hillpark Hotel Tiwi Beach, Sand Island Beach, South Coast, Kenya
PO Box 277, Ukunda 80400, Kenya

Tel	+254 20 2170703
Mobile	+254 722 328365; +254 715 473041
Fax	+254 40 3300041
E-mail	info@hillparktiwibeach.com
Web	www.mawenibeach.com

 VISA  Moi Intl., LS & CH & Intl. 1 hr

Set in beachfront gardens on Sand Island Beach, Hillpark Hotel Tiwi Beach, formerly known as Maweni and Capricho, offers a selection of cottages and hotel rooms. The cottages either face the beach or are surrounded by attractive gardens.

There are 26 self-catering cottages, made up of 1, 2, 3 and 4-bedroom cottages. There are also 17 hotel rooms. All rooms are decorated in Swahili style, with wicker furniture, bright fabrics and aged wooden ornaments. A chef can be provided on request. The restaurant serves a selection of Kenyan and Italian cuisine, as well as seafood. Beach dinners and parties can be arranged. Weddings are planned according to the requirements of the couple. Seminars, conventions, concerts and photos sessions can also be arranged, either on the beach or in the resort.

There are 4 conference halls, the smallest of which seats 40 pax and the largest of which seats 70. The halls are all equipped with aircon, LCD projector, overhead projector, TV, DVD and VCR. The massage parlour offers massage, manicure and pedicure. Boat trips to Shimoni, Wasini Island and Kisite Mpunguti Marine Park can all be arranged. Fishing, scuba diving and snorkelling are also available. Day trips to Shimba Hills and Mwaluganje Elephant Sanctuary can be booked.

Tiwi Villas Tiwi Beach

Tiwi Villas, Tiwi Beach, South Coast, Kenya
PO Box 86775, Mombasa 80100, Kenya
Tel
Mobile +254 727 553173
Fax
E-mail
Web

   Moi Intl., LS & CH & Intl. 1 hr

Perched on a cliff overlooking peaceful Tiwi Beach, Tiwi Villas is a collection of cottages in extensive grounds.

There are 7 2-bedroom cottages, each with fully equipped kitchenette, bathroom and veranda overlooking the beach. There are 5 3-bedroom cottages, set back from the cliff's edge, with kitchenette, bathroom and veranda overlooking the garden. All cottages are whitewashed, with thatched roofs. The restaurant is open sided with views of the sea. It has an international menu with plenty of seafood options such as taffy fish, prawn Masala and fish fillet, as well as stir-fried chicken, pan fried beef and spaghetti carbonara. The bar stocks soft drinks and beers, and the obliging staff are happy to get wine or spirits if required.

The swimming pool, between the cottages and the restaurant, is surrounded by a sunbathing terrace that overlooks the beach. Along the beach, plenty of activities, facilities and amusements are on offer, including snorkelling, boat trips, windsurfing, scuba diving and massage. Nearby hotels and resorts have restaurants, beach bars and beach volleyball.

Swahili House   Tiwi Beach

Swahili House, Tiwi Beach, South Coast, Kenya
PO Box 303, Ukunda 80400, Kenya
Tel
Mobile +254 725 749363; +254 733 995946
Fax
E-mail swahili.house@gmail.com / info@swahilihouse.com
Web www.swahilihouse.com

  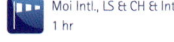 Moi Intl., LS & CH & Intl. 1 hr

On a cliff overlooking the Indian Ocean, Swahili House offers complete privacy and superb views. The house is furnished in the local Swahili Arabic style. The gardens are filled with ancient trees that attract plentiful wildlife including bushbabies, monitor lizards, dik dik, serval cats and mongooses. The main house has 4 bedrooms, 3 of which are en-suite. The dining area looks out over the private swimming pool. The penthouse, known as Naked Africa, can be taken with the house, or separately. It has a large double bedroom, bathroom and kitchen.

Swahili Cottage has 2 double bedrooms. Lofty Cottage has a loft with double bed and a downstairs living room with 2 day beds.

Swahili Villa, set apart from the house and cottages, has 3 spacious en-suite double rooms linked by a freeform sitting area. The bar overlooks the private swimming pool. The villa is tastefully decorated with cream linens, chunky wooden furniture and aged dhow ornaments.

All houses are staffed by a housekeeper and a chef who specialises in seafood and Italian cuisine. The staff can book shopping trips, taxis, excursions and water sports. Local attractions include scenic walks, the Tiwi rock pools and the ancient Congo mosque. A nearby hotel offers windsurfing, diving, squash, tennis and a gym.

Coral Cove Cottages Tiwi Beach

Coral Cove Cottages, Tiwi Beach, South Coast, Kenya
PO Box 600, Ukunda 80400, Kenya

Tel	+254 40 3300010, +254 20 212460
Mobile	+254 733 577708, +254 722 732797
Fax	
E-mail	coralcove@wananchi.com
Web	www.coralcove.tiwibeach.com

   Moi Intl., LS & CH & Intl.
1 hr

Set in 14 acres of lush tropical garden, Coral Cove Cottages are beachfront self-catering cottages. Peaceful Tiwi Beach stretches along the end of the garden.

There are 7 well spaced cottages. Each cottage has 2 bedrooms, a bathroom, open plan sitting and dining room and a fully equipped kitchen. All the verandas face the garden; some also face the beach. Staff to cook, clean and do laundry can be arranged for an additional fee. Fresh fish, seafood, fruit and vegetables are brought to the cottages daily by local vendors. Coral Cove Cottages are owner managed, and the garden is home to a troop of vervet monkeys and a menagerie of pets.

Shopping trips to the local shopping centres can be arranged. Along the beach, plenty of activities, facilities and amusements are on offer, including windsurfing, scuba diving, swimming pool, restaurants, beach bars and beach volleyball. Coral Cove Cottages can also assist with booking safaris, dive courses and car hire.

Twiga Lodge Tiwi Beach

Twiga Lodge, Tiwi Beach, South Coast, Kenya
PO Box 80820, Likoni 80110, Kenya

Tel	
Mobile	+254 721 577614
Fax	
E-mail	twigakenya@gmail.com
Web	www.twigalodge.com

   Moi Intl., LS & CH & Intl.
1 hr

Twiga Lodge is in grounds that extend along the centre of Tiwi Beach. The lodge offers budget accommodation, friendly staff and an extensive campsite. The large grounds are home to many indigenous trees, including a huge baobab, and a troop of vervet monkeys.

There are 18 en-suite budget rooms. These are whitewashed, thatched cottages, with simple furniture and cold showers. The beachfront block opened in 2006, and houses 28 superior rooms. These are fully tiled with a sliding glass door opening onto a balcony that overlooks the beach. They are equipped with twin beds, hot bath and hot shower. There are also 3 cottages, each containing 2 double rooms with simple furniture and cold showers. The large campsite, on the beachfront, is well shaded by numerous trees and has bathroom facilities.

The bar and restaurant overlook the beach. The bar is well stocked with soft drinks, beers, wines and spirits, and plays coastal music. The restaurant is decorated with murals of the giraffes that give the lodge its name. It has a large international menu including full Twiga breakfast, pan fried chicken rosemary, spaghetti with prawns, beef pilau, prawns Masala, fish curry and a selection of snacks. There is also a thatched beachfront lounge.

Beehive Cottages Tiwi Beach

Beehive Cottages, Tiwi Beach, South Coast, Kenya
PO Box 46220, Nairobi 00100, Kenya

Tel	+254 20 3588209
Mobile	+254 722 713478; +254 733 654785
Fax	
E-mail	sales@beehivecottages.com
Web	www.beehivecottages.com

    Moi Intl., LS & CH & Intl.
1 hr

On Tiwi beachfront, Beehive Cottages is a family-run business. There are 2 private self-catering cottages in a 10-acre plot fringed by peaceful Tiwi Beach. The cottages are old colonial houses that have been recently renovated. They are set in beautiful natural surroundings with indigenous palm trees and a number of old trees that attract numerous native birds and wildlife, including bushbabies, vervet monkeys, monitor lizards, mongooses, dik dik and serval cats.

The Honey Comb, on the beachfront, has 4 en-suite double bedrooms. The house also has a fully equipped kitchen, living room and veranda. This attractive whitewashed house has a tall thatched roof and is surrounded by gardens. It is staffed by a housekeeper and chef. The Honey Comb was originally the owners' beach house, and is now available for holiday rent. In the words of the owners: We've loved it for over 20 years, we're sure you will too.

The Forager has 3 double bedrooms and 2 bathrooms. The house also has a fully equipped kitchen, living room and veranda. It is staffed by a housekeeper and chef. Local fishermen and vegetable vendors come to the cottages daily with fresh produce. Local boatmen can arrange boat trips, snorkelling and other excursions.

She She Baharini Beach Hotel Tiwi Beach

She She Baharini Beach Hotel, Tiwi Beach, South Coast, Kenya
PO Box 63230, Nairobi 00619, Kenya

Tel	+254 20 8562025; +254 20 85641597
Mobile	+254 722 511436; +254 735 511436
Fax	
E-mail	info@sheshebeach.com
Web	www.sheshebeach.com

 VISA, MasterCard   Moi Intl., LS & CH & Intl.
1 hr

On Tiwi Beach, She She Baharini Beach Hotel offers the facilities of a resort and a beachfront location.

There are 30 en-suite rooms, made up of 8 doubles, 8 twins, 8 deluxe and 6 seafront. There are 3 rooms to each whitewashed, thatched cottage. All rooms are equipped with aircon and digital safe. The main building houses the reception on the ground floor and a bar on the 1st floor, with satellite TV and views across the compound. The Pool Restaurant serves buffet breakfast, lunch and dinner, and has a selection of pizzas. The Beach Restaurant has an a la carte menu, specialising in Italian cuisine and seafood, including grilled lobster with basmati rice, beef fillet and pasta carbanara. For the freshest seafood, guests are welcome to order their choice of dinner in the morning, and the restaurant will buy it fresh from local fishermen that day. Both Pool Bar and Beach Bar are well stocked, and have a selection of coffees.

The conference hall seats 300 pax, and is equipped with projector and PA system. There are sunbeds and a beach volleyball pitch on the beach in front of the hotel. Tusker Safaris, at reception, can book safaris, excursions, boat trips and watersports.

Amani Tiwi Beach Resort

Tiwi Beach

Amani Tiwi Beach Resort, Tiwi Beach, South Coast, Kenya
PO Box 1877, Ukunda 80400, Kenya

Tel	+44 845 772247
Mobile	
Fax	
E-mail	info@iksat.co.uk
Web	www.amanitiwibeachresort.com

  Moi Intl., LS & CH & Intl.
1 hr

Amani Tiwi Beach Resort is set in 20 acres of lush tropical grounds. The resort was fully refurbished in 2011, and is designed with stunning views of the Indian Ocean.

There are 213 en-suite rooms, made up of 178 standard, 10 premier, 16 superior, 3 junior suites, 2 executive suites and 4 rooms designed for guests with disabilities

The Main Restaurant serves international buffets. Bella Vita is an Italian restaurant located on the beach. Deck Restaurant has an a la carte menu and serves a fusion of seafood and Swahili cuisine. The Coffee Shop serves teas, coffees and light snacks. Wasafri Bar, in the main lobby, has a wide selection of drinks. There are also 2 bars at the poolside, 1 at Bella Vita and 1 at Deck Restaurant. The fully equipped conference hall seats 150 pax. The business centre has internet, fax, photocopier, printer and secretarial services.

The beauty parlour has a range of treatments and massage. There is a gym, library, boutique, car rental and currency exchange. The dive school offers an array of water sports including scuba diving, windsurfing, kayaking and kite surfing. The animation team offers a daily programme of activities. This eco-friendly resort uses solar power, recycles waste, produces compost and grows organic vegetables.

Camp Mwaluganje

Shimba Hills

Camps International, Unit 1 Kingfisher Park, Headlands Business Park, Salisbury Road, Blashford, Ringwood, BH24 4HX, UK

Tel	+254 41 2007761; +254 41 3202056
Mobile	+254 733 989082, +254 733 604422
Fax	
E-mail	dipesh@campsinternational.com
Web	www.campsinternational.com

Ukunda, LS & CH
1 hr

Camp Mwaluganje is operated by Camps International, which supports community and wildlife projects through interaction with adventure tourism. The camp is located in the Mwaluganje Elephant Sanctuary. It is aimed at international volunteers and local school students and interacts closely with the local community and wildlife.

The camp has a collection of dome tents, with nearby external bathroom facilities. The kitchen is stationed beneath a towering baobab tree, and food is served in the shade of the tree. Camp Mwaluganje is involved in a wide range of projects, and develops new initiatives with Mwaluganje Elephant Sanctuary Management. Projects are designed to increase revenue to the local community and protect the elephants by reducing the impact of human wildlife conflict. Current projects include road construction, elephant identification, game trail marking, snare clearing, GPS mapping and the making of elephant dung paper for sale to tourists. Safaris to national parks and other destinations around Kenya can be arranged. Cultural visits to local villages and trips to the coast are also available. Camps International was given the Virgin Holidays Responsible Tourism Award in 2008 and won the Eco Warrior Kenya Award for the Most Sustainable Community Based Tourism Enterprise in 2010.

Mwaluganje Elephant Camp Shimba Hills

Mwaluganje Elephant Camp, Shimba Hills, Kenya
Travellers Beach Hotel and Club, PO Box 87649, Mombasa 80100, Kenya
Tel	+254 41 5485121-6
Mobile	+254 720 648708
Fax	+254 41 5485678; +254 41 5485674
E-mail	travhtls@africaonline.co.ke
Web	www.travellersbeach.com

 VISA, MasterCard, Amex Senator   Ukunda, LS & CH 1 hr

In the Mwaluganje Elephant Sanctuary, Mwaluganje Elephant Camp is a tented camp overlooking a waterhole where elephants frequently come to drink and wallow. The reserve has a variety of landscapes including savannah, forested hills and ponds filled with water lilies.

There are 20 en-suite tents, made up of twins and doubles. One extra bed can be added in each tent. Each tent is equipped with mosquito net, and has a veranda with a view of the forest. A safe is available at reception. The restaurant has a viewing deck overlooking the waterhole. Breakfast, lunch and dinner are served in the restaurant or on the deck. The bar serves soft drinks, beers and spirits. African fish eagles, monitor lizards and hornbills are regular visitors throughout the day, and bushbabies are often seen at night. Evening entertainment can be arranged, such as traditional dancing by Digo and Duruma dancers.

Mwaluganje Elephant Camp is approximately 15km from Kwale town and approximately 55km from Mombasa. Transfers from Moi International Airport or Ukunda airstrip in Diani can be arranged. Mwaluganje Elephant Camp is affiliated to Travellers Beach Hotel and Club in Bamburi. Holidays which combine the 2 hotels can be arranged.

Shimba Shimba Hills

Shimba, Shimba Hills, Kenya
Aberdare Safari Hotels, PO Box 14815, Nairobi 00800, Kenya
Tel	+254 20 4452095-9
Mobile	+254 722 207761
Fax	+254 20 4452102
E-mail	info@aberdaresafarihotels.com
Web	www.aberdaresafarihotels.com

     Ukunda, LS & CH 1 hr

One of the last remaining habitats of the rare Sable antelope, Shimba Hills National Reserve is 192km² of tropical rainforest. The reserve has over 1000 species of plants, some endemic to the area, including the cycad, a palm-like plant. Shimba, a wooden tree lodge overlooking a waterhole, is set in the middle of this forest, near a lush spring.

The 30 rooms are made up of 23 standard rooms, 5 triples and 2 suites. All have balconies with views of the waterhole. There are communal bathroom facilities. The restaurant, located on a covered veranda, overlooks the floodlit waterhole. Jungle Bar opens onto an observation platform. A wooden walkway stretches 120m into the rainforest, ending at an observation point where birds and butterflies abound.

Nearby Sheldrick Falls, a breathtaking 25-meter waterfall with a natural plunge pool, makes a perfect destination for a game walk. A naturalist lectures guests on flora and fauna, before they shower in the spray of the fall or plunge into the pool. Activities include game drives and nature walks. Sundowners at scenic spots are also available. Specialities are bush breakfast, and an authentic African lunch accompanied by colourful traditional Mijikenda dancers. The lodge does not accept children under 5.

KWS, Sable Bandas   Shimba Hills

KWS, Sable Bandas, Shimba Hills, Kenya
Kenya Wildlife Service, PO Box 40241, Nairobi 00100, Kenya

Tel	+254 20 6000800; +254 20 6002345; +254 20 3991000
Mobile	+254 726 610508; +254 726 610509; +254 736 663421
Fax	+254 20 6003792
E-mail	kws@kws.go.ke / reservations@kws.go.ke
Web	www.kws.go.ke

     Ukunda, LS & CH
1 hr

Sable Bandas are owned and managed by Kenya Wildlife Service, KWS. They are situated in Shimba Hills National Reserve. The bandas are in a cool forest clearing, high on a bluff with attractive views over both the rainforest and the coastline in the distance. Sable Bandas are named after the rare Sable antelope which is found in this unique habitat.

There are 4 rondavel bandas. Each banda has 1 twin bedroom, a bathroom and a covered veranda with a dining table and benches. The resident caretaker provides kerosene lamps, mosquito nets, blankets, pillows, bed linen, towels, soap and loo paper. There is a communal kitchen equipped with 3 gas stoves, kitchen utensils, cutlery, crockery and glassware. There is also a communal outdoor barbecue area.

The highlights of Shimba Hills National Reserve include lush coastal forests and spectacular views. The park is also known for the 25-meter Sheldrick Falls. There are driving circuits, nature trails, picnic sites and campsites. As well as the Sable antelope, wildlife includes warthog, giraffe, elephant, leopard, sykes monkeys, colobus monkeys, serval cats, duiker, suni and bush pig. A total of 111 bird species have been recorded here. Shimba Hills are 3km beyond Kwale, and Sable Bandas are 3km from the main gate. Entry to the national reserve is by cash only.

Sable Valley Treehouses   Shimba Hills

Sable Valley Treehouses, Shimba Hills, Kenya
Destination Adventures Ltd, PO Box 5480, Ukunda 80400, Kenya

Tel	+254 40 3203611
Mobile	+254 733 435341
Fax	
E-mail	marketing@destination-adventures.com
Web	www.destination-adventures.com

     Ukunda, LS & CH
50 mins

Elevated from the coastal plain, Sable Valley Treehouses is located high in the Shimba Hills. Named after the rare Sable antelope which is endemic to this area, the retreat is a romantic haven, with access both to a forested wildlife sanctuary and to the coast.

There are 2 exclusive tree houses. Each tree house has been designed and constructed using local materials and resources, and each is equipped with a private Jacuzzi. The generator runs from 6pm to 10pm to power the Jacuzzi; the houses are lit by lanterns and candles. Solid wooden furniture and natural fabrics adorn each house. A butler staffs each house, serving all meals on the balcony, including morning tea, sundowner and candlelit dinner. The Ndovu 4-poster beds can be wheeled onto the balcony for those who wish to sleep beneath the stars. This is an adult only retreat. The retreat is an all inclusive property; meals, facilities, drinks and transfers are all included. Weddings are designed individually to suit the couple's taste. Sable Valley Treehouses can be used as a romantic interlude by guests staying at sister properties Cove Retreat, Gazi Tented Retreat and Galu Beach Retreat.

Sable Fields Shimba Hills

Sable Fields, Shimba Hills, Kenya
PO Box 485, Nanyuki 10400, Kenya
Tel
Mobile +254 720 252700; +254 722 361642; +254 722 237967
Fax
E-mail nasrafield@fieldoutdoor.com
Web www.fieldoutdoor.com

  Shimba Hills, CH
20 mins

On a hilltop on the outer edge of the Shimba Hills National Reserve, Sable Fields has outstanding views of the reserve. Game viewing can be done from the comfort of the balcony.

The retreat comprises the main house and 2 en-suite guest wings. The master suite, in the main house, is intended for a family. It has double and twin beds, bathroom and private terrace. The 2 guest wings each have double and single bed. There is also a swimming pool, central dining and lounge area and main terrace. A resident chef provides all meals if required, or assists in the kitchen with guests on the self-catering option. Shimba Hills National Reserve is the only home in Kenya of the Sable antelope, and is also known for high numbers of elephants. Other nearby sites of interest include Diani and Tiwi Beaches. Excursions to Shimoni and Wasini Island are also possible, as are trips to the Old Town and Fort Jesus in Mombasa.

Sable Fields is owned and managed by Field Outdoor Enterprises, registered in 2008. The company aims to promote and develop ecotourism as an alternative livelihood for pastoralists who many no longer be able to survive on livestock alone.

Camp Muhaka Shimba Hills

Camps International, Unit 1 Kingfisher Park, Headlands Business Park
Salisbury Road, Blashford, Ringwood, BH24 4HX, UK
Tel +254 41 2007761; +254 41 3202056
Mobile +254 733 989082, +254 733 604422
Fax
E-mail dipesh@campsinternational.com
Web www.campsinternational.com

  Ukunda, LS & CH
1 hr

Camp Muhaka is operated by Camps International, which supports community and wildlife projects through interaction with adventure tourism. The camp is located in the heart of a small community, predominantly from the Digo tribe, in the Shimba Hills near the sacred Kaya Muhaka Rainforest. It is aimed at international volunteers and local school students and interacts closely with the local community and Muhaka Primary School. There are 3 thatched bandas, each divided into 2 dorms with a capacity of 8 pax each. Communal bathroom facilities are provided. There is also a kitchen, workshop and laundry block. The large thatched dining area and lounge are close to enormous mango trees and oil palms, home to monkeys and bushbabies. Meals are cooked by the chefs; volunteers are welcome to assist. Camp Muhaka provides an integrated, non-touristy cultural experience. The camp aims to assist the local community with long-term, sustainable development projects. Current projects include school renovation, construction of classrooms, fencing, painting, tree planting, teaching and sports coaching. The camp is also involved in the conservation of the Kaya Muhaka Forest. Camps International was given the Virgin Holidays Responsible Tourism Award in 2008 and won the Eco Warrior Kenya Award for the Most Sustainable Community Based Tourism Enterprise in 2010.

Ocean Bay Hotel Diani

Ocean Bay Hotel, Diani, South Coast, Kenya
PO Box 1151, Ukunda 80400, Kenya
Tel
Mobile +254 722 435576; +254 722 247213
Fax
E-mail oceanbayoliani@yahoo.com / info@oceanbayhoteldiani.com
Web www.oceanbayhoteldiani.com

   Ukunda, LS & CH
20 mins

Ocean Bay Hotel, a short walk from Diani Beach, is entered through an arch of bougainvillea. The hotel offers budget hotel rooms and self-catering apartments, and also has a restaurant and bar.

There are 4 en-suite double rooms. There are also 6 apartments, made up of 4 singles and 2 doubles. Each apartment has a kitchen, dining room, living room and veranda. The restaurant has a Kenyan menu, with some international dishes, such as beef burger, steak and chips, grilled chicken with roast potatoes, chicken curry with rice, beef stew with ugali and spaghetti bolognaise. There is also a selection of snacks including samosas and sandwiches. The bar serves soft drinks, beers and a few spirits. The hotel also has a hair and beauty salon that offers a selection of beauty treatments, as well as manicure and pedicure.

There is a nearby shopping centre, and several nearby restaurants and bars. Tours, excursions and safaris can be booked with local tour agents. Water sports including kite surfing, scuba diving, snorkelling and wind-surfing can be booked on Diani Beach. Boat trips and fishing trips can also be booked locally.

Shambani Cottages   Diani

Shambani Cottages, Diani, South Coast, Kenya
PO Box 947, Ukunda 80400, Kenya
Tel
Mobile +254 720 132116; +254 720 132179
Fax
E-mail info@shambani.com
Web www.shambani.com

  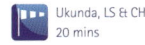 Ukunda, LS & CH
20 mins

Shambani is a collection of villas and cottages not far from Diani Beach. The 12,000 meter² garden is dominated by flamboyant, baobab and palm trees. Resident colobus monkeys inhabit the garden.

There are 2 villas. Flamboyant Villa, named for the 3 large flamboyant trees that surround it, has 2 en-suite bedrooms, dining room, kitchen, outdoor seating area and large terrace. The bedrooms have double beds, mosquito nets and fans. Baobab Villa, overlooking 1 of the 5 baobabs that adorn the garden, has 3 en-suite bedrooms, dining room, kitchen, 2 indoor lounges, outdoor seating area and large terrace. Kidogo Cottage can be taken with either villa, adding an extra bedroom to either.

Simba and Mambo Cottages are twin African style cottages, with stone walls and thatched roofs. The cottages share a kitchen and a large veranda with dining and lounge areas, which overlooks the swimming pool. Twiga Cottage has an en-suite double room, kitchen, dining room and wide veranda with seating. Kidogo Cottage is a studio apartment, accessed by an outdoor staircase. All villas and cottages have housekeeping service. For an additional charge, a chef can be hired. Local fishermen bring seafood to the door daily. South Coast Design, located at reception, can book safaris to destinations around Kenya.

Crossline Villas

Diani

Crossline Villas, Diani, South Coast, Kenya
PO Box 5509, Diani 80401, Kenya

Tel	+39 3488714279
Mobile	+254 725 797406
Fax	
E-mail	alberta47africa@yahoo.it
Web	www.kenyacharmingvillas.com

  Ukunda, LS & CH
20 mins

Crossline Villas are a collection of exclusive villas available for rent. The villas are in a garden bright with bougainvillea, a short distance from Diani Beach. A swimming pool, with pool attendant, is available for the use of guests at all the villas.

Taj Riviera House has 3 double bedrooms, 2 bathrooms, fully equipped kitchen and large veranda. The house is furnished in Zanzibar style, and has daybeds, dining table, card table and bookcase. Grace Villa has 3 double bedrooms, 3 bathrooms, fully equipped kitchen and large veranda. The house is adorned with Lamu furniture and natural fabrics. Ivana's House has 3 bedrooms, fully equipped kitchen and raised terrace with Jacuzzi. Satis Villa has 2 double bedrooms and 1 twin bedroom, 2 bathrooms, fully equipped kitchen and a large terrace furnished for dining. Fabio's House has 3 double en-suite rooms with aircon, fully equipped kitchen and large veranda. Baby cot, babysitter and toys are all available. Afrocharme has 5 en-suite double bedrooms, 2 elegantly furnished lounges with satellite TV and DVD, family room, dining room and terraces. Sofia House has 3 double bedrooms, fully equipped kitchen and open plan living area with terrace.

Each villa has 2 house staff. Chef, babysitter and further house staff can be provided on request.

Jacaranda Indian Ocean Beach Resort

Diani

Jacaranda Indian Ocean Beach Resort, Diani Beach, Kenya
Jacaranda Group of Hotels, PO Box 14287, Nairobi 00800, Kenya

Tel	+254 20 4448713-7
Mobile	+254 733 601613-4, +254 722 205486-7
Fax	+254 20 4445818; +254 20 4448977
E-mail	bookings@jacarandahotels.com
Web	www.jacarandahotels.com/indian-ocean-beach-resort

 VISA, MasterCard    Ukunda, LS & CH
20 mins

Built on the site of a 16th century mosque, Jacaranda Indian Ocean Beach Resort has Arabic architecture and is adorned with antiques from the Sultan of Zanzibar's Palace, including a remarkable chandelier given to the Sultan by British traders for landing rights.

The 100 en-suite deluxe rooms are elegantly furnished, and have minibar, kettle, aircon, safe, hairdryer, smoke detector and private veranda. 25 rooms have ocean views. 1 room is equipped for guests with disabilities. Spices Restaurant serves buffet breakfast and an 8-course table d'hote dinner of coastal specialities. Ocean Terrace, at the poolside, serves light meals and snacks. Bahari Cove serves a la carte seafood on a dhow-shaped floating restaurant. Jungle Village, in traditional Kenyan style bomas, has themed dinners with entertainment. Drinks are served in the Sultan's Lounge, Coconut Willy's pool bar and Dhow Bar on the beach. Wariara Convention Centre seats 180 pax and the Traders Room seats 40. Conference bookings include secretarial support and audio visual equipment.

A daily entertainment programme includes tennis, aerobics, table tennis and volleyball. Golf is available at a nearby Leisure Golf Club. The Kid's Club has a programme for children. A wide variety of water sports are available; non-motorised water sports are included in the rate.

Maisha Marefu House

Diani

Maisha Marefu House, Diani, South Coast, Kenya
PO Box 5785, Ukunda 80400, Kenya

Tel	+32 47 5450045
Mobile	+254 725 825999
Fax	
E-mail	alecvanwijk@skynet.be
Web	www.keniavilla.com

  Ukunda, LS & CH
20 mins

Maisha Marefu House is an elegant private house in an attractive garden, located not far from Diani Beach. The house is fully furnished and fully equipped, and is operated by a team of staff. Its name, Swahili for long life or happy life, aptly describes the atmosphere of the place.

There are 3 en-suite double bedrooms. The master bedroom is on the 1st floor, while 2 other bedrooms are on the ground floor. The house has a living room with satellite TV and music system, bar with open sitting area and a fully equipped kitchen that includes a large American fridge with icemaker. There is also a private swimming pool and Jacuzzi. The house is furnished with traditional Swahili furniture and adorned with antique African artefacts. There is a shaded outdoor dining area near the swimming pool, equipped with internet connection.

The house staff includes a housekeeper, gardener, chef and security guard. Guests can buy their food themselves, or the chef can go shopping for them. Fresh seafood and vegetables are available daily from local vendors. There is also a nearby shopping centre and a selection of restaurants and bars. Tours, excursions and water sports can be booked at local hotels or on Diani Beach.

Tausi Villas

Diani

Tausi Villas, off Diani Beach Road, nr Tausi stage, Diani, Kenya
PO Box 5026, Diani 80400, Kenya

Tel	
Mobile	+254 722 149711; +254 772 046790; +254 722 993167
Fax	
E-mail	reservations@tausiholidayvillas.com
Web	www.tausiholidayvillas.com

  Ukunda, LS & CH
20 mins

Tausi Villas opened in 2010. The whitewashed villas are set in manicured gardens around a swimming pool. The villas are self-catering, and there is also a restaurant on the compound.

There are 14 villas, 2 in each of the 7 houses. The villas have 1, 2 or 3 en-suite double bedrooms, all equipped with mosquito net and fan. The villas also have sitting room, fully equipped kitchenette and balcony. The deluxe villa is more spacious and opens directly onto the swimming pool. The rooftop restaurant overlooks the pool. It serves African and international dishes such as beef stew with chips, grilled fish with rice and a selection of salads. The poolside bar serves soft drinks and beers.

The spa, beneath the restaurant, offers massage, manicure and pedicure. The conference hall seats 20 pax. Conference equipment is not provided but can be hired on request. There is a car available for dropping and picking up guests from destinations in Diani including the Ukunda airstrip. Shops, restaurants, bars and discos are within easy reach of the villas. Water sports, safaris and excursions can be booked at various centres around Diani.

Maimuna Cottages

Diani

Maimuna Cottages, off Diani Beach Road, nr Tausi stage, Diani, Kenya
PO Box 5566, Diani 80400, Kenya
Tel
Mobile +254 717 569770; +254 729 248129
Fax
E-mail info@maimuna.ch
Web www.maimuna.ch

  Ukunda, LS & CH
20 mins

Maimuna Cottages, established in 2009, is a collection of self-catering cottages. Maimuna Cottages Ltd is a collaboration between a Swiss family and a Kenyan family. Their motto is: you feel comfortable with us as our guests and indirectly support the Kenyan family and thus our project.
There are 5 thatched cottages. Some cottages sleep 4 pax, and have a double bedroom, a living room, a kitchen equipped with fridge and electric cooker and a veranda. The remainder sleep 2 pax, and have an open plan bedroom and living room, a kitchen equipped with fridge and electric cooker and a veranda. The family managing the cottages is happy to introduce guests to an authentic Kenyan experience. The compound also has a restaurant which serves breakfast, as well as a gift shop. Shops, restaurants, bars and discos are within easy reach of the cottages, either by private car, taxi or public transport. Water sports centres are also easily accessible, with activities including scuba diving, snorkelling, kite surfing and boat trips. Local travel agents can assist with travel within Kenya, and can book safaris and excursions.

Papatuo Villas

Diani

Papatuo Villas, off Diani Beach Road, nr Tausi stage, Diani, Kenya
PO Box 5717, Diani 80400, Kenya
Tel +254 40 3300144
Mobile +254 721 606534
Fax
E-mail info@papatuo.com
Web www.papatuo.com

  Ukunda, LS & CH
20 mins

Papatuo is a collection of self-catering villas which opened in 2003. It is operated by Papatuo Investment Limited, an Italian society that operates tourism in Africa.
There are 8 whitewashed villas, made up of 2 1-bedroom villas and 6 2-bedroom villas. All villas are whitewashed with tall thatched roofs, and have sitting room with TV and DVD, fully equipped kitchen and veranda adorned with kikoy cushions. All bedrooms are en-suite and have aircon and fan. Chefs can be provided on request.
The round thatched restaurant has an extensive Italian menu, including carpaccio di pesce, spaghetti d'Aragosta, gnocchetti seafood, brasato al vino rosso and rigatoni alla Genovese. There is a wine list and a cocktail menu. There is a coffee bar at the poolside. The cyber café, located in the manager's office, has internet and printing. The boutique stocks a selection of gift items. A shuttle bus goes into Diani every evening, and can drop and pick up guests from restaurants, bars and casinos. Assistance with Italian translation is provided.
Papatuo Investment Limited can book boat trips, water sports, visits to local villages and trips to Mombasa. It can also arrange safaris and excursions around Kenya.

Southern Palms Beach Resort

Diani

Southern Palms Beach Resort, Diani Beach, Kenya
PO Box 363, Ukunda 80400, Kenya

Tel	+254 40 3203721; +254 20 2137555; +254 20 2352666
Mobile	+254 722 203166; +254 733 333366
Fax	+254 40 3203381
E-mail	infodesk@southernpalmskenya.com
Web	www.southernpalmskenya.com

Ukunda, LS & CH
15 mins

Set in 10 acres of mature tropical gardens on Diani Beach, Southern Palms Beach Resort blends traditional Swahili forms with Arabic architecture. The 2 huge freeform swimming pools meander attractively through the resort. The 300 en-suite rooms and the 2 spacious suites feature locally carved Pili Pili 4-poster beds and have tiled ceramic floors. They are equipped with aircon, TV, DVD, telephone, kettle, safe and minibar, and have balconies overlooking the gardens and pool, or the beach.
The Main Restaurant serves breakfast, lunch and themed dinners. Grilled meat, fish and seafood are served in the Manyatta by the pool, or on the beach. The Boriti Snack Bar offers a la carte light lunches. La Via Romana serves Italian dinners and El Nomad serves Lebanese dinners. There are 5 bars, including swim-up bars, the 24-hour Main Bar and Sargile Hookah Bar.
The Sports and Leisure Department has a diverse selection of activities, some included and others costing extra, such as water polo, nature walks, floodlit tennis, volleyball, squash, deep sea fishing, catamaran sailing, water aerobics, scuba diving, windsurfing, pétanque and bird watching. Nightly entertainment includes traditional dancing, acrobatics and local folklore. The Kid's Club has games, films and puzzles.

Hotel Diani Palm Resort

Diani

Hotel Diani Palm Resort, Diani, South Coast, Kenya
PO Box 1091, Ukunda 80400, Kenya

Tel	+254 40 3202523; +254 40 3204043
Mobile	
Fax	+254 40 3203291
E-mail	info@dianipalmhotel.com
Web	www.dianipalmhotel.com

VISA, MasterCard

Ukunda, LS & CH
15 mins

Hotel Diani Palm Resort is a family run hotel not far from Diani Beach. The hotel combines African hospitality with Swiss management.
There are 22 en-suite double rooms. All rooms are equipped with aircon, fridge, TV with local channels, telephone and safe. The rooms are in 2 whitewashed blocks, and all have a balcony overlooking the treeform swimming pool that winds through the garden. The restaurant serves buffet breakfast and dinner. An a la carte menu is available for lunch, including burgers, curries, steaks and stews. Snacks can also be served by the pool. Some evenings, live entertainment such as Maasai dancing is offered after dinner. The Green Palm, a large round bar with open sides and thatched roof, serves soft drinks, beers, spirits and tropical cocktails. The Mzuri Boutique stocks gift items and local artefacts. Foreign exchange, telephone, fax and email are all available at reception. The hotel also has a salon offering haircuts and massage. Shops, restaurants, bars and discos are within easy reach of the resort. Water sports can be booked at a number of centres in Diani. Safaris and excursions to destinations within Kenya can be arranged through reception.

Jambolulu Cottages Diani

Jambolulu Cottages, opp Diani Reef Resort and Spa, Diani, Kenya
PO Box 1342, Ukunda 80400, Kenya

Tel
Mobile +254 724 645753; +254 733 378983
Fax
E-mail jamboluluapt@yahoo.com
Web

  Ukunda, LS & CH
15 mins

Jambolulu Cottages are set either side of a path and surrounded by flowerbeds. The self-catering cottages offer budget accommodation in a convenient location near Diani Complex. The cottages are opposite Diani Reef Resort and Spa; guests staying at the cottages can access the beach by walking through Diani Reef Resort and Spa.

There are 6 cottages. Each cottage has a double bedroom, bathroom, separate WC, fully equipped kitchen, sitting room, dining room and small terrace. An extra bed can be added if required. The cottages are simply furnished, and equipped with fan, mosquito net and TV with local channels. The curtains are printed with African designs. A small garden near reception has a seating area, available for guests who want to eat outside. Nearby Diani Complex has shops and a small supermarket. Nearby restaurants include a Chinese restaurant, an Indian restaurant and several local Kenyan restaurants. Bars, discos and casinos are also within walking distance of the cottages. Tours, excursions and safaris can be booked with local tour agents. Water sports including kite surfing, scuba diving, snorkelling and windsurfing can be booked on Diani Beach. Boat trips and fishing trips can also be booked locally.

Afrochic   Diani

Afrochic, Diani Beach, South Coast, Kenya
Elewana Afrika, PO Box 72630, Nairobi 00200, Kenya

Tel +254 20 3750783, +254 20 3612000
Mobile +254 733 645764, +254 728 781402
Fax +254 20 3751507
E-mail info@elewana.com / reservations@elewana.com
Web www.elewana.com

 All major cards Ukunda, LS & CH
15 mins

Elewana, meaning harmony or understanding in Swahili, alludes to the harmony between the Elewana group of hotels and their surroundings. Afrochic, a small intimate hotel, has elegant Swahili décor and is adorned with coastal lamps, Lamu doors and carved wooden beds. The service is personal and discreet.

The 10 en-suite bedrooms, including a Junior Suite and an Executive Suite, each have their own individual style. All the rooms are spacious, have private balconies and are furnished with attention to detail. They are equipped with aircon, minibar, TV, selection of DVDs, telephone, WiFi, kettle and hairdryer.

Meals are freshly prepared by the chef, and can be served on the beach, in the dining room or on the guests' balcony. The freeform swimming pool is fringed with palm trees, and meanders between the hotel and the beach. The hotel also has a TV lounge and library, and a business centre with computer.

The hotel's concierge can arrange excursions and activities, such as scuba diving, water-skiing, kite surfing, deep sea fishing, dolphin safaris, camel riding and horse riding. Boat trips and safaris can also be arranged. Spa treatments, exercise at a nearby gym and golf at a nearby 18-hole course are available on request.

Bahari Dhow

Diani

Bahari Dhow, Diani Beach, South Coast, Kenya
PO Box 528, Nairobi 00606, Kenya

Tel	+254 40 3202221
Mobile	+254 727 618559, +254 723 411283
Fax	+254 40 3202457
E-mail	reservations@baharidhow.com
Web	www.baharidhow.com

VISA, MasterCard   Ukunda, LS & CH 15 mins

Whitewashed villas on either side of 3 elongated, interlinked swimming pools make up Bahari Dhow. The villas and the pool, surrounded by palm filled gardens and sunbathing deck, extend to the beach.
There are 24 villas in 2 rows, all facing the gardens and swimming pools. The villas are categorised as standard, comfort, deluxe and premium deluxe. Each villa is on 2 floors and has 3 en-suite bedrooms, fully equipped kitchen, dining room, living room and veranda. Each is equipped with satellite TV, telephone and aircon. The villas are staffed by a maid and a chef; guests can discuss their preferred menu with their private chef. Fresh seafood and vegetables are available daily from local vendors.

There is also a beach bar and restaurant, for guests who prefer to eat out. The sheesha lounge, rich with exotic scents, has comfortable cushions and a blend of Middle Eastern and Swahili décor.
Local activities include golf, scuba diving, kite surfing and windsurfing. Deep sea fishing and trips in glass bottomed boats can be arranged. Small 2-seater buggies are available for journeys within Diani. Game drives and safaris to Kenyan national parks can also be arranged here.

Diani Reef Resort and Spa

Diani

Diani Reef Resort and Spa, Diani Beach, South Coast, Kenya
PO Box 35, Ukunda 80400, Kenya

Tel	+254 40 3202723; +254 40 3203308
Mobile	+254 723 786301; +254 723 786305
Fax	+254 40 3202196; +254 40 3202341
E-mail	rsv@dianireef.com / info@dianireef.com
Web	www.dianireef.com

VISA, MasterCard   Ukunda, LS & CH 15 mins

The award winning Diani Reef Resort and Spa offers a wide variety of facilities and activities on Diani Beach.
There are 143 en-suite rooms, made up of 2 presidential suites, 2 penthouse suites, 9 junior suites, 6 deluxe rooms, 104 sea facing rooms and 20 garden facing rooms. All rooms are equipped with aircon, satellite TV, internet, digital safe, minibar, kettle, hairdryer and telephone. The suites are more spacious and include an open plan lounge and dining area, and a Jacuzzi. Coral Rock Café serves buffet with several live cooking stations. Sake Oriental Restaurant specialises in Indian, Chinese and Japanese Teppenyaki cuisine. Fins Seafood and Grill serves sizzling fish and meat. There are also theme nights, and barbecue lunches on Diani Beach. Maya Spa offers a range of wellness therapies. Water sports include scuba diving, windsurfing, kite surfing, jetski and snorkelling. Coco Jumbo Kids' Club has daily activities for children. The resort also has 2 swimming pools, gym, squash court, tennis court, Jacuzzi, night club and casino. Conferences can be arranged in Oyster Conference Hall, Pearl Boardroom or on the beach.
Diani Reef Resort and Spa won the Most Innovative Retreat in the Amarula Best Retreat in Africa awards in 2008. It is featured in Best 100 Retreats in Africa in 2009.

Leisure Lodge Beach & Golf Resort

 Diani

Leisure Lodge Beach & Golf Resort, Diani Beach, Kenya
PO Box 84383, Diani 80401, Kenya

Tel	+254 40 3203624; +254 40 3202620
Mobile	+254 722 206968; +254 716 430670
Fax	+254 40 3202046
E-mail	exec@leisurelodgeresort.com
Web	www.leisurelodgeresort.com

VISA, MasterCard

Ukunda, LS & CH
15 mins

Leisure Lodge Beach & Golf Resort has extensive grounds stretching from the 18-hole golf course to Diani Beach.

The Bahari Wing has 104 en-suite superior rooms with aircon, telephone, satellite TV, safe, minibar, hairdryer and balconies with views of the sea. The Palm Wing has 36 en-suite rooms with twin beds, the same facilities and balconies with views of the garden.

The Bustani Club is in lush tropical gardens with scenic ponds and streams. The 93 en-suite club rooms have a double and single bed, the same facilities plus a seating area and dressing room. The 16 spacious Oasis villas have, in addition, a private pool for each cluster of 4 or 6 villas. The 4 club suites also have living rooms.

Fishermen's Cove Restaurant serves seafood. Cascadas Restaurant serves Italian cuisine. Diani Hotel Restaurant is in a shaded pavilion. The resort also has 3 more restaurants, 7 bars, shops, freeform swimming pools, a bank, a spa and a casino, and provides nightly entertainment such as live bands and cultural shows. A nearby water sports centre can arrange a variety of activities, including scuba diving, kite surfing, windsurfing, kayaking and deep sea fishing. The Jumbo Junior Club has children's activities.

Leopard Beach Resort & Spa

 Diani

Leopard Beach Resort and Spa, Diani Beach, Kenya
PO Box 34, Ukunda 80400, Kenya

Tel	+254 40 3202721; +254 40 3202110-2; +254 20 2728886
Mobile	+254 724 255280
Fax	+254 40 3203424
E-mail	reservations@leopardbeachresort.com
Web	www.leopardbeachresort.com

VISA, MasterCard,
Amex, Eurocard, JCB

Ukunda, LS & CH
15 mins

Leopard Beach Resort and Spa is set in 25 acres of beachfront tropical gardens. The 158 en-suite rooms are made up of 70 standard rooms, 20 superior garden view rooms, 48 superior sea facing rooms, 7 suites, 10 Chui class cottages with private gardens or patios and 3 luxury villas. All rooms are equipped with aircon, satellite TV, telephone, kettle, hairdryer and minibar. The suites also have DVD players, living areas and power-showers or Jacuzzis.

Chui Grill, the award winning Chaines des Rotisseurs restaurant, offers fresh seafood and grills. Horizon Restaurant and Terrace serves buffet breakfast and table d'hote lunch and dinner. Cultural nights take place on the Nyama Choma Terrace, barbecues on Coco Beach and private functions on Kusini Beach. The resort also has Pizza n Pasta Tornati, Tutti Frutti ice cream parlour, Kalani coffee lounge, the Pool Bistro, Mario's aircon cocktail lounge, Marco's alfresco bar and Mahogany disco. The SX PADI centre offers scuba diving, boat trips, kayaking, kite surfing, deep sea fishing and more. The resort also boasts the Uzuri Spa, the Fitness Forest, the Afya Gym, the Athena Conference Centre and the Leopard's Lair Boardroom. Other activities include tennis, water polo, aerobics and beach volleyball. Entertainment includes live bands, acrobatic shows, traditional dancers, magic shows and cabarets.

Warandale Cottages   Diani

Warandale Cottages, nr Colliers Centre, Diani, South Coast, Kenya
PO Box 11, Ukunda 80400, Kenya
Tel
Mobile   +254 724 923585
Fax
E-mail   warandalecottages@yahoo.com
Web   www.warandale.com

         Ukunda, LS & CH
         10 mins

On a coral outcrop overlooking Diani Beach, Warandale Cottages are a collection of attractive and original self-catering cottages. The cottages are all designed slightly differently, with rooms of unusual shapes and interesting local artwork. Warandale Cottages and Kijiji Cottages were originally a single entity, but are now managed separately. The 2 sets of cottages share the same compound, entrance road and swimming pool. Warandale Cottages are 6 cottages. There are 3 1-bedroom cottages, 2 2-bedroom cottages and 1 3-bedroom cottage. All cottages have a fully equipped kitchen, living room and terrace with dining table, chairs and sunbeds. The cottages have terracotta tiled floors, whitewashed walls and thatched roofs. They are surrounded by lush gardens; some overlook the beach while others overlook the gardens. They have bookshelves filled with books, local artefacts and African paintings. A flight of stone steps leads down to the beach. Each cottage is staffed by a housekeeper and chef. Local vendors come to the cottages daily with fresh seafood and vegetables. There is also a nearby shopping centre, and several nearby restaurants and bars. Tours, excursions and water sports can be booked with local tour agents and on Diani Beach.

Kijiji Cottages   Diani

Kijiji Cottages, nr Colliers Centre, Diani Beach, South Coast, Kenya
PO Box 11, Ukunda 80400, Kenya
Tel
Mobile   +254 721 128852; +254 724 255473
Fax
E-mail   info@kijijicottages.com / komba.cottage@yahoo.fr
Web   www.kijijicottages.com / www.kombacottage-kenya.com

         Ukunda, LS & CH
         15 mins

Kijiji Cottages, meaning small village in Swahili, is a collection of attractive self-catering cottages on a coral outcrop overlooking Diani Beach. The cottages are all individually owned, and can be rented either from Kijiji Cottages, or directly from their owners. Kijiji Cottages and Warandale Cottages were originally a single entity, but are now managed separately. The 2 sets of cottages share the same compound, entrance road and swimming pool.
Kijiji Cottages has 6 self-catering cottages; 4 of the cottages can be booked through Kijiji Cottages, while the other 2 can be booked through Komba Cottage. The cottages are whitewashed, with thatched roofs. They have 1, 2 or 3 en-suite bedrooms, fully equipped kitchen, living room and terrace. All the cottages are designed slightly differently, and the furnishings are chosen by their owners. All have bookshelves filled with books and African artefacts and artwork. A flight of stone steps leads down to the beach. Each cottage is staffed by a housekeeper and cook. Security guards patrol the compound.
Local vendors come to the cottages daily with fresh seafood and vegetables. There is also a nearby shopping centre, and several nearby restaurants and bars. Tours, excursions and water sports can be booked with local tour agents and on Diani Beach.

Coral Beach Cottages and Apartments

Diani

Coral Beach Cottages and Apartments, opp Colliers Centre, Diani Beach
PO Box 168, Ukunda 80400, Kenya

Tel	+254 40 3202052; +254 40 3202053
Mobile	+254 733 777176
Fax	+254 40 3202053
E-mail	info@coralbeachcottages.com
Web	www.coralbeachcottages.com

 Ukunda, LS & CH
10 mins

VISA

Coral Beach Cottages and Apartments are in beachfront gardens that fringe Diani Beach. The self-catering cottages surround an attractive freeform swimming pool, while the apartments overlook the garden.

There are 17 cottages and 13 apartments. The cottages are whitewashed, with thatched roofs, and have 1, 2 or 3 en-suite bedrooms. All cottages have a fully equipped kitchen, living room with satellite TV and a large terrace with dining table and chairs. The apartments are in a whitewashed block near reception. They have 1 en-suite bedroom, fully equipped kitchen, living room and balcony with a view of the garden. All bedrooms have either aircon or fan, and are equipped with mosquito nets. The water is heated by solar power, and there is a backup generator. A masseuse offers massage, manicure and pedicure.

African Pot is a round thatched restaurant at the entrance to the compound. The walls are decorated with bright murals of African scenes. The restaurant serves African and Indian dishes such as nyama choma grilled meats, mutton Masala, chicken jeera and grilled fish. The bar has a good selection of soft drinks, beers and spirits, as well as a wine list. Tours, excursions and water sports can all be booked at the nearby Colliers Centre or on Diani Beach.

Diani Campsite and Cottages

Diani

Diani Campsite and Cottages, opp Petro Station, Diani Beach, Kenya
PO Box 5019, Diani 80401, Kenya

Tel	+254 40 3203192
Mobile	+254 722 683900
Fax	
E-mail	dianicampsite@yahoo.com
Web	www.dianicampsite.com

  Ukunda, LS & CH
10 mins

Established in 2003, Diani Campsite and Cottages has a collection of bandas, rooms and tents. Located almost opposite the Petro station in the centre of Diani, the campsite is only a short walk from Diani Beach.

There are 4 1-bedroom bandas, 5 2-bedroom bandas and 1 3-bedroom banda. Each banda is attractively painted and thatched, and has double bedrooms, bathroom, living room and fully equipped kitchen. There is also a block of 4 en-suite rooms. The campsite has a camp house with cooking area, library, showers and WCs. Tents, mattresses and other camping equipment are available for rent.

The thatched open air restaurant is decorated with floor to ceiling murals of African scenes, and is equipped with satellite TV. It serves a broad Kenyan and international menu, including steaks, grilled tuna in garlic butter, prawns pilipili, lobster thermidor, pizzas and nyama choma grilled meats. The bar is well stocked with soft drinks, beers and spirits. There is also a health bar with freshly squeezed fruit juices. Diani Campsite and Cottages tries to make as little impact on the environment as possible; there is a strict policy of keeping the garden free of plastic and all food waste is composted.

Swahili Beach

Diani

Swahili Beach, Diani Beach, South Coast, Kenya
PO Box 5202, Diani 80401, Kenya

Tel	+254 40 3201130; +254 40 3201140
Mobile	+254 733 834325; +254 722 610549; +254 726 067757
Fax	+254 40 3201133
E-mail	reservations@swahilibeach.com
Web	www.swahilibeach.com

VISA, MasterCard   Ukunda, LS & CH 10 mins

Swahili Beach, a luxurious and sophisticated resort, was established in 2011. The resort blends the architecture of the East African coast with the influences of Arabia, India and Zanzibar. It was designed with state of the art technologies to ensure minimum ecological impact.

There are 140 en-suite rooms, made up of 16 standard, 110 superior and 14 executive suites. All rooms are furnished with Swahili furniture and equipped with flat screen TV, minibar, electronic safe, WiFi and aircon. Standard rooms have views of the gardens and cascading swimming pools. Superior rooms have views of the ocean and include an extended sitting room. Executive suites have views of the ocean and include a lounge, dining veranda and private kitchen.

The Majilis serves buffet; East to East serves a fusion of Indian and Swahili cuisine; the Champagne and Oyster Bar serves seafood; Baharini serves Italian cuisine. The many bars include a swim-up poolside bar.

The Spa and Fitness Centre has 6 treatment rooms and a wide selection of treatments. The gym has cardiovascular machines, isotonic equipment and weights. The 2 fully equipped conference rooms seat 150 pax and 50 pax. There is also a hair and beauty salon, children's club and water sports centre offering a full range of beach and ocean activities.

LTI Kaskazi Beach Hotel

Diani

LTI Kaskazi Beach Hotel, Diani Beach, South Coast, Kenya
PO Box 135, Ukunda 80400, Kenya

Tel	+254 40 3203725; +254 40 3203771-9
Mobile	+254 40 3300114
Fax	+254 40 3202233
E-mail	sales@kaskazibeachhotel.com
Web	www.kaskazibeachhotel.com

 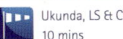

VISA, MasterCard   Ukunda, LS & CH 10 mins

Built in Moorish style, LTI Kaskazi Beach Hotel has white walls set with graceful arches. The hotel is in a horseshoe shape around its swimming pool and landscaped garden, and faces directly onto Diani Beach.

There are 191 en-suite rooms, all with aircon, telephone, safe rental, wooden floors, sitting area, furnished balconies and mini fridges. Some of the rooms have a sea view and others overlook the gardens. Karibu Restaurant serves buffet breakfast, lunch, tea and dinner. Aladdin's Grill Room serves a la carte dinners, reservation necessary. Drinks are served in the Lounge Bar, the Cocktail Bar and the Beach Bar. An entertainment team offers a variety of activities including sports and games during the day and shows at night.

The hotel has an open lobby, cyber café, boutique, hairdresser, gift shop and TV room. The freeform swimming pool is large enough for sporting activities. The conference room seats 80 pax and the boardroom seats 50, theatre style. Both are equipped with audio visual equipment including projector and PA system. The hotel also has teambuilding facilities. Nearby water sports and activity centres offer a range of land and water activities, including scuba diving, quad biking, kite surfing, windsurfing and dhow boat trips.

Alfajiri Villas Diani

Alfajiri Villas, Diani Beach, South Coast, Kenya
PO Box 454, Ukunda 80400, Kenya

Tel	+254 40 3202630; +39 3485100972
Mobile	+254 733 630491; +254 722 727876
Fax	+254 40 3202218
E-mail	molinaro@africaonline.co.ke
Web	www.alfajirivillas.com

 All major cards   Ukunda, LS & CH
10 mins

Alfajiri Villas are 3 elegant villas on coral cliffs, with magnificent views of the coastline. The villas are adorned with Lamu doors, African artefacts and flowing fabrics.

The Cliff Villa, Caribbean style, has 2 double bedrooms, 1 twin room and 1 triple room, all en-suite with aircon. It also has a dining room, sitting room, kitchen and a large veranda. The Garden Villa, African style and adorned with African artefacts, has 4 en-suite double bedrooms. The Beach Villa has 4 en-suite double bedrooms. Chic furniture and artefacts have been collected from around the world. Each villa has a private swimming pool and massage gazebo.

The villas are serviced by 25 staff. Meals are prepared according to the guests' requirements. Fresh seafood, such as crab, prawns, fish and lobster, is brought from the beach daily. Parma ham and cheeses are flown in from Europe, while fresh salads, vegetables and fruits are picked locally. Activities included in the rate are massage, yoga, reflexology, snorkelling, boat trips, windsurfing, gym, sauna, tennis, squash and golf inclusive of green fees and clubs. A vehicle is available for local excursions. Other water sports, safaris and excursions can be arranged.

Alfajiri won the 2002 Harpers and Queen Award for the private villa providing the best service worldwide.

Diani Forest Lodge Diani

Diani Forest Lodge, off Mombasa-Diani Highway, Diani, Kenya
PO Box 1005, Ukunda 80400, Kenya

Tel	
Mobile	+254 733 791685
Fax	
E-mail	enkironji@yahoo.com
Web	

   Ukunda, LS & CH
30 mins

Diani Forest Lodge offers conferences and seminars in the forest not far from Diani Beach. The lodge is located just off the Diani-Mombasa Highway, almost opposite the Diani junction. It is surrounded by coastal forest and local villages.

There are 66 en-suite rooms, made up of doubles and twins. The restaurant serves a predominantly Kenyan menu, with a few international dishes. Dishes include stews, curries, salads, sandwiches and nyama choma grilled meats served with ugali, chips or chapatti. There are 3 conference rooms. The largest seats 100 pax, another seats 60 and the smallest seats 30. Conference equipment is not provided; projector and PA system should be hired externally if required. Workshops, seminars and functions can be catered for.

The shops, restaurants, bars and discos of Diani are within easy reach of the lodge, either by private car, taxi or public transport. Water sports centres are also easily accessible, with activities including scuba diving, snorkelling, kite surfing and boat trips. Local travel agents can assist with travel within Kenya, and can book safaris and excursions.

PrideInn Hotel Diani

Diani

PrideInn Hotel Diani, Diani, South Coast, Kenya
PO Box 66969, Nairobi 00200, Kenya
Tel	+254 20 8000415-6
Mobile	+254 725 497815
Fax	
E-mail	stay@prideinn.co.ke
Web	www.prideinn.co.ke

     Ukunda, LS & CH
10 mins

PrideInn Hotel Diani is a whitewashed building in Diani, entered through a white arch printed with the name PrideInn Hotel Diani. Its location makes it convenient for all the shops, businesses, restaurants and bars of this vibrant strip of coast.

There are singles, doubles and family rooms. All rooms are en-suite, and some have aircon. They are furnished with polished wooden beds and adorned with bright coastal fabrics. The swimming pool is surrounded by a sunbathing deck, and shaded by palm trees and thatched sun umbrellas. The thatched lounge beside the pool, furnished with coastal sofas and armchairs, makes a restful place to spend the day. The restaurant has a varied international menu, including Indian and Swahili cuisines, as well as seafood and popular international dishes. There is a secure car park. PrideInn Hotel Diani's sister hotels are PrideInn Hotel Nairobi, PrideInn Hotel Mombasa and PrideInn Hotel Nyali, all part of the Glory Safaris group. Glory Safaris also offers car hire on a short or long-term basis, and runs a driving school. Glory Safaris books tours and safaris and has a selection of activity packages in Kenya and Tanzania.

Simba Village

Diani

Simba Village, nr Diani Beach Shopping Centre, Diani, South Coast
PO Box 5703, Ukunda 80400, Kenya
Tel	+254 40 3202334
Mobile	+254 738 079390; +254 737 450917
Fax	+254 40 3202334
E-mail	office@simba-apartments.com
Web	www.simba-apartments.com

 Ukunda, LS & CH
10 mins

Simba Village is a charming apartment complex, designed in Moorish style. The self-catering apartments are set in tropical gardens, and face onto a swimming pool. The compound is located next to Diani Beach Shopping Centre, near Ukunda Airstrip, which makes it convenient for the shops, businesses, restaurants and bars of Diani.

There are 13 apartments, made up of 9 studios, 2 suites and 2 deluxe apartments. The studios are open plan, and have an en-suite bedroom and fully equipped kitchen. The suites have an en-suite double room, fully equipped kitchen and living room. The deluxe apartments have 3 bedrooms, 1 of which is en-suite and the other 2 sharing a bathroom, a fully equipped kitchen and a living room. A housekeeper is available for cleaning and changing towels and bed linen. Water and electricity are charged based on consumption. Satellite TV packages are also available and charged extra. The apartments are available on a weekly or monthly basis. Tours, excursions and safaris can be booked with local tour agents. Water sports including kite surfing, scuba diving, snorkelling and windsurfing can be booked on Diani Beach. Boat trips and fishing trips can also be booked locally.

Watano House

Diani

Watano House, opp Diani Beach Shopping Centre, Diani, South Coast
PO Box 252, Ukunda 80400, Kenya
Tel
Mobile +254 720 293156
Fax
E-mail info@watanohouse.com
Web www.watanohouse.com

   Ukunda, LS & CH
10 mins

One of the original houses in Diani, Watano House is an attractive and spacious beachfront villa. Behind Watano House, also with access to the beach, are 2 smaller cottages available for rent. The compound can be taken as a whole, or the house and cottages can be taken separately. Watano House has 8 bedrooms, made up of 7 en-suite double rooms, and a room with bunk beds adjoining the master bedroom, suitable for children. All rooms have fans and mosquito nets; 1 room has aircon. There is a large open plan living and dining area, a fully equipped kitchen and a sea facing veranda running the length of the house. The swimming pool, sunbathing terrace and garden all overlook the beach. The house is staffed with housekeeper, gardener, security guard and chef. Local vendors bring fresh fish, seafood and vegetables to the house daily. Guests are welcome to discuss their preferred menu with the chef.

Dolly house is a 1-room studio with 4-poster bed, fridge, gas cooker, bathroom and veranda. The Gatehouse has 2 twin bedrooms, fully equipped kitchen, bathroom and outside living and dining area. Both cottages are equipped with fans, mosquito nets, towels and bed linen. Water sports, trips and excursions can be booked in Diani.

Diani Sea Resort

Diani

Diani Sea Resort, Diani Beach, South Coast, Kenya
PO Box 37, Ukunda 80400, Kenya
Tel +254 40 3203438
Mobile +254 711 387028
Fax +254 40 3203439
E-mail dianisea@africaonline.co.ke
Web www.dianisea.com

 VISA, MasterCard    Ukunda, LS & CH
10 mins

Diani Sea Resort is set in 4½ hectares of tropical gardens overlooking Diani Beach.
There are 170 en-suite rooms in 2 and 3-floor buildings that face onto palm filled gardens. The superior rooms, with either double or twin beds, have a terrace or balcony, mosquito net, satellite TV and aircon. The family rooms have an additional bedroom. The suites are on the 2nd floor, with balconies overlooking the seafront.
Pwani Restaurant, in the main building, serves buffet breakfast and lunch. Dinner is a themed buffet, except on Saturday when a candlelit, a la carte dinner is served. The Mawimbi restaurant, between the pool and the sunbathing area, serves snacks throughout the day, and Italian dinners for which reservation is necessary.
The large swimming pool surrounds a small island of tropical flowers; the top pool has a slide. The resort also has 2 tennis courts, squash courts, table tennis and mini-golf. The animation team organises activities throughout the day, such as volleyball, football, cultural shows, bingo, acrobatics and a barbecue accompanied by a live band. The resort's reservation desk can book safaris to other parts of Kenya. Nearby water sports centres provide equipment for various beach and ocean activities.

WaterLovers

Diani

WaterLovers, Diani Beach, South Coast, Kenya
PO Box 5444, Diani 80401, Kenya

Tel	+39 348 3009785
Mobile	+254 735 790535; +254 727 008840
Fax	
E-mail	info@waterlovers.it
Web	www.waterlovers.it

 VISA, MasterCard

 Ukunda, LS & CH
10 mins

Combining Mediterranean and Swahili styles, WaterLovers is a charming, small hotel on Diani's beachfront. The hotel provides chic décor and personal service.

The 6 split-level cottages are equipped with aircon, fan, mosquito nets, security box, kettles and SIM cards for guests to use in their personal mobile phones. Both double and triple rooms are available. The cottages are furnished with Swahili and Arabic designs and each has a private veranda overlooking the ocean. The self-catering villa can sleep 8 guests. It has 2 en-suite double bedrooms on the ground floor, a spacious en-suite bedroom with two double beds on the upper floor gallery, a dining area and a fully equipped open kitchen. A private chef can be provided on request. Tides Restaurant has whitewashed Greek style arcades set with wooden ceiling beams. The menu changes daily, with dishes such as roasted pumpkin ravioli in crab and fish ragout and passion fruit mousse with white chocolate flakes. Ocean Spirit Bar serves cocktails, fresh fruit juices and aperitifs, and overlooks both the turtle shaped infinity pool and the beach. The hotel can book boat trips, fishing, snorkelling, visits to golf courses or trips to the marine park on request.

Asha Cottage

Diani

Asha Cottage, Diani Beach, South Coast, Kenya
PO Box 5107, Diani 80401, Kenya

Tel	
Mobile	+254 723 644945; +254 727 624626
Fax	
E-mail	info@ashacottages.com
Web	www.ashacottages.com

 VISA

 Ukunda, LS & CH
10 mins

Asha Cottage is a seafront, family-run cottage with a commitment to responsible tourism. The cottage is built in Swahili style in an acre of attractive beachfront gardens. There are 5 en-suite bedrooms, each decorated with a combination of African fabrics, Afghan rugs and European art. They have terracotta tiles and solid wooden furniture, and are equipped with mosquito net, fan and aircon. The veranda has a communal seating area and overlooks the swimming pool. The Ledge serves table d'hote lunch and dinner, offering a selection of homemade soups, salads and seafood. The menu changes daily. The garden gazebo offers a range of beauty treatments, such as full body massage, back, neck and shoulder massage, manicure, pedicure and reflexology. The snooker room has aircon and a selection of books. An ngalawa boat is available for excursions and snorkelling. Asha Cottage can arrange trips to Shimba Hills, Wasini Island and Kisite Mpunguti Marine Park, as well as safaris to destinations in Kenya. Asha Cottage uses solar power, recycles waste, collects rainwater and composts food waste. It also donates a fixed percentage of its profit to 2 organisations working to protect the environment and support social development. The Asha Boutique hosts the Social Responsibility Corner which provides information about these organisations.

Diani Marine Divers Village

Diani

Diani Marine Divers Village, Diani Beach, South Coast, Kenya
Diani Marine Ltd, PO Box 340, Ukunda 80400, Kenya
Tel +254 40 3202367; +254 40 3203451
Mobile
Fax +254 40 3203452
E-mail info@dianimarine.com
Web www.dianimarine.com

VISA, MasterCard   Ukunda, LS & CH 15 mins

Based around a PADI 5 star dive centre, Diani Marine Divers Village has both rooms and cottages set in tropical gardens. The centre has 3 dive boats and modern equipment, and is also involved in the protection of marine life. The Village consists of 10 en-suite rooms set around an open courtyard, made up of 7 doubles, 2 twins and 1 triple. The rooms all have fans, and some also have fridge and basin. Breakfast is served in a breakfast pavilion, equipped with WiFi.

Colobus House, on the beachfront, has terrace stairs leading directly to the beach. Villa Rosa, somewhat smaller, is set back from the beach. Both houses have 2 ground floor en-suite double rooms with aircon, and 2 1st floor rooms with fan, as well as a living area, dining room and fully equipped kitchen. The Honeymoon Suite has an en-suite double room, living area, open plan kitchen and top floor with romantic double bath. The Safari Tent has an en-suite double room on a wooden platform, with canvas walls and thatched roof.

There is also a swimming pool surrounded by thatched sun umbrellas, pool bar, boutique and massage services. The centre has implemented waste disposal projects, and composts food waste.

Stilts

Diani

Stilts, Diani, South Coast, Kenya
PO Box 5324, Diani 80401, Kenya
Tel
Mobile +254 722 523278; +254 722 823258
Fax
E-mail stiltsdiani@hotmail.com
Web www.stiltsdiani.com

         Ukunda, LS & CH 15 mins

Stilts is an eco-camp and campsite, situated in lush forest near Diani Beach. The camp has budget accommodation for adventurous travellers. There are 2 stone cottages with thatched roofs. Each of these has an en-suite double room and a terrace. There are 5 bandas, raised on stilts, with bamboo walls and simple verandas. There are 8 tents, made up of 6 doubles and 2 singles. 1 tent is shaded by a thatched roof, while the others are in brush woodland. There is also a campsite. A large communal bathroom block is available for guests staying in the bandas and tents, with a laundry area at one end.

A bar and restaurant, high on stilts, serves an international menu including fillet steak, marinated fish fillet, calamari, curries, spaghetti bolognaise and sandwiches. Beneath the restaurant is a strong room, with a safety deposit box allocated to each guest.

The forested garden has stone pathways and a barbecue area.

A noticeboard gives information on local tours, water sports, activities and events. Stilts Diani offers a 5-day trip on a catamaran to Stilts Kiwayu. Stilts is across the road from Forty Thieves Beach Bar; access to the beach is through the bar.

Baobab Beach Cottage
& Desert Rose Beach Cottage

Diani

Baobab & Desert Rose Beach Cottages, Diani, Kenya
Ali Barbour's Group, PO Box 53, Ukunda 80400, Kenya

Tel	+254 40 3202163
Mobile	+254 720 843585; +254 714 456130; +254 710 171303
Fax	+254 40 3202223
E-mail	tracy@flamboyantdiani.com / info@alibarbours.com
Web	www.dianibeachkenya.com

 All major cards   Ukunda, LS & CH 15 mins

Baobab Beach Cottage & Desert Rose Beach Cottage are 2 attractive self-catering cottages in lush gardens. They are set back from Diani Beach, which is approximately 50 metres from the cottages.

Baobab Beach Cottage has 4 en-suite double bedrooms, equipped with fans. The sitting room and veranda overlook the gardens and beyond, the Indian Ocean. Desert Rose Beach Cottage has 2 en-suite double bedrooms and 1 en-suite triple room, all with fans. The spacious lounge is equipped with a bar. The veranda overlooks the gardens, and beyond, the Indian Ocean.

Both cottages have fully equipped kitchens, hot water and generator. All the rooms are equipped with mosquito nets and bed linen. The cottages are each staffed with a cook and cleaners. Guests can discuss their preferred menu with the cook; fresh seafood and vegetables are brought daily by local vendors. Guests staying at the cottages are welcome to use the tennis court and squash court at neighbouring Flamboyant Boutique Hotel. Situated in the centre of Diani, the cottages are within easy reach of shops, restaurants, bars, dive centres and a golf course. Water sports, deep sea fishing and safaris to other destinations in Kenya can be arranged at centres nearby.

Flamboyant Boutique Hotel

Diani

Flamboyant Boutique Hotel, Diani, South Coast, Kenya
Ali Barbour's Group, PO Box 53, Ukunda 80400, Kenya

Tel	+254 40 3202163
Mobile	+254 720 843585; +254 714 456130; +254 710 171303
Fax	+254 40 3202223
E-mail	tracy@flamboyantdiani.com / info@alibarbours.com
Web	www.dianibeachkenya.com

 All major cards   Ukunda, LS & CH 15 mins

Named after the vivid tree in its luxuriant garden, Flamboyant Boutique Hotel was a family house that has been redesigned as an elegant small hotel. The hotel is family run and offers privacy, quality service and attention to detail.

The 10 en-suite rooms are made up of 2 honeymoon suites and 8 standard rooms. 9 rooms have a sea view while 1 has a courtyard view. The rooms can be doubles, twins or triples, and all have aircon, fan, safe, hairdryer, WiFi and power sockets. The cuisine is mainly seafood and includes Swahili coastal specialities. International cuisine and traditional Kenyan dishes are also served.

The hotel has squash and tennis courts, snooker table, barbecue area, large swimming pool and smaller paddling pool. For an extra charge, water sports, deep sea fishing and safaris to other destinations in Kenya can be arranged. The hotel's central location in Diani gives it easy access to shops, restaurants, bars, water sports centres and a golf course.

Flamboyant Boutique Hotel is a romantic venue for weddings, anniversaries and birthdays. The thatched gazebo overlooking the Indian Ocean makes a lovely venue for private parties. The hotel arranges the décor, ceremony and catering according to each individual's preference.

Manyatta Green

Diani

Manyatta Green, Diani, South Coast, Kenya
PO Box 1892, Ukunda 80400, Kenya
Tel
Mobile +254 710 110443
Fax
E-mail
Web

Ukunda, LS & CH
20 mins

Manyatta Green is painted the vivid green that gave it its name. On the opposite side of the road from the beach, Manyatta Green offers budget accommodation not far from the beach. The bar and restaurant face the road; the bright green façade and tall thatched roof cannot be missed. There are 7 apartments in 3 cottages. The apartments are also bright green with thatched roofs. Each apartment has a double bedroom, bathroom, living room, kitchenette and veranda. The bedrooms are equipped with mosquito net and fan. The kitchenettes are equipped with gas cooker, fridge, crockery, cutlery and glassware. The living rooms have sofa, table, armchair and TV with local channels.

The verandas are furnished with plastic garden furniture.

The roadside bar and restaurant has a predominantly Kenyan menu with a few international dishes, such as nyama choma grilled meats with ugali, pan fried goat with chips, spaghetti bolognaise, beef stew with mashed potatoes and Masala chips. The bar serves soft drinks, beers and a few spirits. Guests in the apartments are welcome to order room service from the restaurant. There is also plentiful parking between the road, the bar and the cottages. Shops, restaurants, bars, discos and water sports centres are within easy reach of Manyatta Green.

Diani Sea Lodge

Diani

Diani Sea Lodge, Diani Beach, South Coast, Kenya
PO Box 37, Ukunda 80400, Kenya
Tel +254 40 3203438
Mobile +254 711 387199
Fax +254 40 3203439
E-mail dianisea@africaonline.co.ke
Web www.dianisea.com / www.kenya-hotels.de

 VISA, MasterCard

 Ukunda, LS & CH
15 mins

Set in lush beachfront gardens, Diani Sea Lodge offers a wide selection of activities. The bungalow-style rooms face the garden, the freeform swimming pool or the beach.

There are 161 en-suite rooms, made up of standard, superior, bahari and family rooms. All rooms are fully tiled, and have 4-poster bed, armchairs, coffee table, hairdryer, safe and aircon. Bahari rooms also have king size bed, minibar, satellite TV and their verandas have sea views. The family rooms consist of a double room with adjoining single room. The restaurant serves table d'hote, with dishes such as grilled seafish fillet and roast lamb. Twice a week, barbecues are served, and once a week

is African night. The romantic private dinner for 2 includes lobster, and ends with an Irish coffee and cheese plate. There is also a main bar, pool bar and snack restaurant.

Sports facilities include tennis court, table tennis table, dartboard, pool table and crazy golf course. The health club offers massage and other treatments. The kids' club has an adventure walk, painting and treasure hunt. Daily activities run from 10am to 9pm, and include beach volleyball, pool gymnastics and Beats of Africa. A live band plays on Wednesdays. A travel desk books excursions and safaris. Curios are sold at the poolside every Thursday.

The Sands at Nomad

Diani

The Sands at Nomad, Diani Beach, South Coast, Kenya
PO Box 5066, Diani 80401, Kenya

Tel	
Mobile	+254 725 373888; +254 733 373888; +254 724 262426
Fax	
E-mail	reservations@thesandsatnomad.com
Web	www.thesandsatnomad.com

VISA, MasterCard

Ukunda, LS & CH
20 mins

Originally known for Nomad, its popular beach bar and restaurant, The Sands at Nomad is an elegant boutique hotel. The Venetian stucco building is adorned with traditional Swahili furniture and hand-carved African artefacts. The hotel is set in 25 acres of indigenous coastal forest stretching along Diani Beach.

There are 18 en-suite rooms, 7 beach cottages and 12 luxury suites. All rooms are individually designed, and equipped with aircon, satellite TV and minibar. The suites also have private Jacuzzi, panoramic terrace and large sitting room.

Nomad Beach Bar and Restaurant serves tropical buffet breakfast.

Lunch and dinner offer both a la carte and buffet, with a wide selection of international dishes including seafood, pizzas and pastas. The Juice Bar has freshly squeezed fruit juices and Italian ice cream. The Red Pepper Restaurant serves traditional Kenyan cuisine. Exclusive garden or beachfront barbecues can be arranged.

Forest Breeze offers massage, manicure, pedicure and a selection of beauty treatments. Diving the Crab, in front of the hotel, offers dive courses, wreck exploration and whale shark spotting. Other water sports such as kite surfing, windsurfing, kayaking and deep sea fishing are also available.

Ocean Village Club

Diani

Ocean Village Club, Diani Beach, South Coast, Kenya
PO Box 88, Ukunda 80400, Kenya

Tel	+254 20 2080964
Mobile	+254 735 632188
Fax	+254 20 3502778
E-mail	generalmanager@oceanvillageclubkenya.com
Web	www.oceanvillageclubkenya.com

VISA, MasterCard

Ukunda, LS & CH
20 mins

Ocean Village Club is set in lush tropical gardens on Diani Beach. The club has a selection of whitewashed bungalows of various sizes, and a wide variety of activities and facilities.

There are 36 bungalows, made up of 11 1-bedroom bungalows, 17 2-bedroom bungalows and 8 3-bedroom bungalows. All bungalows have verandas overlooking the gardens. They are furnished with handmade furniture made from local wood, and equipped with mosquito net and aircon. Makuti Restaurant, a large structure of timber and thatch, serves buffet breakfast and dinner. Sails Restaurant, overlooking the sea, serves seafood. The Pool Bar and Sails Bar are both well stocked with soft drinks,

beers, wines and spirits. There is also a TV lounge bar, with a satellite TV showing sports, news and films.

The resort has a swimming pool surrounded by sunbeds, floodlit tennis courts and a curio shop. Sports offered include volleyball, waterpolo, table tennis, darts, petanque and aquagym. The animation team offers a selection of games and shows, including tribal dancing, acrobatic shows, live bands and Swahili lessons. There is also a fitness centre, massage salon and African hairdresser. For an extra charge, safaris, excursions, snorkelling, scuba diving and windsurfing can be arranged. An 18-hole golf course is located near the resort.

507

Papillon Lagoon Reef Hotel   Diani

Papillon Lagoon Reef Hotel, Diani Beach, South Coast, Kenya
Rex Resorts, PO Box 5292, Diani 80401, Kenya

Tel	+254 20 2331338
Mobile	+254 725 204777; +254 733 202213
Fax	+254 20 2331337
E-mail	safari.uk@rexsafaris.com
Web	www.rexresorts.com/papillon_lagoon_reef

VISA, MasterCard   Ukunda, LS & CH 20 mins

Papillon Lagoon Reef Hotel is an all inclusive resort on Diani Beach. The hotel has Swahili style architecture and is set in manicured gardens studded with ancient baobabs.

The 119 en-suite rooms are made up of 25 cottage rooms, 76 garden rooms and 18 beachfront rooms. The cottage rooms have 3 or 4 beds, aircon, telephone, safe, hairdryer and balconies overlooking the garden. The garden rooms are twins or doubles with the same facilities as cottage rooms. The beachfront rooms have 4-poster beds, aircon, fridge, TV, telephone, safe, hairdryer and balconies overlooking the beach.

Baobab Restaurant serves buffets of international and Kenyan cuisine.

Zig Zag Bar and Restaurant serves breakfast, lunch and barbecues by the pool, and has nightly entertainment such as live bands, traditional dancing and acrobatic shows. The Pool Bar has a counter that guests can swim to and the Beach Bar is at the beachfront. Jasmini Room is available for conferences of 70 pax.

Windsurfing, snorkelling and beach fishing are included in the rate. Other activities available for an additional cost include scuba diving, floodlit tennis, water-skiing, sports tuition and car hire. Children's activities include table tennis, pool, bar football, board games, beach football and volleyball.

Baobab Beach Resort & Spa   Diani

Baobab Beach Resort & Spa, Diani Beach, South Coast, Kenya
PO Box 32, Ukunda 80400, Kenya

Tel	+254 20 2057094-7
Mobile	+254 754 222061-3; +254 786 333303; +254 789 333303
Fax	+254 20 2057092
E-mail	reservations@baobab-beach-resort.com
Web	www.baobab-beach-resort.com

VISA, MasterCard, Amex Travellers Cheques   Ukunda, LS & CH 20 mins

Set in indigenous forests, Baobab Beach Resort & Spa is surrounded by grounds humming with over 100 species of birds, 4 species of monkeys and other forest dwelling wildlife. The resort won the TUI Environmental Champion Award in 2006 and 2007.

The Baobab main building has 87 sea facing rooms. There are also 68 garden bungalows with a garden view and 28 superior bungalows with partial sea view. The new Maridadi Wing has 36 superior rooms, 8 deluxe rooms and 12 deluxe bungalows, all with views of the sea or the 3-tier cascading pool. All rooms are en-suite and well equipped. Interconnecting rooms and rooms for guests with disabilities are available. Karibu Restaurant serves buffet breakfast, lunch and dinner, and has evening entertainment. Maridadi Restaurant, overlooking the beach, serves light lunches and Asian buffet dinners. Marhaba Restaurant, not included in full board, serves a la carte seafood. Jambo Pool Bar has seats in the pool and beside it. Porini Amphitheatre is an open air disco. Afya Bora Wellness Club and Spa has a fully equipped gym and offers treatments including aromatic massage, mud wrap and Jacuzzi. Complimentary activities include archery, aquafit, beach volleyball and tennis. Activities available for a surcharge include scuba diving, deep sea fishing, sailing and golf.

Galu Beach Retreat

Galu

Galu Beach Retreat, Galu Beach, South Coast, Kenya
Destination Adventures Ltd., PO Box 5480, Ukunda 80400, Kenya
Tel +254 40 3203611
Mobile +254 733 435341
Fax
E-mail reservations@destination-adventures.com
Web www.destination-adventures.com

Ukunda, LS & CH
20 mins

Galu Beach Retreat is a boutique hotel on Galu Beach. As well as striking beach views, the retreat offers yoga sessions and private seafood dinners. Galu Beach Retreat was formerly called Shaanti Holistic Retreat. There are 8 en-suite rooms and 2 luxury suites. All the rooms have glass fronts with views of the beach. They are furnished with Lamu furniture including 4-poster beds and adorned with Moroccan fabrics. The suites have a raised bedroom looking onto the beach through a circular window, a living room with 2 Lamu sofas and a walk-in dressing room. Breakfast is served by a personal butler on the guests' veranda.

A circular cocktail bar is located at the beachfront. The restaurant, over the bar, gives panoramic views of the beach and serves an international menu including vegetarian options and seafood. A small thatched rondavel in the garden can be booked for private lobster dinners with advance notice. This is an adult only retreat.

Morning and evening yoga sessions with a yogi from India take place on a sea facing platform and are open to all. The retreat also has an ocean view Jacuzzi and beachfront star baths. Massage rondavals beside the swimming pool offer treatments such as Swedish massage, aromatherapy, reflexology and facials.

Four Twenty South

Galu

Four Twenty South, Galu Beach, South Coast, Kenya
PO Box 5015, Diani 80400, Kenya
Tel
Mobile +254 722 901806
Fax
E-mail info@fourtwentysouth.com
Web www.fourtwentysouth.com

Ukunda, LS & CH
20 mins

Four Twenty South is named for its latitude, since at the time it was built there was nothing on the site to locate it. This delightful collection of beachfront cottages was built in the 1950s, and has been run by the same family since 1966.

There are 6 well-spaced cottages in palm fringed gardens facing the beach. The cottages have 2, 3 or 4 bedrooms, kitchen, living room, dining room and veranda. They are elegantly furnished with solid wooden furniture, cream linens and ornamental lamps. Each cottage is comprehensively equipped, down to the beach towels, and staffed by a maid and chef. The kitchens are fully equipped, including condiments like spices, olive oil and balsamic vinegar. The rooms are cooled by fans, and have games such as scrabble, chess and backgammon. Mobile telephone line and internet connection are available on request. Waste is disposed of responsibly, and food waste is composted for the lush gardens.

The cottages recreate the era in which they were established. There is no aircon, swimming pool or television. Fresh fish, seafood, fruit and vegetables are brought to the door by local vendors. Guests make their own timetables and create their menus with their private chef.

Diani Beachalets

Galu

Diani Beachalets, Galu Beach, South Coast, Kenya
PO Box 5076, Diani 80400, Kenya

Tel	+254 40 3202180
Mobile	+254 734 408324
Fax	
E-mail	info@dianibeachalets.com
Web	www.dianibeachalets.com

   Ukunda, LS & CH
20 mins

Diani Beachalets is a collection of self-catering bandas and cottages located in beachfront gardens. The cottages offer budget accommodation on Galu Beach.

There are 6 bandas, 4 1-bedroom cottages, 5 2-bedroom cottages, 2 3-bedroom cottages and 1 4-bedroom cottage. The bandas have communal facilities, including kitchen, showers and WC. The cottages have whitewashed exteriors and red tiled roofs. All cottages face the gardens which have a wide variety of birds, lizards and monkeys; some also face the sea. Each cottage has a living area and a simple kitchen. Cooks and cleaners are available on request at a daily rate. A shop on site sells a selection of food and toiletries, as well as soft drinks, beers, wines and spirits. Local vendors bring fresh fruit, vegetables and fish to the cottages every day.

Shops, restaurants, bars and discos are within easy reach of the cottages, either by private car, taxi or public transport. Water sports centres are also easily accessible, with activities including scuba diving, snorkelling, kite surfing and boat trips. Local travel agents can assist with travel within Kenya, and can book safaris and excursions.

Malaika Holiday Villas

Galu

Malaika Holiday Villas, Galu, South Coast, Kenya
PO Box 1063, Ukunda 80400, Kenya

Tel	
Mobile	+254 729 812073
Fax	
E-mail	info@malaikaholidayvillas.com
Web	www.malaikaholidayvillas.com

  Ukunda, LS & CH
25 mins

Set in manicured lawns with stone pathways and large shady trees, Malaika Holiday Villas take their name from the Swahili for little angels. The self-catering cottages surround a swimming pool and a children's playground, and are located a short distance from Diani Beach.

There are 4 cottages, made up of 2 2-bedroom cottages and 2 1-bedroom cottages. The cottage exteriors are forest green with white finishing, and are topped with high thatched roofs to maximise the breeze. All the cottages are fully furnished with local furniture, and contain en-suite bedrooms, a sitting room, fully equipped kitchen and veranda. They have tiled floors, and are equipped with TV, fridge and fan. There is a backup generator in case of power cuts. The cottages can be taken on a short, medium or long-term basis. Staff to cook, clean and babysit can be arranged for a surcharge.

For those who choose not to cook, there is a restaurant with an international menu and a bar with a selection of soft drinks, beers and spirits. Shops, restaurants, bars and discos are within easy reach of the cottages, either by private car, taxi or public transport. A full range of water sports is available on Diani Beach.

Turawa Galu

Turawa, Galu, South Coast, Kenya
PO Box 5246, Diani 80400, Kenya
Tel
Mobile   +254 724 414244; +254 716 820390
Fax
E-mail   info@kenya-urlaub.com
Web   www.kenya-urlaub.com

      Ukunda, LS & CH
                                       25 mins

Turawa, meaning swamp of buffalo in German, is a long low house containing self-catering apartments. The whitewashed house with thatched roof has a long veranda which runs the length of the house. The garden is bright with bougainvillea.

There are 3 apartments. All contain 2 en-suite double bedrooms and an open plan kitchen and living room. The apartments are equipped with fan, safe, fridge and bed linen, and adorned with local furniture and accessories. In the centre of the house is a large, well equipped kitchen and a communal sitting room, equipped with sofas, books, TV with local channels and a selection of DVDs.

The apartments are let on a weekly basis. This includes daily cleaning, use of the garden and garden furniture and the car park. Laundry, dry cleaning, massage and a private cook can be arranged for a surcharge. Shops, restaurants, bars and discos are within easy reach of the house, either by private car, taxi or public transport. Water sports including scuba diving, kite surfing, kayaking and boat trips are available on Diani Beach, a short distance away. Turawa can arrange airport transfers, as well as excursions and safaris to places of interest in Kenya.

Almanara Diani Beach Resort Galu

Almanara Diani Beach Resort, Galu Beach, South Coast, Kenya
PO Box 5468, Diani 80401, Kenya
Tel   +254 20 2138501-3; +254 20 2138505
Mobile   +254 720 779228
Fax   +254 20 2138504
E-mail   info@almanararesort.com
Web   www.almanararesort.com

 VISA, MasterCard   Ukunda, LS & CH
                                                25 mins

Almanara Diani Beach Resort is an exclusive collection of private villas in lush beachfront gardens.

The 6 executive villas each have 3 en-suite double bedrooms, an open plan dining and living area, a study area with PC, printer, WiFi and international telephone, a fully stocked kitchen, a rooftop terrace and a spacious veranda. The master bedroom has a safe and a flat screen satellite TV with DVD player. A chef, maid and waiter are allocated to each villa. The Presidential Villa is entered by way of a magnificent glass walkway over a Koi pond. It has 5 ocean view double bedrooms, 7 bathrooms, a fully equipped study, WiFi throughout, a private gym, a games room, a massage room, a private infinity swimming pool, a Jacuzzi and a team of staff including chef, maid, waiters and security guards. Guests have the use of a chauffeur-driven Toyota VX land cruiser.

Sails, a beachfront bar and restaurant, serves haute cuisine and specialises in seafood. There is also a swimming pool with sunken pool bar and a Jacuzzi. The Cloud Nine Health Spa provides a full range of treatments. The KiLeo Water Sports Centre has courses and equipment for hire. The Wasi Wasi Wenu, Almanara's own ngalawa, is available for boat rides.

South Coast

 Accommodation Guide   511

Galu Sea Lodge Galu

Galu Sea Lodge, Galu Beach, South Coast, Kenya
PO Box 5556, Diani 80401, Kenya

Tel	+254 40 3203307
Mobile	+254 727 300166; +254 733 624515
Fax	
E-mail	galusealodge@hotgossip.co.ke
Web	www.galusealodge.net

 VISA    Ukunda, LS & CH 25 mins

Galu Sea Lodge is a collection of self-catering cottages in attractive gardens sloping down to Galu Beach. The swimming pool, at the foot of the gardens, is surrounded by a sundeck overlooking the beach.

There are 7 2-floor cottages, all whitewashed with thatched roofs. On the ground floor, each cottage has a sitting room, dining room and kitchen fully equipped for 6 pax, including gas cooker, fridge, crockery and cutlery. There is also a WC and a veranda with a view. On the 1st floor, each cottage has 3 double bedrooms, 2 bathrooms and a large balcony overlooking the beach. Each cottage is staffed by a housekeeper and chef. Fresh fish, seafood, fruit and vegetables are brought to the door by local vendors. Guests make their own timetables and create their menus with their private chef.

The cottages are equipped with WiFi. The manager can assist with booking safaris and other excursions. Shops, restaurants, bars and discos are within easy reach of the cottages, either by private car, taxi or public transport. Water sports centres are also easily accessible, with activities including scuba diving, snorkelling, kite surfing, deep sea fishing and boat trips.

Simba and Oryx Cottages Galu

Simba and Oryx Cottages, Galu Beach, South Coast, Kenya
PO Box 5305, Diani 80401, Kenya

Tel	
Mobile	+254 727 299911
Fax	
E-mail	info@simba-oryx.com
Web	www.simba-oryx.com

       Ukunda, LS & CH 25 mins

Simba and Oryx, or Lion and Oryx, is a name taken from the local story of a lioness that found and took care of an abandoned baby oryx. They are also the 2 favourite animals of the cottages' owner. Located on Galu Beach, at the southern end of Diani Beach, Simba and Oryx Cottages are 2 rows of self-catering, whitewashed thatched cottages in beachfront gardens. The 10 self-catering cottages sleep between 2 and 6 guests. The larger cottages have 2 triple bedrooms and the smaller ones have 1 double bedroom. Each cottage is furnished in coastal African style with comfortable Mwule beds, and has an open plan dining and sitting room and a granite kitchen equipped with gas cooker, fridge, crockery and cutlery.

Bed linen, towels and mosquito nets are also provided. The cottages all have verandas overlooking the beach and plentiful parking.

Activities include swimming, snorkelling and long beach walks. It is possible to book boat rides, deep sea fishing and diving with local boat operators. Trips to the Shimba Hills National Reserve and boat trips to Wasini Island for snorkelling and swimming with dolphins can be booked at nearby travel agents. Shops, restaurants, bars and discos are within easy reach of the cottages, either by private car, taxi or public transport.

Mzima

Galu

Mzima, Galu Beach, South Coast, Kenya
PO Box 5625, Diani 80401, Kenya
Tel
Mobile +254 724 699240
Fax
E-mail info@mzima.co.ke
Web www.mzima.co.ke

 VISA, MasterCard   Ukunda, LS & CH 25 mins

With a name that means embodied perfection in Swahili, Mzima offers luxury, wellness and balanced living. Mzima was established in 2011 and combines coastal architecture with that of ancient Rome. The resort faces directly onto Galu Beach, and is surrounded by lush tropical gardens and a swimming pool. There are 5 en-suite double rooms. The rooms are adorned with Asian and Swahili handcrafted furniture and equipped with aircon and WiFi. Frangipani Cottage is a self-catering cottage, with a double and twin room, bathroom, living room with satellite TV, dining room, fully equipped kitchen and veranda. The cottage also has a plunge pool and barbecue area.

The resort serves a fusion of local and continental cuisine. Breakfast and lunch are made up of fresh, healthy dishes and dinner is table d'hote specialising in fish and seafood. The spa offers massage, manicure, pedicure, aromatherapy and reflexology. The main house has a reading room with flat screen satellite TV and DVD.

Activities include zumba, yoga, water aerobics, bicycling to Kaya Forest and sundowners. Water sports include kite surfing, windsurfing, scuba diving, snorkelling, dhow cruises, horse riding and boat trips to Funzi Island and Wasini Island. Participation in local community projects and visits to local schools, villages and trading centres can be arranged.

Sentido Neptune Paradise Beach Resort

Galu

Sentido Neptune Paradise Beach Resort, Galu Beach, Kenya
PO Box 696, Ukunda 80400, Kenya
Tel +254 40 3202350
Mobile +254 716 016000; +254 731 609881
Fax +254 20 3549979
E-mail info.neptuneparadise@sentidohotels.com
Web www.sentidohotels.com

VISA, MasterCard   Ukunda, LS & CH 25 mins

Set in 25 acres of tropical gardens, Sentido Neptune Paradise Beach Resort has a wide selection of facilities and activities.

The 92 en-suite superior rooms are housed in whitewashed thatched cottages, and equipped with telephone, satellite TV, WiFi, safe, kettle, aircon and hairdryer, and have a balcony or terrace.

The main restaurant seats 200 pax and serves international buffets. Olive Kitchen, an a la carte restaurant, serves seafood. The resort also has a snack bar, pool bar and boat bar. The spa offers massages and beauty treatments. The Miniclub organises games and activities for children aged between 4 and 12 in the playground and in the children's section of the pool.

The resort, together with adjoining sister resort, Sentido Neptune Village Beach Resort, offers a wide variety of sports and water sports including aerobics, aquagym, beginners' diving, tennis, table tennis, beach volleyball, darts and mini golf. For an extra charge, windsurfing, surfing, snorkelling, scuba diving and deep sea fishing can be arranged. The resort has bikes for rent. Trips to a nearby golf course, safaris and other excursions can also be arranged. A daily newsletter gives information on the region and the day's activities and entertainment programme. A holiday concierge assists guests with the planning of their activities.

Sentido Neptune Village Beach Resort

Galu

Sentido Neptune Village Beach Resort, Galu Beach, Kenya
PO Box 696, Ukunda 80400, Kenya

Tel	+254 40 3300046
Mobile	+254 716 016000; +254 731 609871
Fax	+254 20 3549979
E-mail	info.neptunevillage@sentidohotels.com
Web	www.sentidohotels.com

 VISA, MasterCard  Ukunda, LS & CH 25 min

In tropical gardens on Galu Beach, Sentido Neptune Village Beach Resort has a wide selection of facilities and activities.

The 166 en-suite rooms are made up of 90 standard rooms, including 15 interconnecting rooms for families, 66 superior rooms and 2 junior suites. The rooms are all equipped with telephone, satellite TV, safe and aircon, and have a balcony or terrace. The superior rooms are more spacious and also have kettles and hairdryers.

The main restaurant seats 230 pax and serves buffet breakfast, lunch and dinner. There is also an a la carte restaurant, a snack menu and 2 bars. An entertainment team provides activities during the day and shows at night. Activities include aerobics, aquagym, beginner's diving in the pool, snorkelling, tennis, table tennis, beach volleyball, darts, billiards, boccia and mini golf. Massage, windsurfing, surfing and PADI scuba diving are available for a supplementary charge. Trips to a nearby 18-hole golf course, safaris and other excursions can also be arranged. The Miniclub provides entertainment for children aged 4 to 12. The resort prints a daily newsletter with information on the region and the day's entertainment. A holiday concierge assists guests with the planning of their activities.

Sentido Neptune Palm Beach Resort

Galu

Sentido Neptune Palm Beach Resort, Galu Beach, Kenya
PO Box 696, Ukunda 80400, Kenya

Tel	+254 40 3300046
Mobile	+254 716 016000; +254 731 609871
Fax	+254 20 3549979
E-mail	reservations.neptunepalmbeach@sentidohotels.com
Web	www.sentidohotels.com

VISA, MasterCard  Ukunda, LS & CH 25 mins

Sentido Neptune Palm Beach Resort opened in 2006. Thatched cottages, in traditional Swahili and Lamu design, are set in tropical gardens on Galu Beach.

There are 60 en-suite deluxe rooms, 4 in each cottage. Each room has a sitting area, telephone, satellite TV, WiFi, safe, kettle, aircon, hairdryer and veranda. 48 rooms have a garden view and 12 have a sea view.

The Main Restaurant seats 86 pax. Located next to the freeform swimming pool, it serves international buffets. The a la carte restaurant is furnished with Lamu beds, library and hookah pipes. There is also a snack bar and 2 bars. The Miniclub provides entertainment for children aged between 4 and 12. Childcare can also be arranged. The resort prints a daily newsletter with information on the region and details of the day's activities and entertainment programme. A holiday concierge assists guests with the planning of their activities during their stay.

Adjoining sister hotel, Sentido Neptune Village Beach Resort offers water sports and an extensive programme of activities. It has a spa with massages and a range of beauty treatments. Trips to an 18-hole golf course, safaris and excursions to other destinations in Kenya can also be booked.

Lantana Galu Beach

Galu

Lantana Galu Beach, South Coast, Kenya
PO Box 5728, Diani 80401, Kenya
Tel   +254 20 2604434
Mobile   +254 714 315151; +254 738 650828
Fax
E-mail   info@lantana-galu-beach.co.ke
Web   www.lantana-galu-beach.com

VISA, MasterCard   Ukunda, LS & CH
25 mins

Lantana Galu Beach, on Galu beachfront, is a collection of luxury villas, apartments, bungalows and penthouses in landscaped gardens. The contemporary Swahili architecture, traditional carved furniture and coral walls create an atmosphere that is both lavish and modern. The accommodation is all self-catering, with housekeeping service. The 20 villas have 3 en-suite bedrooms, each with private balcony, fully equipped kitchen, sitting room, dining room and barazza-style rooftop terrace. Each has a 3-floor entrance hall with central fountain which enhances the impression of space and light. The 20 apartments have 2 or 3 en-suite bedrooms, open plan sitting and dining room and fully equipped kitchen.

The 3 bungalows are identical in design to the apartments, but open directly onto the gardens. The 4 penthouses have 1 en-suite bedroom, open plan living area and vast rooftop terrace with Jacuzzi and bar. All are equipped with satellite TV, DVD and WiFi. There is a beachside swimming pool, garden swimming pool, beachfront restaurant and coffee bar. The spa offers a selection of treatments and therapies including holistic massage, aromatherapy facials and nail therapies. The gym is fully equipped with state of the art fitness machines. Lantana Galu Beach also has a business centre and convenience shop. The concierge service can assist with booking taxis, trips, excursions and water sports.

Tropical Garden

Galu

Tropical Garden, Galu, South Coast, Kenya
PO Box 5401, Ukunda 80400, Kenya
Tel
Mobile   +254 728 583431
Fax
E-mail   metrinamulavu@yahoo.com
Web   www.tropical-garden-kenya.de

Ukunda, LS & CH
25 mins

Tropical Garden, a short walk from Galu Beach, is a collection of thatched bandas around a lush garden. A swimming pool surrounded by thatched sun umbrellas lies at the foot of the garden. Tropical Garden offers budget accommodation and friendly service.
There are 7 en-suite bandas, made up of 5 doubles and 2 triples. Each one contains a bedroom, bathroom and veranda. All the bandas are adorned with murals in bright colours depicting African scenes and animals, and furnished with simple wooden furniture and bright local fabrics.
The restaurant is an open sided, high roofed building serving African dishes and seafood. African murals cover the walls. The restaurant can be used for meetings. There is also a children's play area. Local activities include scuba diving, snorkelling and boat trips. Shops, restaurants, bars and discos are within easy reach of the bandas, either by private car, taxi or public transport. Tropical Garden can arrange airport transfers, as well as excursions and safaris to places of interest in Kenya.

Kusini Cottages

Galu

Kusini Cottages, Galu Beach, South Coast, Kenya
PO Box 5414, Diani 80401, Kenya

Tel	+254 40 3202996
Mobile	+254 721 652787
Fax	
E-mail	info@kusinibeachcottages.com
Web	www.kusinibeachcottages.com

VISA, MasterCard

Ukunda, LS & CH
25 mins

A charming collection of self-catering cottages, Kusini Cottages are beachfront on Galu Beach. The infinity pool, watched over by the thatched beach bar, appears to tumble onto the beach. The cottages opened in 2006. There are 5 cottages, made up of 1 1-bedroom, 1 2-bedroom and 3 3-bedroom cottages. All bedrooms are en-suite. The cottages have large sitting rooms and their open air kitchens are fully equipped including all crockery, cutlery and glassware. They are whitewashed, with thatched roofs and wooden shutters. Each cottage is individually designed, and adorned with coastal furniture and stylish African artefacts. Most of the large open air balconies have a beach view, and all are equipped with dining table and chairs. Each cottage is staffed by a room steward and chef. Kusini Cottages have reduced their impact on the environment as much as possible, and are powered by solar power.

The gardens are well maintained and dotted with palm trees. The swimming pool has a separate children's area. There is also a beach bar and a thatched beachfront lounge with comfortable sofas and armchairs covered with bright cushions. Excursions and safaris to other Kenyan destinations can be booked through Safi Safaris, located on site.

Pinewood Village

Galu

Pinewood Village, Galu Beach, South Coast, Kenya
PO Box 190, Diani 80401, Kenya

Tel	+254 40 3300045; +254 40 3300038; +254 20 2080981-3
Mobile	+254 734 699723; +254 723 957080
Fax	+254 40 3300045
E-mail	info@pinewood-beach.com
Web	www.pinewood-beach.com

VISA, MasterCard

Ukunda, LS & CH
40 mins

Situated on the beachfront, Pinewood Village is known for its personal service and its fully equipped water sports centre.

The 38 en-suite 1st floor rooms and the 20 en-suite ground floor suites are gathered in clusters around the gardens. The 36 deluxe rooms overlook the garden while the 2 executive rooms look onto the seafront. The 18 suites have large verandas overlooking the garden and the 2 executive suites have large seafront verandas. All the suites have a living room and kitchen, complete with the services of a personal chef for dinner.

Bahari Restaurant serves breakfast and dinner; Tamu Snack Grill serves lunch and afternoon tea; Jahazi Bistro serves lunch and Peponi Restaurant serves barbeques and theme dinners. Drinks are served in the Pool Bar, the Jahazi Beach Bar and the Lounge Bar.

The Aqualand Water Sports Centre offers a huge variety of activities, including glass bottomed boat trips, snorkelling, kite surfing and windsurfing. Other facilities include the Amani Gym, tennis, table tennis, squash and swimming pool with Jacuzzi. Beach games and camel riding are also available. The fully equipped business centre ensures that guests can keep up with work, while the Amani Spa assists them to truly relax.

Camp Makongeni

Makongeni

Camps International, Unit 1 Kingfisher Park, Headlands Business Park, Salisbury Road, Blashford, Ringwood, BH24 4HX, UK

Tel	+254 41 2007761; +254 41 3202056
Mobile	+254 733 989082; +254 733 604422
Fax	
E-mail	dipesh@campsinternational.com
Web	www.campsinternational.com

      Ukunda, LS & CH
1 hr

Camp Makongeni is operated by Camps International, which supports community and wildlife projects through interaction with adventure tourism. The camp is located in Makongeni Village, a small community, predominantly from the Digo tribe, in the Shimba Hills. It is aimed at international volunteers and local school students and interacts closely with the local community.

There are 4 thatched cottages, in traditional coastal style. The chef caters for all tastes, and uses fresh local produce. The camp has a minivan and 4WD vehicle. Local taxis are available to travel between the camp and the beach.

Camp Makongeni provides an integrated, non-touristy cultural experience. The camp aims to assist the local community with long-term, sustainable development projects. The core focus is on education and initiatives that benefit the school. Current projects include teaching, construction and renovation of classrooms, painting and fencing, desk making, sports and coaching. Tree planting and agricultural activities are also in progress. Camps International was given the Virgin Holidays Responsible Tourism Award in 2008 and won the Eco Warrior Kenya Award for the Most Sustainable Community Based Tourism Enterprise in 2010.

Kinondo Kwetu

Kinondo

Kinondo Kwetu, Kinondo Beach, South Coast, Kenya
Cheli & Peacock, PO Box 743, Nairobi 00517, Kenya

Tel	+254 20 6004054/3; +254 20 6003090/1
Mobile	+254 733 490234; +254 724 255375
Fax	+254 20 6004050; +254 20 6003066
E-mail	safaris@chelipeacock.co.ke / info@kinondo-kwetu.com
Web	www.chelipeacock.com / www.kinondo-kwetu.com

      Ukunda, LS & CH
50 mins

Located on a tranquil private beach south of Diani, Kinondo Kwetu is surrounded by holy forests and sacred land. Kinondo Kwetu is both an all inclusive luxury resort and a serene retreat.

Mama Taa Villa has 6 suites, 3 upstairs and 3 downstairs. Mama Tina Villa has 1 en-suite double room and 2 single rooms with a shared bathroom. Shimba, Twiga and Songoro are 3 double cottages with king size beds and en-suite bathrooms. Mbuyu cottage has a double bedroom and a connecting single bedroom with a shared bathroom. Ubani beach house is a double storey cottage with a double en-suite bedroom upstairs and a double and single bedroom downstairs. Private entrances mean that each floor can be taken separately or the house can be rented as a whole. Lunches and dinners are served alfresco, and are created from locally-grown fruits and vegetables as well as fresh fish and seafood. At Kinondo Kwetu, guests can indulge in the luxury of doing nothing at all, or can enter into a myriad of beach activities. Scuba diving, snorkelling, boat trips, deep sea fishing and kite surfing are all available. Tennis, horse riding and Finnish sauna are also on offer. Cultural visits to Kinondo village and game drives in Shimba Hills National Reserve can be arranged.

Galu Kinondo Beach House Kinondo

Galu Kinondo Beach House, Kinondo Beach, Kenya
Lamu Homes & Safaris Ltd, PO Box 772, Nairobi 00606, Kenya
Tel	+254 20 4446384; +254 20 4447397
Mobile	
Fax	
E-mail	info@lamuhomes.com
Web	www.lamuhomes.com

  Ukunda, LS & CH
50 mins

Galu Kinondo Beach House is a private house set in a 3-acre tropical garden. The house is whitewashed and has a thatched roof; its swimming pool and garden overlook the seafront.
There are 5 en-suite bedrooms, kitchen, dining room and veranda with seating area. The large swimming pool is on the beachfront. Bed linen, towels, mosquito nets, crockery, cutlery and glassware are all provided. The house is staffed by housekeeper, chef, gardener and night guard. Guests are welcome to discuss their preferred menus with the chef. A small, friendly dog lives on site. A backup generator is available in case of power cuts. Guests are recommended to buy drinking water, as well as fruit, vegetables and any other food they might need. The chef can assist with ordering fish and seafood from local fishermen. The house is located at the south end of Galu and Kinondo Beaches. Drive to the south end of Diani Beach and continue into Galu. The house is 4.3km past the end of the tarmac, past Pinewood Village and Kinondo Kwetu, just after the Kaya Kinondo Sacred Forest site.

Cove Retreat Kinondo

Cove Retreat, Kinondo Beach, South Coast, Kenya
Destination Adventures Ltd, PO Box 5480, Ukunda 80400, Kenya
Tel	+254 40 3203611
Mobile	+254 733 435341
Fax	
E-mail	reservations@destination-adventures.com
Web	www.destination-adventures.com

  Ukunda, LS & CH
50 mins

Situated in a private cove alongside a fishing community, Cove Retreat is a unique collection of tree houses. Its rustic design and secluded location make it a true retreat from modern living.
There are 6 tree houses, each in its own baobab tree. Each tree house has its own Jacuzzi, terrace and bathroom with sea view. Jicho Bar serves soft drinks, wines, beers, spirits and cocktails. The Sea View Restaurant has an a la carte menu; guests can eat in the restaurant or in their tree house. The infinity pool has a sundeck and bar seats. Health and beauty treatments are given in the guests' tree house. This is an adult only retreat. The retreat is all inclusive; meals, facilities, drinks and transfers are included. Local excursions for snorkelling, sailing and mangrove trips can be arranged with the local community in dug out canoes and outriggers. Bush walks and visits to the nearby village are also available. Sport fishing and scuba diving can be arranged externally. Weddings are designed individually to suit the couple's taste. The retreat supports the local community by leasing its land and has built a landing site for fishermen and a primary school.

Gazi Tented Retreat   Gazi Bay

Gazi Tented Retreat, Gazi Bay, South Coast, Kenya
Destination Adventures Ltd, PO Box 5480, Ukunda 80400, Kenya
Tel   +254 40 3203611
Mobile   +254 733 435341
Fax
E-mail   reservations@destination-adventures.com
Web   www.destination-adventures.com

 Ukunda, LS & CH
40 mins

Set in remote and unspoilt Gazi Bay, Gazi Tented Retreat is a beachfront tented camp. Palm studded gardens slope down to the beach.

There are 8 en-suite Bedouin style tents overlooking the circular swimming pool and sundeck. Each tent has a stone floor and thatched roof, and is furnished with solid wooden furniture including a 4-poster bed. A separate Swahili style lounge area has a minibar. Each tent is also equipped with aircon, and a romantic shower. The generator runs from 6pm to 6am. This is an adult only retreat.

The Sea View Restaurant serves a la carte breakfast, light lunch and table d'hote dinner. The bar is stocked with soft drinks, juices, beers, wines, spirits and cocktails. The retreat is an all inclusive property; meals, facilities, drinks and transfers are all included. Activities include snorkelling off the sand banks, walking in the mangroves and visits to the local village. Inshore and sport fishing, and scuba diving can be booked and paid for locally. Local fishermen also provide boat trips in the mangroves and bird watching. Weddings are designed individually to suit the couple's taste. The retreat supports the local community by operating its mangrove project. It has also built a kindergarten school.

The Sands   Chale Island
at Chale Island

The Sands at Chale Island, Chale Island, South Coast, Kenya
PO Box 5066, Diani 80401, Kenya
Tel
Mobile   +254 725 373888; +254 733 373888; +254 724 262426
Fax
E-mail   chale@thesandsatnomad.com
Web   www.thesandsatchaleisland.com

Ukunda, LS & CH
1 hr

Chale Island, about 50km south of Mombasa, is a stunning island fringed by white sand beaches and a coral reef. At its centre is a tidal salt water lake surrounded by mangroves. The Sands at Chale Island is a contemporary mix of Swahili structures, Italian stucco, Lamu furniture and African art. There are 16 tower rooms, in 2 towers. Each room is semi-circular, with Swahili day beds on sea facing verandas. There are 2 penthouse suites, with en-suite double room, sitting room, veranda and rooftop Jacuzzi. All rooms are equipped with aircon, satellite TV, DVD, telephone, internet, safe, minibar and hairdryer. There are 9 standard bandas, 14 superior bandas and 6 Chale bandas with Jacuzzis. There are also 2 over-water bandas on the northwest of the island, raised on stilts over the sea. There is 1 luxury suite on the rocks, joined to the island by a stone bridge, ideal for honeymooners.

The main restaurant serves Italian cuisine and seafood. The a la carte restaurant is located on the inland lake. There is also a well equipped water sports centre, a PADI scuba diving centre, a spa and 2 boutiques. Boat trips and shopping trips to Diani are available. Safaris and excursions to destinations in Kenya can be arranged.

Msambweni Beach House and Private Villas

Msambweni

Msambweni Beach House and Private Villas, Msambweni Beach
PO Box 51, Msambweni 80404, Kenya

Tel	+254 20 3577093
Mobile	+254 723 697346
Fax	+254 20 2137599
E-mail	info@msambweni-beach-house.com
Web	www.msambweni-beach-house.com

 VISA, MasterCard, Amex   Ukunda, LS & CH
1 hr

Meaning land of the Sable antelope, Msambweni Beach House and Private Villas is as striking as this rare creature. The Arabic architecture of the house sets whitewashed walls, high arches and turreted roofs against the bright colours of the coast. A 25m infinity pool and the winding jetty end in a lovely sundowner spot, raised on a cliff overlooking the Indian Ocean. The main house has 3 en-suite rooms with private verandas, a luxury tented room and 2 extra rooms on the 2nd floor. The sitting areas are adorned with pale linen curtains and embroidered cushions and gently lit by Lamu lamps on wooden tables. The 3 Lamu villas have their own infinity pools and Jacuzzis facing the sea. A private cook and waiter staff these villas.

Children are not allowed unless the house is taken exclusively.
The main dining area serves seafood and Swahili dishes, as well as Belgian and French cuisine, prepared by kitchen staff trained by a celebrity Belgian chef.
Activities include snorkelling, fishing, kite surfing, windsurfing, beach volleyball, badminton, croquet and mountain biking. Scuba diving, deep sea fishing, tennis and golf can also be booked from here. Nearby attractions include Kisite Mpunguti Marine Park, where guests can dive with sea turtles and swim with dolphins, and Shimba Hills National Reserve, where the rare Sable antelope is still found.

Funzi Keys

Funzi Island

Funzi Keys, Funzi Island, South Coast, Kenya
PO Box 95573, Mombasa, Kenya

Tel	
Mobile	+254 733 900446; +254 733 900582
Fax	
E-mail	torriani@funzikeys.com / info@funzikeys.com
Web	www.funzikeys.com

VISA, MasterCard, Amex  Funzi Island, CH
5 mins

Tucked away on an idyllic island, Funzi Keys is a remote and exclusive resort. Funzi Keys, surrounded by water on its own private peninsular, offers luxurious seclusion. There are 9 seafront cottages, including 2 cottages designed for families. There are also 8 sea view cottages. The spacious cottages have stone walls, thatched roofs and netted windows. The rooms are individually designed, furnished with hand-carved 4-poster beds, and adorned with wooden artefacts and colourful fabrics. All cottages are equipped with fan, safe, kettle, hairdryer, cool box and beach accessories, and have private verandas.
The Main Restaurant, over the bar, has views of the sunset across the sea. It serves a selection of freshly caught seafood and locally grown fruit and vegetables. The large freeform swimming pool is surrounded by a Mazeras deck with Poolside Restaurant. Massage, manicure and pedicure are available. Activities include sailing, creek fishing, windsurfing and canoeing. Boat trips up the Ramisi River or Funzi Creek provide glimpses of kingfishers, crocodiles and even dolphins. Deep sea fishing and scuba diving in the Pemba Channel can be arranged locally. Tatler twice voted Funzi Keys 1 of the top 101 hotels in the world, and Conde Nast Traveller voted it 1 of the top 6 private island resorts in the world.

Mwazaro Mangrove Lodge Shimoni

Mwazaro Mangrove Lodge, Mwazaro Beach, nr Shimoni, South Coast
PO Box 14, Shimoni 80409, Kenya
Tel   +49 341 25980150
Mobile
Fax   +49 341 2598099150
E-mail   info@keniabeach.de
Web   www.keniabeach.de/en

             Ukunda, LS & CH
                                                   1.5 hrs

It is said that a missionary proclaimed, on reaching Mwazaro Beach: Where God makes holidays. Mwazaro, meaning Place for Praying in the ancient language of the coastal region, is a holy place for the Digo people who continue to pray at the Holy Baobab. This attractive and spiritual beach is the location for Mwazaro Mangrove Lodge.

There are 10 Palm Cottages, built of palm fronds, with lovely views of the sea. External bathroom facilities are available. There are also some new Coral Houses, with en-suite bathrooms. The lodge is eco-friendly, and is powered by solar and wind energy. The chef studied traditional cuisine and the art of spice in Zanzibar, and the cuisine is created from fresh ingredients and coastal spices.

Activities include boat trips, fishing and cultural visits to fishing villages. Day trips to nearby sites of interest can be arranged. The mangrove forest at Ramisi River can be seen by boat; rare species of animals include crocodiles and giant lizards. Speedboat trips to Funzi Bay for sport fishing are available; dolphins frequently follow the boat and whale sharks and humpback whales have been seen in season. Kisite Mpunguti Marine Park offers diving, snorkling and boat trips. Shimoni fishing village, a 1hr walk from Mwazaro, is famous for its historical slave caves.

Shimoni Reef Lodge   Shimoni

Shimoni Reef Lodge, Shimoni, South Coast, Kenya
PO Box 82234, Mombasa 80100, Kenya
Tel   +254 40 52015; +254 41 471771
Mobile   +254 733 939359; +254 738 880228
Fax   +254 41 473969
E-mail   info@shimonireeflodge.com
Web   www.shimonireeflodge.com

 VISA, MasterCard   Ukunda, LS & CH
                                                                        1.5 hrs

Shimoni Reef was originally an outpost base for One Earth Safaris, the first company to really explore these waters, diving in the Pemba Channel and investigating the outer reefs. Now Shimoni Reef Lodge gives guests the chance to experience this pristine ocean reserve.

The lodge has 6 Swahili style cottages, 1 self-catering 2-bedroom house and 1 rooftop suite overlooking the Wasini Channel. The garden has views of the Indian Ocean, Wasini Island and Usambari Mountains in Tanzania. The cottages can be booked individually, or the lodge can be taken exclusively. Guests discuss their food preferences with the cooks and design their own menus. A myriad of water sports is on offer, including scuba diving, snorkelling, fishing, swimming with dolphins and boat trips to the islands. A traditional dhow is available for private excursions. Shimoni, meaning the place of the caves in Swahili, has much history. The caves were used as a holding pen for slaves before they were shipped to Zanzibar. Rusted chains remain to remind guests of these horrors, but today, a visit to the caves contributes positively to the support of the community. Other trips include exploring the nature trails of the forest reserve and boat trips through Kisite Mpunguti Marine Park, a 39km² paradise of marine life and aquatic birds.

Shimoni Gardens Resort Shimoni

Shimoni Gardens Resort, Shimoni, South Coast, Kenya
Tomasi Holidays, PO Box 99190, Mombasa 80107, Kenya
Tel   +254 20 2039284
Mobile +254 712 918589
Fax
E-mail sales@shimonigardens.com
Web   www.shimonigardens.com

                         Ukunda, LS & CH
                                            1.5 hrs

Shimoni Gardens Resort is located in the heart of the coastal forest of Shimoni. Kisite Mpunguti Marine Park, off the coast at Shimoni, covers a marine area with 4 small islands surrounded by coral reef. The major attractions are dolphins and coral gardens.
There are 6 tree rooms with panoramic views of Wasini Island and Wasini Channel. There are also 16 en-suite double rooms, with whitewashed walls and thatched roofs. The resort has a conference hall, pool table, dartboard and board games.
Visitors can visit the Shimoni caves, once holding pens for thousands of slaves awaiting shipment to the infamous Zanzibar slave market.

The caves are managed by the Shimoni community and proceeds go to community based activities. The mangrove bridge is a boardwalk with views of fossilised corals and dense mangrove forest. Rare migratory birds and sea birds are often found here. Other activities available for a surcharge include dhow boat trips, snorkelling, diving and swimming with dolphins. Abundant marine life includes trigger fish, moray eel and angelfish. Humpback whales and whale sharks are seasonal. The resort offers a selection of short and longer term excursions, such as a 2-day trip to Shimba Hills National Reserve and a full day dhow excursion.

KWS, Shimoni Bandas Shimoni

KWS, Shimoni Bandas, Shimoni, South Coast, Kenya
Kenya Wildlife Service, PO Box 40241, Nairobi 00100, Kenya
Tel   +254 20 6000800; +254 20 6002345; +254 20 3991000
Mobile +254 726 610508; +254 726 610509; +254 736 663421
Fax   +254 20 6003792
E-mail kws@kws.go.ke / reservations@kws.go.ke
Web   www.kws.go.ke

                        Ukunda, LS & CH
                                            1.5 hrs

Kisite Mpunguti Marine Park, off the coast at Shimoni, covers a marine area with 4 small islands surrounded by coral reef. The major attractions are dolphins and coral gardens. The site is excellent for snorkelling, diving and bird watching. More than 250 fish species have been recorded here. Large colonies of sea birds are seen, and significant numbers of crab plover and roseate tern migrate annually from Europe to nest here. Owned by the Kenya Wildlife Service, KWS, Shimoni Bandas provide budget self-catering accommodation in the coastal forest at Shimoni. There are 7 simple twin bandas; 3 bandas are en-suite and 4 share communal bathroom facilities. The communal dining area is equipped

with tables and chairs. The communal kitchen is equipped with stove, utensils, cutlery, crockery and glassware. The resident caretaker provides bed linen, mosquito nets and towels. The bandas are located in the KWS compound, 200 meters from the main Shimoni pier. The park does not operate the SafariCard system; entry is by cash only.
Water sports and other activities can be booked locally. Bird watching, snorkelling, scuba diving and dolphin watching are recommended. Licences for filming can be obtained from KWS.

Mpunguti Lodge

Wasini Island

Mpunguti Lodge, Wasini Island, South Coast, Kenya
PO Box 19, Shimoni 80409, Kenya
Tel
Mobile +254 722 566623
Fax
E-mail mohammedmasoud@yahoo.com
Web

   Ukunda, LS & CH
2 hrs

Wasini Island lies a short distance south of Shimoni. The island is sparsely populated, and has no roads; the fishing villages of Wasini and Mkwiro are the 2 centres. The Swahili ruins, approximately 400 years old, are recommended. There is also an exposed coral reef at the end of Wasini village. Wasini Island is close to the Kisite Mpunguti Marine Park, an area of 4 islands surrounded by coral reef which provides some of the best snorkelling in Kenya.

Mpunguti Lodge has 10 en-suite rooms, 3 of which have views of the sea. There are also 18 rooms with outside bathroom facilities. The restaurant, overlooking the sea, serves traditional Swahili cuisine, and has a number of vegetarian, seafood and meat options. The campsite has a capacity of 10 tents, and is equipped with bathroom facilities. Wasini Island has no electricity. In the evening a generator powers the lights; water is heated by solar power. A team of 10 staff serves the lodge.

Mpunguti Lodge is known for its excursions to the pristine marine park south of Wasini Island. Park fees are paid to Kenya Wildlife Service, KWS. The voyage can be enjoyed in either a traditional dhow or a motorboat. Refreshments and snorkelling equipment are provided.

Blue Cottage

Wasini Island

Blue Cottage, Wasini Island, South Coast, Kenya
PO Box 42547, Mombasa 80100, Kenya
Tel
Mobile +254 722 532230
Fax
E-mail post@orangebrixx.com
Web

  Ukunda, LS & CH
2 hrs

Wasini Island lies a short distance south of Shimoni. The island is sparsely populated, and has no roads; the fishing villages of Wasini and Mkwiro are the 2 centres. The Swahili ruins, approximately 400 years old, are recommended. There is also an exposed coral reef at the end of Wasini village. Wasini Island is close to the Kisite Mpunguti Marine Park, an area of 4 islands surrounded by coral reef which provides some of the best snorkelling in Kenya.

Blue Cottage is a rustic cottage built in traditional Swahili style. The cottage accommodates up to 3 pax, and has a kitchenette, bathroom and veranda. The cottage is surrounded by garden and directly overlooks the sea, with private access to the beach. There is also a banda with 1 double bedroom. There is no electricity on Wasini Island. Lighting and cooking are provided by gas and kerosene. Tents can be provided, inclusive of bed linen and mattress.

At nearby Mpunguti Lodge, excursions to the pristine marine park south of Wasini Island can be booked. Park fees are paid to Kenya Wildlife Service, KWS. The voyage can be enjoyed in either a traditional dhow or a motorboat. Refreshments and snorkelling equipment are provided.

Ngarawa, local boat – Photo © www.sokomoto.com

Index to all camps, lodges, hotels & resorts

748 Camp   146

A
Abbey Resort   285
Abdul's Eco Nest   371
Aberdare Country Club   84
Acacia Camp   27
Acacia House   262
Acaluma Camp   258
African Heritage House   37
African Pearl Hotel   401
Afrochic   494
Alakara Hotel   166
Alfajiri Villas   500
Al Hamra   423
Alia Bay Guest House   147
Almanara Diani Beach Resort   511
Almond Resort   156
Amani Mara   255
Amani Tiwi Beach Resort   485
Amber House   369
Amboseli Porini Camp   321
Amboseli Serena Lodge   323
Amboseli Sopa Lodge   327
Amu House   375
Aqua Lodge   301
Aquarius Beach Resort   419
Arabuko Jamii Villas   426
Ascot Residence   418
Asha Cottage   503
Ashnil Aruba Lodge   352
Ashnil Mara Camp   241
Ashnil Samburu Camp   136

B
Baba's   442
Bahari Beach Hotel   454
Bahari Dhow   495
Bahati House   379
Baitil Aman   384
Bamburi Beach Hotel   445
Bamburi Chalets   442
Banana House   380
Banana Leaf Hotel   78
Baobab Beach Cottage & Desert Rose Beach Cottage   505
Baobab Beach Resort & Spa   508
Baobab Holiday Resort   448
Baobab Lodge Resort   428
Basecamp   233
Basecamp Dorobo Bush Camp   260
Basecamp Wilderness   213
Bateleur Camp   244
Batian Grand Hotel   79
Batian Guest House   95
Baytil Ajaib   373
Beach House   388
Beachview Cottages   417
Beehive Cottages   484
Beverly Key Club   404
Beyt Salaam   364
Big Time Safari Camp   225
Bilashaka Lodge   300
Black Leopard Retreat   228
Blue Bay Village   420
Blue Cottage   523
Blue Marlin Resort   402
Blue Post Hotel   72
Blu Key Beach Club   409
Bluu Nile Hotel   200
Bobong Camp   155
Boko Boko   433
Bomen Hotel   134
Boni House   59
Bontana Hotel   284
Borana   125
Brackenhurst Conference Centre   58
Buffalo Bay Motel   74
Burch's Camp   305
Bush Adventures   123
Bush Buck Camp   261
Bustani Café & Bookshop   373

C
Camp Carnelley's   310
Campi ya Kanzi   339
Camp Makongeni   517
Camp Malta   74
Camp Muhaka   488
Camp Mwaluganje   485
Camp North   145
Camp Oloshaiki   233
Camp Tsavo   331
Castle Forest Lodge   75
Castle Royal Hotel   472
Casuarina Rest House   370
Centre of Origin at Makena's Hills   115
Champali Camp   362
Cheetah Tented Camp   252
Che Shale   399
Chester Hotel   285

 Accommodation Guide

Chiky Villa   416
Chui   327
Chui Lodge   313
Club Rio   473
Cool Breeze Hotel   467
Coral Beach Cottages and Apartments   498
Coral Cove Cottages   483
Coral Key Beach Resort   405
Cottars 1920s Camp   228
Country House Inn   37
Country Lodge Hotel   55
Cove Retreat   518
Crater Lake Permanent Tented Camp and Sanctuary   315
Crayfish Camp   309
Crossline Villas   490
Crowne Plaza   63
Crystal Bay   415

D

Dafina Holiday Cottage   299
Dancourt Hotel   440
Danpark Hotel and Apartments   436
Darajani Hotel   468
David Livingstone Safari Resort   266
Deloraine House   278
Delta Crescent Wildlife Sanctuary   169
Delta Dunes Lodge   398
Desert Rose   151
Diamond Beach Village   390
Diamonds Dream of Africa   408
Diamonds Malindi Beach   407
Diani Beachalets   510
Diani Campsite and Cottages   498
Diani Forest Lodge   500
Diani Marine Divers Village   504
Diani Reef Resort and Spa   495
Diani Sea Lodge   506
Diani Sea Resort   502
Duma Camp   265

E

Eden Parlour Restaurant and Hotel   451
Eden Roc Hotel   402
Elangata Olerai Luxury Camp   227
Eldoret Club   175
Eldoret Wagon Hotel   171
Elementaita Country Lodge   293
Elephant Bedroom Camp   136
Elephant Castle Hotel   78
Elephant Pepper Camp   253
Elephant Watch Camp   139
El Karama Eco Lodge   122
Elsamere   312

Elsa's Kopje   103
Enashipai Resort and Spa   306
Enasoit   123
Enchoro Wildlife Camp   225
Encounter Mara   259
Enkare   317
Enkewa Mara Camp   227
Enkolong Tented Camp   220
Entim   240
Entumoto   222
Epiya Chapeyu Tented Safari Camp   347
Equator Chalet   91
Eros Hotel   286
Excellent Magere Guest House   192
Exploreans Mara Rianta Camp   266

F

Fairmont Mara Safari Club   263
Fairmont Mount Kenya Safari Club   94
Fairmont The Norfolk   44
Fairview Hotel   55
Fatuma's Tower   382
Fig Tree Camp   235
Fig Tree House   430
Finch Hattons   336
Fischer's Tower   304
Fish Eagle Inn   311
Fisherman's Camp   311
Fishing Lodge & Tusk Camp   83
Flamboyant Boutique Hotel   505
Flamingo Camp and Cottages   293
Flamingo Hill Camp   288
Fourteen Falls Lodge   72
Four Twenty South   509
Frog Guesthouse   423
Funzi Keys   520

G

Galdessa Camp   346
Galdessa Private Camp   347
Galu Beach Retreat   509
Galu Kinondo Beach House   518
Galu Sea Lodge   512
Garden House   386
Garoda Resort   424
Gazi Tented Retreat   519
Gemina Court   63
Giraffe Manor   31
Giriama Residence   416
Glory Grand Hotel   471
Glory Holiday Resort   449
Gogar Farm   279
Golf Hotel   180

Governors' Camp   243
Governors' Il Moran Camp   243
Governors' Private Camp   242
Gray's Oak Hotel   28
Great Rift Valley Lodge & Golf Resort   298
Green Hills Hotel   79
Grogan's Castle   335

H

Hapa Hapa Restaurant   366
Hemingways Resort   421
Hennessis Hotel   56
Heron Hotel   53
Hill Park Hotel   62
Hillpark Hotel Tiwi Beach   481
Hills Country Lodge   195
Hillside Villa   184
Hilton Hotel   50
Hippo Point   314
Hogmead   33
Homa Bay Tourist Hotel   202
Hotel Ambassadeur   49
Hotel Beograda   190
Hotel California   145
Hotel Cathay   284
Hotel Dados   200
Hotel Diani Palm Resort   493
Hotel Dorse   471
Hotel Genevieve   286
Hotel Hippo Buck   202
Hotel Incredible   98
Hotel Kunste   282
Hotel La Mada   61
Hotel Mamba   185
Hotel Perch   187
Hotel Royal Spring   287
Hotel Sapphire   469
Hotel Sirikwa   172
Hotel Starbucks   77
Hotel Three Steers   98
Hotel Titanic   428
Hotel Vunduba   186
House of Waine   31

I

Ibis Hotel Karatina 1   76
Ibis Hotel Karatina 2   77
Ibis Hotel Nanyuki   91
Ibis Hotel Nyeri   80
Ilkeliani Camp   232
Il Ngwesi   124
Impala Safari Lodge   349
Impala Wildlife Lodge   226

Imperial Hotel   188
Indiana Beach Apartment Hotel   444
InterContinental   51
Isacheno Bandas. *See* KEEP
Isiolo Transit Hotel   133
Island Camp   275
Isukuti Houses   181
Ivory Resort Hotel   80
Izaak Walton Inn   106

J

Jacaranda Beach Resort   413
Jacaranda Hotel   43
Jacaranda Indian Ocean Beach Resort   490
Jacqueline's House   253
Jacyjoka Apartments   455
Jambo House   376
Jambolulu Cottages   494
Jannataan   386
Jannat House   371
Jazz Restaurant and Hotel   198
Jehovah Jire Hotel   165
JK Mara Camp   234
Joy's Camp   134
Jua Kali House   417
Jumuia Conference and Beach Resort   435
Jumuia Conference and Country Home, Nairobi   57
Jumuia Guest House   185
Jumuia Guest House, Nakuru   287
Jungle Green Bar & Grill   101

K

Kahama Hotel   444
Kakamega Sports Club   180
Kalacha Camp   149
Kamboyo Guest House   339
Kamsons Villa and Cottages   437
Kapkuro Bandas   170
Karen Blixen Camp   250
Karen Blixen Coffee Garden   30
Karibuni Lodge   168
Karibuni Villas   400
Kasigau Conservation Trust   332
Kauro Guest House   153
Keekorok Lodge   229
KEEP   182
Kembu Cottages Campsite and Farmstay   279
Kensington Mara West   245
Kentmere Club   58
Ken Trout   95
Kenvash Hotel   302
Kenya Bay Beach Hotel   443
Kenya Comfort Hotel   52

Kenya Comfort Hotel Suites   45
Kericho Club   195
Kerio View   175
Kiangazi House   312
Kiboko Bay Resort   193
Kibo Safari Camp   324
Kibo Villa   322
Kichakani Camp   236
Kicheche Bush Camp   255
Kicheche Laikipia Camp   89
Kicheche Mara Camp   265
Kicheche Valley Camp   258
Kichwa Tembo   245
Kifaru House   127
Kigio Wildlife Camp   296
Kigotho's Hotel and Apartments   453
Kijani House   377
Kijiji Cottages   497
Kilaguni Serena Safari Lodge   338
Kileleoni Mara Guest House   267
Kilifi Bay Beach Resort   427
Kilili Baharini Resort & Spa   408
Kilima Camp   246
Kilimanjaro & Kibo Guest Houses   326
Kilima Safari Camp   324
Kimana Mara Camp   218
Kimugu River Lodge   197
Kingfisher   434
Kinna Bandas   103
Kinondo Kwetu   517
Kipepeo Guest House   363
Kipini Conservancy House   399
Kipini Tana River Lodge   398
Kipungani Explorer   392
Kisindi Lodge and Spa   201
Kisiwani House   383
Kisumu Beach Resort   186
Kisumu Hotel   189
Kitale Club   168
Kitale Highview Hotel   166
Kitani Lodge   337
Kitendentini Bahari Hotel   368
Kitich Camp   153
Kitsapu Cottages   425
Kivi Milimani   52
Kivulini Bahari   460
Kivulini Beach Resort   411
Kivu Retreat   288
Kiwayu Safari Village   362
Kizingo   391
Kizingoni Beach Villas   391
Klique Hotel   173
Koija Starbeds   119
Koitoboss Guest House   170
Kongoni Camp   92

Kongoni Lodge   313
Kusini Cottages   516
Kuwinda Camp   356
Kweisos House   194
Kweto Beach Resort   480
KWS   83, 95, 96, 102, 103, 147, 164, 170, 181, 203
290, 326, 327, 334, 339, 487, 522

L

La Belle Inn   302
Laico Regency   49
Lake Baringo Club   277
Lake Bogoria Spa Resort   278
Lake Elementaita Lodge   295
Lake Elmenteita Luxury Camp   292
Lake Jipe Bandas   334
Lake Naivasha Country Club   306
Lake Naivasha Panorama Park   303
Lake Naivasha Resort   304
Lake Naivasha Sopa Resort   307
Lake Nakuru Flamingo Lodge   289
Lake Nakuru Lodge   291
Lakeside Tourist Lodge   301
Lake Turkana Koobi Fora Bandas   147
Lakira Camp   289
Lamu Archipelago Villa   368
Lamu House   365
Lamu Palace Hotel   367
Lantana Galu Beach   515
Laragai House   126
Larsen's Camp   137
Lavender Gardens Hotel   333
Lawford's   403
Leisure Lodge Beach & Golf Resort   496
Lelechwa Cottage   115
Leleshwa Camp   216
Lelin Campsite and Bandas   176
Lemarti's Camp   119
Lenana Mount Hotel   54
Leopard Beach Resort & Spa   496
Leopard Rock Lodge   104
Lewa House   128
Lewa Safari Camp   126
Lewa Wilderness   127
Lion in the Sun   410
Lion's Bluff   334
Little Governors' Camp   244
Little Naibor   239
Little Nile Guest House   203
Little Olarro   214
Loisaba   118
Loisiijo Lodge   316
Loldia House   299
Longonot Ranch House   308

Lonno Lodge 413
Losho Mara Camp 224
Lotus Hotel 474
LTI Kaskazi Beach Hotel 499
Ltorec 457

M

Maasai Ostrich Resort 27
Macushla House 32
Magharibi Luxury Suites 199
Magline Guest House 193
Mago Guest House 183
Maili Saba Camp 280
Maimuna Cottages 492
Maina Highway Hotel 107
Maisha Marefu House 491
Maji Moto Eco Camp 212
Makuti Villas Resort 429
Makwetu Resort 458
Malaika Holiday Villas 510
Malewa Wildlife Lodge 297
Malu Lodge 297
Mamba Village 457
Manda Bay 389
Man Eaters Camp 346
Manfriday's Mida Creek 427
Manson Hotel 472
Manyatta Camp 351
Manyatta Green 506
Mara Bush Camp 238
Mara Bush House 217
Mara Bushtops Camp 217
Mara Eden Safari Camp 231
Mara Enkipai Safari Camp 248
Mara Explorer 236
Mara House 263
Mara Intrepids 237
Mara Kima Camp 234
Maralal Safari Lodge 154
Mara Leisure Camp 231
Mara Ngenche 241
Mara Plains Camp 257
Mara Porini Camp 213
Mara Serena Safari Lodge 242
Mara Simba Lodge 230
Mara Siria 246
Mara Sokonoi 223
Mara Springs Safari Camp 219
Mara Timbo Camp 249
Mara Under Canvas 215
Marble Arch Hotel 46
Marich Pass Field Studies Centre 163
Marina Lodge 305
Marriott Hotel 1/8

Marsabit Lodge 150
Masai Mara Manyatta Camp 224
Masai Mara Sopa Lodge 223
Masinga Dam Resort 109
Matira Bush Camp 237
Matrix Beach House 431
Mbweha Camp 291
Mei Place 449
Merica Hotel 283
Meridian Court Hotel 46
Meru County Hotel 99
Meru Mt Kenya Lodge 105
Meru Safari Hotel 99
Mfangano Island Camp 204
Mida Ecocamp 426
Mid Africa Hotel 167
Midland Hotel 283
Midview Hotel 456
Milele Beach Hotel 448
Milele Hotel 56
Milele Resort Presbyterian Guest House 282
Milimani Resort & Annex 191
Millbrook Hotel 437
Mnarani Club 429
Mnarani House 379
Moffat Court Apartments 456
Mombasa Beach Apartments 453
Mombasa Beach Hotel 454
Mombasa Continental Resort 438
Morendat Training and Conference Centre 298
Mountain Rock Lodge 86
Mpata Safari Club 247
Mpunguti Lodge 523
Msafini Hotel 381
Msafiri House 76
Msambweni Beach House and Private Villas 520
Msoloni Village 412
Mt Elgon Lodge 169
Mt Mtelo Cottages and Campsite 163
Mugunda House 281
Mukima House 93
Mukutan Retreat 116
Munira Island Camp 363
Murera Bandas 102
Murera Springs Eco Lodge 101
Mutamaiyu House 116
Mwaluganje Elephant Camp 486
Mwazaro Mangrove Lodge 521
Mzima 513

N

Naboisho Camp 259
Naiberi River Campsite & Resort 177
Naibor 239

Nairobi Mamba Village   34
Nairobi Pacific Hotel   47
Nairobi Safari Club   45
Nairobi Serena Hotel   51
Nairobi Tented Camp   35
Naishi Guest House   290
Namanga River Lodge   321
Nandi Bears Club   183
Nanyuki River Camel Camp   93
Naro Moru River Lodge   86
Nawaitorong Lodge   148
Ndololo Safari Camp   353
New Bahati Lodge   366
New HillCrest Hotel   40
New Palm Tree Hotel   473
New Victoria Hotel   187
Ngare Serian   251
Ngerende Island Lodge   264
Ngobit River Lodge   90
Ngong Bounty Hotel   30
Ngong Hills Hotel   65
Ngong House   33
Ngulia Safari Lodge   337
Ngutuni Safari Lodge   353
Nkorombo Mobile Camp   249
NMK   147, 315
Nomad Palace Hotel   156
North Coast Beach Hotel   433
Nyali Beach Holiday Resort   459
Nyali Chalets   450
Nyali International Beach Hotel   461
Nyali Luxury Beach Apartments   459
Nyanza Club   190
Nyumbu Camp   260

O

Oakwood Hotel   48
Oasis Eco Camp   295
Oasis Lodge   149
Ocean Bay Hotel   489
Ocean Beach Resort and Spa   410
Ocean Breeze   414
Ocean Sports Resort   421
Ocean Village Club   507
Offbeat Mara Camp   254
Offbeat Meru Camp   104
Olarro   214
Oldarpoi Mara Community Camp   220
Old Moses and Shipton's Mountain Huts   96
Ol Donyo Wuas   340
Olerai House   300
Ole Sereni   36
Ol Gaboli Community Lodge   121
Olive Gardens Hotel   39

Ol Malo   117
Ol Malo House   117
Ol Moran   226
Oloika Guest House   316
Olonana   248
Olorgesailie Bandas   315
Ol Pejeta Bush Camp   88
Ol Pejeta House   88
Ol Seki Hemingways Mara   215
Ol Tome Mara Magic   221
Ol Tukai Lodge   323
Olumara Tented Camp   254
Oreteti Tented Camp   124
Oribi Guest House   203
Osoita Lodge   28
Outspan Hotel   81
Owoods Lodge & Annex   108

P

Palacina Suites   38
Palm Beach House   374
Palm House   387
Palm Shade Camp   150
Panari Hotel   35
Panaroma Gardens Hotel   468
Panesic Hotel   107
Papatuo Villas   492
Papillon   443
Papillon Lagoon Reef Hotel   508
Pa Pweza Adamsville Beach Suites   447
Paradise Beach Resort   432
Paris Hotel   47
Park Villa Hotel   171
Patterson's Safari Camp   345
Pelican House   90
Peponi Cottages   418
Peponi Hotel   378
Petleys   365
Petuscha Garden Lodge   439
Philadelphia Retreat and Conference Centre   109
Pig and Whistle Resort   100
Pinewood   167
Pinewood Village   516
Plaza Beach Hotel   440
Poa Place Resort   174
Pole Pole Guest House   372
Porini Lion Camp   256
Porini Rhino Camp   89
PrideInn Hotel Diani   501
PrideInn Hotel Mombasa   470
PrideInn Hotel Nairobi   42
PrideInn Hotel Nyali   450
Private Mara Camp   240

R

Rangeland Hotel and Campsite 133
Rapids Camp 75
Ratna Serviced Apartments 460
Ray's Place Inn 197
RedCourt Hotel 36
Red Elephant Lodge 350
Reef Hotel 452
Rekero 238
Relax Inn 178
Rhino River Camp 102
Rhino Valley Lodge 338
Rhino Watch Camp & Lodge 84
Richard's Camp 264
Richard's Private Camp 257
Rick Seaside Villas 451
Riuki Cultural Centre 73
Riverside Camp 235
Roberts' Camp 276
Rock House 32
Rockside Camp 331
Rondo Retreat 182
Royal Court Hotel 470
Royal Gede Resort 425
Royal Mara Safari Lodge 252
Royal Reserve Safari and Beach Club 435
Rusinga Island Lodge 204
Rutundu Log Cabins 97

S

Sable Bandas 487
Sable Fields 488
Sable Valley Treehouses 487
Sabuk 118
Sabuk Guest House 73
Safari Park Hotel 61
Sagala Lodge 354
Sagret Hotel 53
Sailfish Club 403
Sai Rock Hotel & Spa 446
Sakina House 384
Salama Beach Resort 434
Sala's Camp 229
Salt Springs Mara Camp 247
Samaki House 369
Samatian Island Lodge 275
Samburu Game Lodge 138
Samburu Intrepids 139
Samburu Simba Lodge 135
Samburu Sopa Lodge 138
Samburu Sports Centre and Guest Lodges 151
Sanana 458
Sandai Homestay & Cottages 82
Sandalwood 29

Sandavy Guest House 40
Sandies Coconut Village 406
Sandies Tropical Village 407
Sand Island Beach Cottages 481
Sangare Tented Camp 85
Sankara 42
Sarara Camp 154
Sarova Lion Hill Game Lodge 290
Sarova Mara Game Camp 230
Sarova Panafric 54
Sarova Salt Lick Game Lodge 332
Sarova Shaba Game Lodge 135
Sarova Stanley 48
Sarova Taita Hills Game Lodge 333
Sarova Whitesands Beach Resort and Spa 446
Saruni 261
Saruni Samburu 137
Saruni Wild 262
Sasaab 140
Satao 354
Satao Elerai Safari Camp 326
Savana Executive Hotel 201
Savannah 420
Sawela Lodge 307
Scorpio Villas 404
Seasons Hotel 212
Seaview Resort 401
Sego Safari Lodge 176
Sekenani Camp 222
Semadep Safari Camp 219
Sentido Neptune Beach Resort 441
Sentido Neptune Palm Beach Resort 514
Sentido Neptune Paradise Beach Resort 513
Sentido Neptune Village Beach Resort 514
Sentrim 680 44
Sentrim Amboseli Camp 325
Sentrim Boulevard 50
Sentrim Mara 221
Sentrim Tarhi Eco Camp 352
Serena Beach Hotel and Spa 436
Serena Mountain Lodge 97
Serian 251
Severin Safari Camp 336
Severin Sea Lodge 441
Shambani Cottages 489
Shela House 387
Shella Bahari Guest House 378
Shella Island Hotel 382
Shella Pwani Guest House 388
Shella Royal House 385
Shella Sea Breeze Guest House 380
She She Baharini Beach Hotel 484
Sheywe Centre 179
Shimba 486
Shimoni Bandas 522

Shimoni Gardens Resort   522
Shimoni Reef Lodge   521
Siana Springs Tented Camp   216
Siaya Guest House   179
Silole Sanctuary   34
Silver Springs Hotel   38
Simba and Oryx Cottages   512
Simba Lodge   308
Simba & Nyati   327
Simba & Nyati Bandas   327
Simba Village   501
Sirikoi   128
Sirikwa Safaris   164
Sirimon Bandas   96
Sleeping Warrior Camp   294
Sleeping Warrior Lodge   296
Slopes Villa Hotel   106
Soi Safari Lodge   276
Solio Lodge   85
Sonia Hotel and Apartments   438
Sosian   120
Southern Dream   389
Southern Palms Beach Resort   493
Southern Sun Mayfair   43
Sportsview Hotel   62
Spurwing Camp   218
St Anna Guest House   192
Star Guest House   383
Stem Hotel   281
Stephanie Beach Resort   409
Stilts   504
Stone House   374
Stopover Guest House Lamu Old Town   364
Stopover Guest House Shela   377
Stopover Hotel   108
Subira House   376
Subukia Bandas   280
Suguroi Hill Tree House   250
Suhufi Palace Hotel   469
Sultan's Palace   370
Sunbird Lodge   292
Sun N Sand Beach Resort   432
Sun Palm Hotel   415
Sunrise Resort Apartments and Spa   452
Sunsail Hotel   367
Sunset Hotel   191
Sunset House   381
Sunset Key Cottages   405
Swahili Beach   499
Swahili House   482
Sweetwaters Tented Camp   87

T

Takaungu Cottages   430
Takaungu House   431
Tamarind Garden   277
Tamarind Village   461
Tassia   125
Tausi Villas   491
Tawi Lodge   325
Tea Hotel   196
Tea Planters' Inn   184
Teavale Guest House   196
Tembo Village   414
Temple Point Resort   424
The Ark   83
The Driftwood Beach Club   406
The Duke of Breeze   188
The Exotic House   194
The Gables   41
The King Post   41
The Lolldaiga Institute   122
The Majlis   390
The Methodist Guest House and Conference Centre   39
The New Big Tree   447
The Nobel Conference Centre   174
The Sanctuary at Ol Lentille   120
The Sands at Chale Island   519
The Sands at Nomad   507
The Sportsman's Arms   92
The Woburn Residence Club   400
Thomson's Falls Lodge   87
Tijara Beach Boutique Hotel   480
Timau River Lodge   94
Tipilikwani Camp   232
Tiwi Villas   482
Top Camp   310
Topi House   256
Tortilis Camp   322
Trackmark   146
Transit Motel   105
Travellers Beach Hotel and Club   445
Tree Top House   164
Treetops   82
Tribe   59
Trinity Resort   439
Trisan Hotel   65
Tropical Garden   515
Tsavo Buffalo Camp   355
Tsavo Lodge   350
Tsavo Mashariki   349
Tsavo River Hill   355
Tsavo Safari Camp   345
Tudor Water Sports   467
Turawa   511
Turkwell Lodge   148
Turtle Bay Beach Club   422

Twiga Hotel 411
Twiga House 314
Twiga Lodge 483
Twiga Resort 177

U
Udo Bandas 181
Ufanisi Resort 198
Utalii Hotel 60

V
View Point Lodge 294
Villas Watamu 422
Vision Gate Hotel 165
Voi Safari Lodge 348
Voi Wildlife Lodge 351
Voyager Beach Resort 455
Voyager Ziwani 335

W
Wajir Guest House 152
Wajir Hilton Palace 152
Wakumbe Camp 121
Warandale Cottages 497
Watamu Adventist Beach Resort and Campsite 419
Watano House 502
WaterLovers 503
Westwood Hotel 81
Whirlspring Hotel 189
Whistling Thorns 29
White Beach Palace 412
White Castle Motel 173
White Highlands Inn 172
White House 385
White Star Hotel 100
Wida Highway Motel 57
Wildebeest Camp 64
Wildebeeste Art Workshop & Gallery 375
Windsor Golf and Country Club 60
Woodmere 64

Y
Yare Safaris Hostel and Campsite 155
Yellow Green Hotel 303
YMCA Naivasha Camp 309
Yumbe Villa and Yumbe House 372

Z
Zomeni Lion Hill Lodge 348
Zonic Hotel 199

Lions in the Maasai Mara – Photo © Tamara Britten

Gede Ruins – Photo © www.sokomoto.com

Lake Turkana, nr Nabiyotum Crater – Photo © www.yellowwings.com